STITCHES

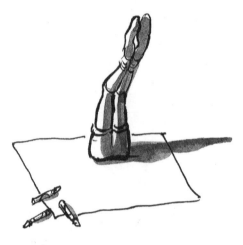

STITCHES

a memoir...

DAVID SMALL

McClelland & Stewart

A cataloguing record for this publication is available from Library and Archives Canada.

ISBN 978-0-7710-8110-1

We acknowledge the financial support of the Government of Canada through the Book Publishing Industry Development Program and that of the Government of Ontario through the Ontario Media Development Corporation's Ontario Book Initiative. We further acknowledge the support of the Canada Council for the Arts and the Ontario Arts Council for our publishing program.

Book design by Paul Buckley

Printed and bound in the United States of America

McClelland & Stewart Ltd.
75 Sherbourne Street
Toronto, Ontario
M5A 2P9

www.mcclelland.com

1 2 3 4 5   13 12 11 10 09

To Mark Stewart Guin and to my brother, Ted

STITCHES

I WAS SIX

DETROIT

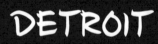

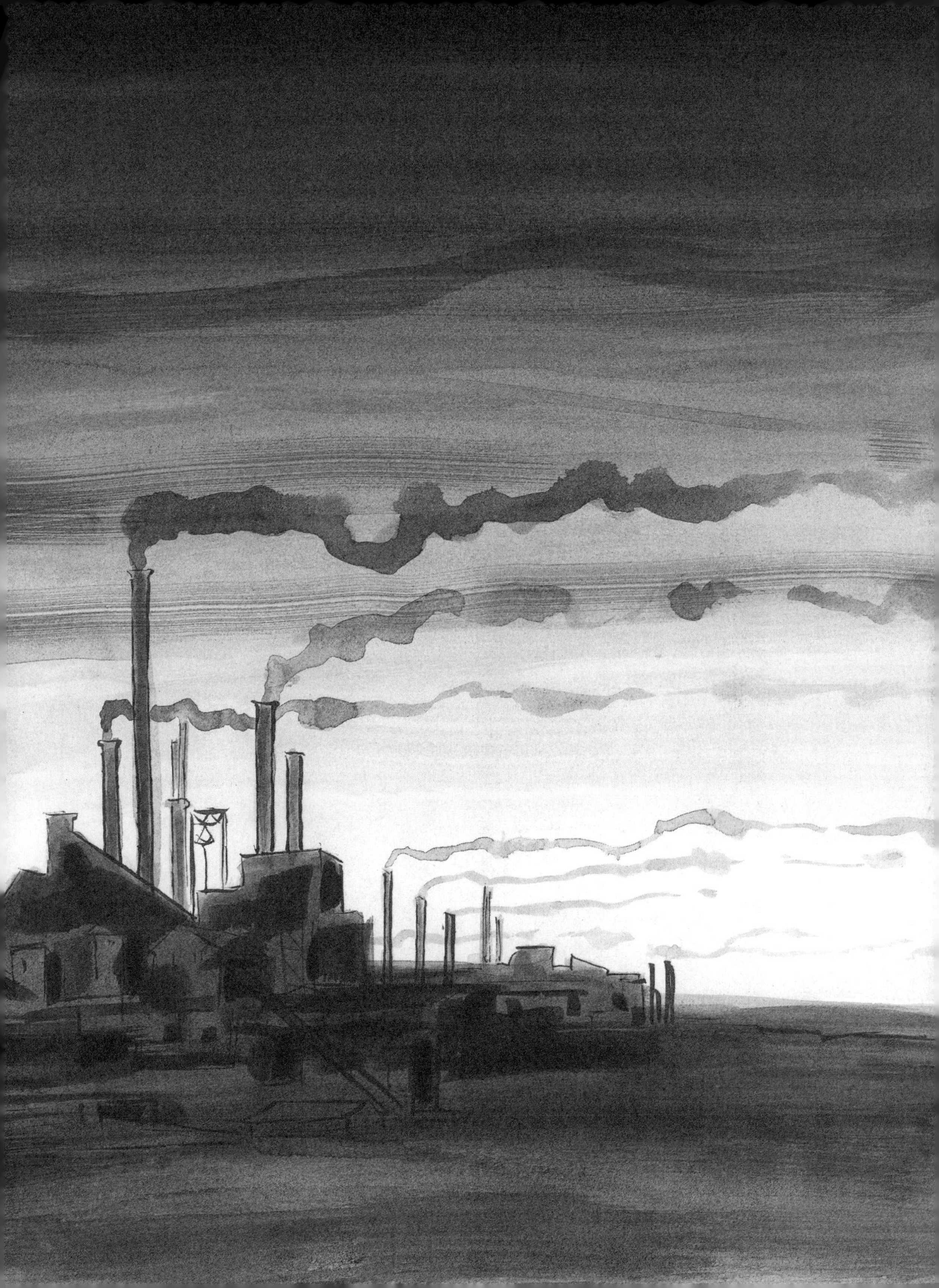

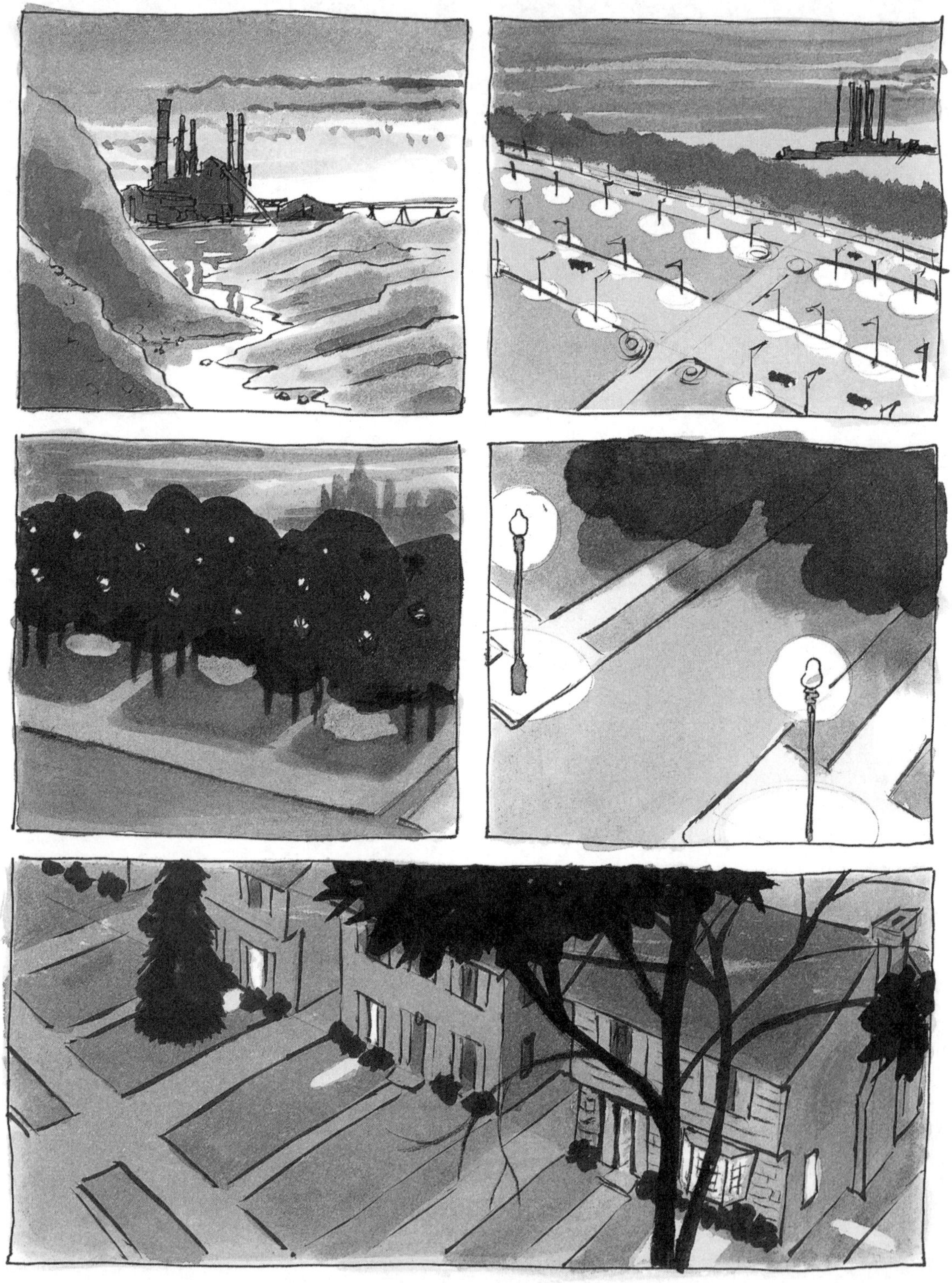

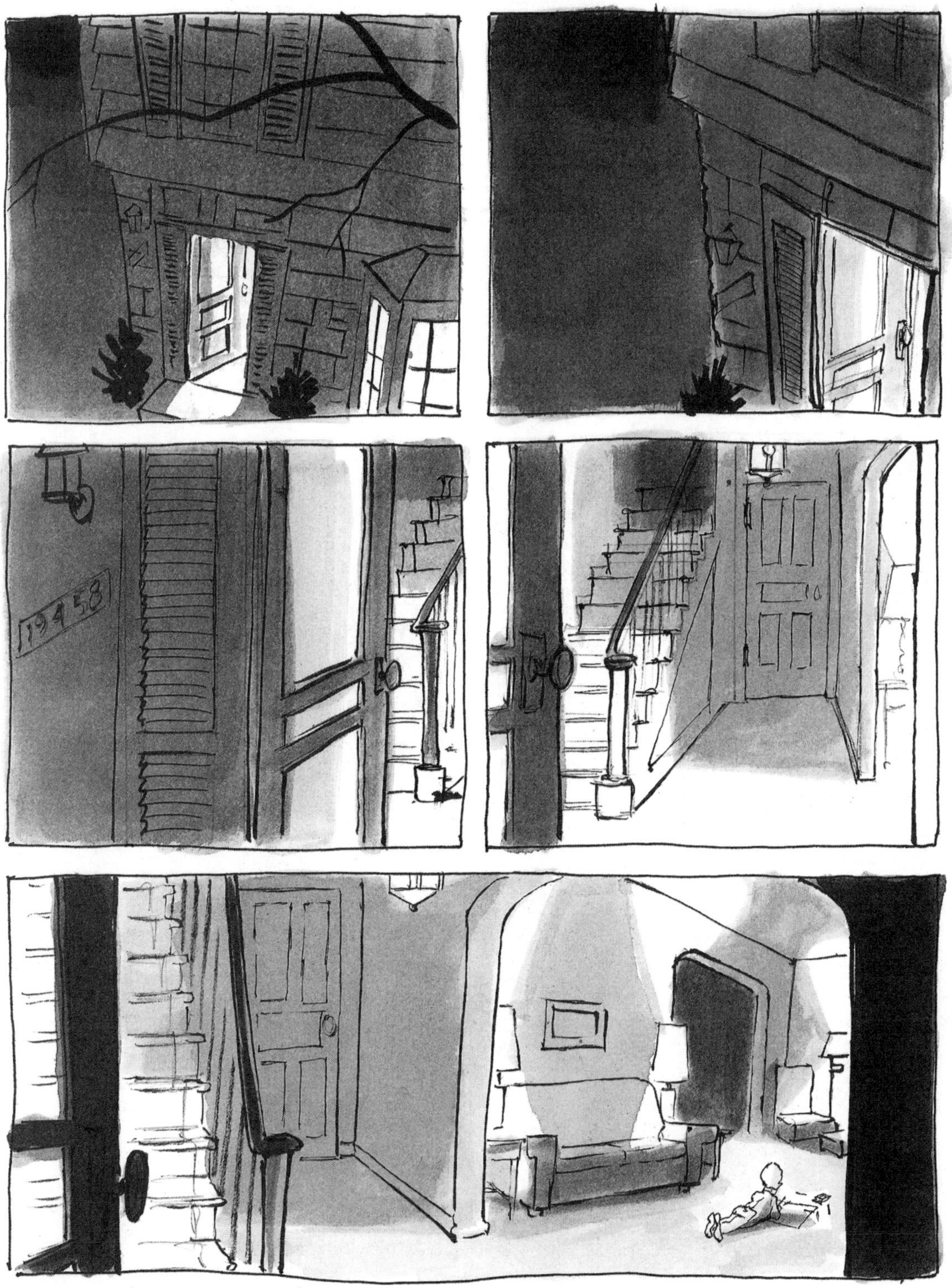
19458

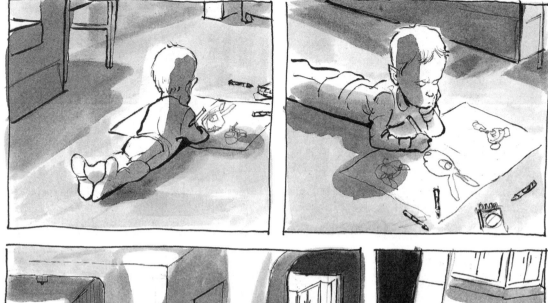

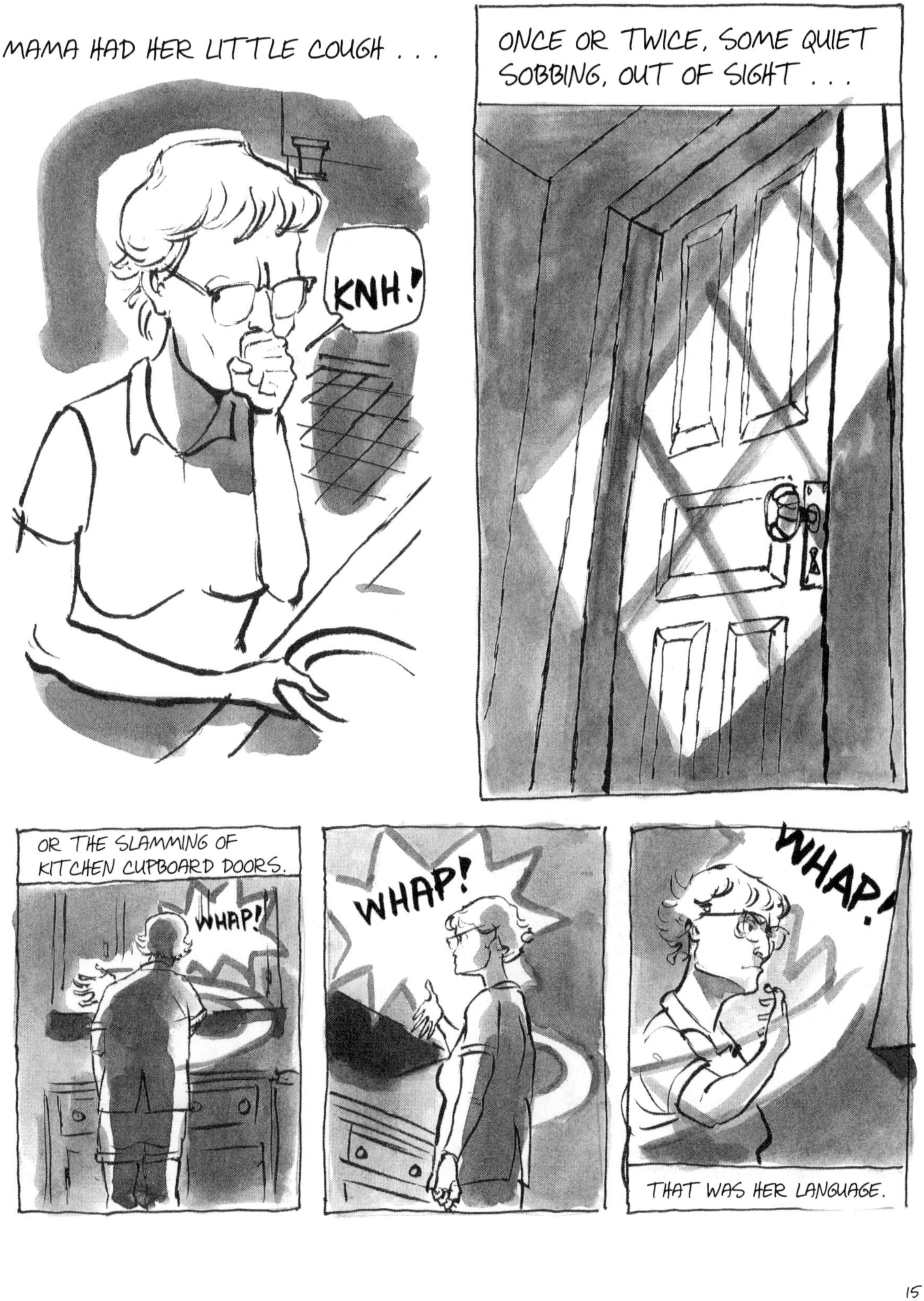
MAMA HAD HER LITTLE COUGH . . .
KNH!
ONCE OR TWICE, SOME QUIET SOBBING, OUT OF SIGHT . . .
OR THE SLAMMING OF KITCHEN CUPBOARD DOORS.
WHAP!
WHAP!
WHAP!
THAT WAS HER LANGUAGE.

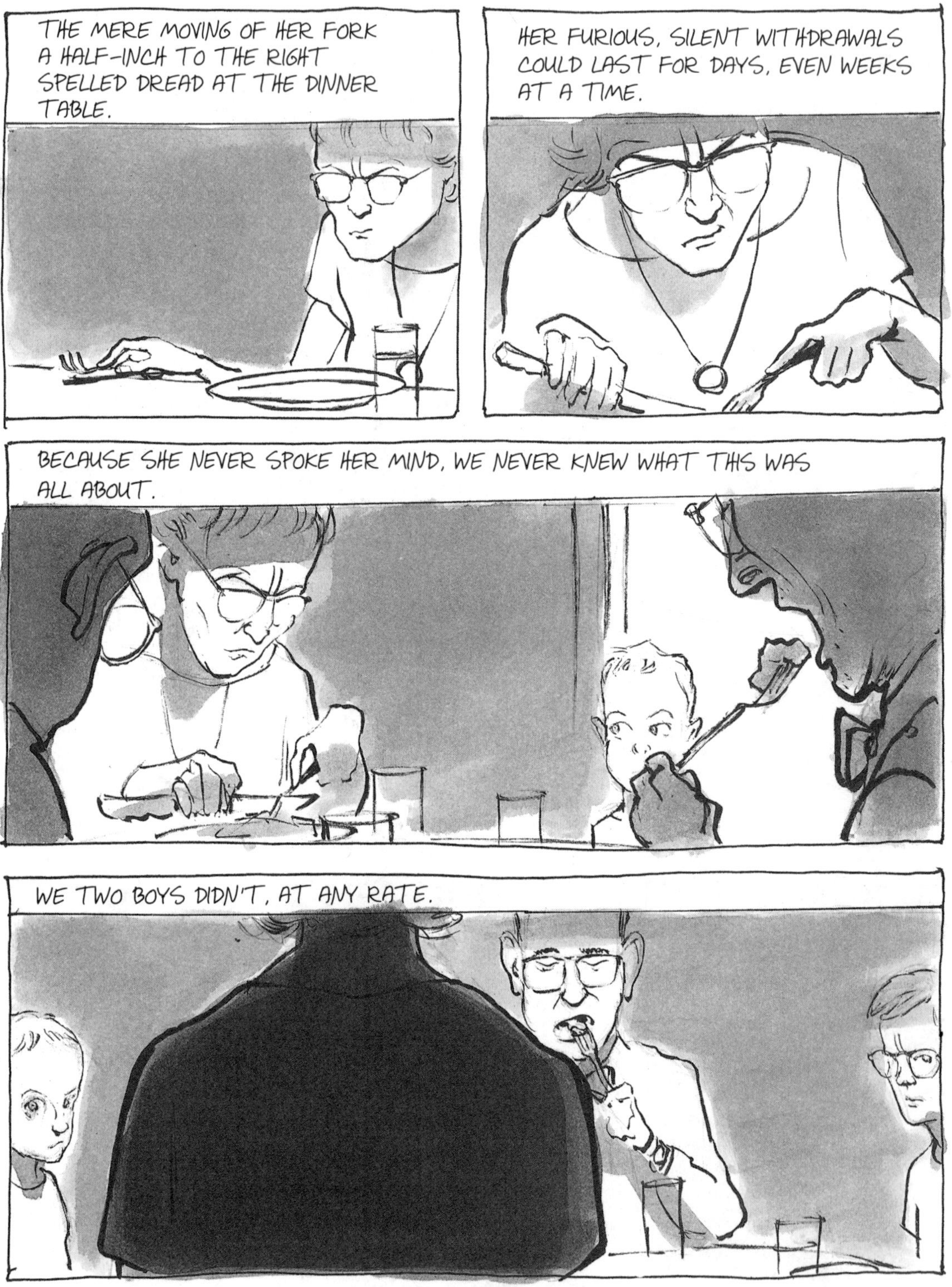
THE MERE MOVING OF HER FORK A HALF-INCH TO THE RIGHT SPELLED DREAD AT THE DINNER TABLE.
HER FURIOUS, SILENT WITHDRAWALS COULD LAST FOR DAYS, EVEN WEEKS AT A TIME.
BECAUSE SHE NEVER SPOKE HER MIND, WE NEVER KNEW WHAT THIS WAS ALL ABOUT.
WE TWO BOYS DIDN'T, AT ANY RATE.

DAD, HOME FROM WORK, WENT DOWN TO THE BASEMENT AND THUMPED A PUNCHING BAG. THAT WAS HIS LANGUAGE.

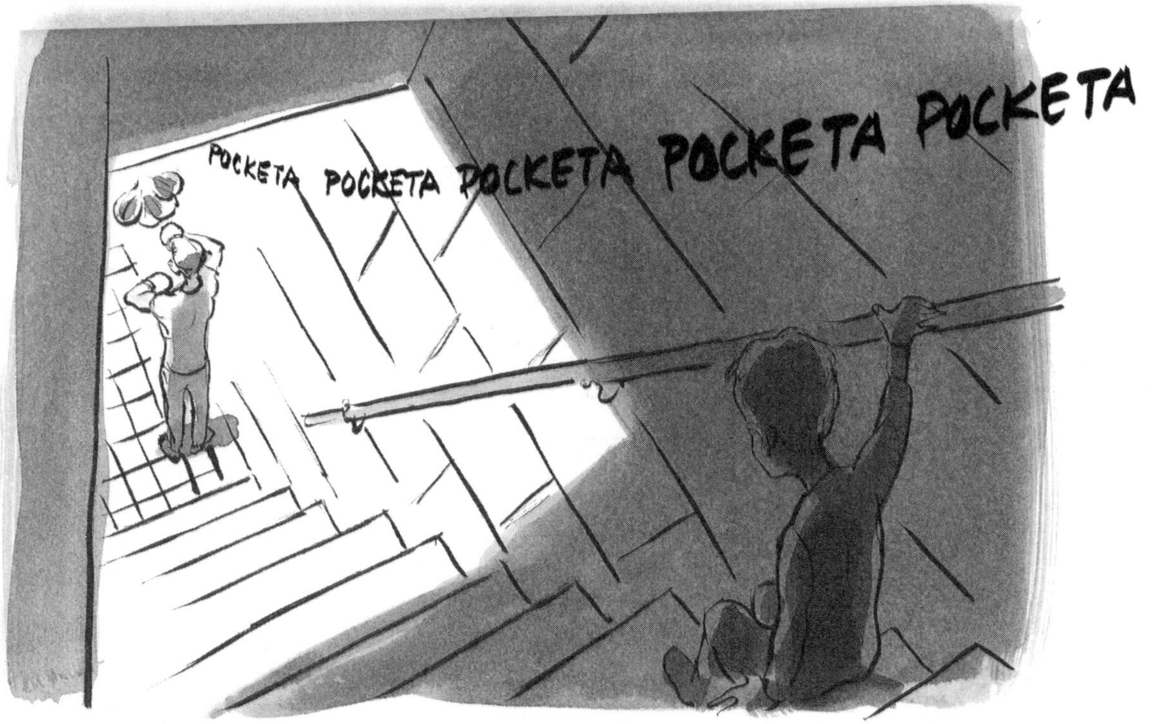
POCKETA POCKETA POCKETA POCKETA POCKETA POCKETA

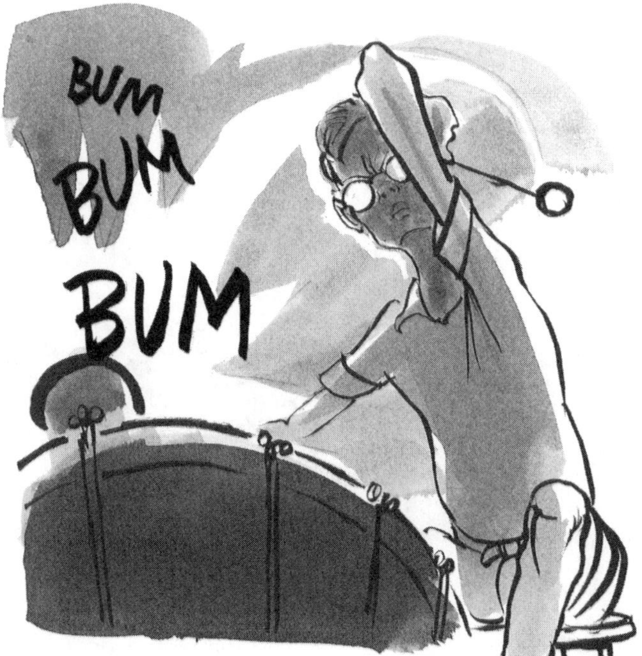
BUM
BUM
BUM

MY BROTHER, TED, BEAT ON HIS DRUM.

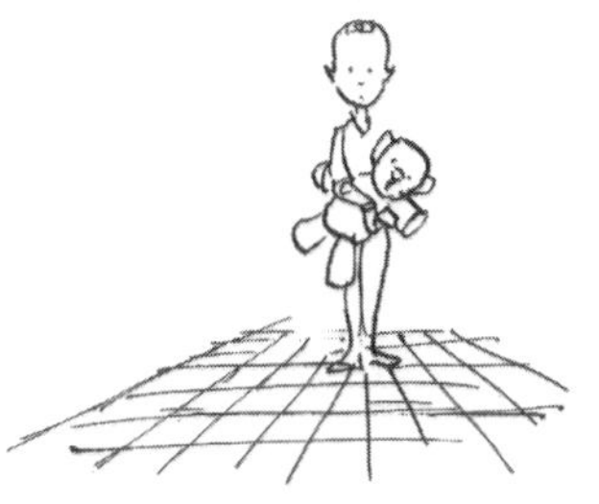

AND I, TOO, HAD LEARNED
A WAY OF EXPRESSING MYSELF
WORDLESSLY . . .

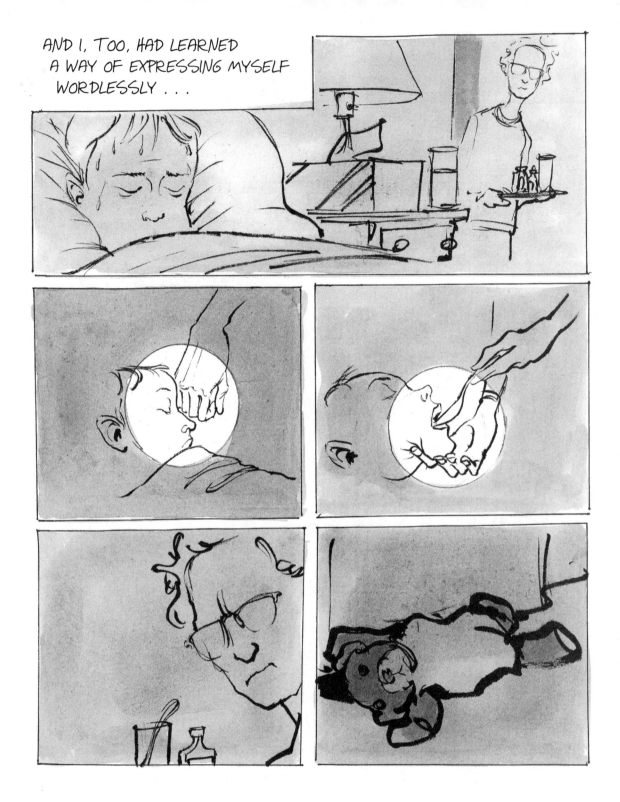

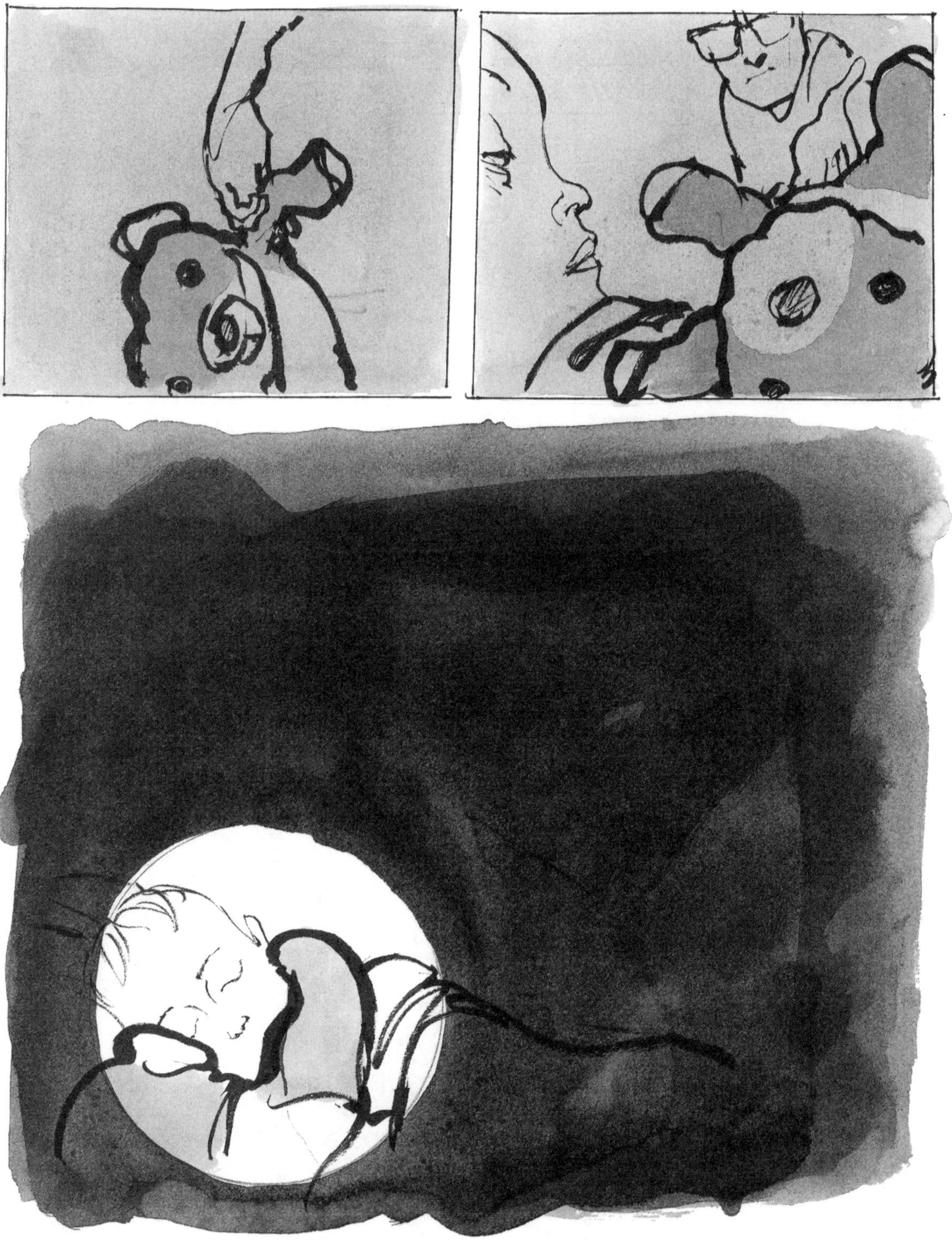

GETTING SICK, THAT WAS MY LANGUAGE.

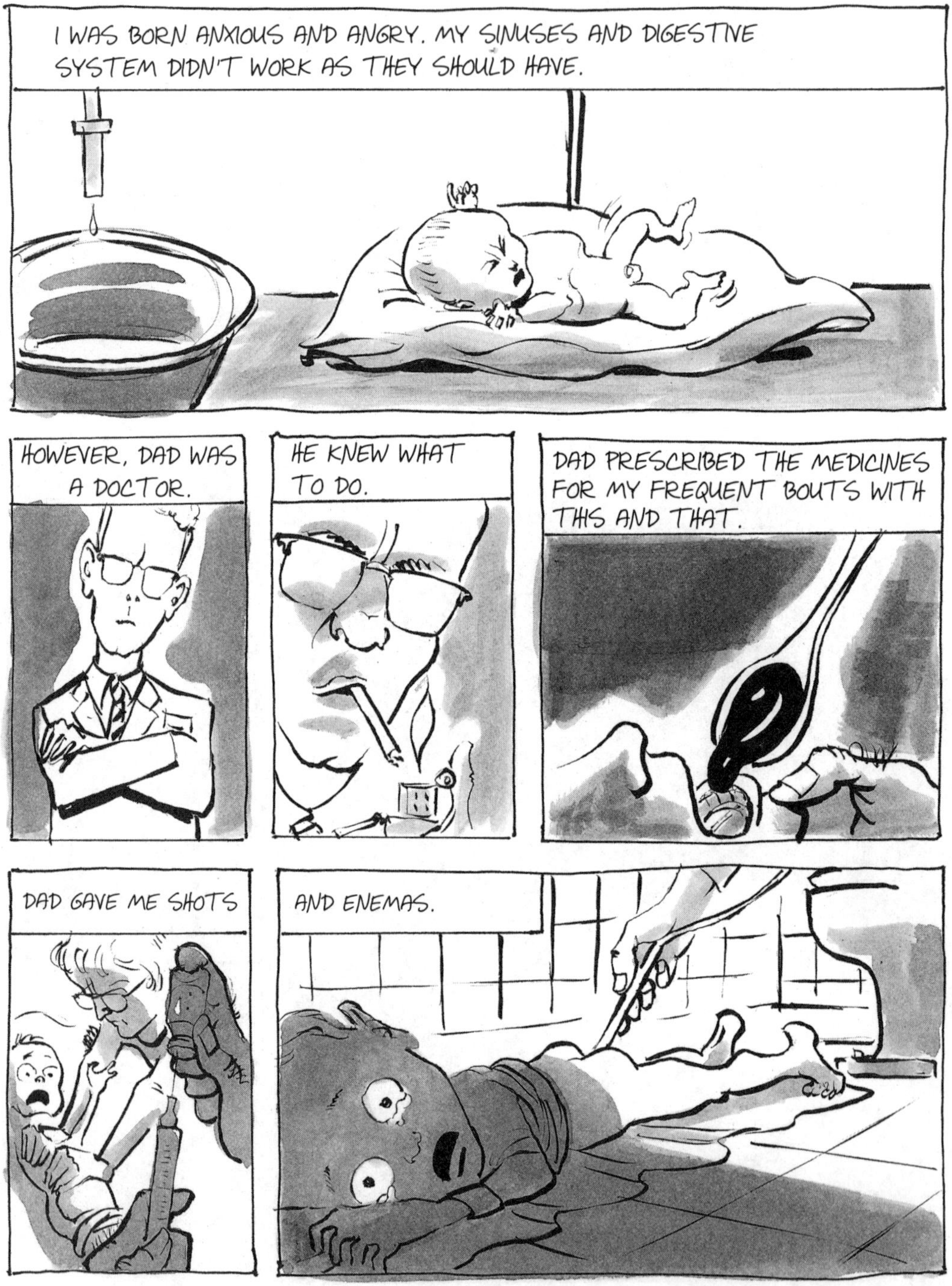
I WAS BORN ANXIOUS AND ANGRY. MY SINUSES AND DIGESTIVE SYSTEM DIDN'T WORK AS THEY SHOULD HAVE.
HOWEVER, DAD WAS A DOCTOR.
HE KNEW WHAT TO DO.
DAD PRESCRIBED THE MEDICINES FOR MY FREQUENT BOUTS WITH THIS AND THAT.
DAD GAVE ME SHOTS
AND ENEMAS.

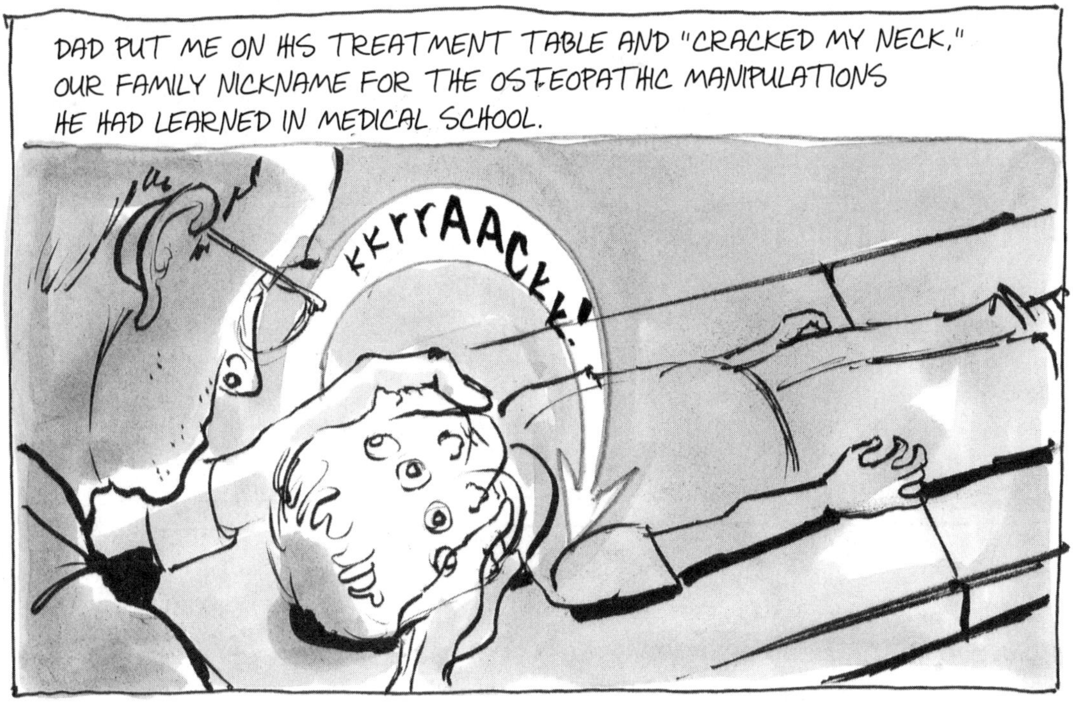
DAD PUT ME ON HIS TREATMENT TABLE AND "CRACKED MY NECK," OUR FAMILY NICKNAME FOR THE OSTEOPATHIC MANIPULATIONS HE HAD LEARNED IN MEDICAL SCHOOL.
KKrrAACKK!

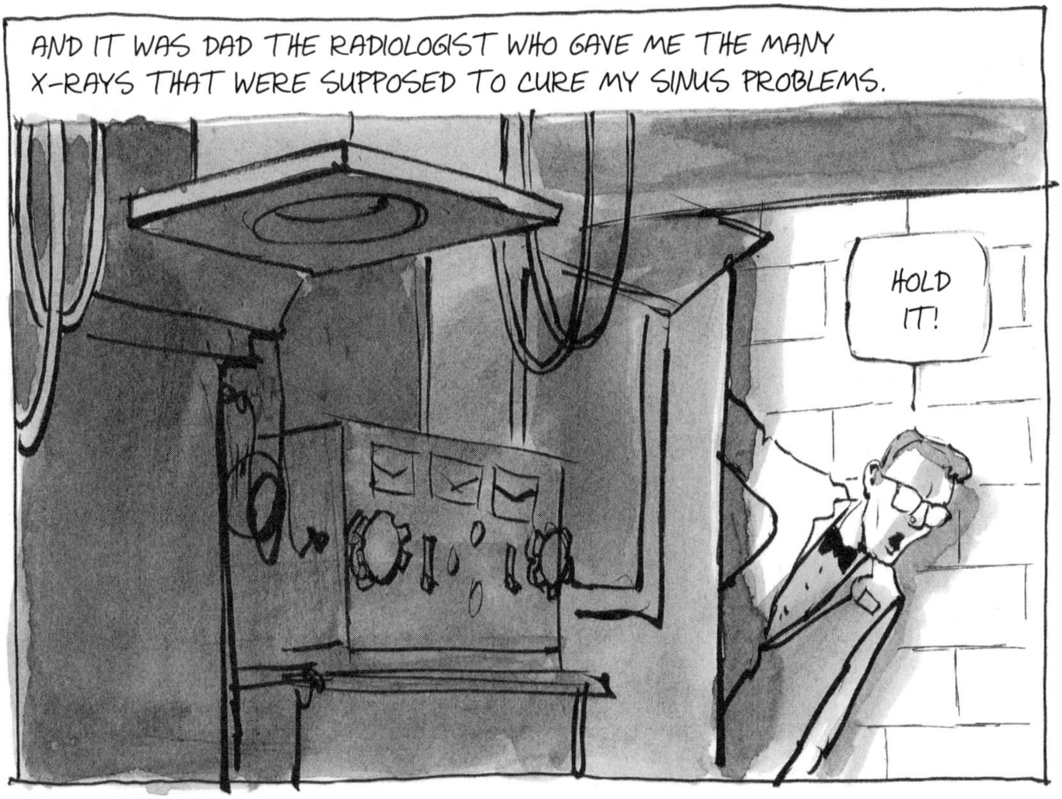
AND IT WAS DAD THE RADIOLOGIST WHO GAVE ME THE MANY X-RAYS THAT WERE SUPPOSED TO CURE MY SINUS PROBLEMS.
HOLD IT!

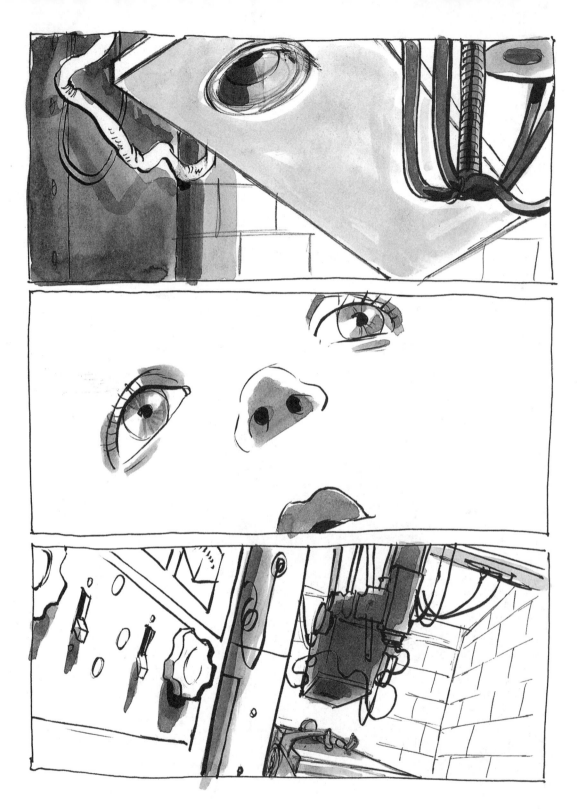

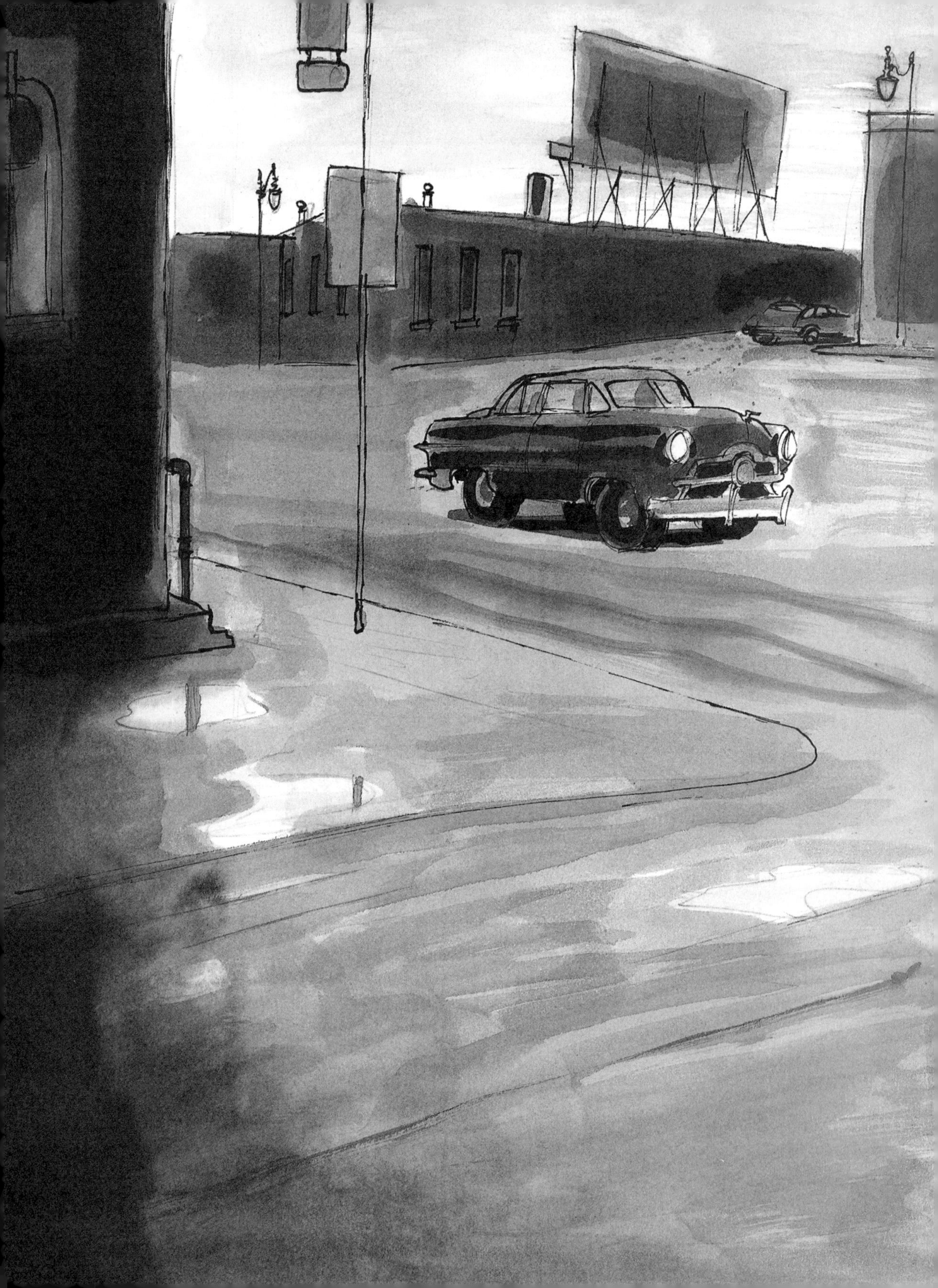

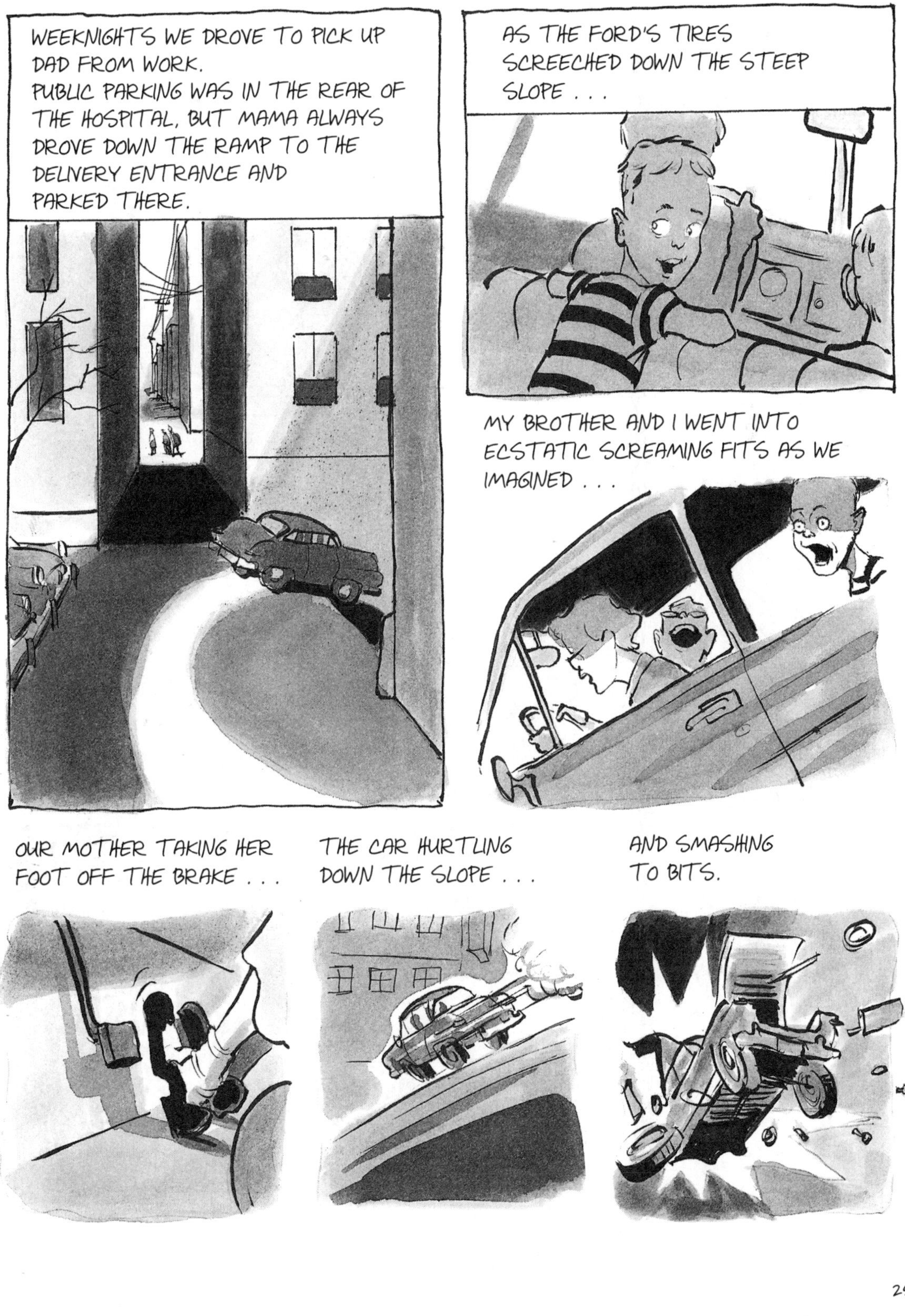
WEEKNIGHTS WE DROVE TO PICK UP DAD FROM WORK.
PUBLIC PARKING WAS IN THE REAR OF THE HOSPITAL, BUT MAMA ALWAYS DROVE DOWN THE RAMP TO THE DELIVERY ENTRANCE AND PARKED THERE.
AS THE FORD'S TIRES SCREECHED DOWN THE STEEP SLOPE . . .
MY BROTHER AND I WENT INTO ECSTATIC SCREAMING FITS AS WE IMAGINED . . .
OUR MOTHER TAKING HER FOOT OFF THE BRAKE . . .
THE CAR HURTLING DOWN THE SLOPE . . .
AND SMASHING TO BITS.

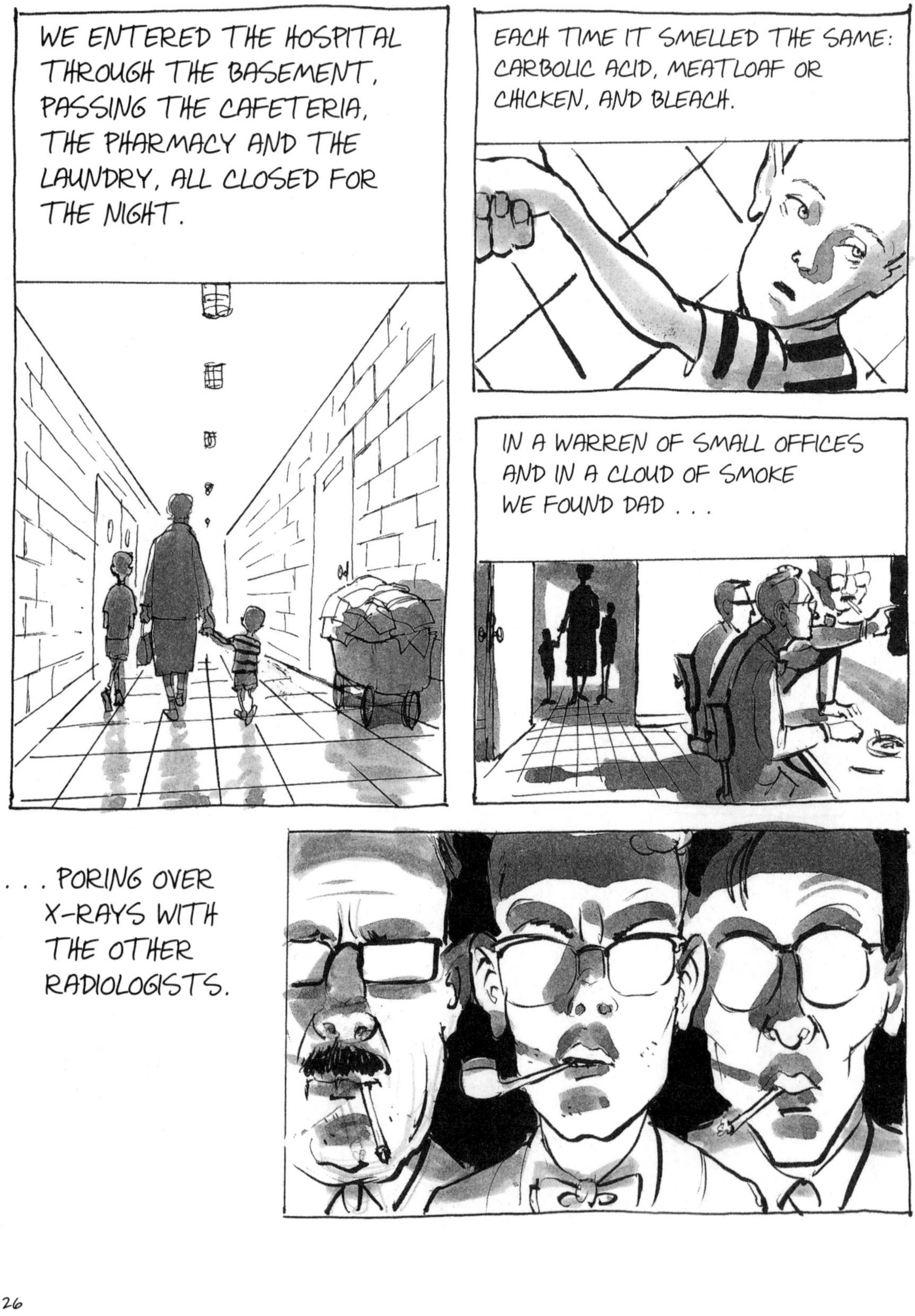
WE ENTERED THE HOSPITAL THROUGH THE BASEMENT, PASSING THE CAFETERIA, THE PHARMACY AND THE LAUNDRY, ALL CLOSED FOR THE NIGHT.
EACH TIME IT SMELLED THE SAME: CARBOLIC ACID, MEATLOAF OR CHICKEN, AND BLEACH.
IN A WARREN OF SMALL OFFICES AND IN A CLOUD OF SMOKE WE FOUND DAD . . .
. . . PORING OVER X-RAYS WITH THE OTHER RADIOLOGISTS.

TO ME, DAD AND HIS COLLEAGUES SEEMED LIKE THE HEROIC MEN FEATURED IN THE ADS IN **LIFE** MAGAZINE, MARCHING BRAVELY INTO THE BRIGHT AND SHINING FUTURE.

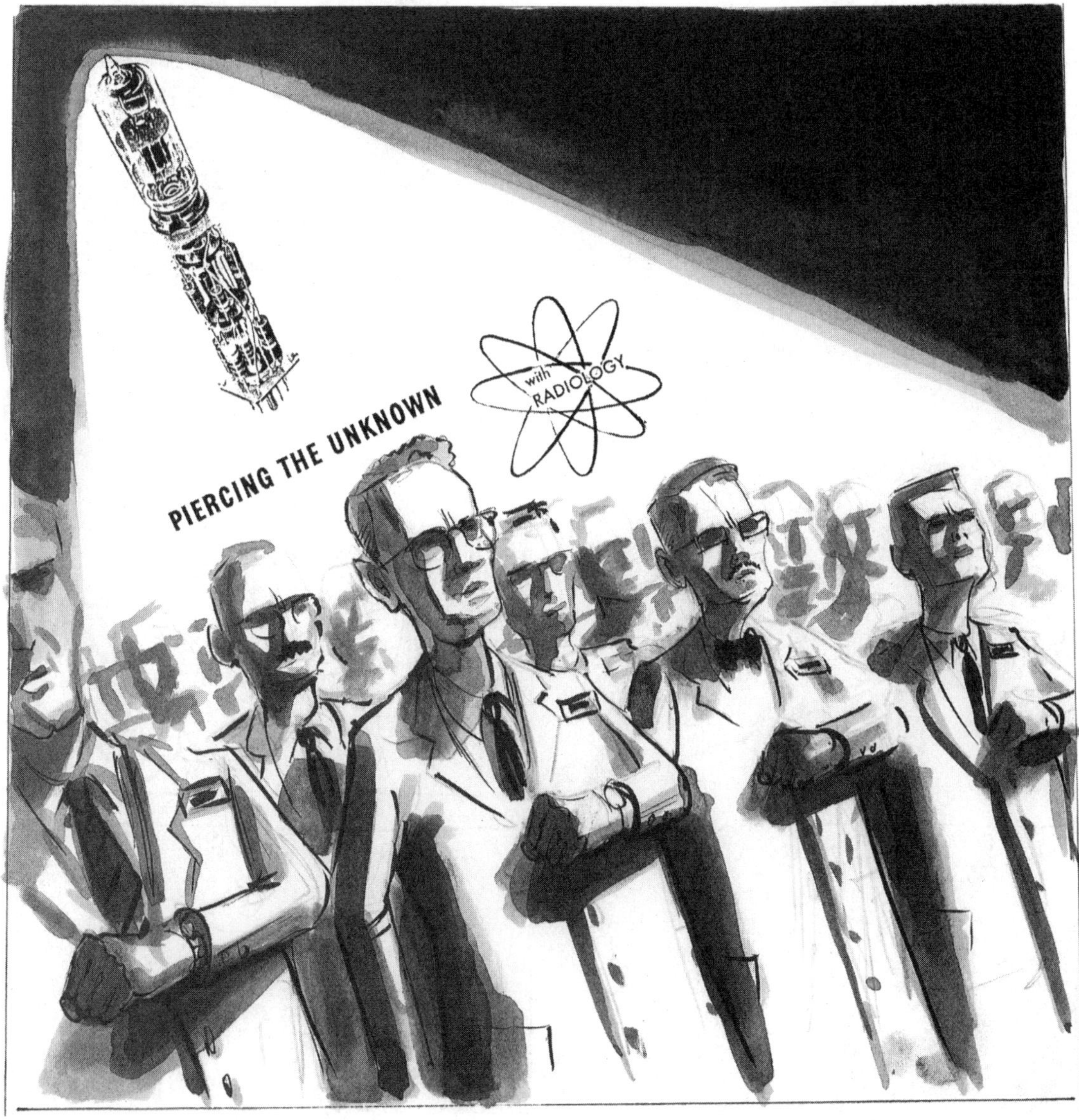
with
RADIOLOGY
PIERCING THE UNKNOWN

THEY WERE SOLDIERS OF SCIENCE, AND THEIR WEAPON WAS THE X-RAY. X-RAYS COULD SEE THROUGH CLOTHES, SKIN, EVEN METAL. THEY WERE MIRACULOUS WONDER RAYS THAT WOULD CURE ANYTHING.

MY BROTHER AND I LIKED
SEEING THE X-RAYS OF
LITTLE KIDS' STOMACHS, THE
STUFF THEY HAD SWALLOWED LIKE
KEYS AND POP BEADS . . .

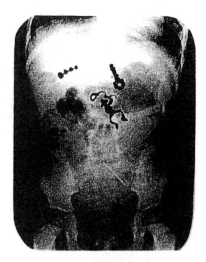

. . . AND CRACKER-JACK PRIZES.

I'LL BE A WHILE,
BETTY, BOYS . . .

TAKE A SEAT IN
MY OFFICE.

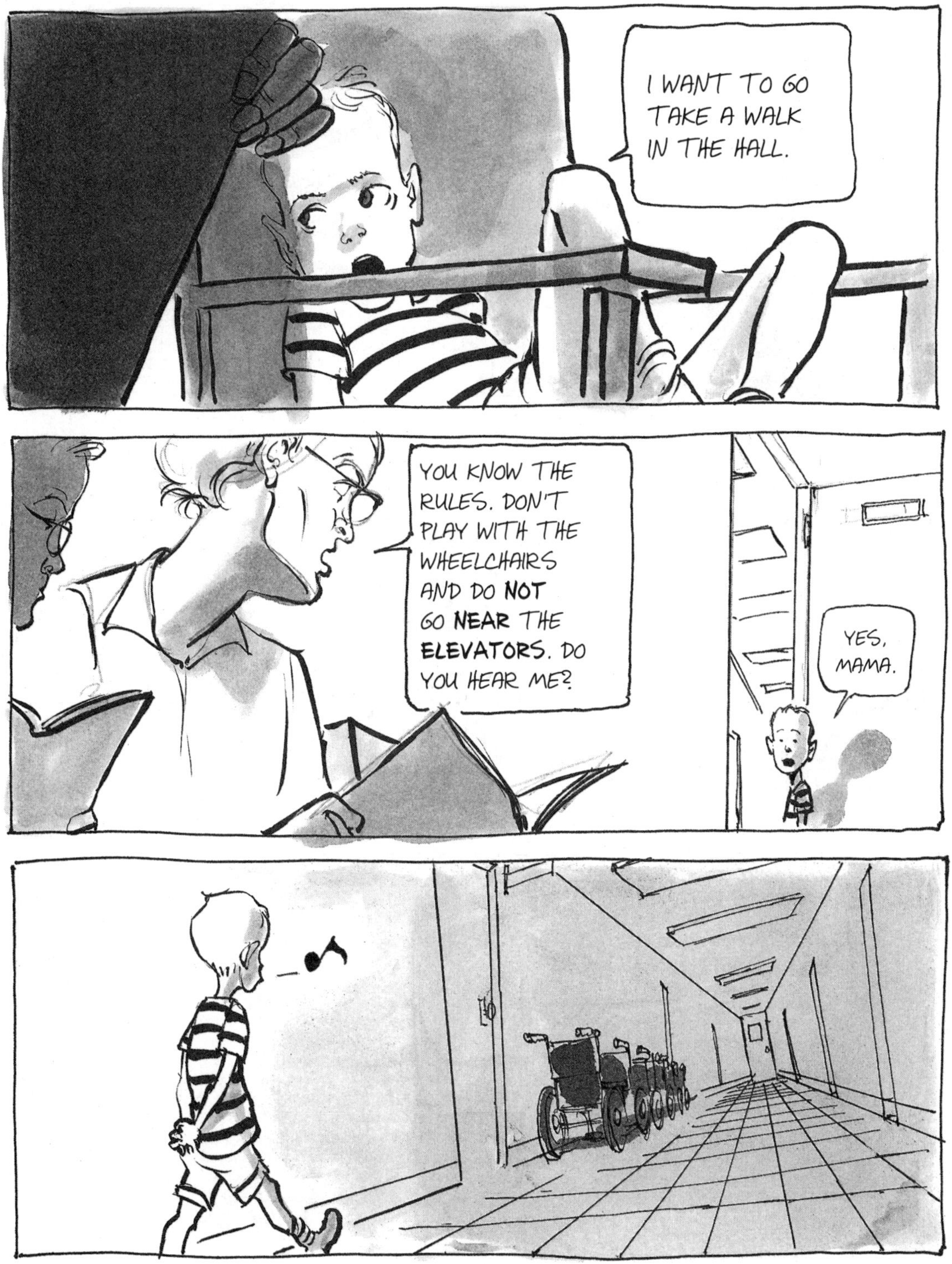
I WANT TO GO TAKE A WALK IN THE HALL.
YOU KNOW THE RULES. DON'T PLAY WITH THE WHEELCHAIRS AND DO **NOT** GO **NEAR** THE **ELEVATORS**. DO YOU HEAR ME?
YES, MAMA.

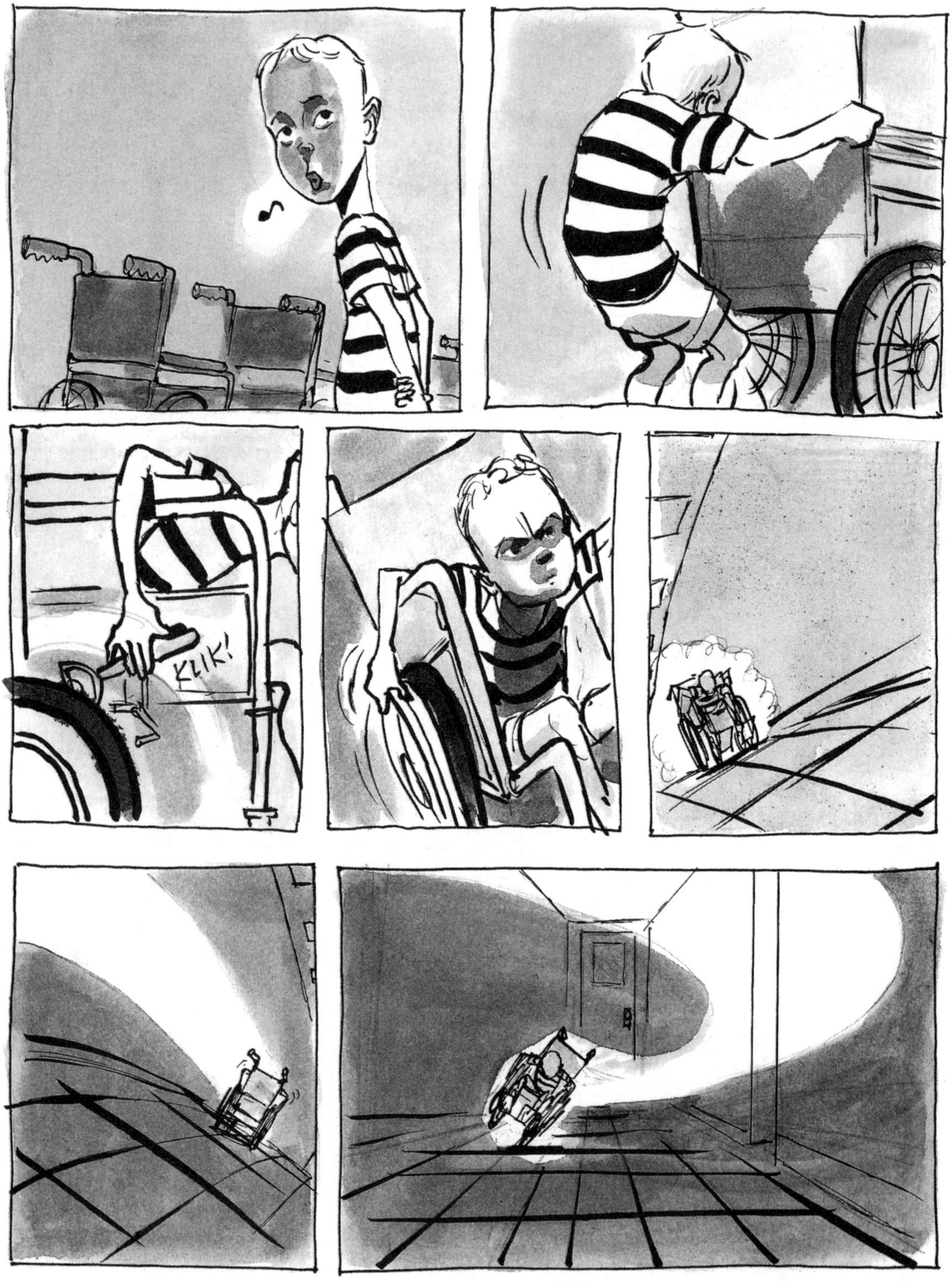
KLIK!

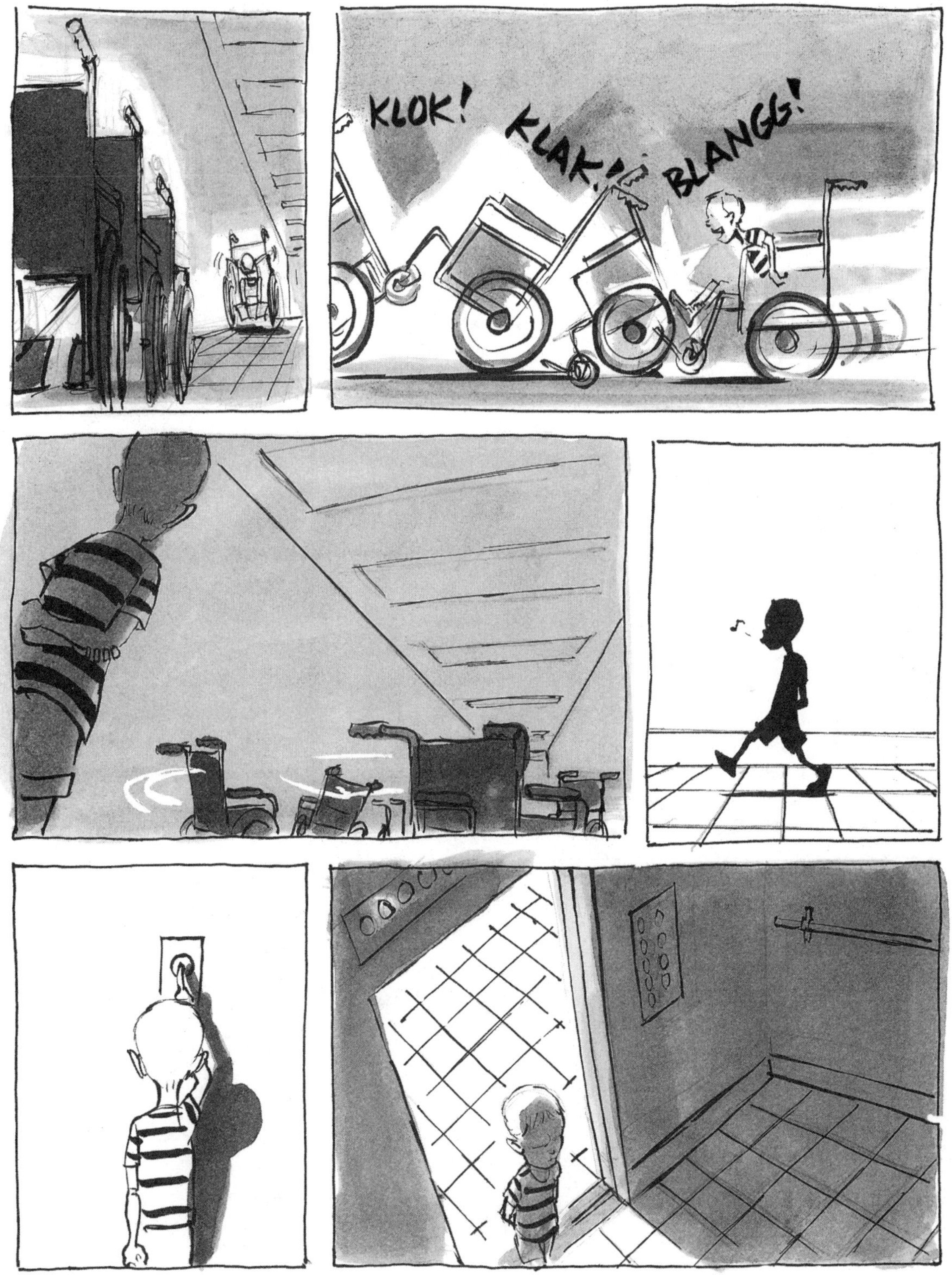
KLOK!
KLAK!
BLANGG!

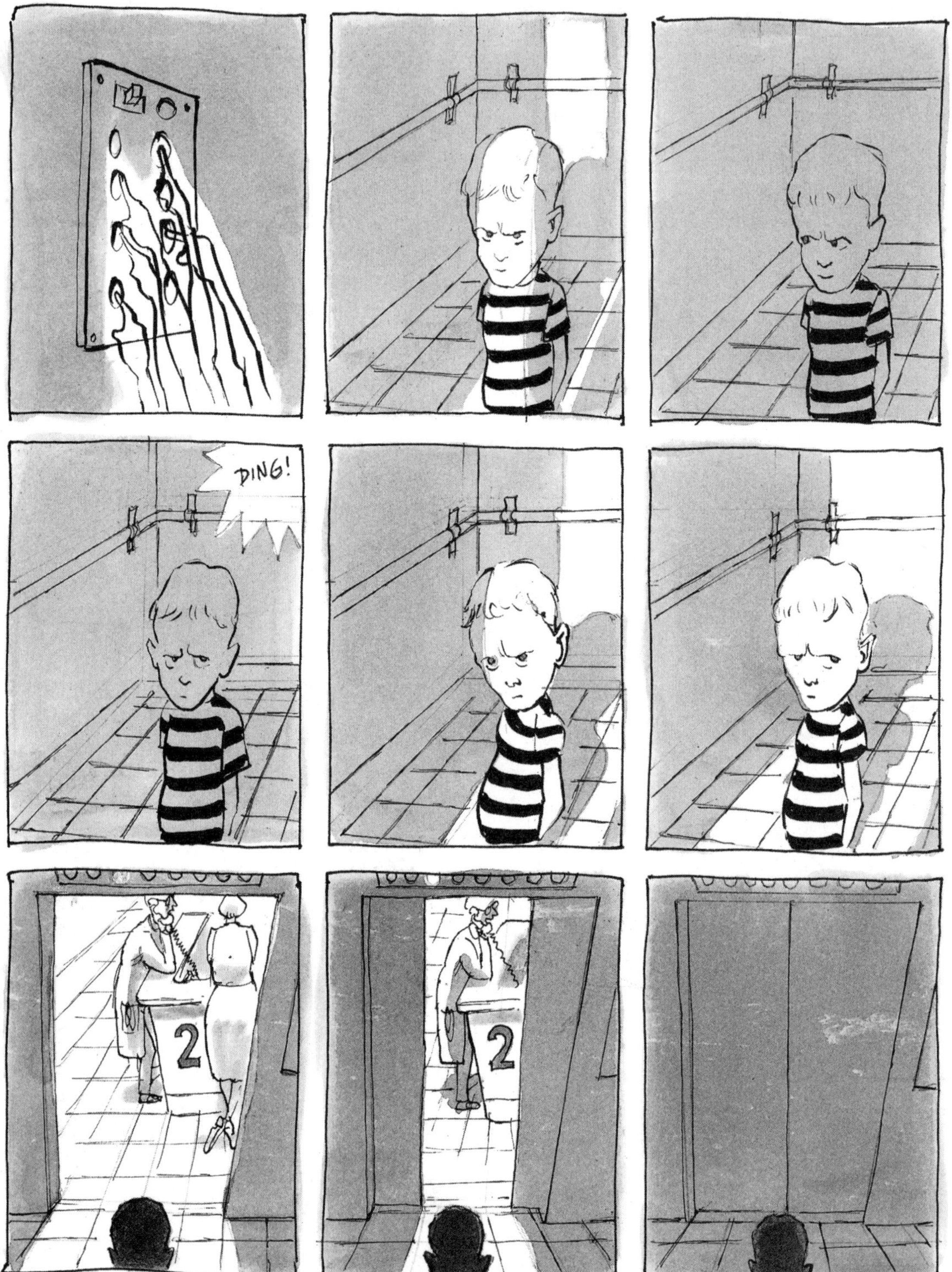
DING!
2
2

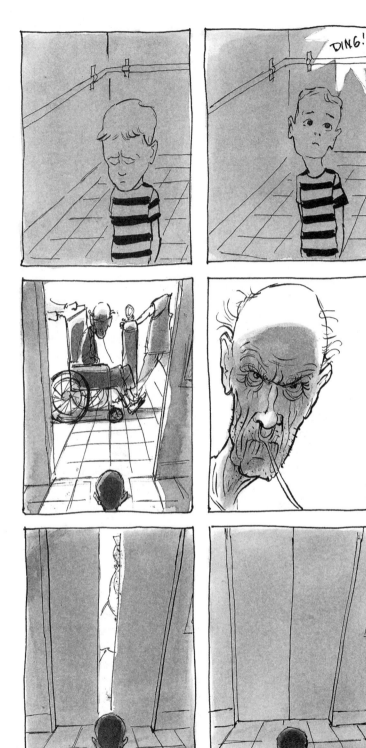

DING!
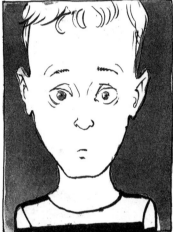

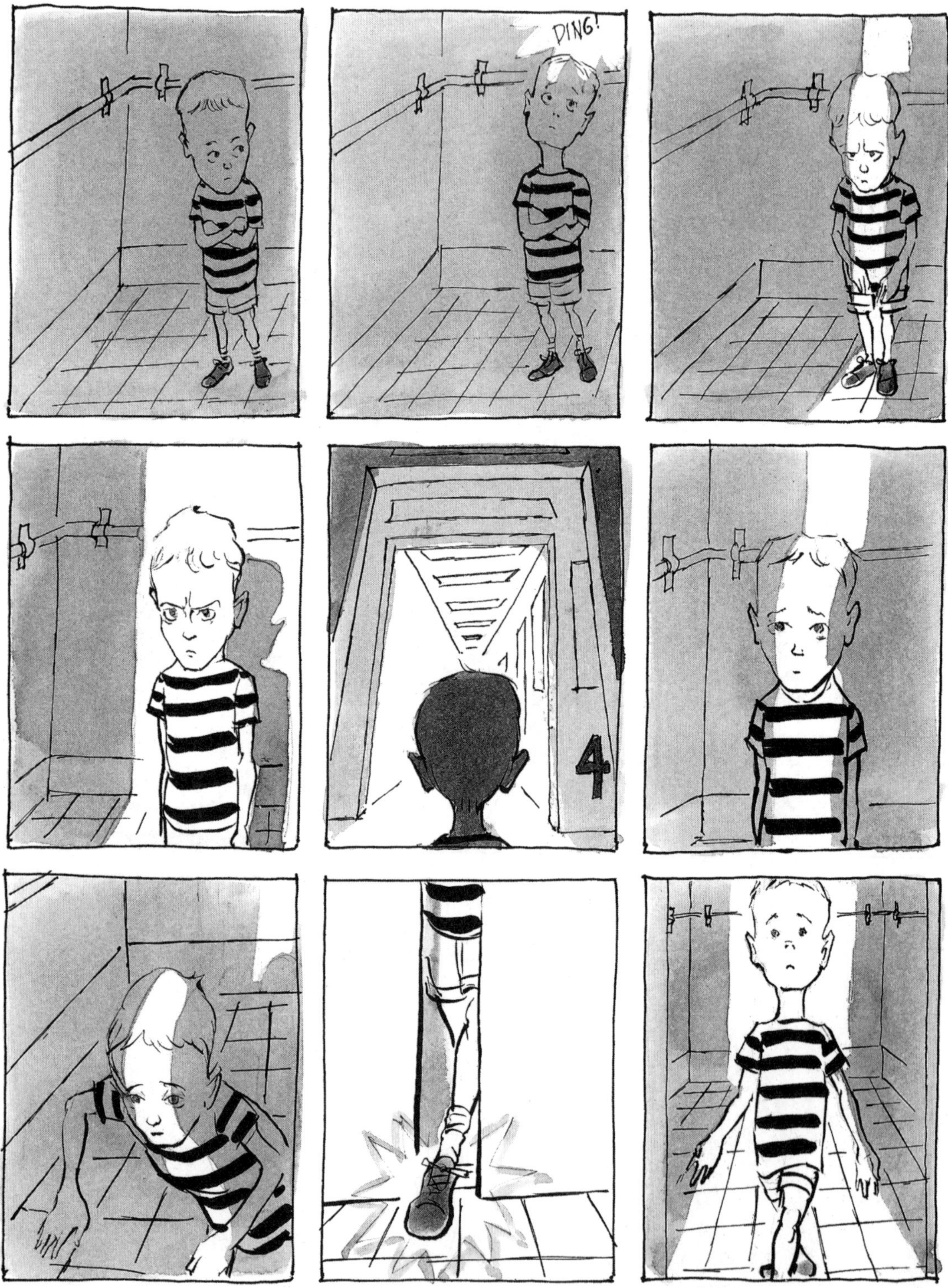
DING!

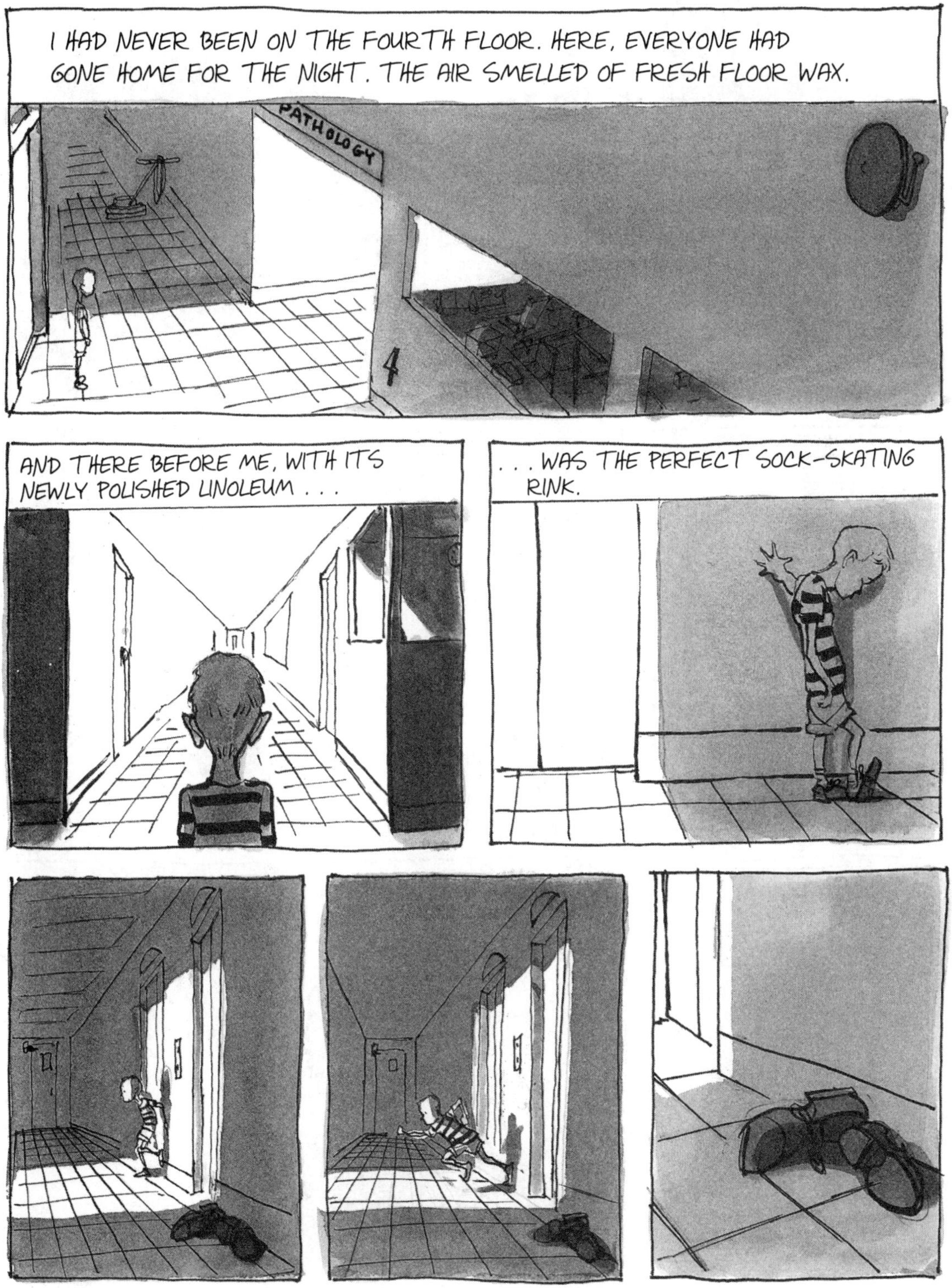
I HAD NEVER BEEN ON THE FOURTH FLOOR. HERE, EVERYONE HAD GONE HOME FOR THE NIGHT. THE AIR SMELLED OF FRESH FLOOR WAX.
PATHOLOGY
4
AND THERE BEFORE ME, WITH ITS NEWLY POLISHED LINOLEUM . . .
. . . WAS THE PERFECT SOCK-SKATING RINK.

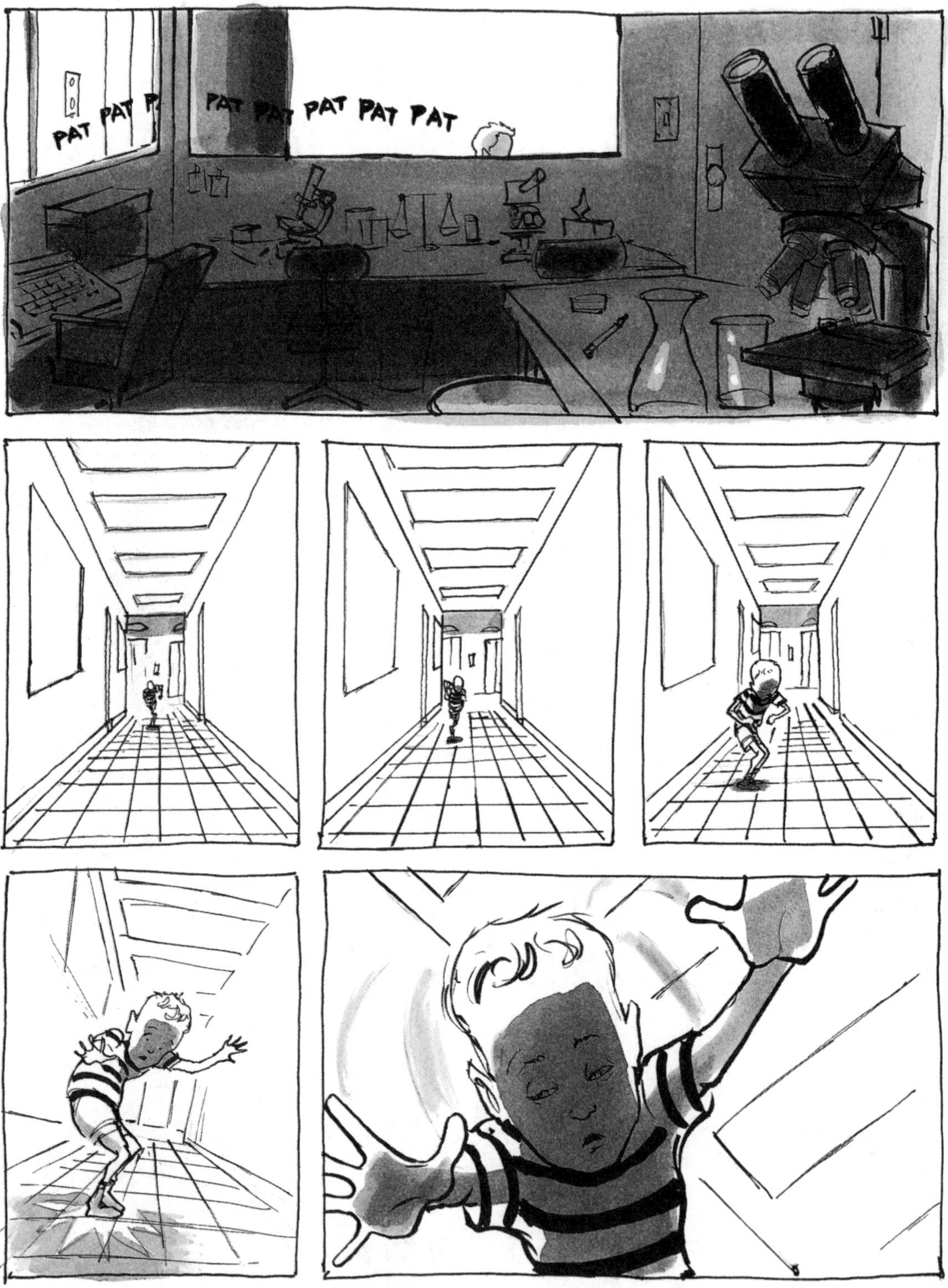
PAT PAT PA
PAT PAT PAT PAT PAT

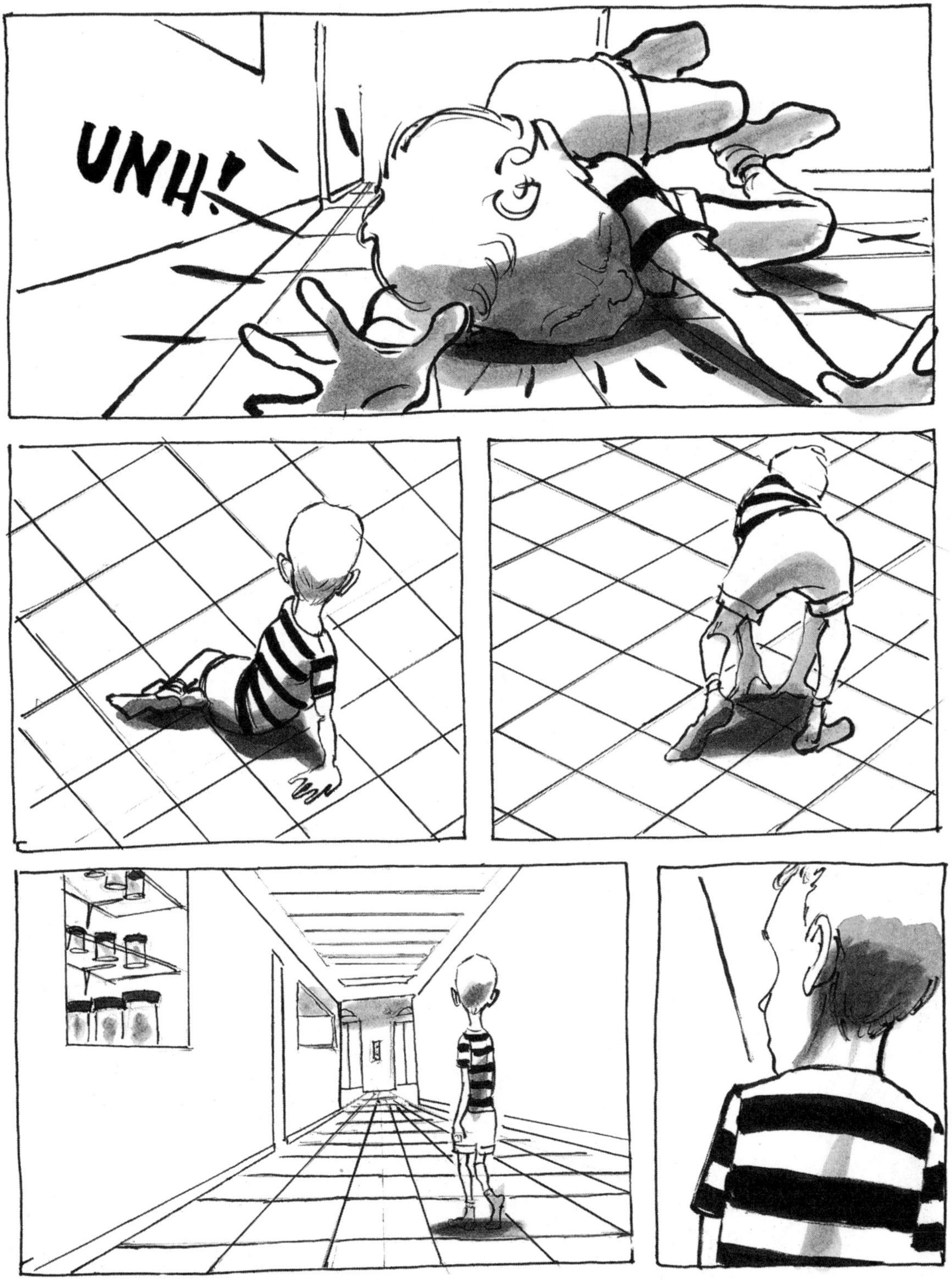
UNH!

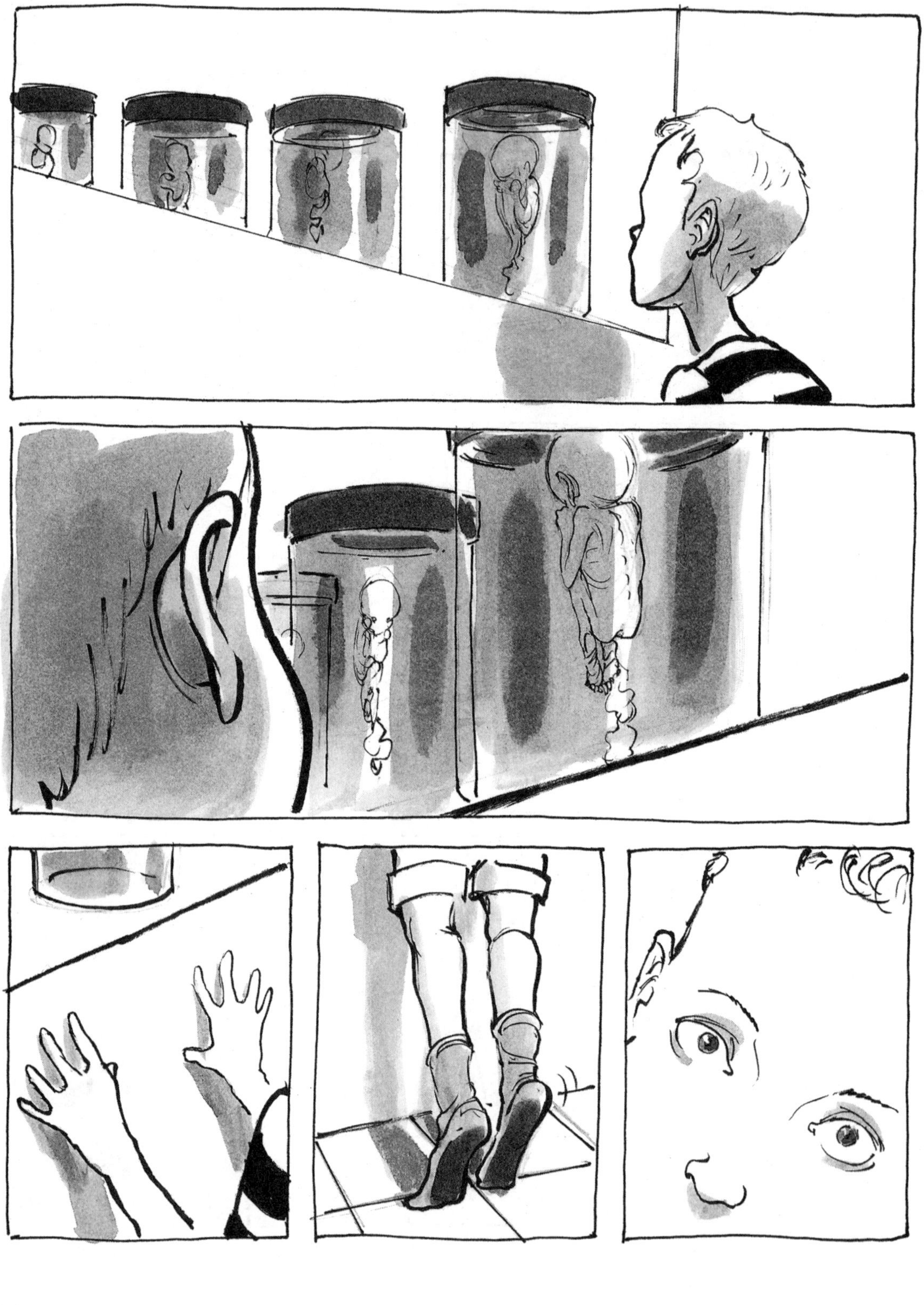

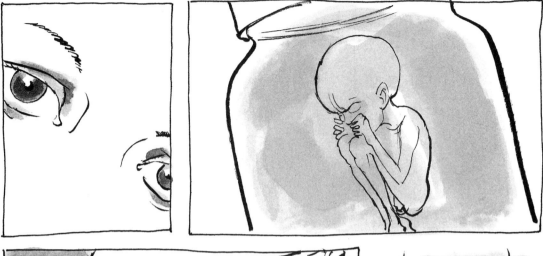

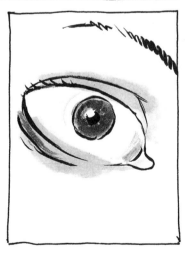

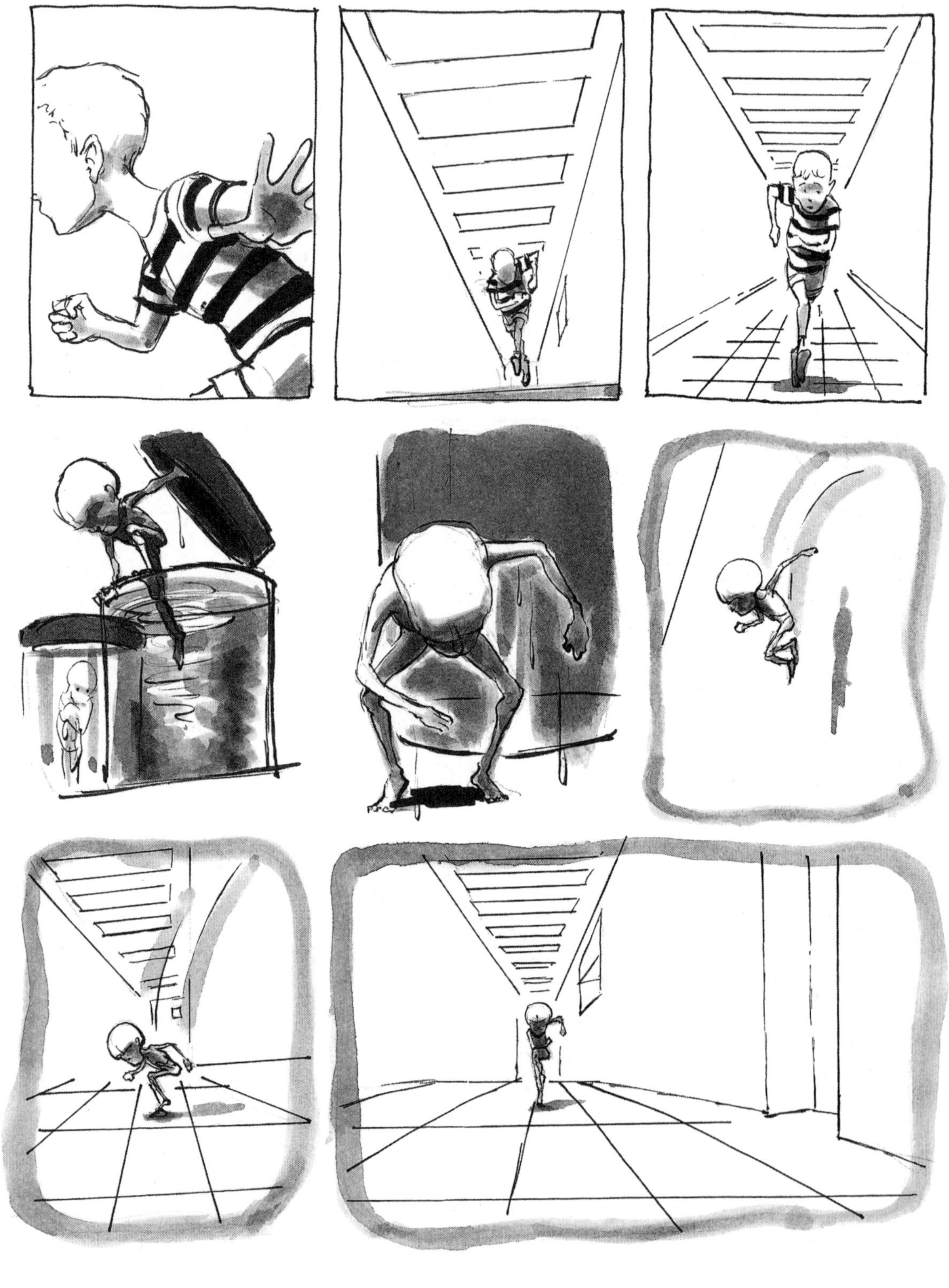

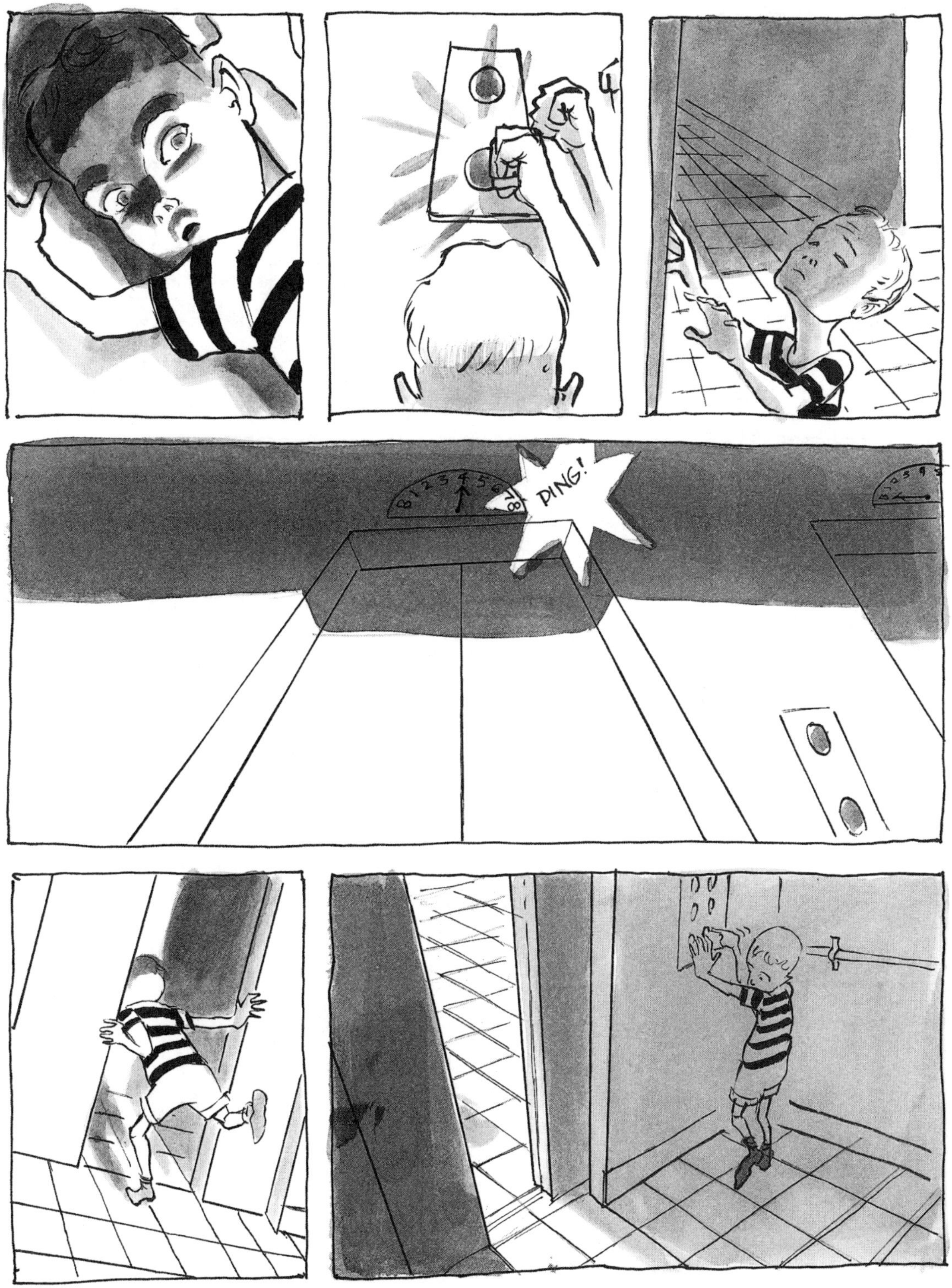
DING!

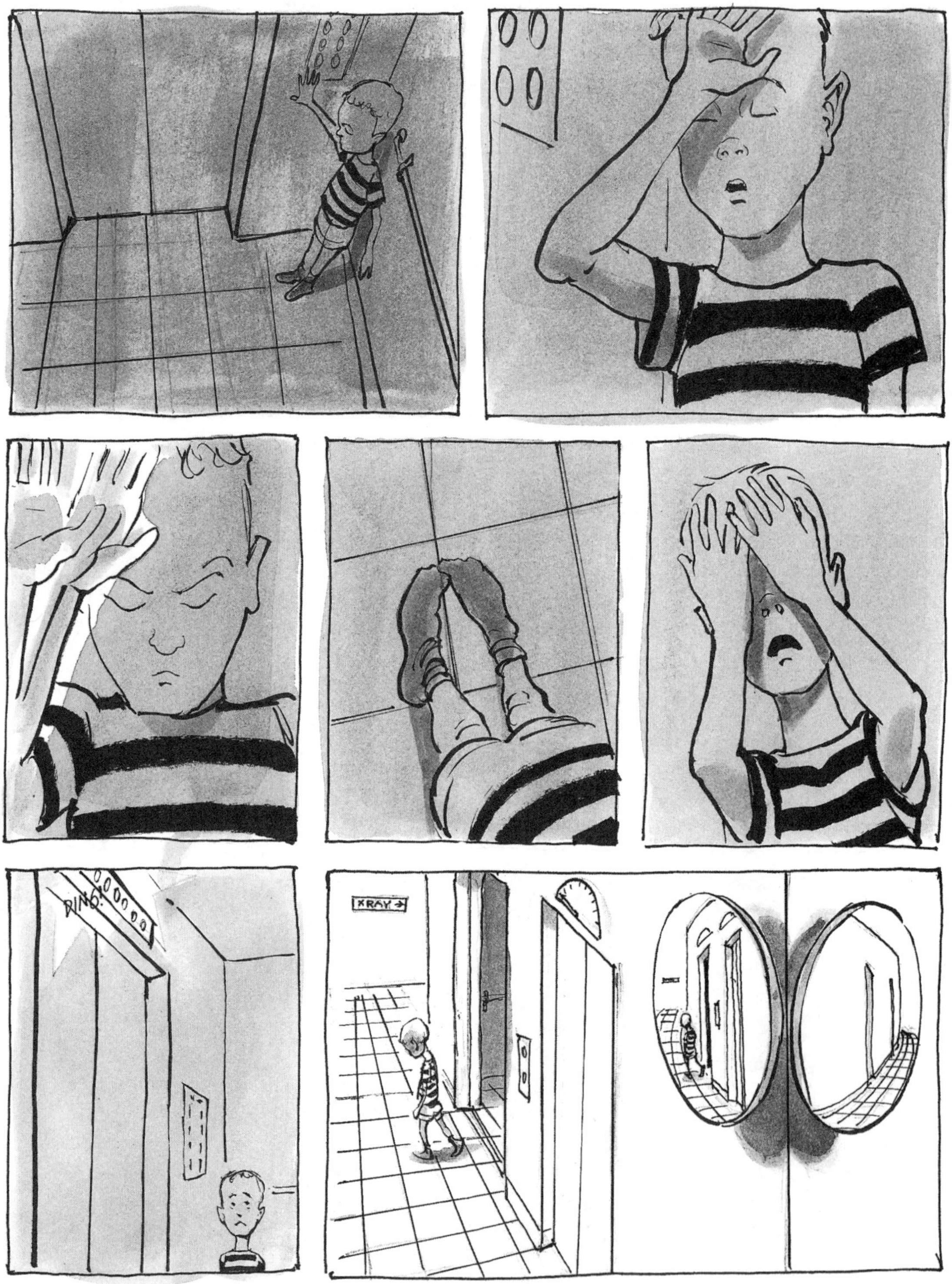
DING!
X RAY →

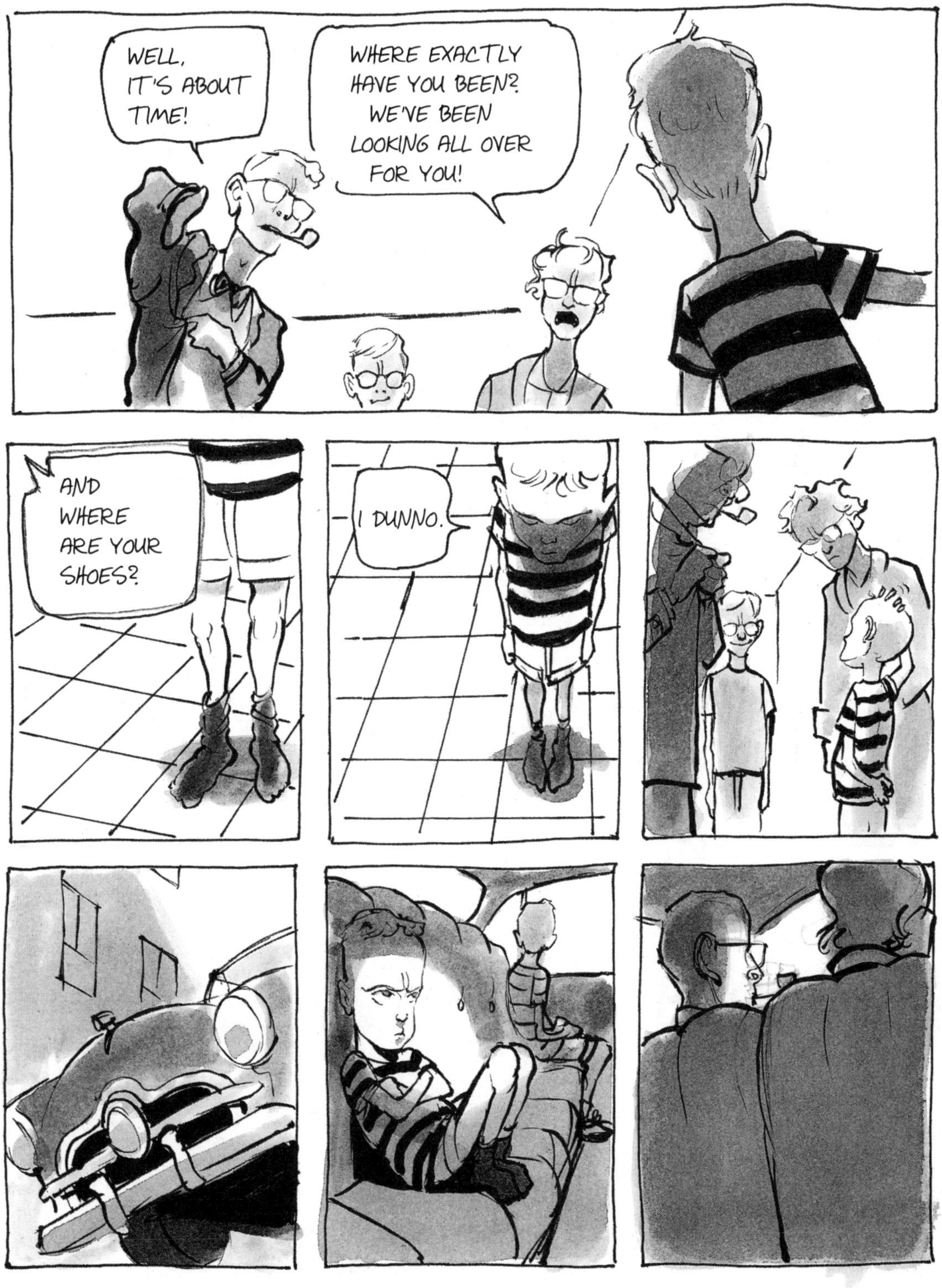
WELL, IT'S ABOUT TIME!
WHERE EXACTLY HAVE YOU BEEN? WE'VE BEEN LOOKING ALL OVER FOR YOU!
AND WHERE ARE YOUR SHOES?
I DUNNO.

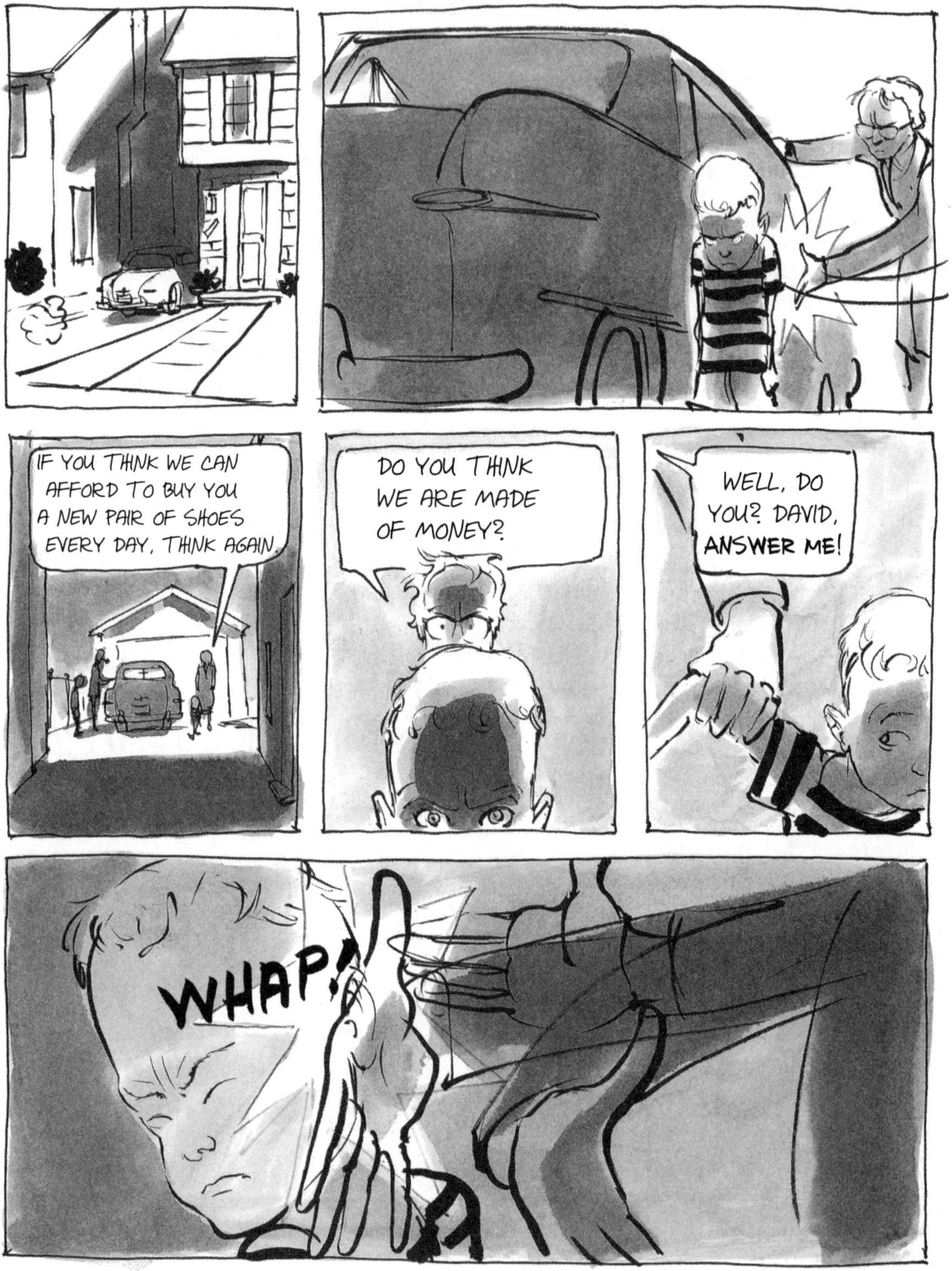
IF YOU THINK WE CAN AFFORD TO BUY YOU A NEW PAIR OF SHOES EVERY DAY, THINK AGAIN.
DO YOU THINK WE ARE MADE OF MONEY?
WELL, DO YOU? DAVID, ANSWER ME!
WHAP!

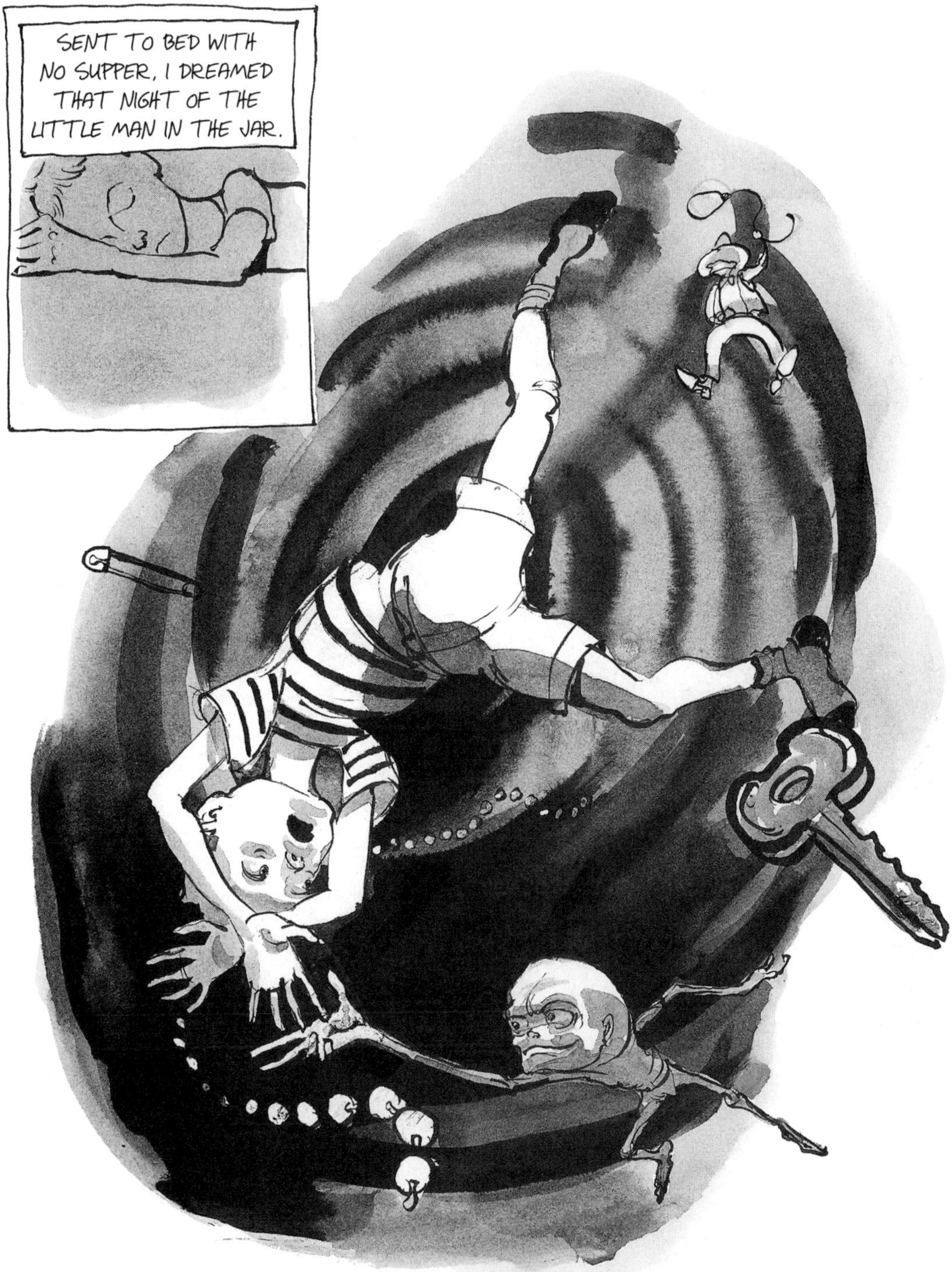
SENT TO BED WITH NO SUPPER, I DREAMED THAT NIGHT OF THE LITTLE MAN IN THE JAR.

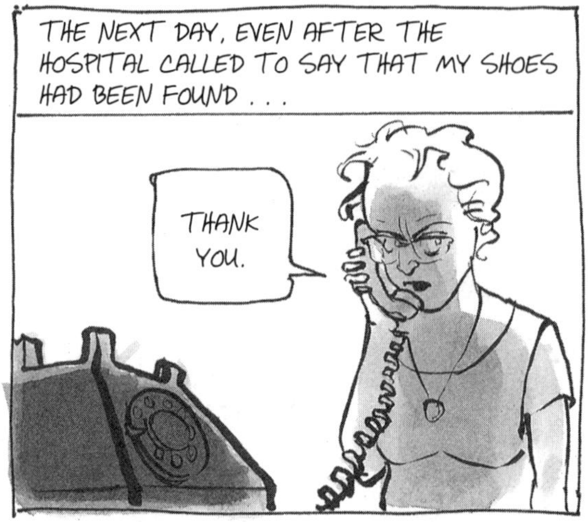
THE NEXT DAY, EVEN AFTER THE HOSPITAL CALLED TO SAY THAT MY SHOES HAD BEEN FOUND . . .
THANK YOU.

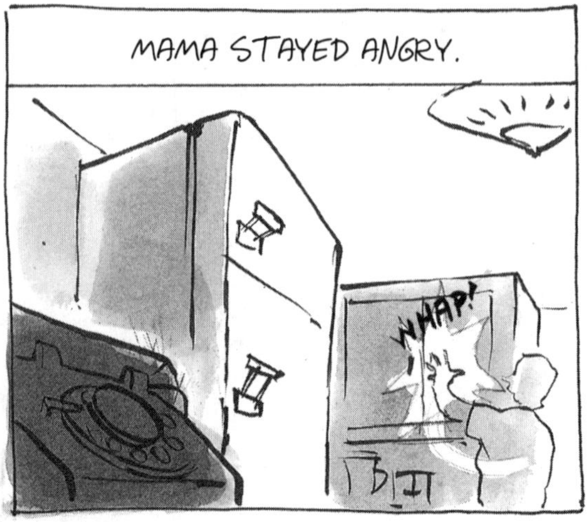
MAMA STAYED ANGRY.
WHAP!

HER SILENT FURY WAS LIKE A BLACK TIDAL WAVE.
EITHER YOU GET OUT OF THE WAY, OR . . .

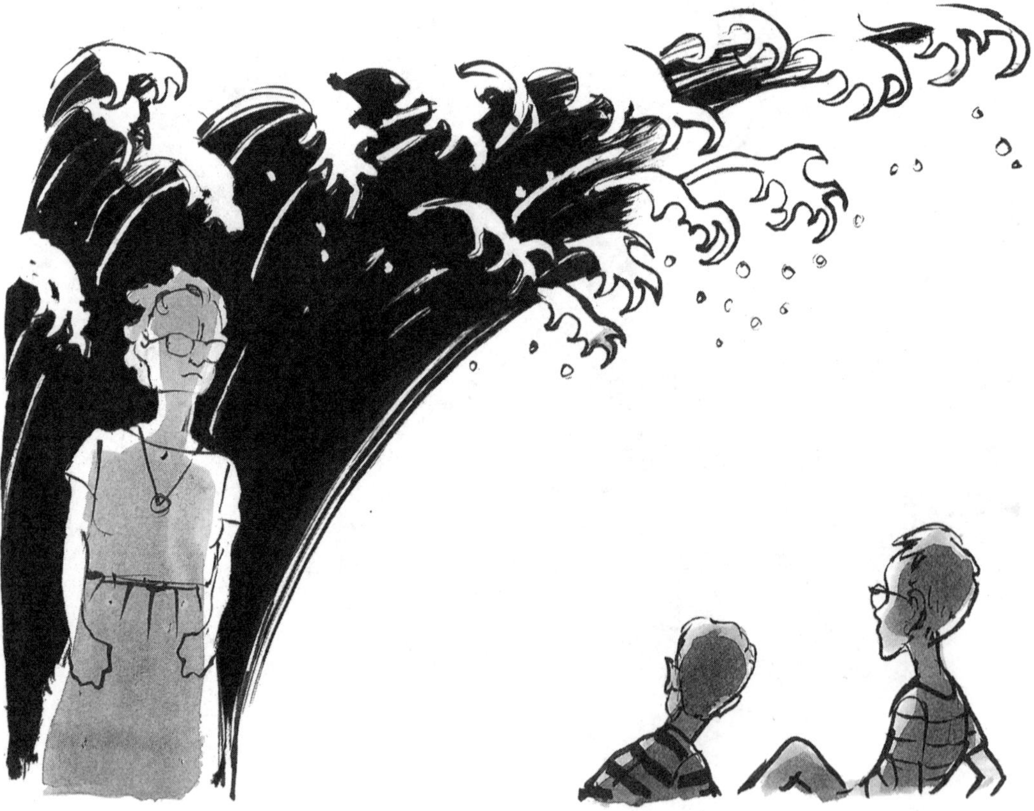

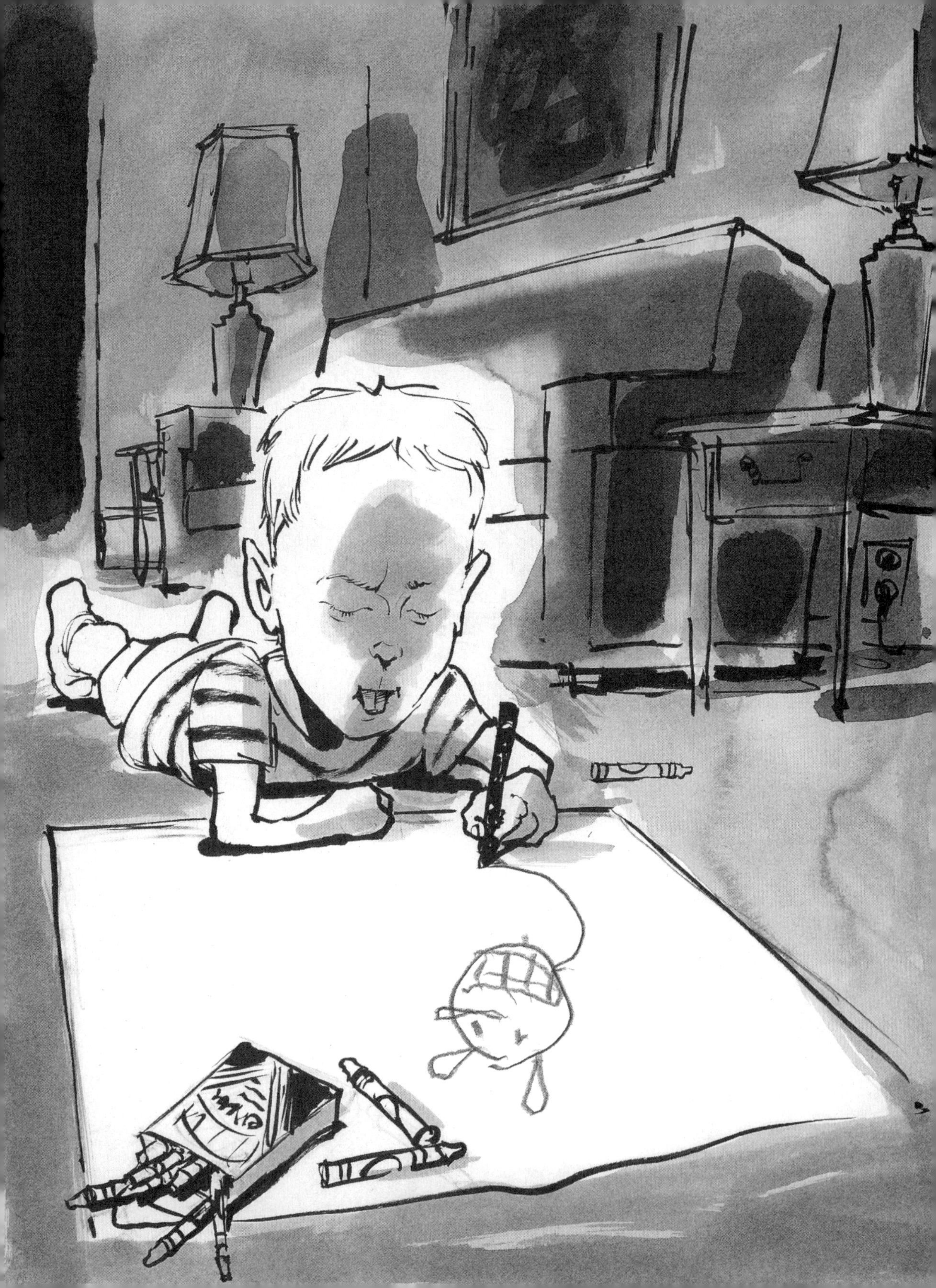

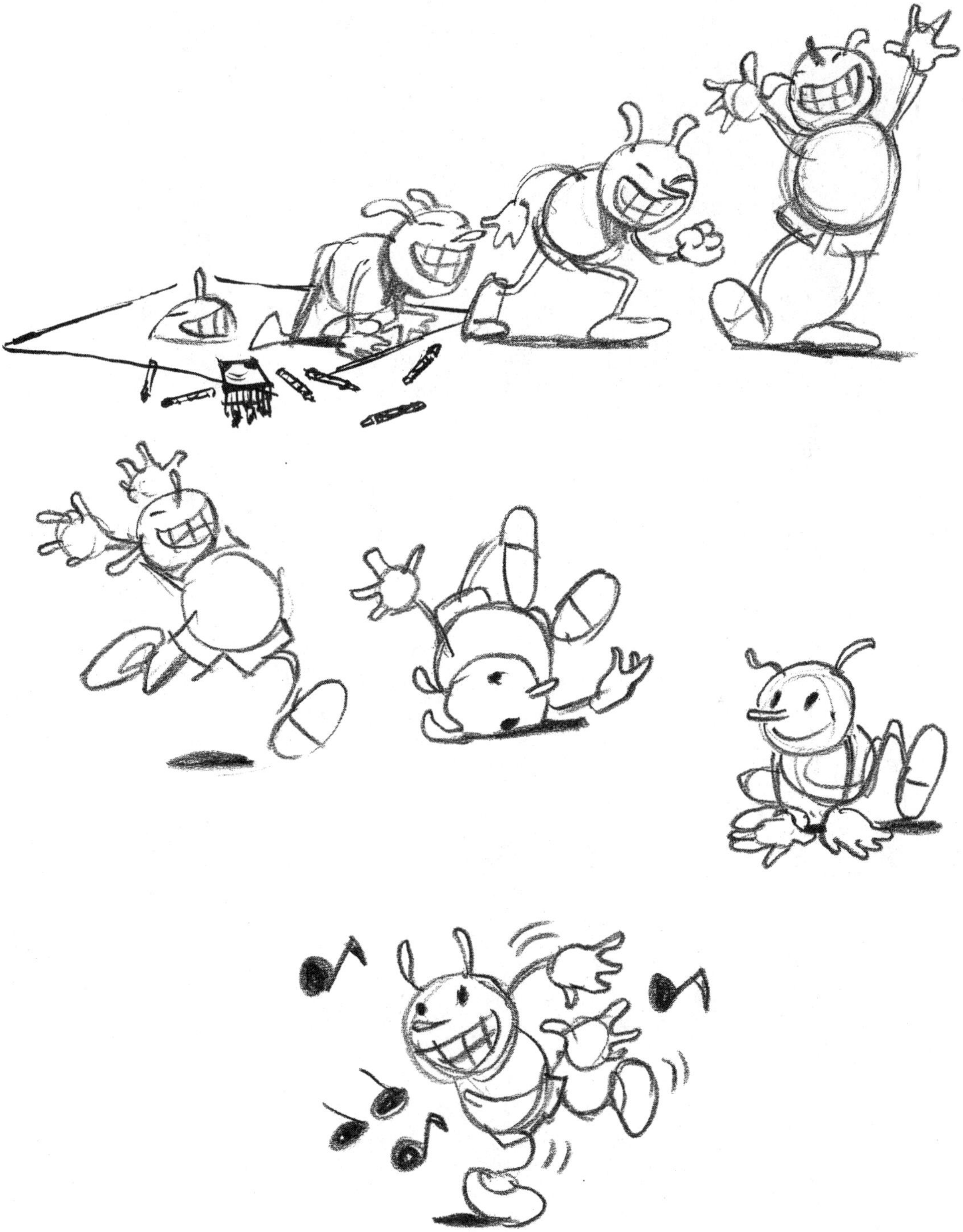

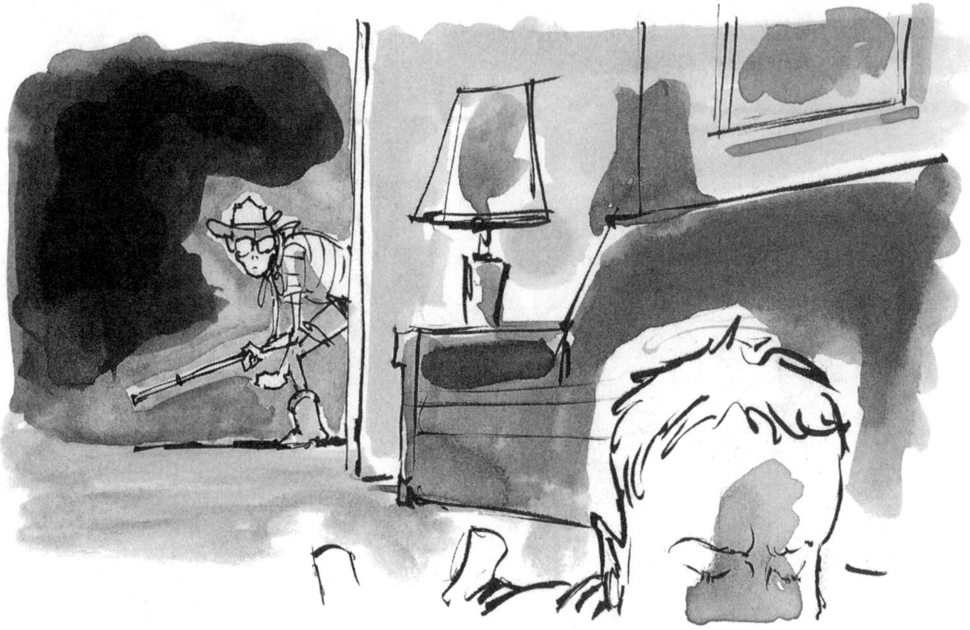

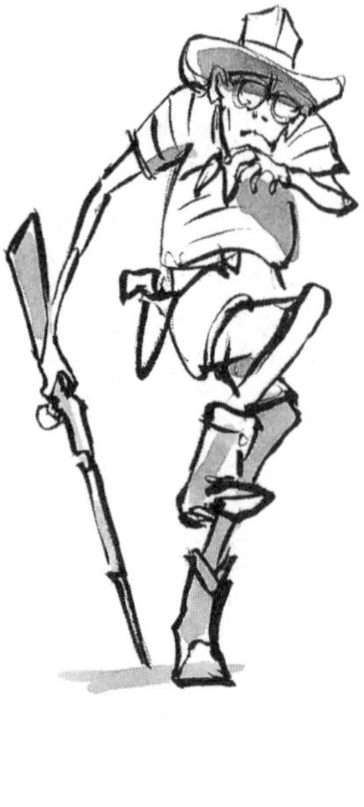

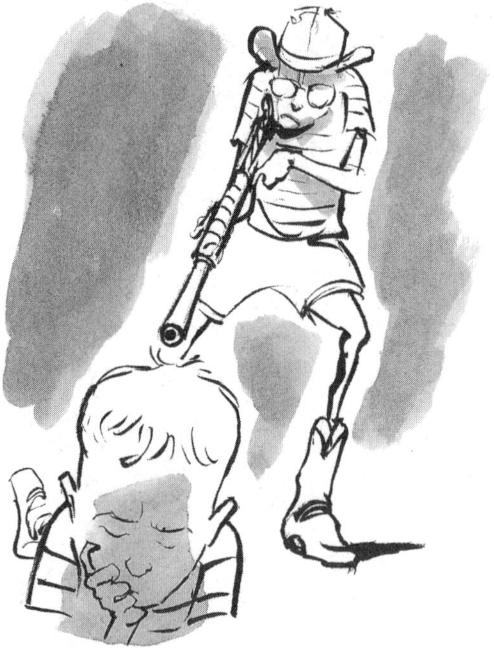

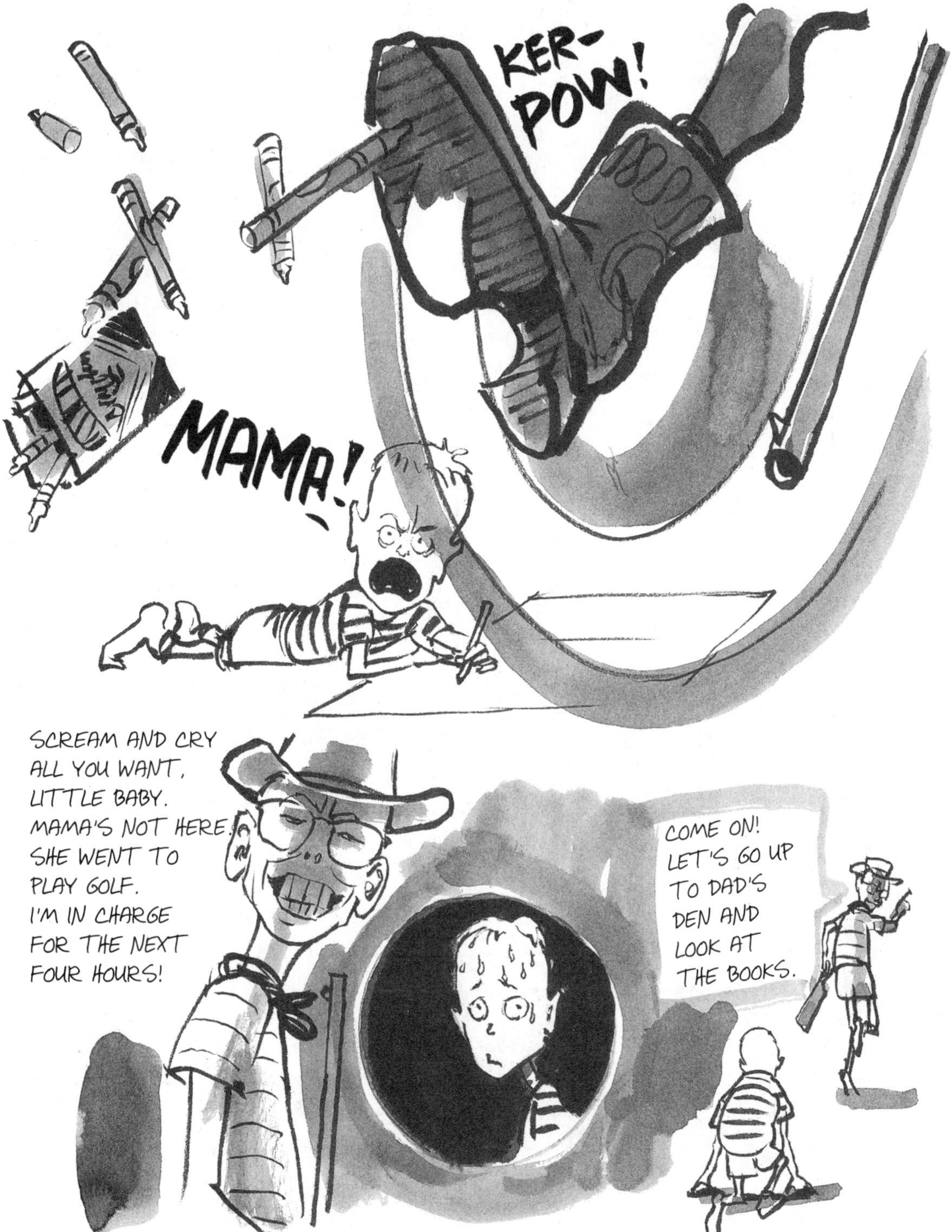
KER-POW!
MAMA!
SCREAM AND CRY ALL YOU WANT, LITTLE BABY. MAMA'S NOT HERE. SHE WENT TO PLAY GOLF. I'M IN CHARGE FOR THE NEXT FOUR HOURS!
COME ON! LET'S GO UP TO DAD'S DEN AND LOOK AT THE BOOKS.

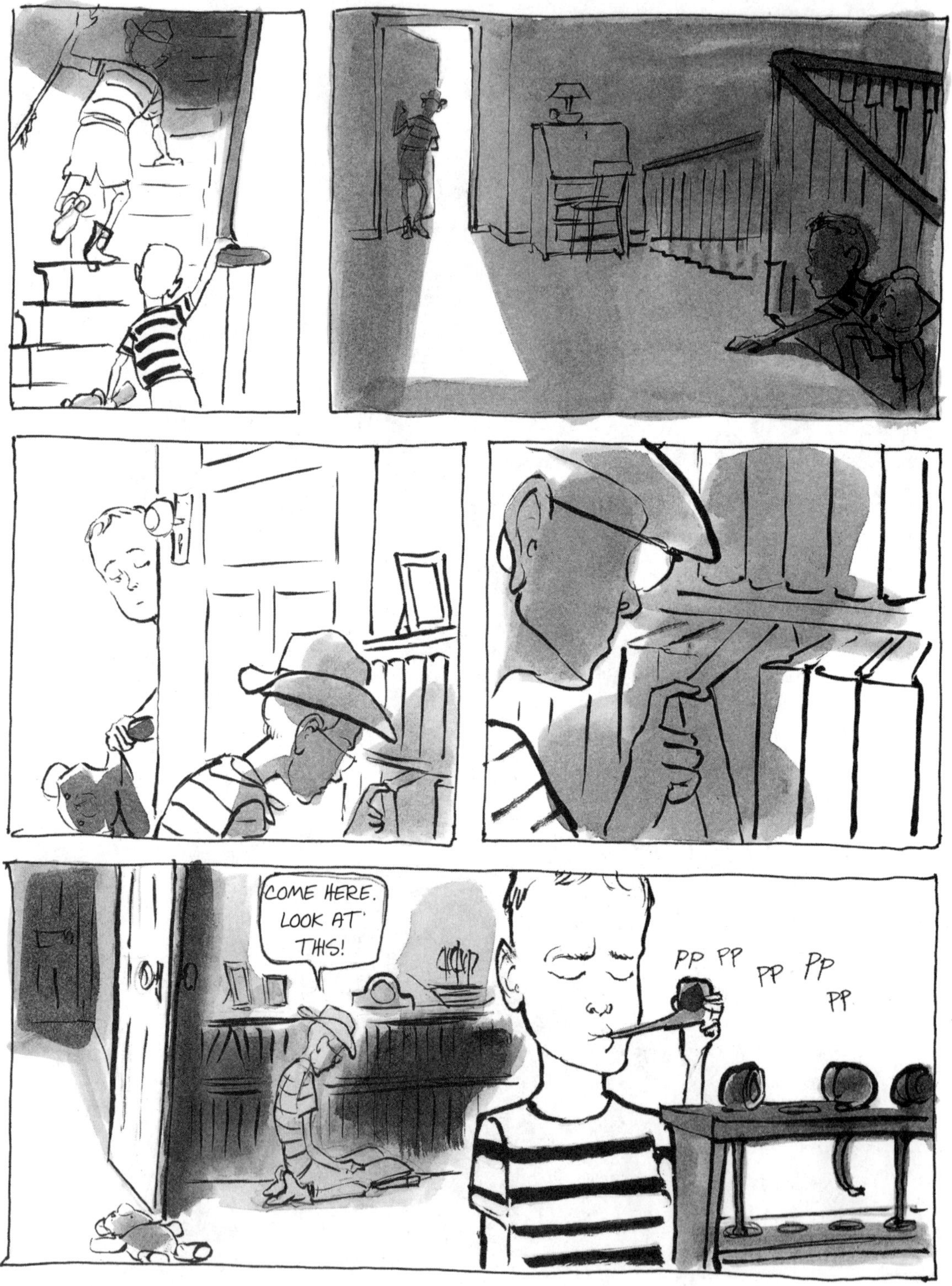
COME HERE. LOOK AT THIS!
PP PP PP PP PP

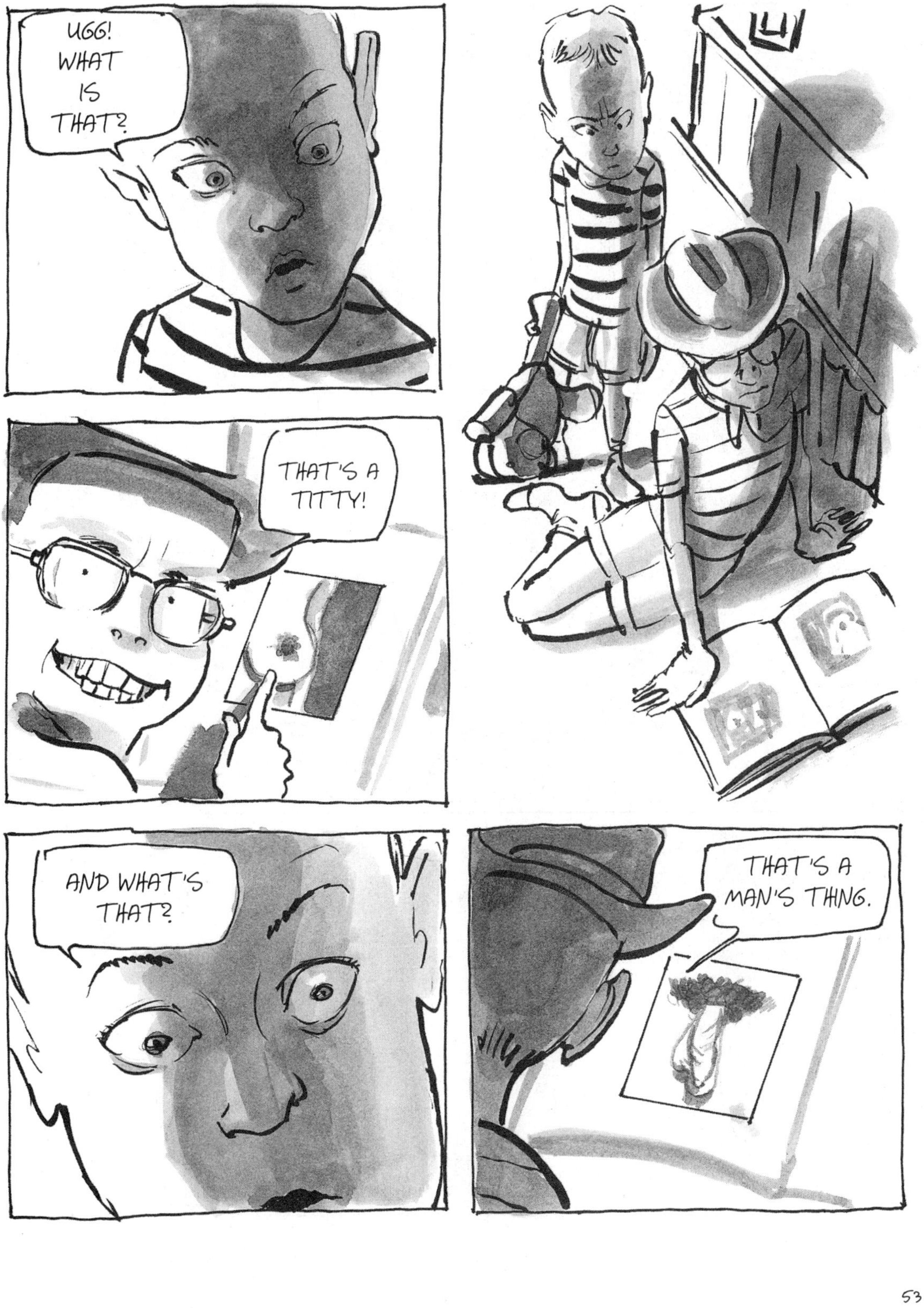
UGG! WHAT IS THAT?
THAT'S A TITTY!
AND WHAT'S THAT?
THAT'S A MAN'S THING.

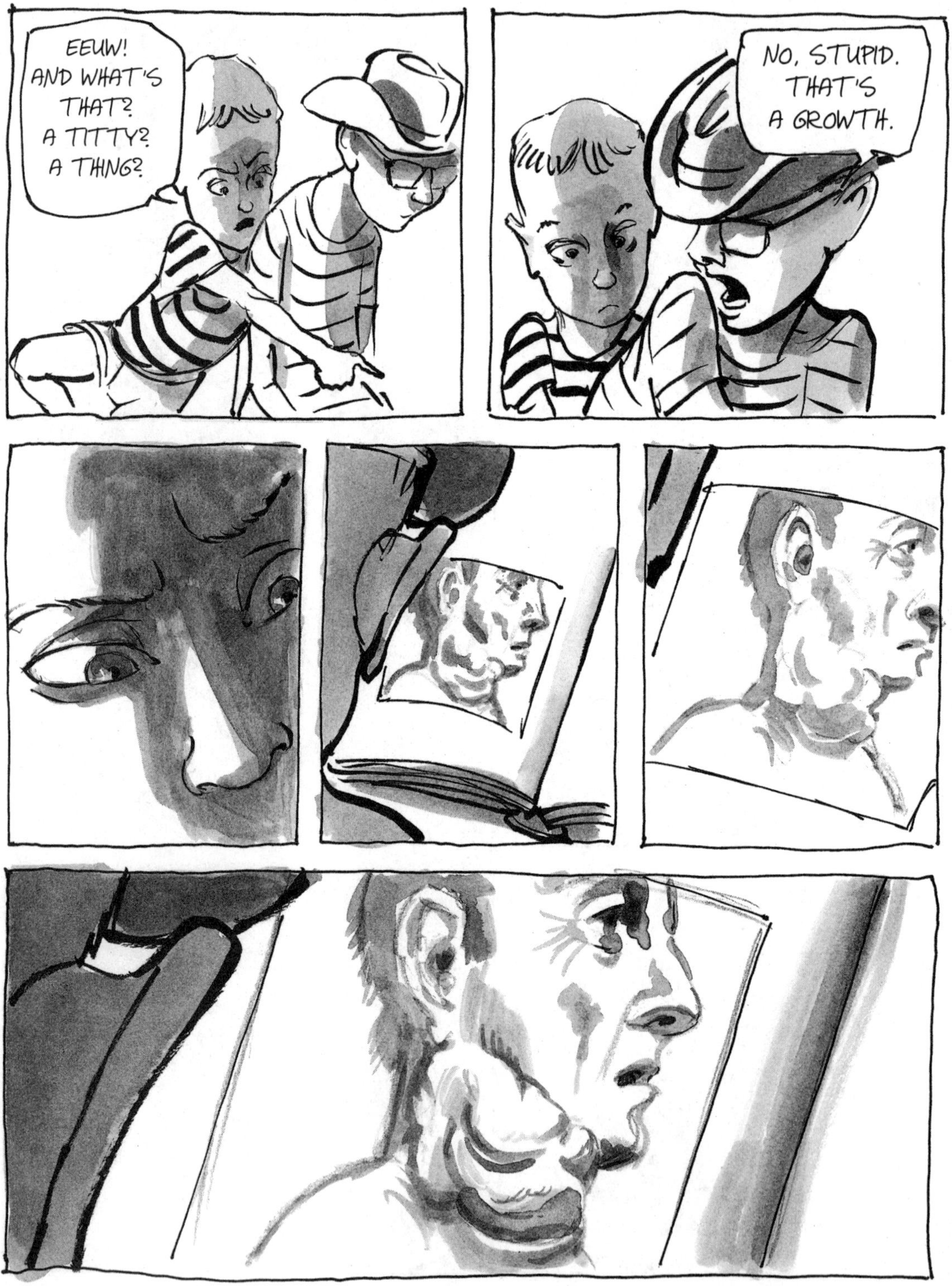
EEUW! AND WHAT'S THAT? A TITTY? A THING?
NO, STUPID. THAT'S A GROWTH.

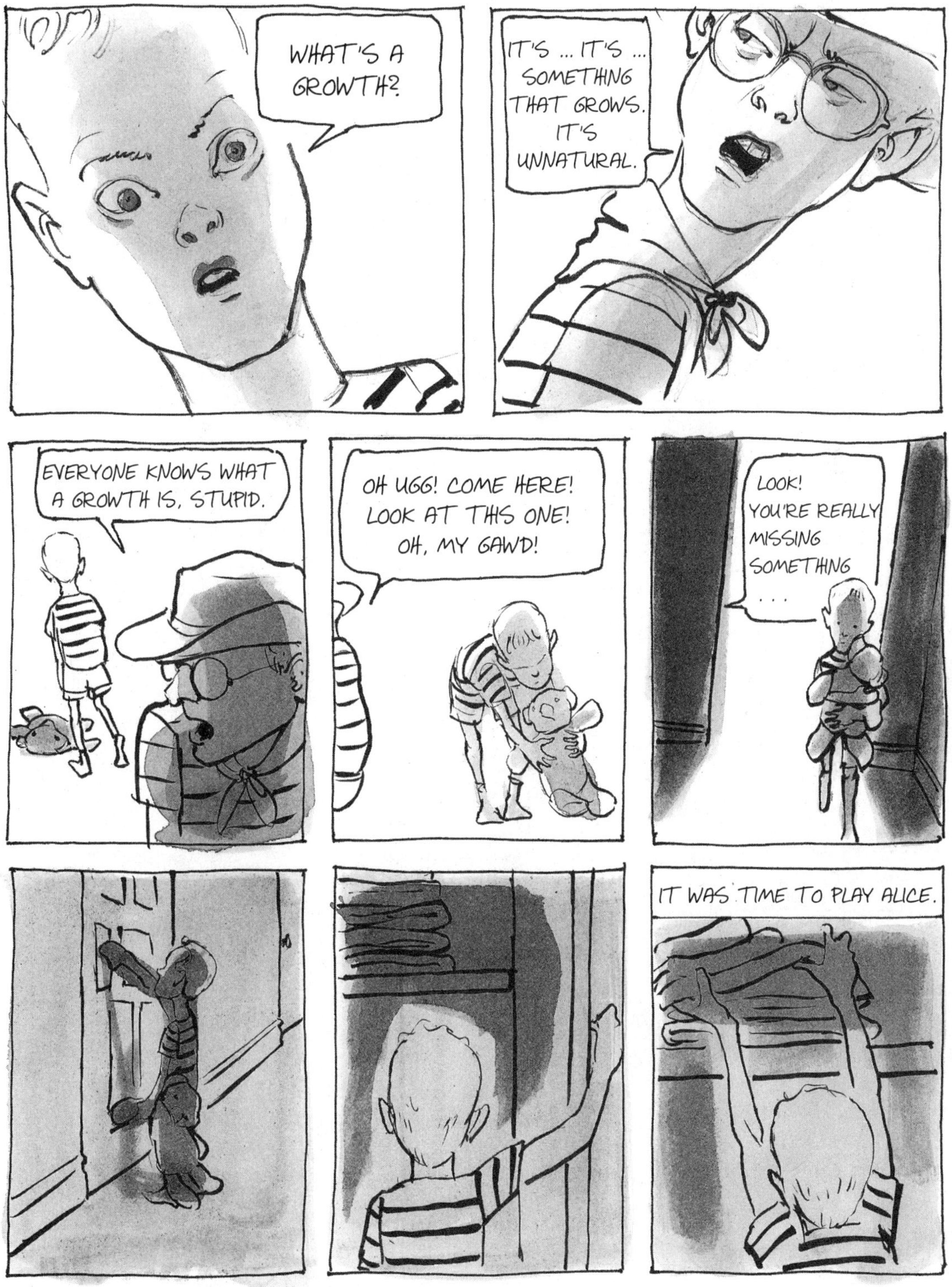
WHAT'S A GROWTH?
IT'S ... IT'S ... SOMETHING THAT GROWS. IT'S UNNATURAL.
EVERYONE KNOWS WHAT A GROWTH IS, STUPID.
OH UGG! COME HERE! LOOK AT THIS ONE! OH, MY GAWD!
LOOK! YOU'RE REALLY MISSING SOMETHING . . .
IT WAS TIME TO PLAY ALICE.

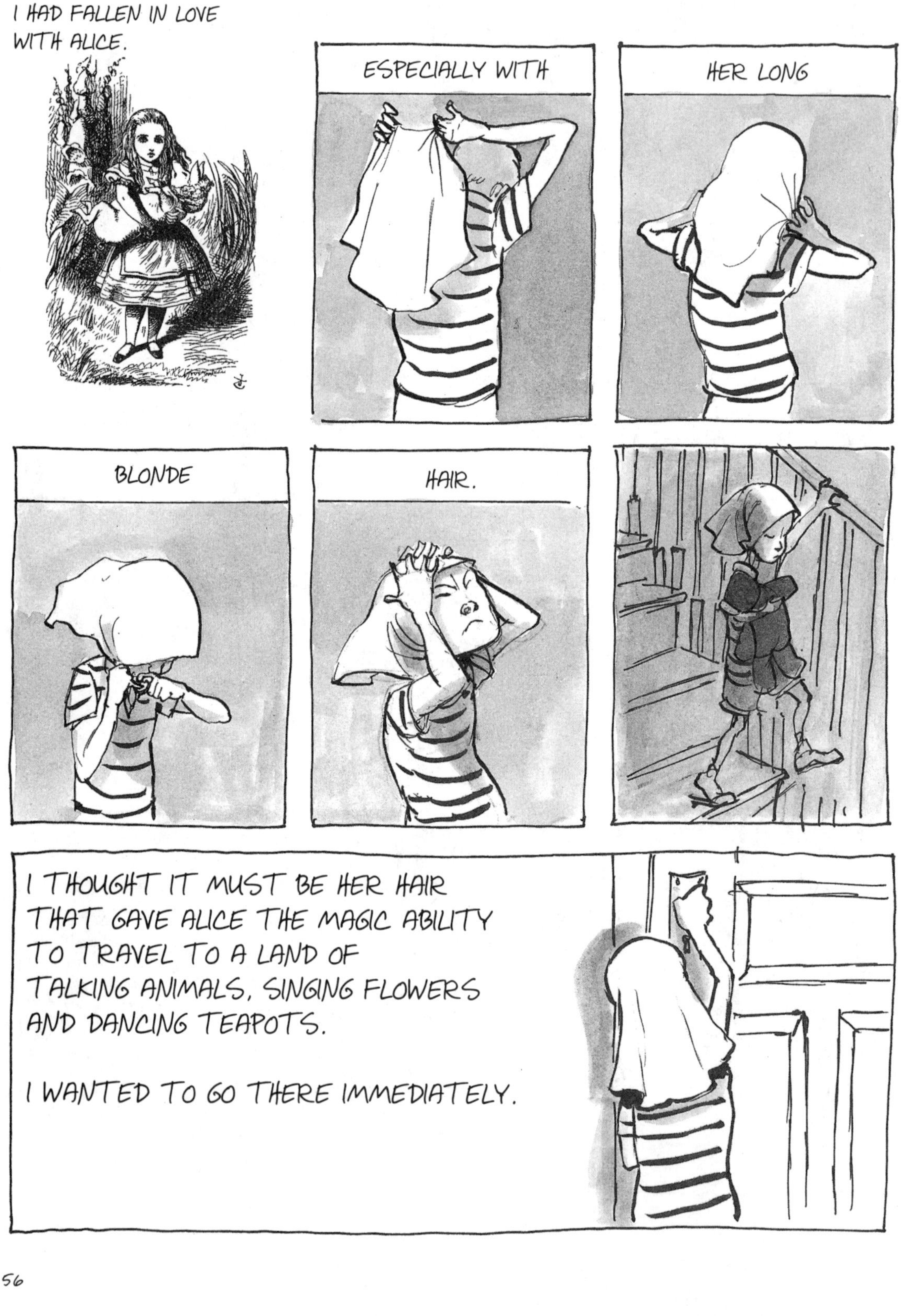
I HAD FALLEN IN LOVE WITH ALICE.
ESPECIALLY WITH
HER LONG
BLONDE
HAIR.
I THOUGHT IT MUST BE HER HAIR THAT GAVE ALICE THE MAGIC ABILITY TO TRAVEL TO A LAND OF TALKING ANIMALS, SINGING FLOWERS AND DANCING TEAPOTS.
I WANTED TO GO THERE IMMEDIATELY.

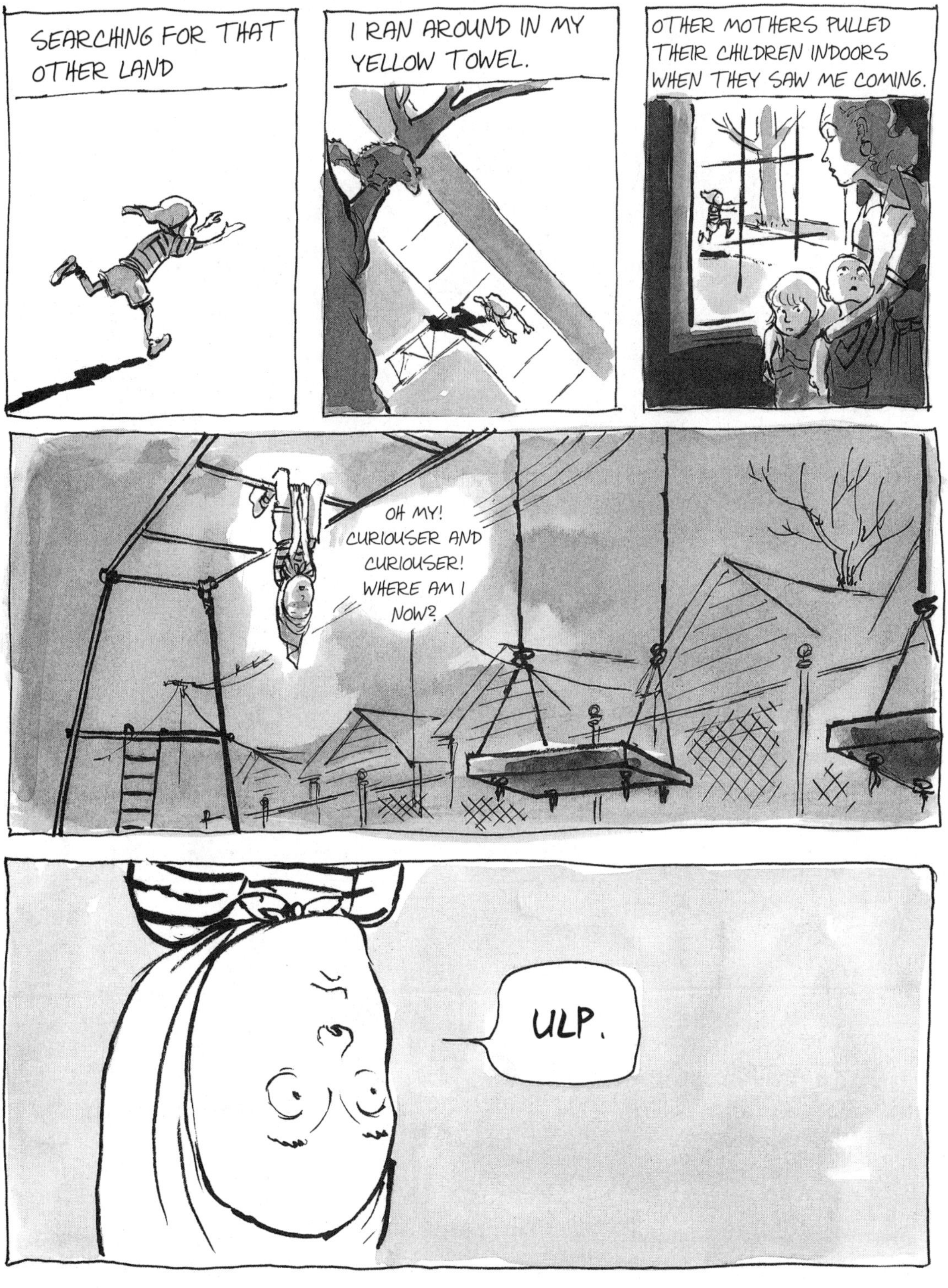
SEARCHING FOR THAT OTHER LAND
I RAN AROUND IN MY YELLOW TOWEL.
OTHER MOTHERS PULLED THEIR CHILDREN INDOORS WHEN THEY SAW ME COMING.
OH MY! CURIOUSER AND CURIOUSER! WHERE AM I NOW?
ULP.

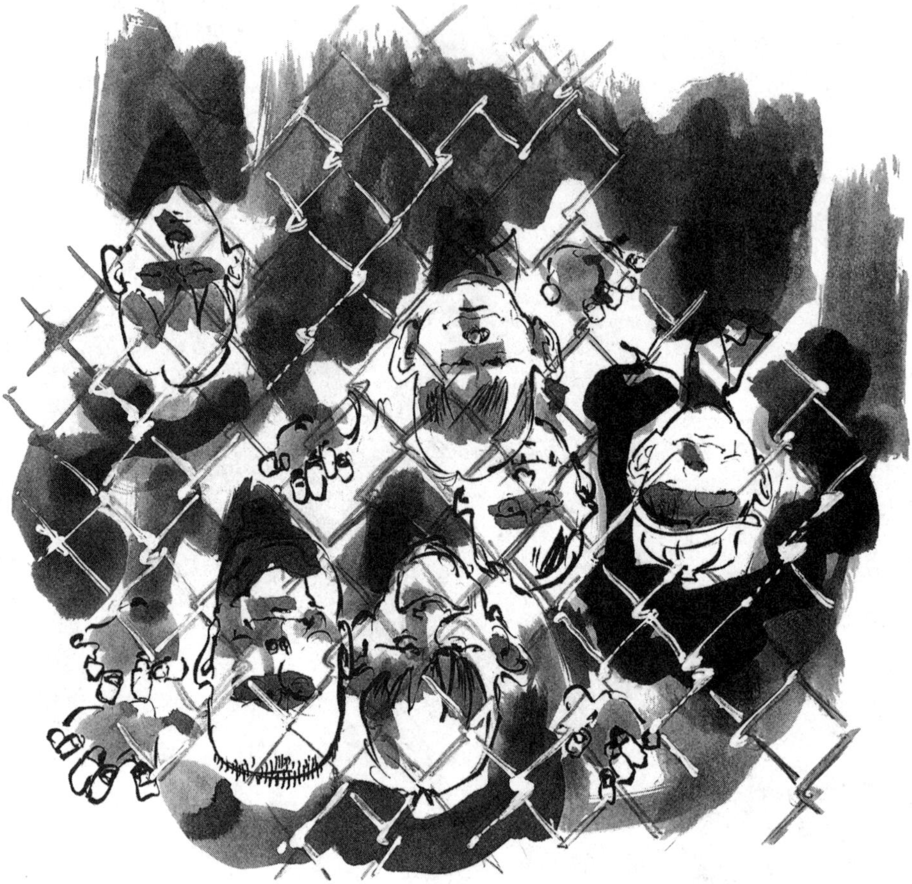

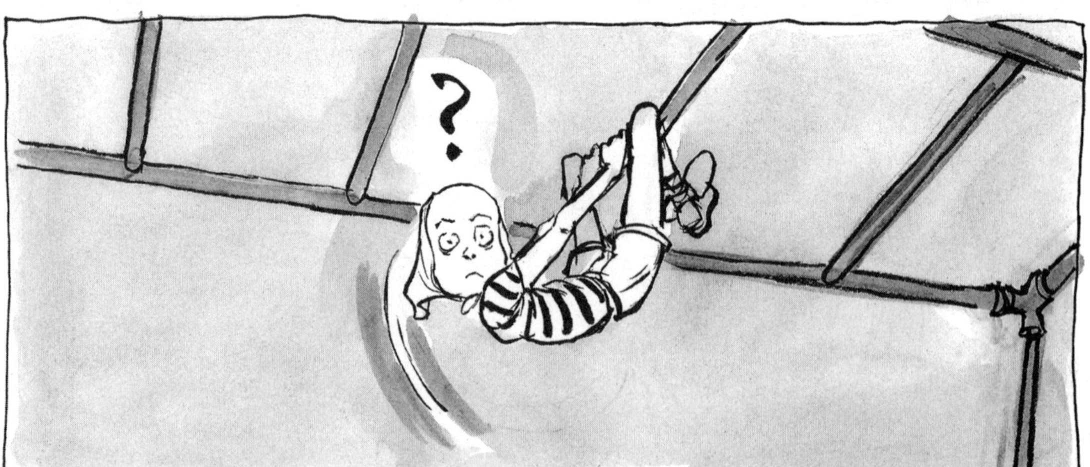
?

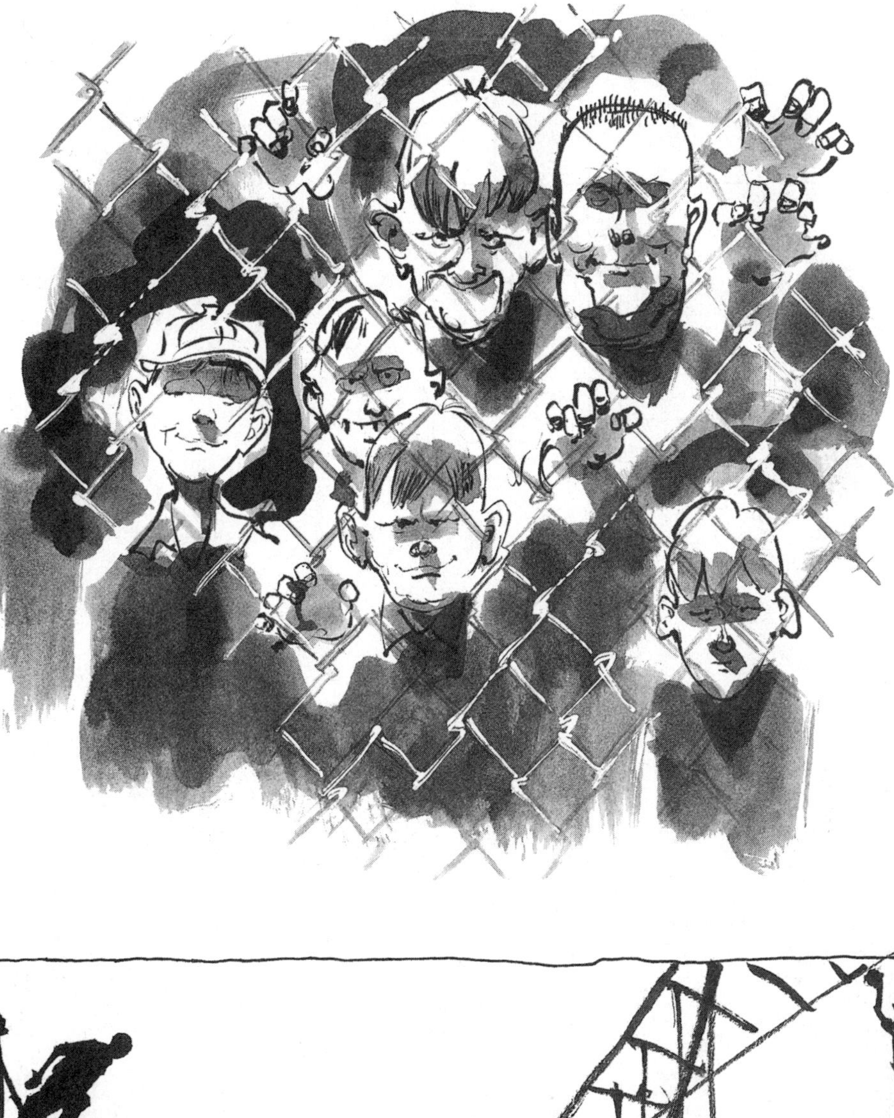

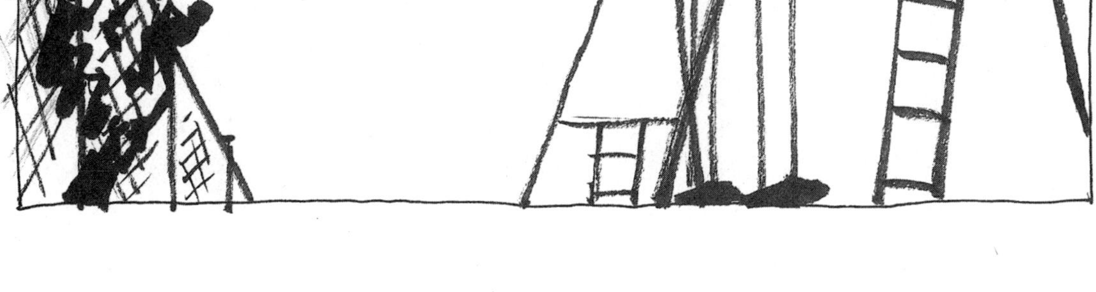

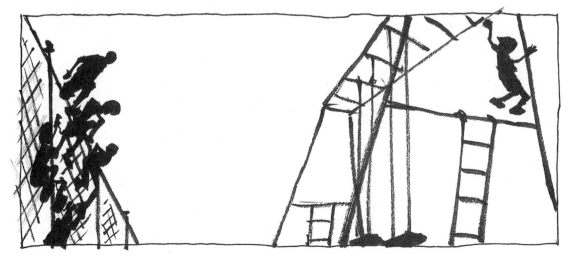

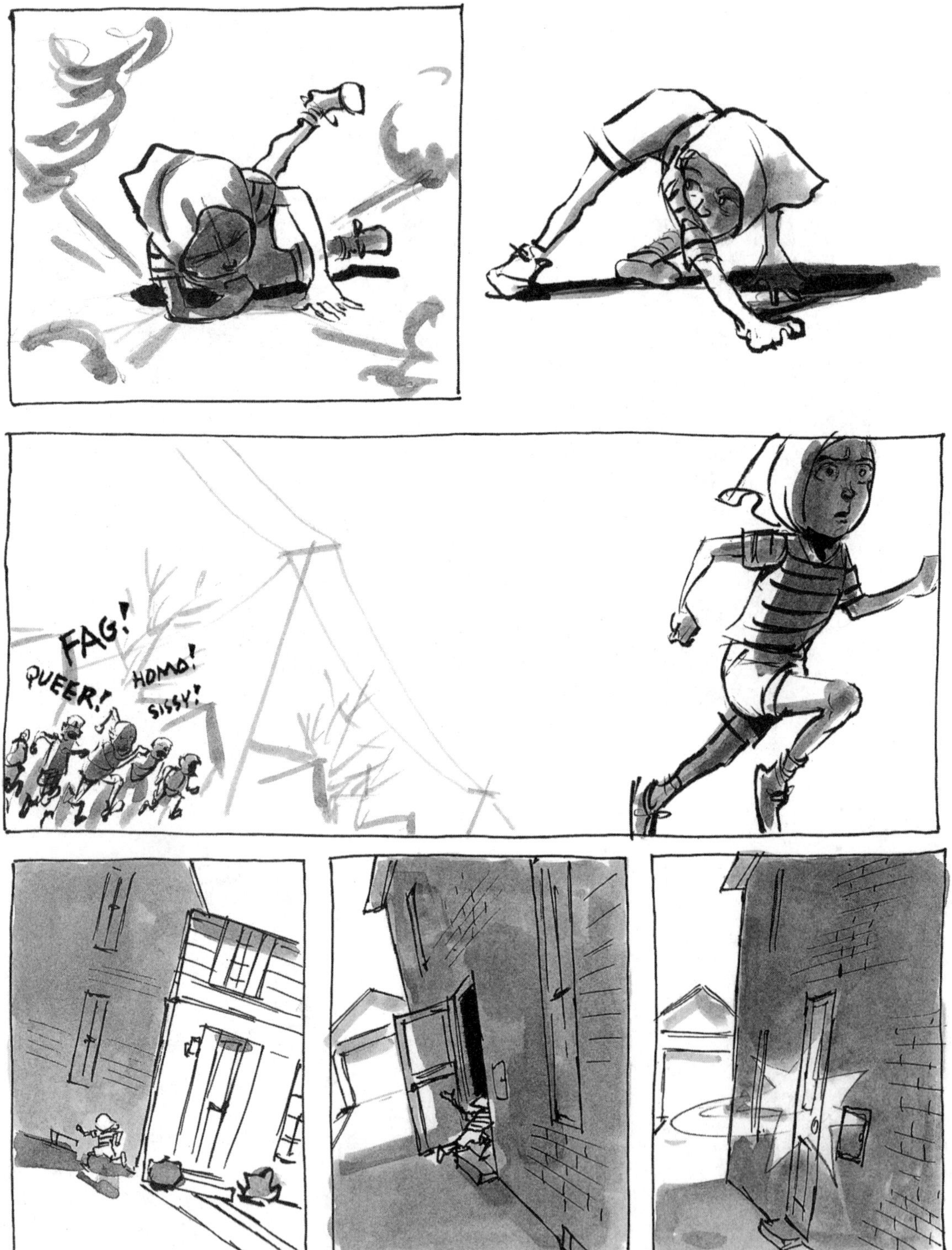
FAG!
QUEER!
HOMO!
SISSY!

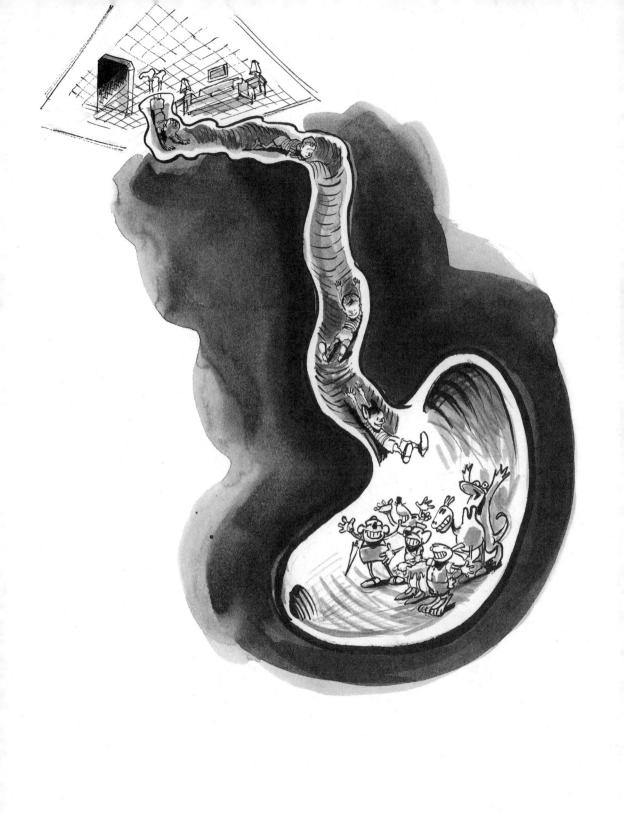

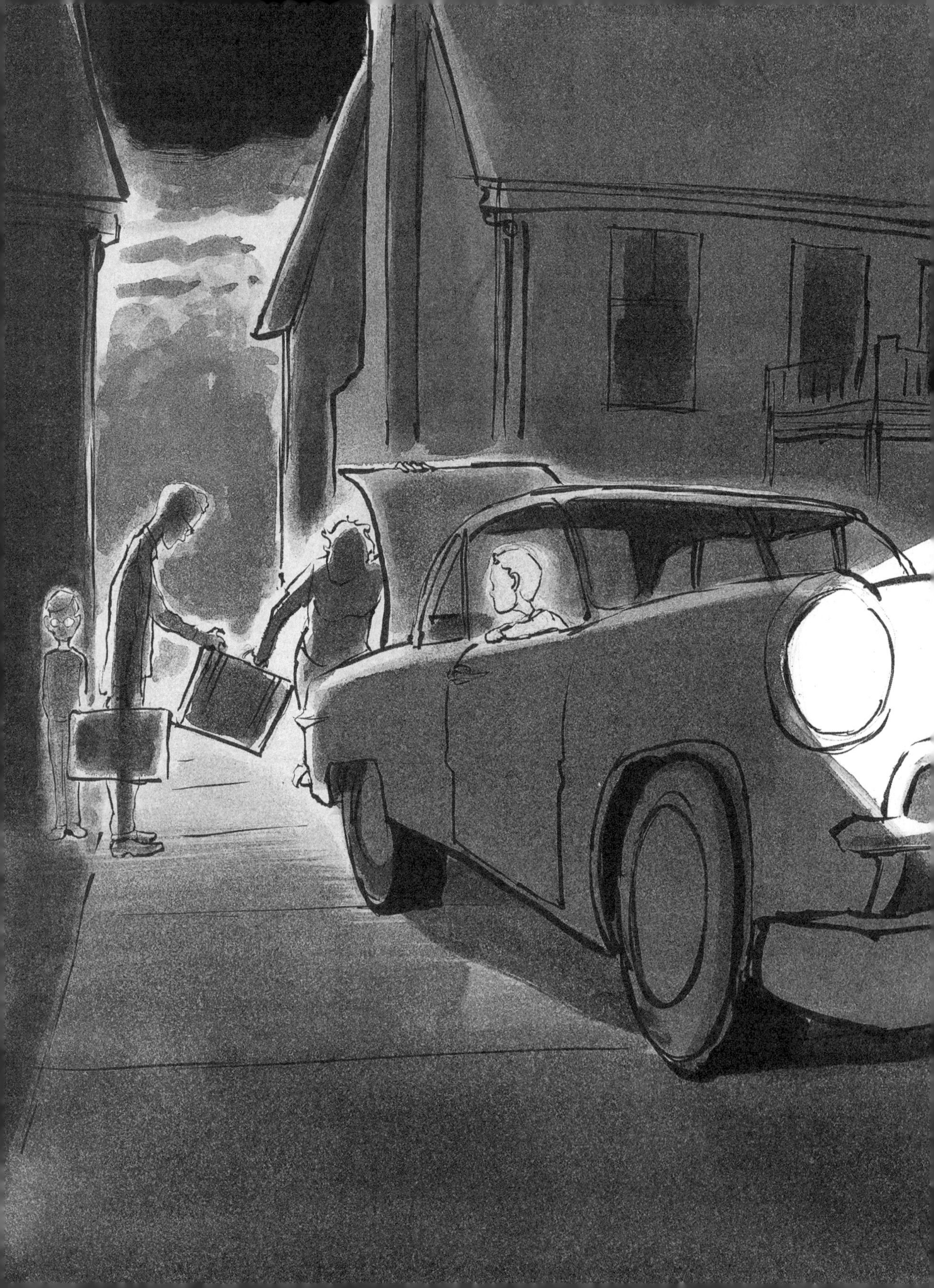

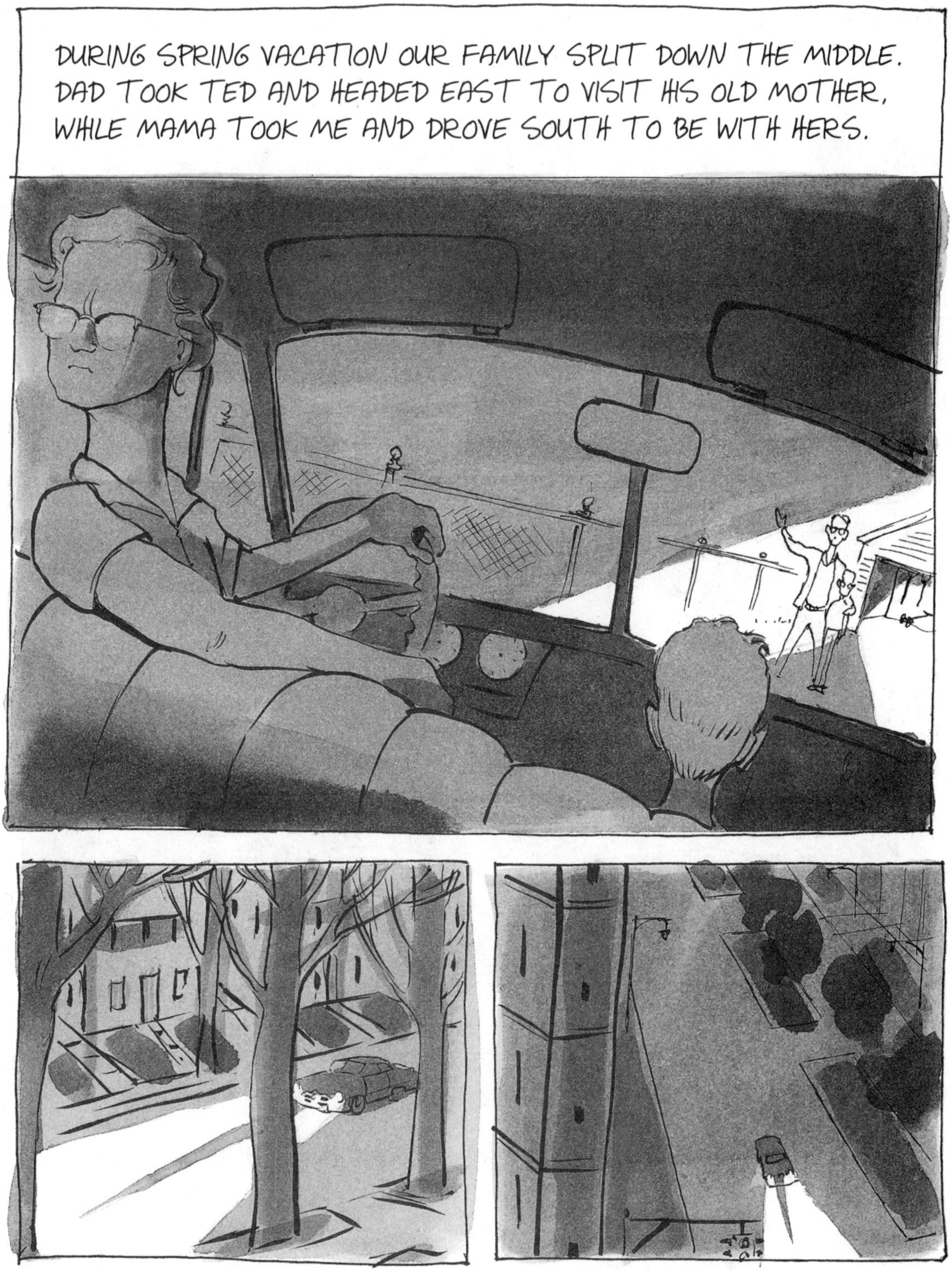
DURING SPRING VACATION OUR FAMILY SPLIT DOWN THE MIDDLE. DAD TOOK TED AND HEADED EAST TO VISIT HIS OLD MOTHER, WHILE MAMA TOOK ME AND DROVE SOUTH TO BE WITH HERS.

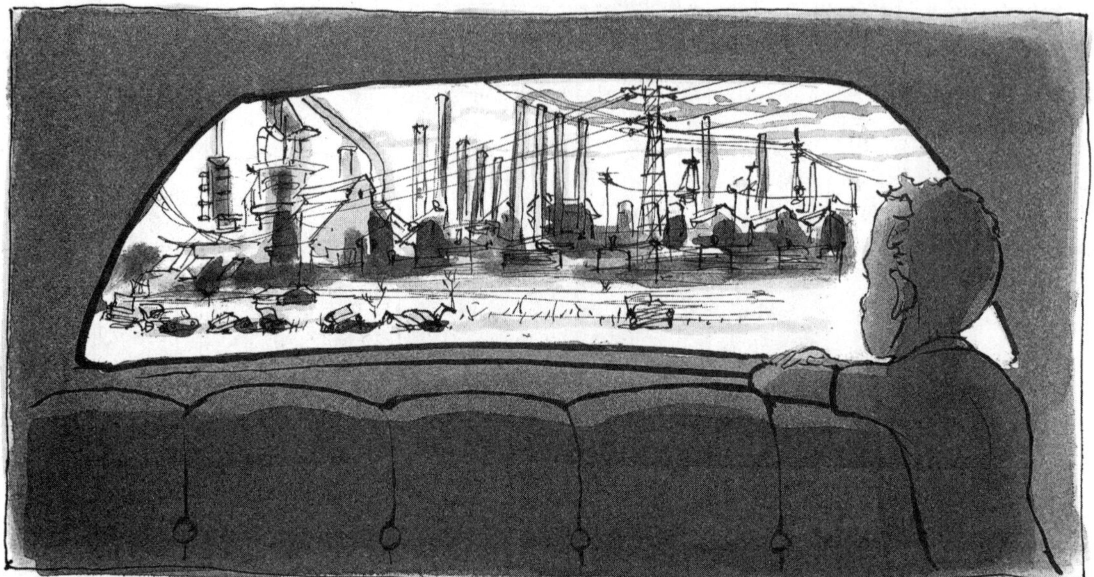

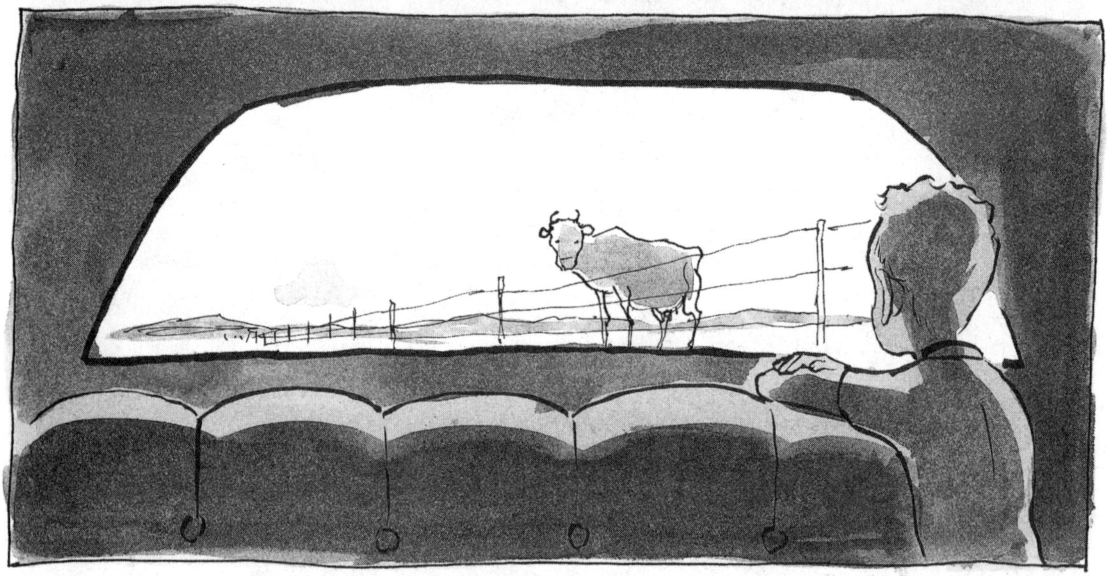

IT WAS A LONG TRIP BETWEEN DETROIT AND SOUTHEASTERN INDIANA ON TWO-LANE ROADS ALL THE WAY.

THERE WAS NO RADIO IN THE CAR, AND NO AIR-CONDITIONING.

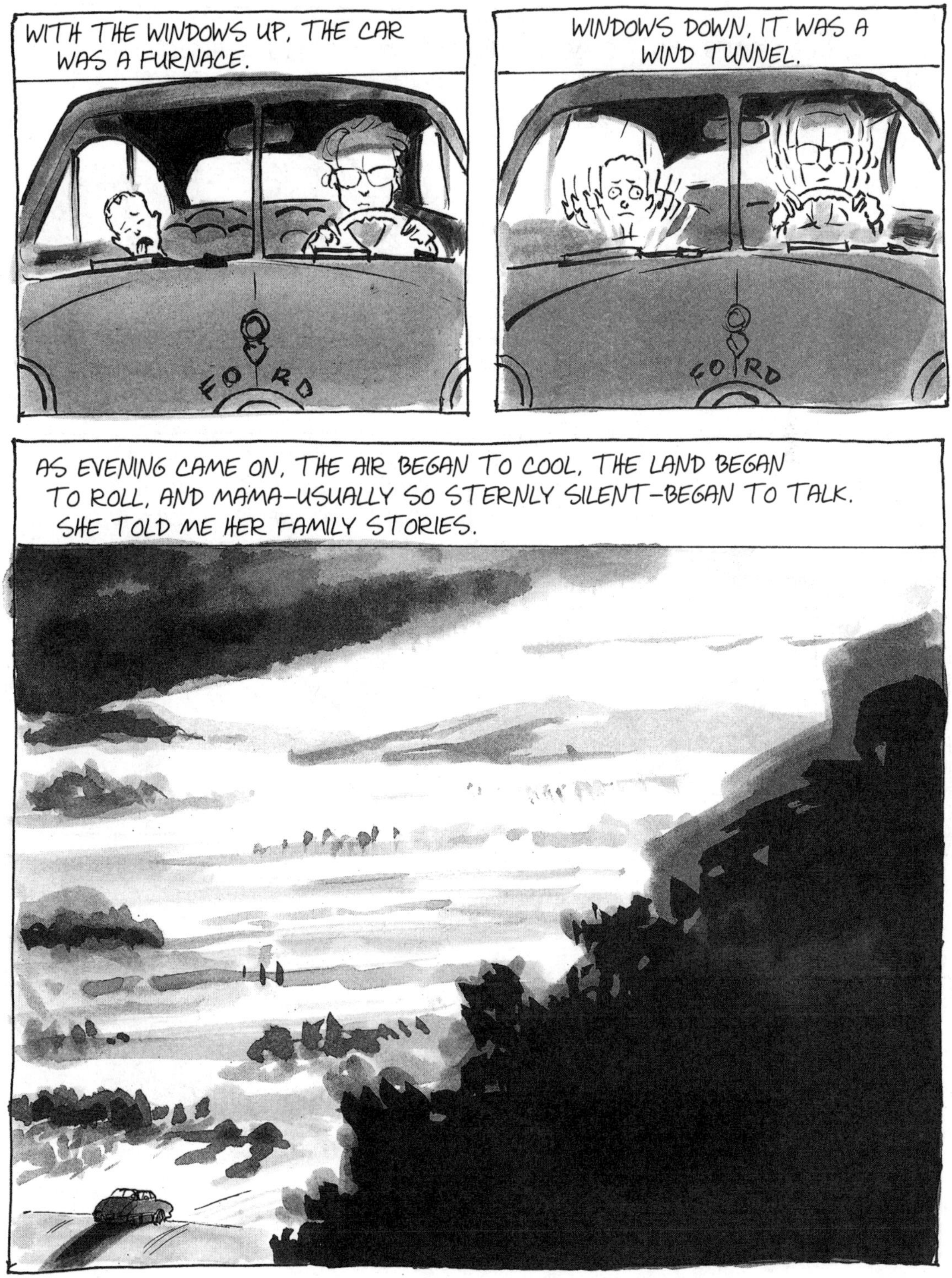
WITH THE WINDOWS UP, THE CAR WAS A FURNACE.
WINDOWS DOWN, IT WAS A WIND TUNNEL.
FORD
FORD
AS EVENING CAME ON, THE AIR BEGAN TO COOL, THE LAND BEGAN TO ROLL, AND MAMA–USUALLY SO STERNLY SILENT–BEGAN TO TALK. SHE TOLD ME HER FAMILY STORIES.

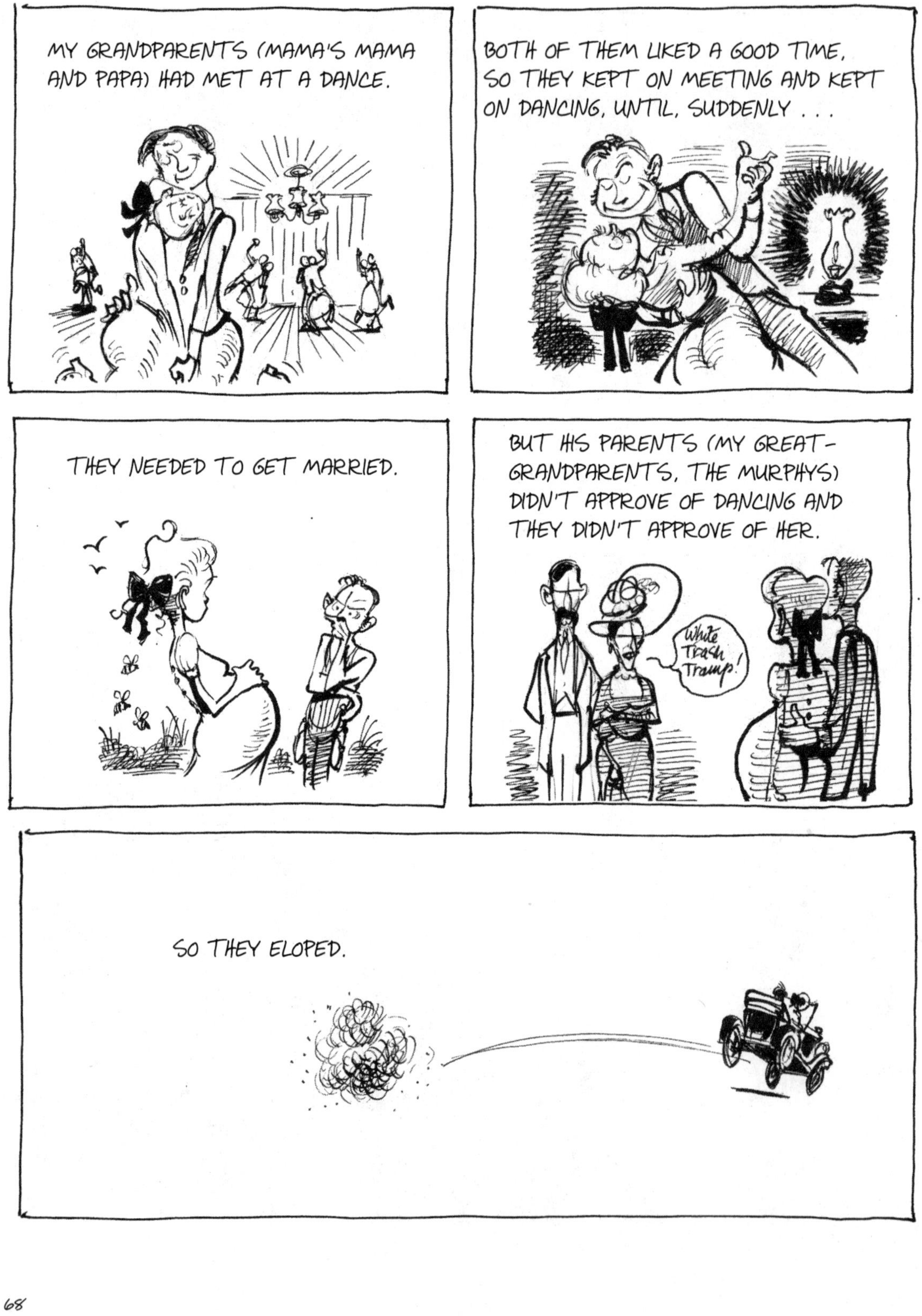
MY GRANDPARENTS (MAMA'S MAMA AND PAPA) HAD MET AT A DANCE.
BOTH OF THEM LIKED A GOOD TIME, SO THEY KEPT ON MEETING AND KEPT ON DANCING, UNTIL, SUDDENLY . . .
THEY NEEDED TO GET MARRIED.
BUT HIS PARENTS (MY GREAT-GRANDPARENTS, THE MURPHYS) DIDN'T APPROVE OF DANCING AND THEY DIDN'T APPROVE OF HER.
White Trash Tramp!
SO THEY ELOPED.

NOW MAN AND WIFE, THEY MOVED INTO A ONE-ROOM CABIN ON THE BACK OF THE MURPHY PROPERTY. BECAUSE THE MURPHYS WOULD NOT ALLOW GRANDMA TO HAVE HER BABY IN THEIR HOUSE, MAMA WAS BORN IN THAT CABIN.

THE DOCTOR COULD NOT FIND HER HEARTBEAT. HE BELIEVED SHE WAS DEAD, YET SOMEHOW STILL BREATHING.

THEN HE DISCOVERED HER HEART. IT WAS OVER ON THE WRONG SIDE OF HER CHEST.

MAMA'S FATHER DIED WHEN SHE WAS TEN. HE AND TWO FRIENDS HAD BEEN OUT DRINKING AND, WHILE DRIVING HOME IN THE DARK, SAILED OVER A CLIFF.

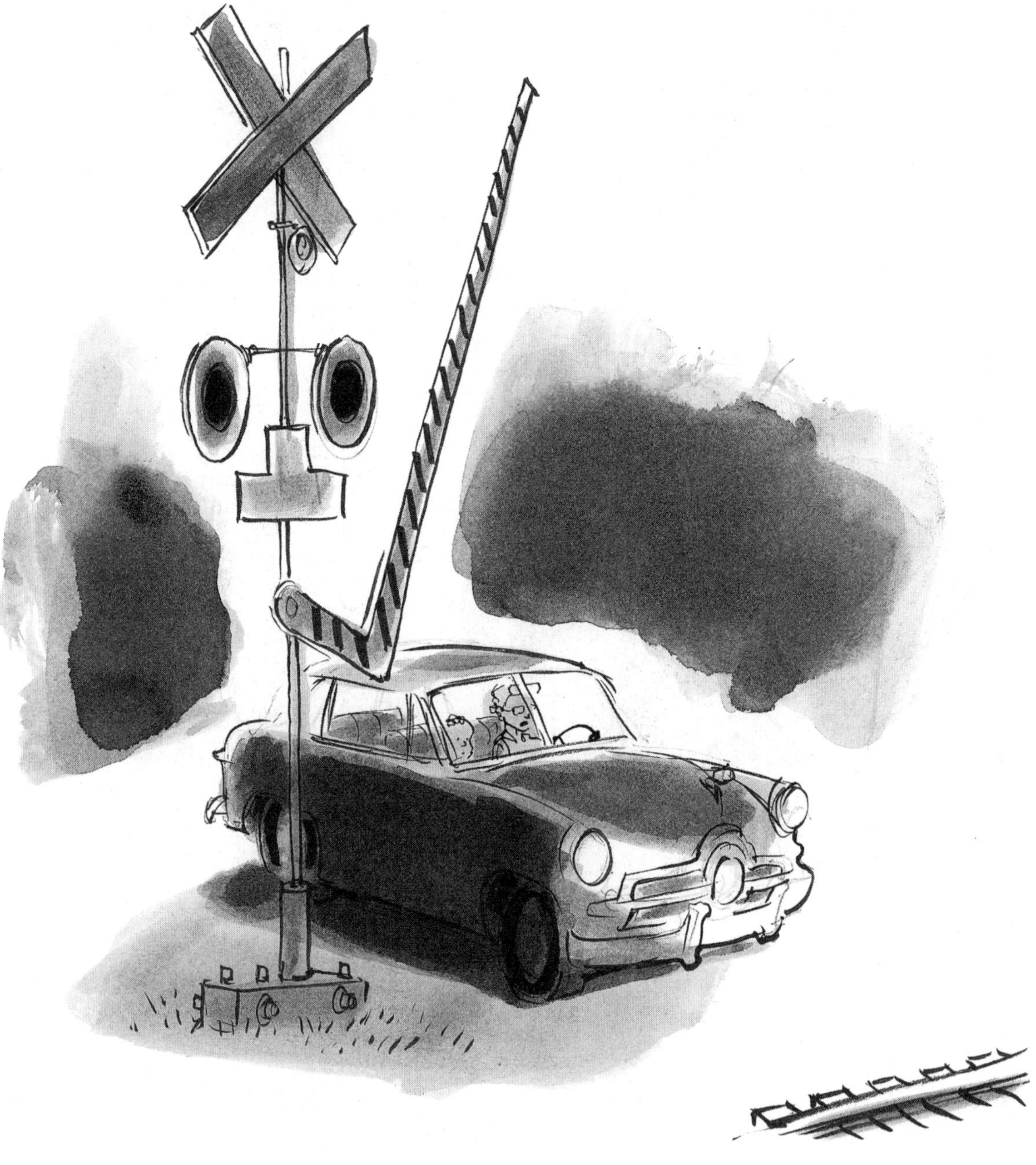

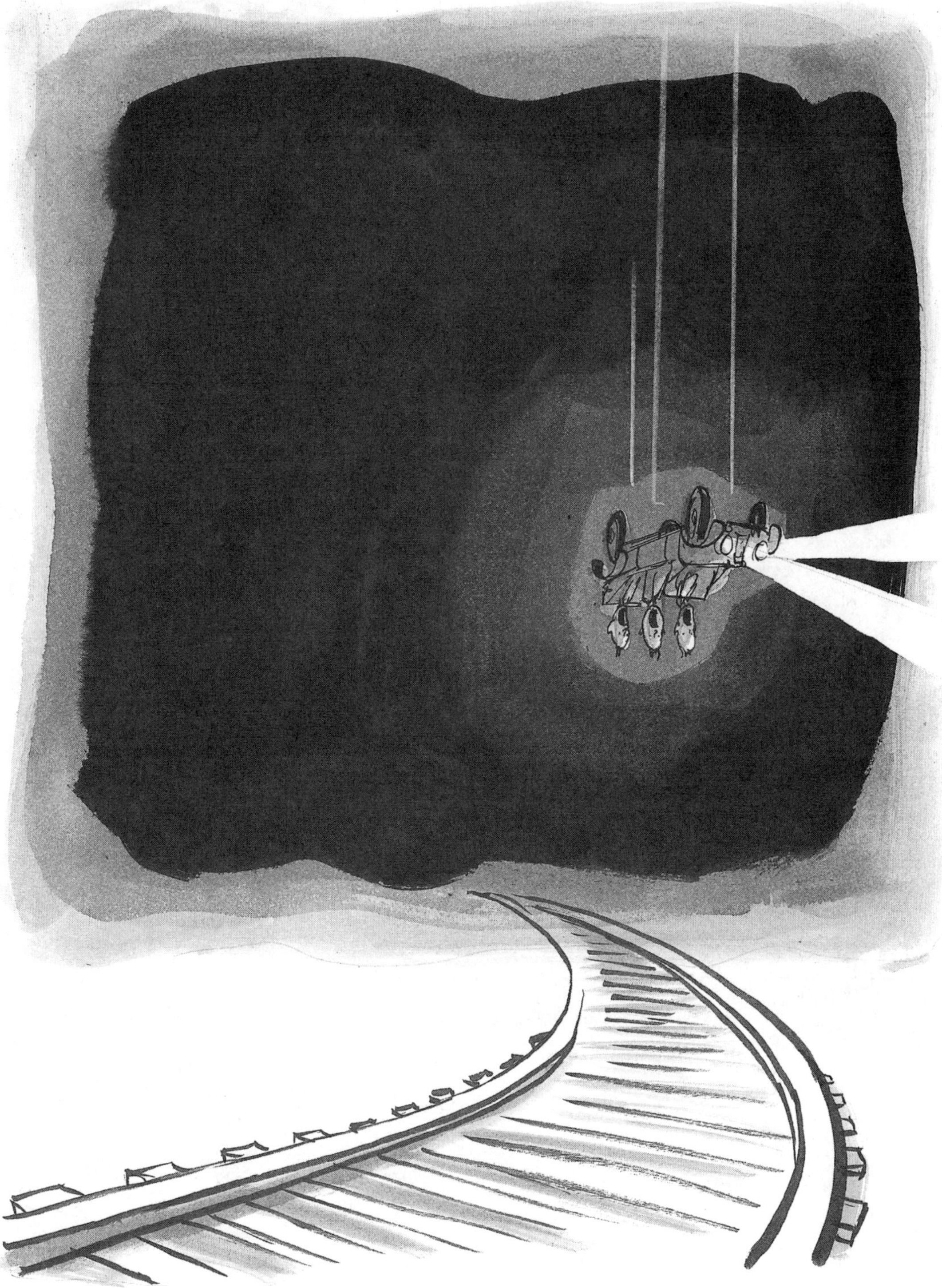

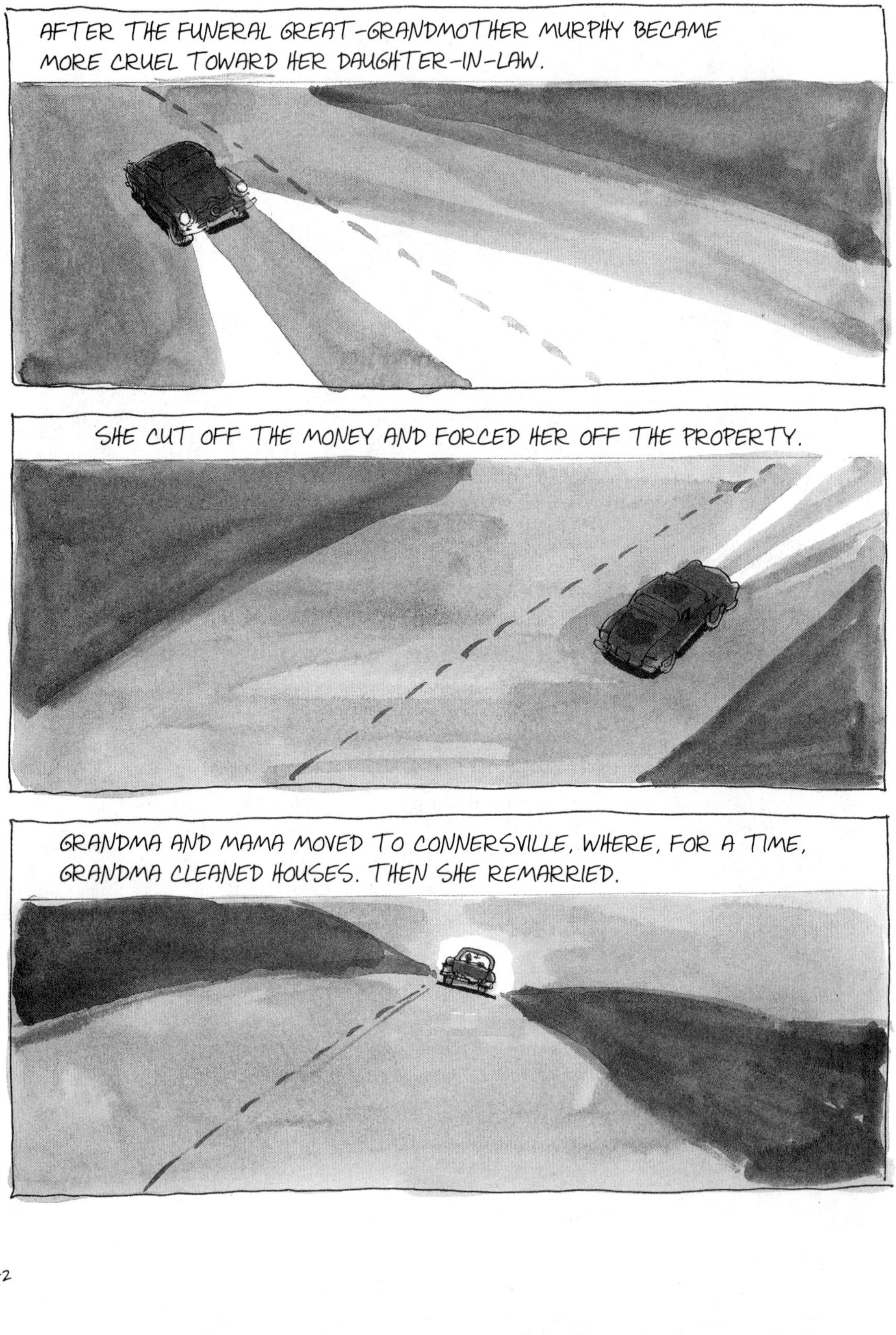
AFTER THE FUNERAL GREAT-GRANDMOTHER MURPHY BECAME MORE CRUEL TOWARD HER DAUGHTER-IN-LAW.
SHE CUT OFF THE MONEY AND FORCED HER OFF THE PROPERTY.
GRANDMA AND MAMA MOVED TO CONNERSVILLE, WHERE, FOR A TIME, GRANDMA CLEANED HOUSES. THEN SHE REMARRIED.

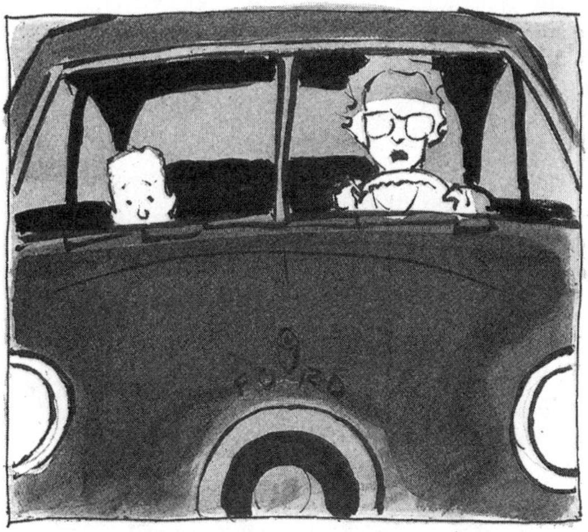
FORD

GREAT-GRANDFATHER
MURPHY TRIED TO KILL HIMSELF
BY DRINKING DRANO.

ALTHOUGH HE LIVED, HE
NEVER SPOKE ANOTHER
WORD. THE POISON
HAD EATEN AWAY HIS
VOCAL CORDS.

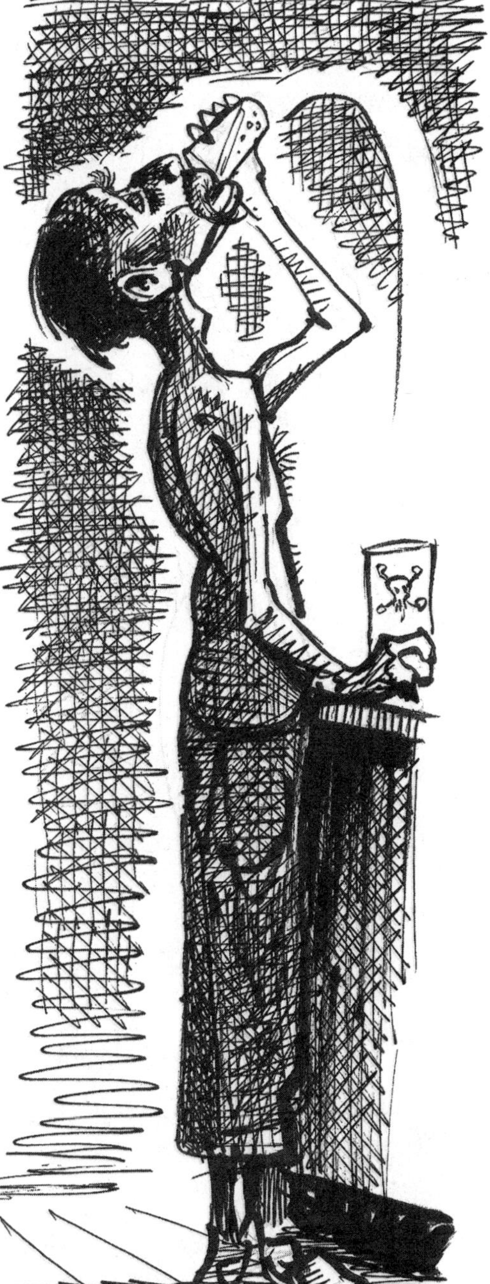

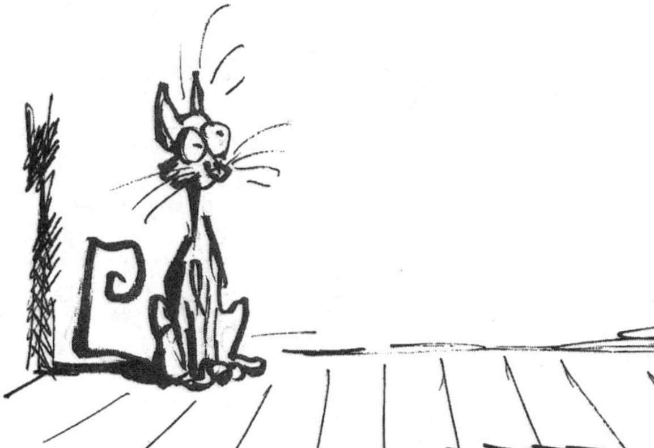

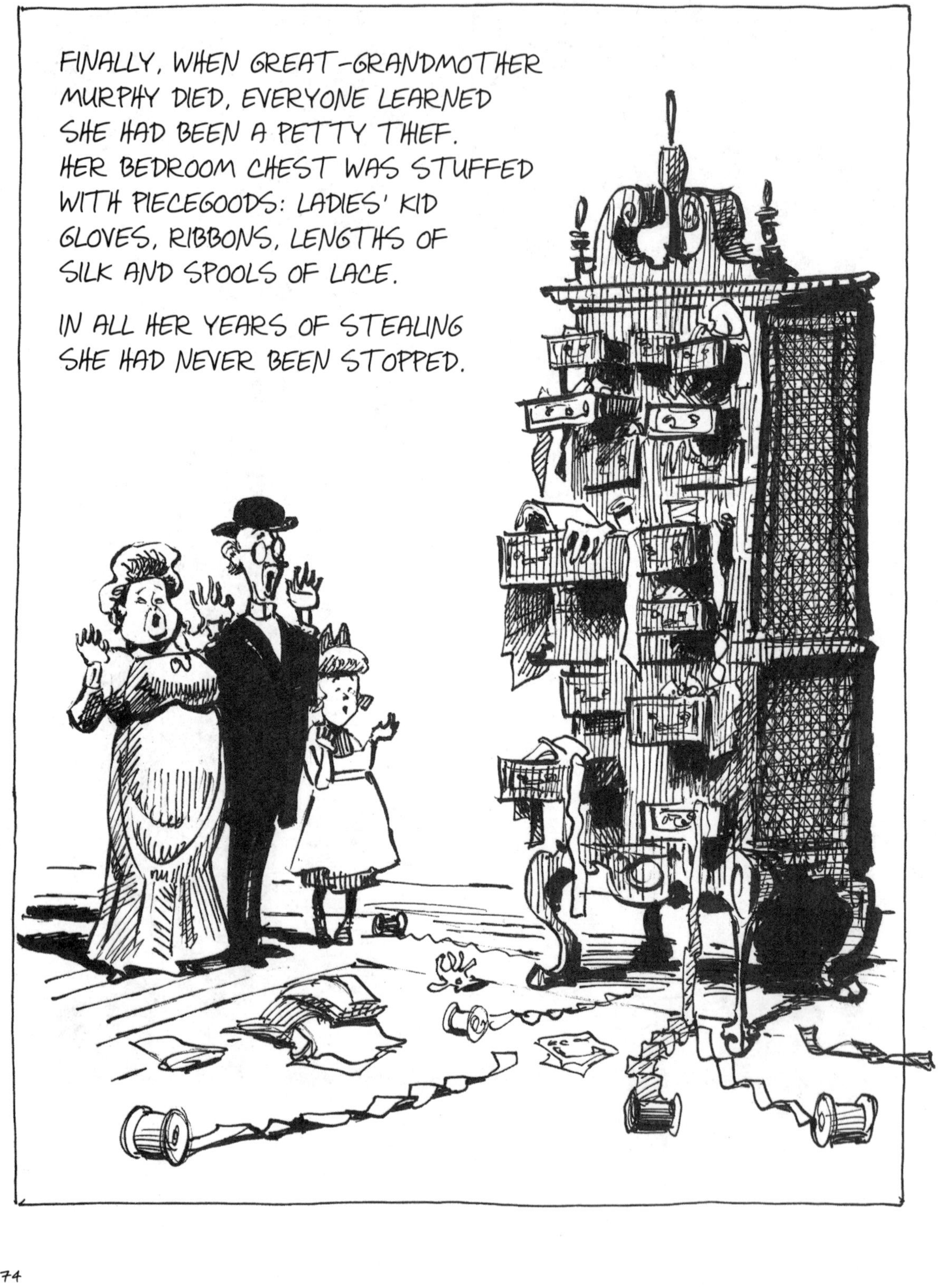
FINALLY, WHEN GREAT-GRANDMOTHER MURPHY DIED, EVERYONE LEARNED SHE HAD BEEN A PETTY THIEF. HER BEDROOM CHEST WAS STUFFED WITH PIECEGOODS: LADIES' KID GLOVES, RIBBONS, LENGTHS OF SILK AND SPOOLS OF LACE.
IN ALL HER YEARS OF STEALING SHE HAD NEVER BEEN STOPPED.

AFTER EACH OF HER VISITS
TO THE DRY-GOODS STORE,
THE OWNER WOULD CALL
MR. MURPHY, WHO
PROMPTLY (AND OF COURSE,
QUIETLY) CAME DOWN
AND PAID THE BILL.

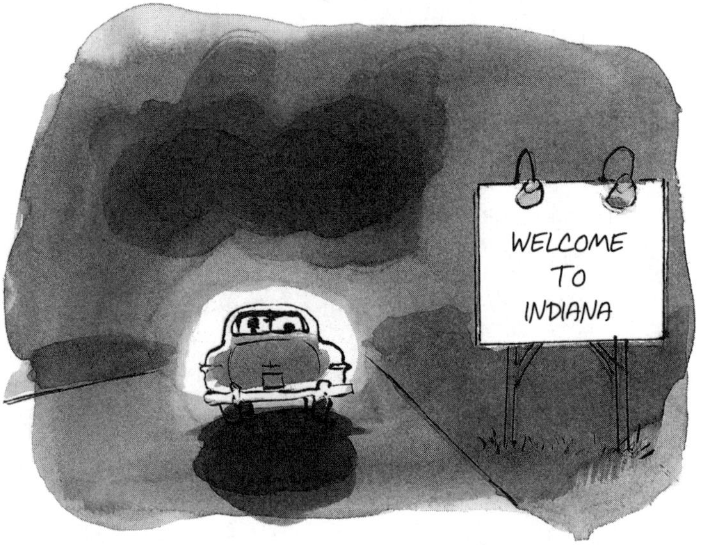
WELCOME
TO
INDIANA

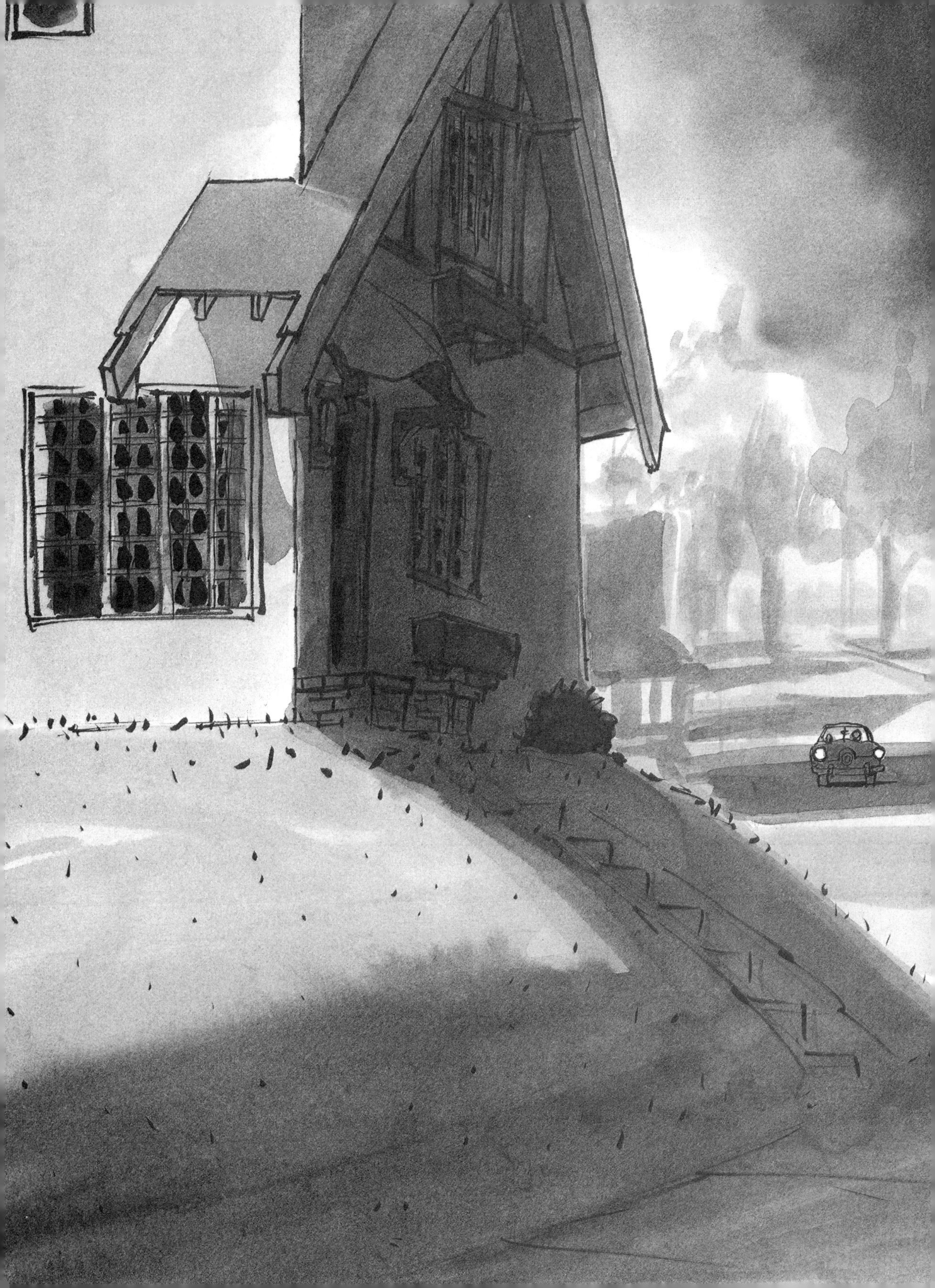

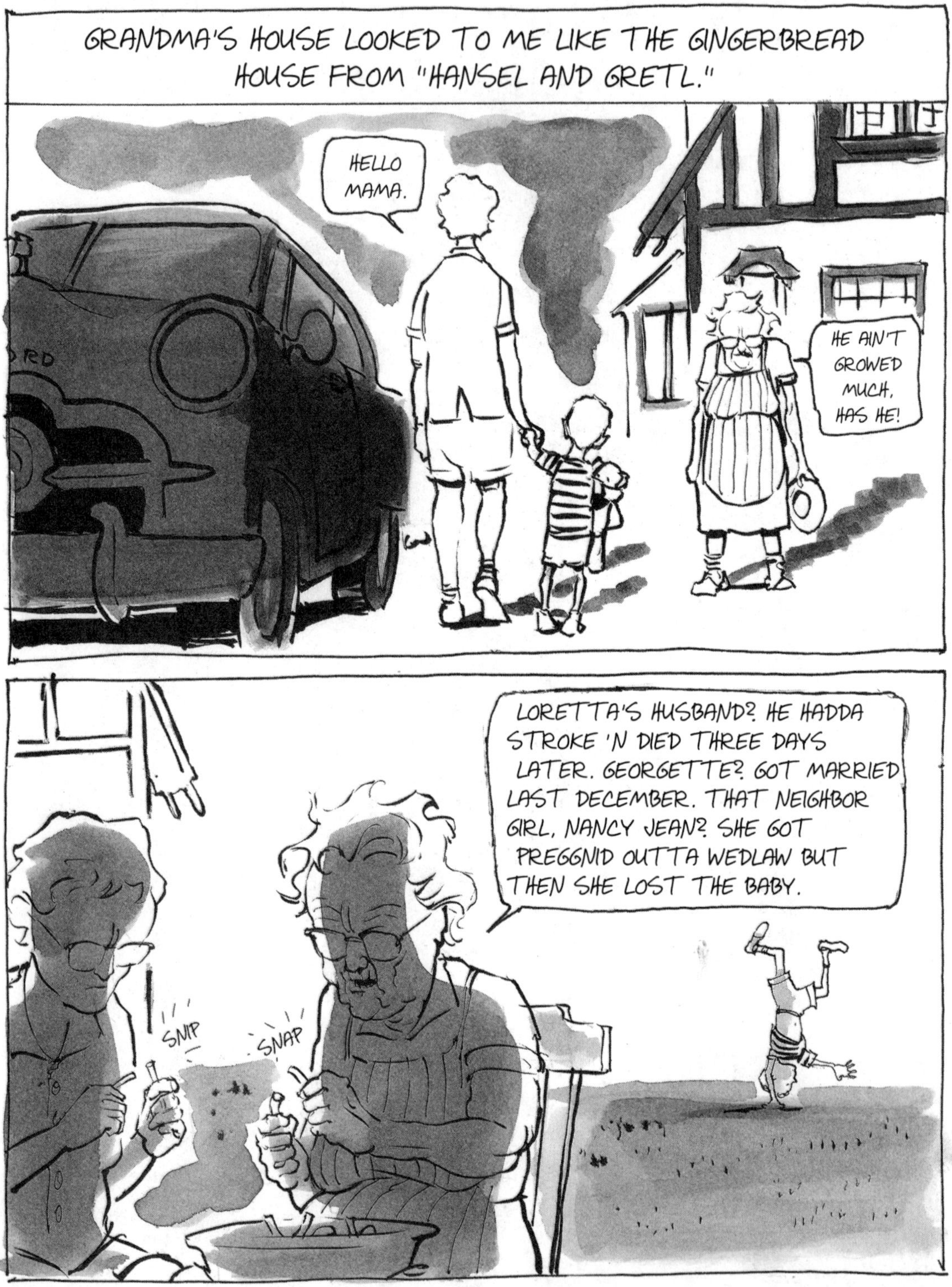
GRANDMA'S HOUSE LOOKED TO ME LIKE THE GINGERBREAD HOUSE FROM "HANSEL AND GRETL."
HELLO MAMA.
HE AIN'T GROWED MUCH, HAS HE!
LORETTA'S HUSBAND? HE HADDA STROKE 'N DIED THREE DAYS LATER. GEORGETTE? GOT MARRIED LAST DECEMBER. THAT NEIGHBOR GIRL, NANCY JEAN? SHE GOT PREGGNID OUTTA WEDLAW BUT THEN SHE LOST THE BABY.
SNIP
SNAP

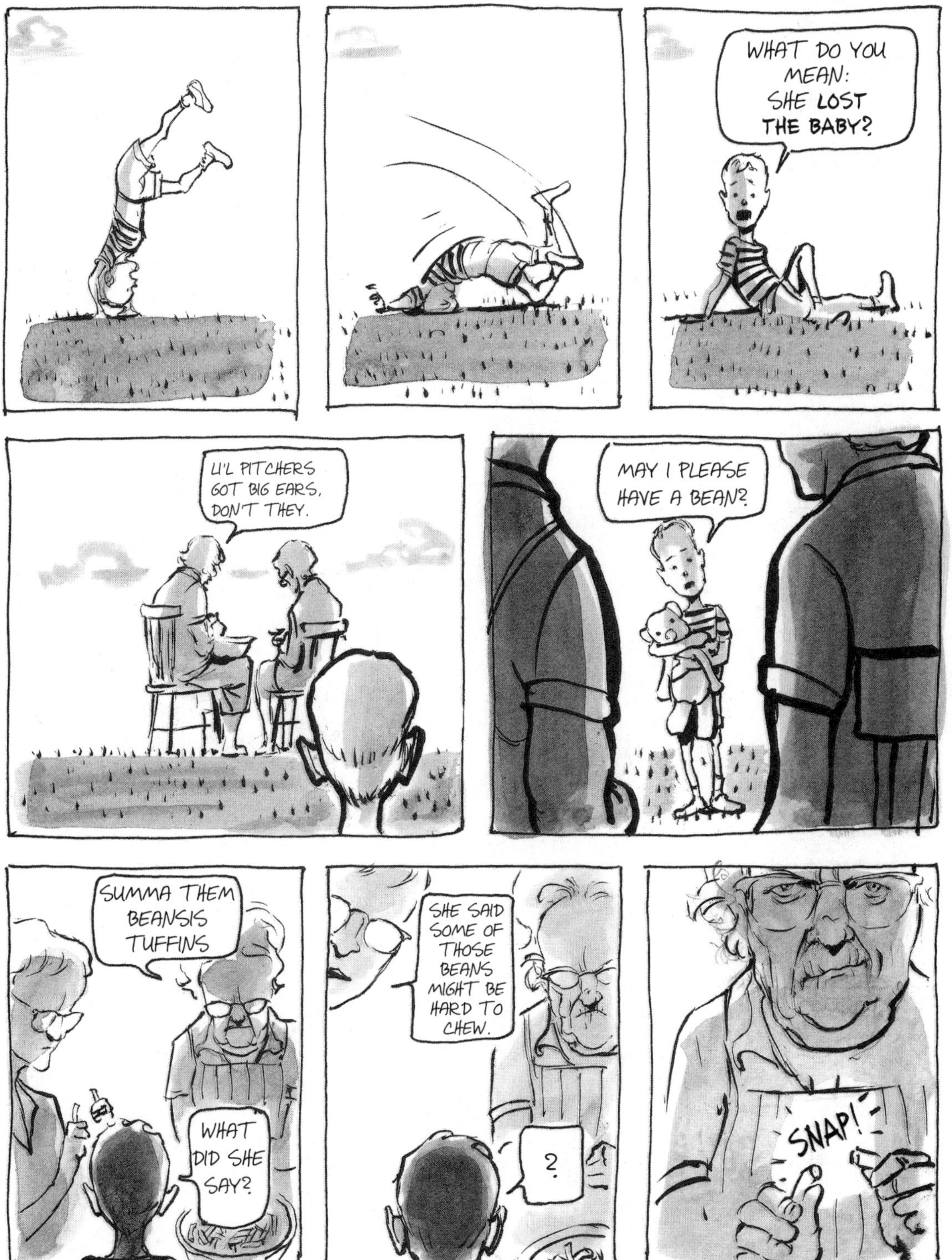

WHAT DO YOU MEAN: SHE LOST THE BABY?
LI'L PITCHERS GOT BIG EARS, DON'T THEY.
MAY I PLEASE HAVE A BEAN?
SUMMA THEM BEANSIS TUFFINS
WHAT DID SHE SAY?
SHE SAID SOME OF THOSE BEANS MIGHT BE HARD TO CHEW.
?
SNAP!

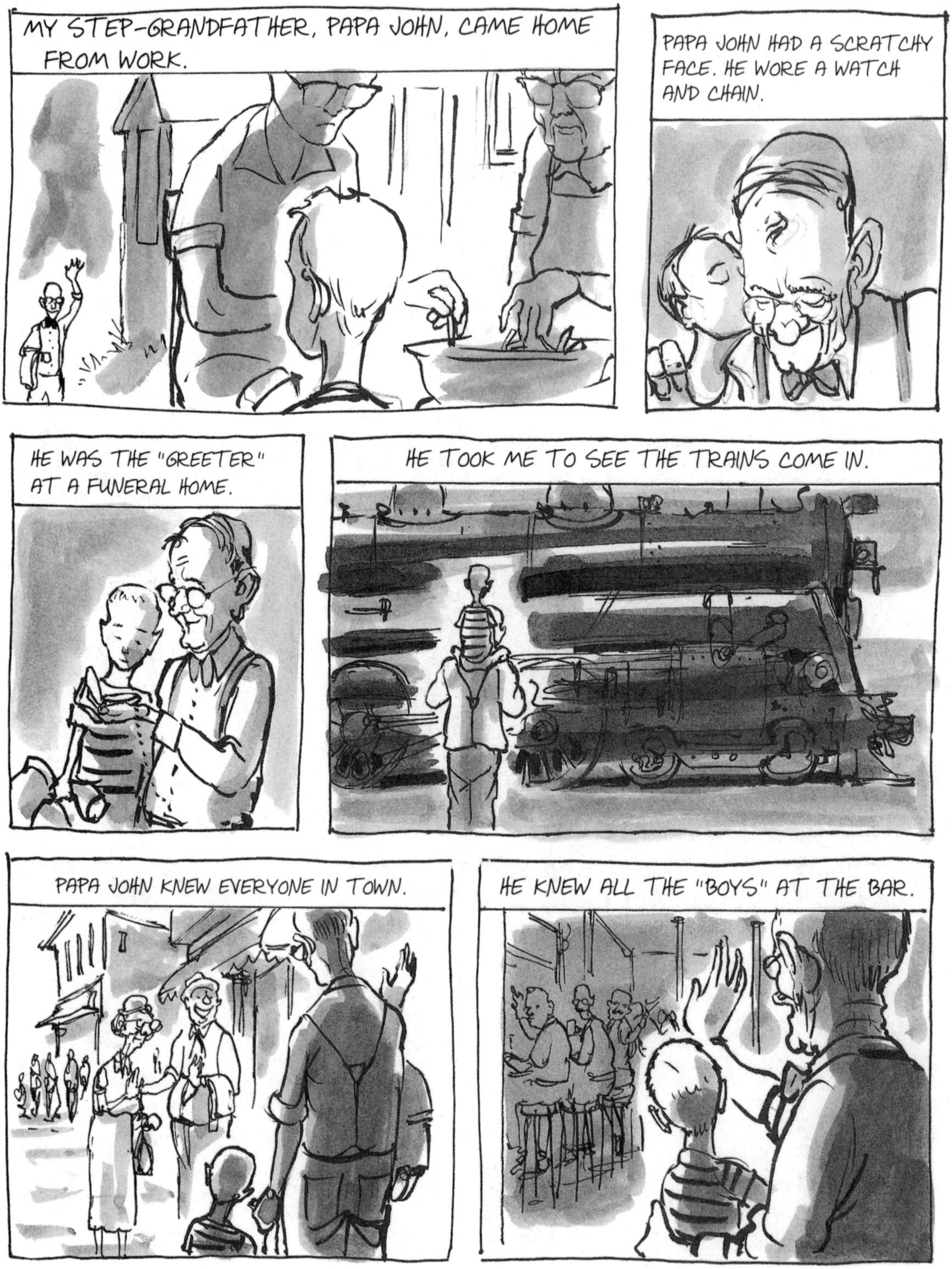
MY STEP-GRANDFATHER, PAPA JOHN, CAME HOME FROM WORK.
PAPA JOHN HAD A SCRATCHY FACE. HE WORE A WATCH AND CHAIN.
HE WAS THE "GREETER" AT A FUNERAL HOME.
HE TOOK ME TO SEE THE TRAINS COME IN.
PAPA JOHN KNEW EVERYONE IN TOWN.
HE KNEW ALL THE "BOYS" AT THE BAR.

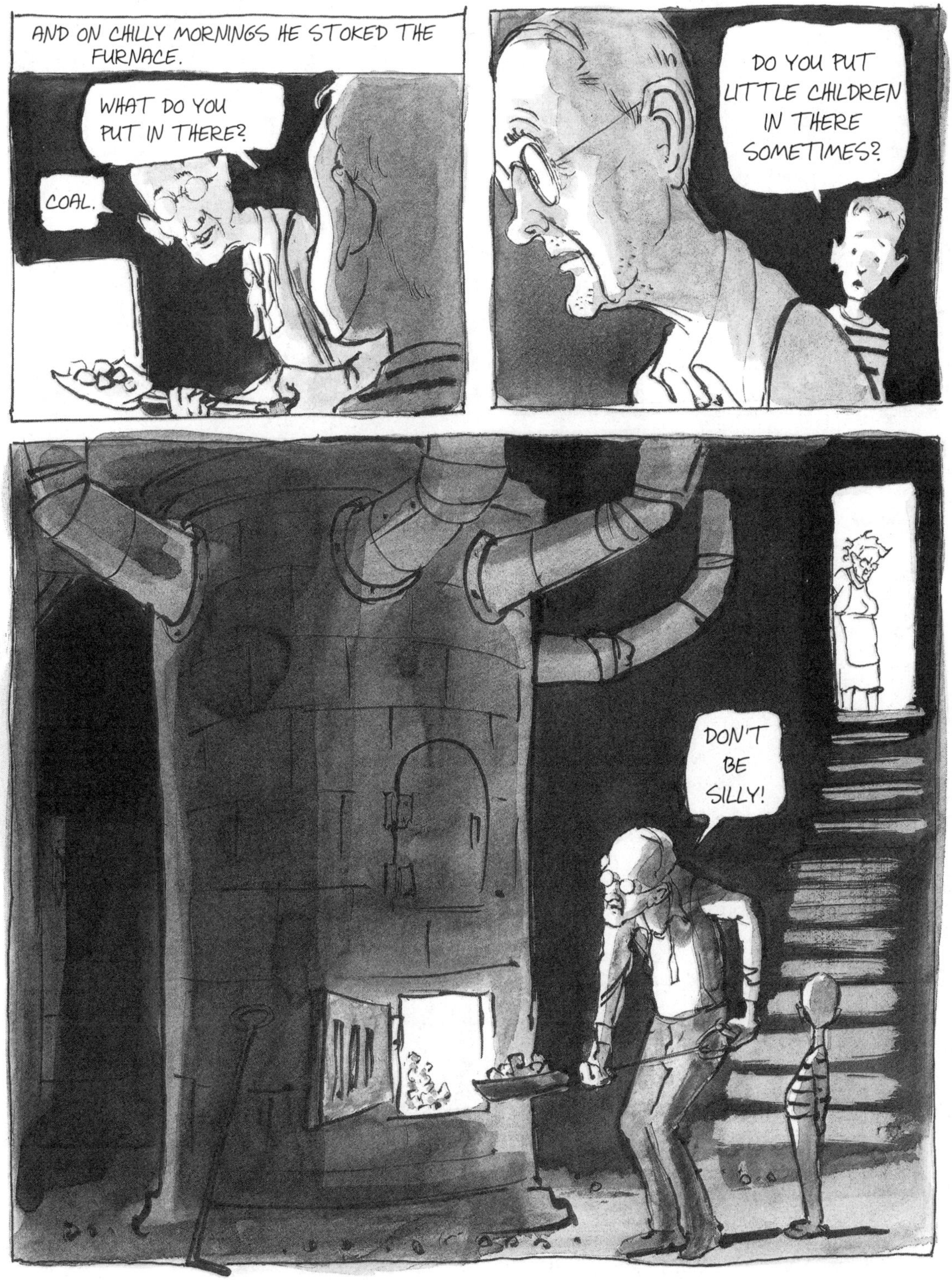
AND ON CHILLY MORNINGS HE STOKED THE FURNACE.
WHAT DO YOU PUT IN THERE?
COAL.
DO YOU PUT LITTLE CHILDREN IN THERE SOMETIMES?
DON'T BE SILLY!

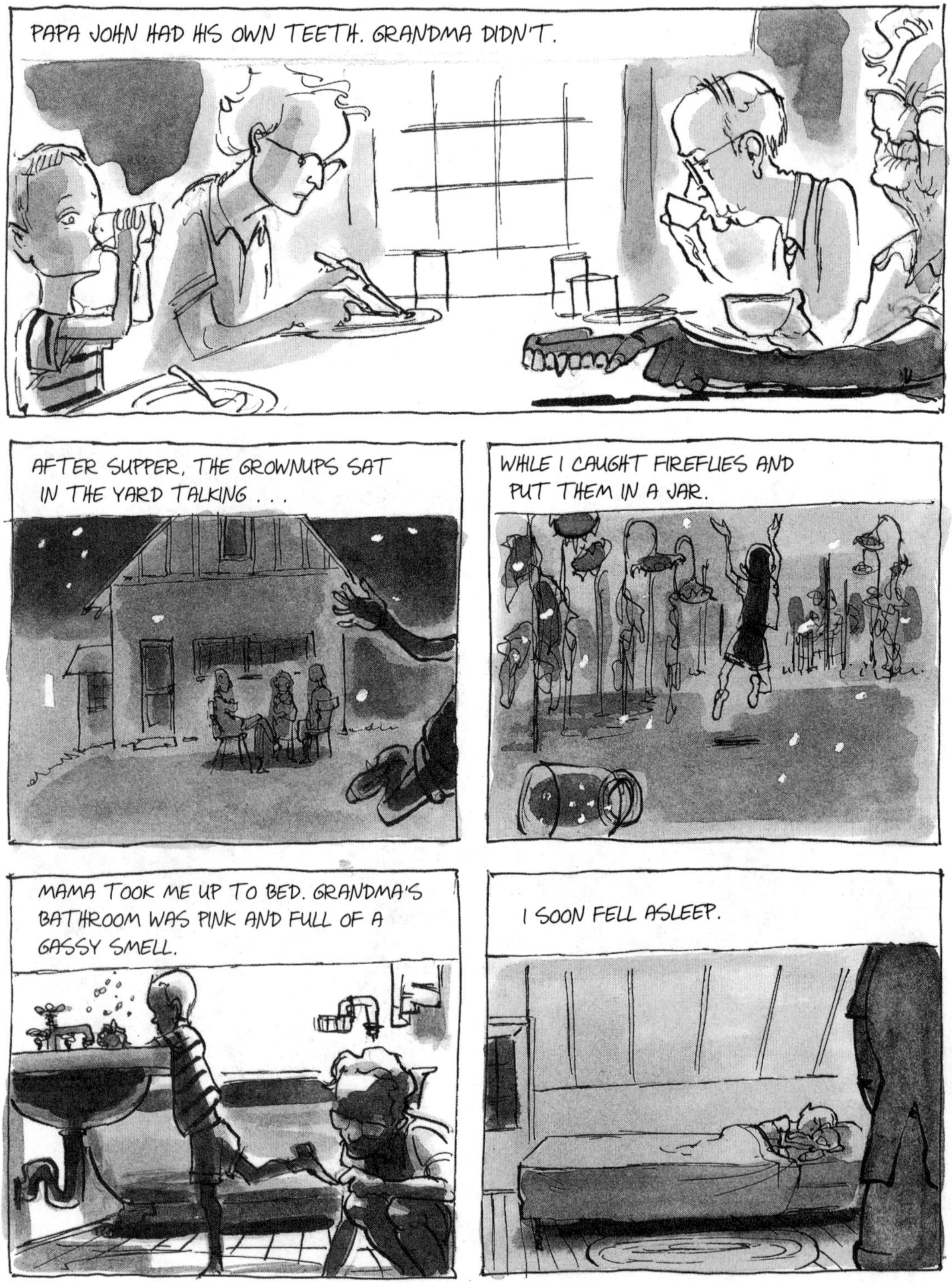
PAPA JOHN HAD HIS OWN TEETH. GRANDMA DIDN'T.
AFTER SUPPER, THE GROWNUPS SAT IN THE YARD TALKING . . .
WHILE I CAUGHT FIREFLIES AND PUT THEM IN A JAR.
MAMA TOOK ME UP TO BED. GRANDMA'S BATHROOM WAS PINK AND FULL OF A GASSY SMELL.
I SOON FELL ASLEEP.

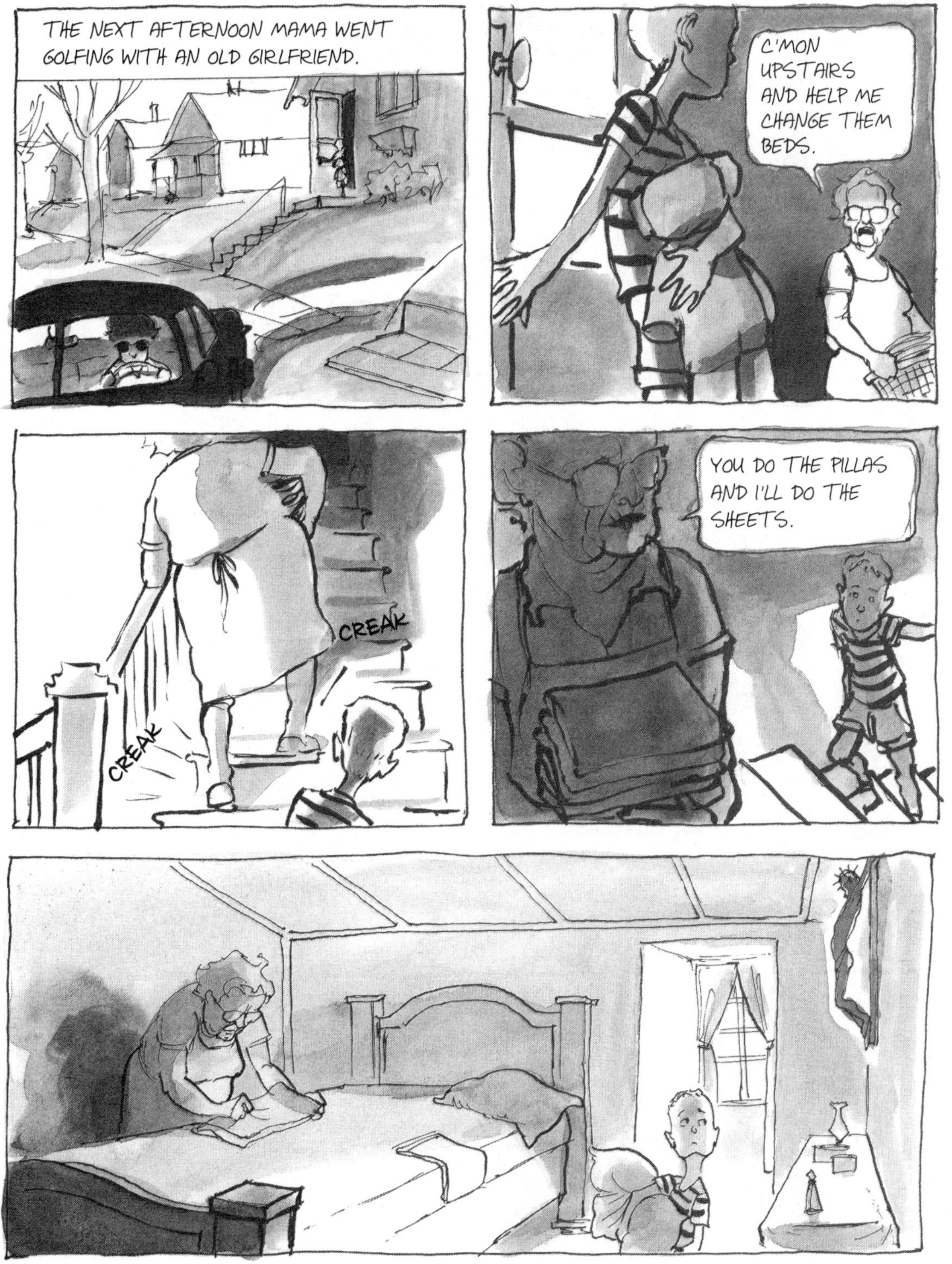
THE NEXT AFTERNOON MAMA WENT GOLFING WITH AN OLD GIRLFRIEND.
C'MON UPSTAIRS AND HELP ME CHANGE THEM BEDS.
CREAK
CREAK
YOU DO THE PILLAS AND I'LL DO THE SHEETS.

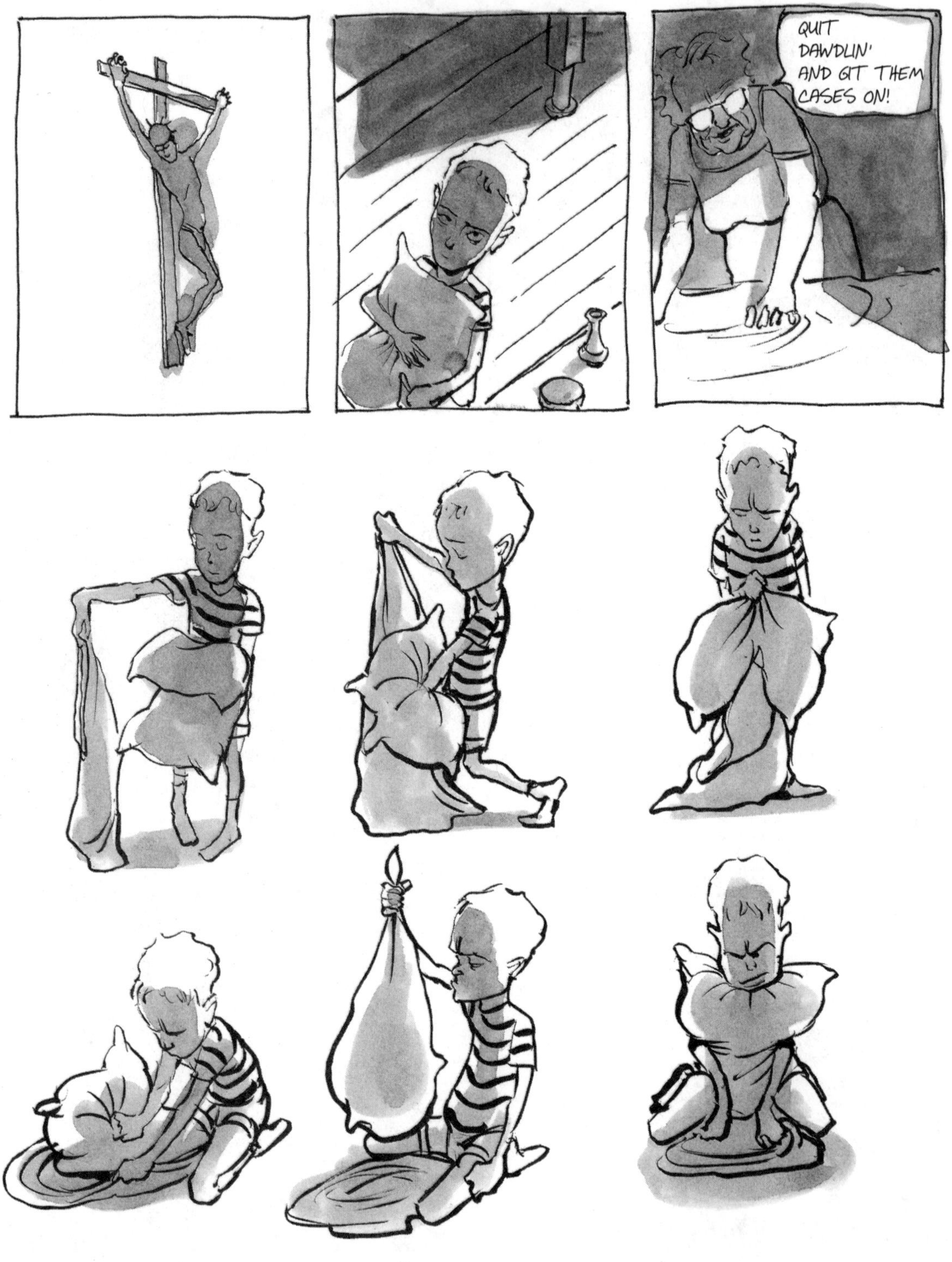
QUIT DAWDLIN' AND GIT THEM CASES ON!

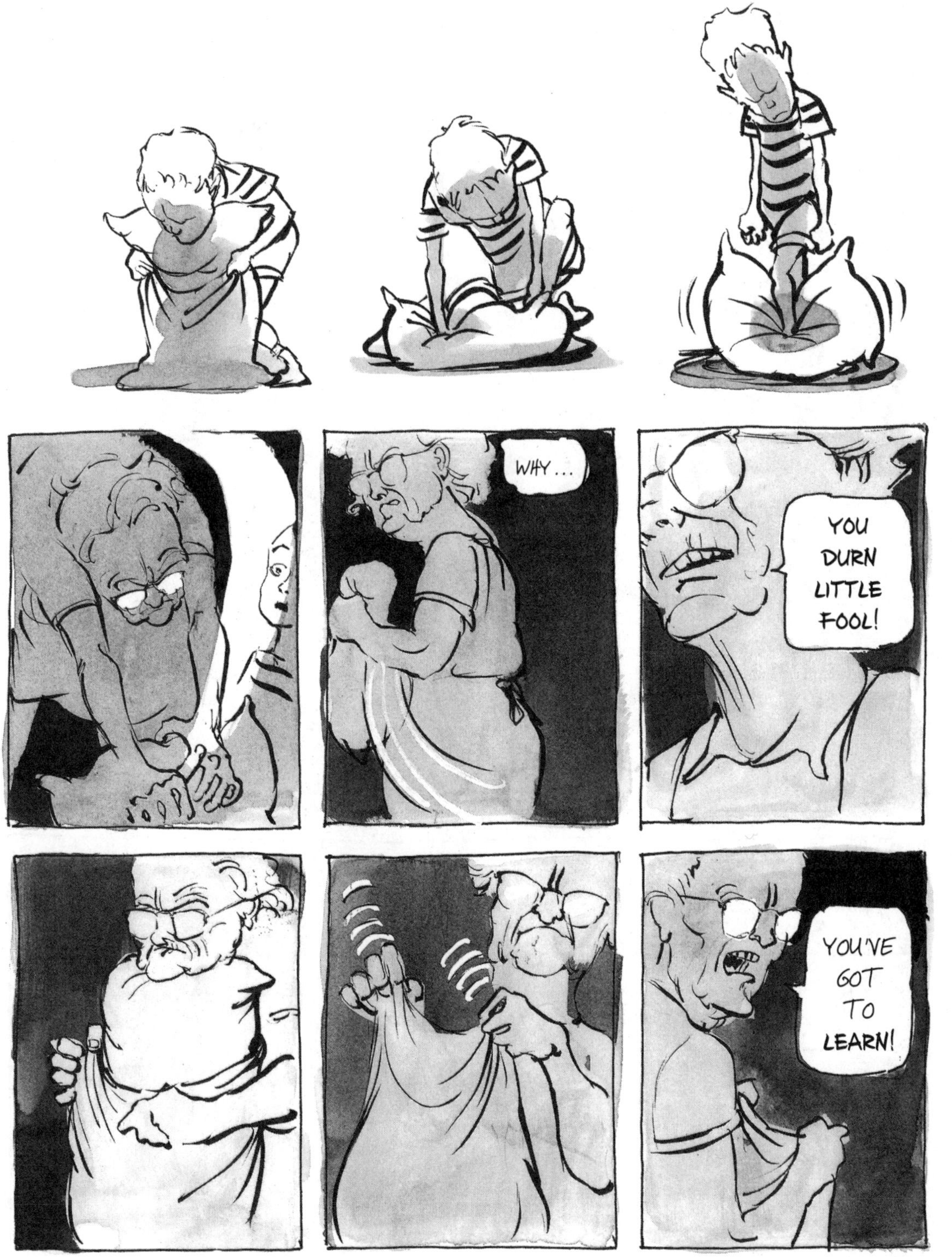
WHY...
YOU DURN LITTLE FOOL!
YOU'VE GOT TO LEARN!

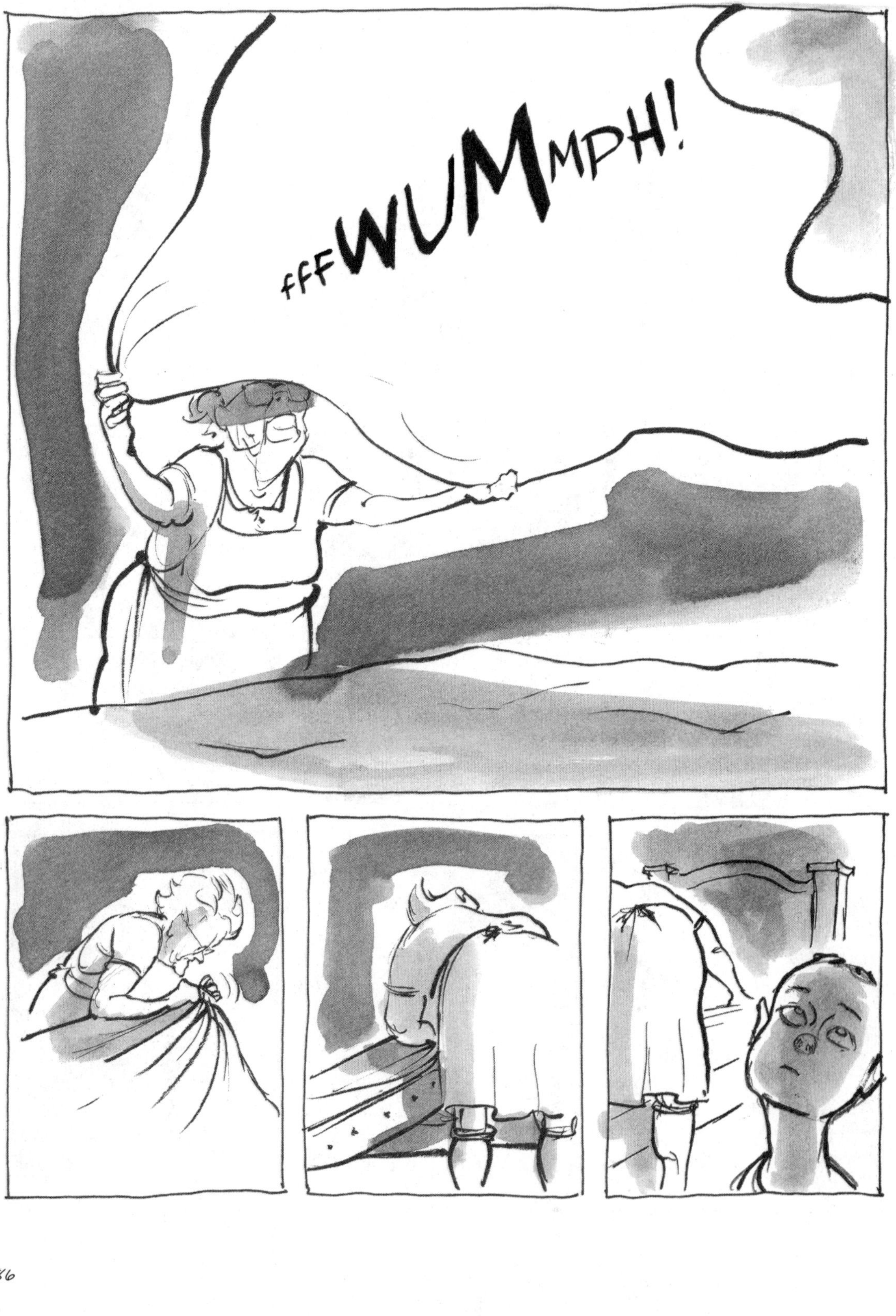
fffWUMMPH!

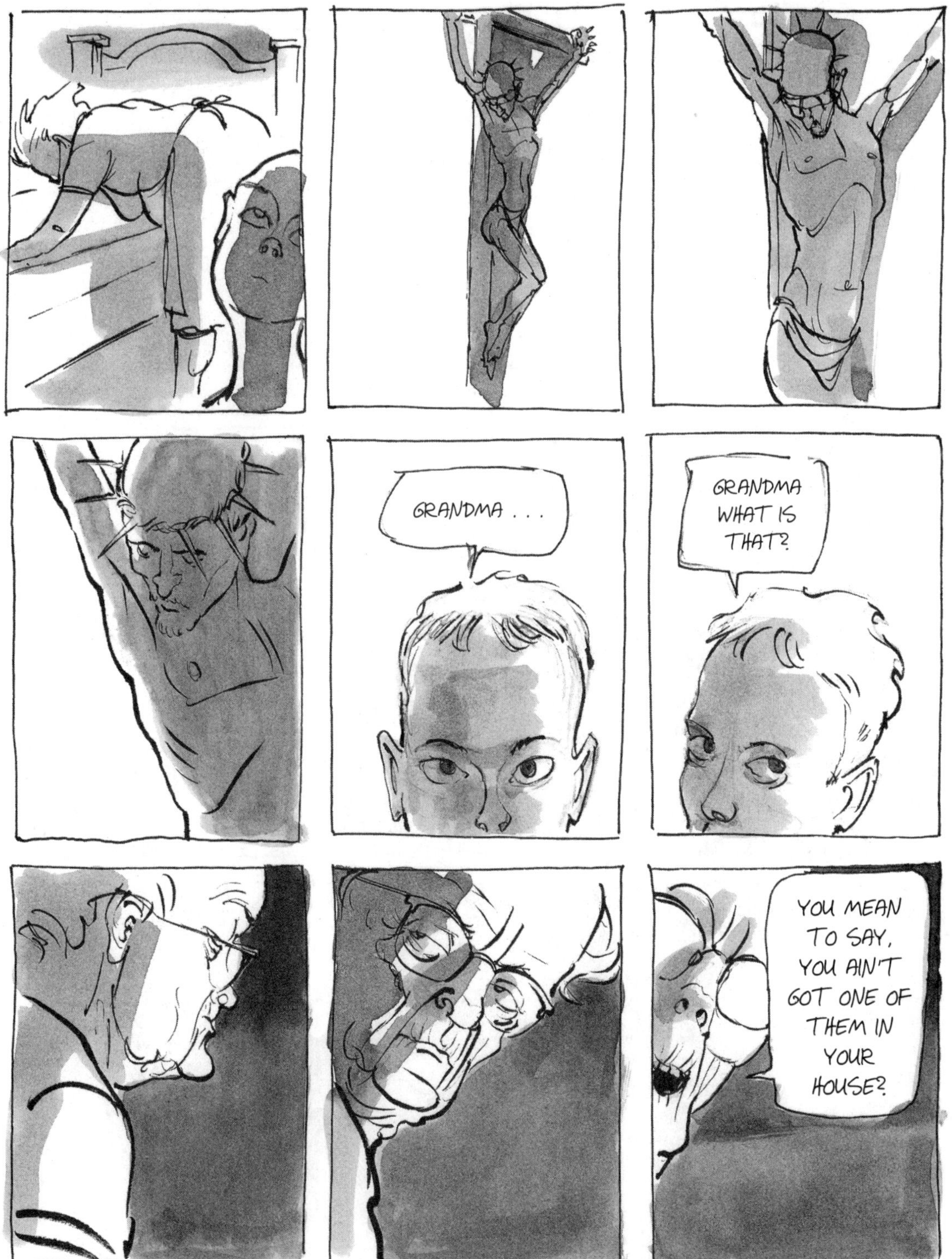
GRANDMA . . .
GRANDMA WHAT IS THAT?
YOU MEAN TO SAY, YOU AIN'T GOT ONE OF THEM IN YOUR HOUSE?

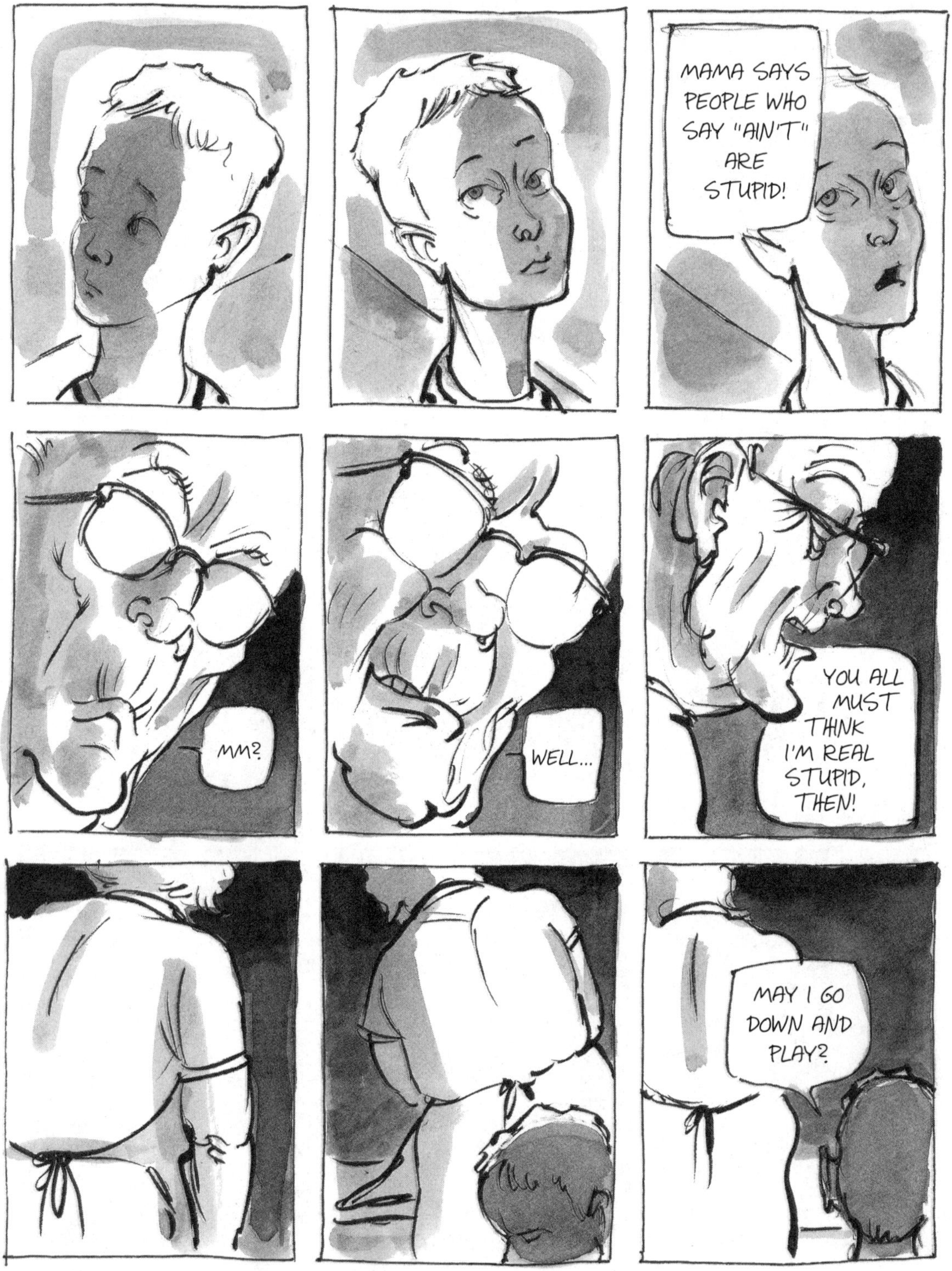
MAMA SAYS PEOPLE WHO SAY "AIN'T" ARE STUPID!
MM?
WELL...
YOU ALL MUST THINK I'M REAL STUPID, THEN!
MAY I GO DOWN AND PLAY?

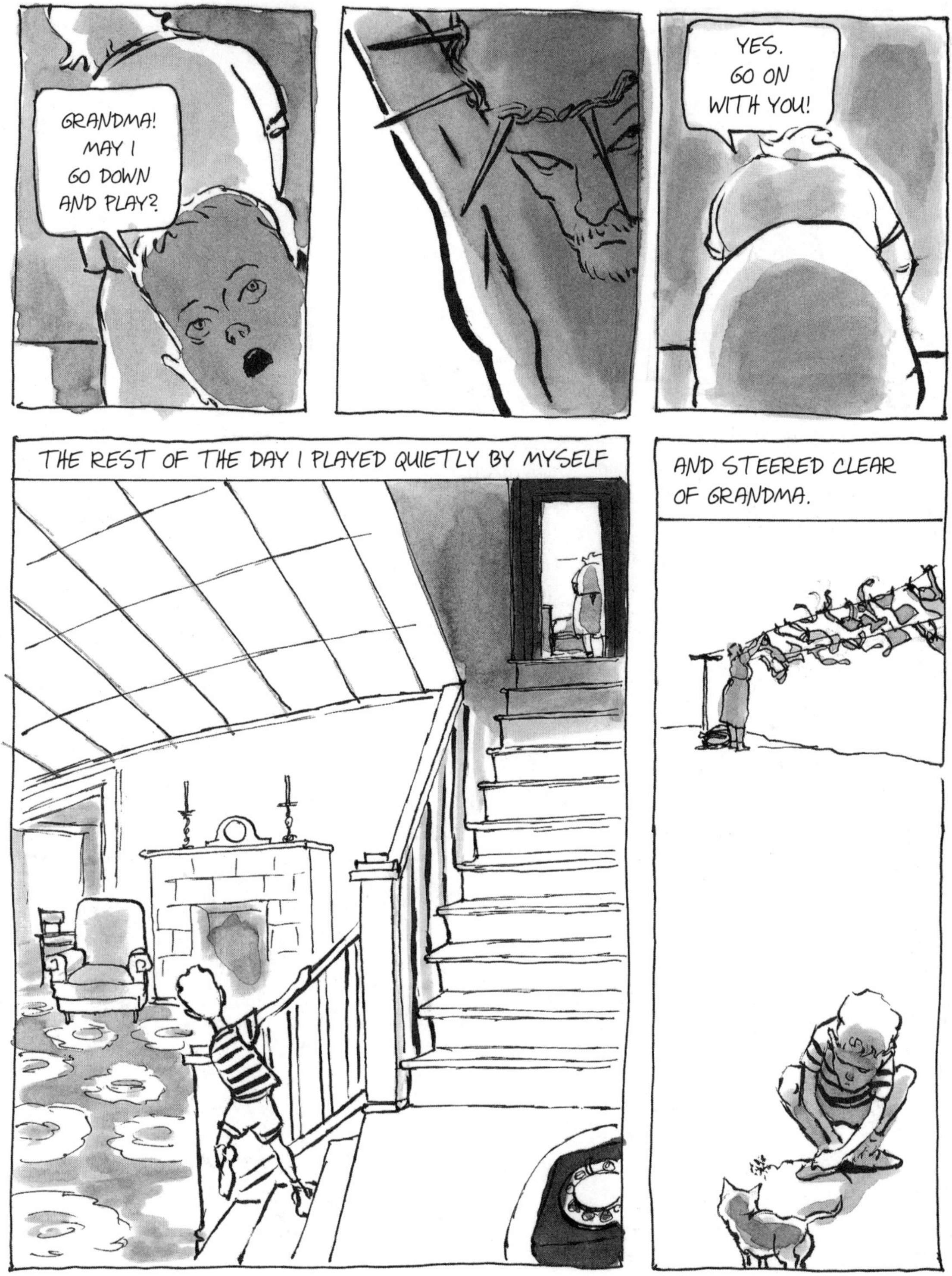
GRANDMA! MAY I GO DOWN AND PLAY?
YES. GO ON WITH YOU!
THE REST OF THE DAY I PLAYED QUIETLY BY MYSELF
AND STEERED CLEAR OF GRANDMA.

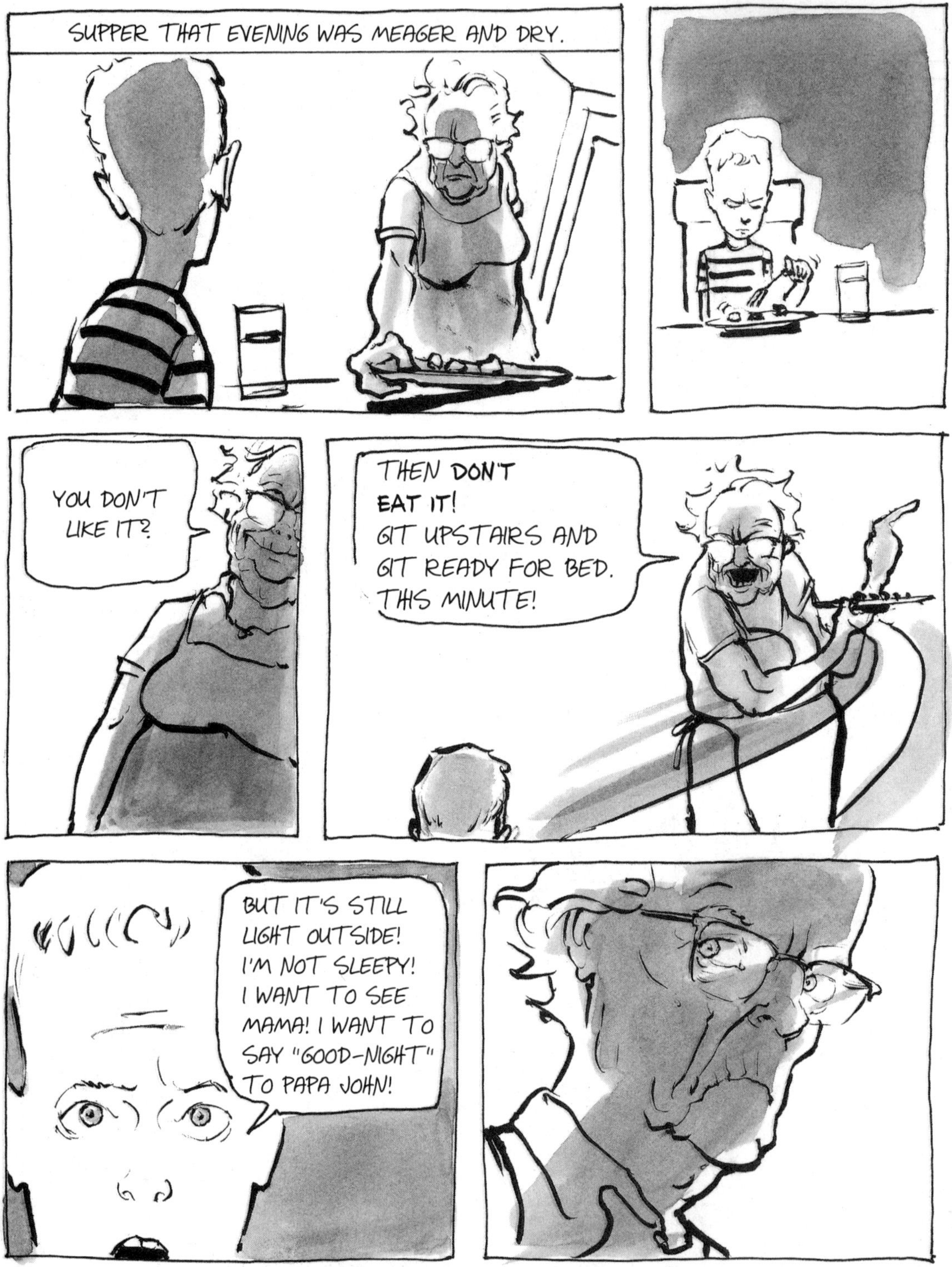
SUPPER THAT EVENING WAS MEAGER AND DRY.
YOU DON'T LIKE IT?
THEN DON'T EAT IT! GIT UPSTAIRS AND GIT READY FOR BED. THIS MINUTE!
BUT IT'S STILL LIGHT OUTSIDE! I'M NOT SLEEPY! I WANT TO SEE MAMA! I WANT TO SAY "GOOD-NIGHT" TO PAPA JOHN!

I SAID GIT. NO BACK-TALK!

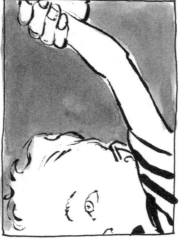

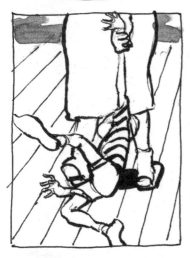

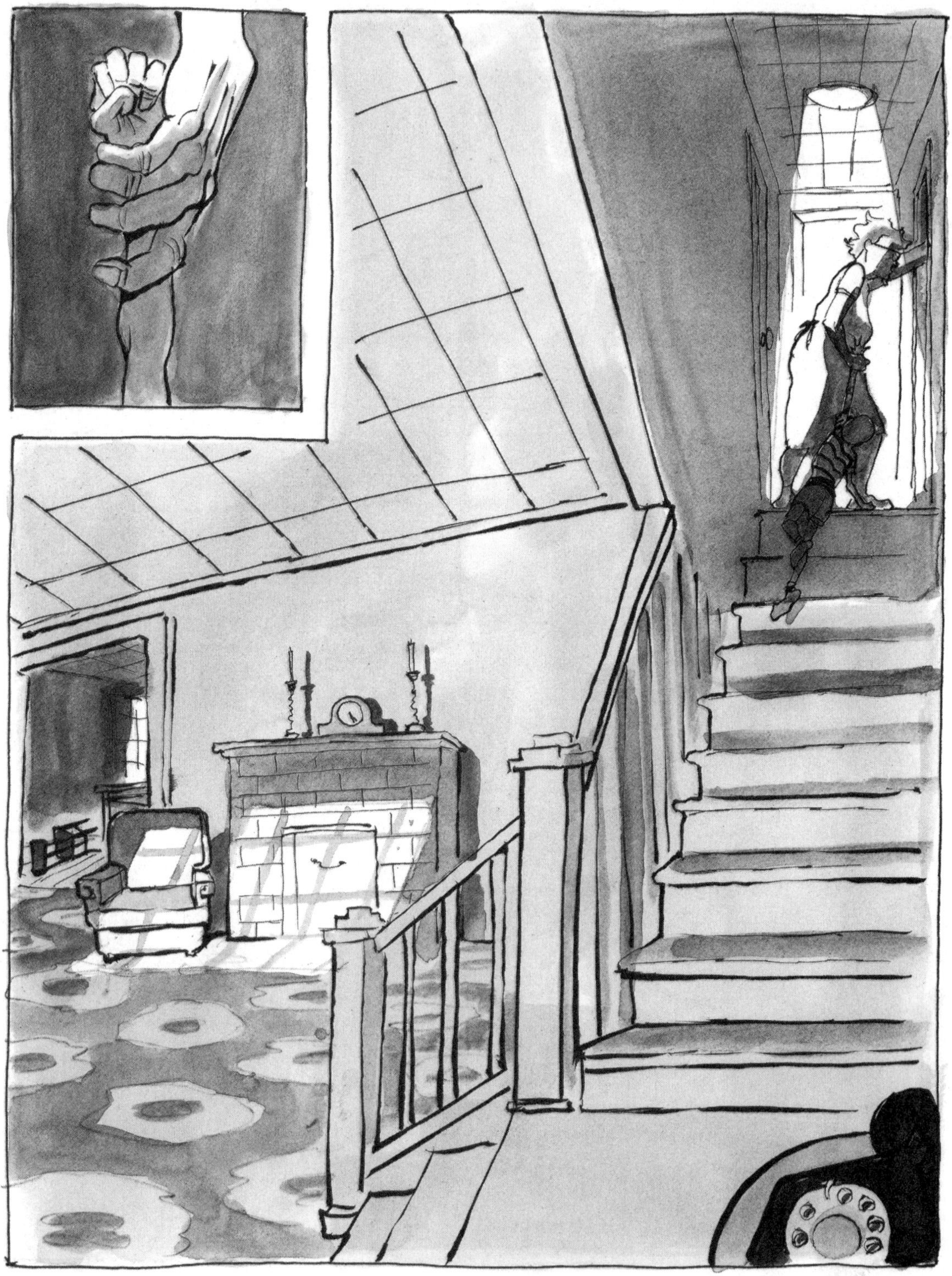

FIRST WE'RE GONNA WARSH YER HANDS.
SSSSSSSSS
SSSSSSSSSSSS
SSSSSSS
SSSSS

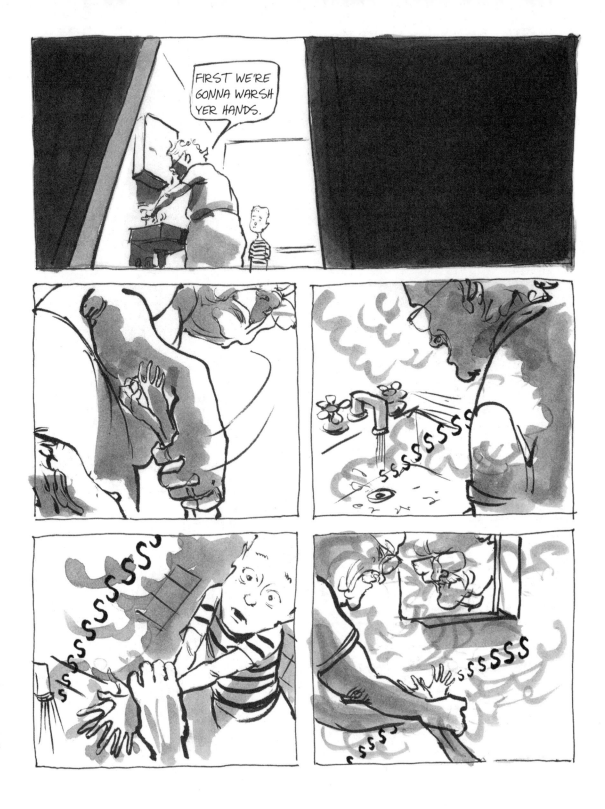

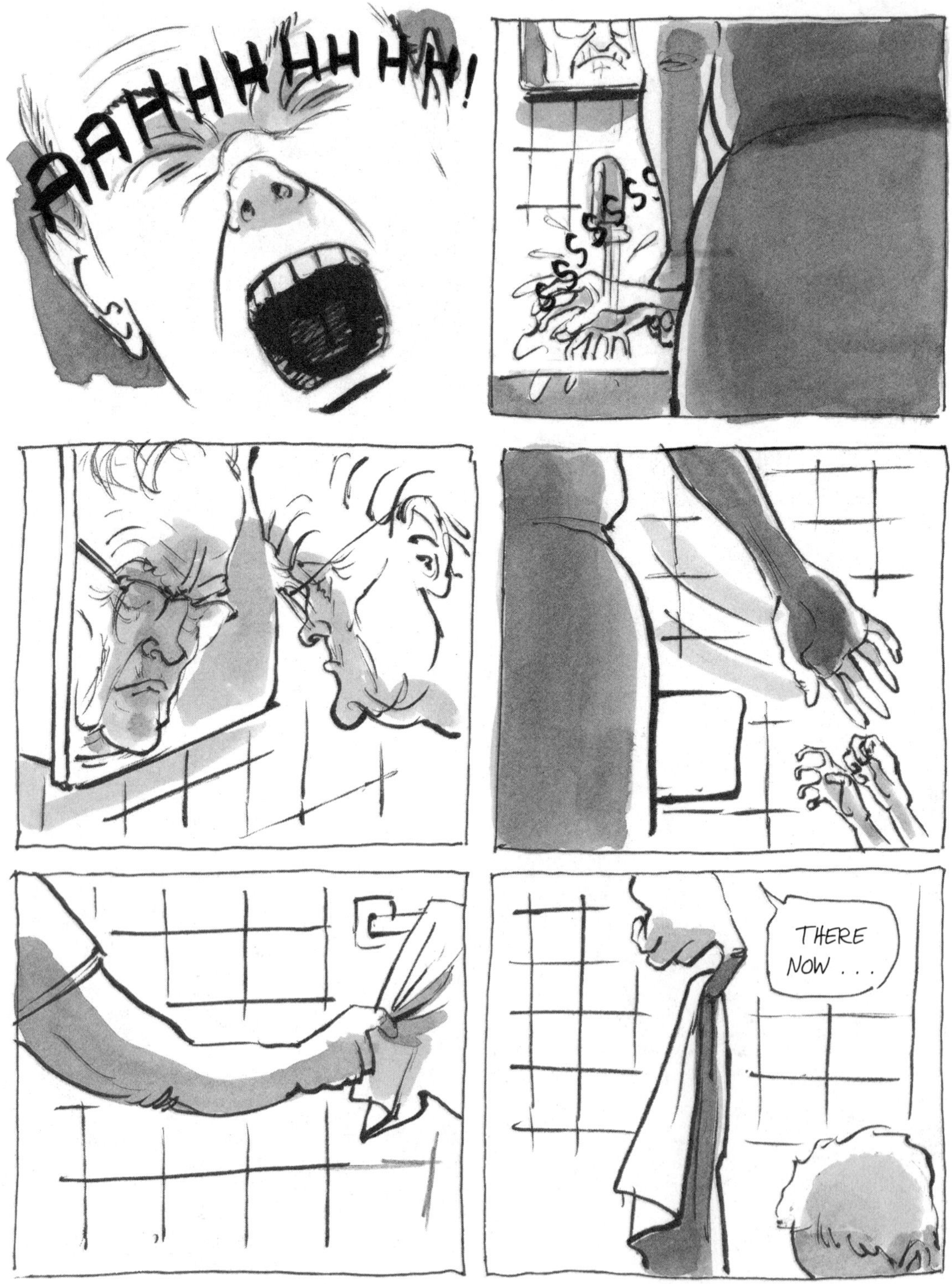
AAHHHHHHHHH!
SSSSSSS
THERE NOW . . .

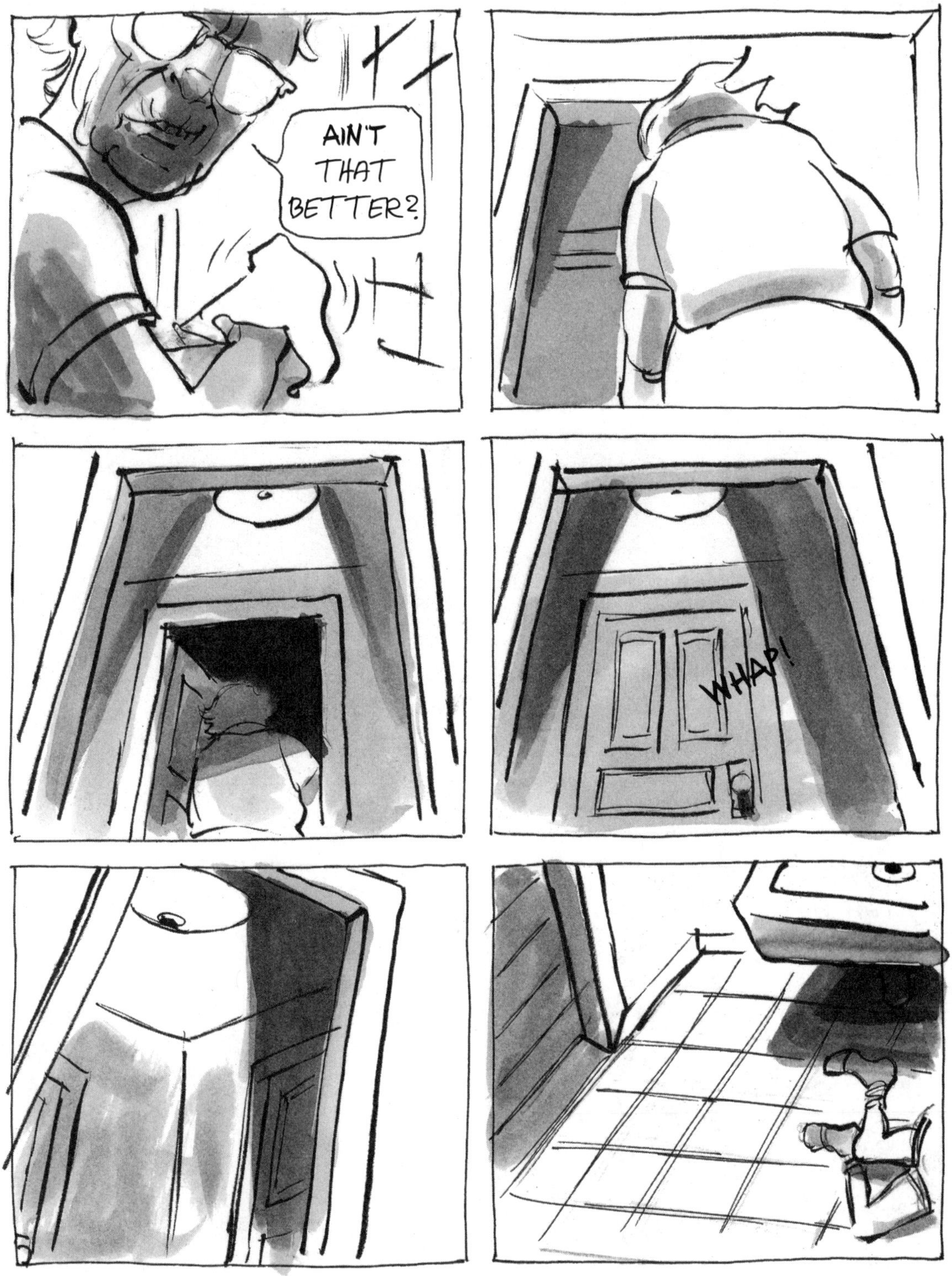
AIN'T THAT BETTER?
WHAP!

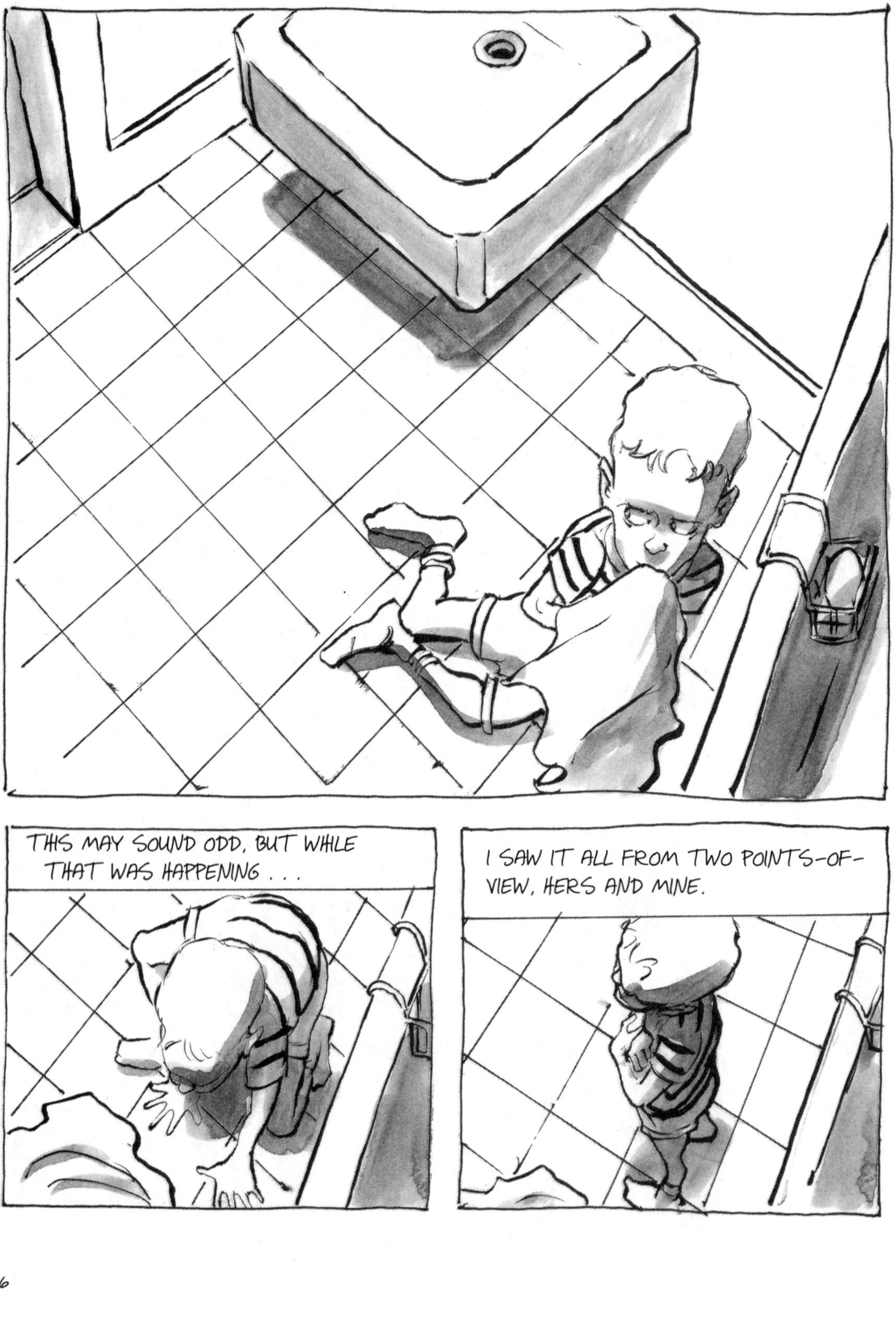
THIS MAY SOUND ODD, BUT WHILE THAT WAS HAPPENING . . .
I SAW IT ALL FROM TWO POINTS-OF-VIEW, HERS AND MINE.

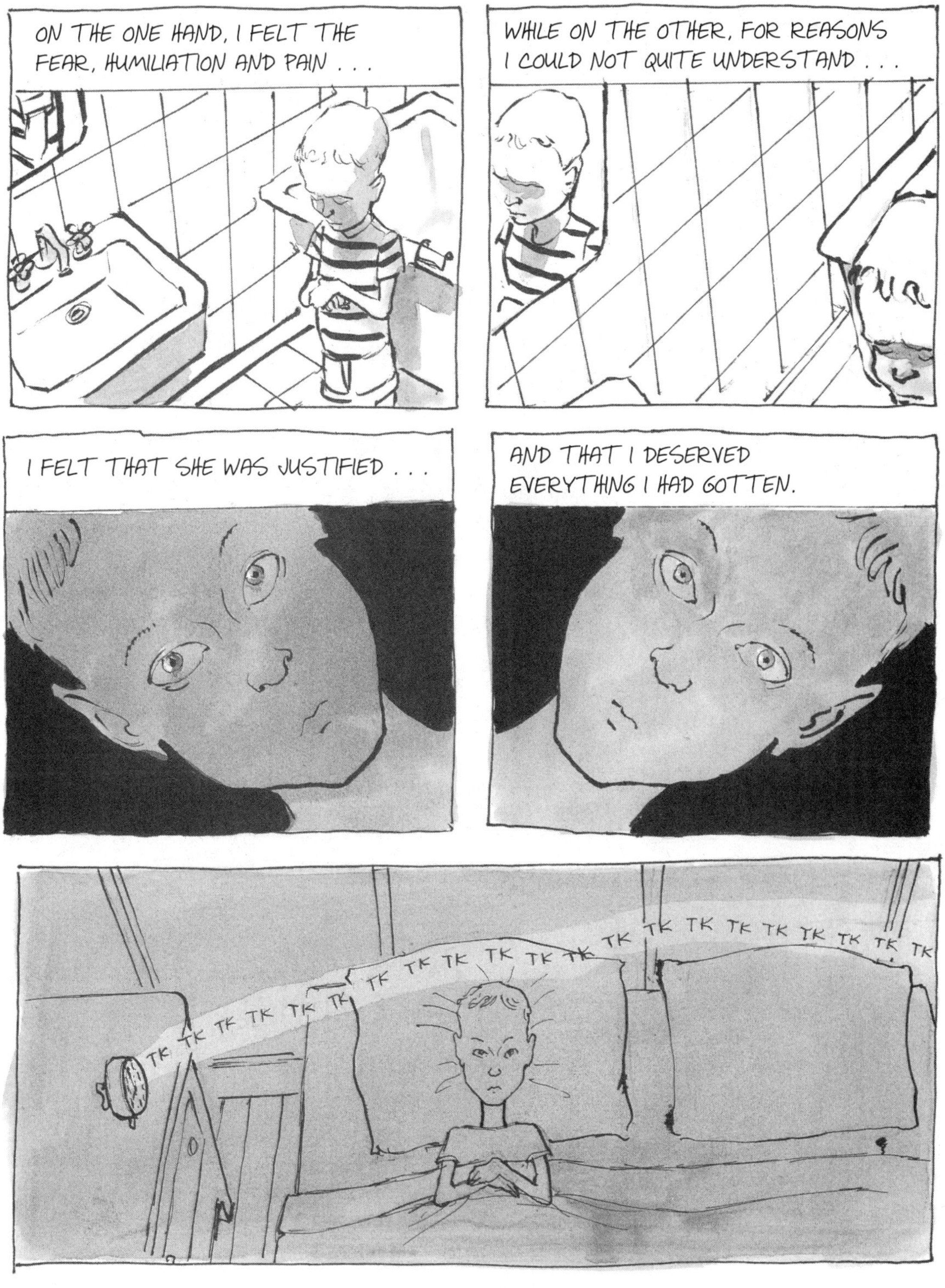
ON THE ONE HAND, I FELT THE FEAR, HUMILIATION AND PAIN . . .
WHILE ON THE OTHER, FOR REASONS I COULD NOT QUITE UNDERSTAND . . .
I FELT THAT SHE WAS JUSTIFIED . . .
AND THAT I DESERVED EVERYTHING I HAD GOTTEN.
TK TK TK TK TK TK TK TK TK TK TK TK TK TK TK TK TK TK TK TK TK TK TK

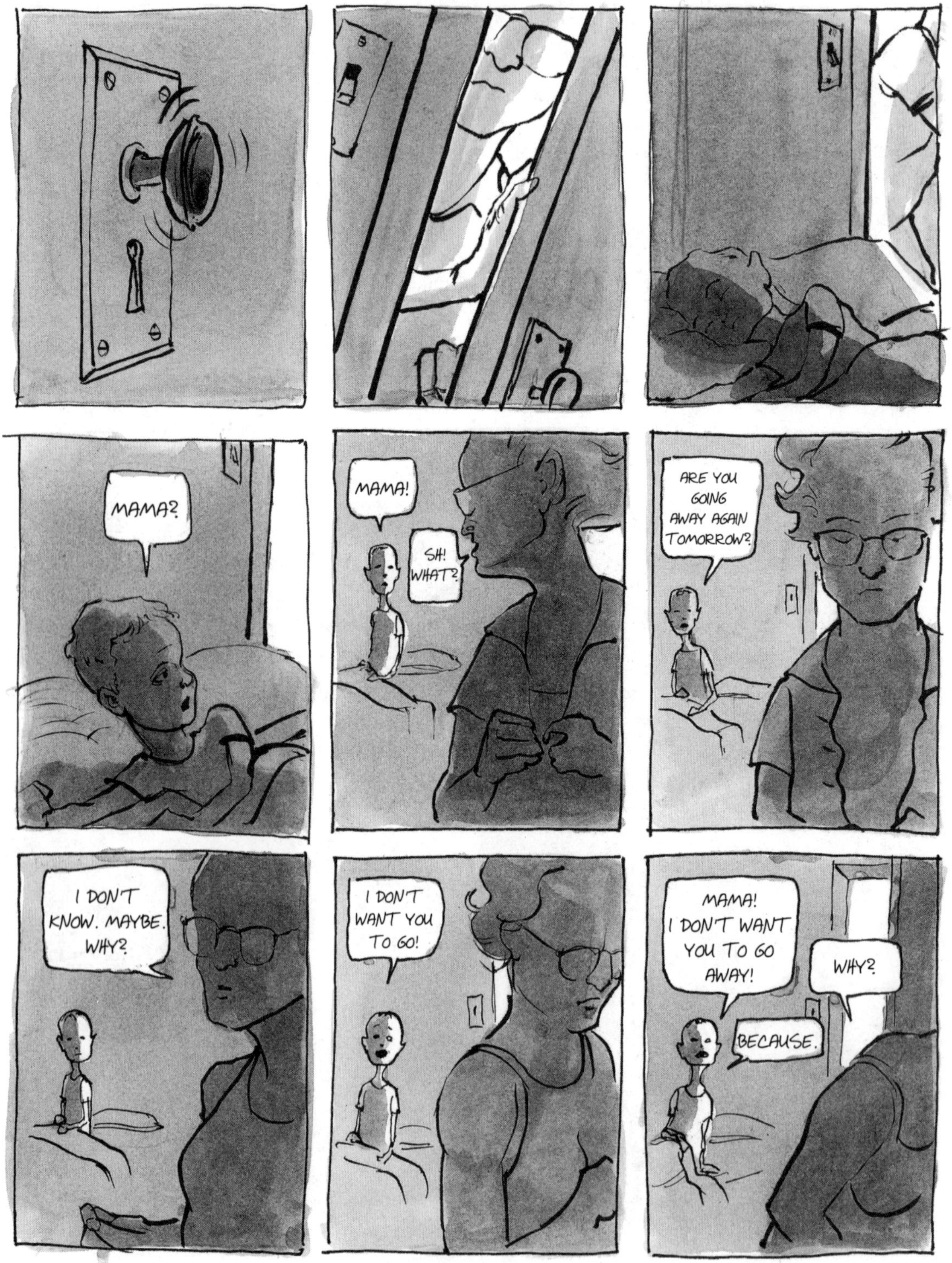
MAMA?
MAMA!
SH! WHAT?
ARE YOU GOING AWAY AGAIN TOMORROW?
I DON'T KNOW. MAYBE. WHY?
I DON'T WANT YOU TO GO!
MAMA! I DON'T WANT YOU TO GO AWAY!
WHY?
BECAUSE.

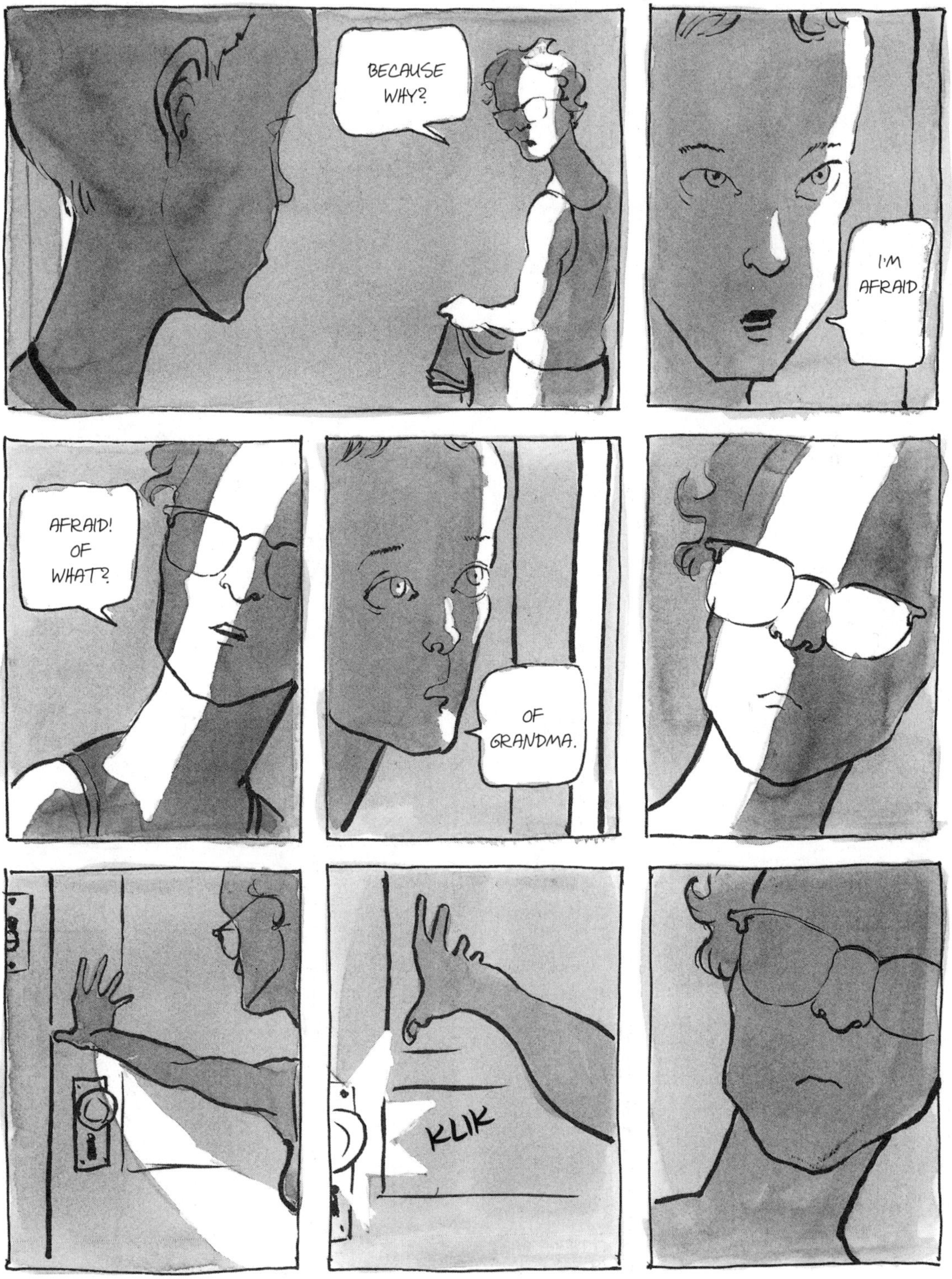
BECAUSE WHY?
I'M AFRAID.
AFRAID! OF WHAT?
OF GRANDMA.
KLIK

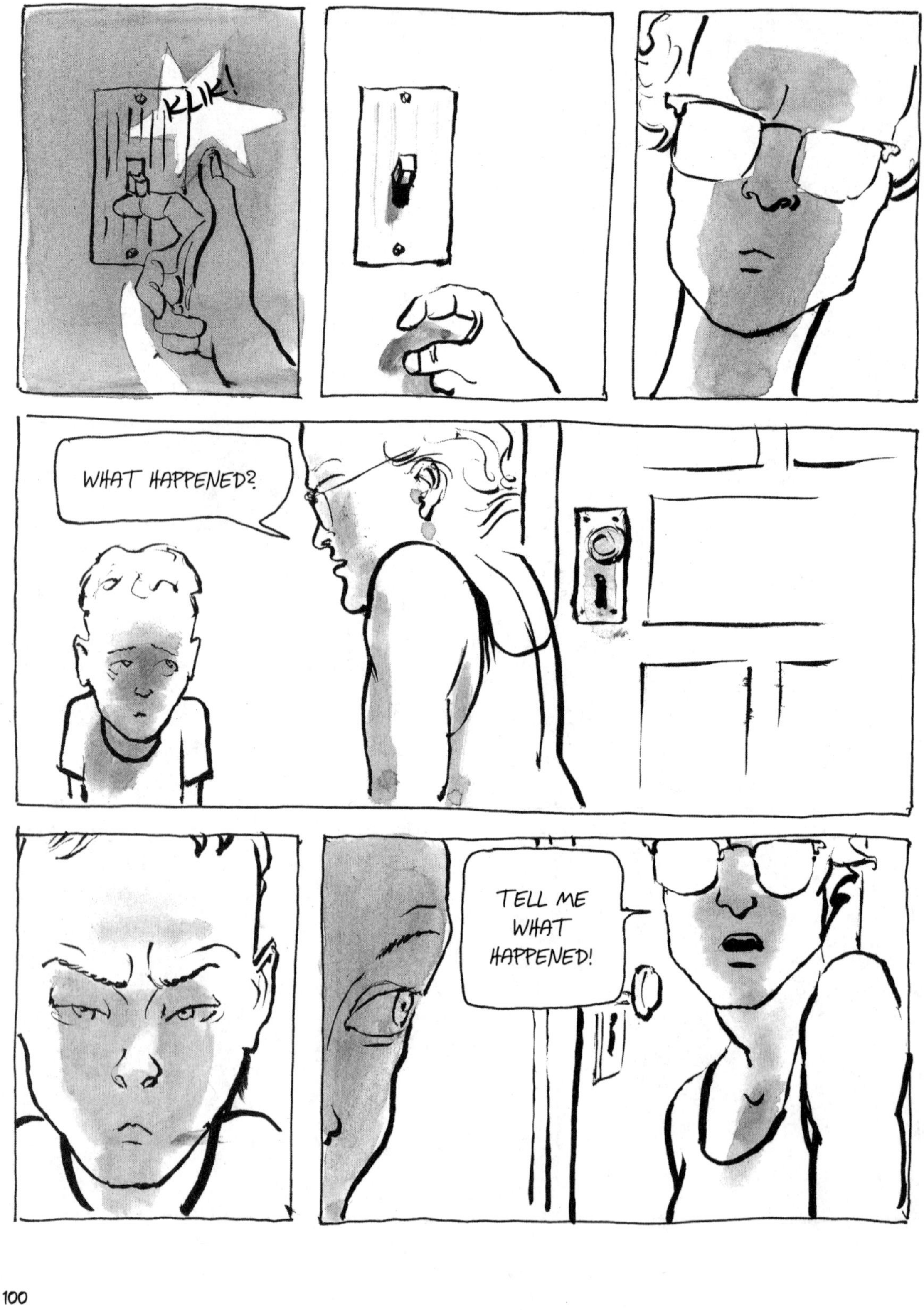
KLIK!
WHAT HAPPENED?
TELL ME WHAT HAPPENED!

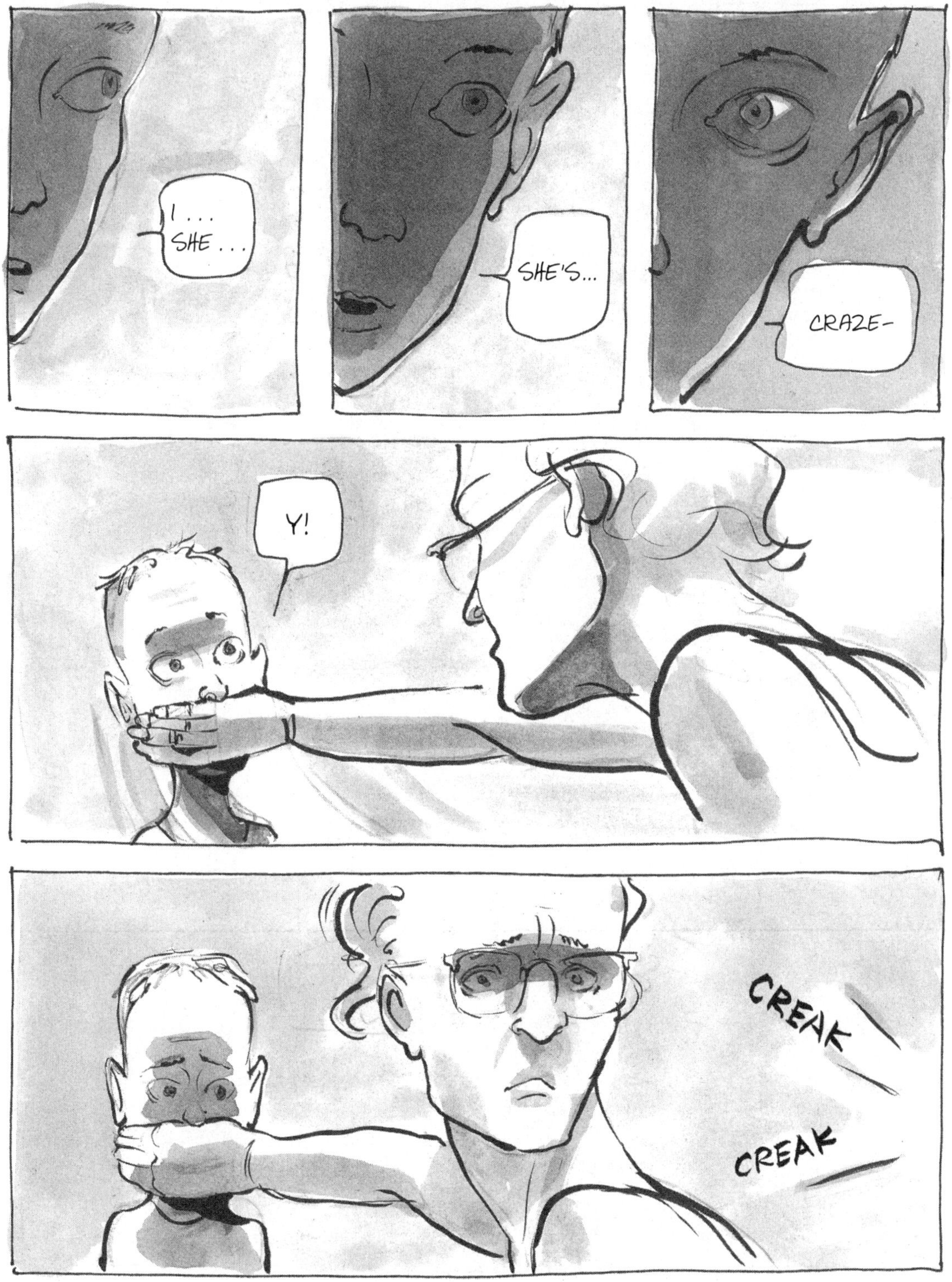
I . . .
SHE . . .
SHE'S...
CRAZE-
Y!
CREAK
CREAK

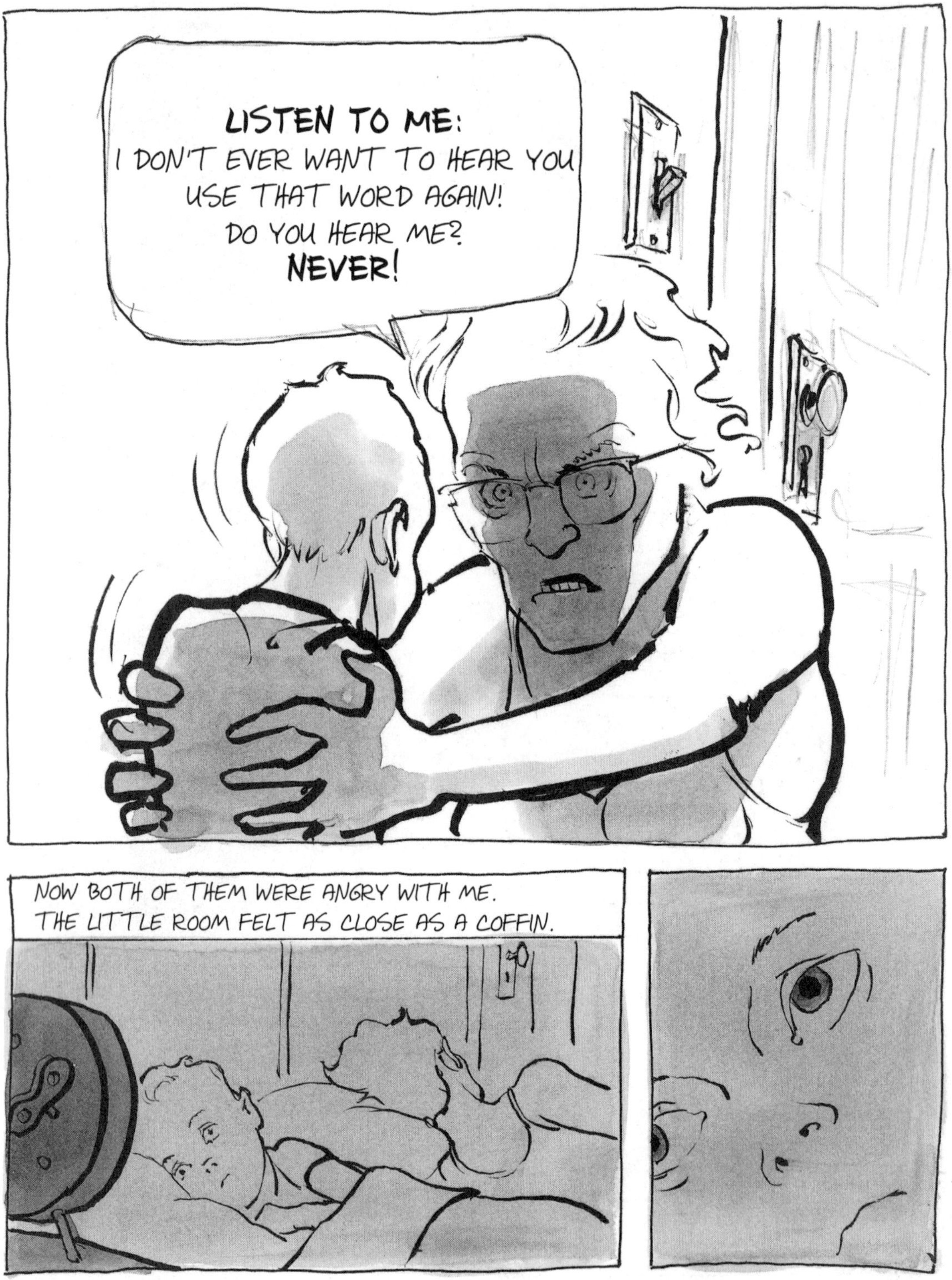
LISTEN TO ME:
I DON'T EVER WANT TO HEAR YOU USE THAT WORD AGAIN! DO YOU HEAR ME? NEVER!
NOW BOTH OF THEM WERE ANGRY WITH ME. THE LITTLE ROOM FELT AS CLOSE AS A COFFIN.

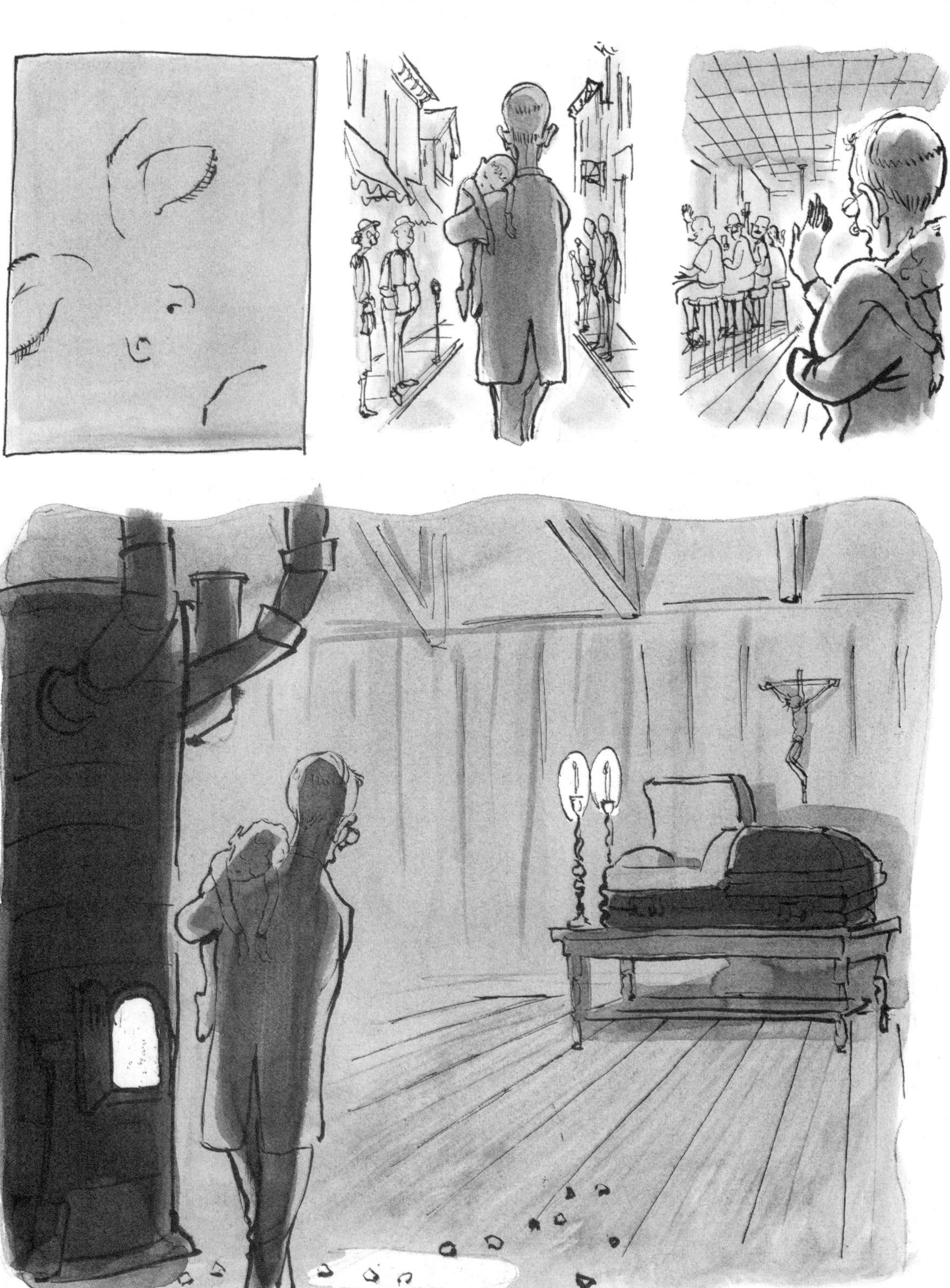

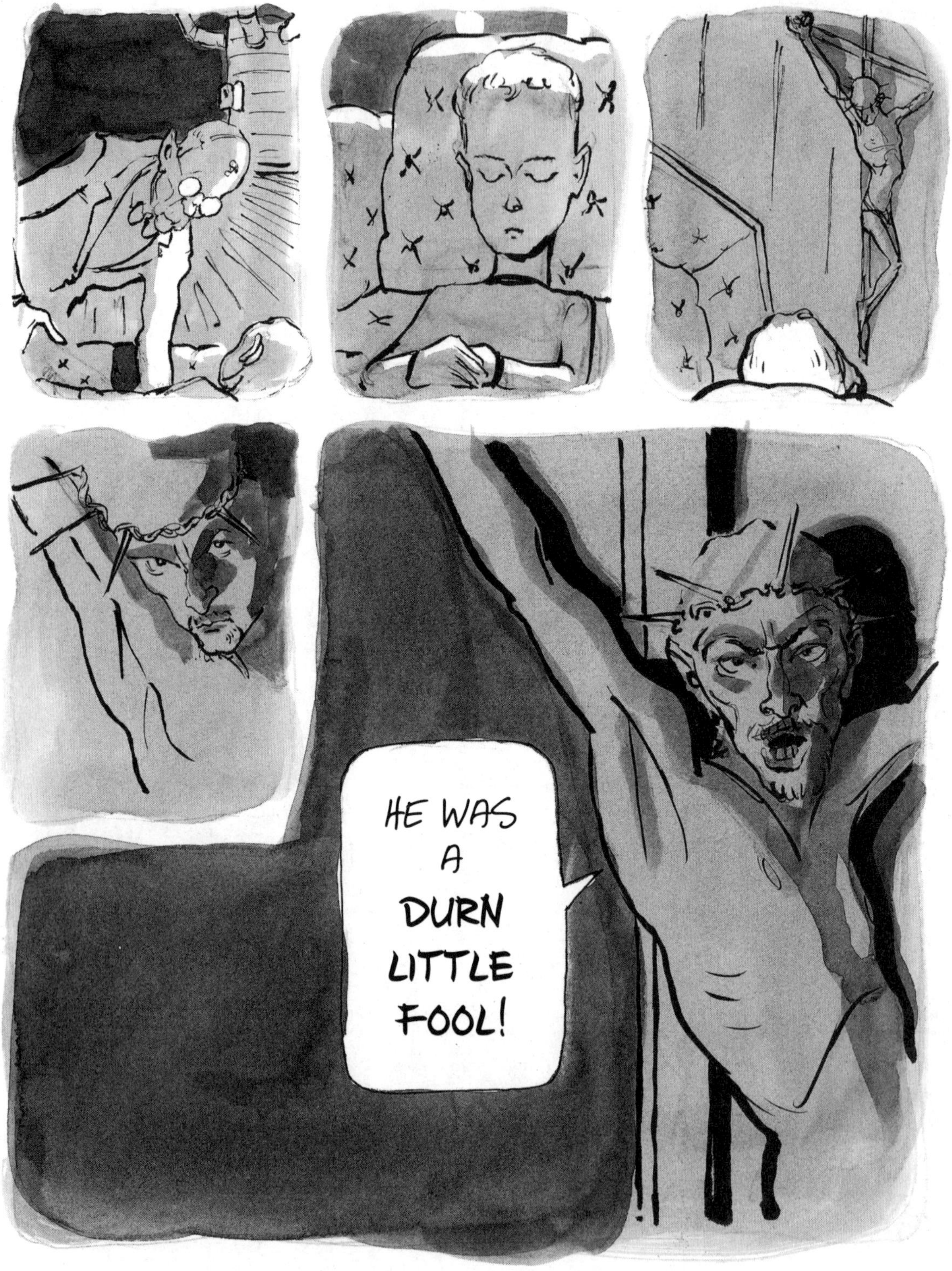
HE WAS A DURN LITTLE FOOL!

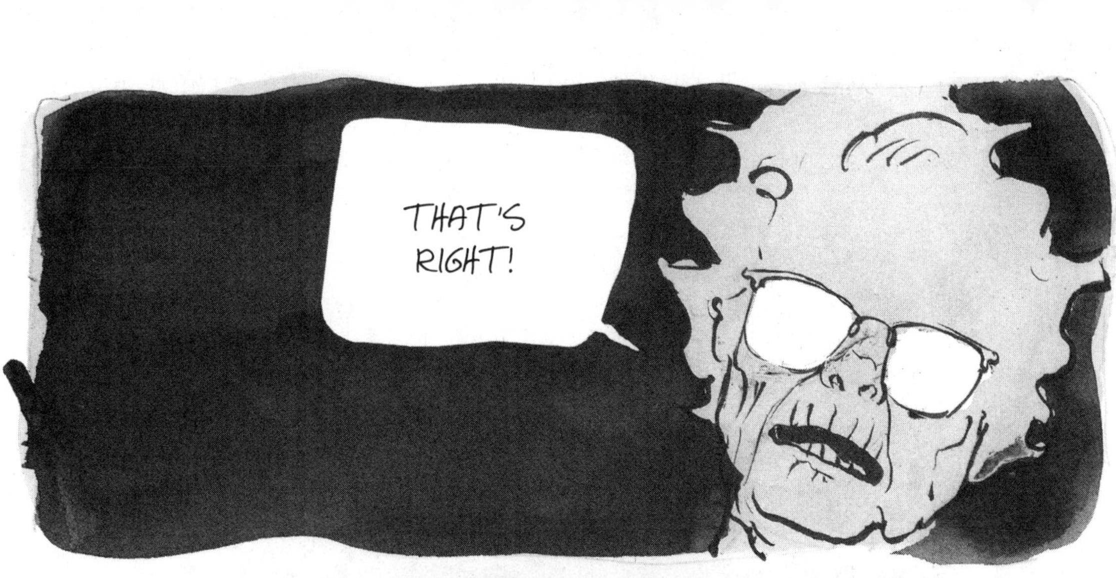
THAT'S RIGHT!

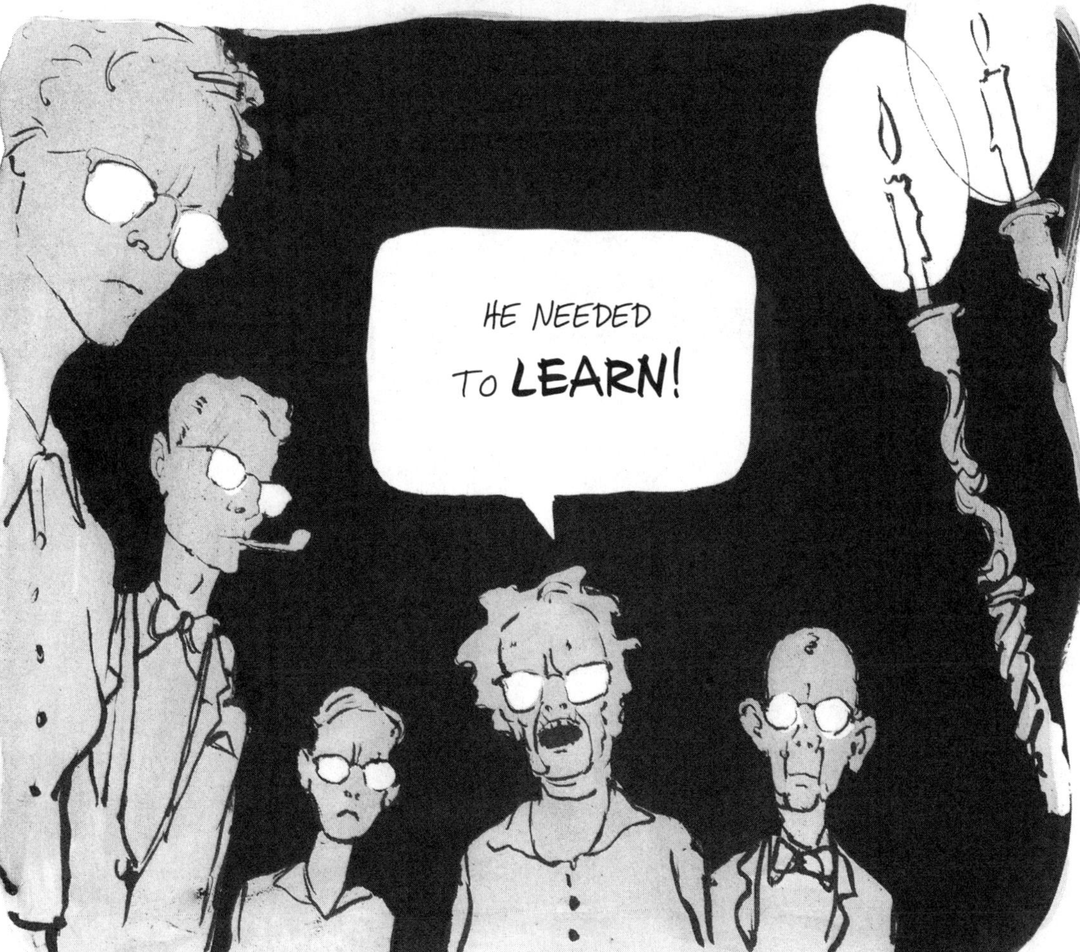
HE NEEDED TO LEARN!

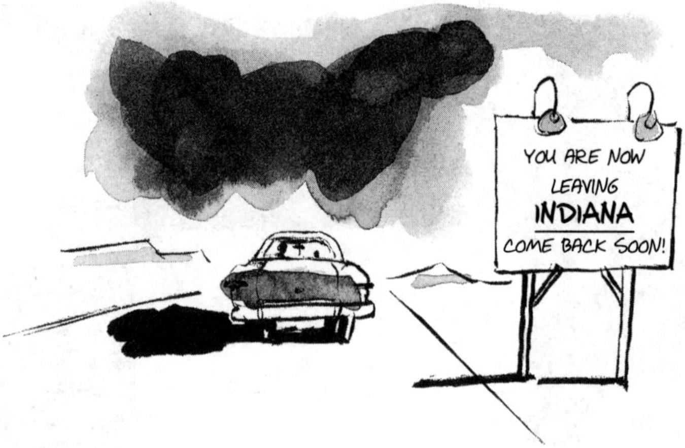
YOU ARE NOW
LEAVING
INDIANA
COME BACK SOON!

I WAS ELEVEN

DETROIT

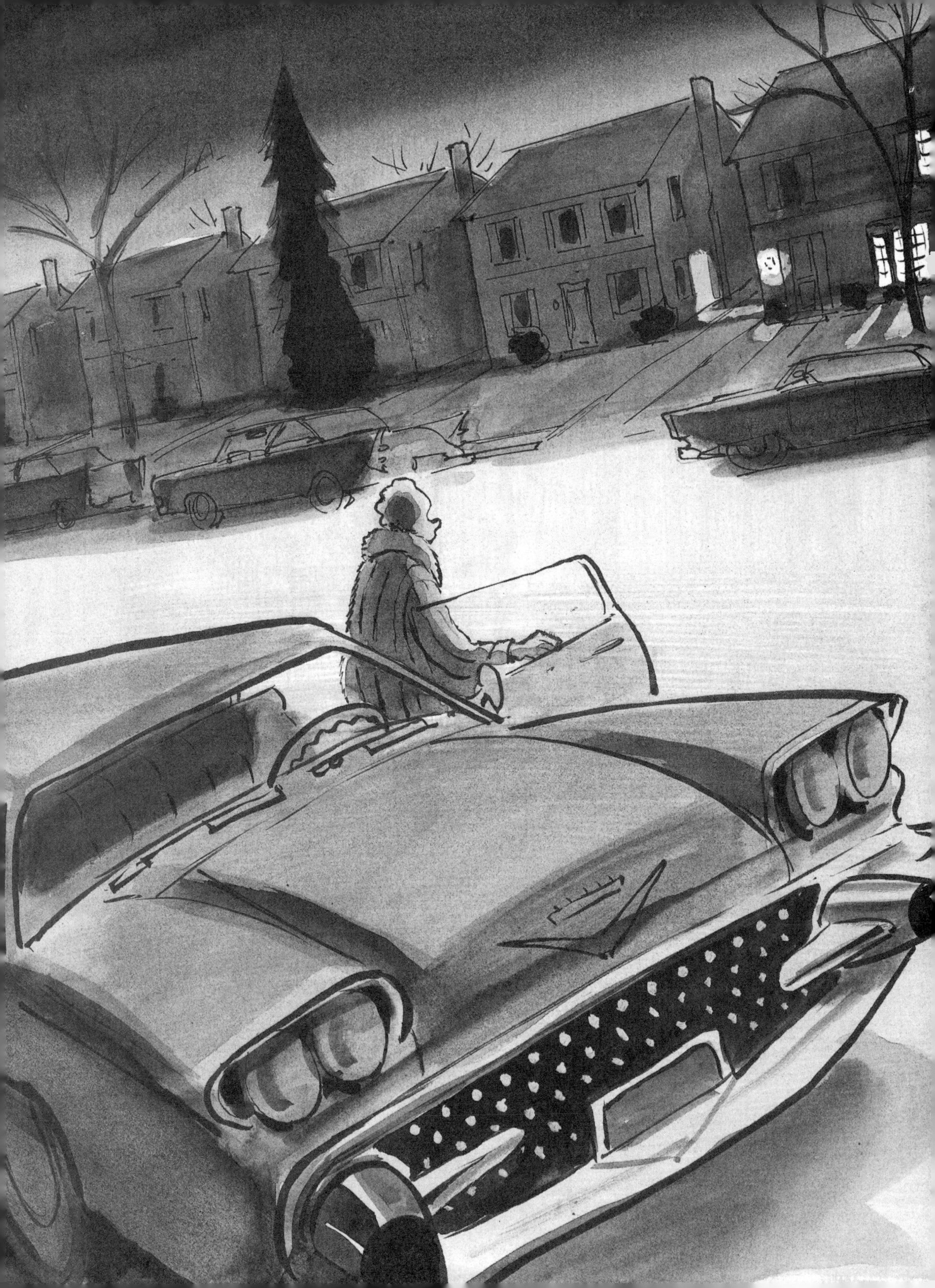

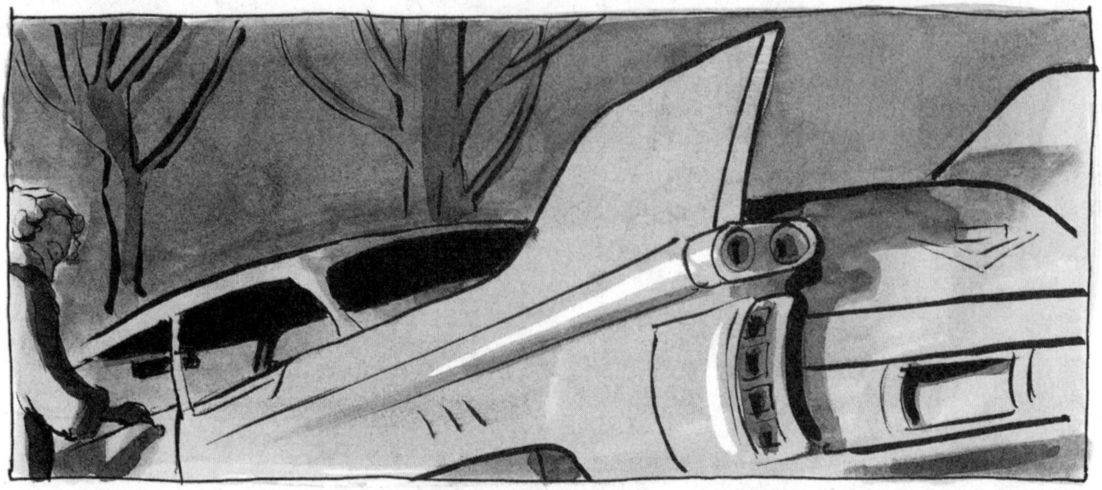

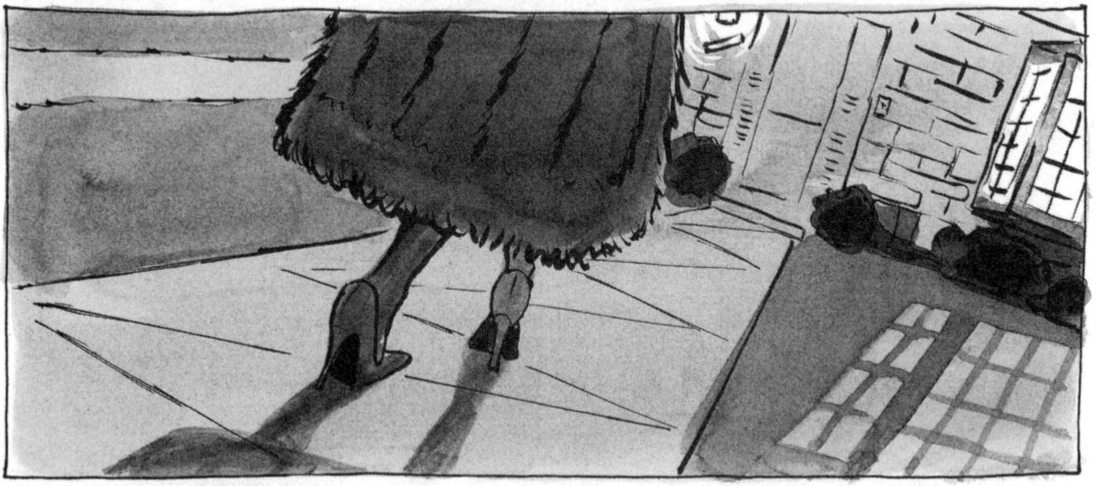

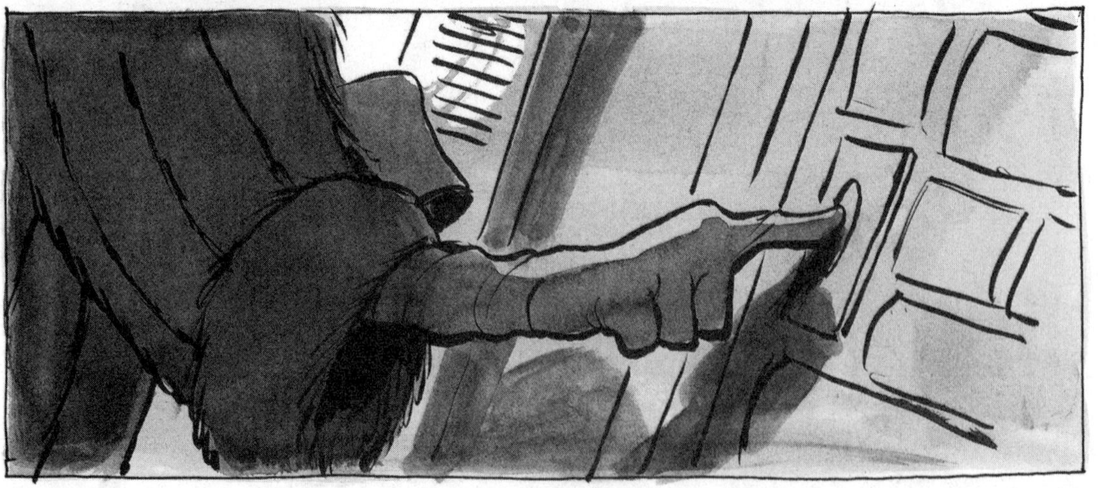

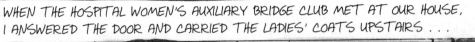

WHEN THE HOSPITAL WOMEN'S AUXILIARY BRIDGE CLUB MET AT OUR HOUSE,
I ANSWERED THE DOOR AND CARRIED THE LADIES' COATS UPSTAIRS . . .

WHY, DAVID! HOW YOU'VE GROWN!

. . A JOB I LIKED BECAUSE IT INVOLVED CARRYING MRS. DILLON'S MINK.

I HAD A MAD CRUSH ON MRS. DILLON.

THE WIFE OF A SURGEON, SHE HAD FOR ME AN ALMOST SUPERNATURAL GLAMOUR AND SOPHISTICATION.

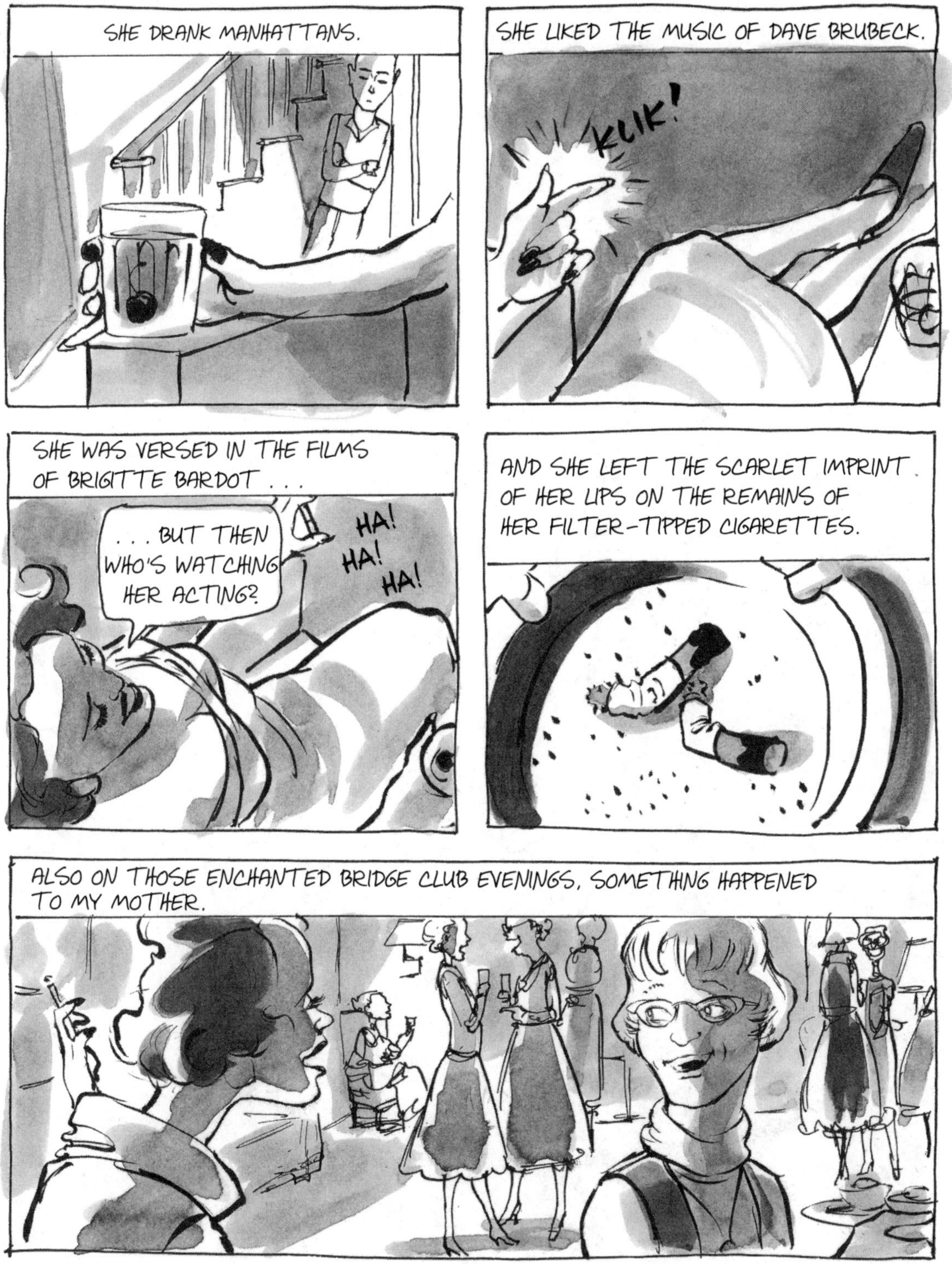
SHE DRANK MANHATTANS.
SHE LIKED THE MUSIC OF DAVE BRUBECK.
KLIK!
SHE WAS VERSED IN THE FILMS OF BRIGITTE BARDOT . . .
. . . BUT THEN WHO'S WATCHING HER ACTING?
HA! HA! HA!
AND SHE LEFT THE SCARLET IMPRINT OF HER LIPS ON THE REMAINS OF HER FILTER-TIPPED CIGARETTES.
ALSO ON THOSE ENCHANTED BRIDGE CLUB EVENINGS, SOMETHING HAPPENED TO MY MOTHER.

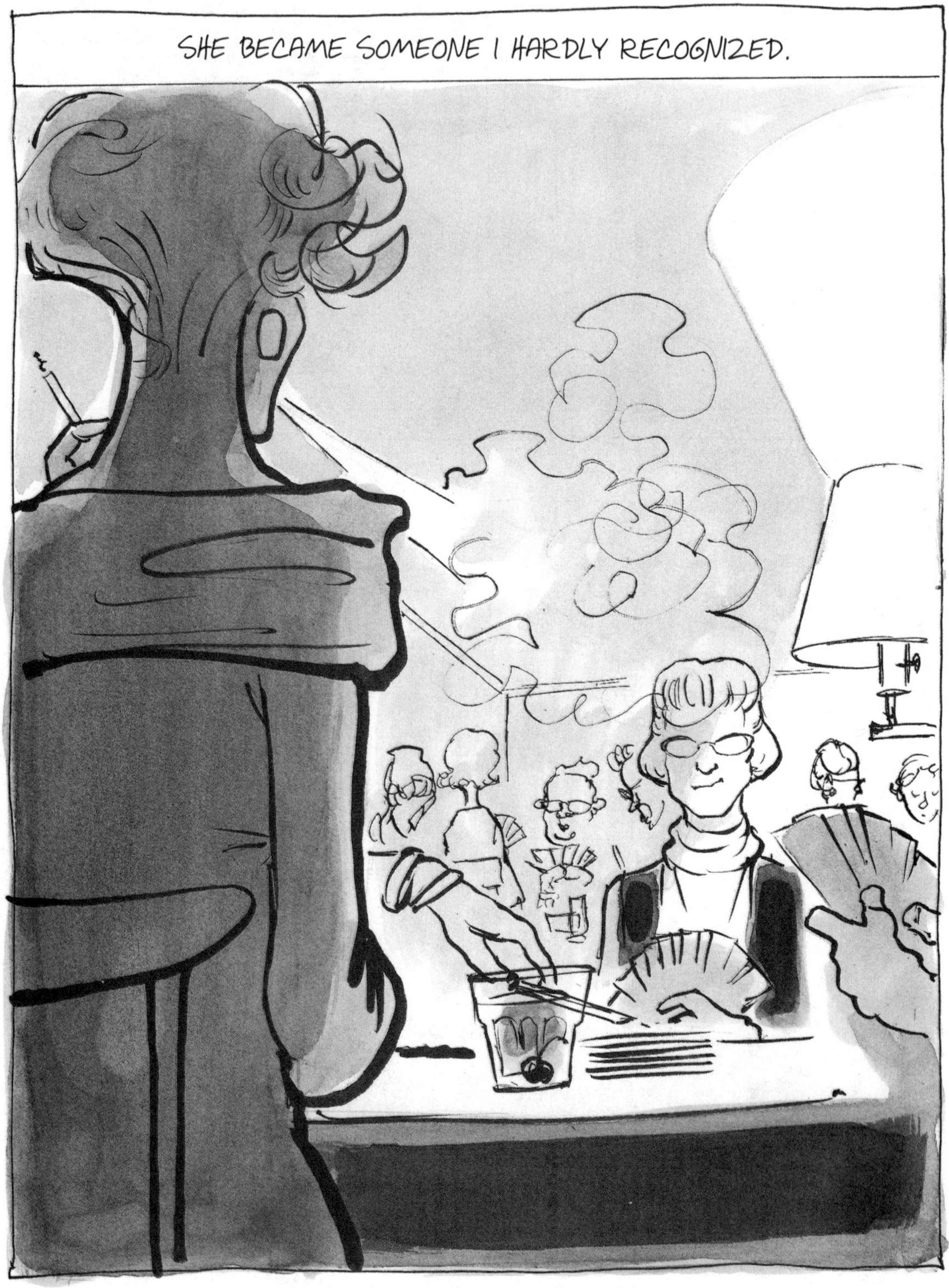
SHE BECAME SOMEONE I HARDLY RECOGNIZED.

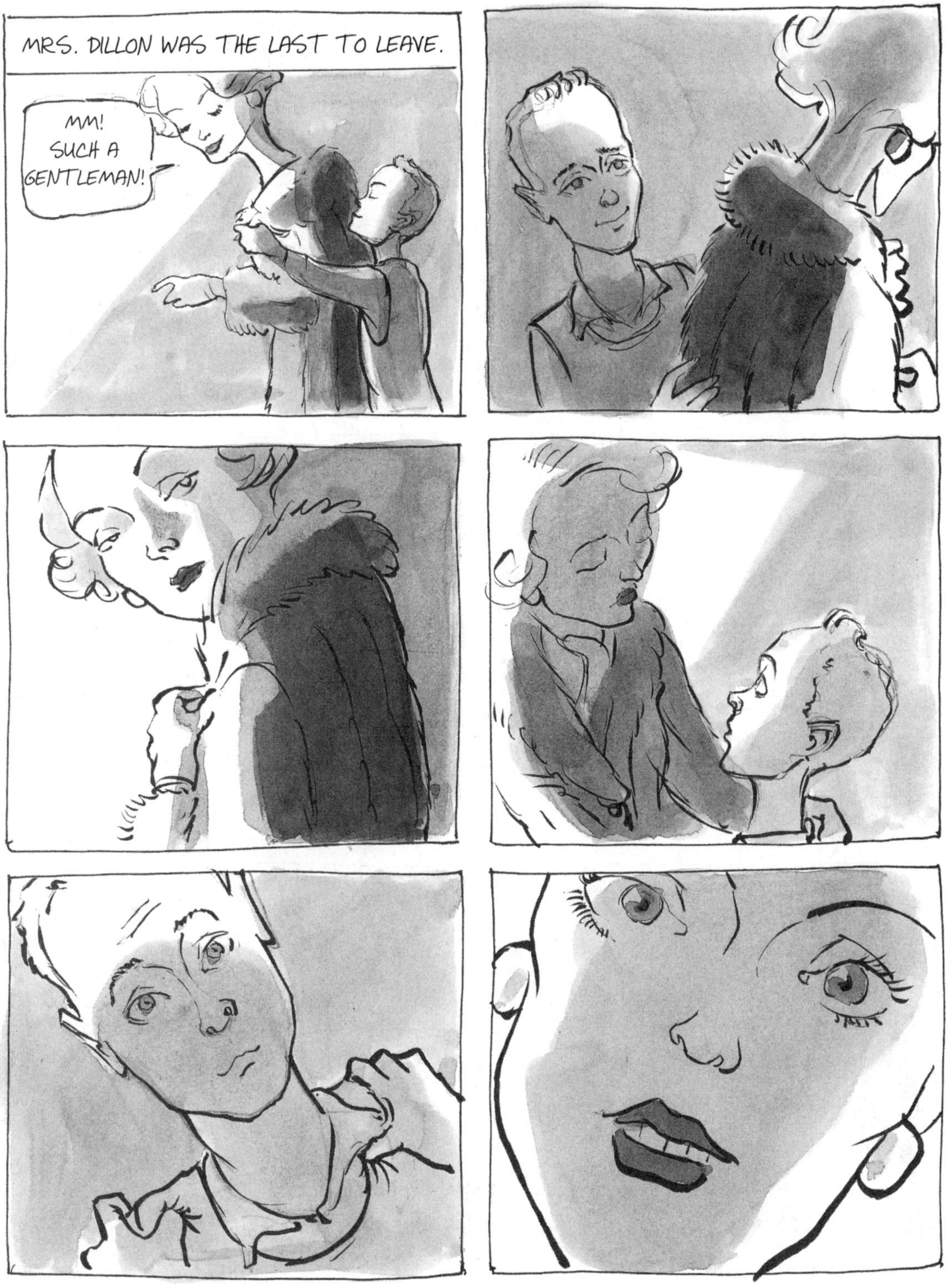
MRS. DILLON WAS THE LAST TO LEAVE.
MM! SUCH A GENTLEMAN!

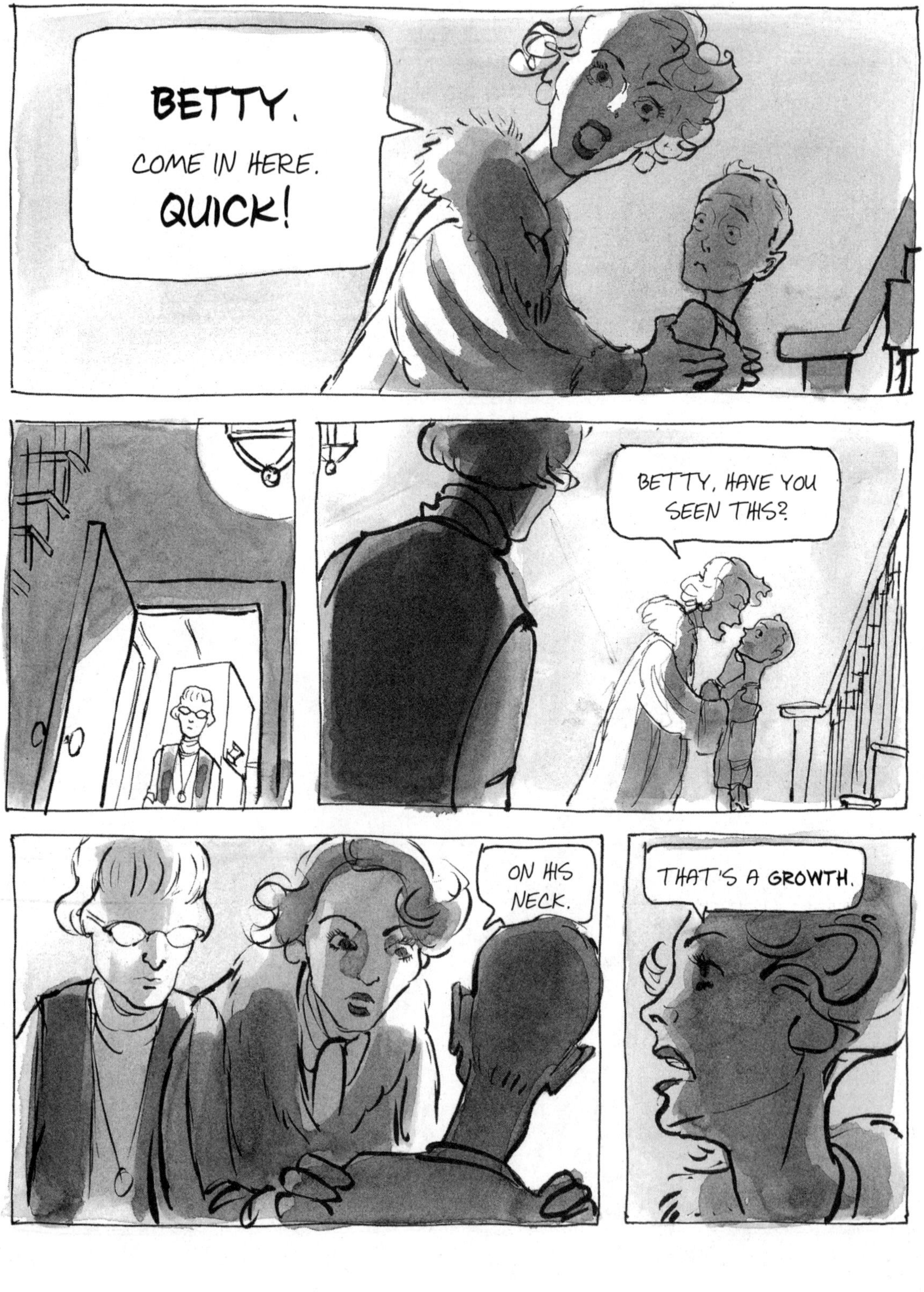
BETTY.
COME IN HERE.
QUICK!
BETTY, HAVE YOU SEEN THIS?
ON HIS NECK.
THAT'S A GROWTH.

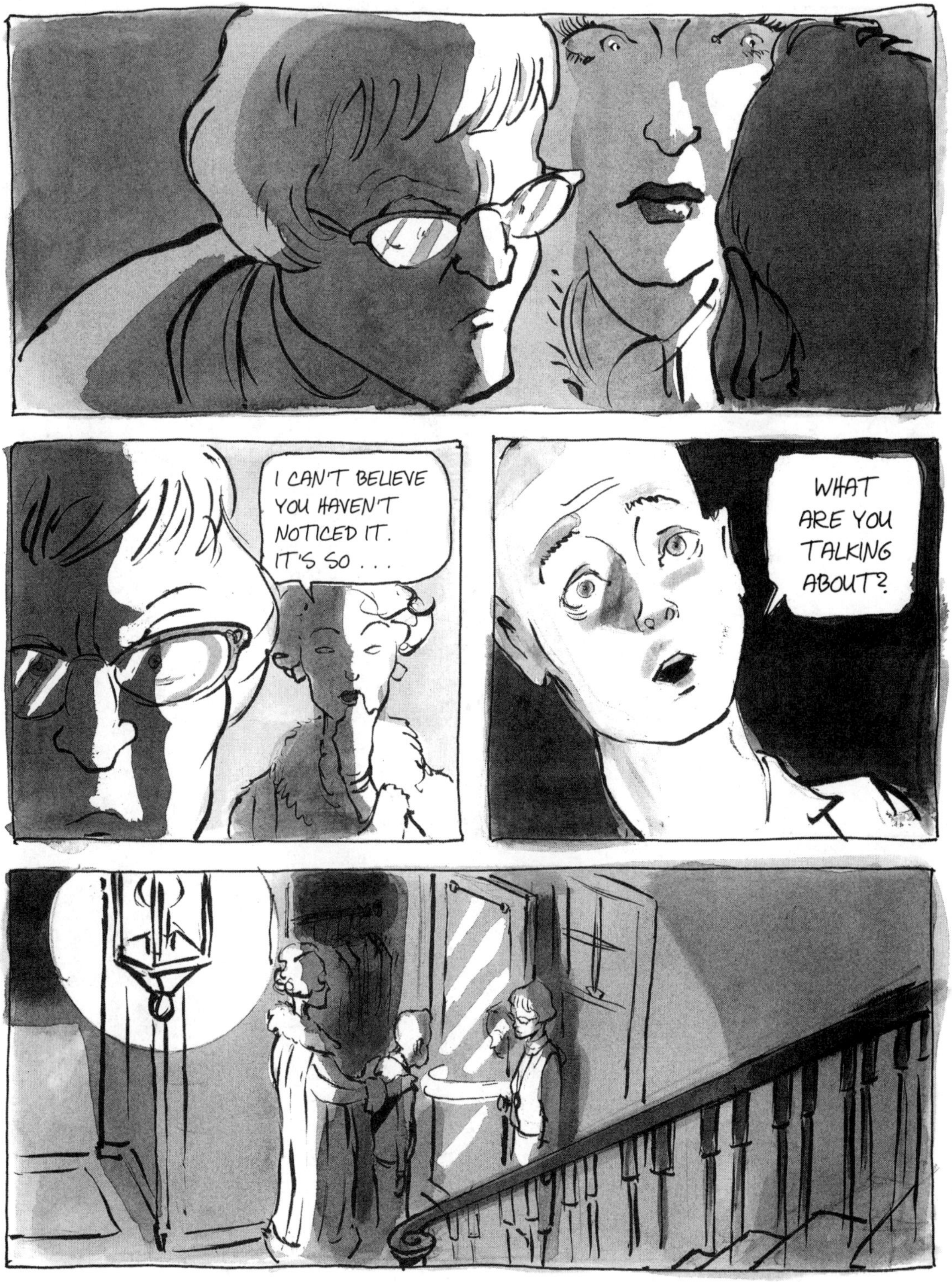
I CAN'T BELIEVE YOU HAVEN'T NOTICED IT. IT'S SO . . .
WHAT ARE YOU TALKING ABOUT?

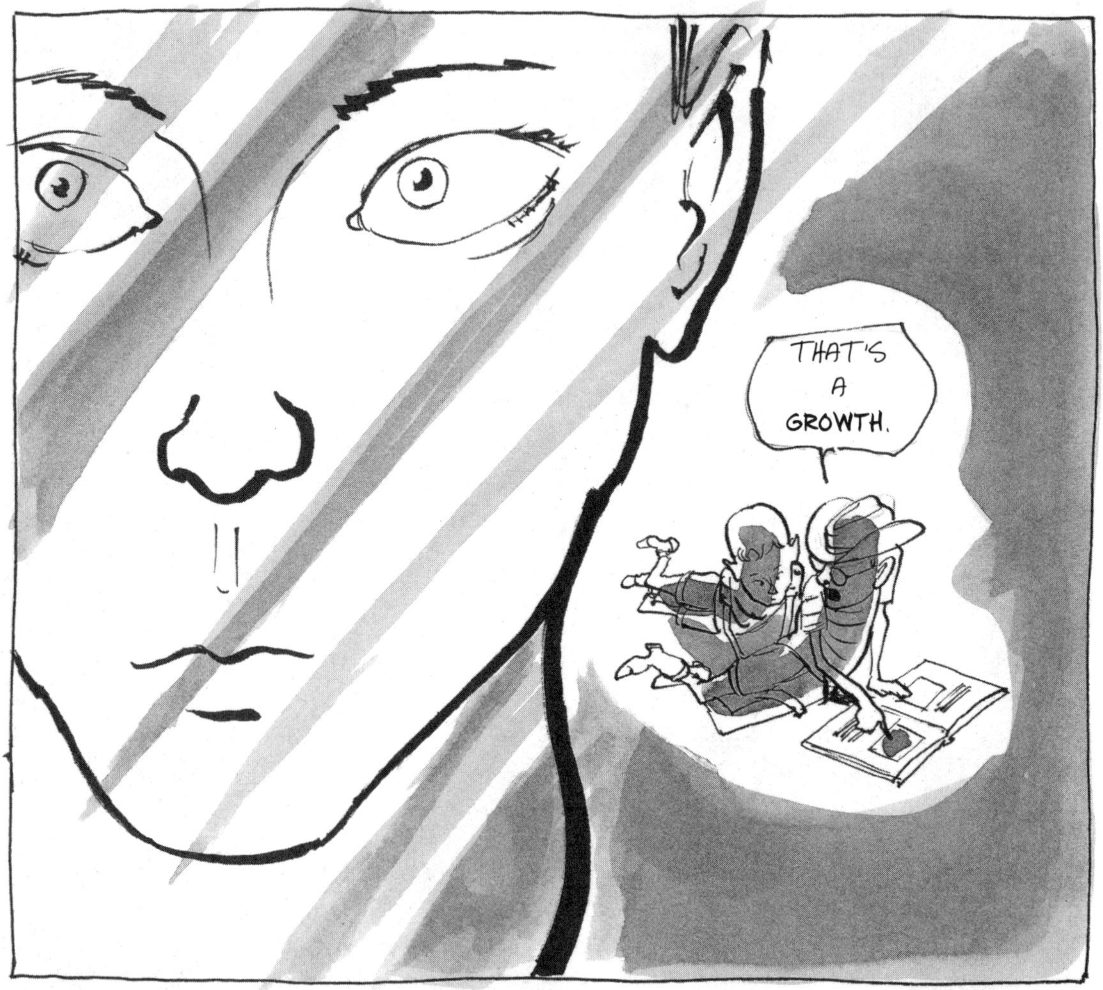
THAT'S A GROWTH.

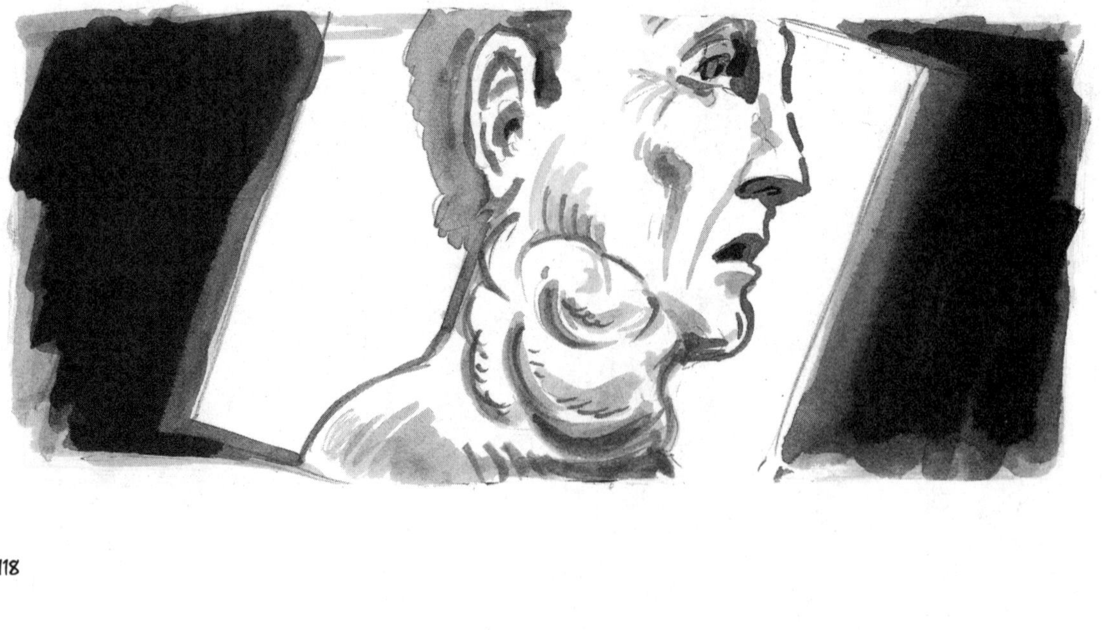

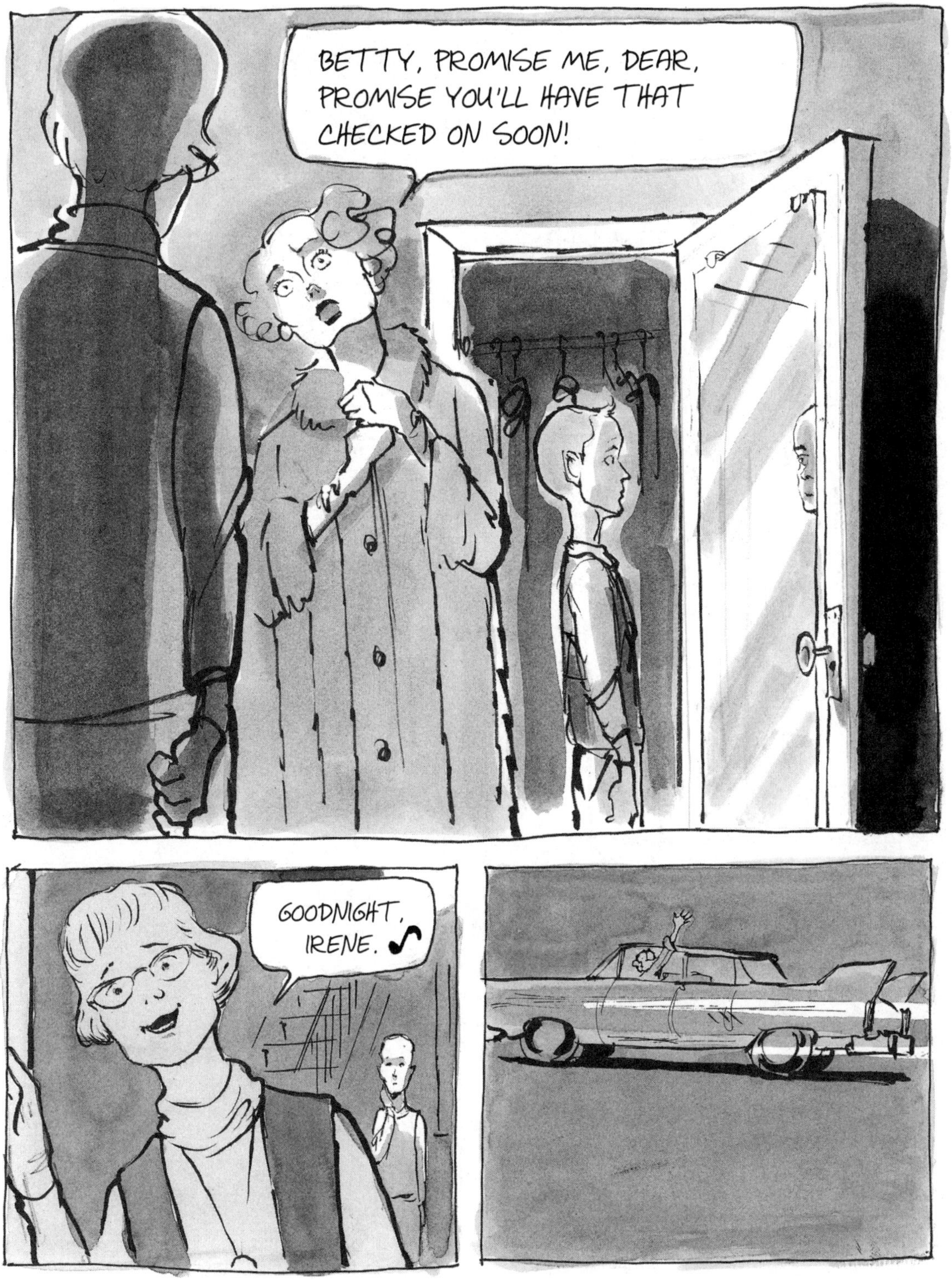
BETTY, PROMISE ME, DEAR, PROMISE YOU'LL HAVE THAT CHECKED ON SOON!
GOODNIGHT, IRENE. ♪

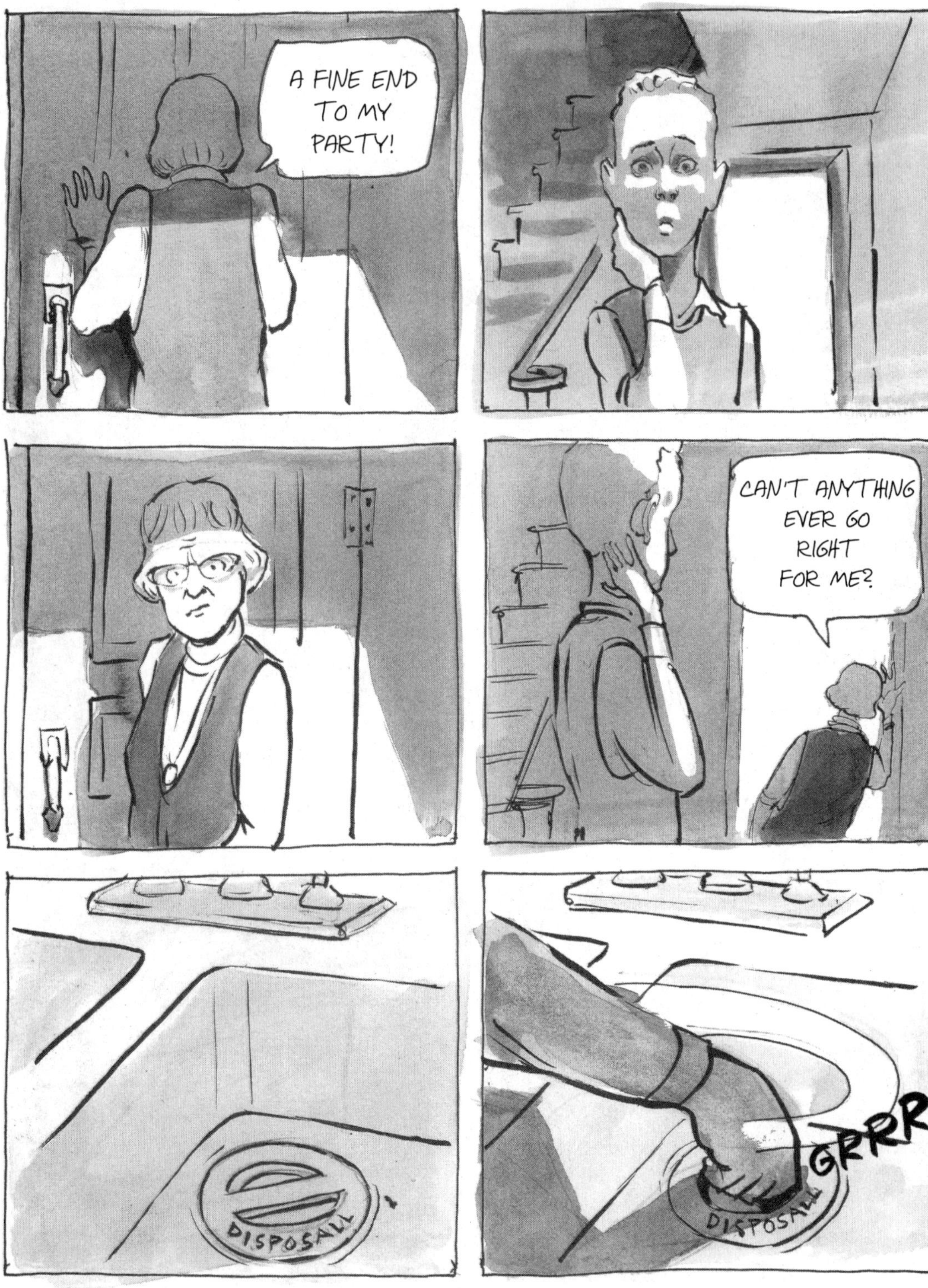
A FINE END TO MY PARTY!
CAN'T ANYTHING EVER GO RIGHT FOR ME?
DISPOSALL
DISPOSALL
GRRR

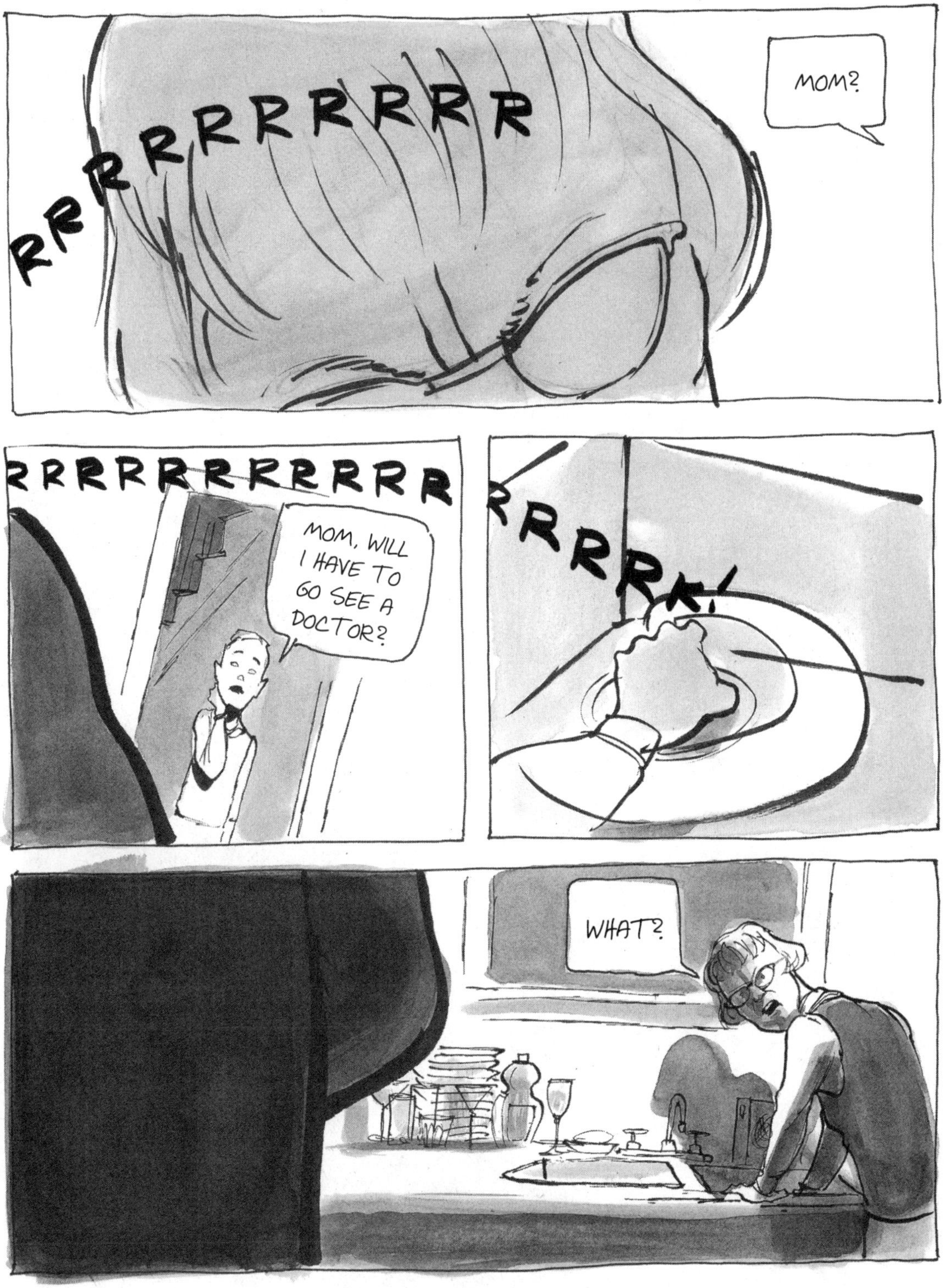
RRRRRRRRRRR
MOM?
RRRRRRRRRRRR
MOM, WILL I HAVE TO GO SEE A DOCTOR?
RRRRK!
WHAT?

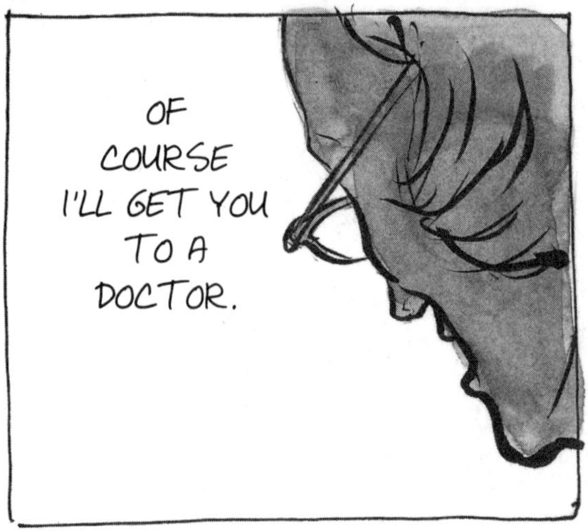
OF COURSE I'LL GET YOU TO A DOCTOR.

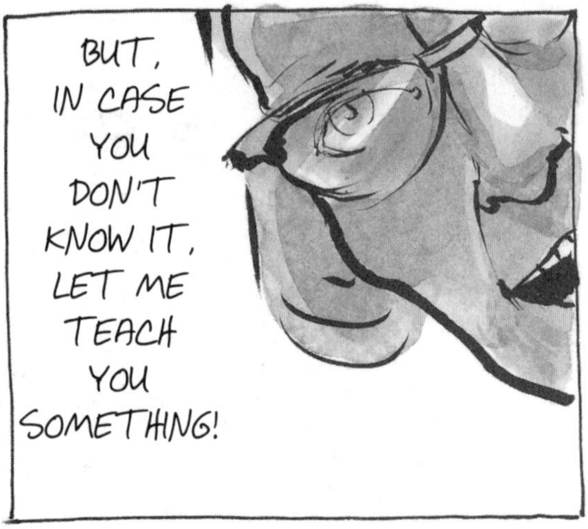
BUT, IN CASE YOU DON'T KNOW IT, LET ME TEACH YOU SOMETHING!

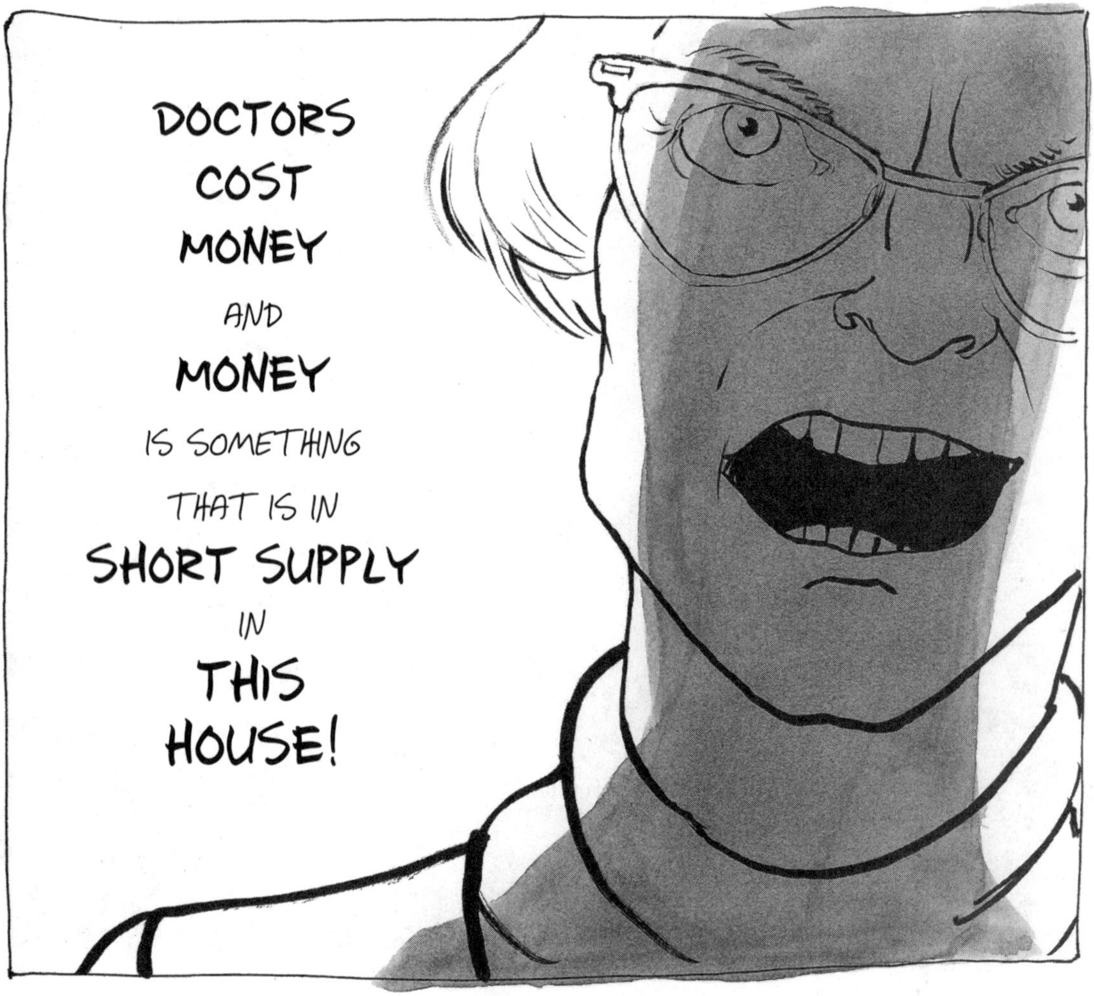
DOCTORS COST MONEY AND MONEY IS SOMETHING THAT IS IN SHORT SUPPLY IN THIS HOUSE!

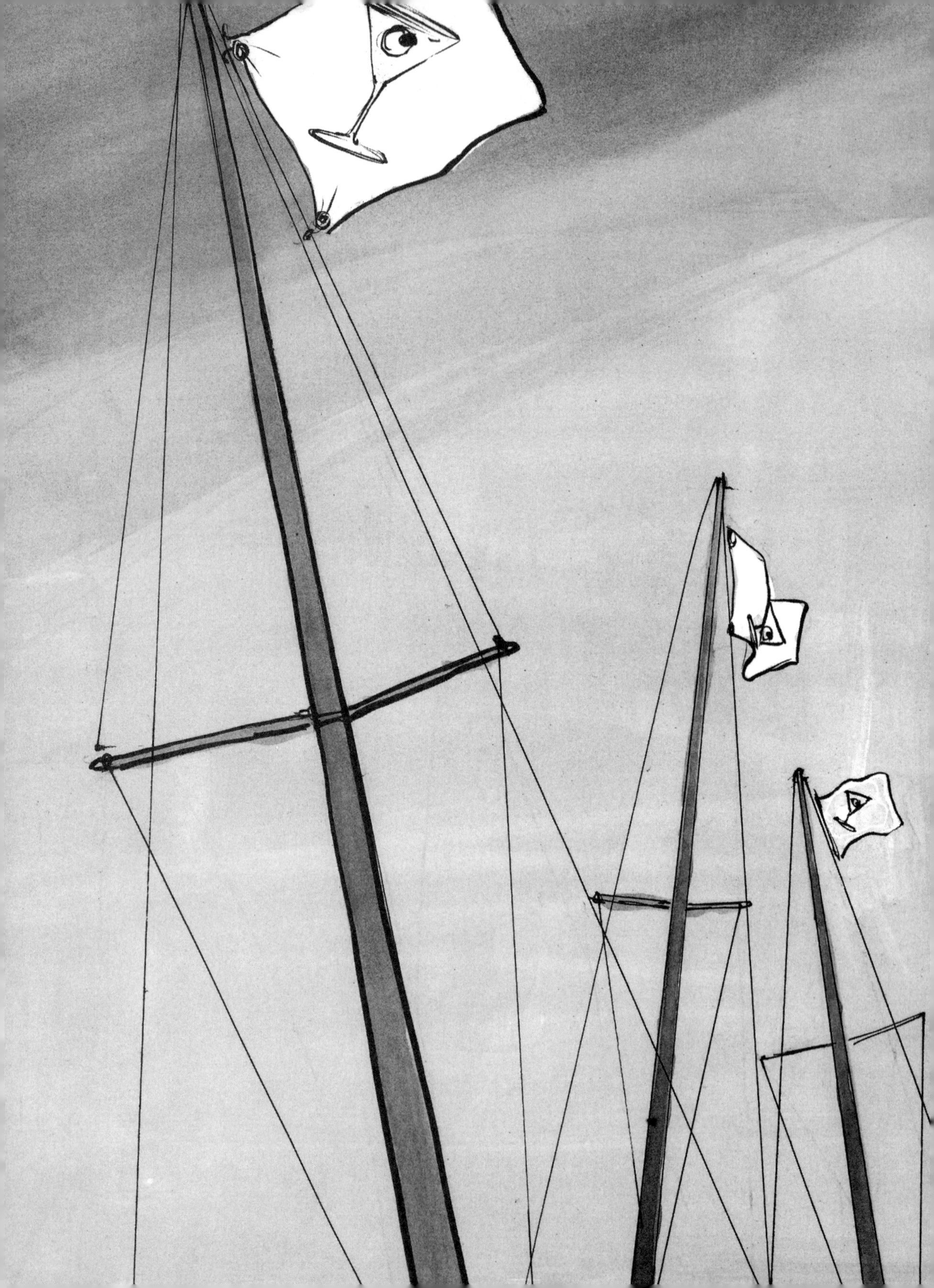

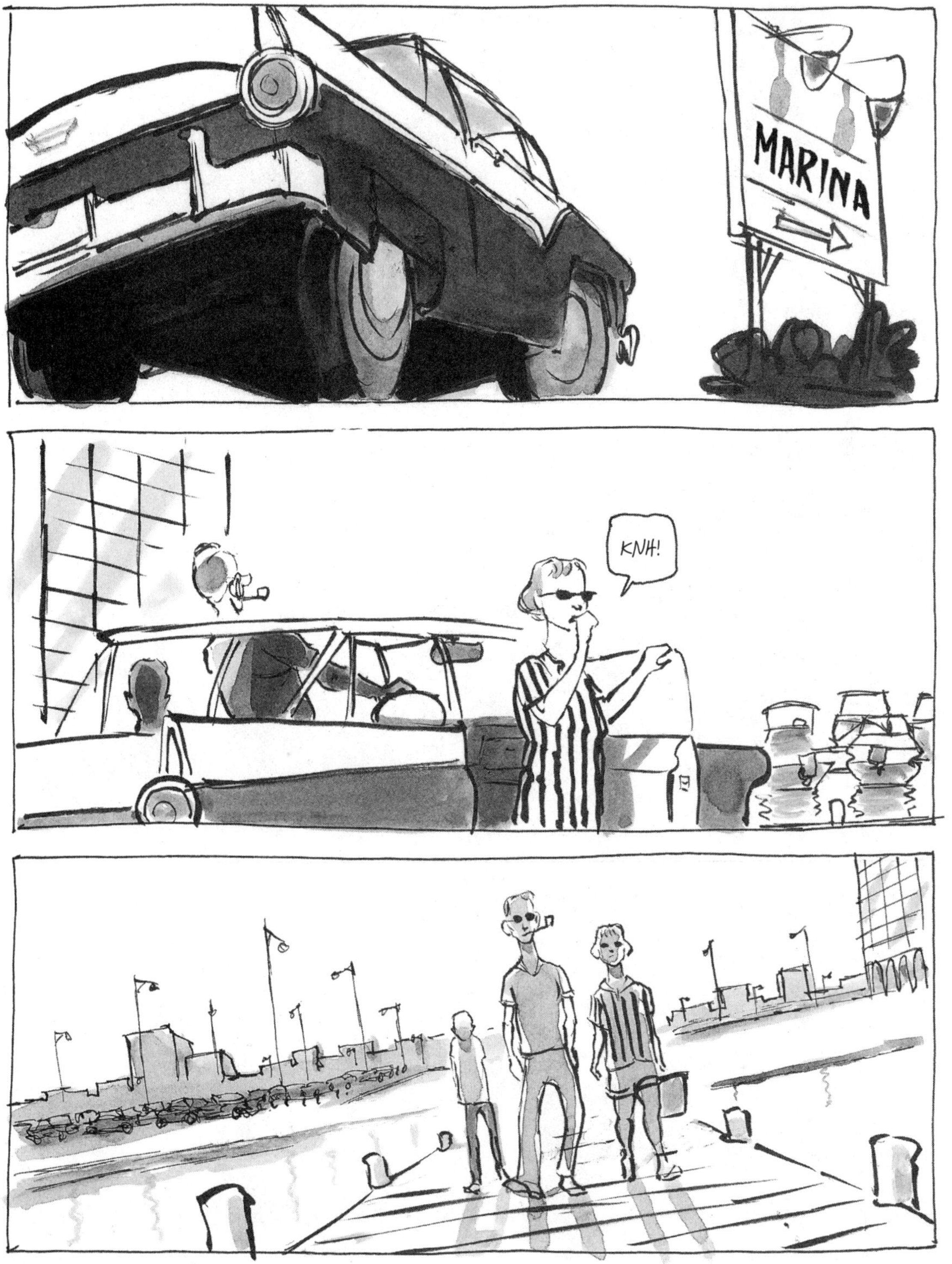
MARINA
KNH!

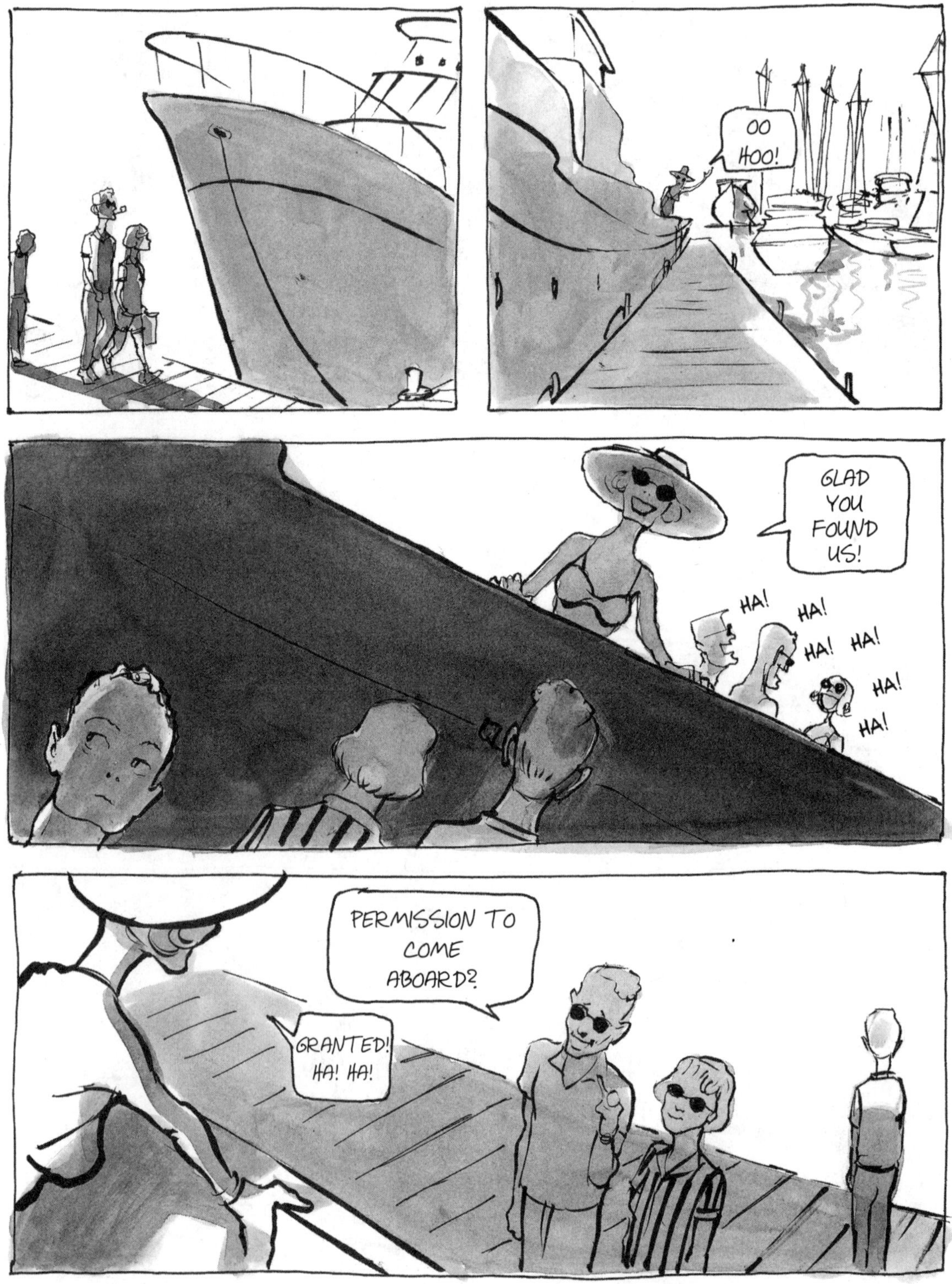
OO HOO!
GLAD YOU FOUND US!
HA! HA! HA! HA! HA! HA!
PERMISSION TO COME ABOARD?
GRANTED! HA! HA!

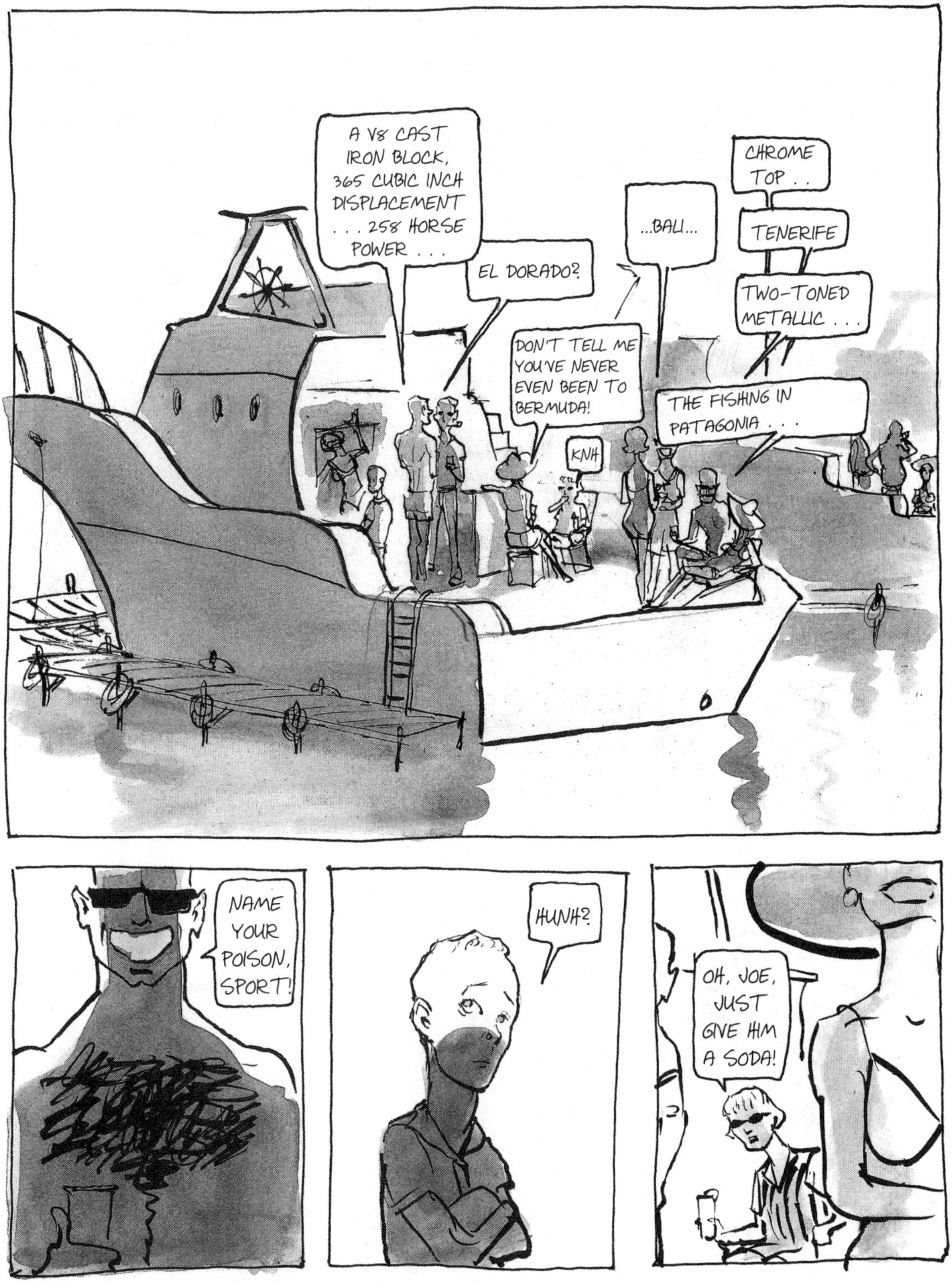
A V8 CAST IRON BLOCK, 365 CUBIC INCH DISPLACEMENT . . . 258 HORSE POWER . . .
EL DORADO?
DON'T TELL ME YOU'VE NEVER EVEN BEEN TO BERMUDA!
KNH
...BALI...
CHROME TOP . .
TENERIFE
TWO-TONED METALLIC . . .
THE FISHING IN PATAGONIA . . .
NAME YOUR POISON, SPORT!
HUNH?
OH, JOE, JUST GIVE HIM A SODA!

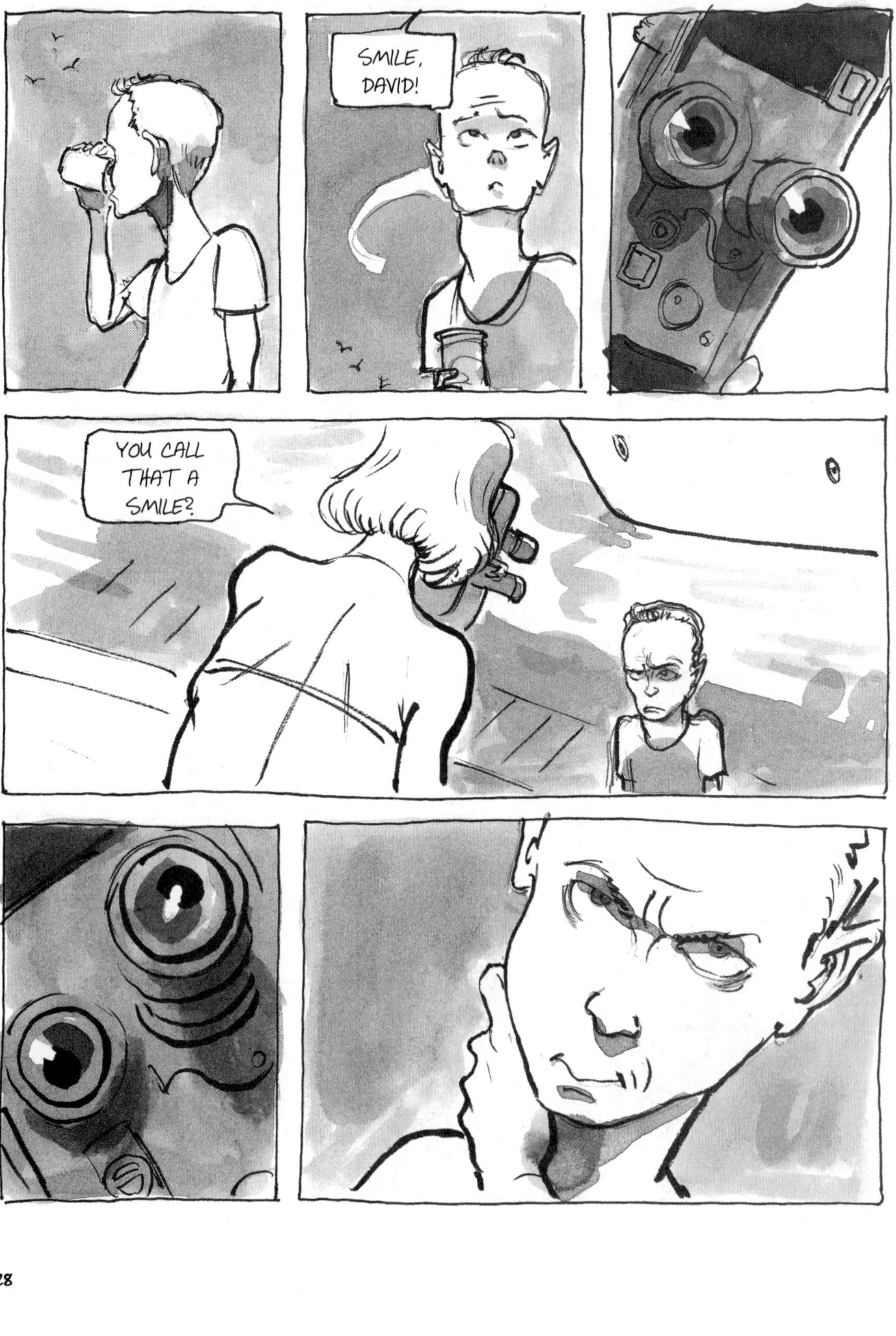
SMILE, DAVID!
YOU CALL THAT A SMILE?

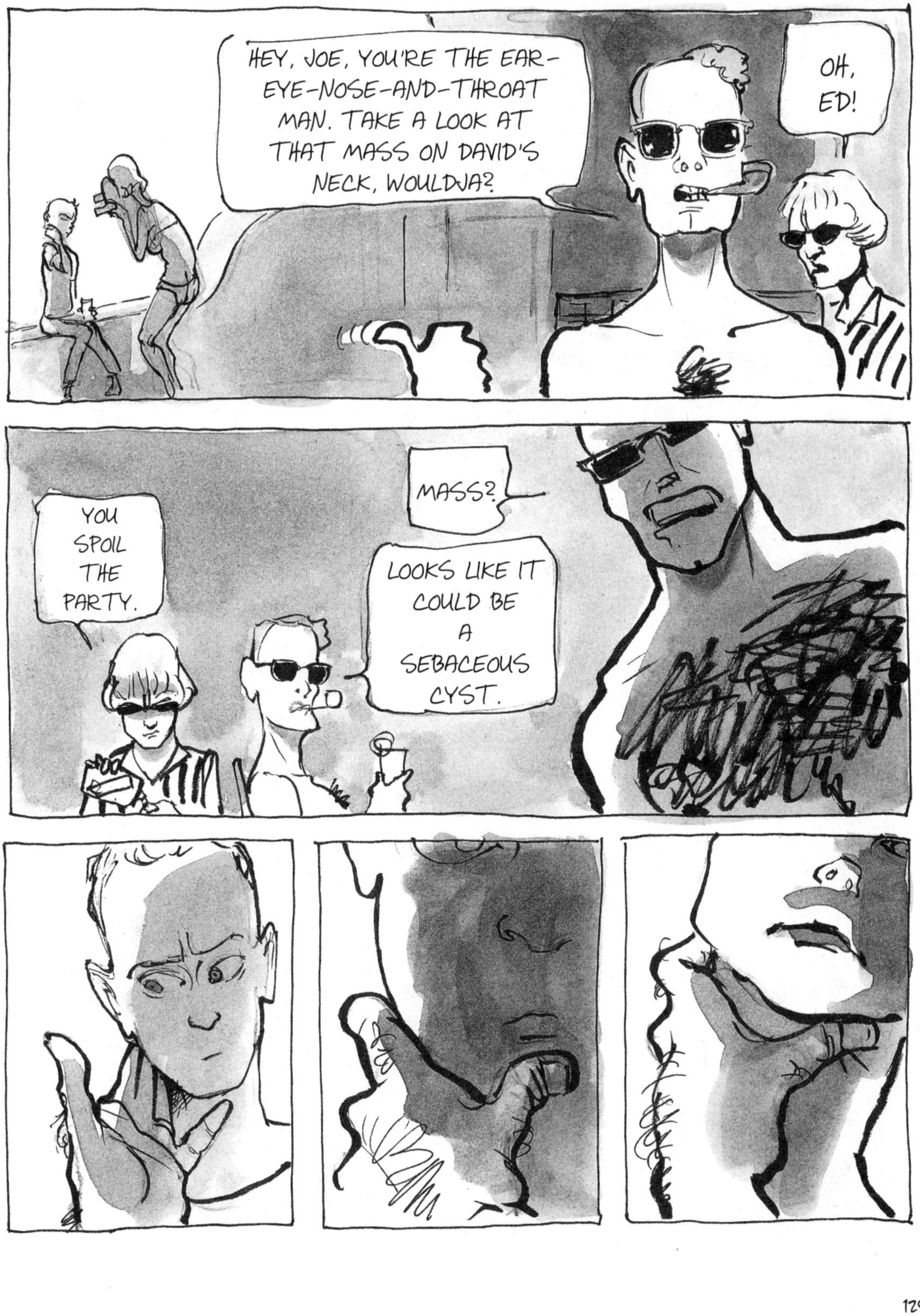
HEY, JOE, YOU'RE THE EAR-EYE-NOSE-AND-THROAT MAN. TAKE A LOOK AT THAT MASS ON DAVID'S NECK, WOULDJA?
OH, ED!
YOU SPOIL THE PARTY.
MASS?
LOOKS LIKE IT COULD BE A SEBACEOUS CYST.

HOLD STILL THERE,
SPORT.
HMM.
YOUR GUESS IS AS
GOOD AS MINE.
BETTER HAVE BETTY
CALL MY OFFICE,
MAKE AN APPOINTMENT,
NEXT WEEK.

AND HEY,
ED . . .
YOU'RE THE
X-RAY MAN.
GET ME SOME
SHOTS OF
THAT AREA,
WOULDJA?

HA!   HA!   HA!

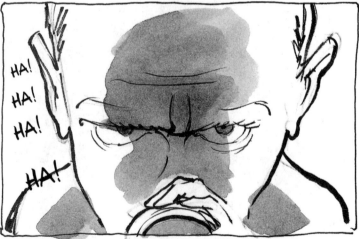

HA!
HA!
HA!

HA!

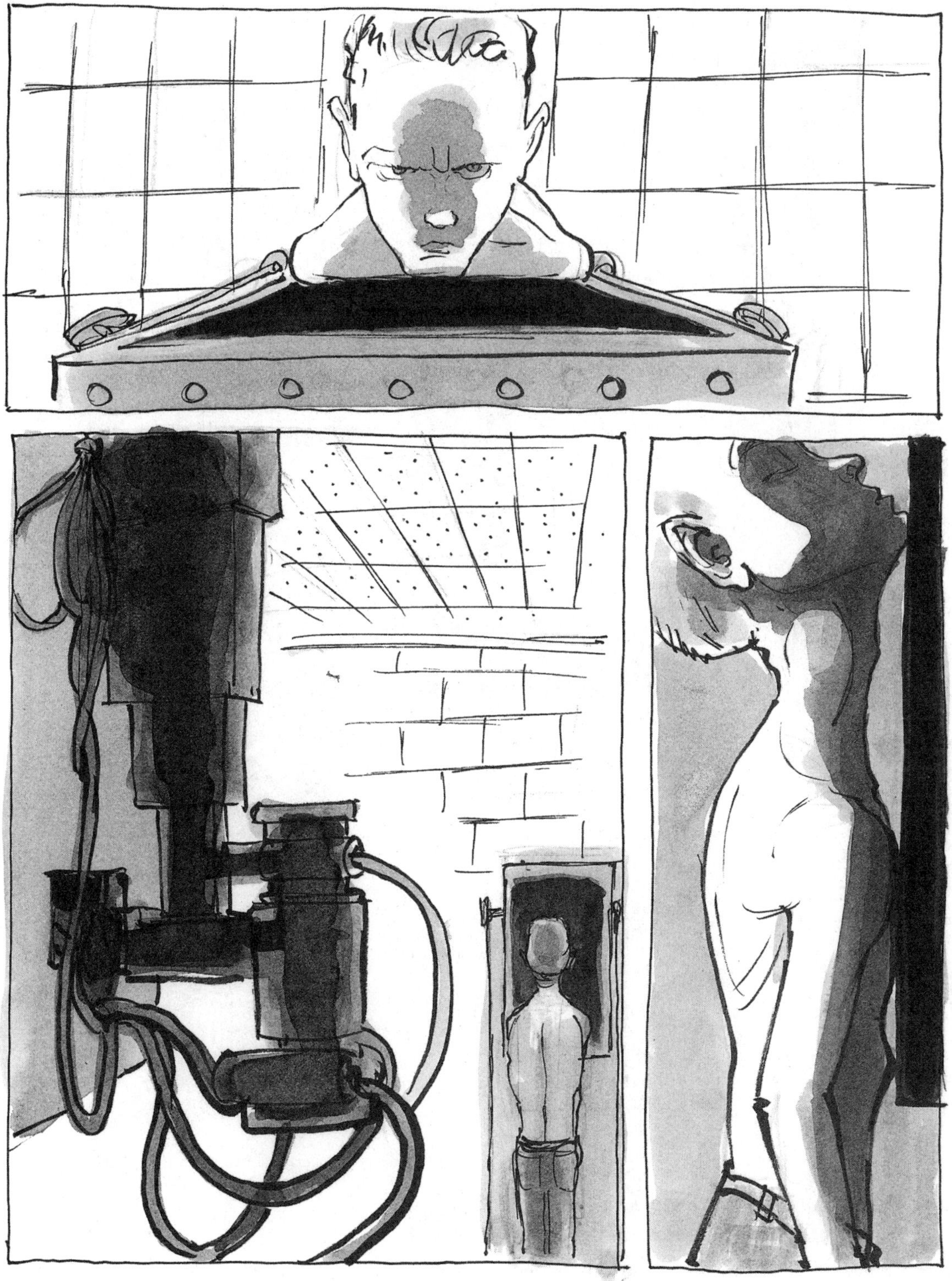

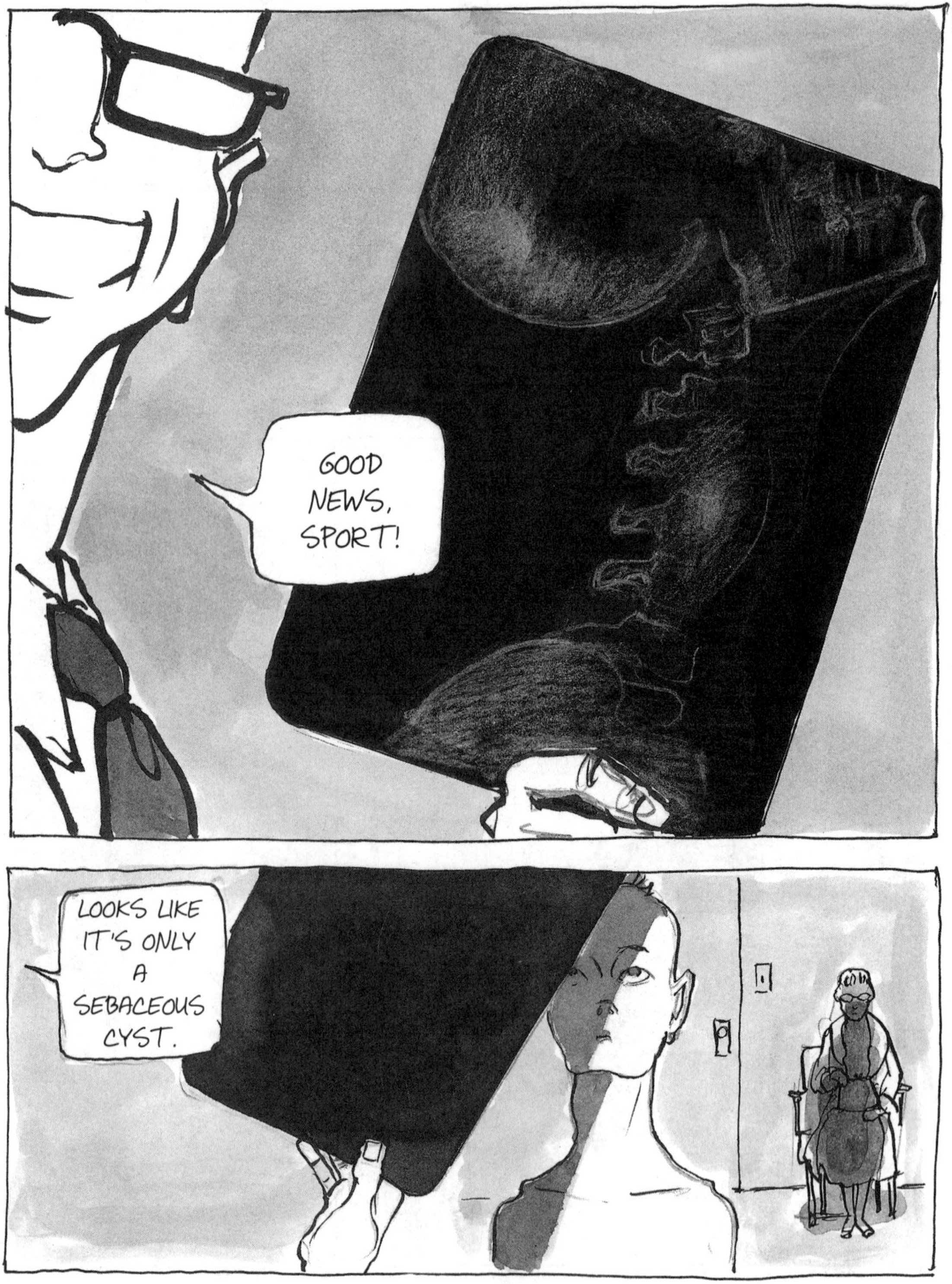
GOOD NEWS, SPORT!
LOOKS LIKE IT'S ONLY A SEBACEOUS CYST.

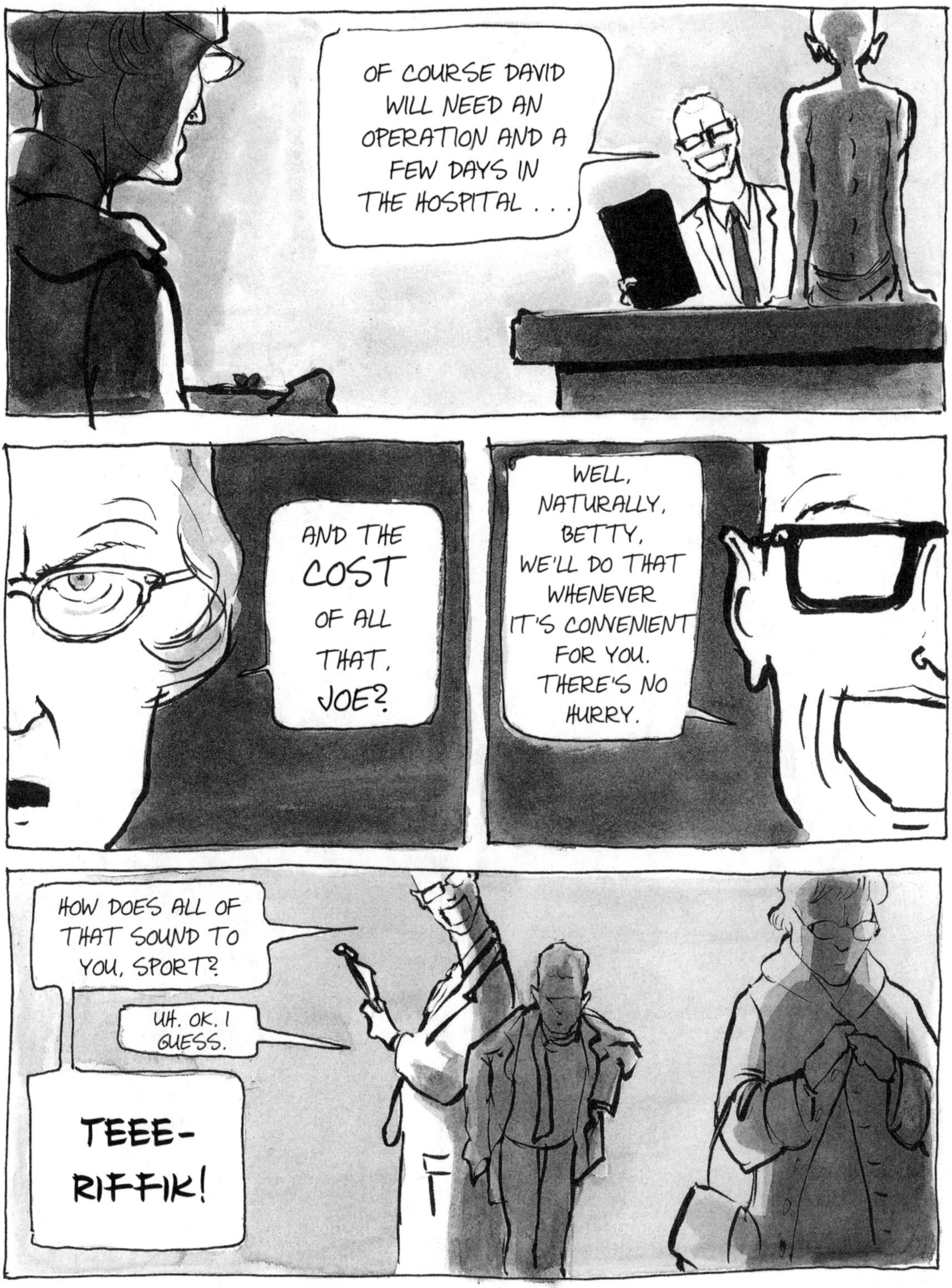
OF COURSE DAVID WILL NEED AN OPERATION AND A FEW DAYS IN THE HOSPITAL . . .
AND THE COST OF ALL THAT, JOE?
WELL, NATURALLY, BETTY, WE'LL DO THAT WHENEVER IT'S CONVENIENT FOR YOU. THERE'S NO HURRY.
HOW DOES ALL OF THAT SOUND TO YOU, SPORT?
UH. OK. I GUESS.
TEEE-RIFFIK!

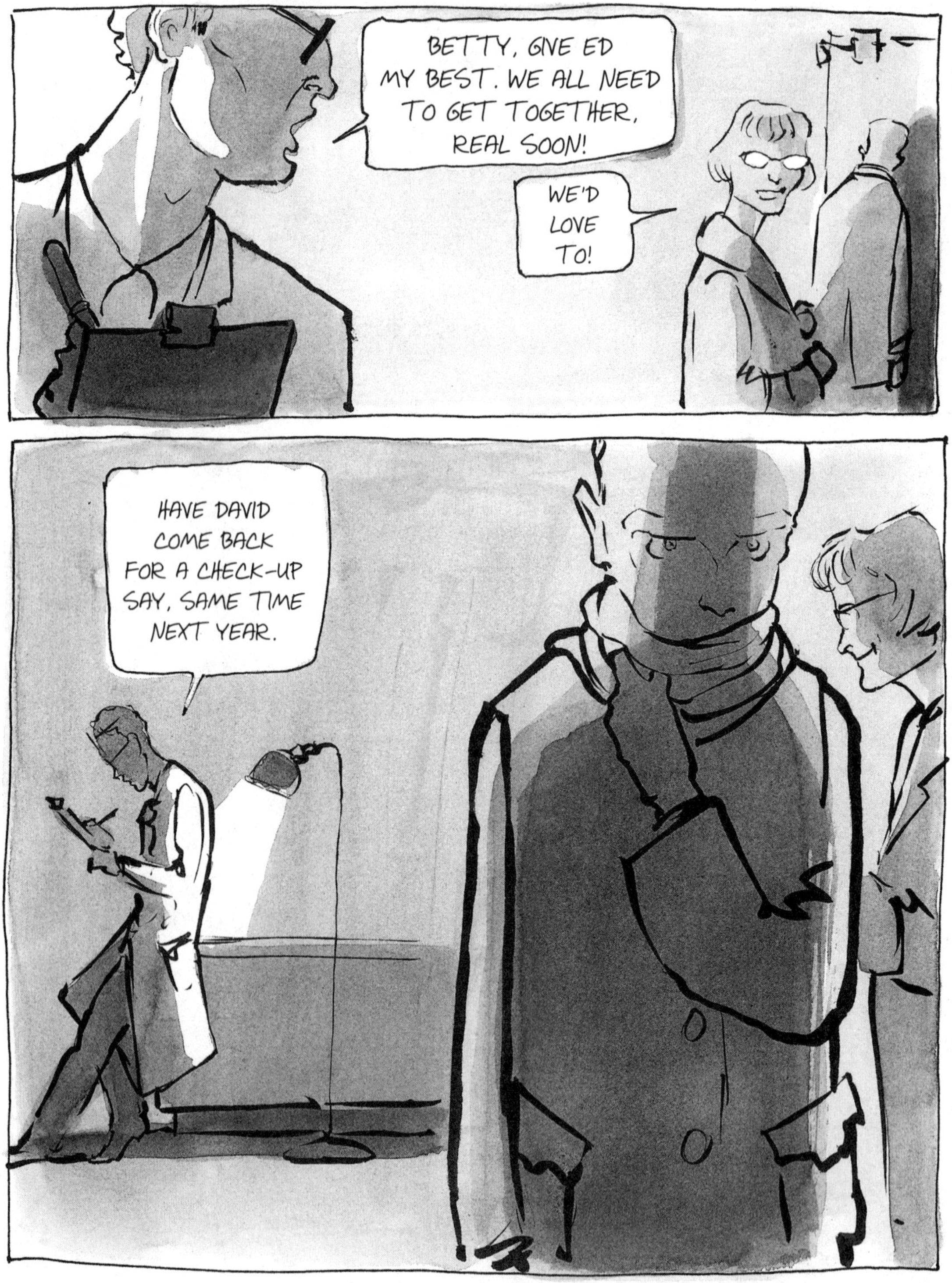
BETTY, GIVE ED MY BEST. WE ALL NEED TO GET TOGETHER, REAL SOON!
WE'D LOVE TO!
HAVE DAVID COME BACK FOR A CHECK-UP SAY, SAME TIME NEXT YEAR.

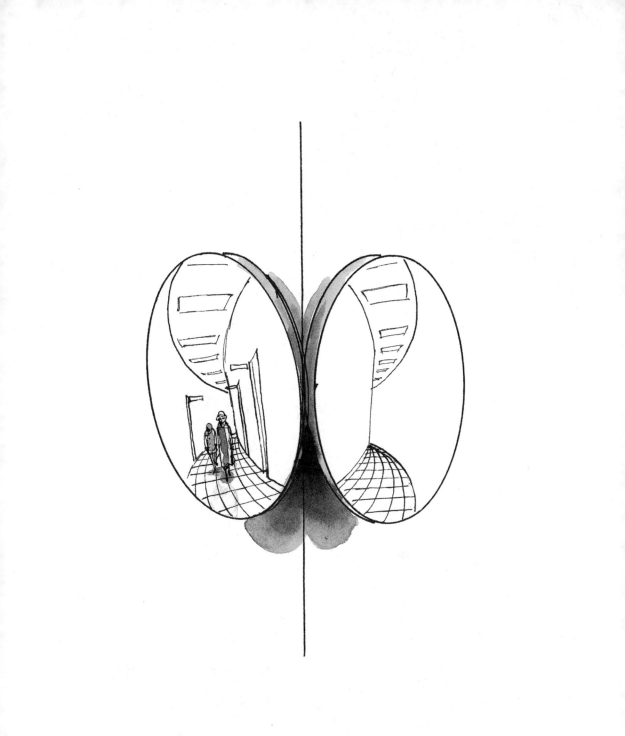

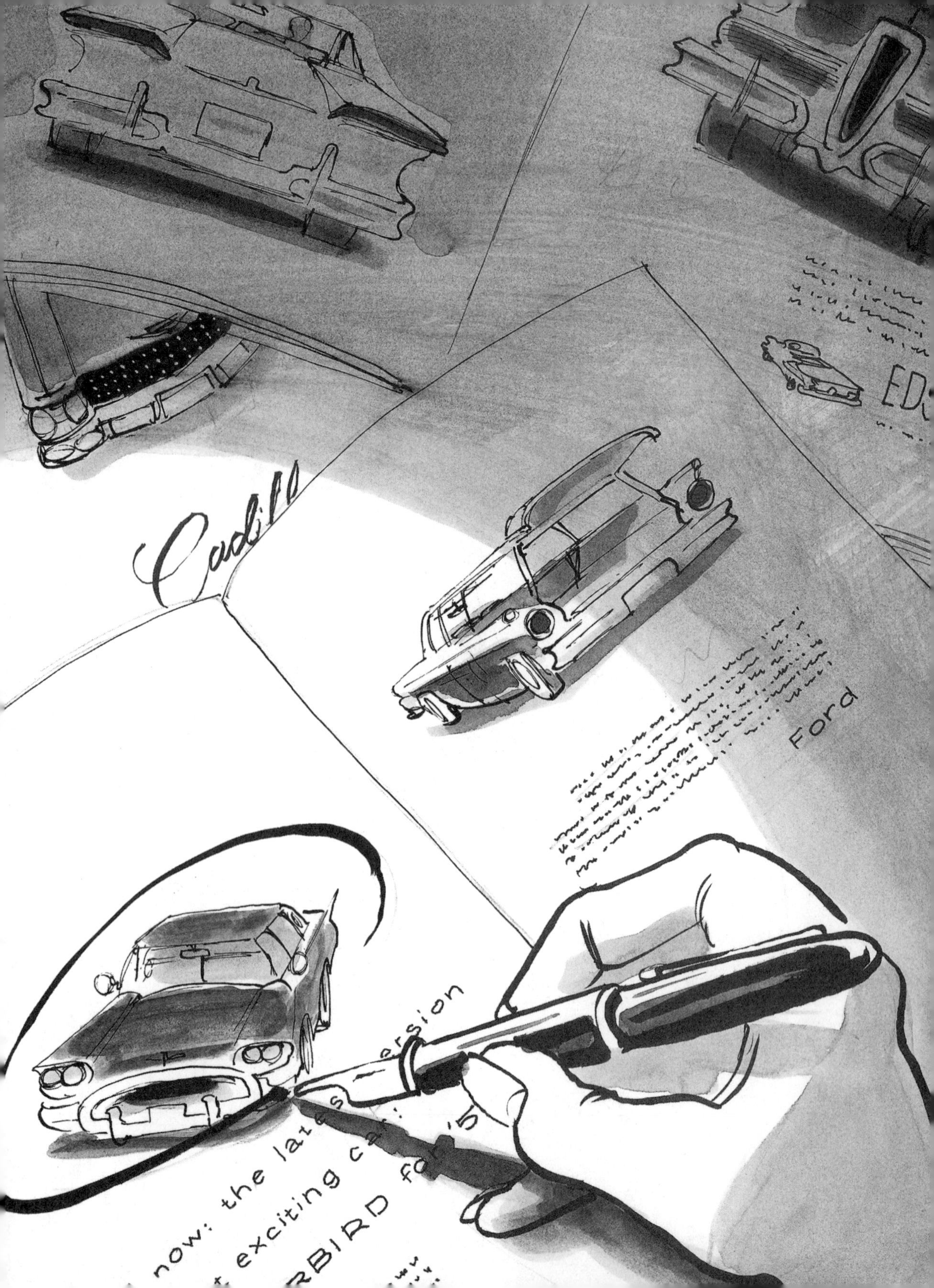
Cadill
Ford
now: the late
ersion
exciting c
RBIRD fo '5

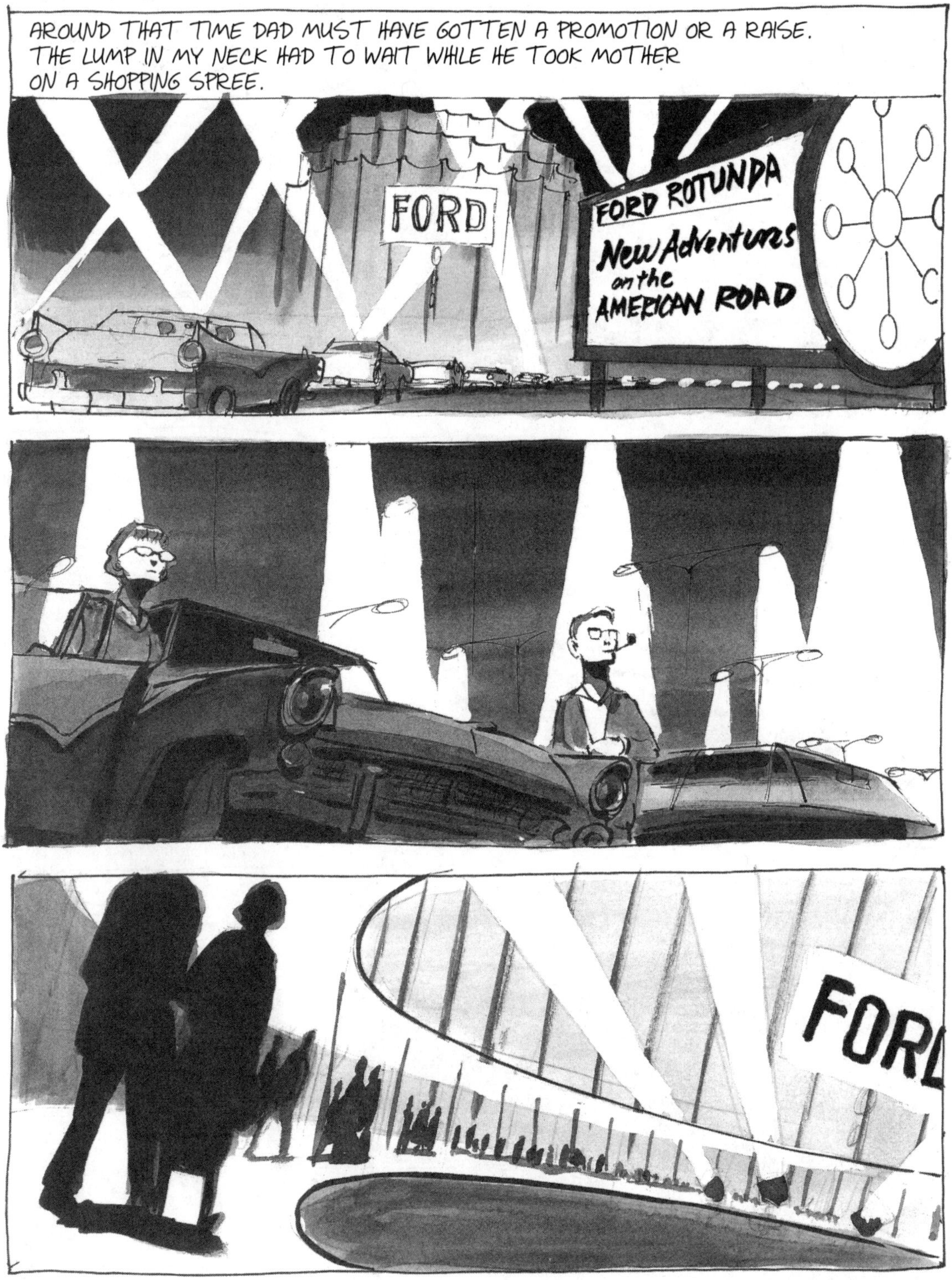
AROUND THAT TIME DAD MUST HAVE GOTTEN A PROMOTION OR A RAISE. THE LUMP IN MY NECK HAD TO WAIT WHILE HE TOOK MOTHER ON A SHOPPING SPREE.
FORD
FORD ROTUNDA
New Adventures on the AMERICAN ROAD
FORD

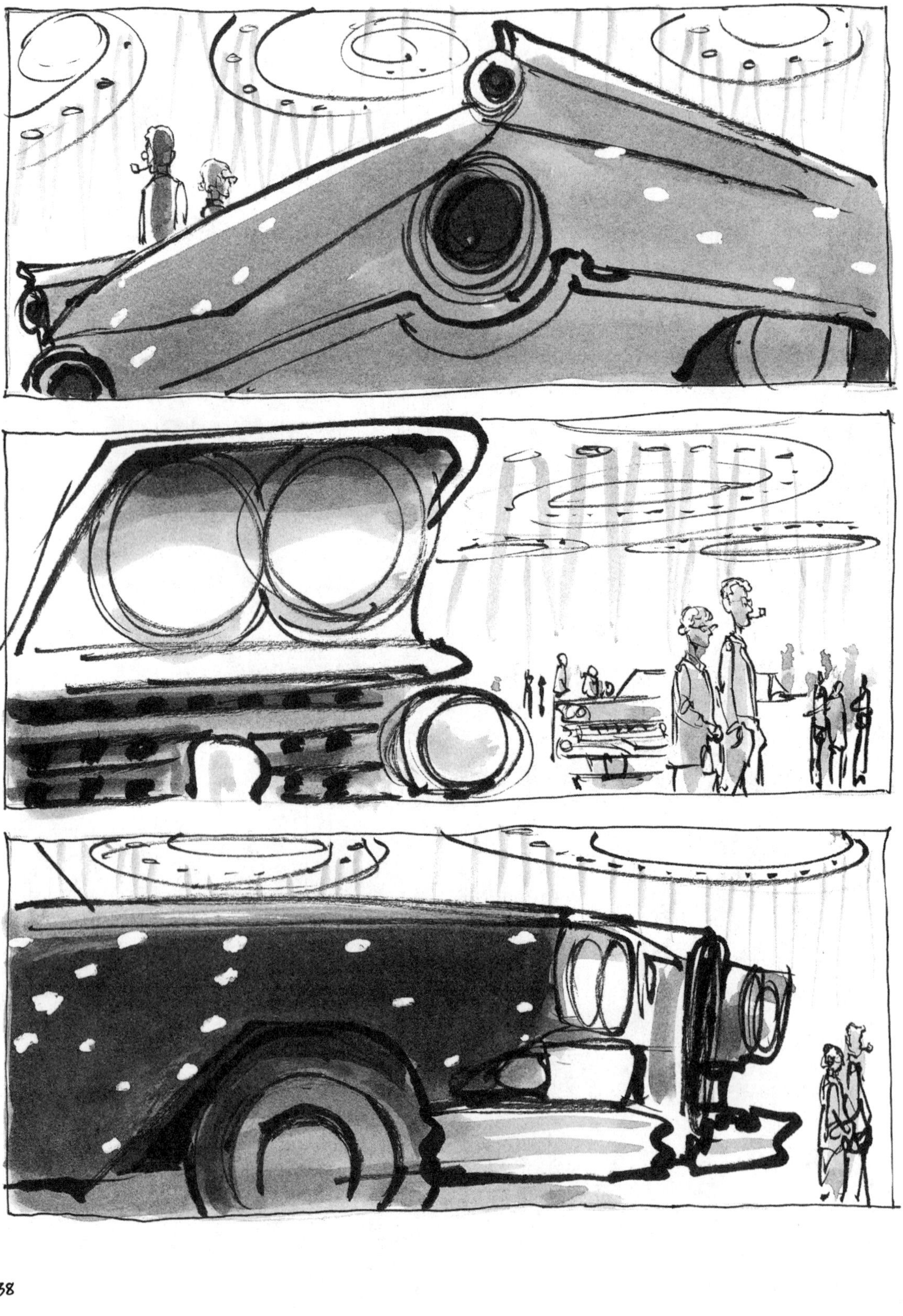

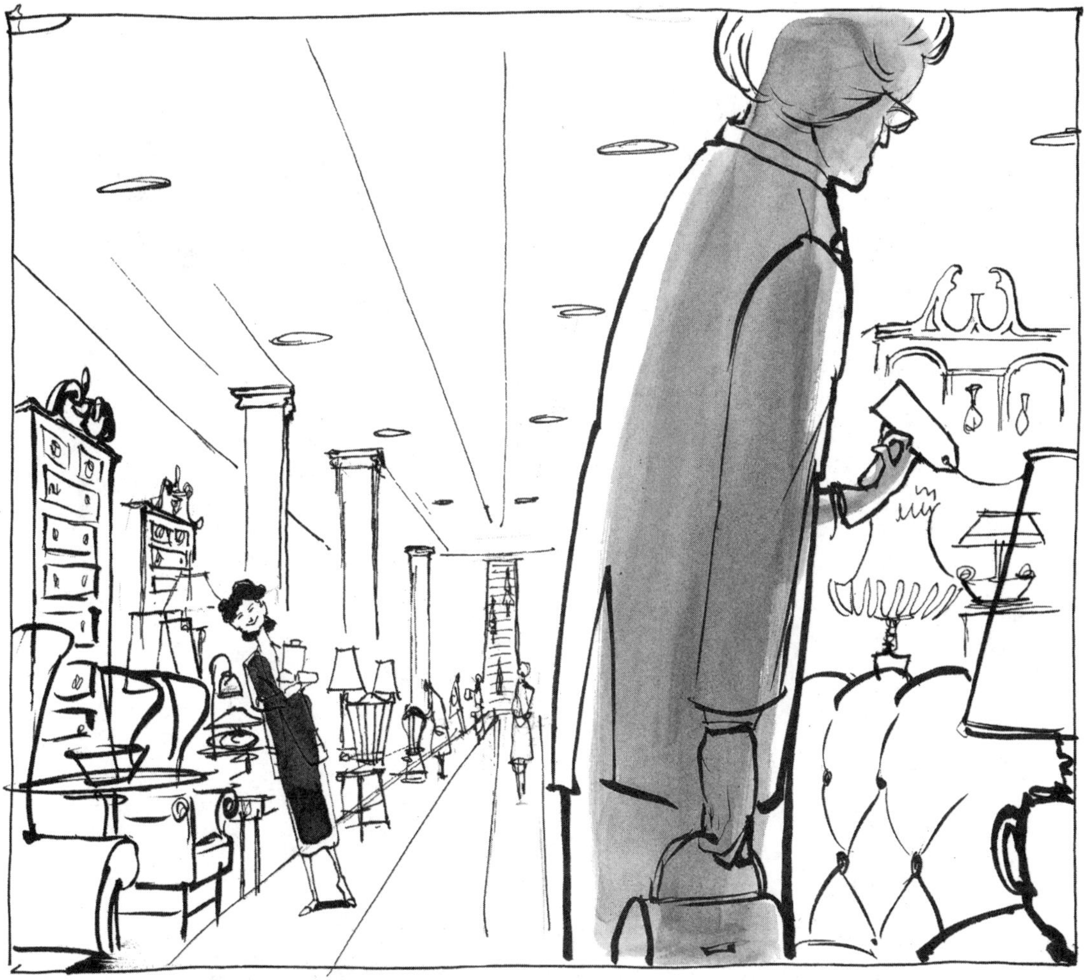

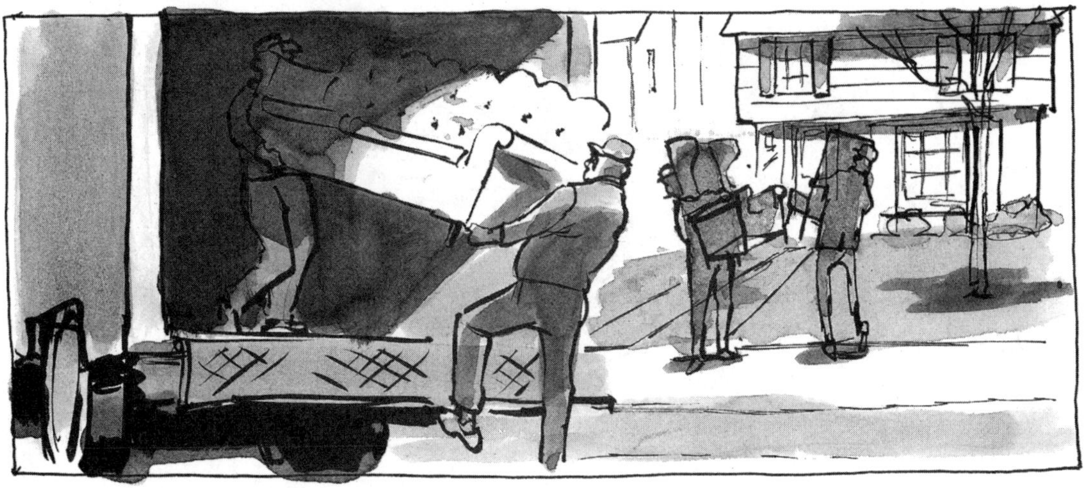

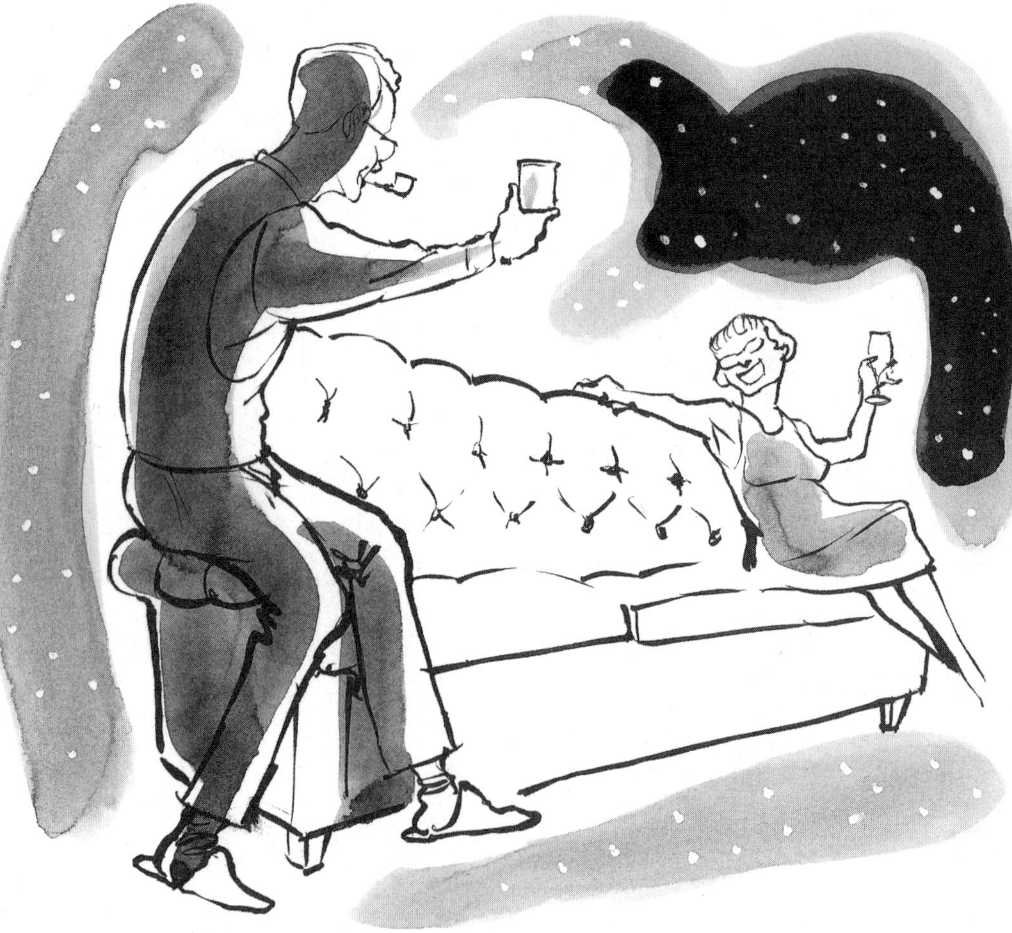

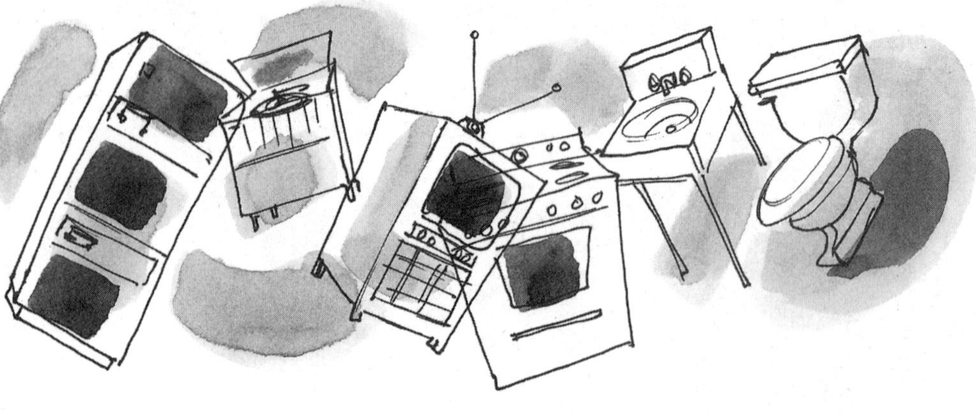

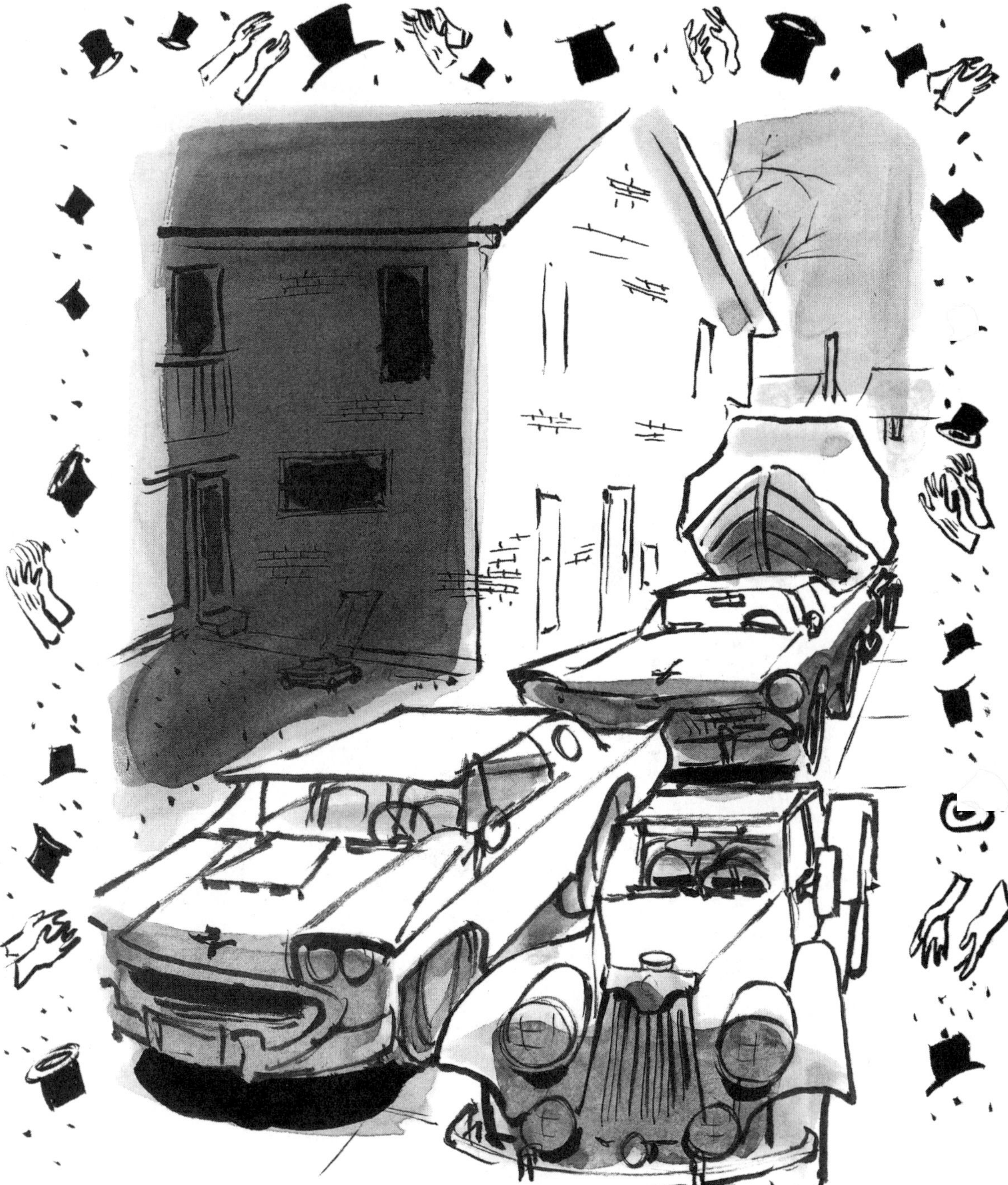

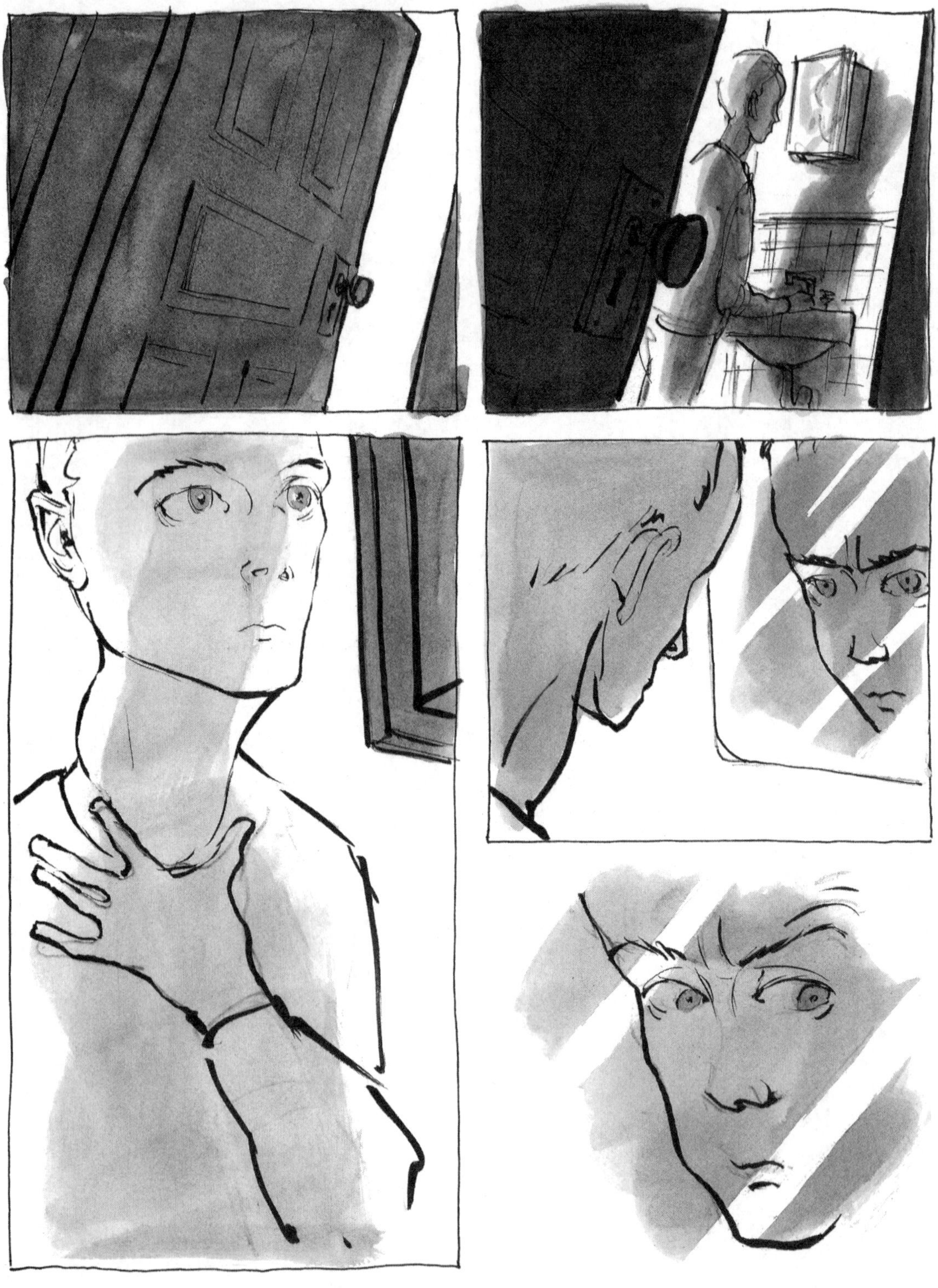

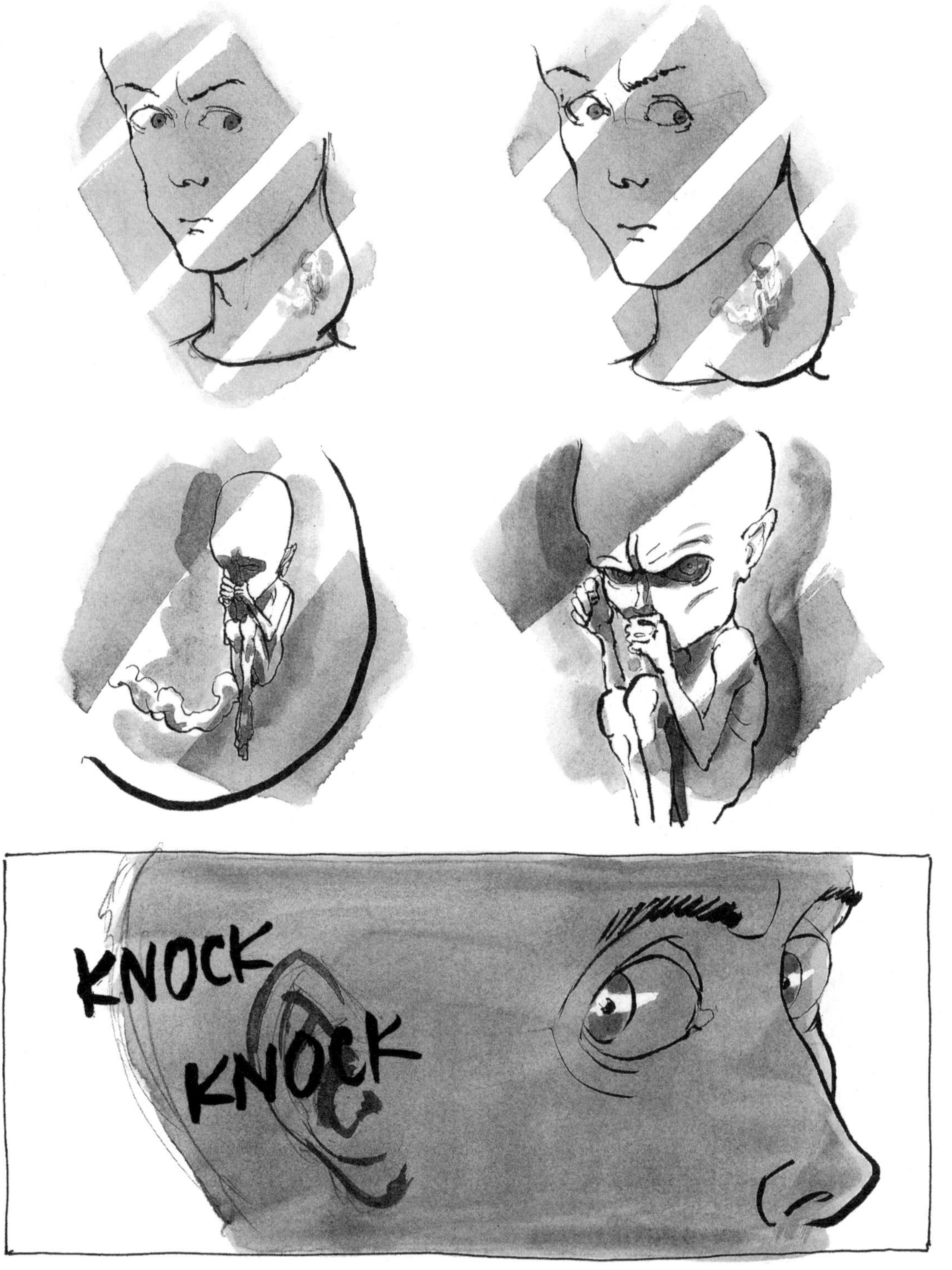
KNOCK
KNOCK

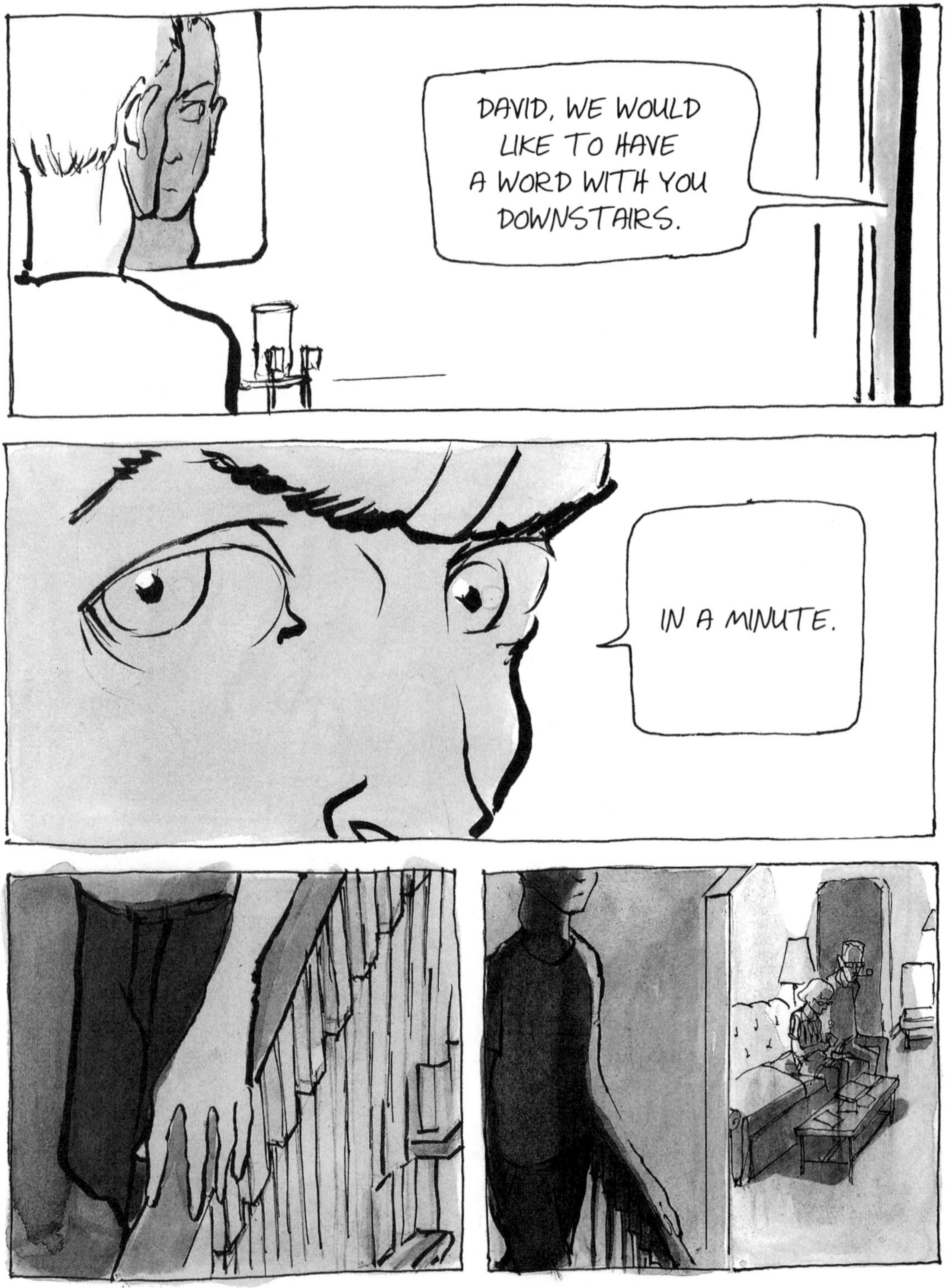
DAVID, WE WOULD LIKE TO HAVE A WORD WITH YOU DOWNSTAIRS.
IN A MINUTE.

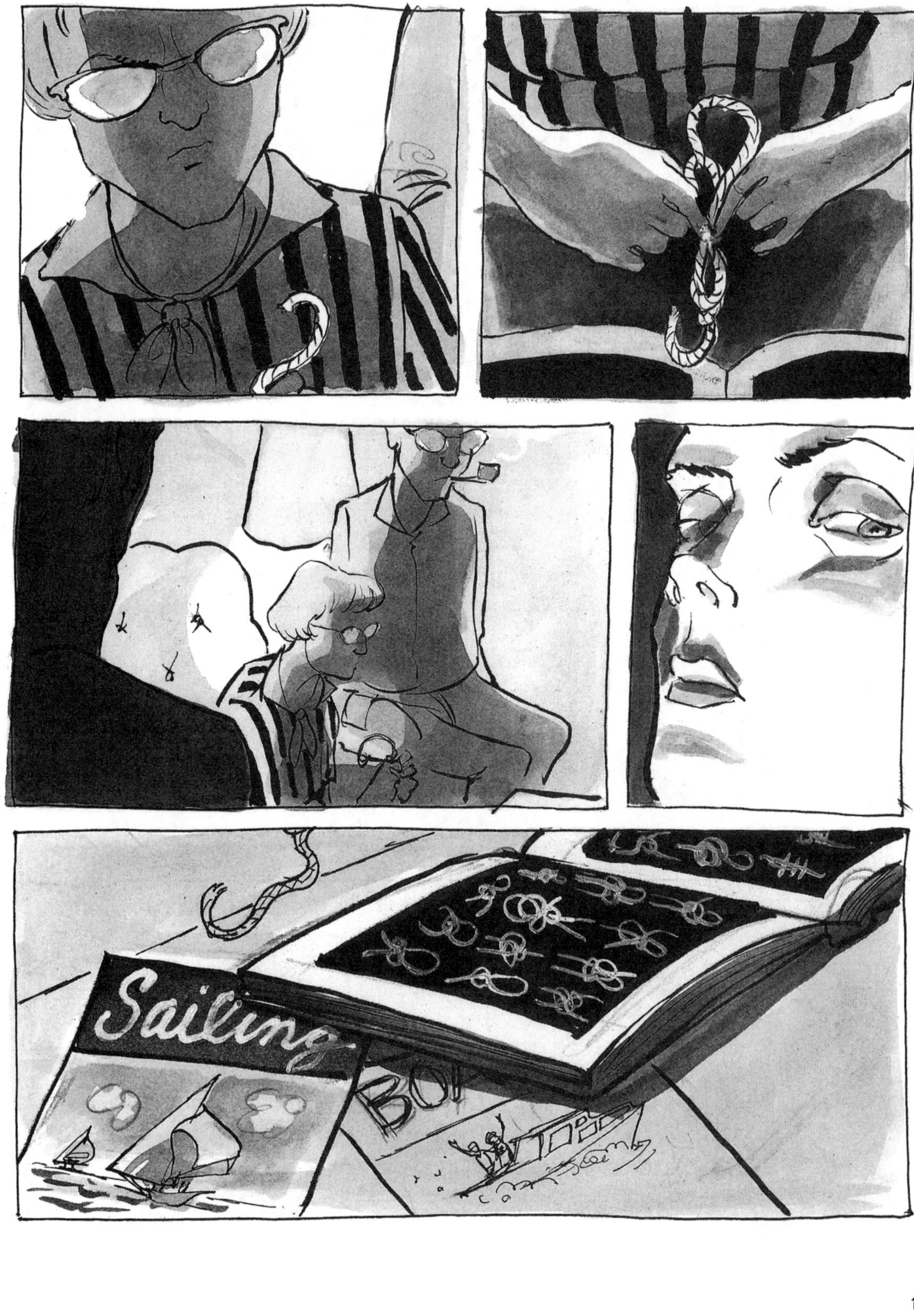
Sailing

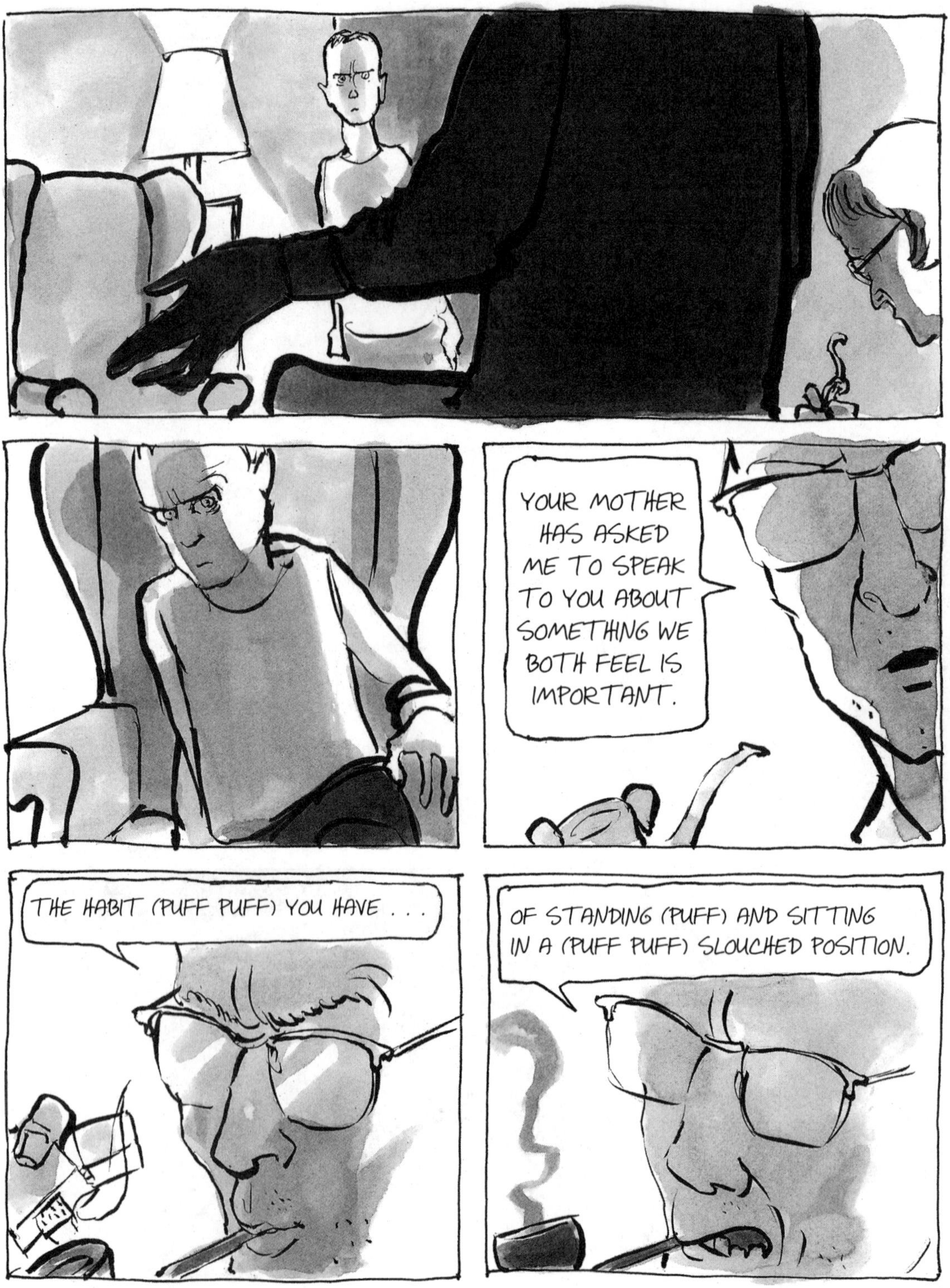
YOUR MOTHER HAS ASKED ME TO SPEAK TO YOU ABOUT SOMETHING WE BOTH FEEL IS IMPORTANT.
THE HABIT (PUFF PUFF) YOU HAVE . . .
OF STANDING (PUFF) AND SITTING IN A (PUFF PUFF) SLOUCHED POSITION.

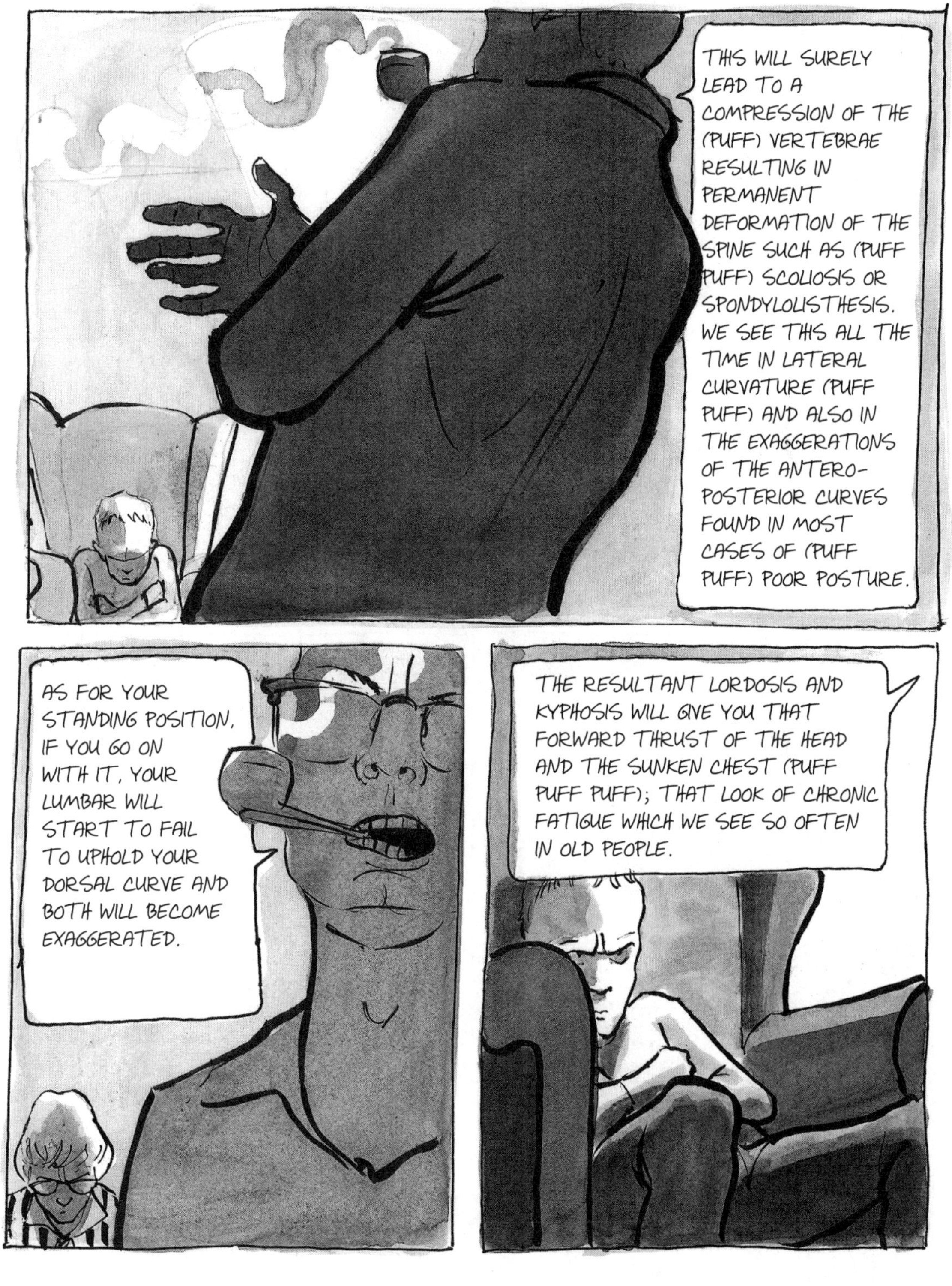
THIS WILL SURELY LEAD TO A COMPRESSION OF THE (PUFF) VERTEBRAE RESULTING IN PERMANENT DEFORMATION OF THE SPINE SUCH AS (PUFF PUFF) SCOLIOSIS OR SPONDYLOLISTHESIS. WE SEE THIS ALL THE TIME IN LATERAL CURVATURE (PUFF PUFF) AND ALSO IN THE EXAGGERATIONS OF THE ANTERO-POSTERIOR CURVES FOUND IN MOST CASES OF (PUFF PUFF) POOR POSTURE.
AS FOR YOUR STANDING POSITION, IF YOU GO ON WITH IT, YOUR LUMBAR WILL START TO FAIL TO UPHOLD YOUR DORSAL CURVE AND BOTH WILL BECOME EXAGGERATED.
THE RESULTANT LORDOSIS AND KYPHOSIS WILL GIVE YOU THAT FORWARD THRUST OF THE HEAD AND THE SUNKEN CHEST (PUFF PUFF PUFF); THAT LOOK OF CHRONIC FATIGUE WHICH WE SEE SO OFTEN IN OLD PEOPLE.

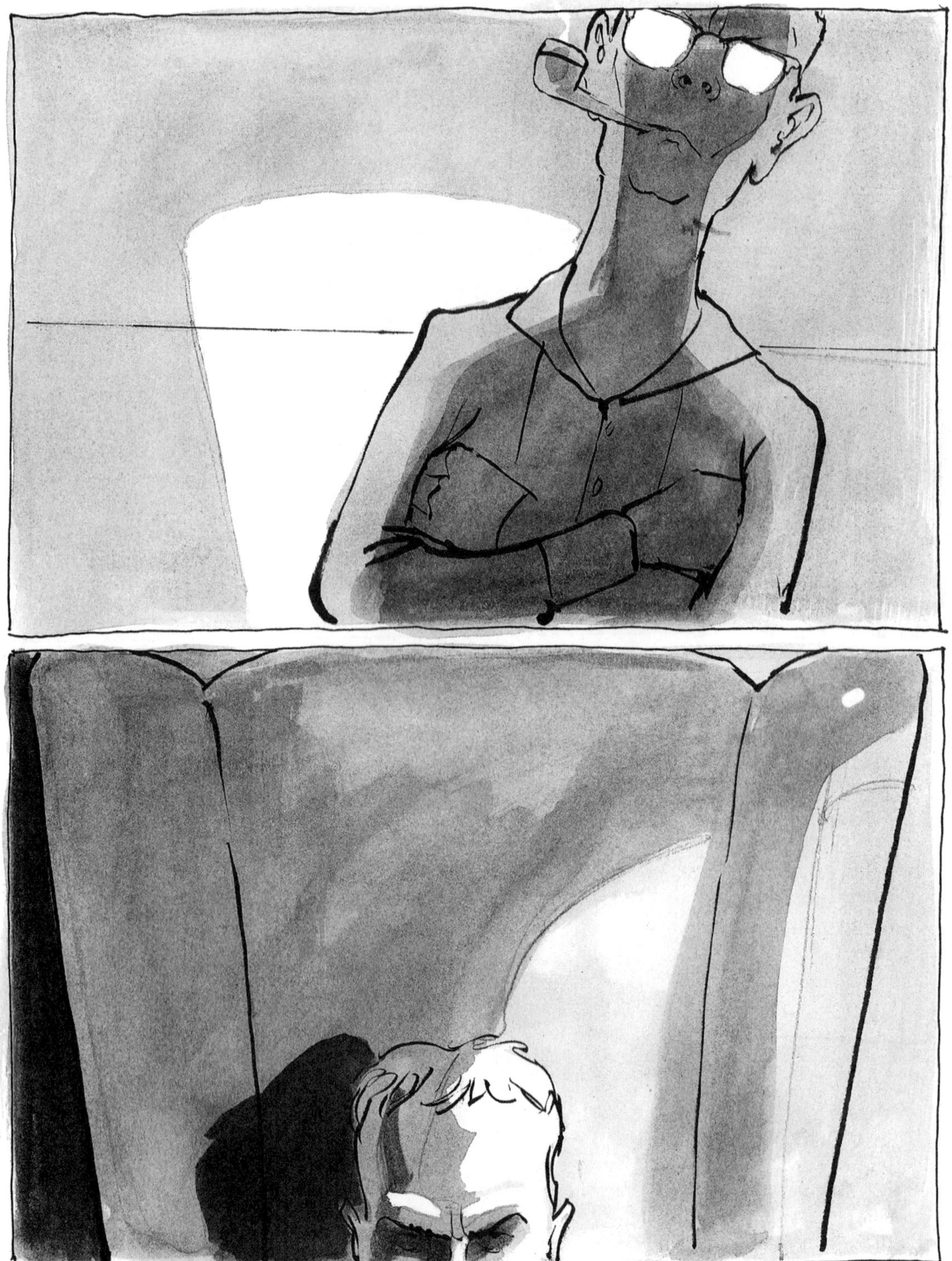

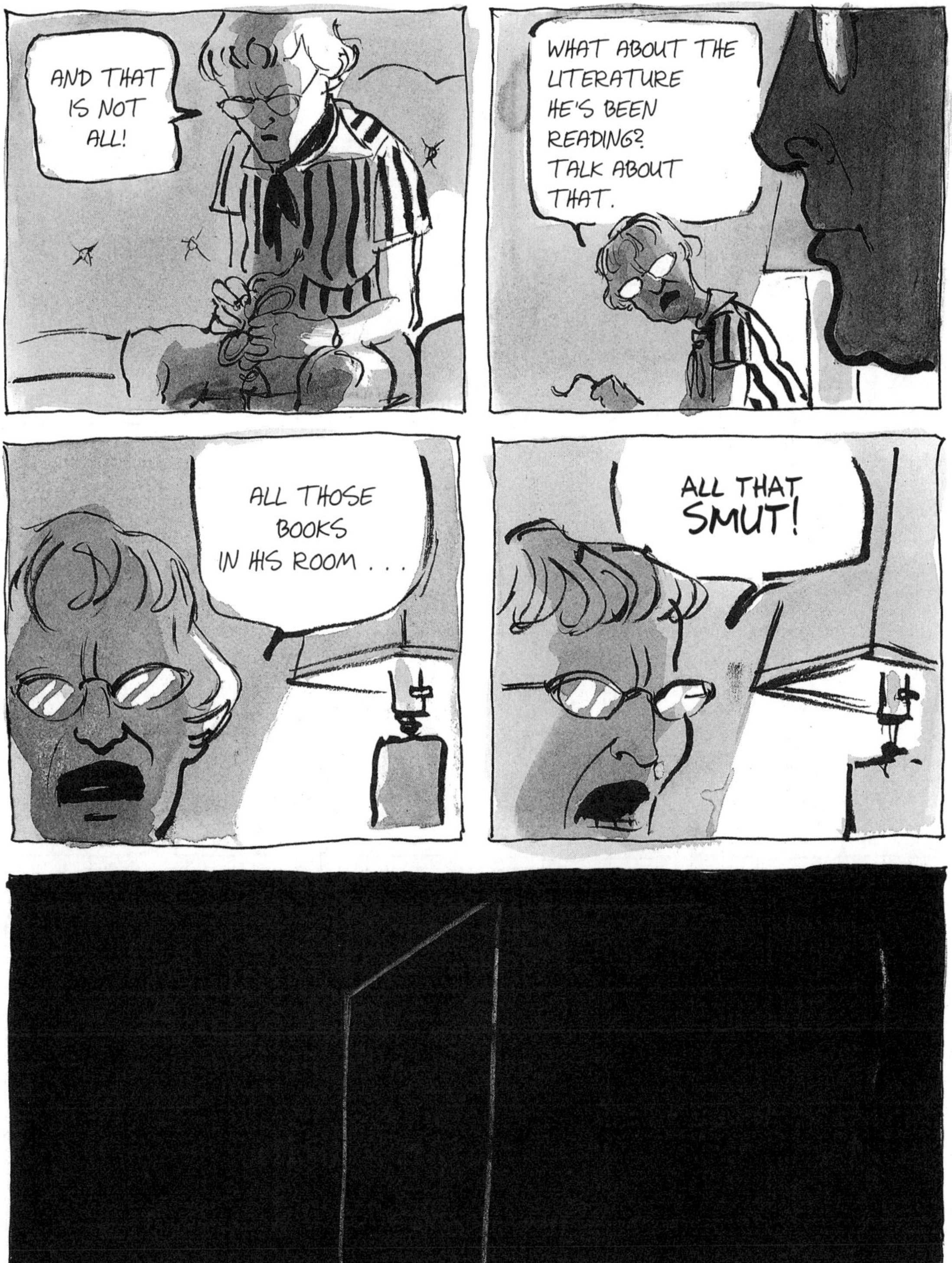
AND THAT IS NOT ALL!
WHAT ABOUT THE LITERATURE HE'S BEEN READING? TALK ABOUT THAT.
ALL THOSE BOOKS IN HIS ROOM . . .
ALL THAT SMUT!

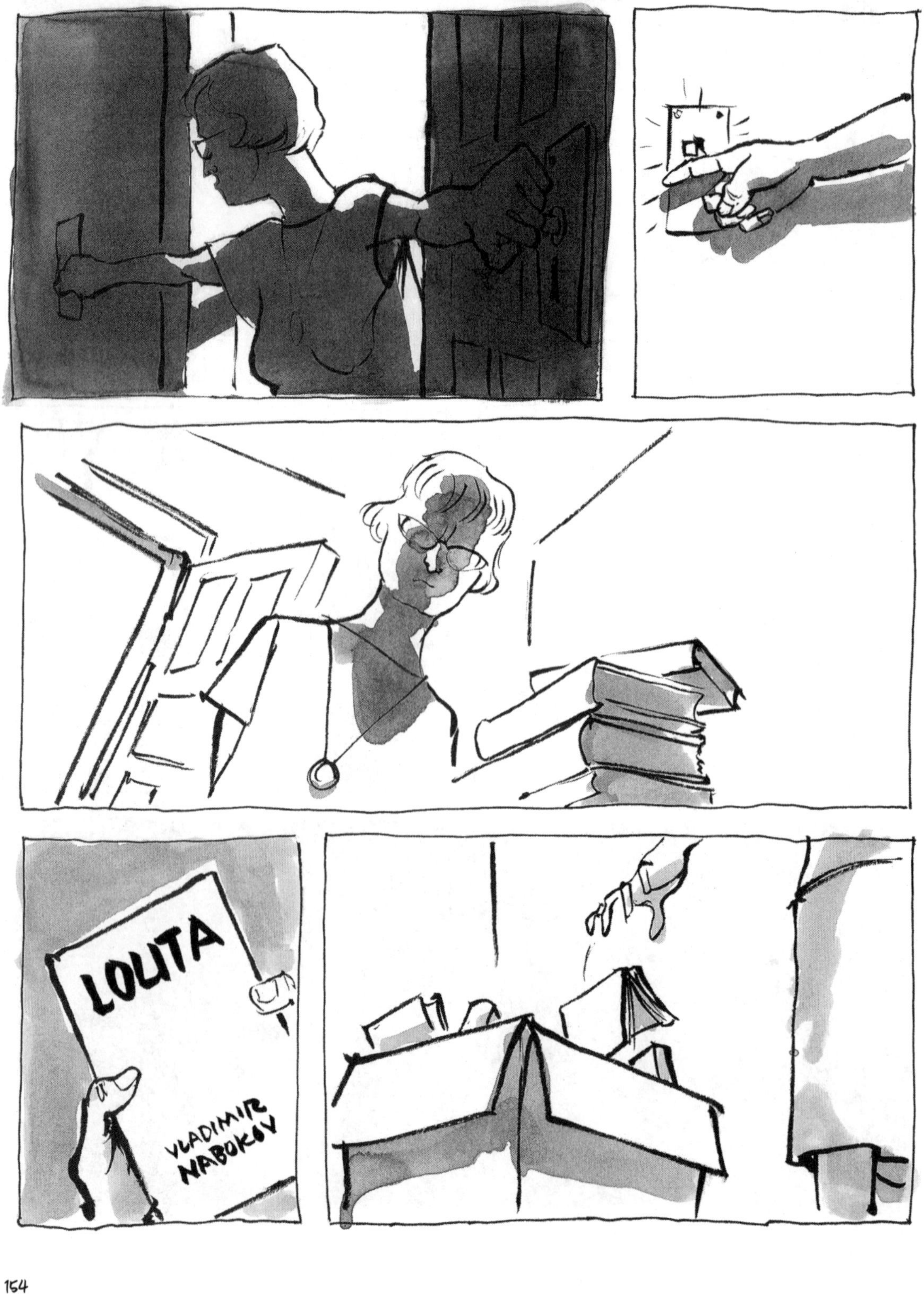
LOLITA
VLADIMIR NABOKOV

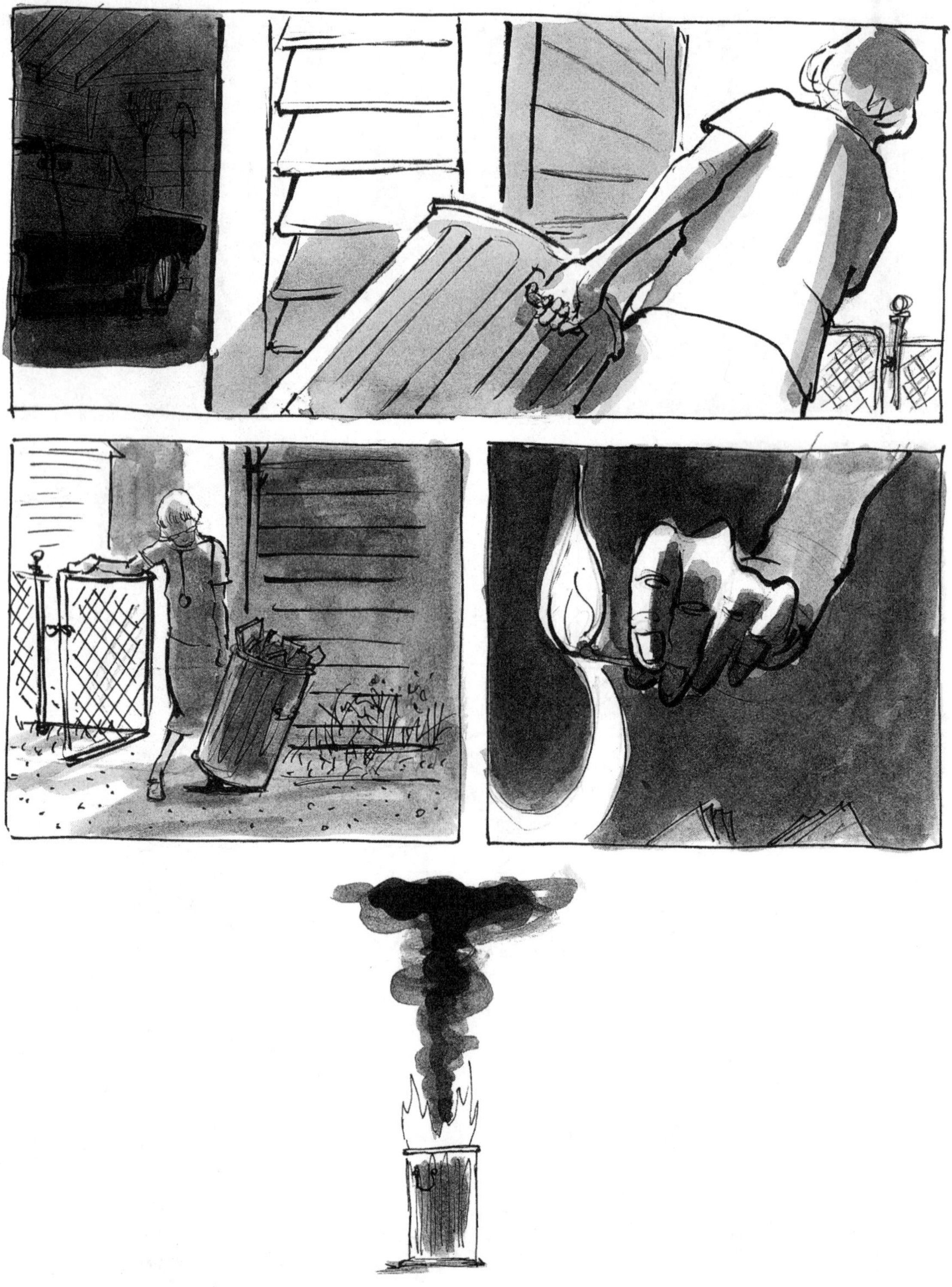

THREE AND A HALF
YEARS
AFTER THE FIRST
DIAGNOSIS

I WAS FOURTEEN

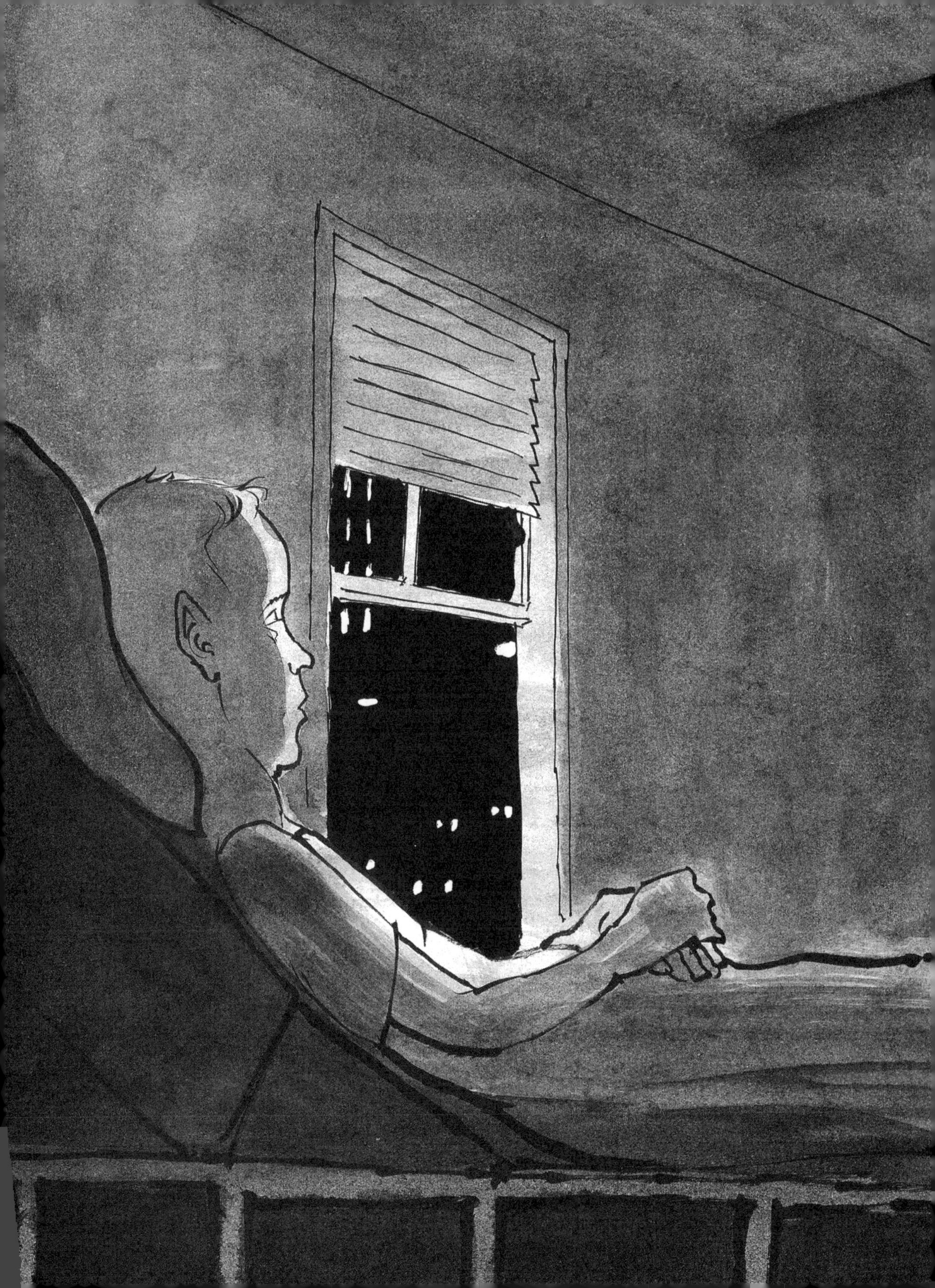

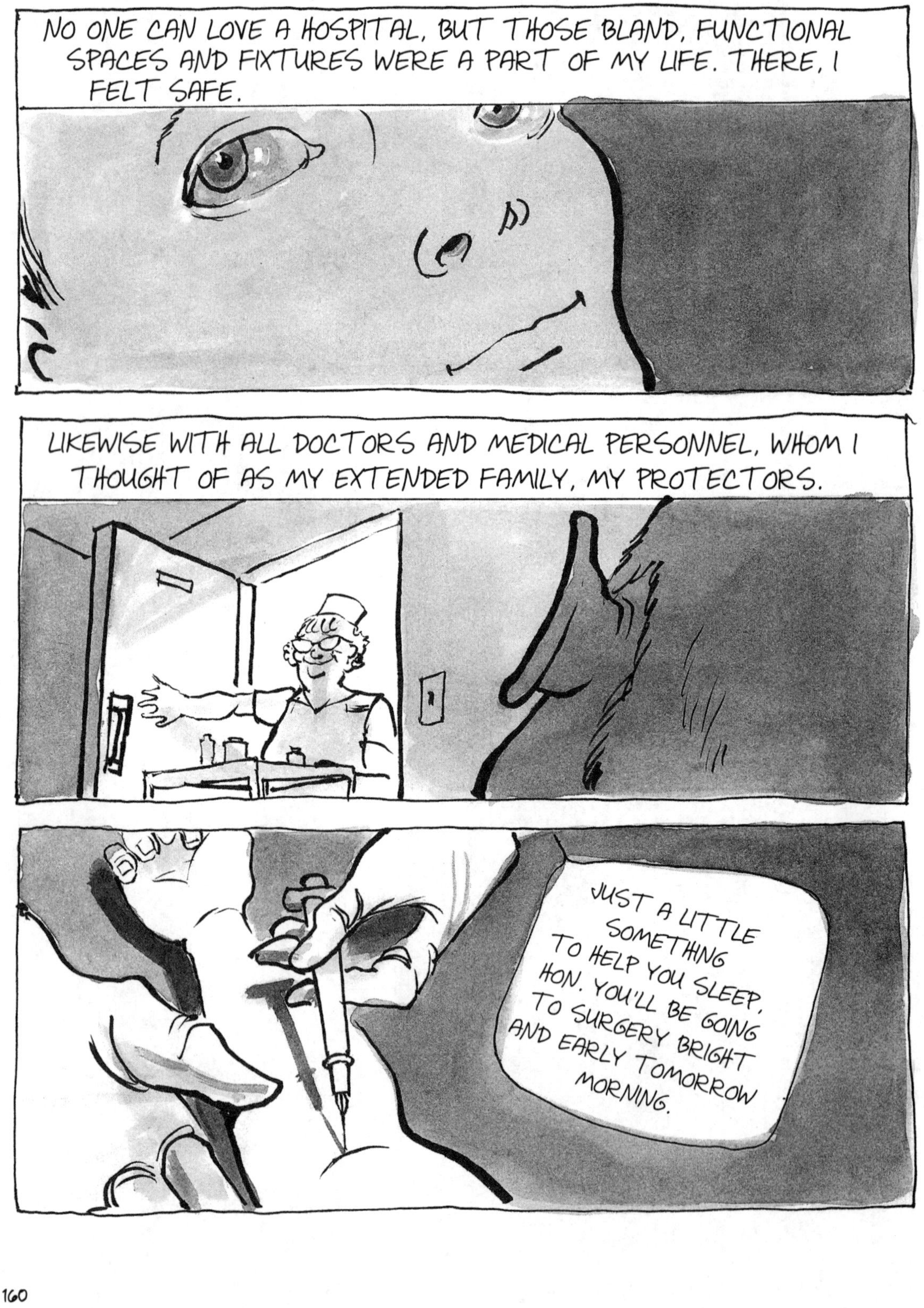
NO ONE CAN LOVE A HOSPITAL, BUT THOSE BLAND, FUNCTIONAL SPACES AND FIXTURES WERE A PART OF MY LIFE. THERE, I FELT SAFE.
LIKEWISE WITH ALL DOCTORS AND MEDICAL PERSONNEL, WHOM I THOUGHT OF AS MY EXTENDED FAMILY, MY PROTECTORS.
JUST A LITTLE SOMETHING TO HELP YOU SLEEP, HON. YOU'LL BE GOING TO SURGERY BRIGHT AND EARLY TOMORROW MORNING.

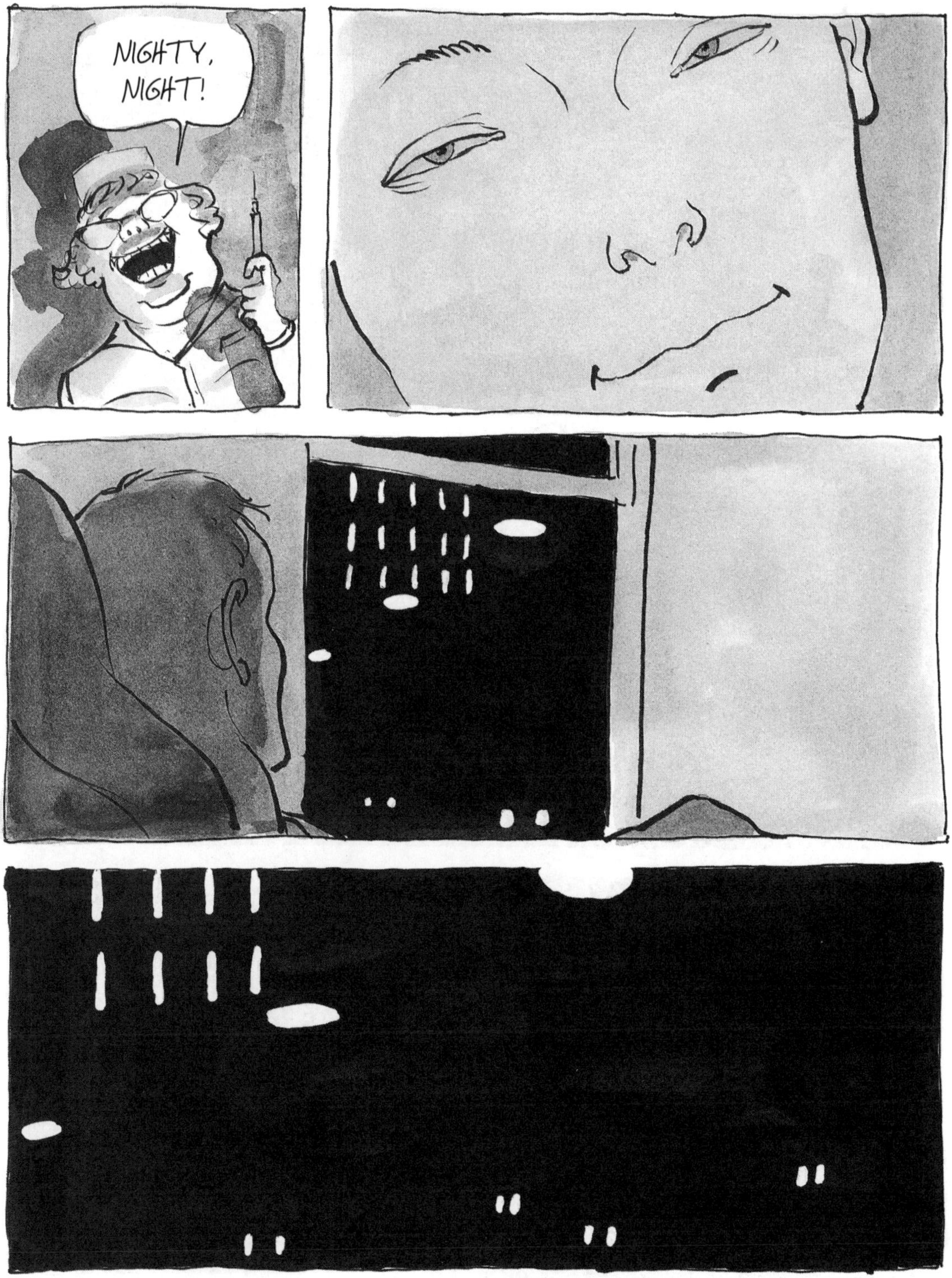
NIGHTY, NIGHT!

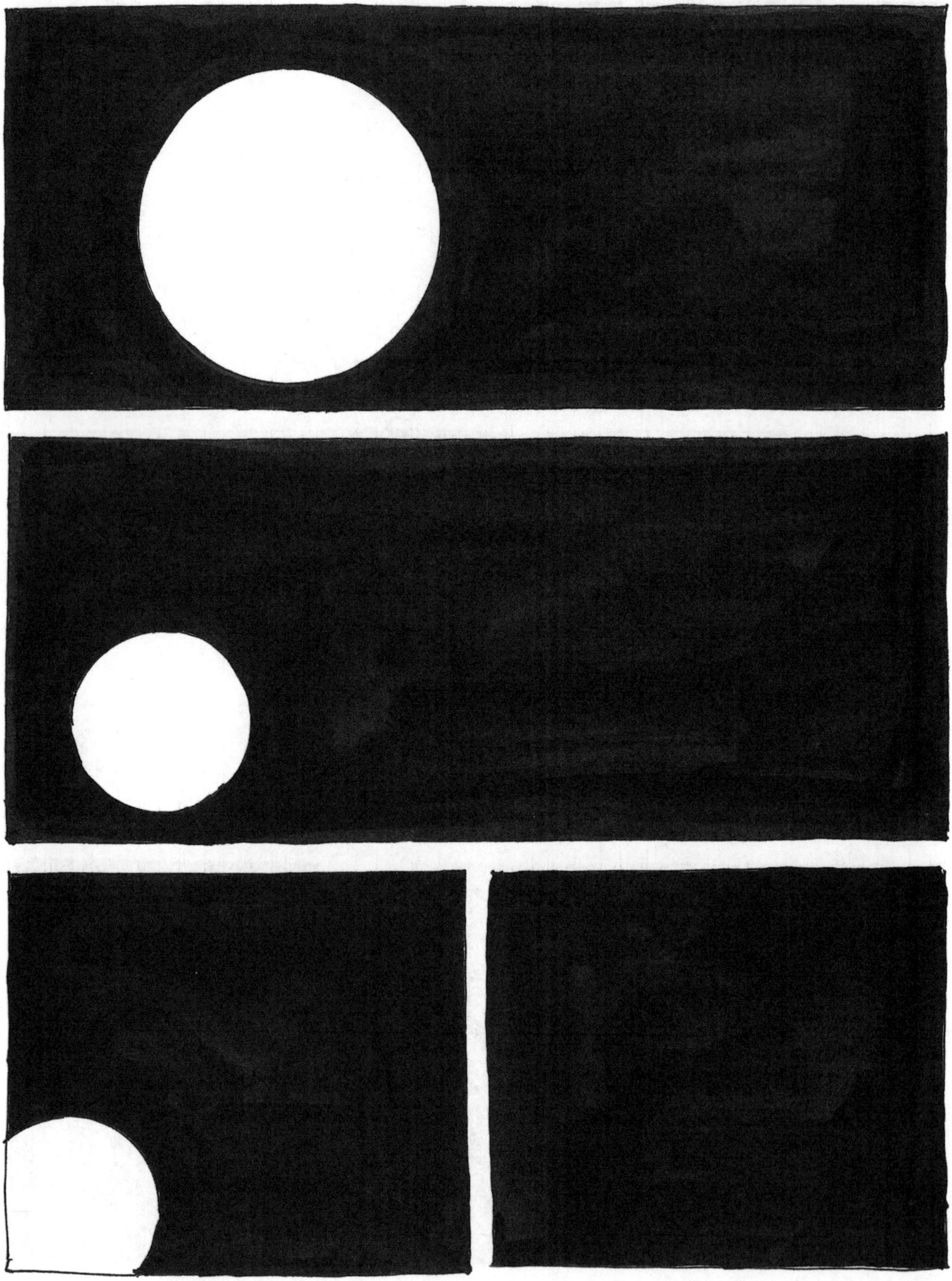

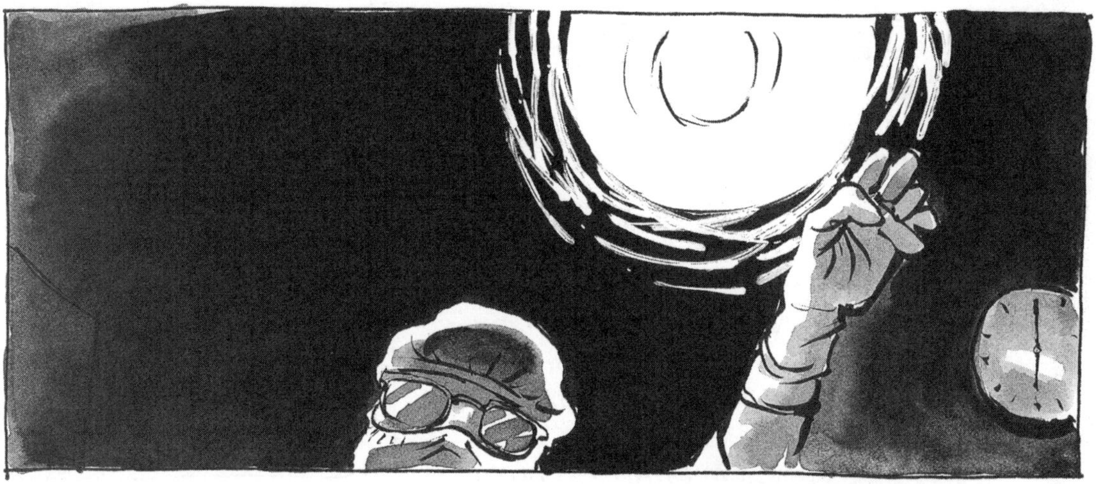
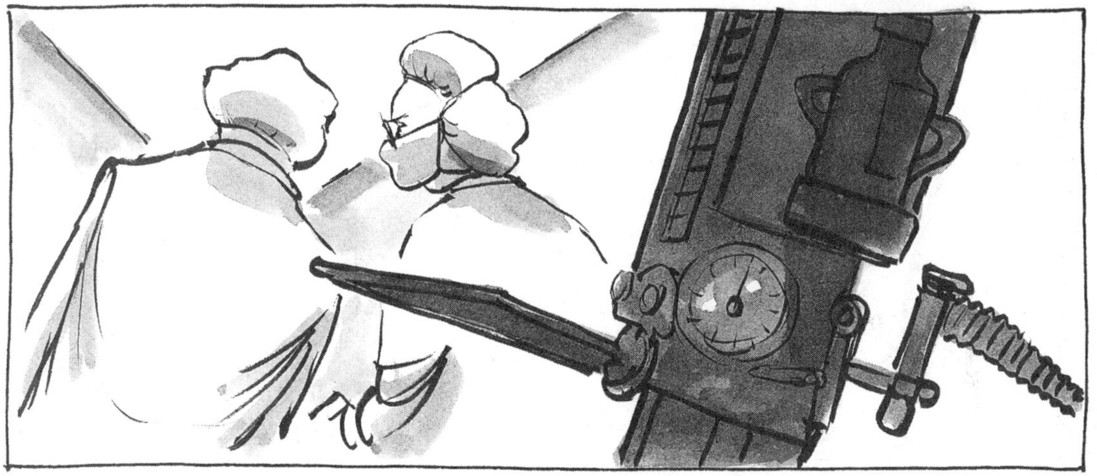
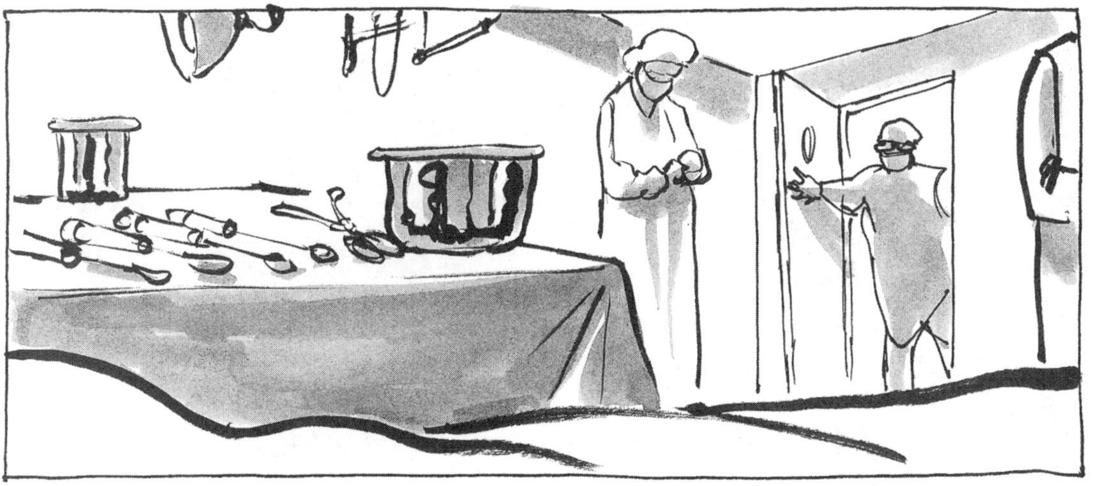

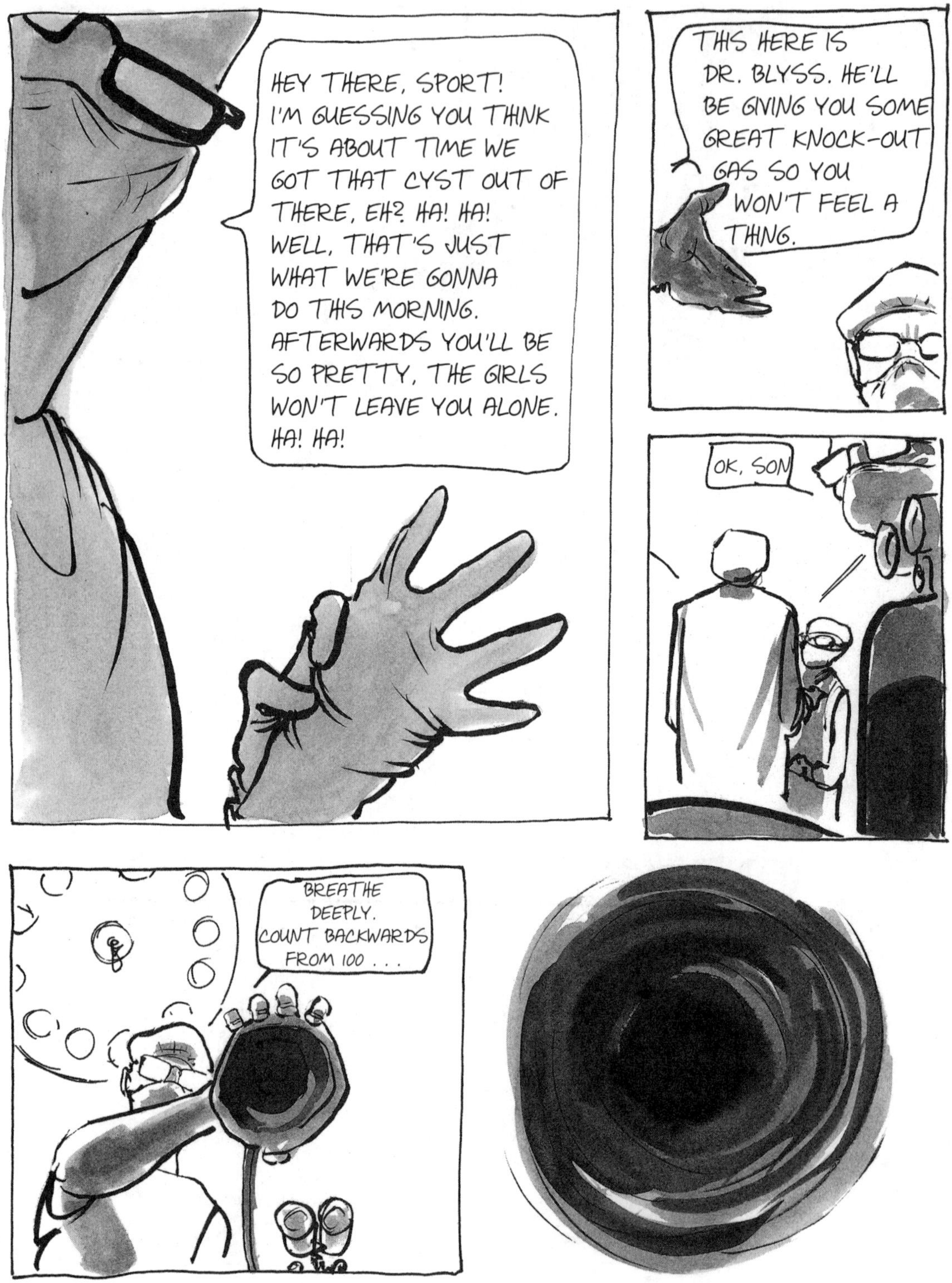
HEY THERE, SPORT! I'M GUESSING YOU THINK IT'S ABOUT TIME WE GOT THAT CYST OUT OF THERE, EH? HA! HA! WELL, THAT'S JUST WHAT WE'RE GONNA DO THIS MORNING. AFTERWARDS YOU'LL BE SO PRETTY, THE GIRLS WON'T LEAVE YOU ALONE. HA! HA!
THIS HERE IS DR. BLYSS. HE'LL BE GIVING YOU SOME GREAT KNOCK-OUT GAS SO YOU WON'T FEEL A THING.
OK, SON
BREATHE DEEPLY. COUNT BACKWARDS FROM 100 . . .

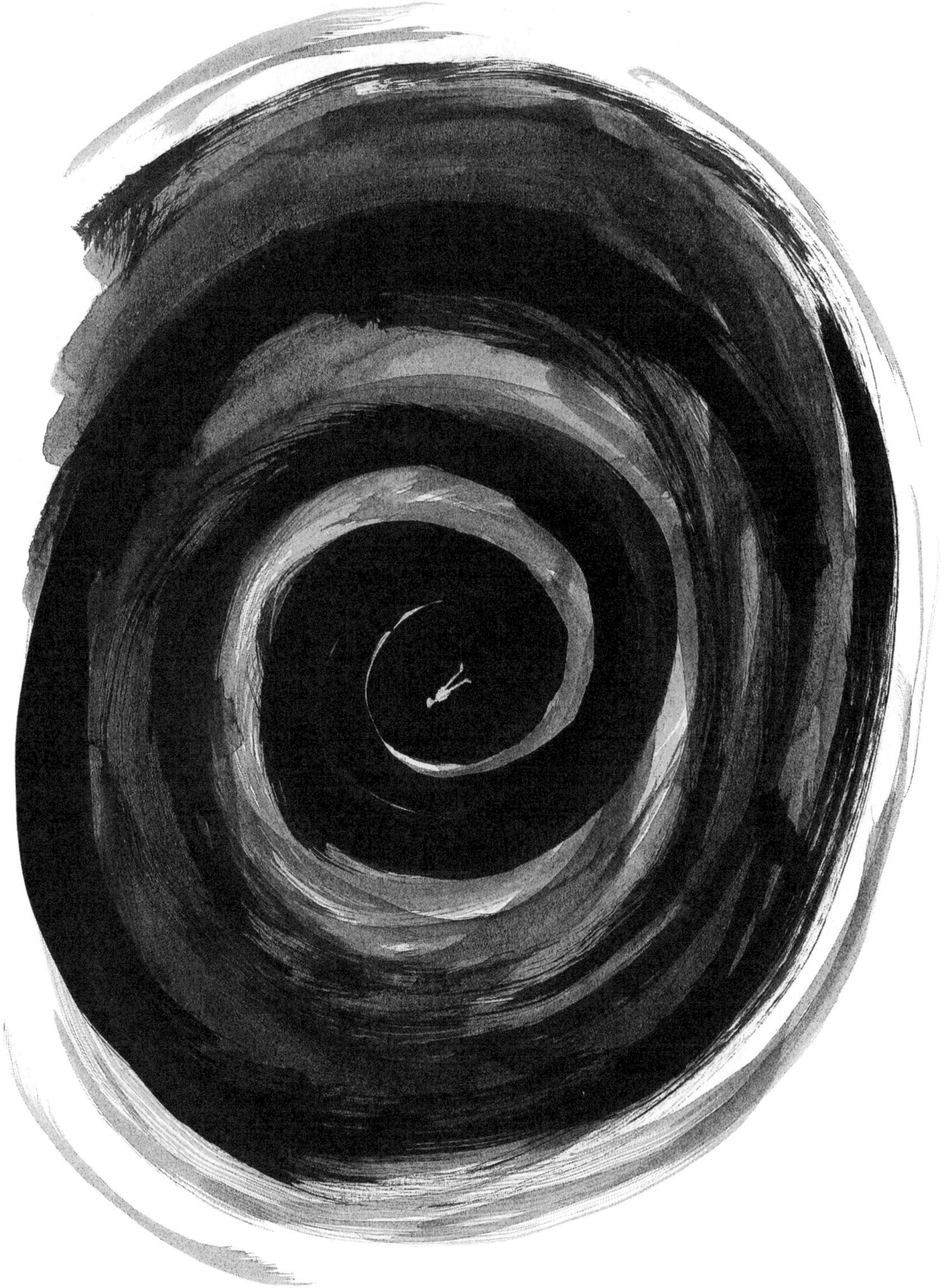

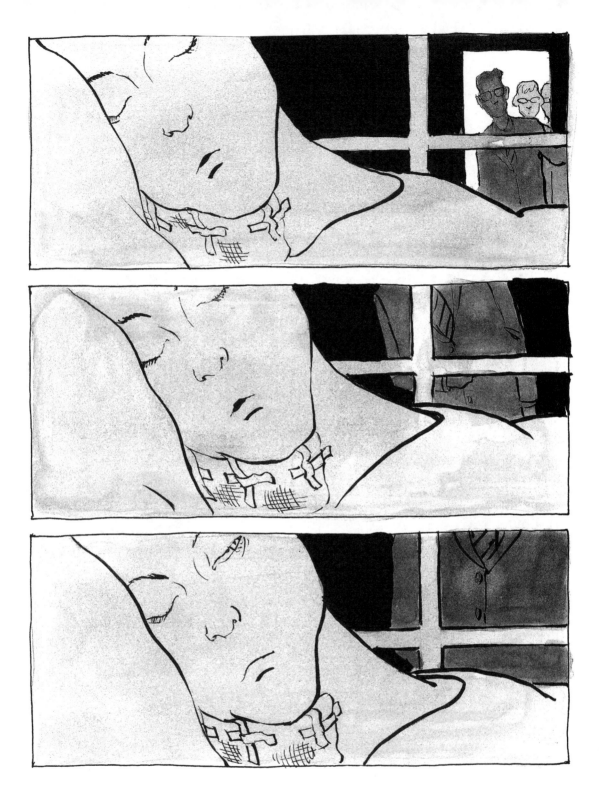

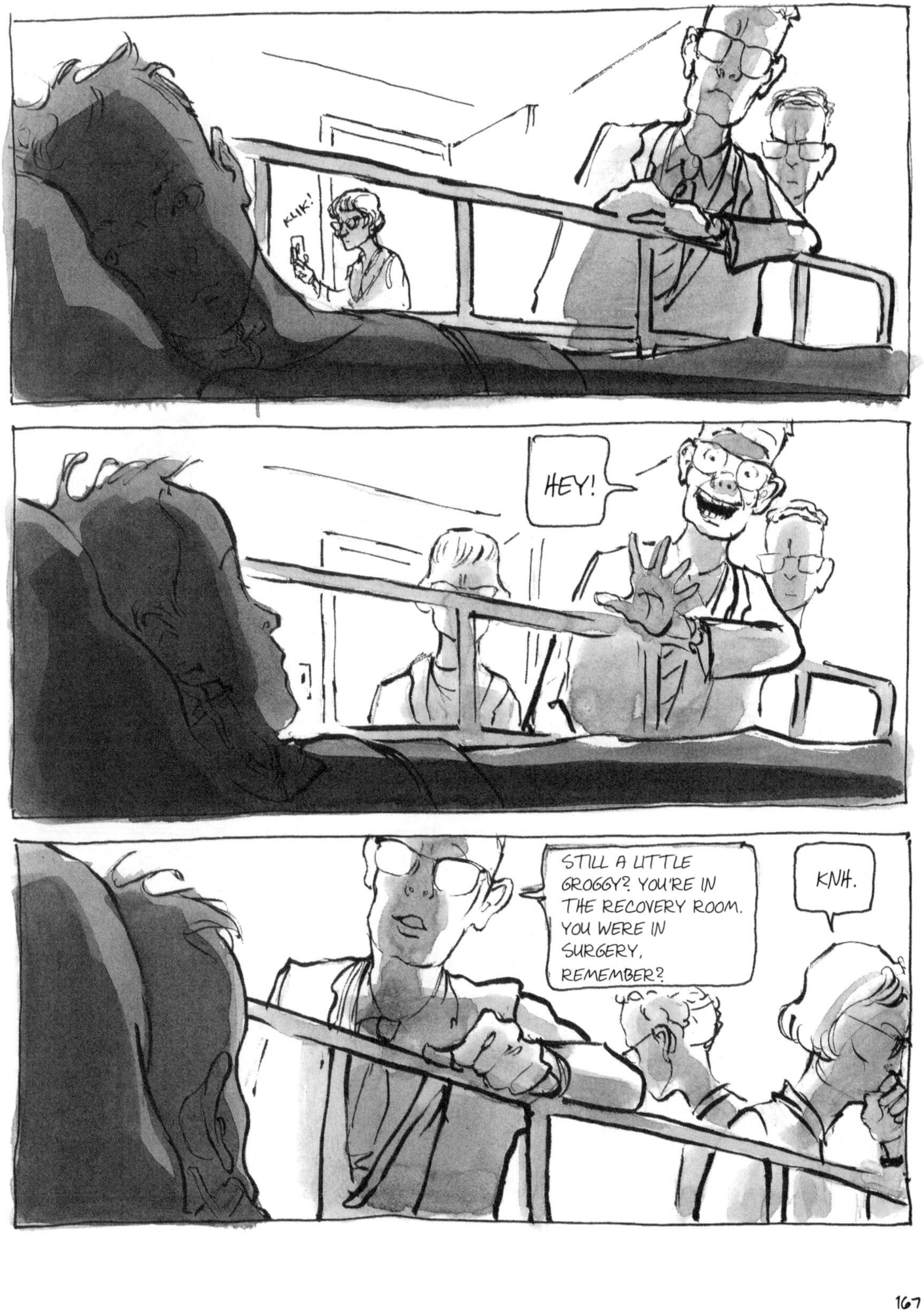
KLIK!
HEY!
STILL A LITTLE GROGGY? YOU'RE IN THE RECOVERY ROOM. YOU WERE IN SURGERY, REMEMBER?
KNH.

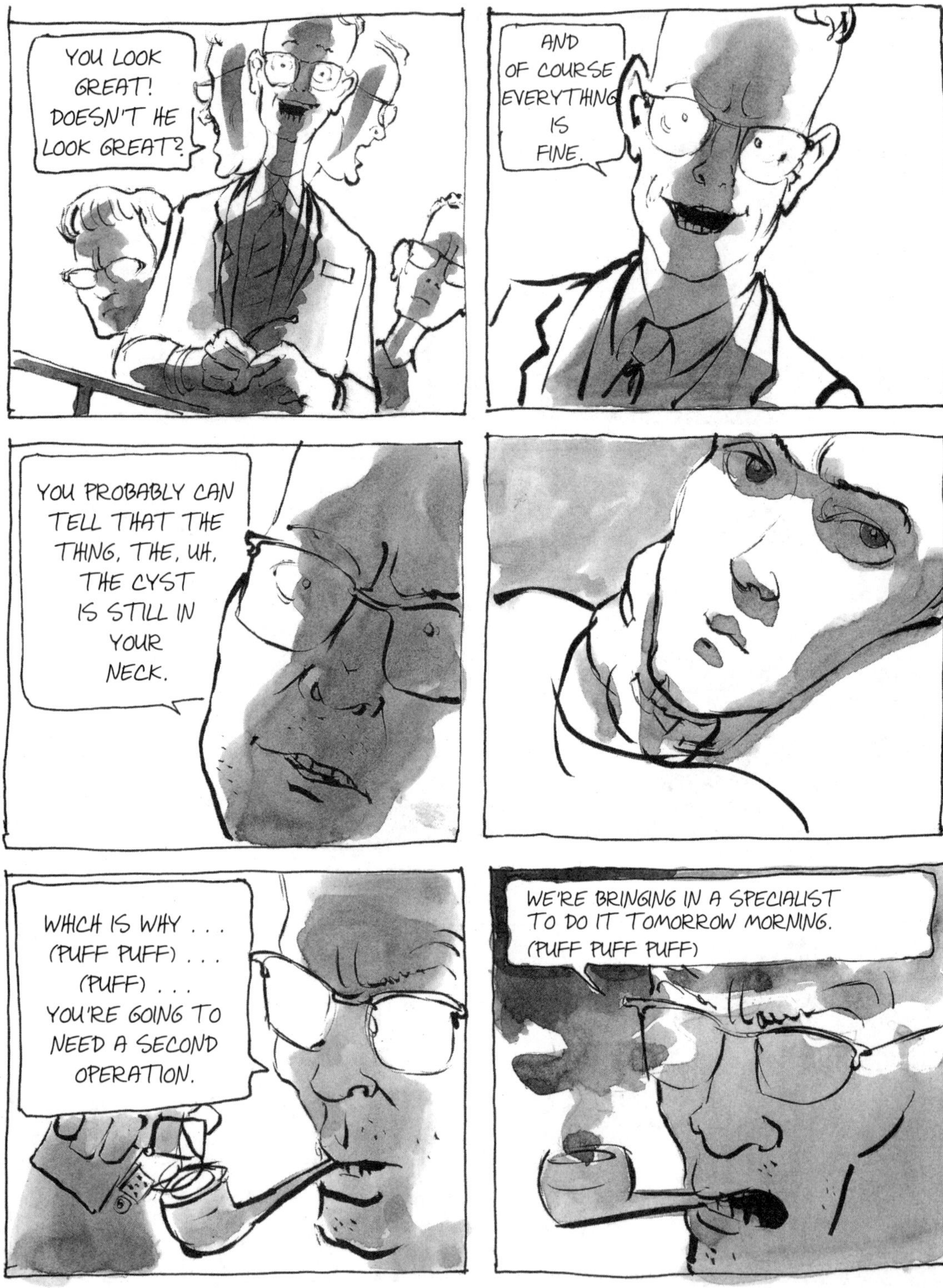
YOU LOOK GREAT! DOESN'T HE LOOK GREAT?
AND OF COURSE EVERYTHING IS FINE.
YOU PROBABLY CAN TELL THAT THE THING, THE, UH, THE CYST IS STILL IN YOUR NECK.
WHICH IS WHY . . . (PUFF PUFF) . . . (PUFF) . . . YOU'RE GOING TO NEED A SECOND OPERATION.
WE'RE BRINGING IN A SPECIALIST TO DO IT TOMORROW MORNING. (PUFF PUFF PUFF)

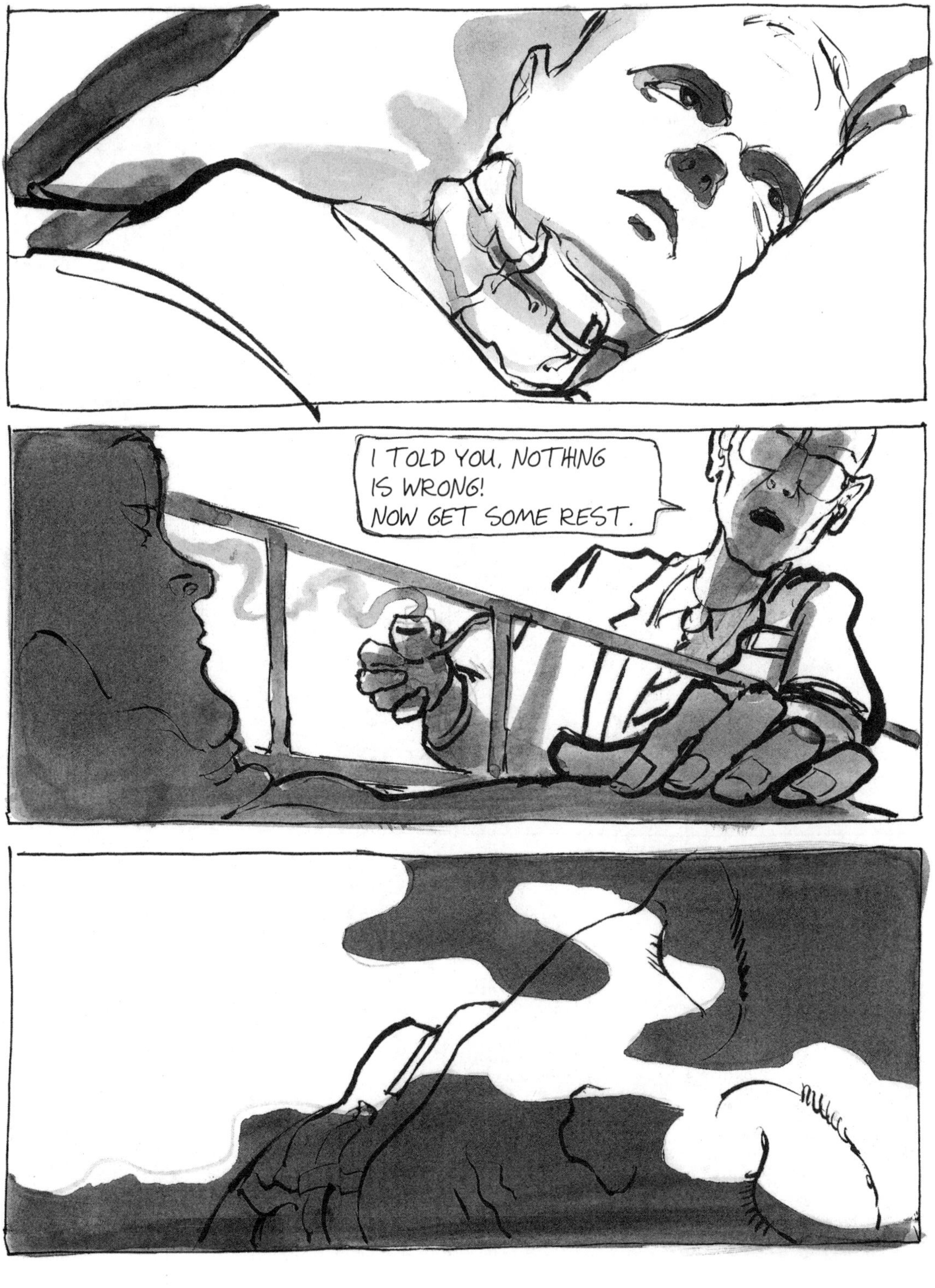
I TOLD YOU, NOTHING IS WRONG! NOW GET SOME REST.

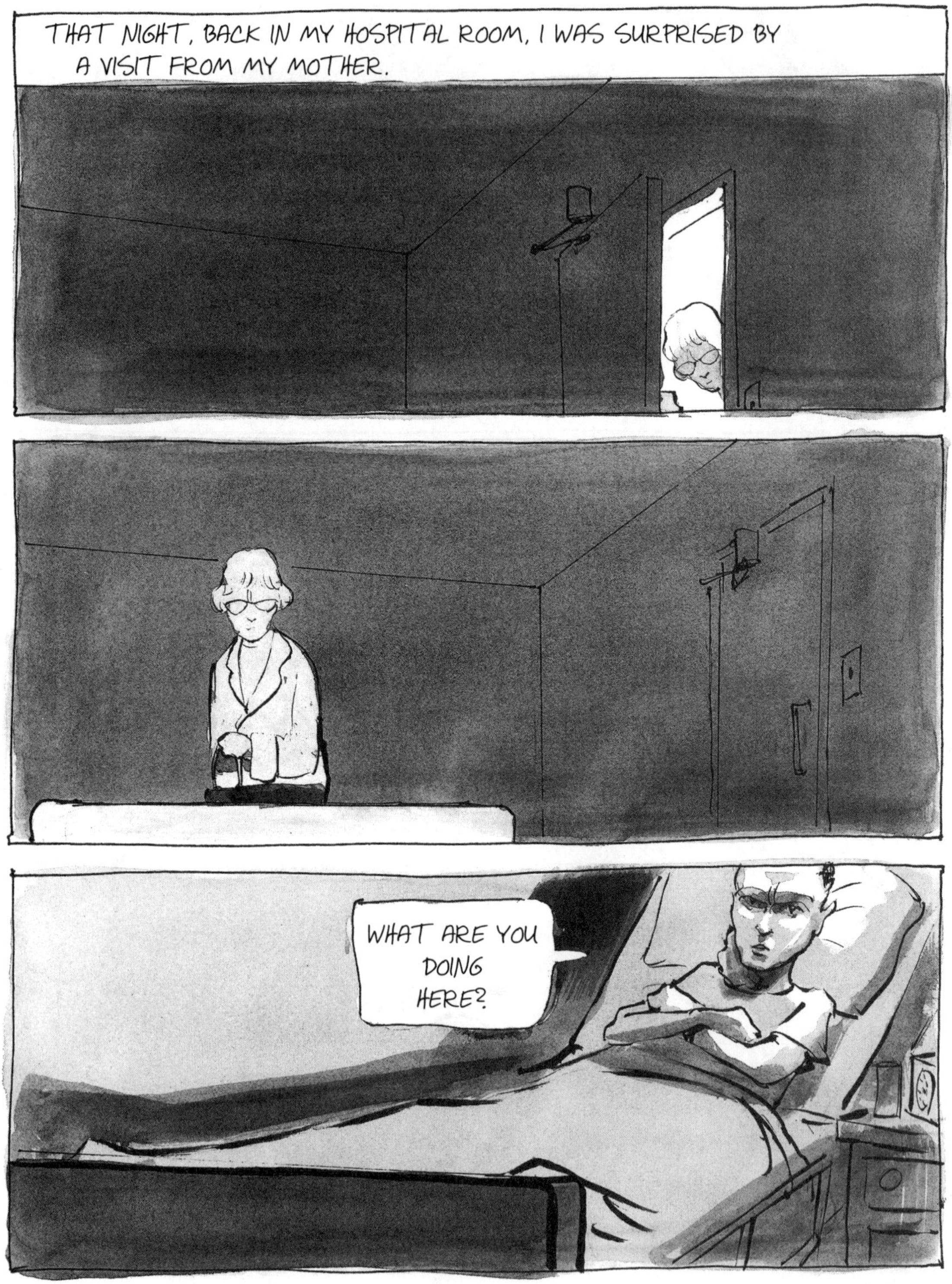
THAT NIGHT, BACK IN MY HOSPITAL ROOM, I WAS SURPRISED BY A VISIT FROM MY MOTHER.
WHAT ARE YOU DOING HERE?

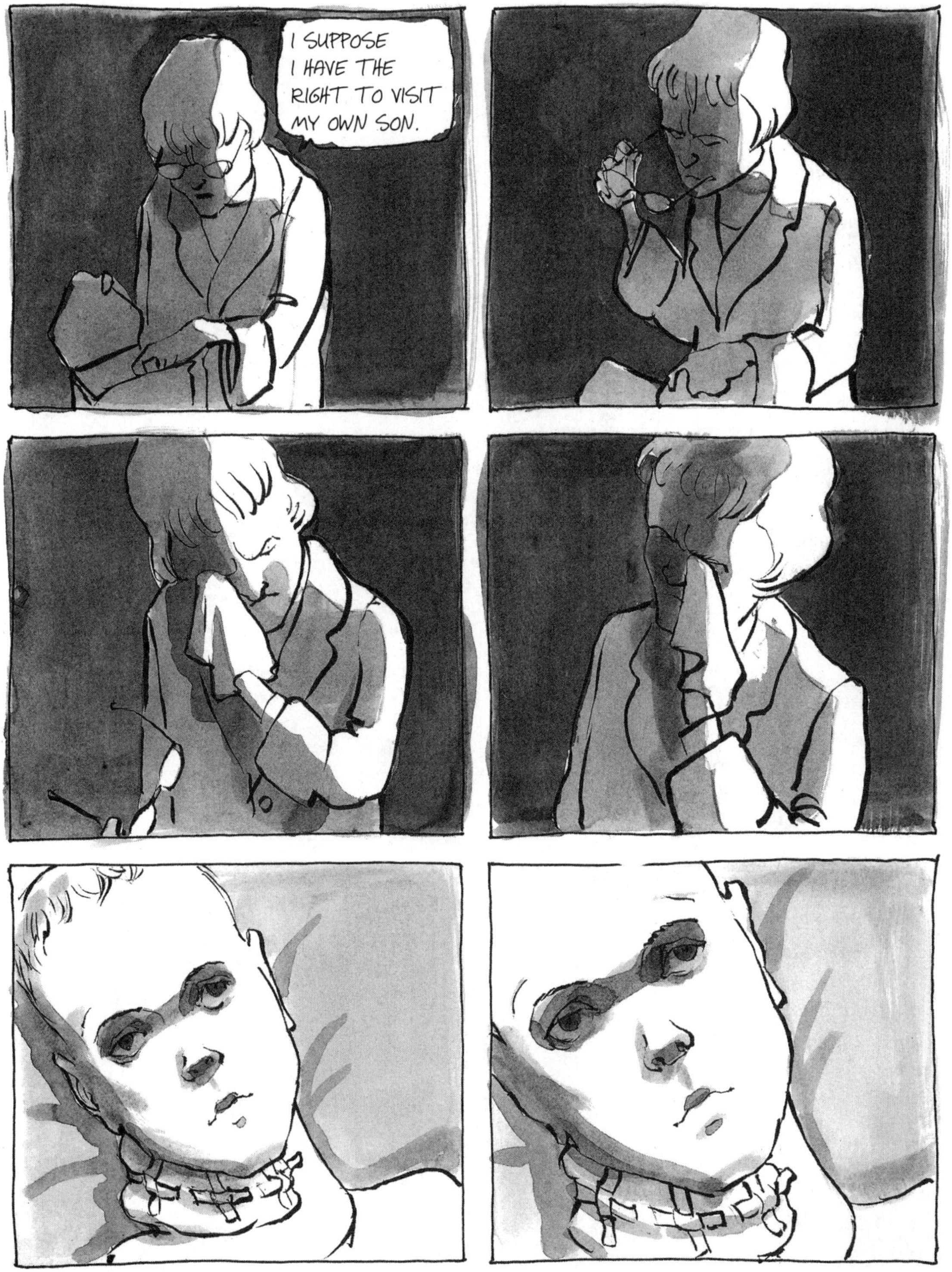
I SUPPOSE I HAVE THE RIGHT TO VISIT MY OWN SON.

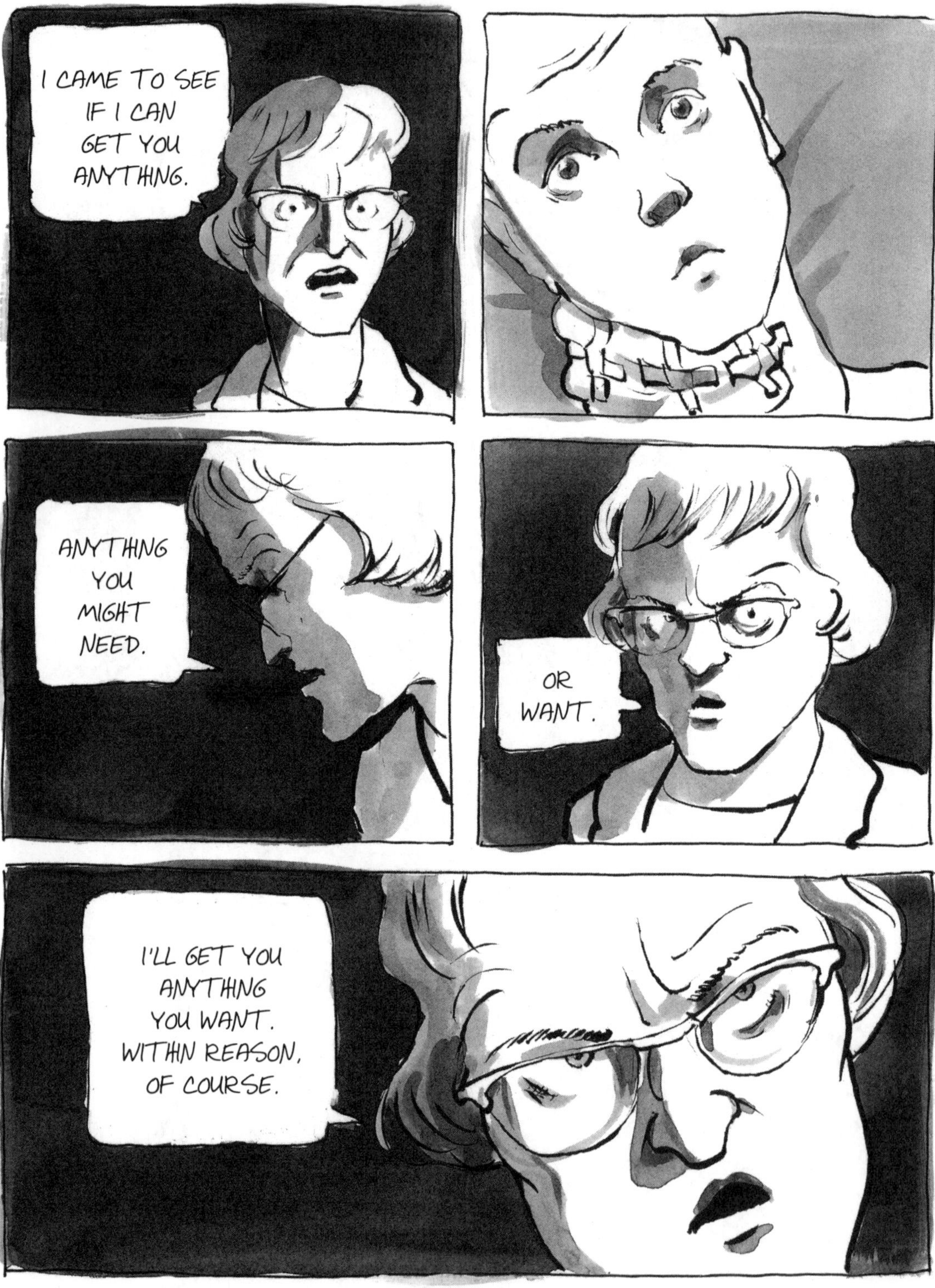
I CAME TO SEE IF I CAN GET YOU ANYTHING.
ANYTHING YOU MIGHT NEED.
OR WANT.
I'LL GET YOU ANYTHING YOU WANT. WITHIN REASON, OF COURSE.

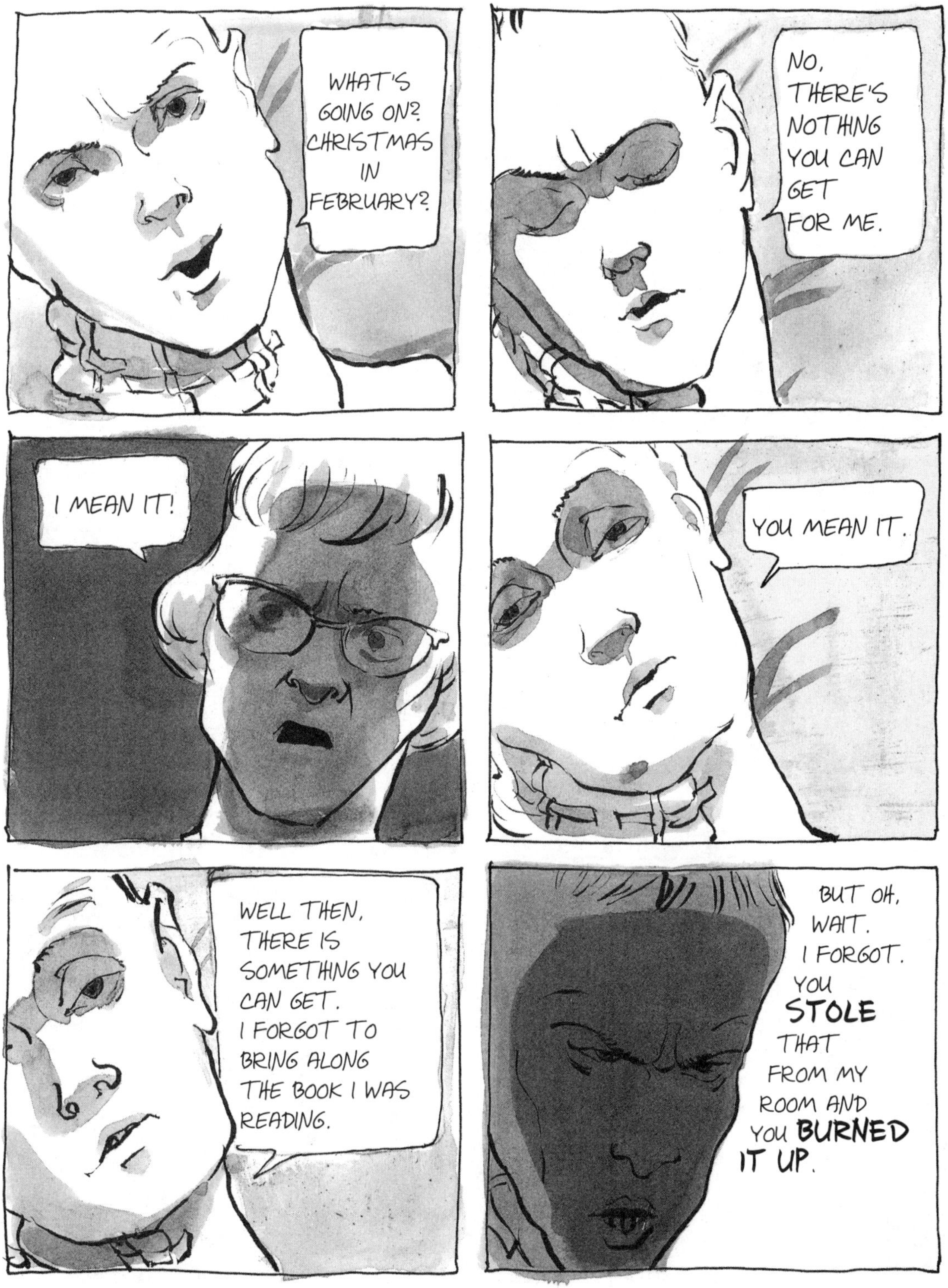
WHAT'S GOING ON? CHRISTMAS IN FEBRUARY?
NO, THERE'S NOTHING YOU CAN GET FOR ME.
I MEAN IT!
YOU MEAN IT.
WELL THEN, THERE IS SOMETHING YOU CAN GET. I FORGOT TO BRING ALONG THE BOOK I WAS READING.
BUT OH, WAIT. I FORGOT. YOU STOLE THAT FROM MY ROOM AND YOU BURNED IT UP.

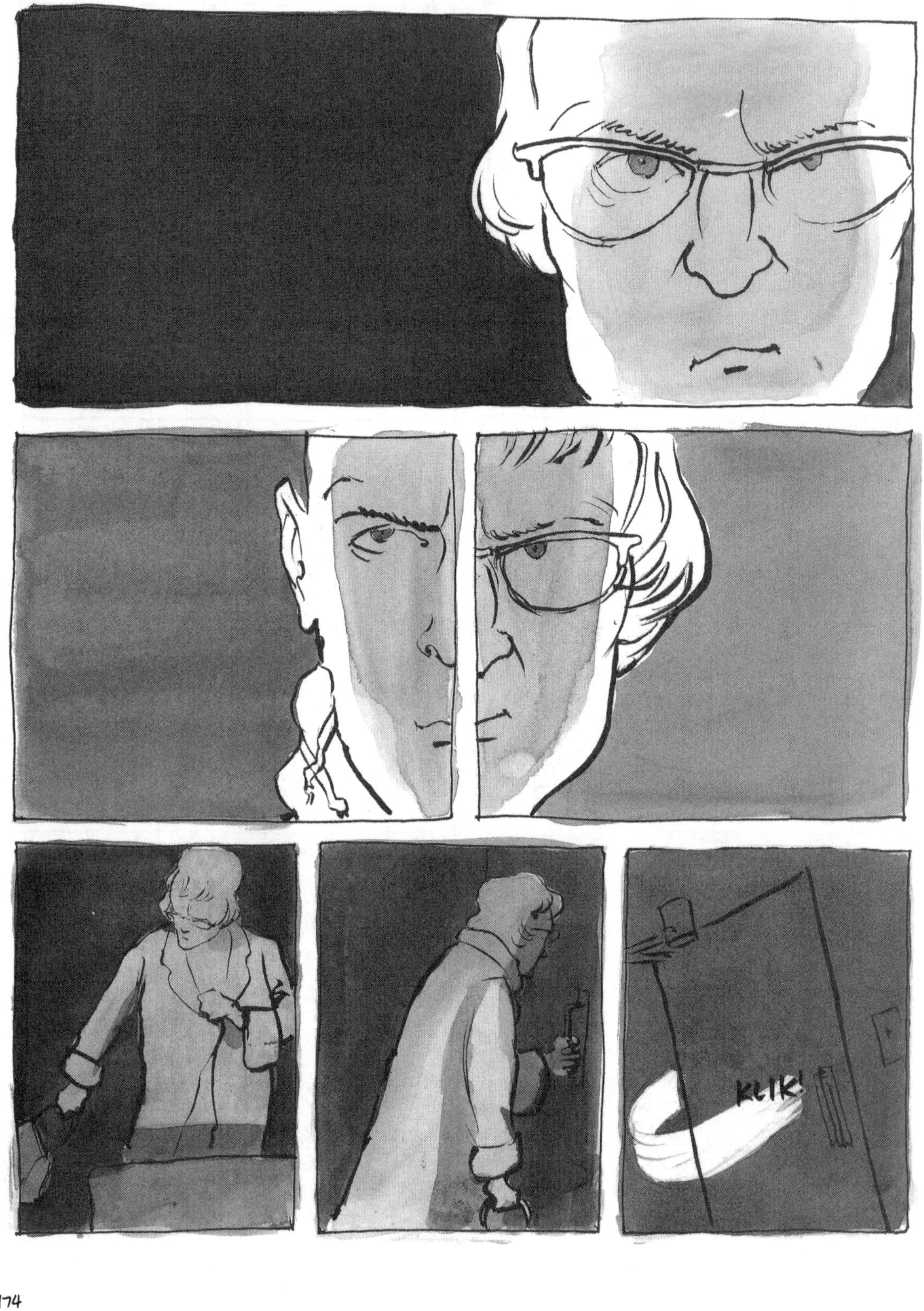
KLIK!

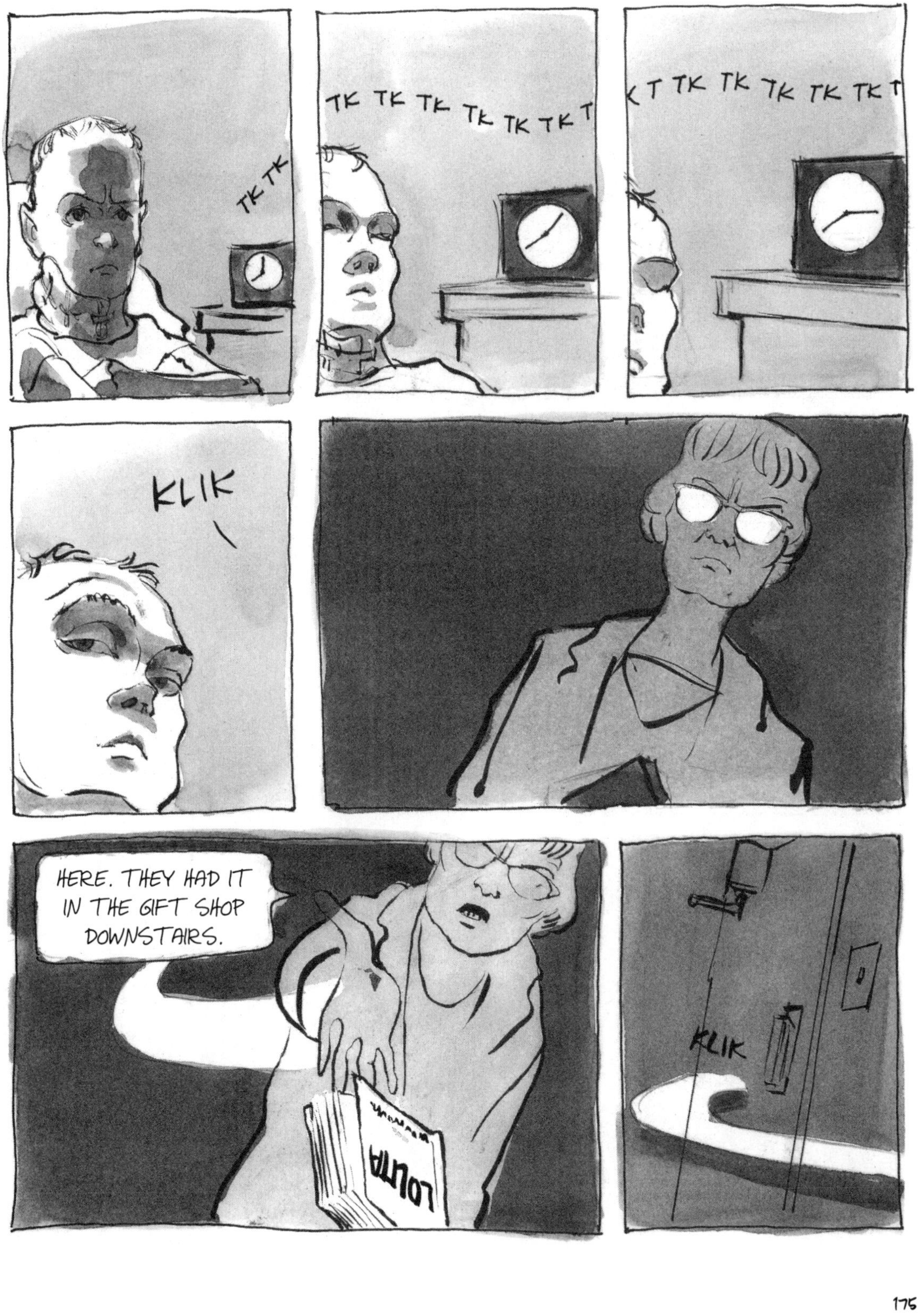
TK TK
TK TK TK TK TK TK T
K T TK TK TK TK TK T
KLIK
HERE. THEY HAD IT IN THE GIFT SHOP DOWNSTAIRS.
LOLITA
KLIK

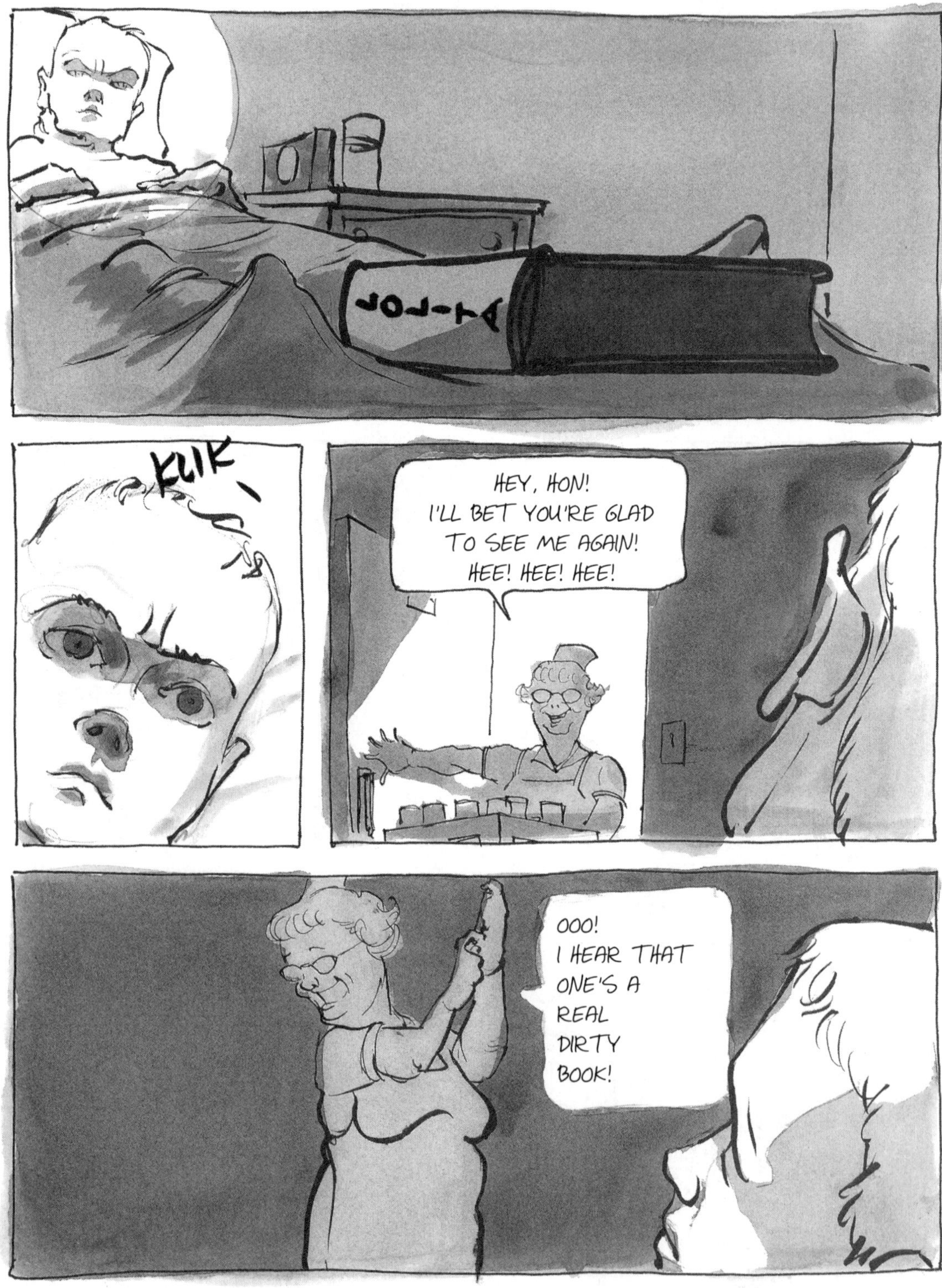
KLIK
HEY, HON! I'LL BET YOU'RE GLAD TO SEE ME AGAIN! HEE! HEE! HEE!
OOO! I HEAR THAT ONE'S A REAL DIRTY BOOK!

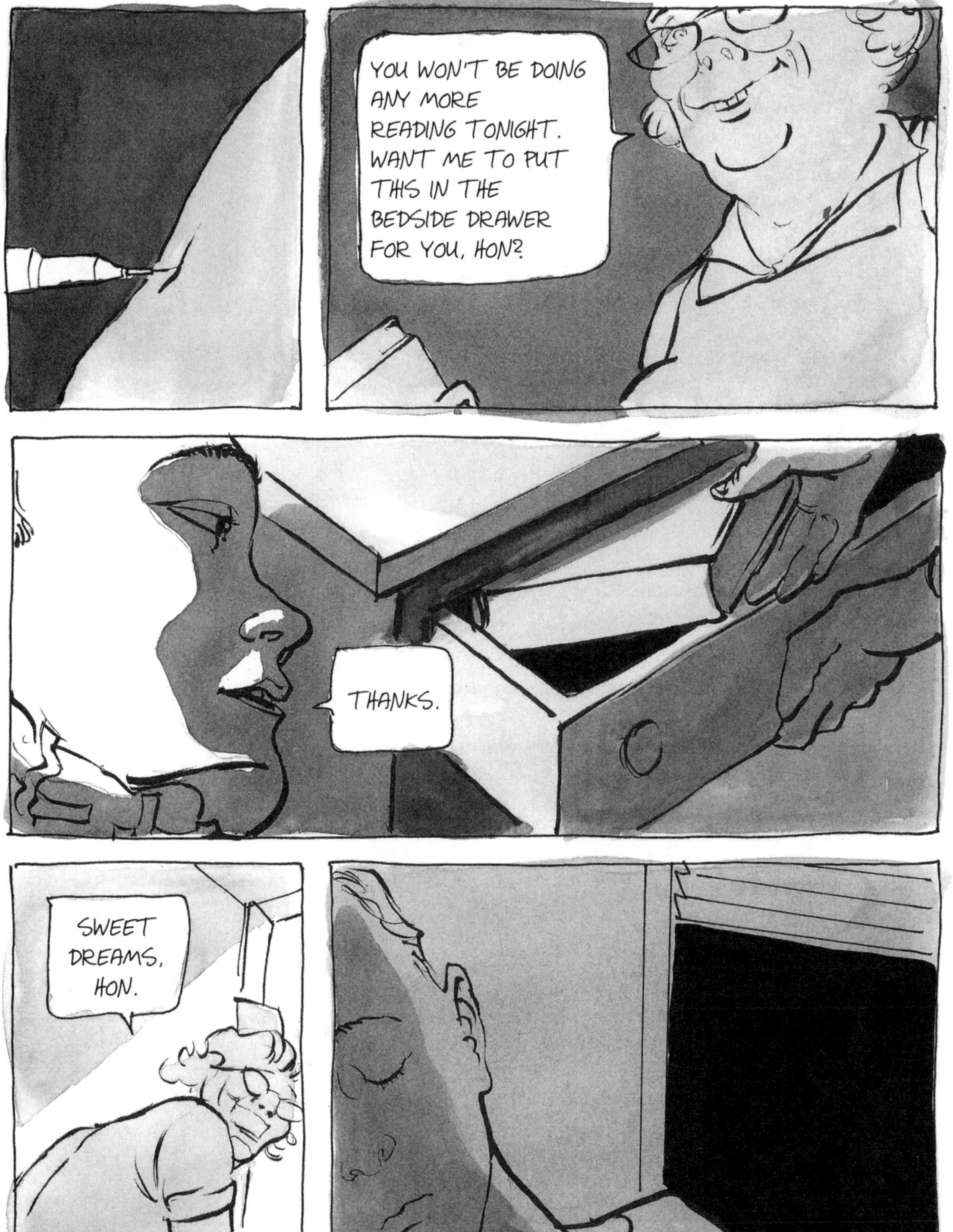
YOU WON'T BE DOING ANY MORE READING TONIGHT. WANT ME TO PUT THIS IN THE BEDSIDE DRAWER FOR YOU, HON?
THANKS.
SWEET DREAMS, HON.

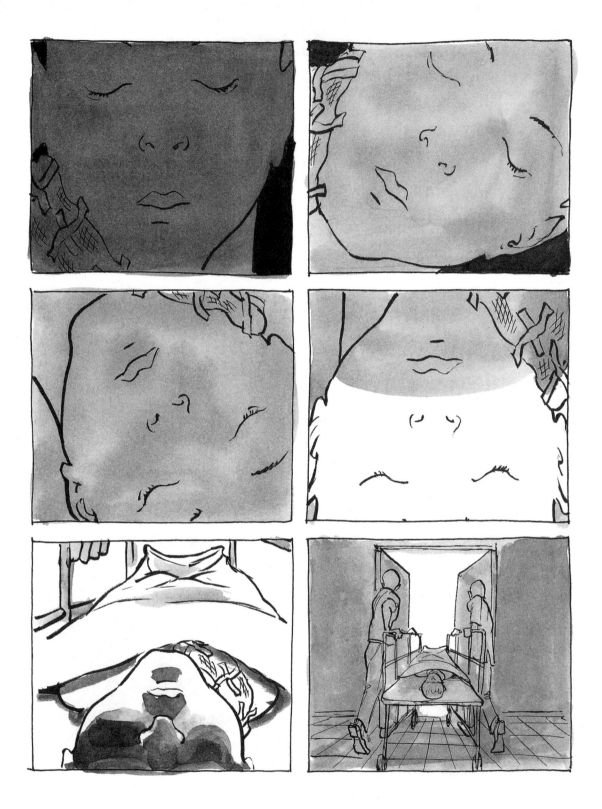

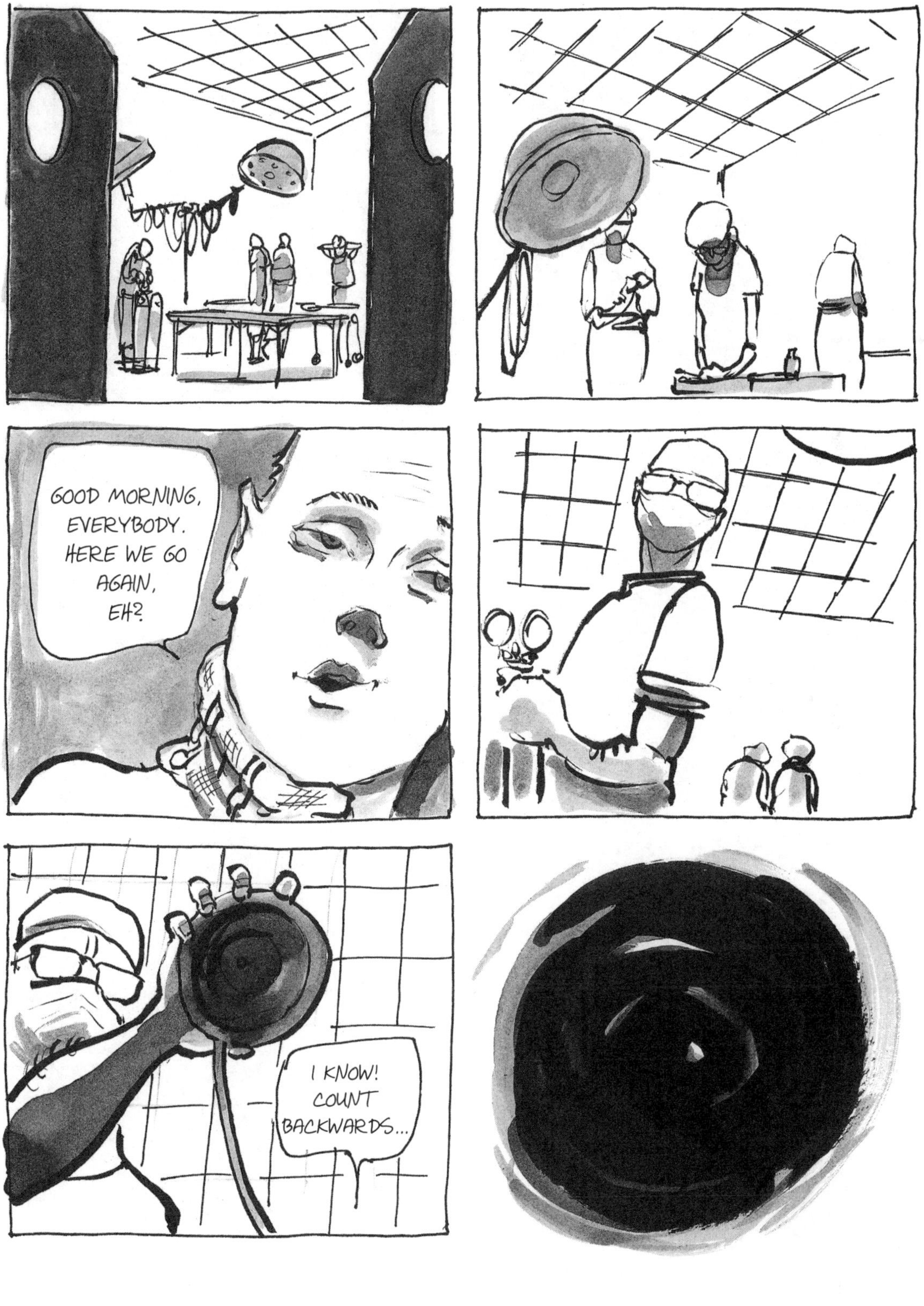
GOOD MORNING, EVERYBODY. HERE WE GO AGAIN, EH?
I KNOW! COUNT BACKWARDS...

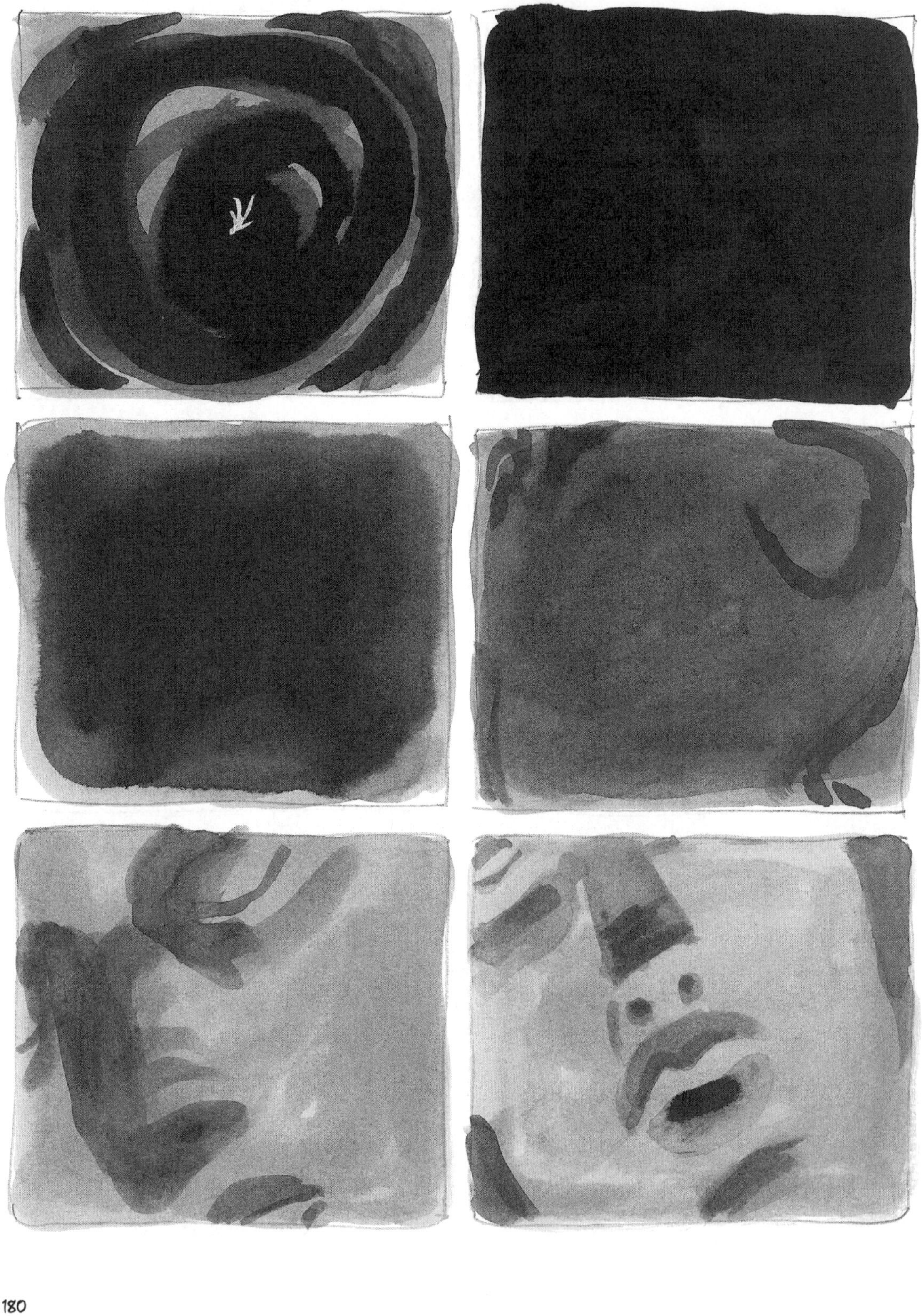

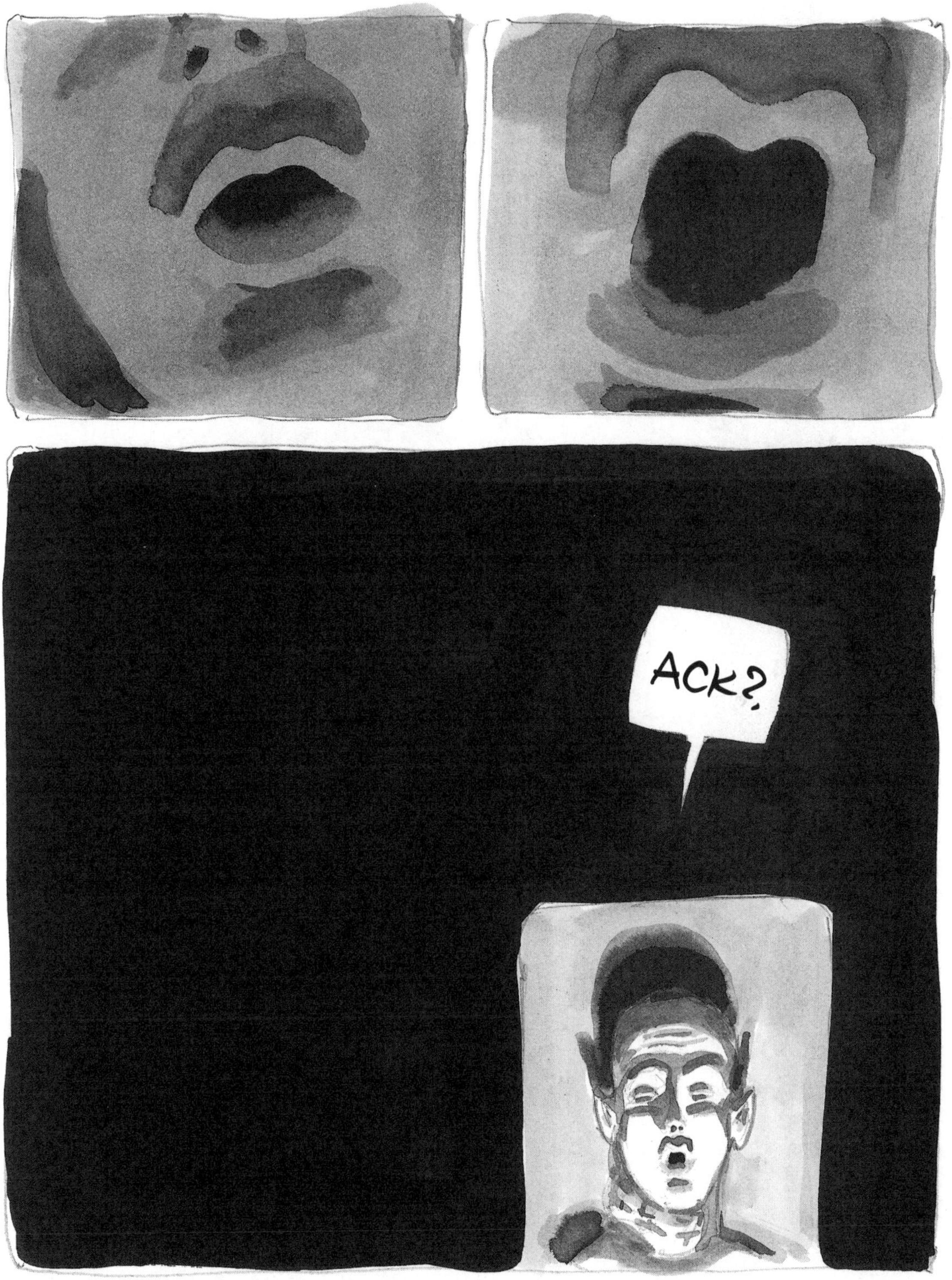
ACK?

STEP INSIDE YOUR MOUTH WITH ME FOR A MOMENT, WON'T YOU?

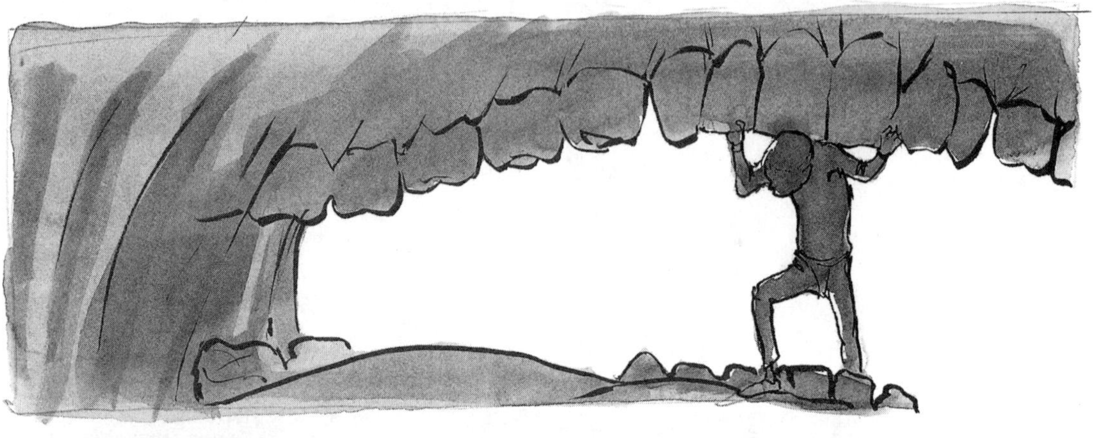

CAREFUL ON THE TONGUE! IT'S SLIPPERY!

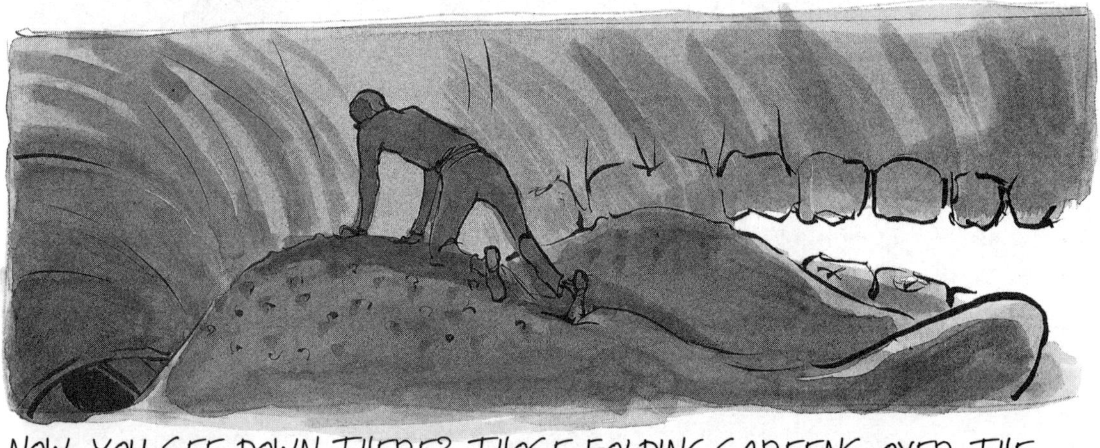

NOW, YOU SEE DOWN THERE? THOSE FOLDING SCREENS OVER THE TUNNEL OF YOUR THROAT? THOSE ARE YOUR VOCAL CORDS. WHEN AIR FLOWS OVER THEM THEY VIBRATE LIKE THE STRINGS ON A CELLO.

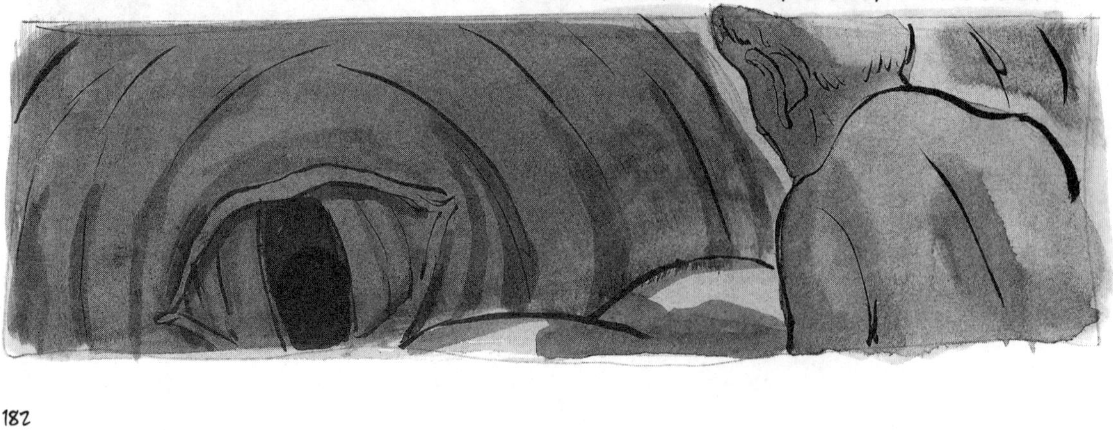

YOUR VOCAL CORDS MAKE THE SOUNDS OF YOUR VOICE,
YOUR CURSES AND YOUR PRAYERS.

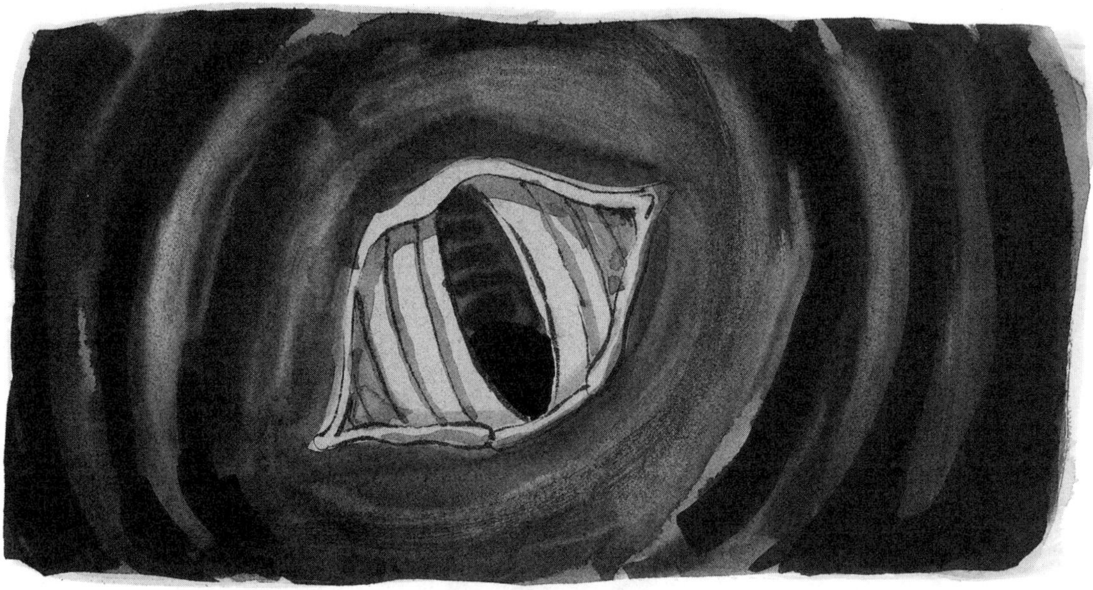

WHEN I WOKE UP FROM OPERATION #2, I HAD ONLY ONE
VOCAL CORD, AND WITH ONLY ONE VOCAL CORD THE SOUND YOU MAKE IS . . .

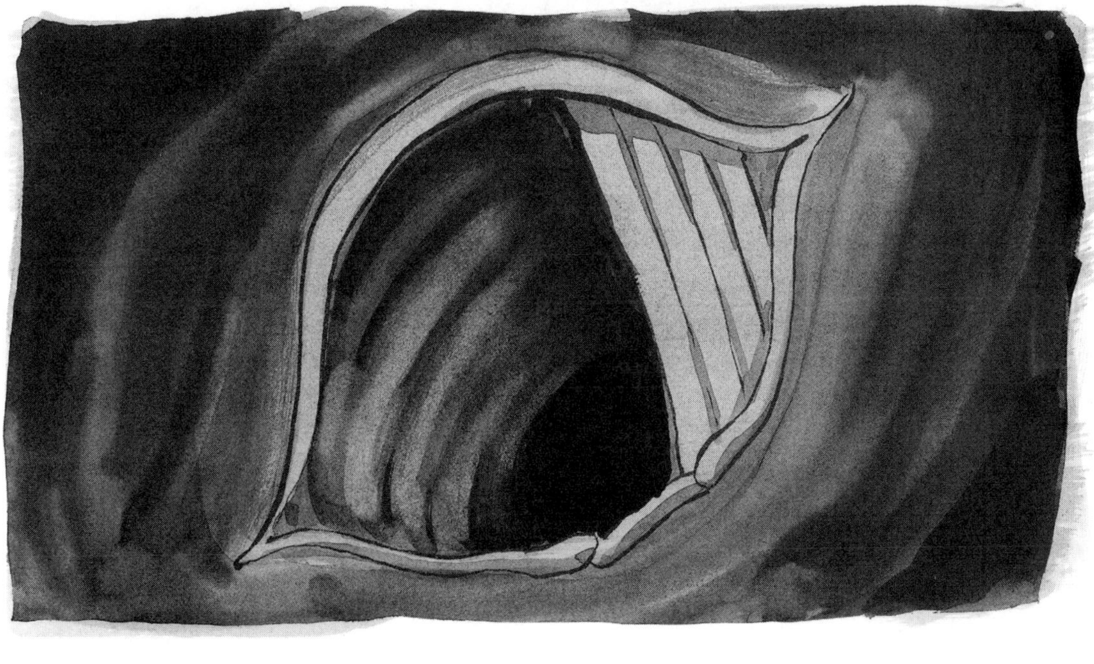

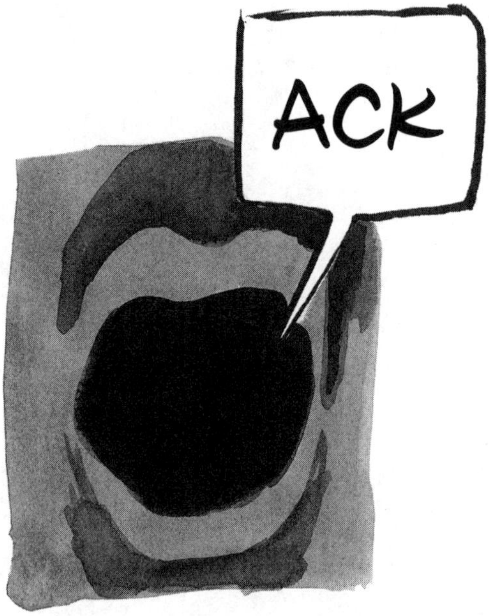
ACK

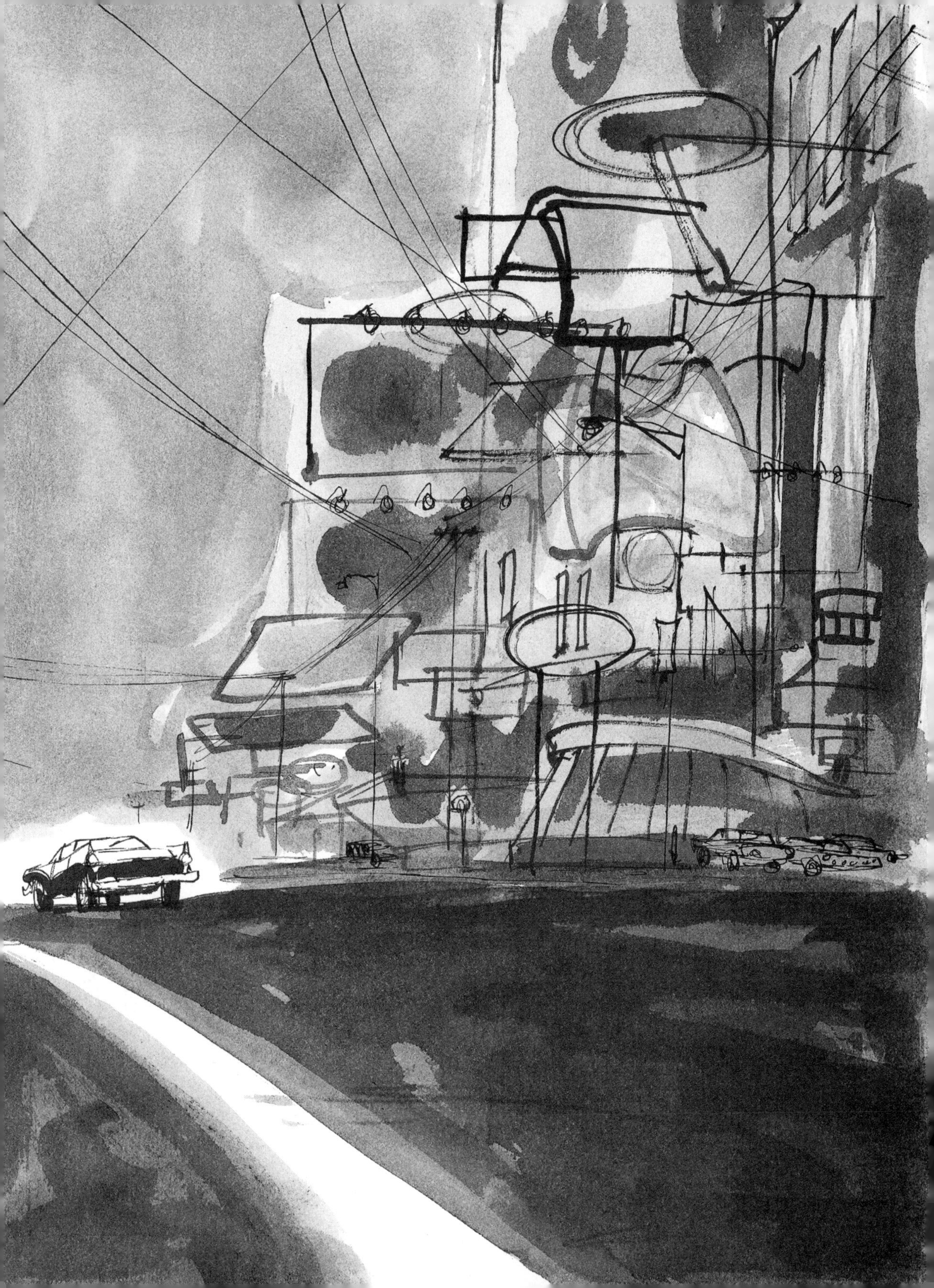

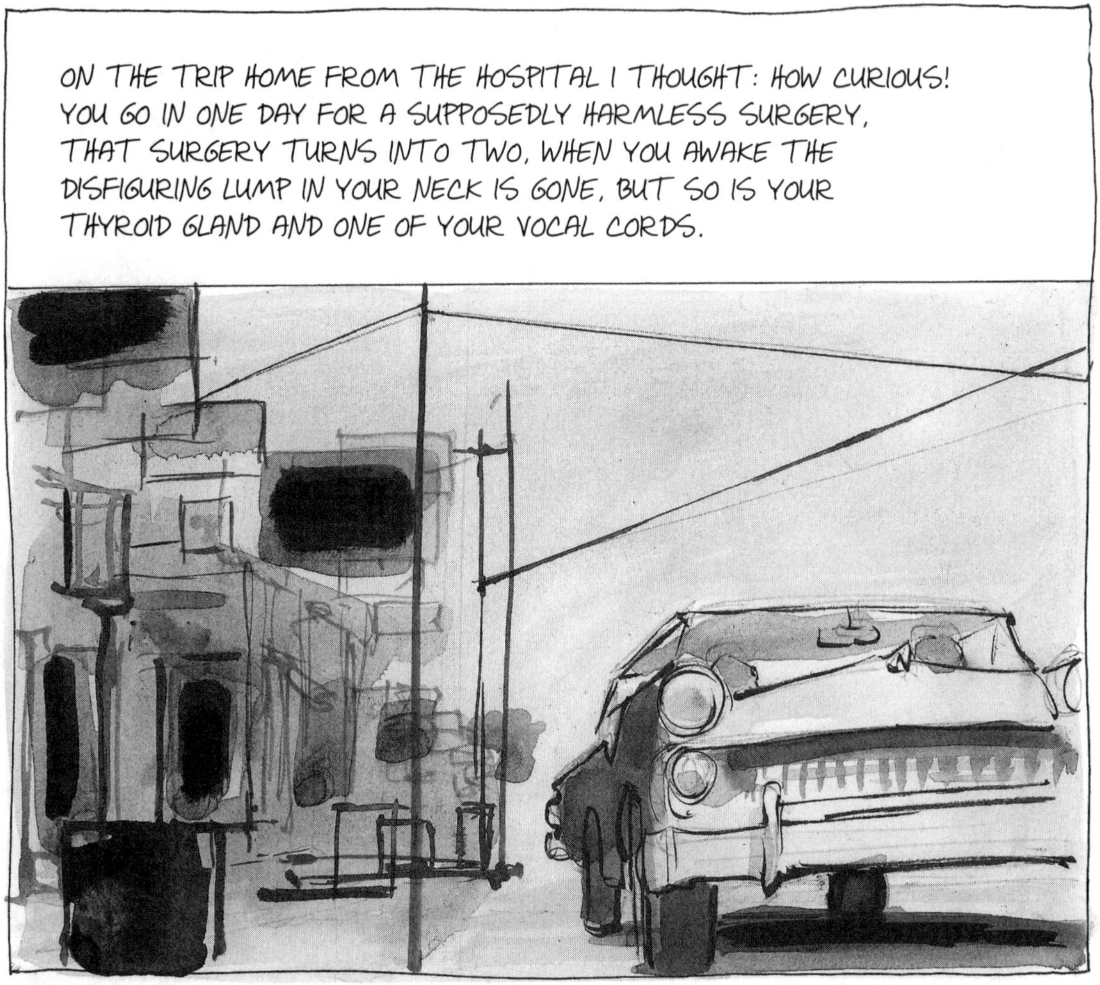
ON THE TRIP HOME FROM THE HOSPITAL I THOUGHT: HOW CURIOUS! YOU GO IN ONE DAY FOR A SUPPOSEDLY HARMLESS SURGERY, THAT SURGERY TURNS INTO TWO, WHEN YOU AWAKE THE DISFIGURING LUMP IN YOUR NECK IS GONE, BUT SO IS YOUR THYROID GLAND AND ONE OF YOUR VOCAL CORDS.

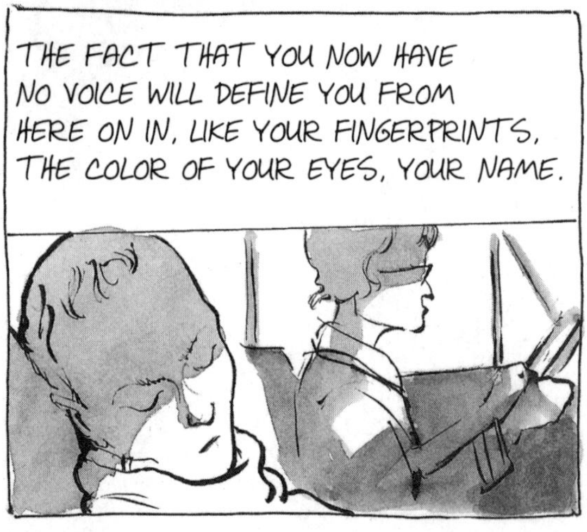
THE FACT THAT YOU NOW HAVE NO VOICE WILL DEFINE YOU FROM HERE ON IN, LIKE YOUR FINGERPRINTS, THE COLOR OF YOUR EYES, YOUR NAME.

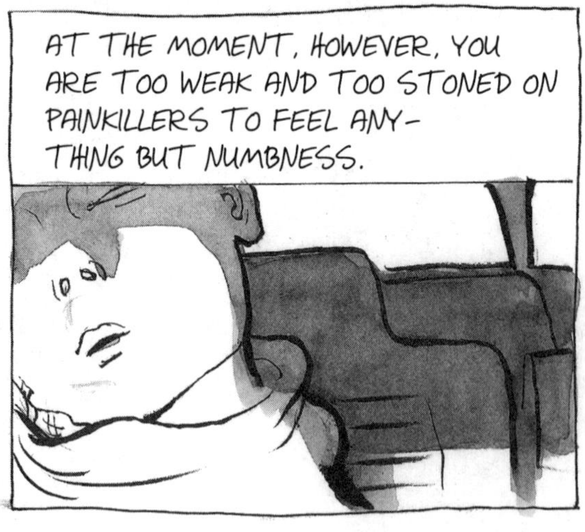
AT THE MOMENT, HOWEVER, YOU ARE TOO WEAK AND TOO STONED ON PAINKILLERS TO FEEL ANY-THING BUT NUMBNESS.

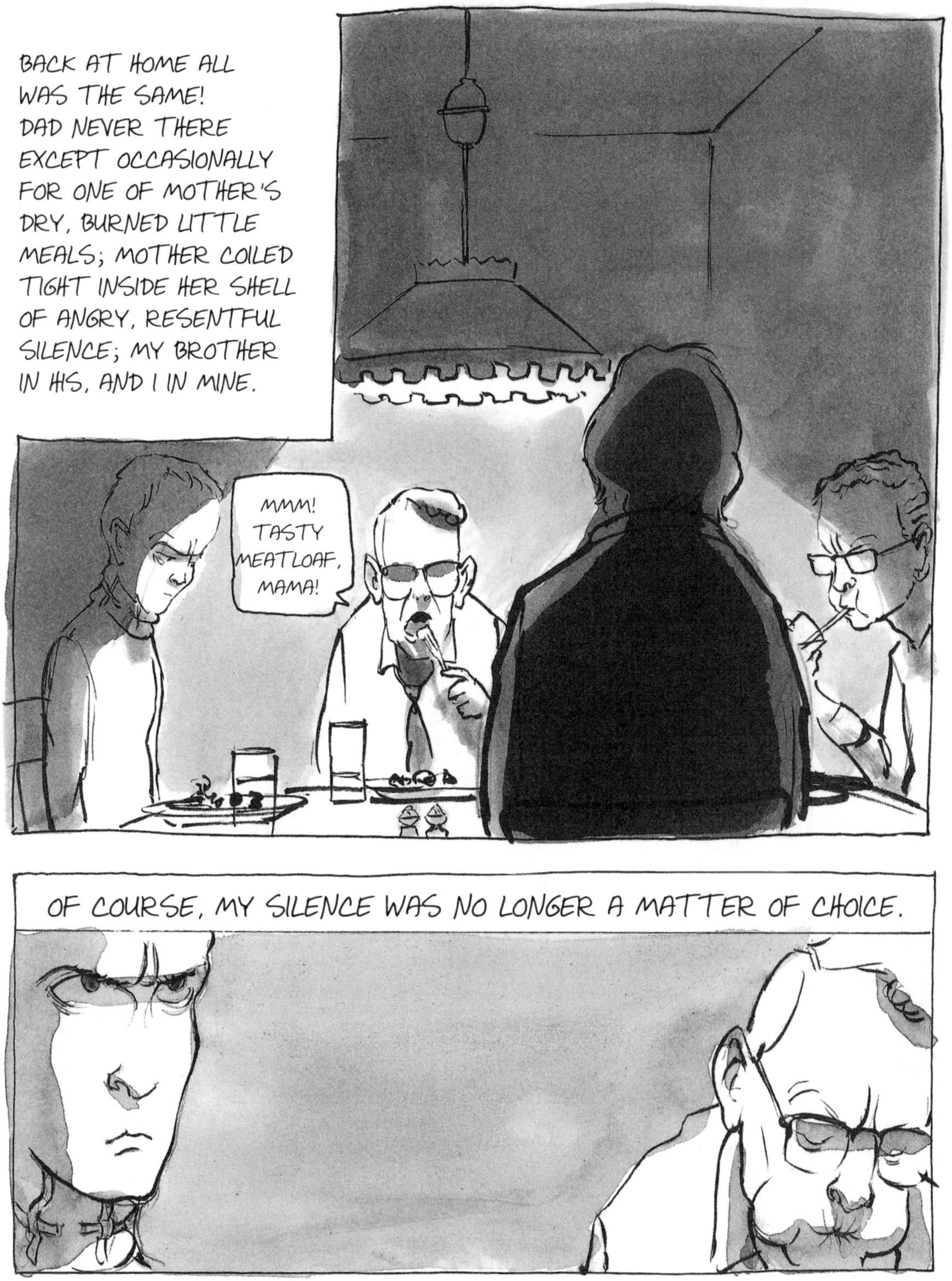
BACK AT HOME ALL WAS THE SAME! DAD NEVER THERE EXCEPT OCCASIONALLY FOR ONE OF MOTHER'S DRY, BURNED LITTLE MEALS; MOTHER COILED TIGHT INSIDE HER SHELL OF ANGRY, RESENTFUL SILENCE; MY BROTHER IN HIS, AND I IN MINE.
MMM! TASTY MEATLOAF, MAMA!
OF COURSE, MY SILENCE WAS NO LONGER A MATTER OF CHOICE.

AFTER DINNER CAME THE SOUNDS OF MOTHER IN THE KITCHEN "TAKING CARE OF" THE DISHES . . .

WHAP!

KLANG!

CRASH!

. . . OF MY BROTHER SLAMMING AWAY AT HIS DRUMS IN THE BASEMENT . . .

BA-DA
BING BAM!

BUM BUM BUM BUM BUM BUM BUM BUM

. . . AND THE SQUEAL OF DAD'S TIRES AS HE PEELED OUT DOWN PINEHURST AVENUE.

SKREEEEEEEeeeeeeeeee!

eeeee
laggggg!

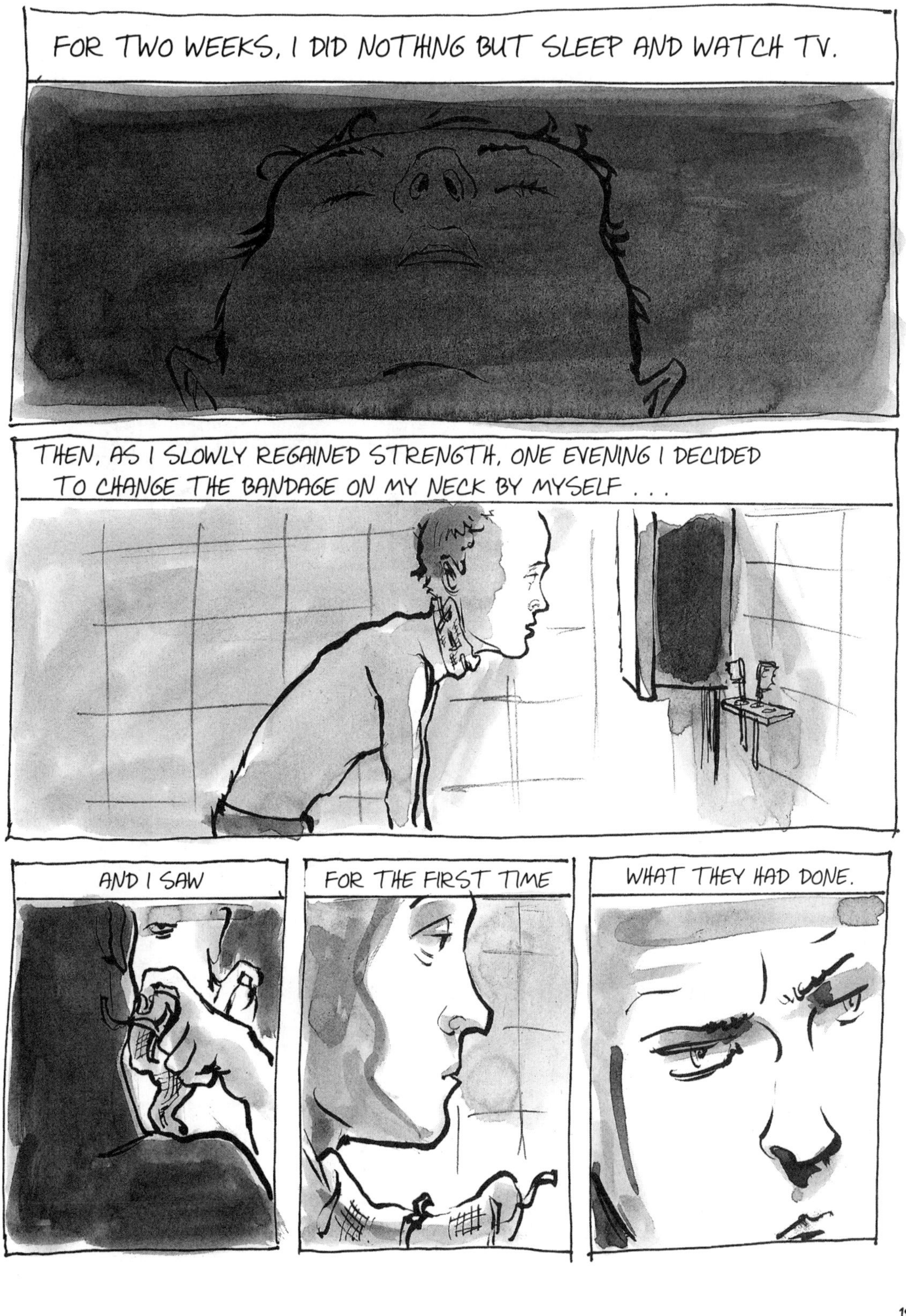
FOR TWO WEEKS, I DID NOTHING BUT SLEEP AND WATCH TV.
THEN, AS I SLOWLY REGAINED STRENGTH, ONE EVENING I DECIDED TO CHANGE THE BANDAGE ON MY NECK BY MYSELF . . .
AND I SAW
FOR THE FIRST TIME
WHAT THEY HAD DONE.

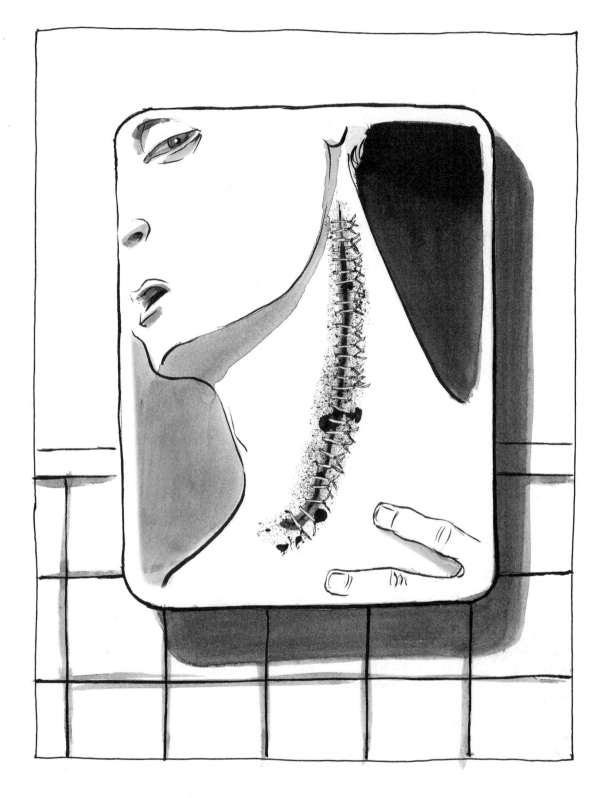

A CRUSTED BLACK TRACK OF STITCHES; MY SMOOTH YOUNG THROAT SLASHED AND LACED BACK UP LIKE A BLOODY BOOT.

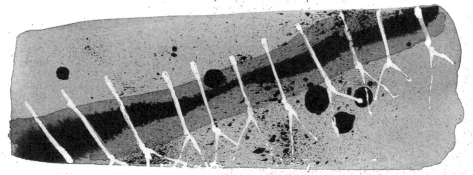

"SURELY THIS IS NOT ME."   "NO, FRIEND. IT SURELY IS."

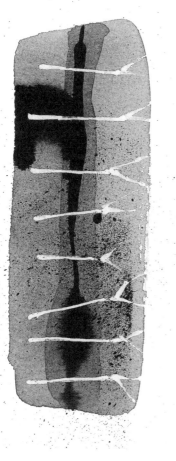
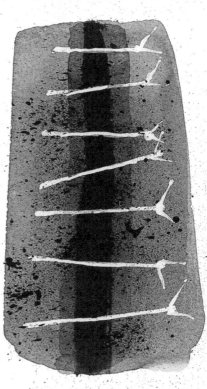

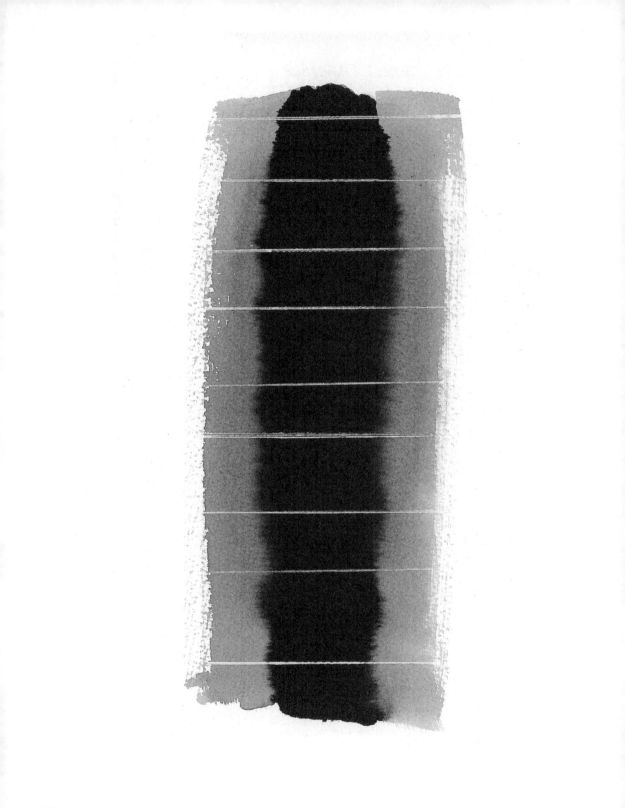

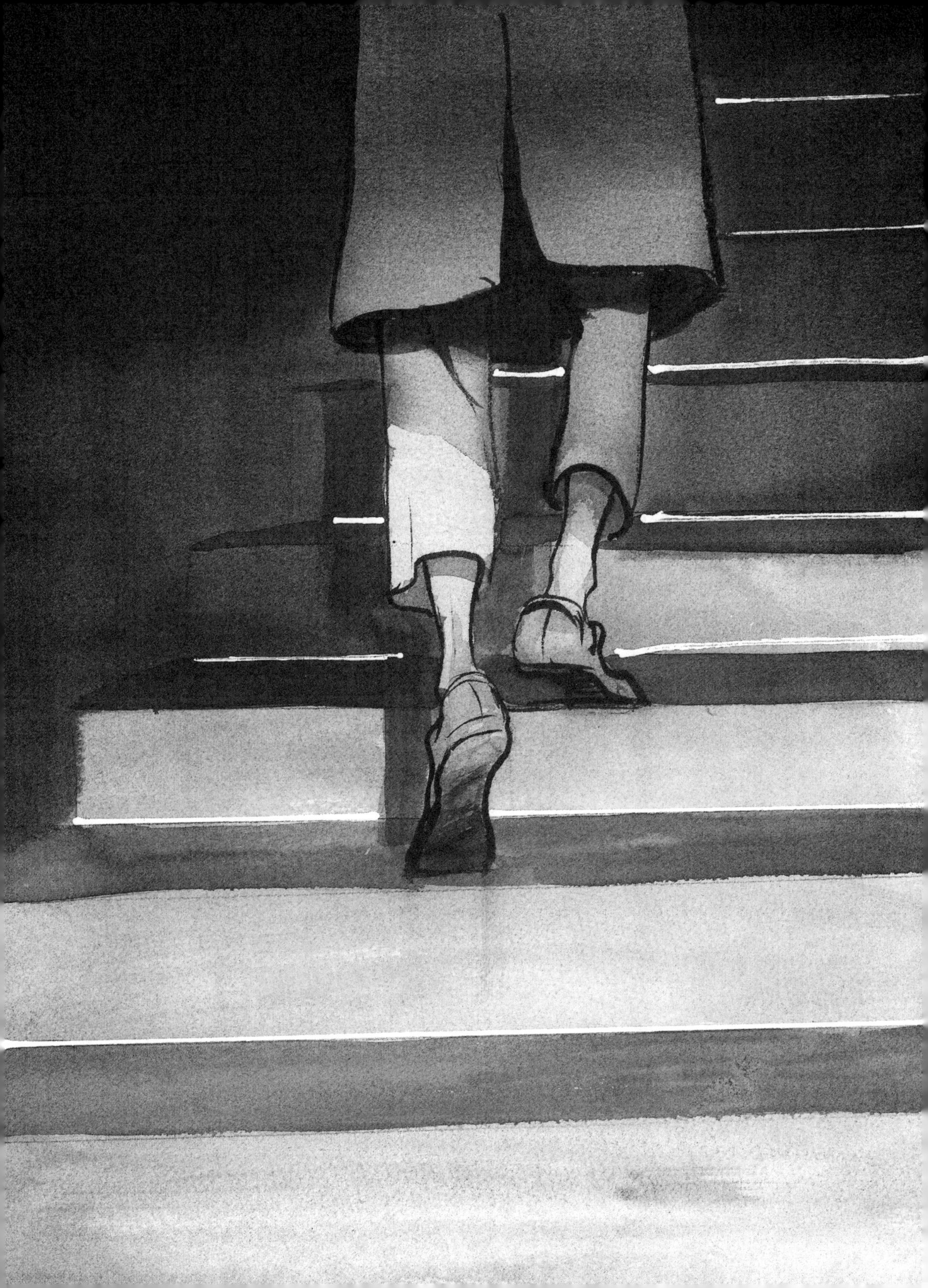

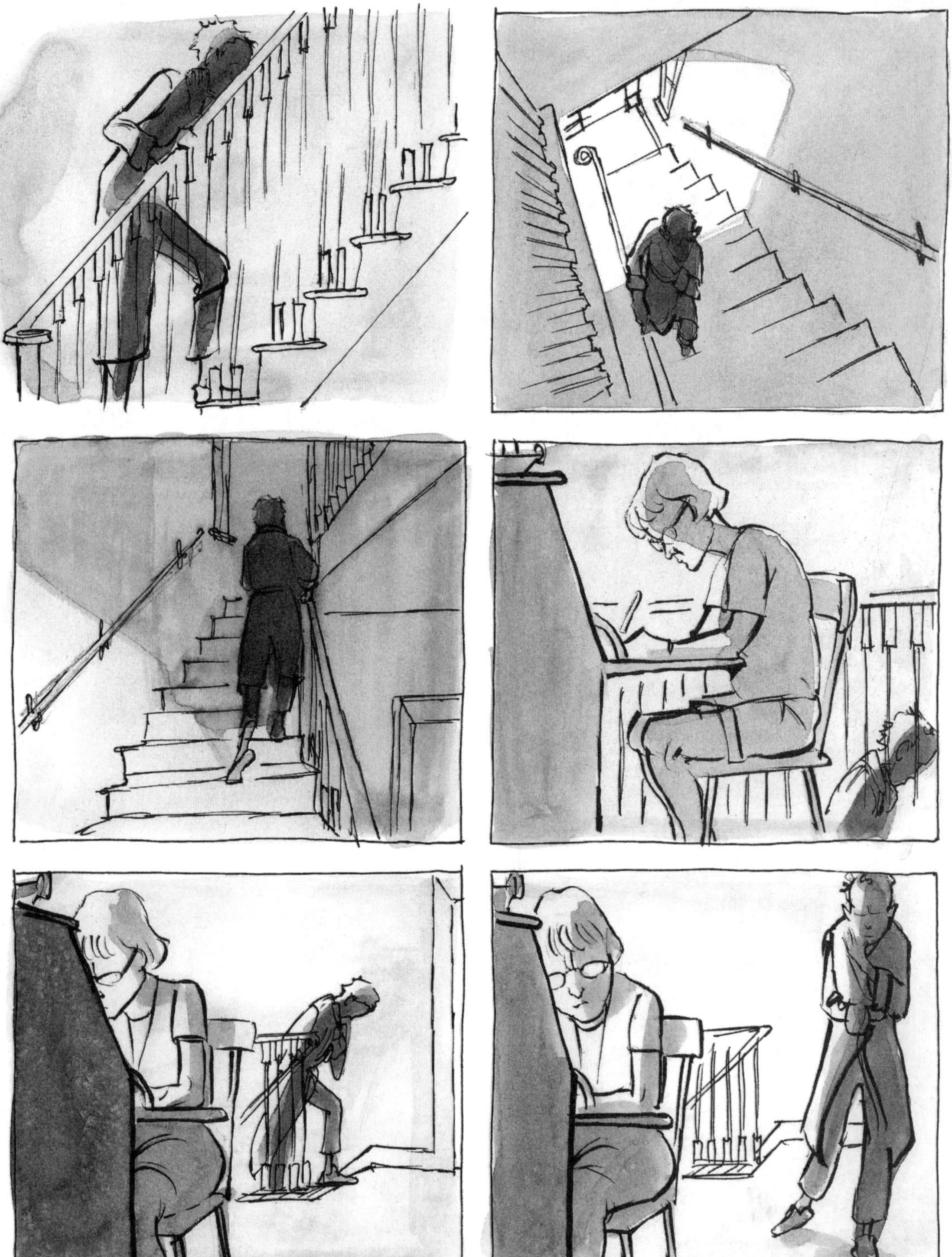

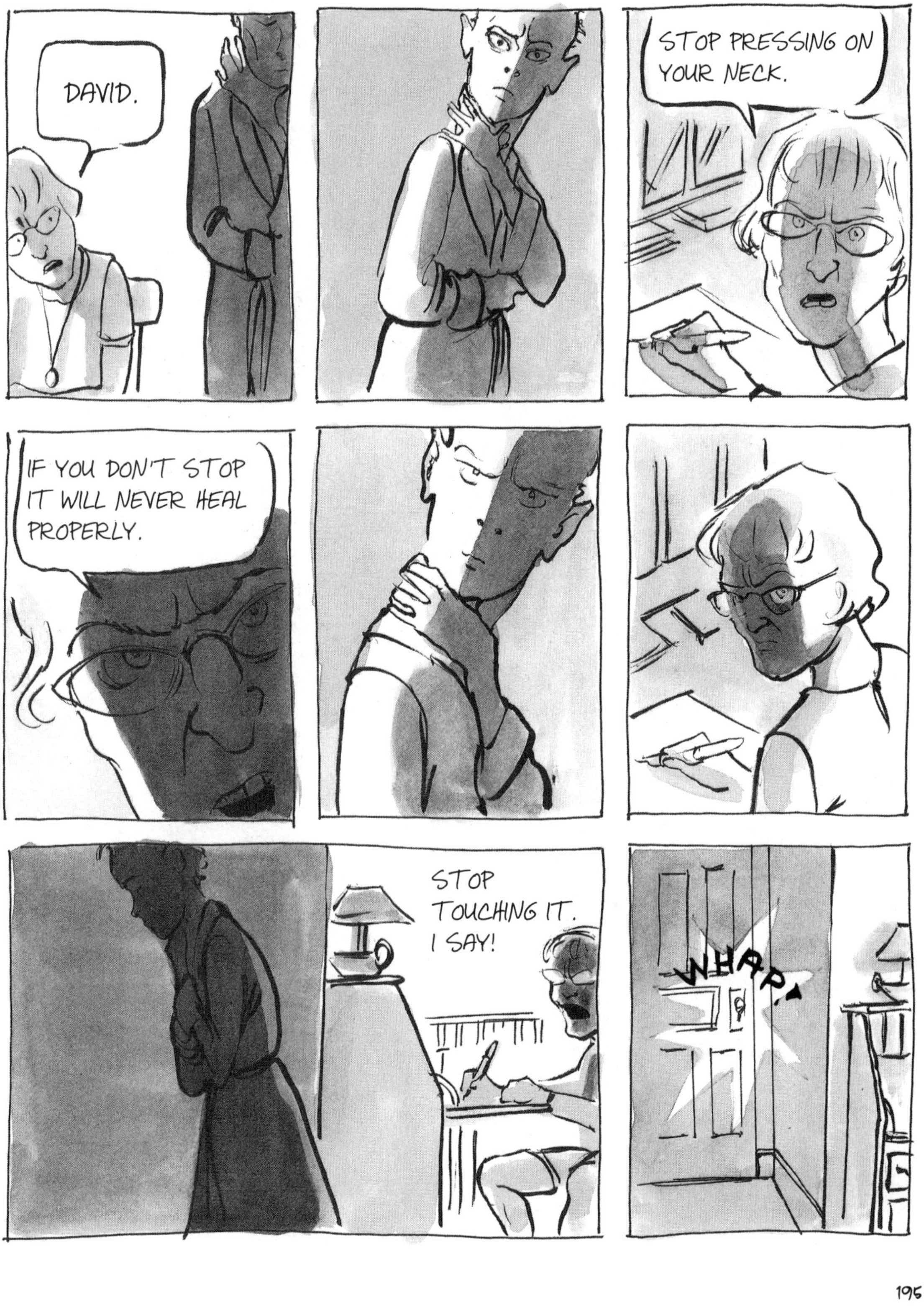
DAVID.
STOP PRESSING ON YOUR NECK.
IF YOU DON'T STOP IT WILL NEVER HEAL PROPERLY.
STOP TOUCHING IT. I SAY!
WHAP!

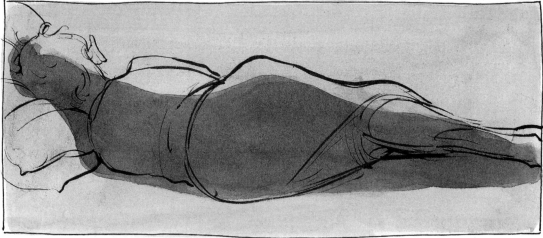

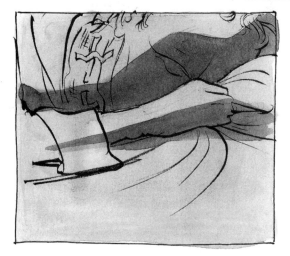

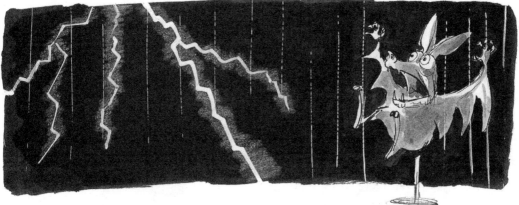

MAMA!

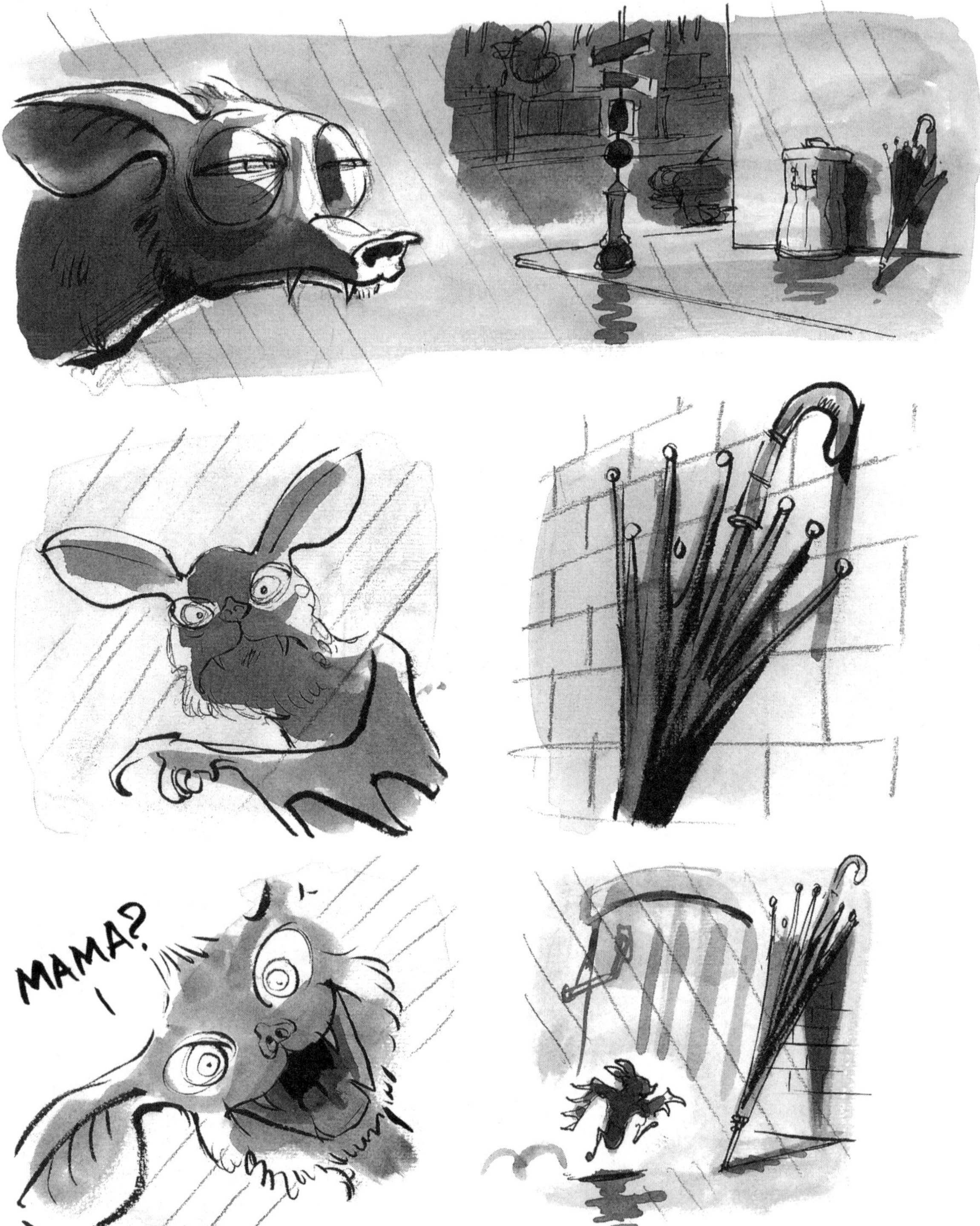
MAMA?

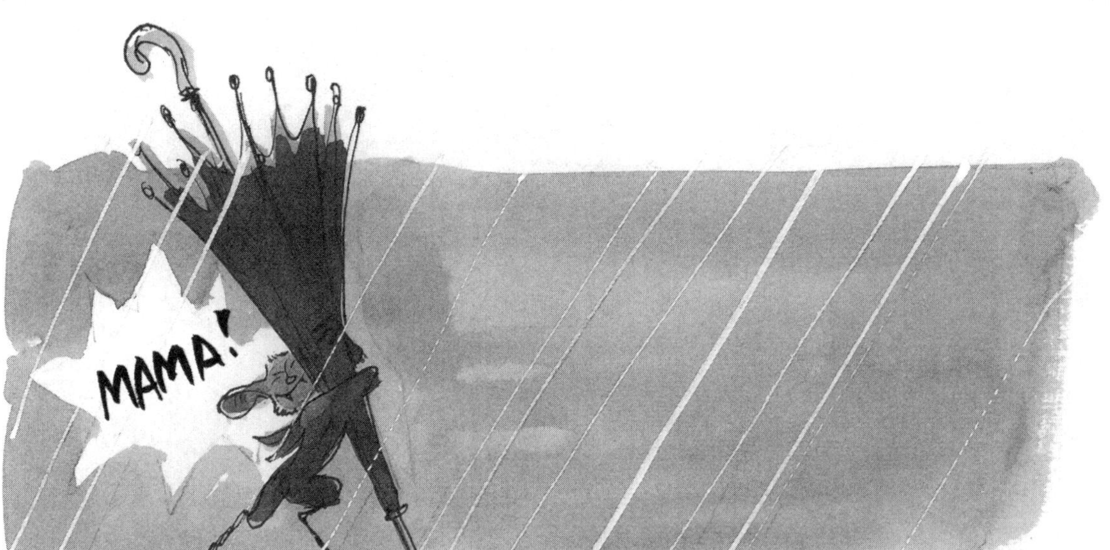
MAMA!

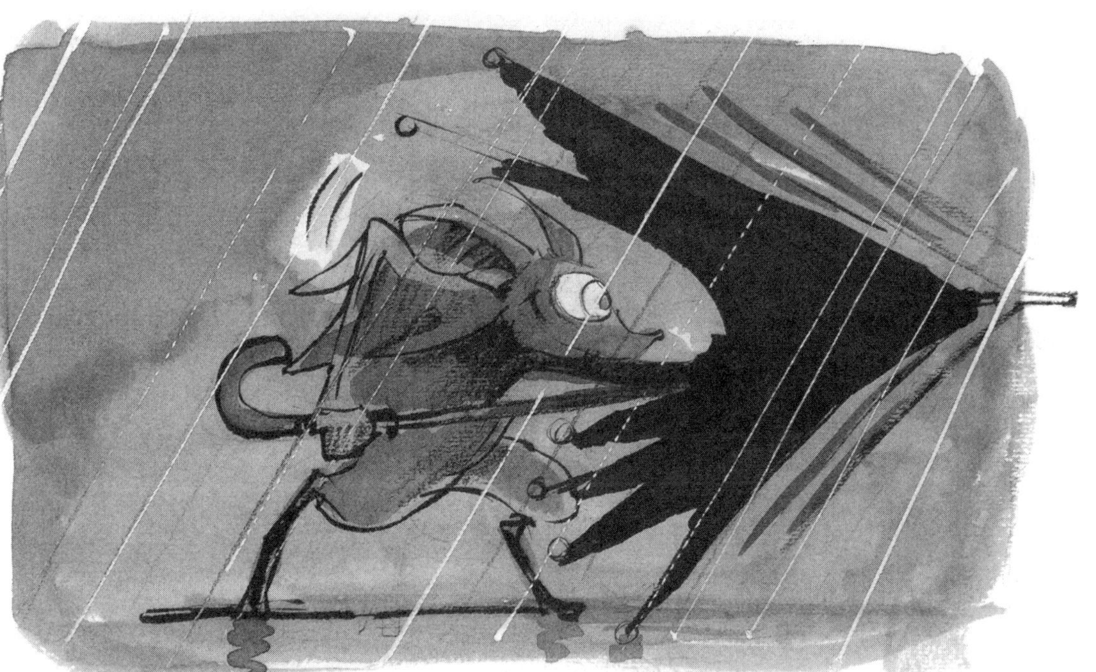

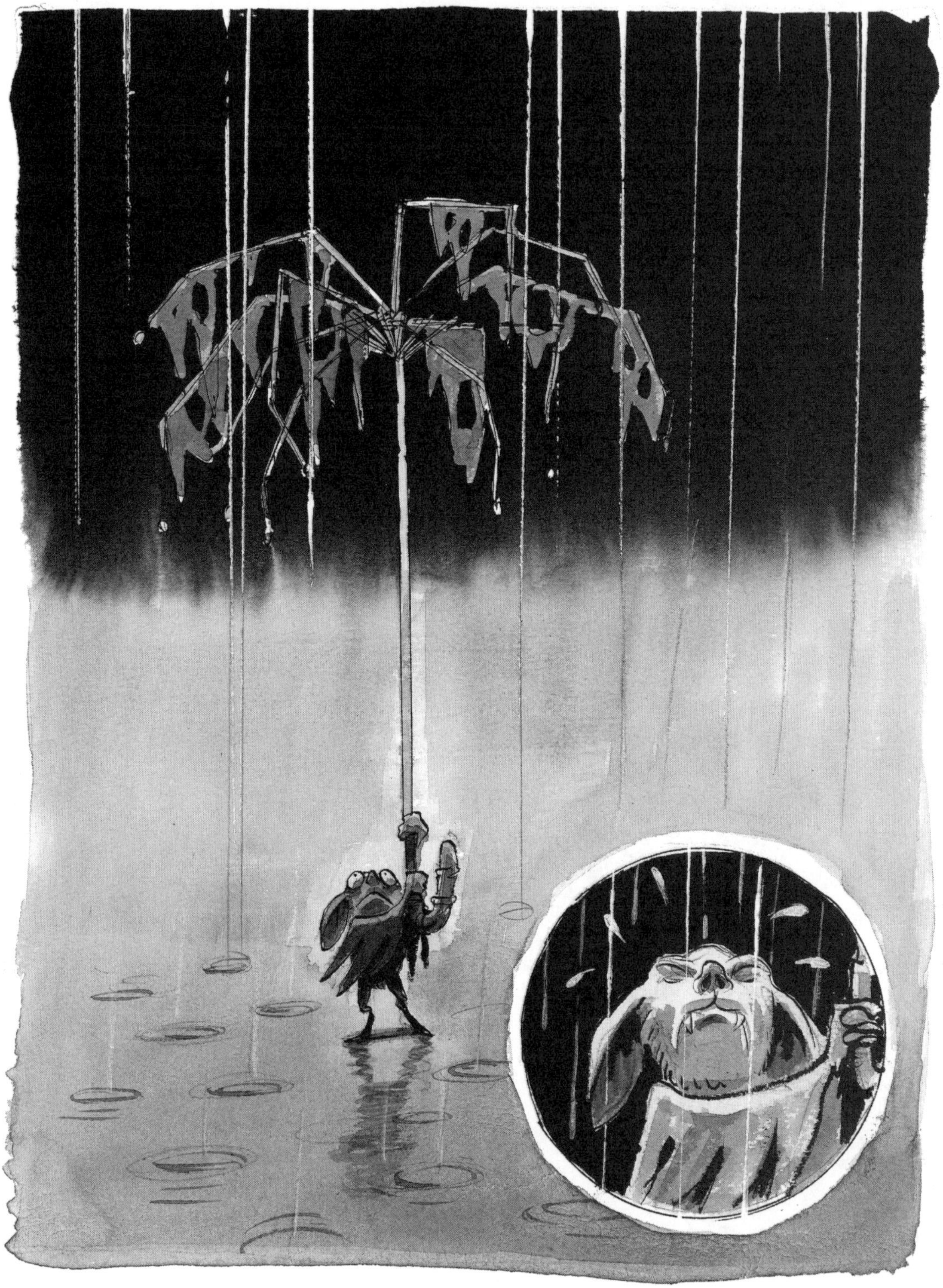

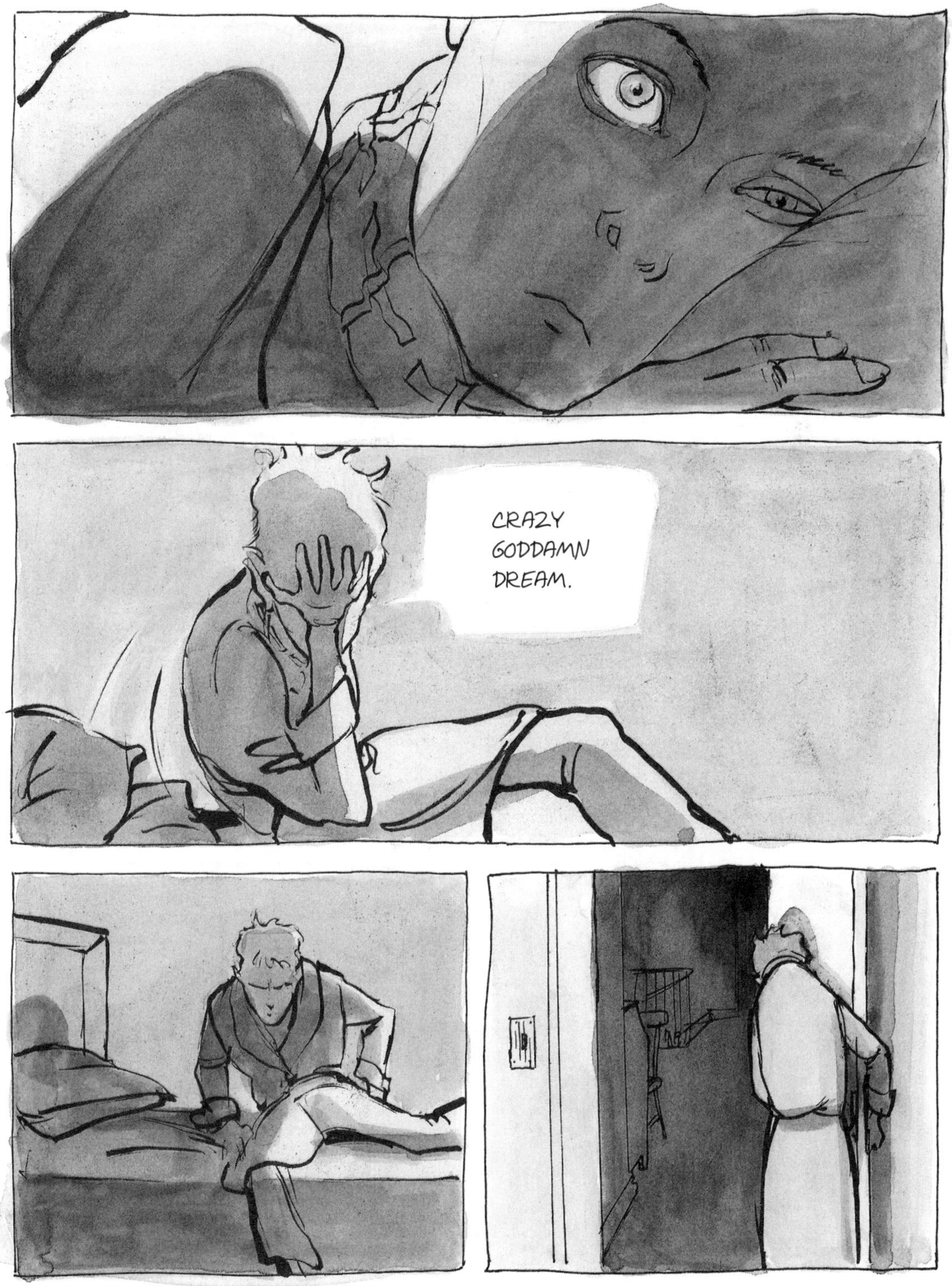
CRAZY GODDAMN DREAM.

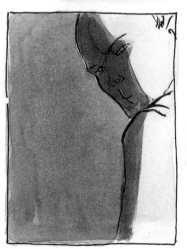

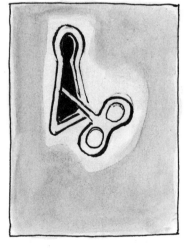

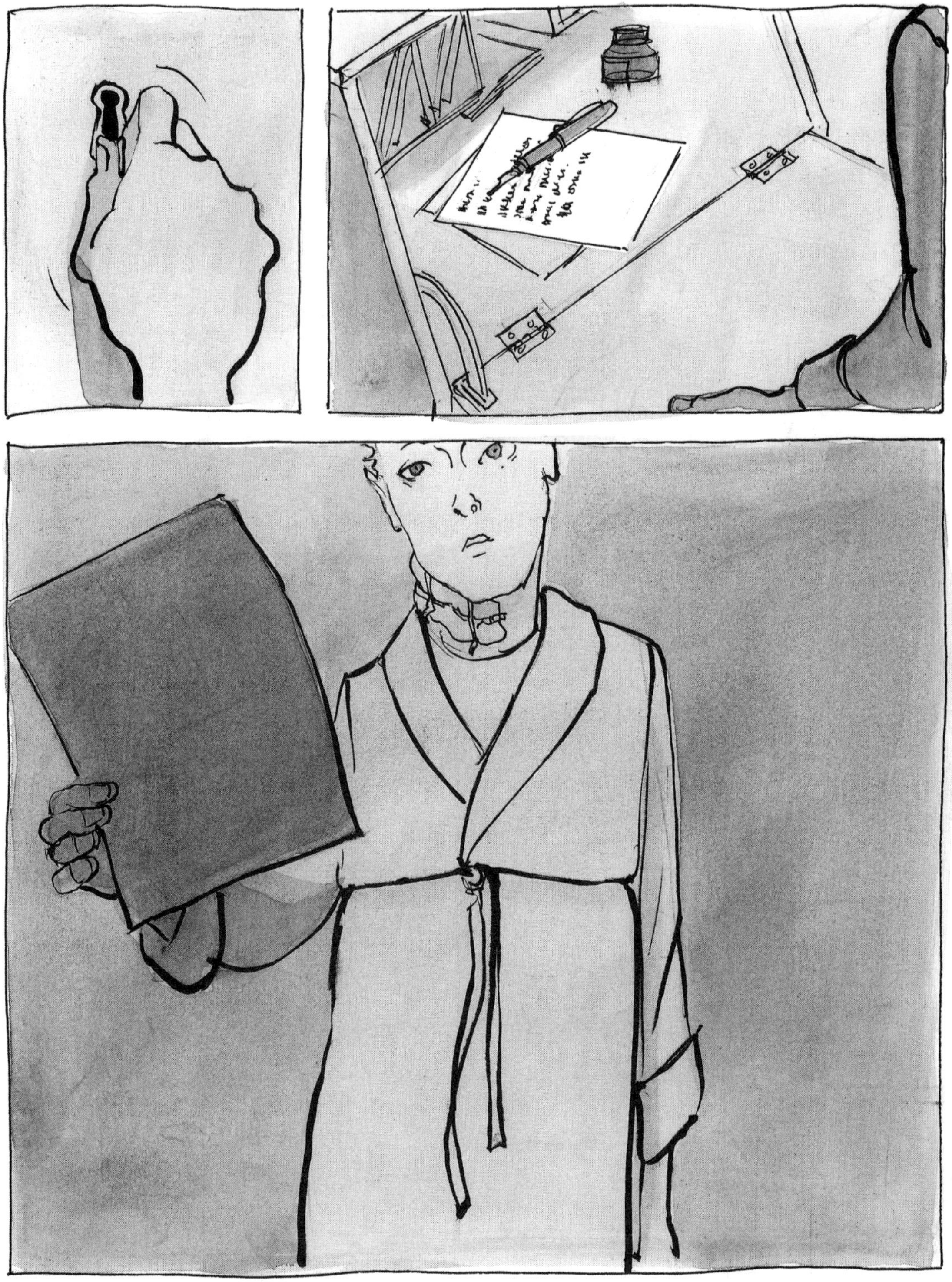

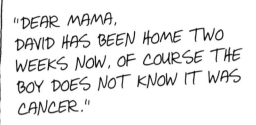

"DEAR MAMA,
DAVID HAS BEEN HOME TWO
WEEKS NOW, OF COURSE THE
BOY DOES NOT KNOW IT WAS
CANCER."

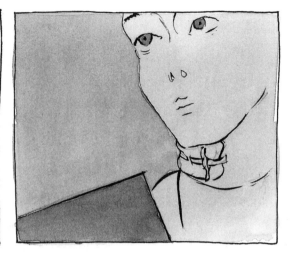

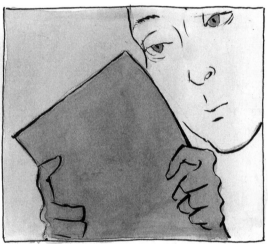

"OF COURSE THE BOY . . .

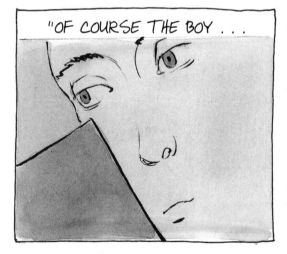

. . . DOES NOT KNOW . . ."

THE BOY.

THE BOY.

THE. BOY. DOES. NOT.

KNOW.

OF COURSE THE BOY DOES NOT KNOW IT WAS CANCER.

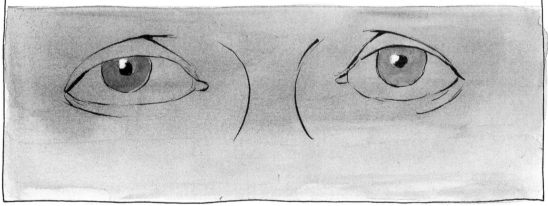

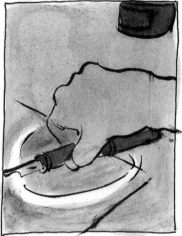
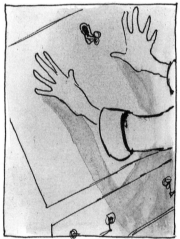

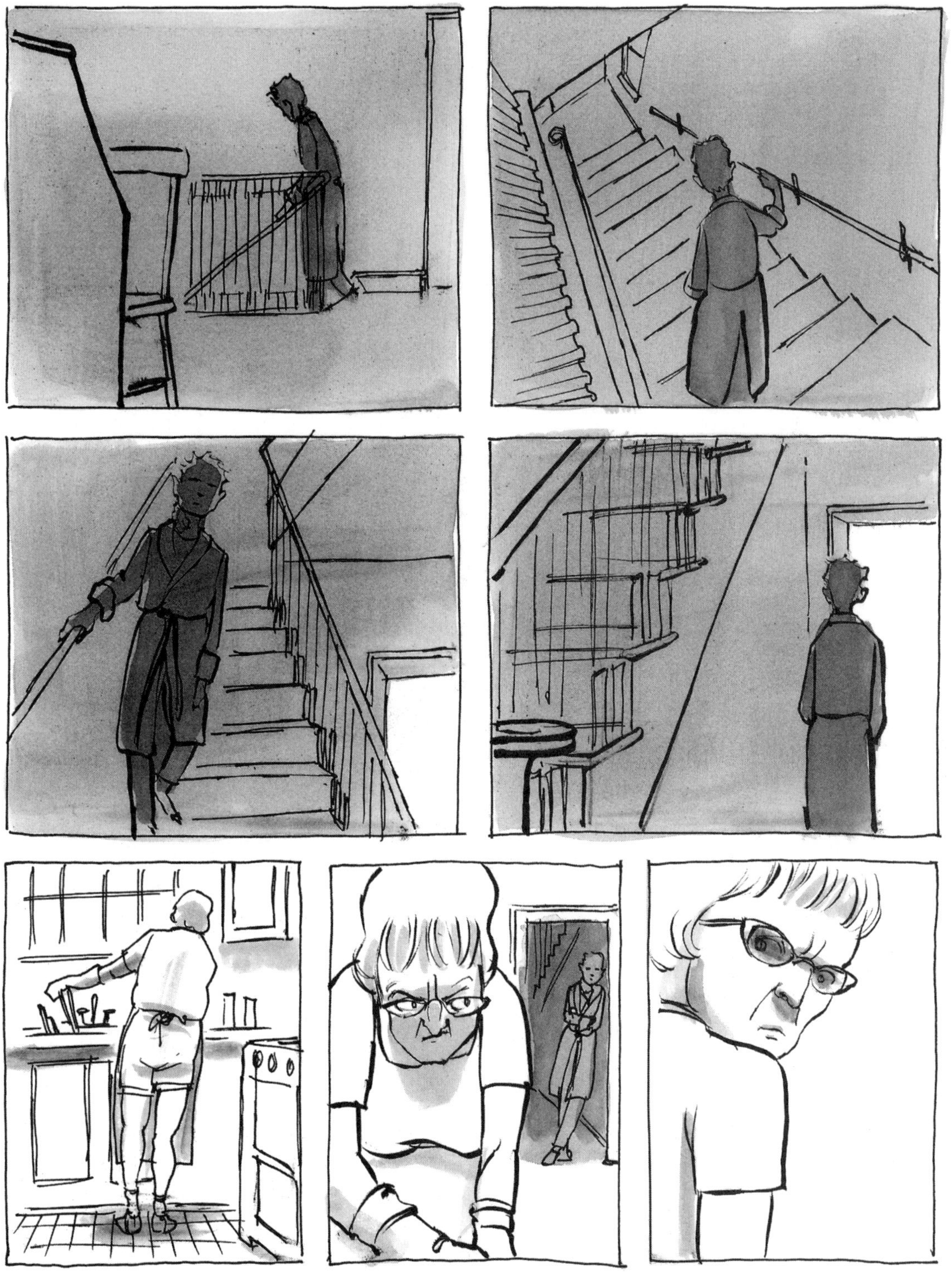

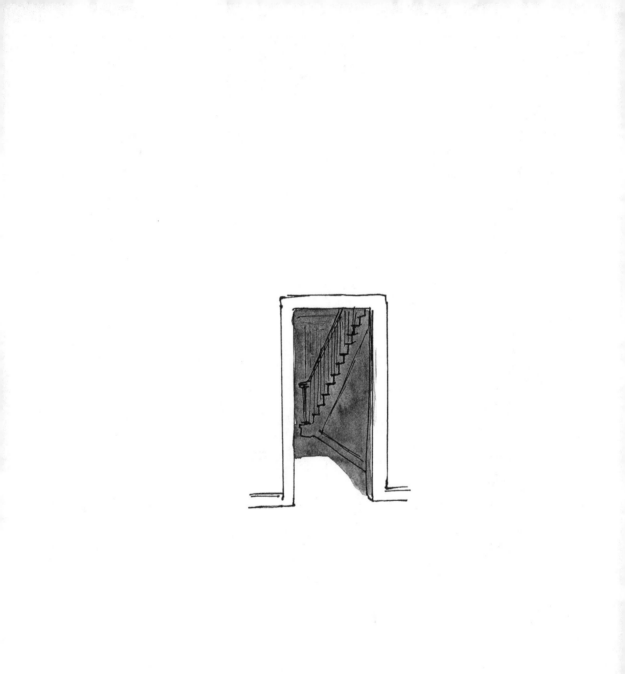

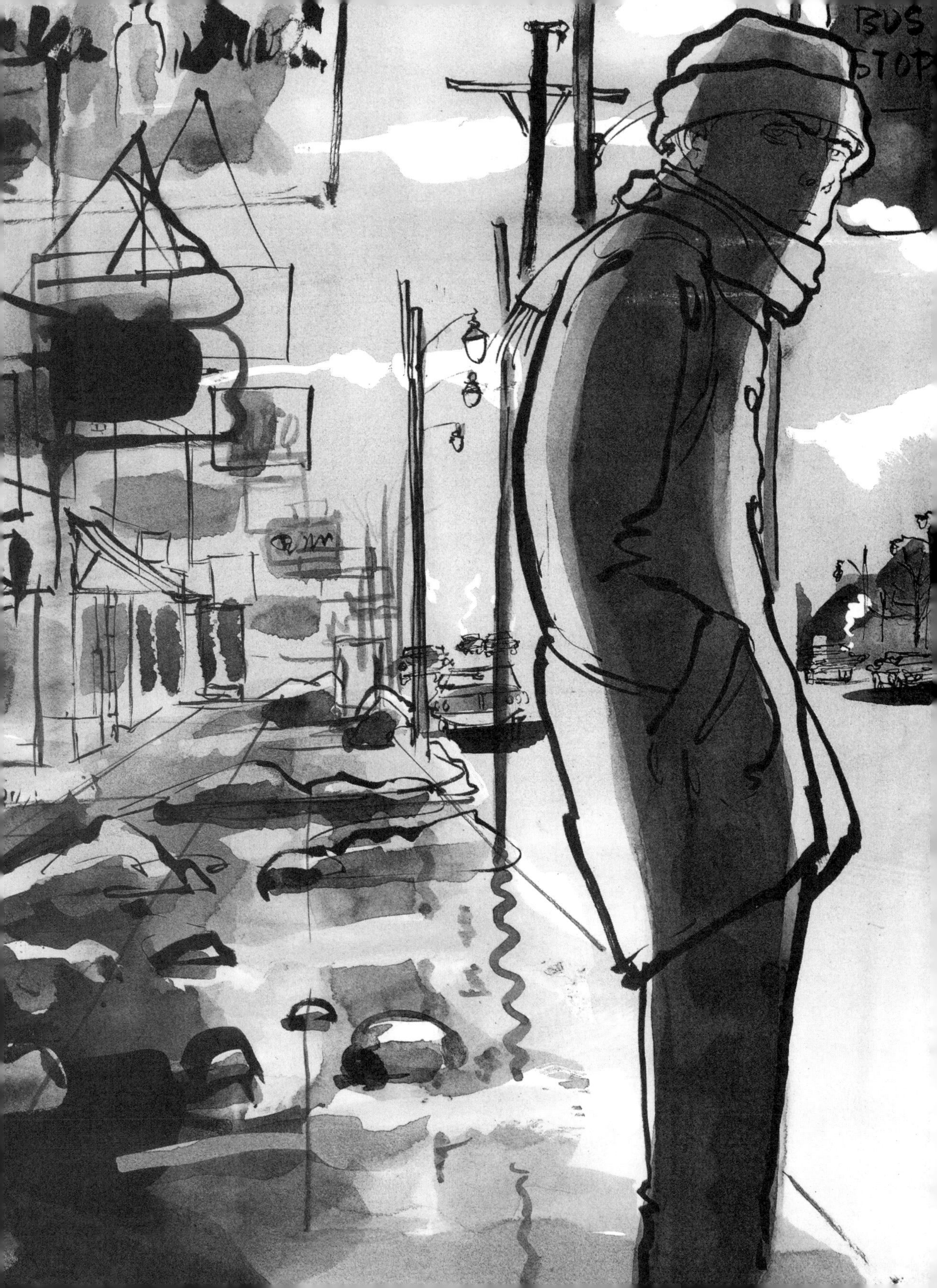
BUS
STOP

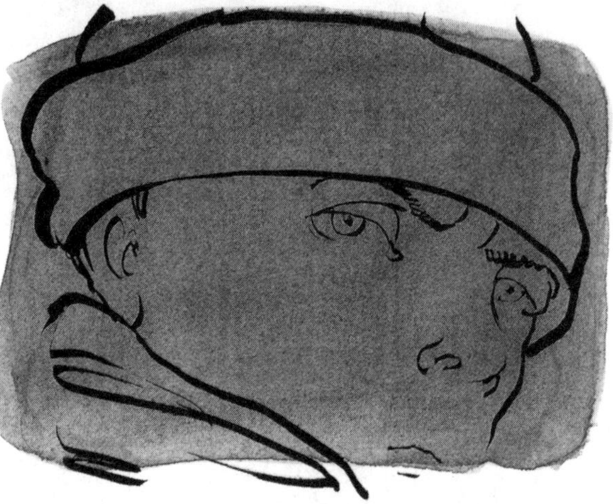

SUDDENLY THINGS BEGAN MAKING SENSE: THE NECESSITY FOR TWO OPERATIONS, THE LOSS OF MY THYROID AND VOCAL CORD. THEN, AFTER THE FIRST SURGERY, MY PARENTS' WEIRD ATTEMPTS TO RALLY AND TO PLAY THE ROLE OF A REAL FAMILY.

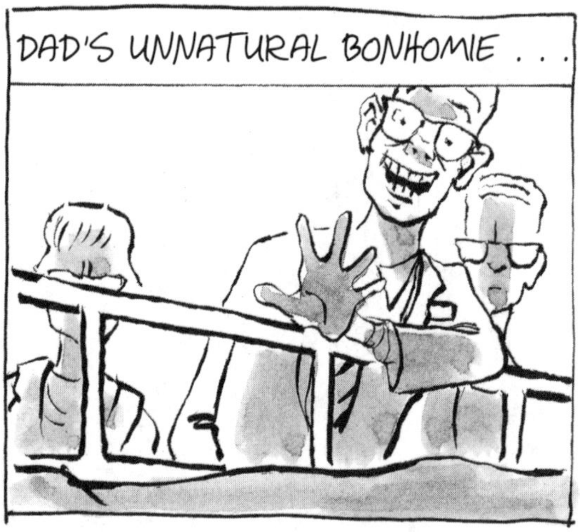
DAD'S UNNATURAL BONHOMIE . . .

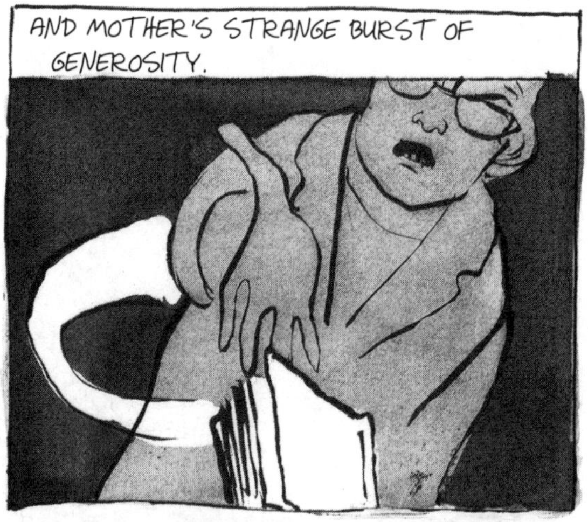
AND MOTHER'S STRANGE BURST OF GENEROSITY.

ABOVE ALL, I RECALLED WAKING UP FROM THE SECOND SURGERY AND REACHING OUT FOR THAT BOOK, SYMBOL OF MY LIBERATION.

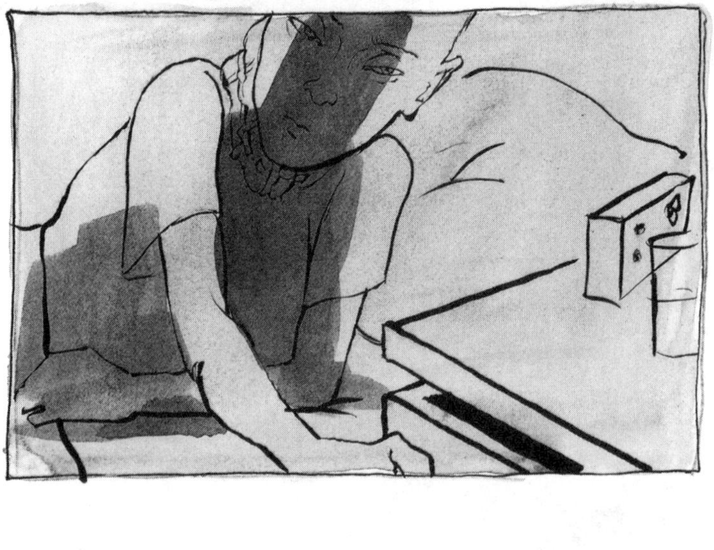

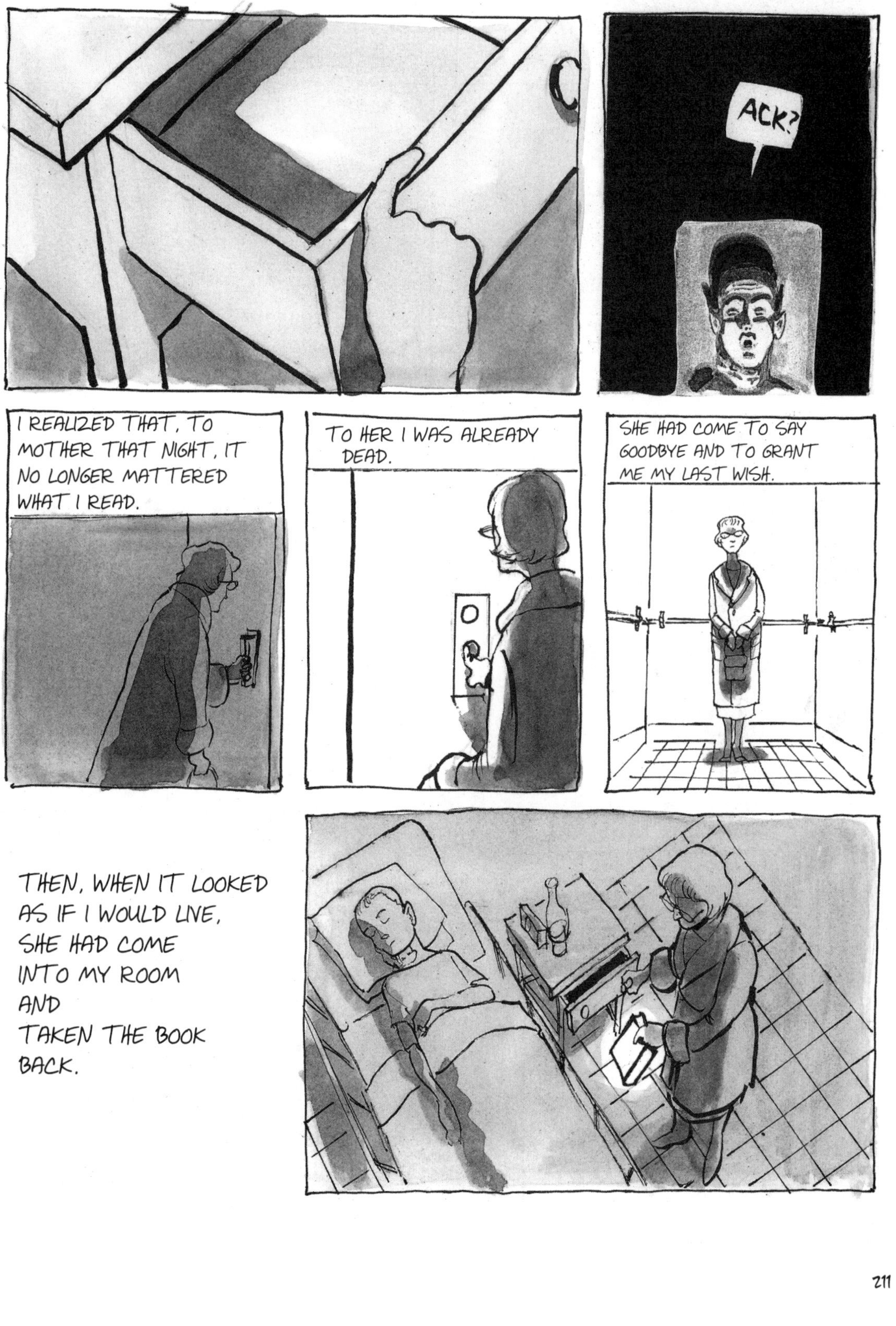
ACK?
I REALIZED THAT, TO MOTHER THAT NIGHT, IT NO LONGER MATTERED WHAT I READ.
TO HER I WAS ALREADY DEAD.
SHE HAD COME TO SAY GOODBYE AND TO GRANT ME MY LAST WISH.
THEN, WHEN IT LOOKED AS IF I WOULD LIVE, SHE HAD COME INTO MY ROOM AND TAKEN THE BOOK BACK.

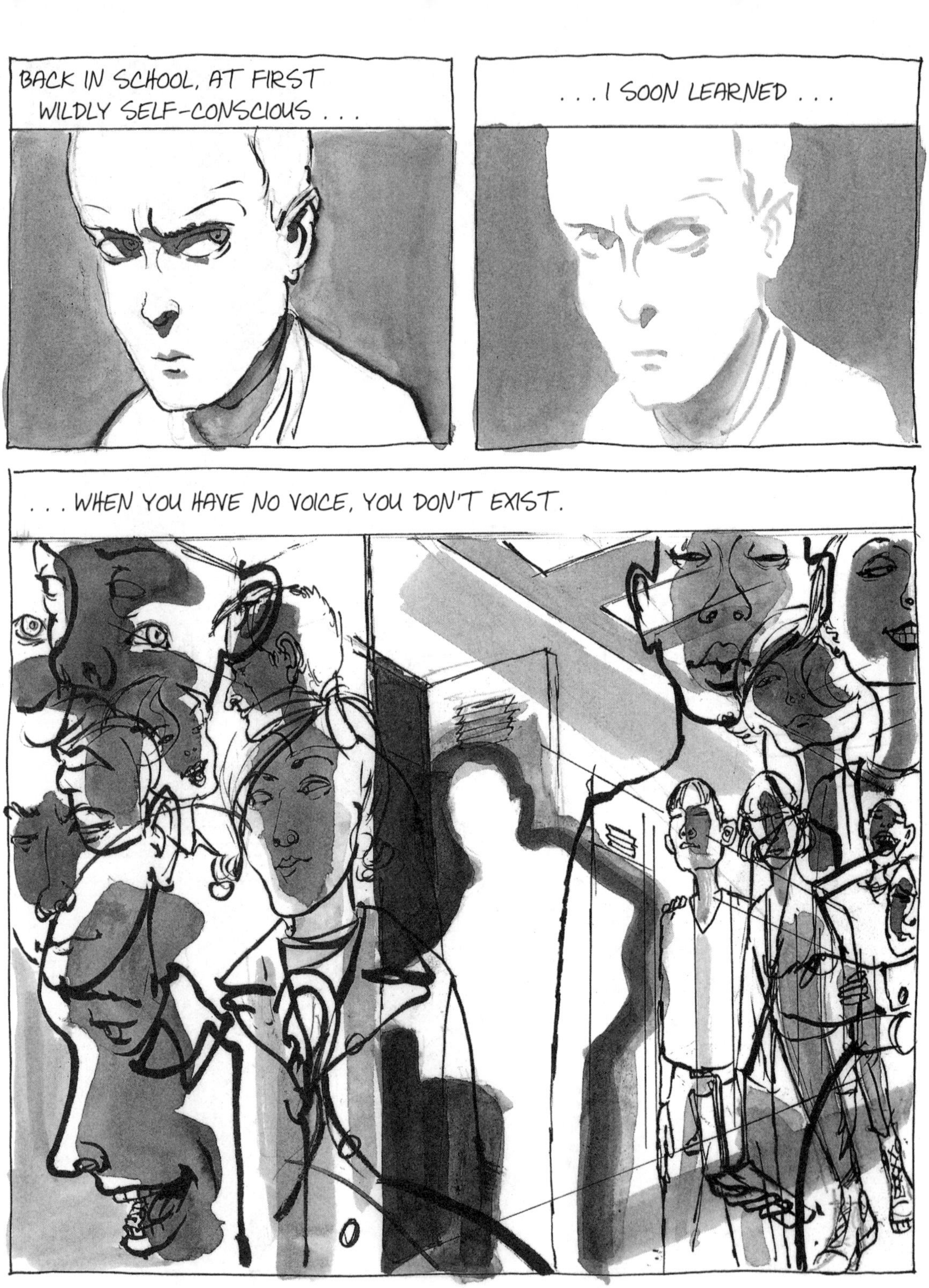
BACK IN SCHOOL, AT FIRST WILDLY SELF-CONSCIOUS . . .
. . . I SOON LEARNED . . .
. . . WHEN YOU HAVE NO VOICE, YOU DON'T EXIST.

EVEN AMONG MY OLD FRIENDS I FELT INVISIBLE, A SHADOW FLICKERING AROUND THE EDGES OF EVERY EVENT.

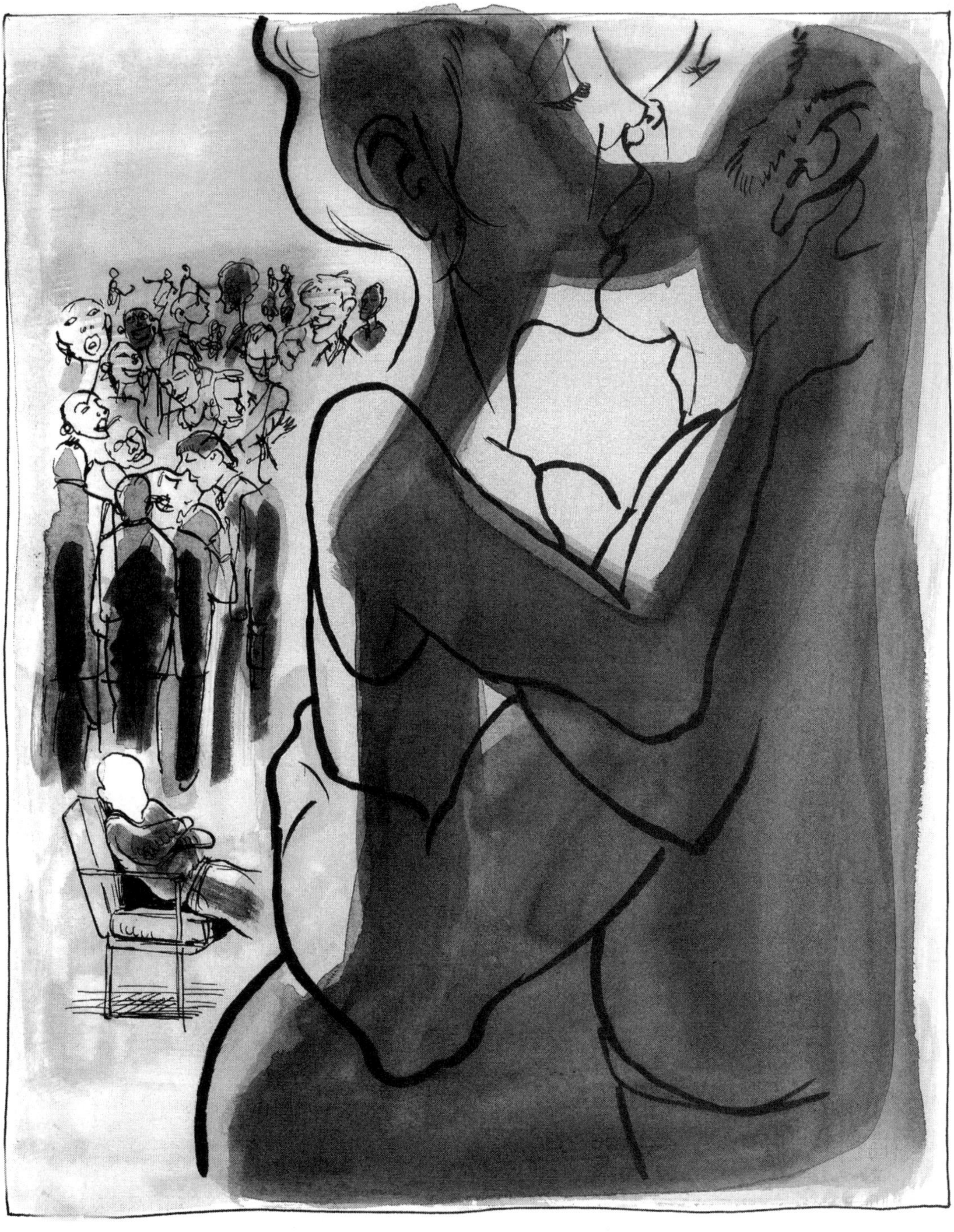

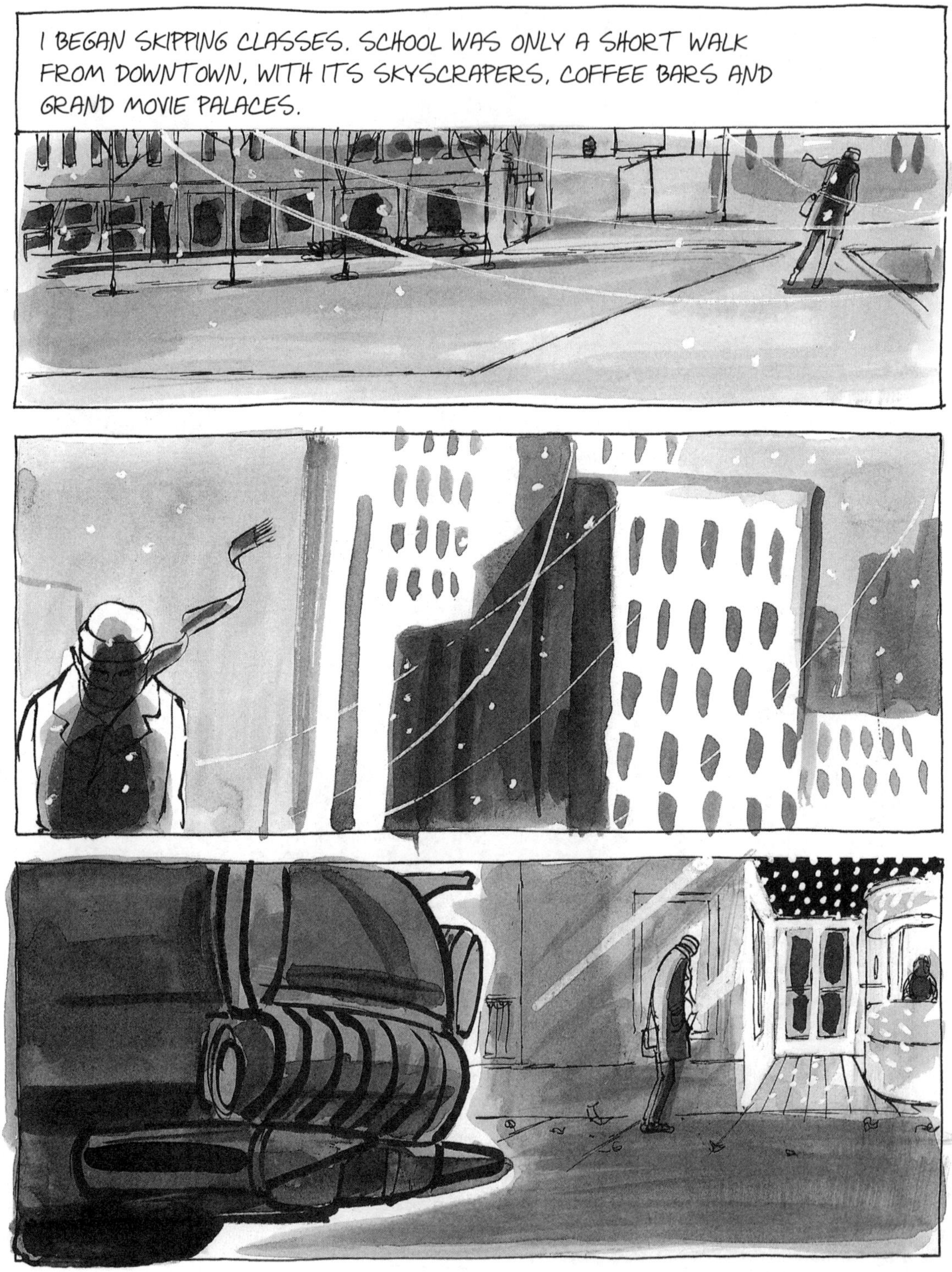
I BEGAN SKIPPING CLASSES. SCHOOL WAS ONLY A SHORT WALK FROM DOWNTOWN, WITH ITS SKYSCRAPERS, COFFEE BARS AND GRAND MOVIE PALACES.

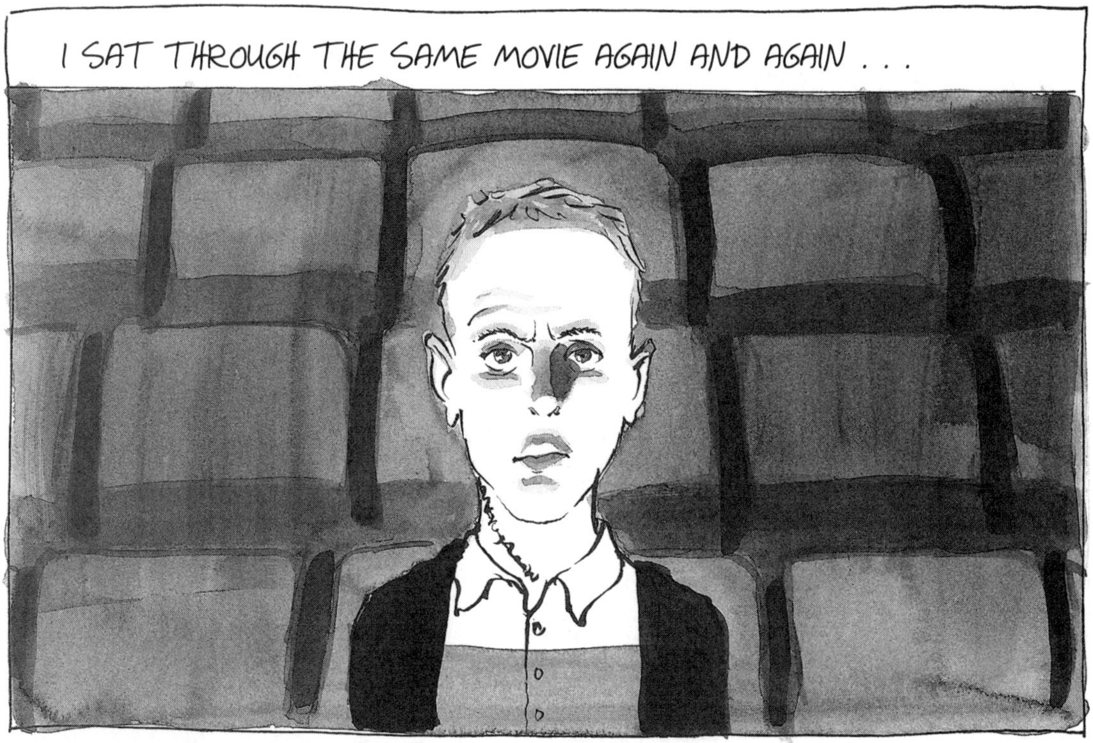
I SAT THROUGH THE SAME MOVIE AGAIN AND AGAIN . . .

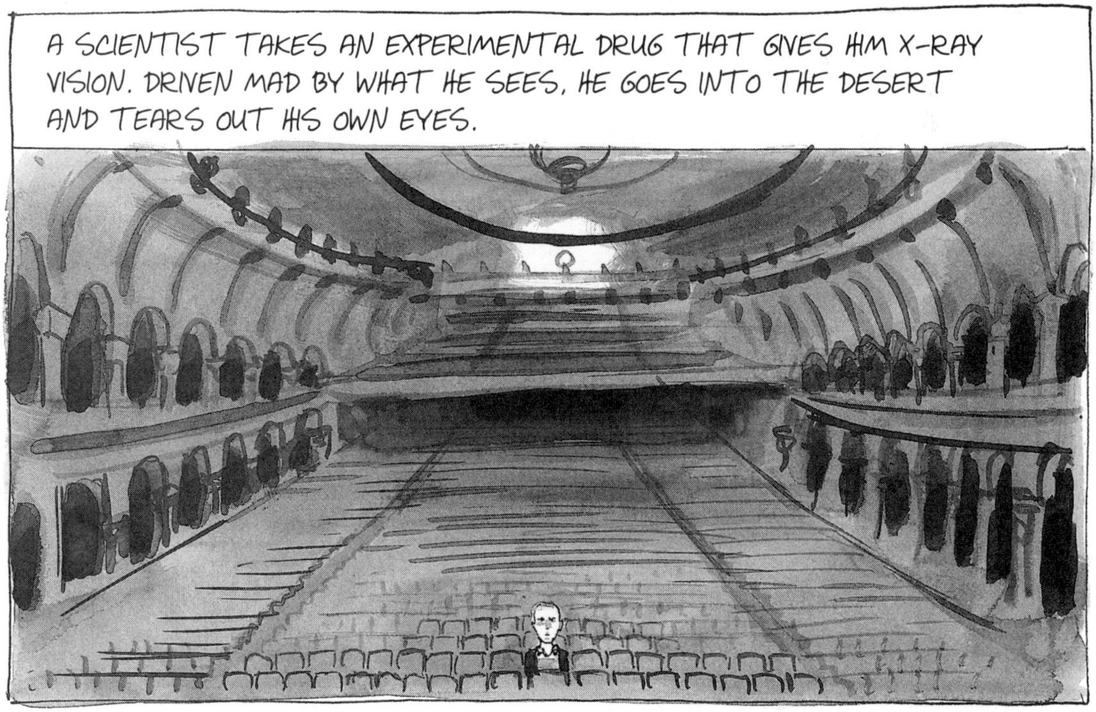
A SCIENTIST TAKES AN EXPERIMENTAL DRUG THAT GIVES HIM X-RAY VISION. DRIVEN MAD BY WHAT HE SEES, HE GOES INTO THE DESERT AND TEARS OUT HIS OWN EYES.

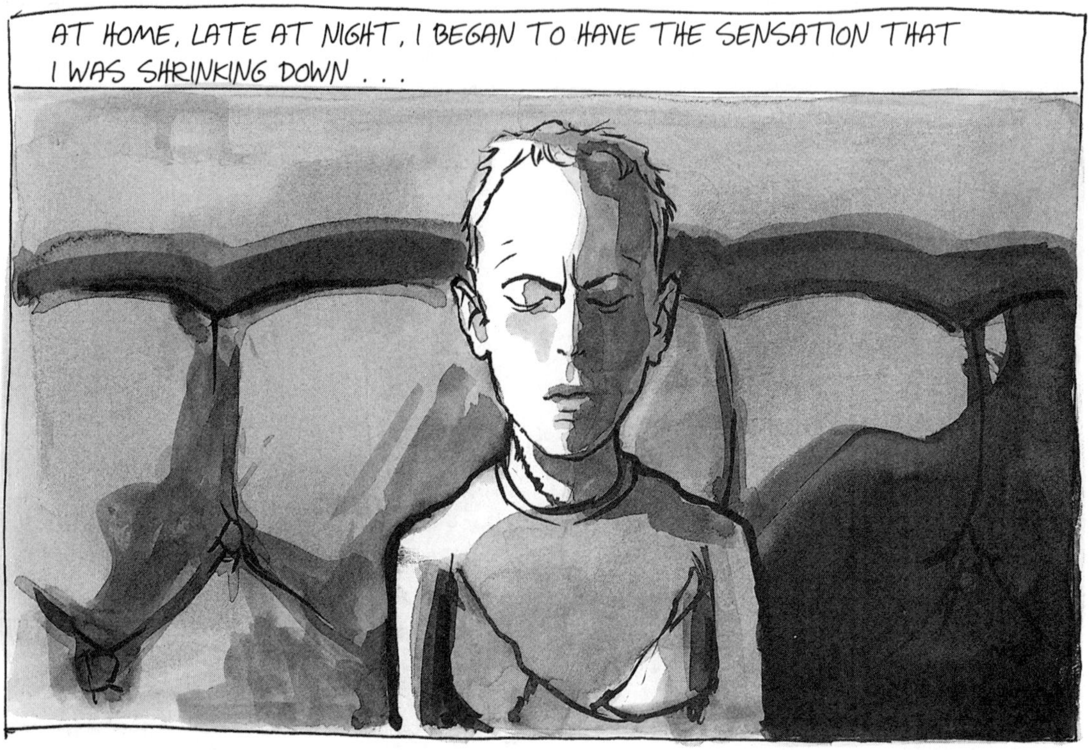
AT HOME, LATE AT NIGHT, I BEGAN TO HAVE THE SENSATION THAT I WAS SHRINKING DOWN . . .

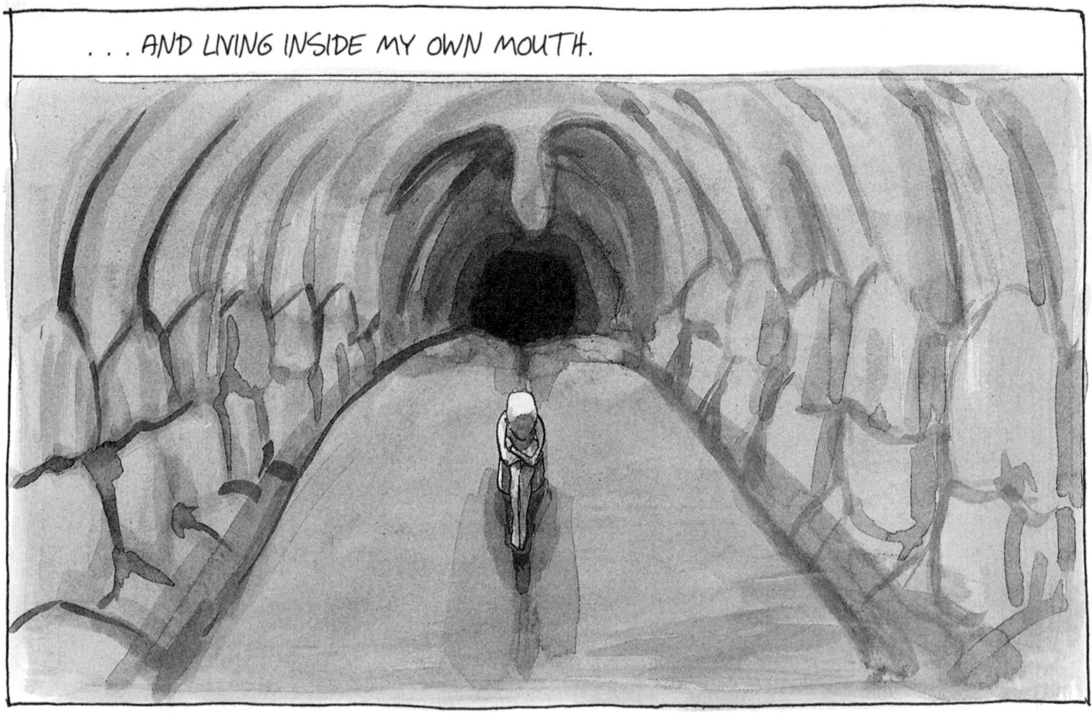
. . . AND LIVING INSIDE MY OWN MOUTH.

. . A HOT, MOIST CAVERN, IN WHICH EVERYTHING I THOUGHT, EVERY WORD THAT CAME INTO MY BRAIN, WAS THUNDEROUSLY SHOUTED BACK AT ME.

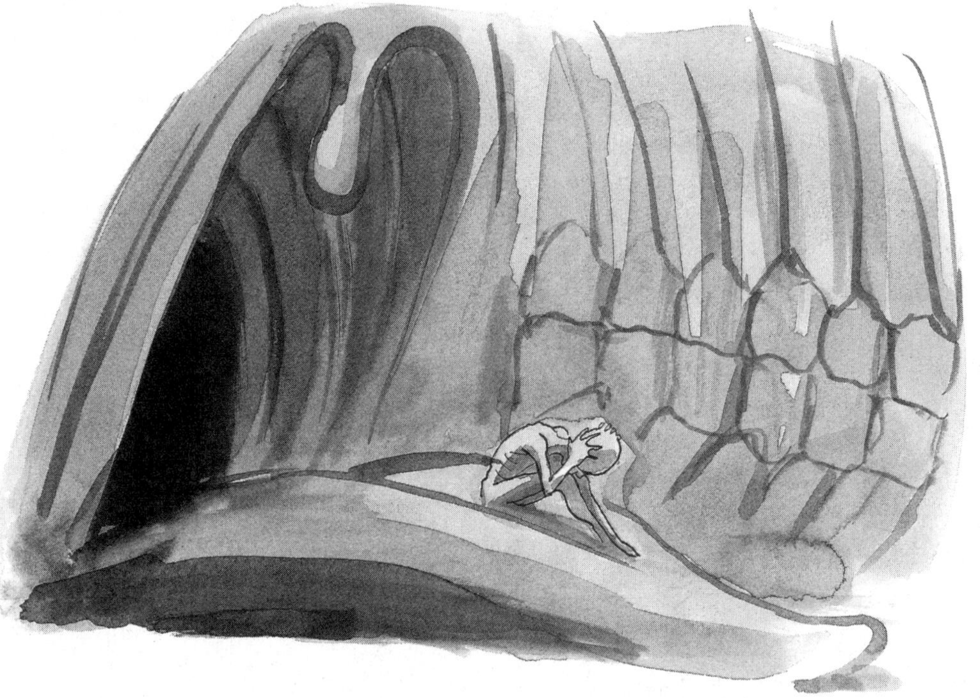

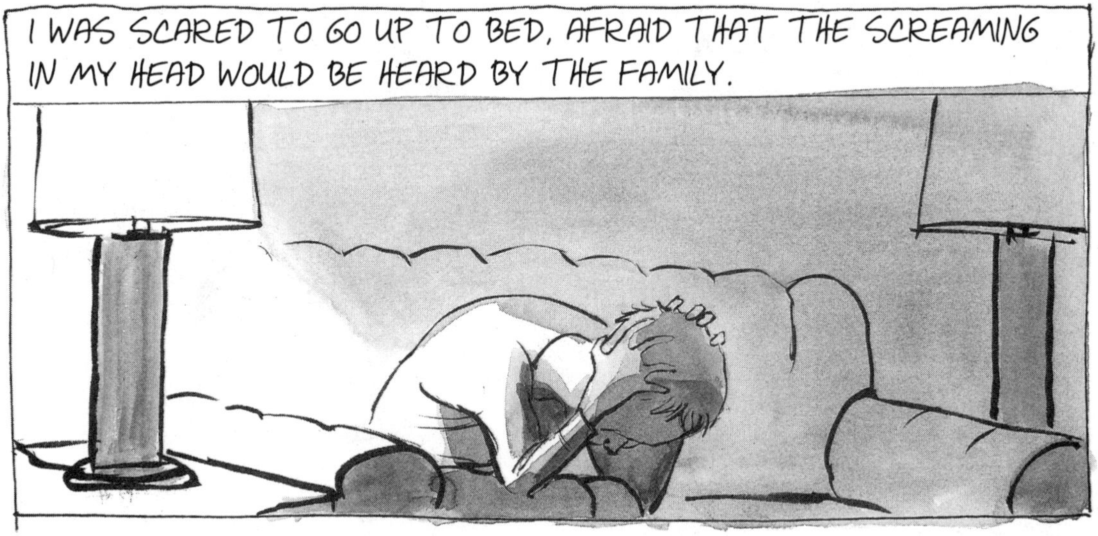
I WAS SCARED TO GO UP TO BED, AFRAID THAT THE SCREAMING IN MY HEAD WOULD BE HEARD BY THE FAMILY.

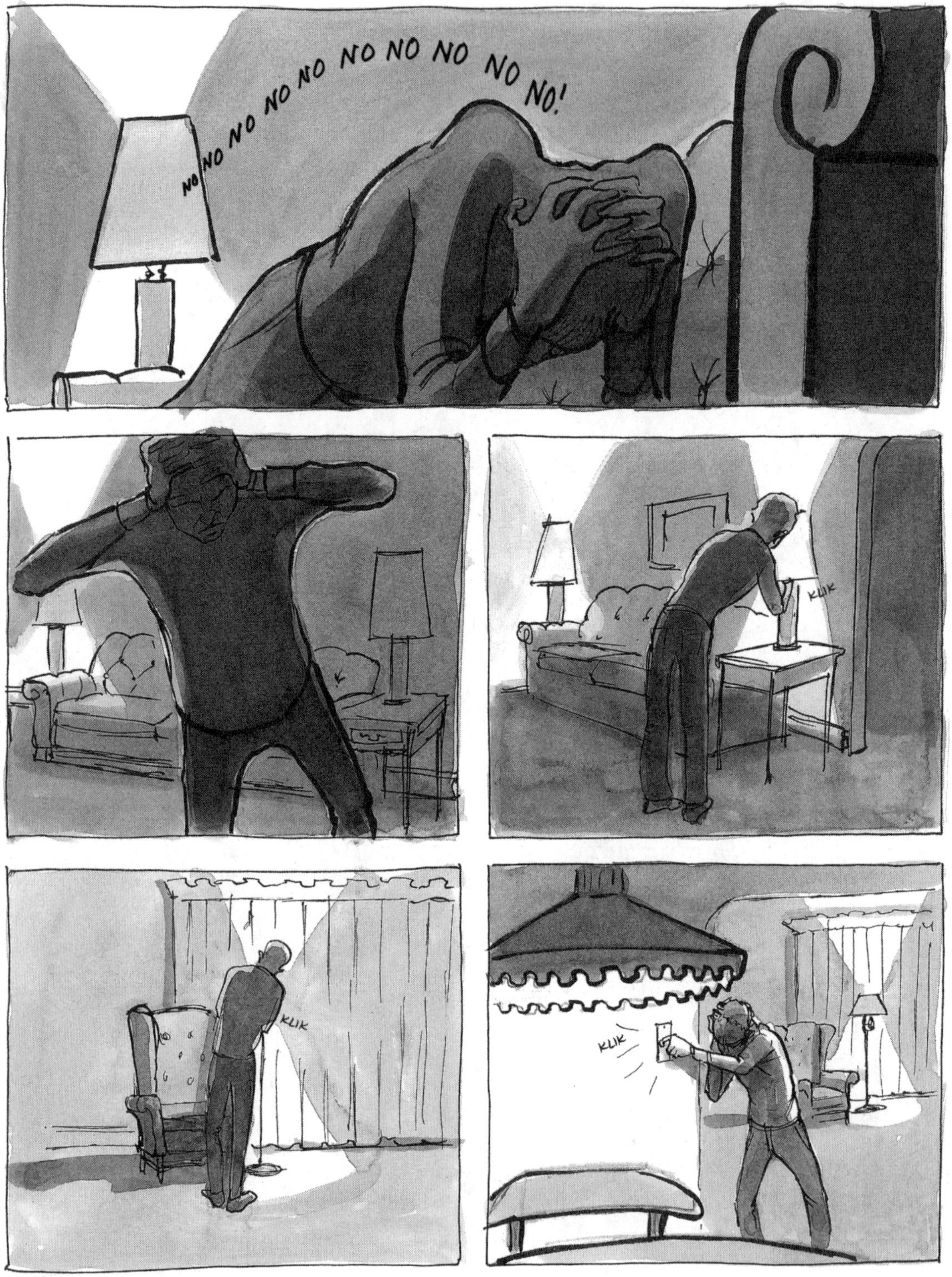
NO NO NO NO NO NO NO NO NO NO!
KLIK
KLIK
KLIK

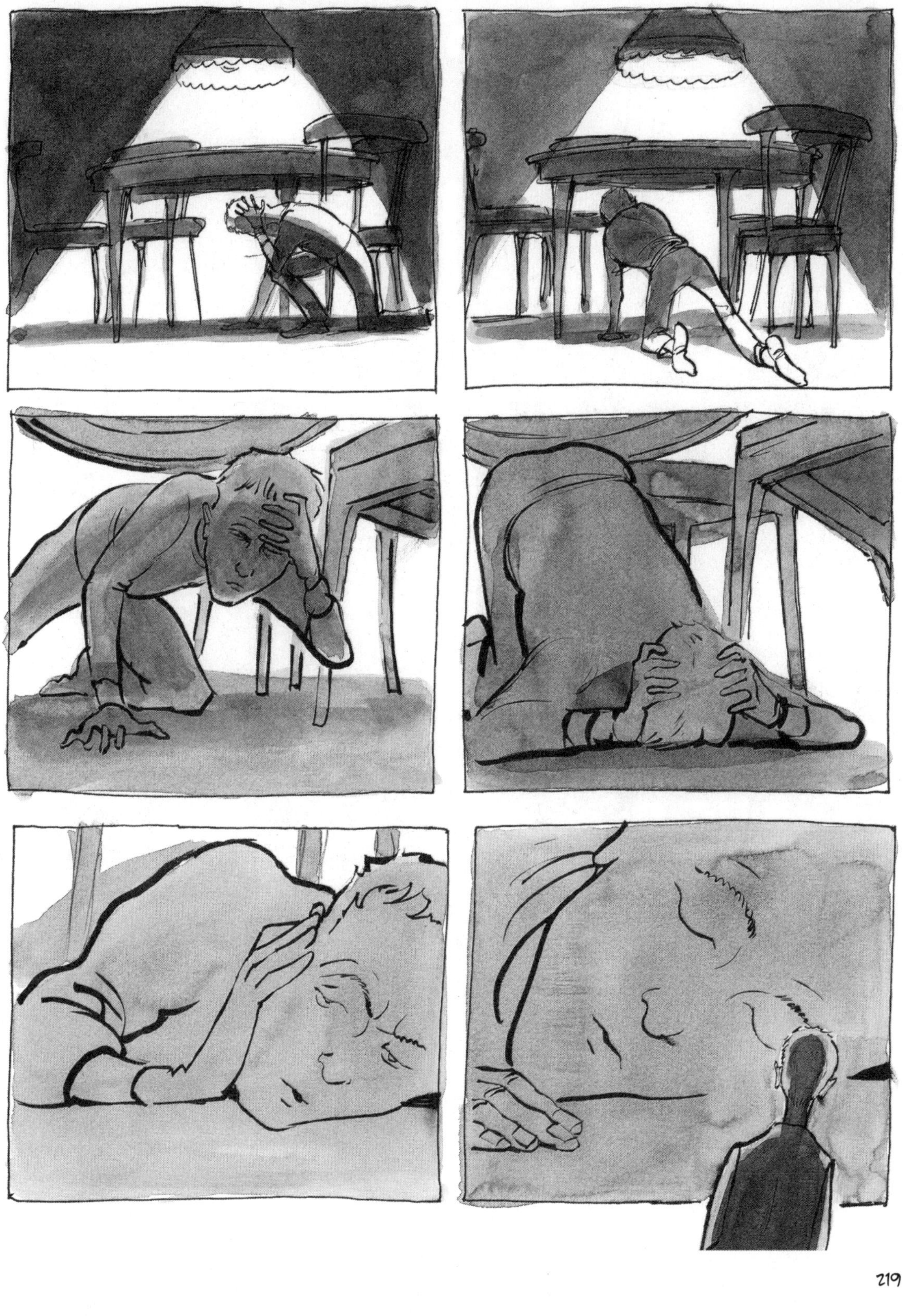

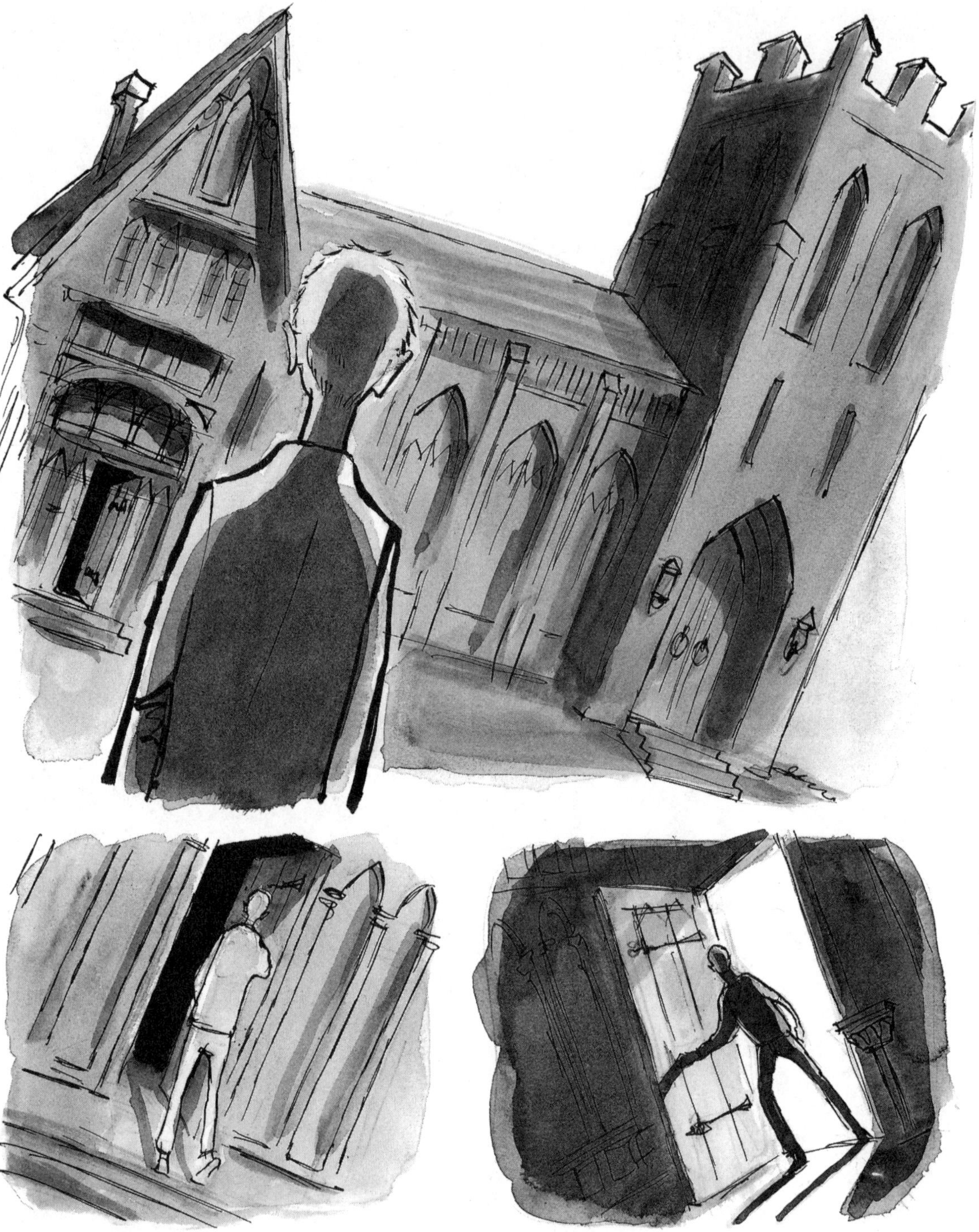

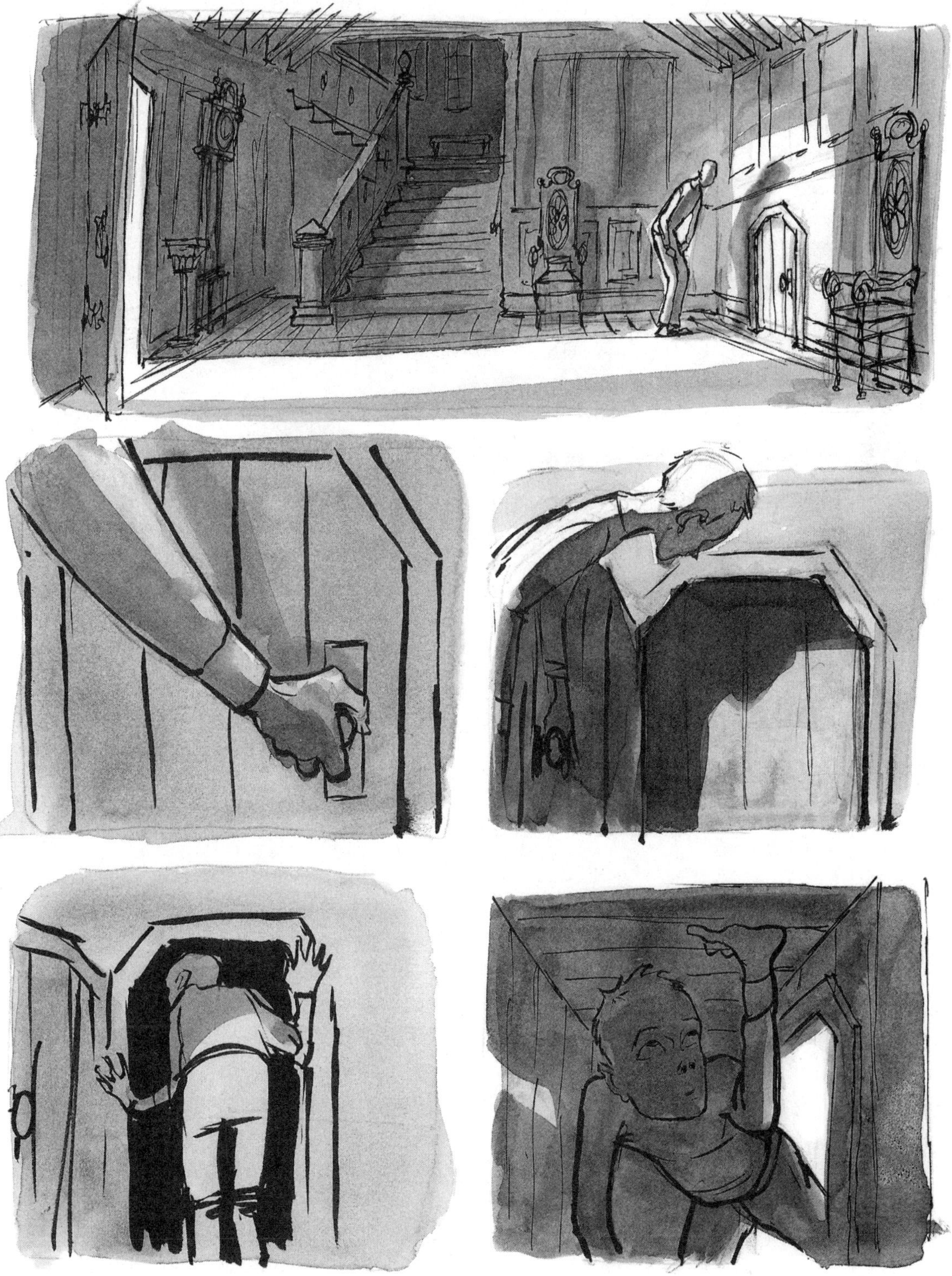

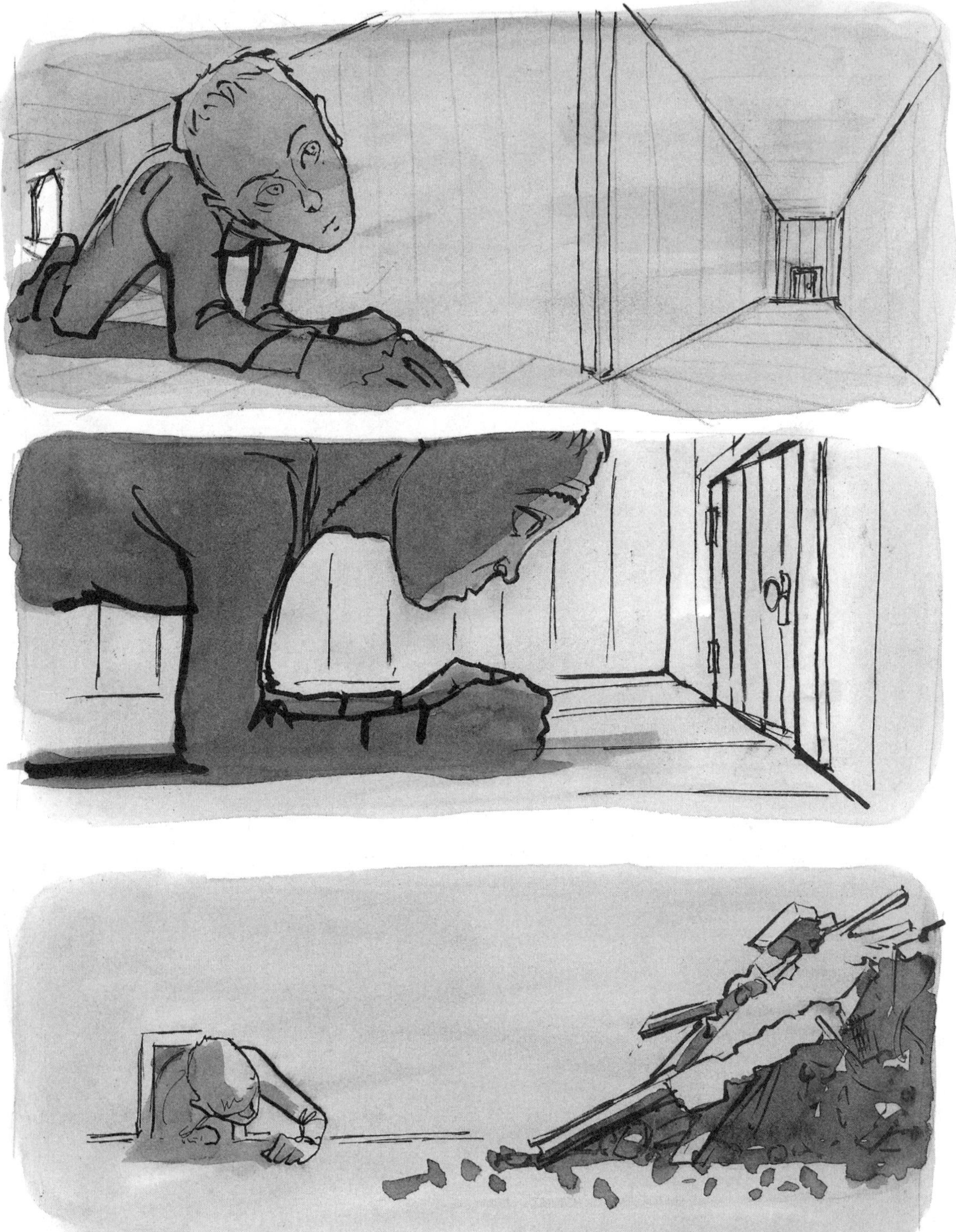

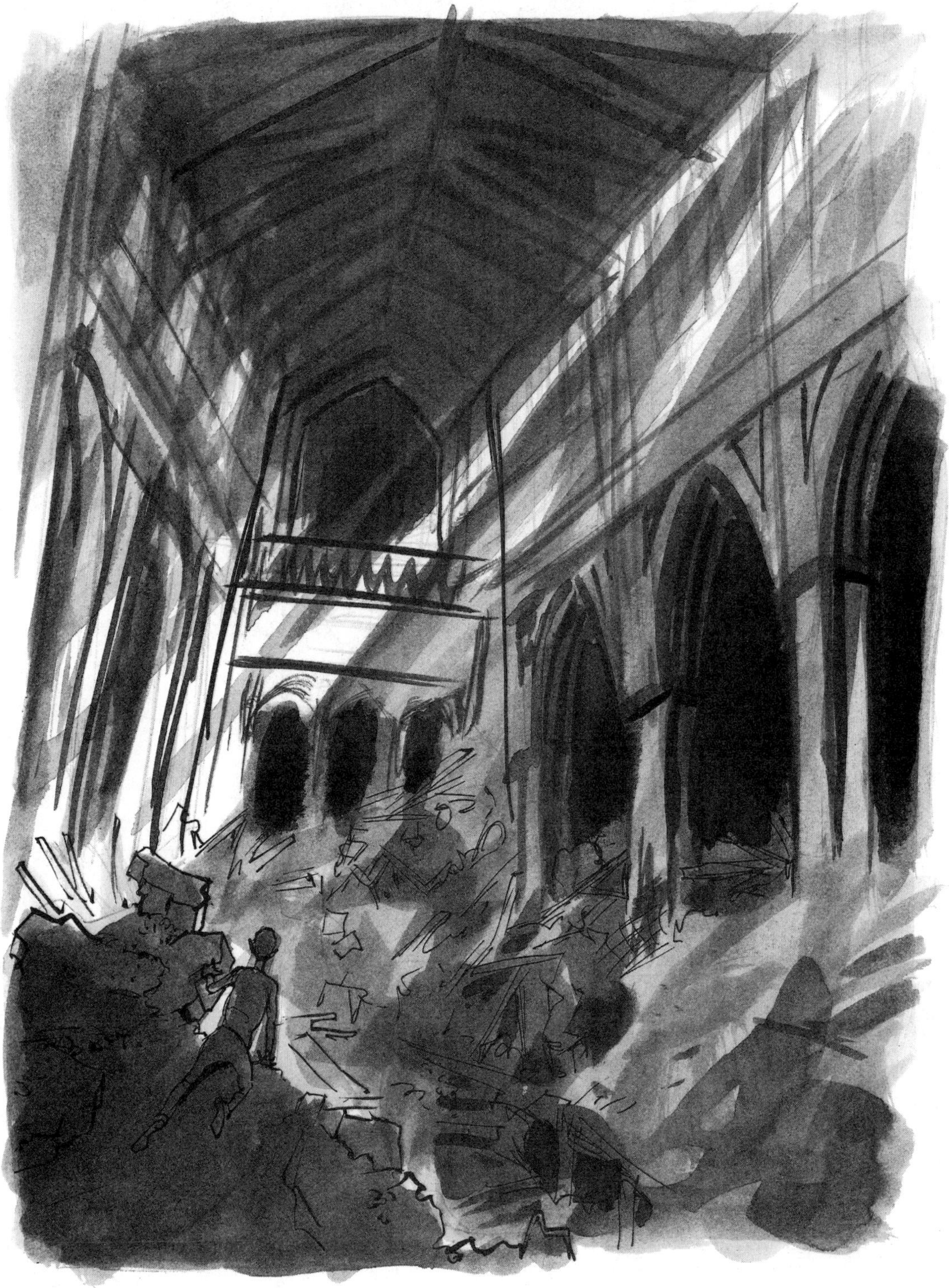

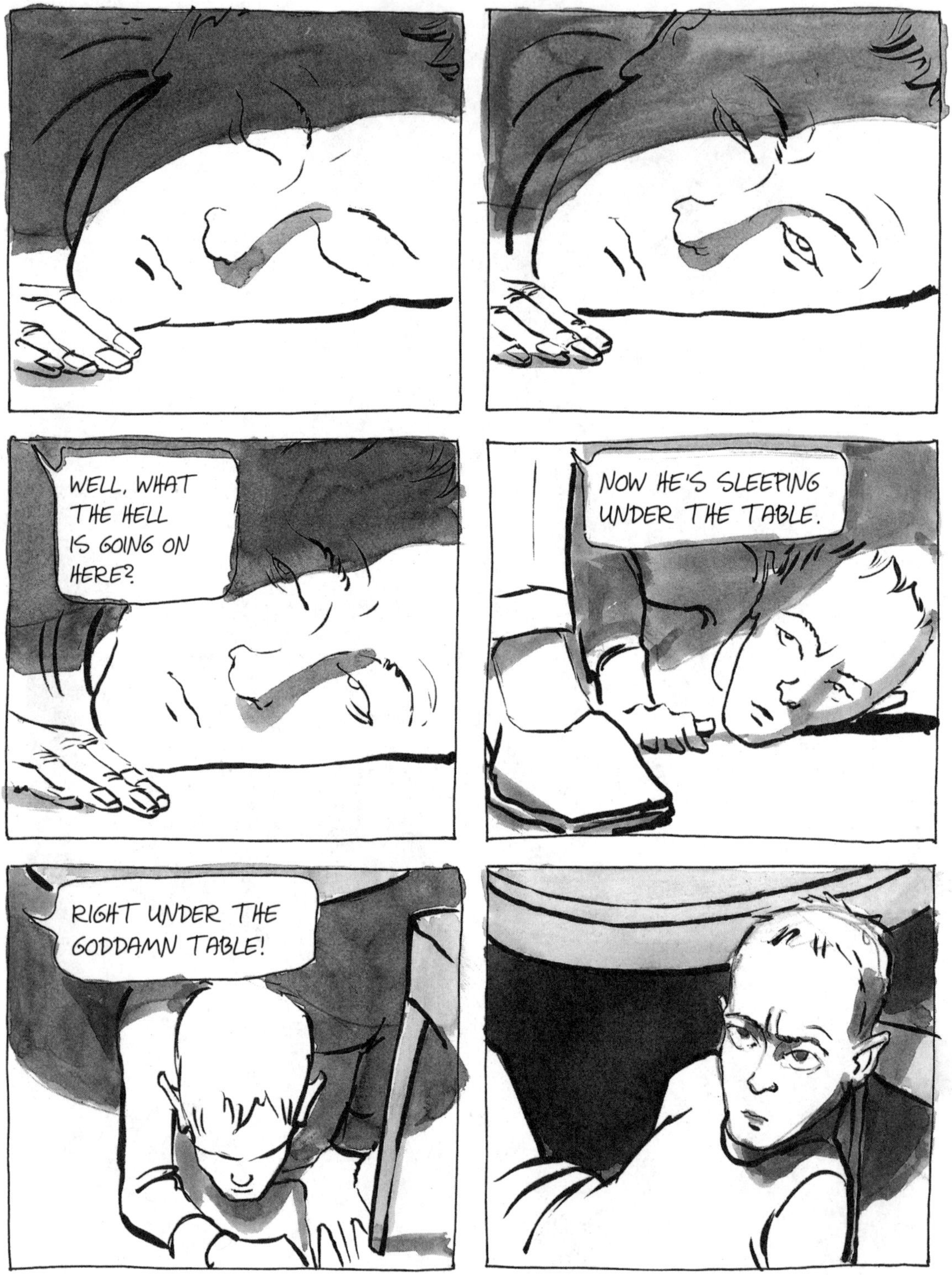
WELL, WHAT THE HELL IS GOING ON HERE?
NOW HE'S SLEEPING UNDER THE TABLE.
RIGHT UNDER THE GODDAMN TABLE!

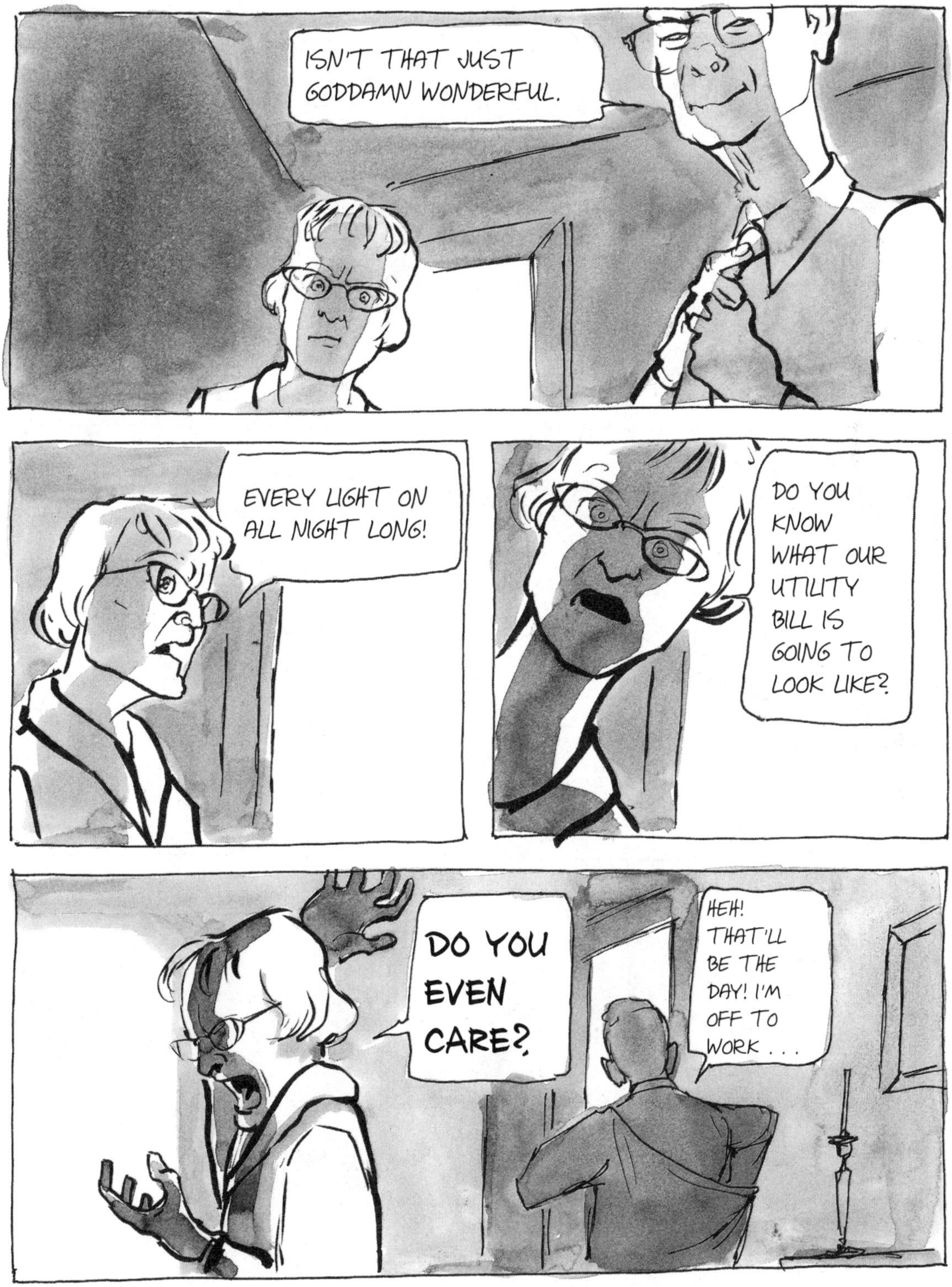
ISN'T THAT JUST GODDAMN WONDERFUL.
EVERY LIGHT ON ALL NIGHT LONG!
DO YOU KNOW WHAT OUR UTILITY BILL IS GOING TO LOOK LIKE?
DO YOU EVEN CARE?
HEH! THAT'LL BE THE DAY! I'M OFF TO WORK . . .

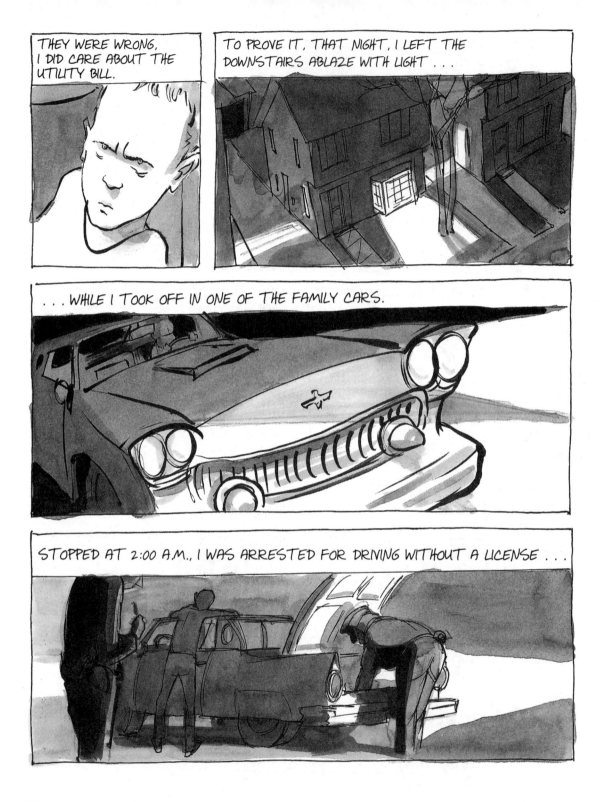

THEY WERE WRONG, I DID CARE ABOUT THE UTILITY BILL.

TO PROVE IT, THAT NIGHT, I LEFT THE DOWNSTAIRS ABLAZE WITH LIGHT . . .

. . . WHILE I TOOK OFF IN ONE OF THE FAMILY CARS.

STOPPED AT 2:00 A.M., I WAS ARRESTED FOR DRIVING WITHOUT A LICENSE . . .

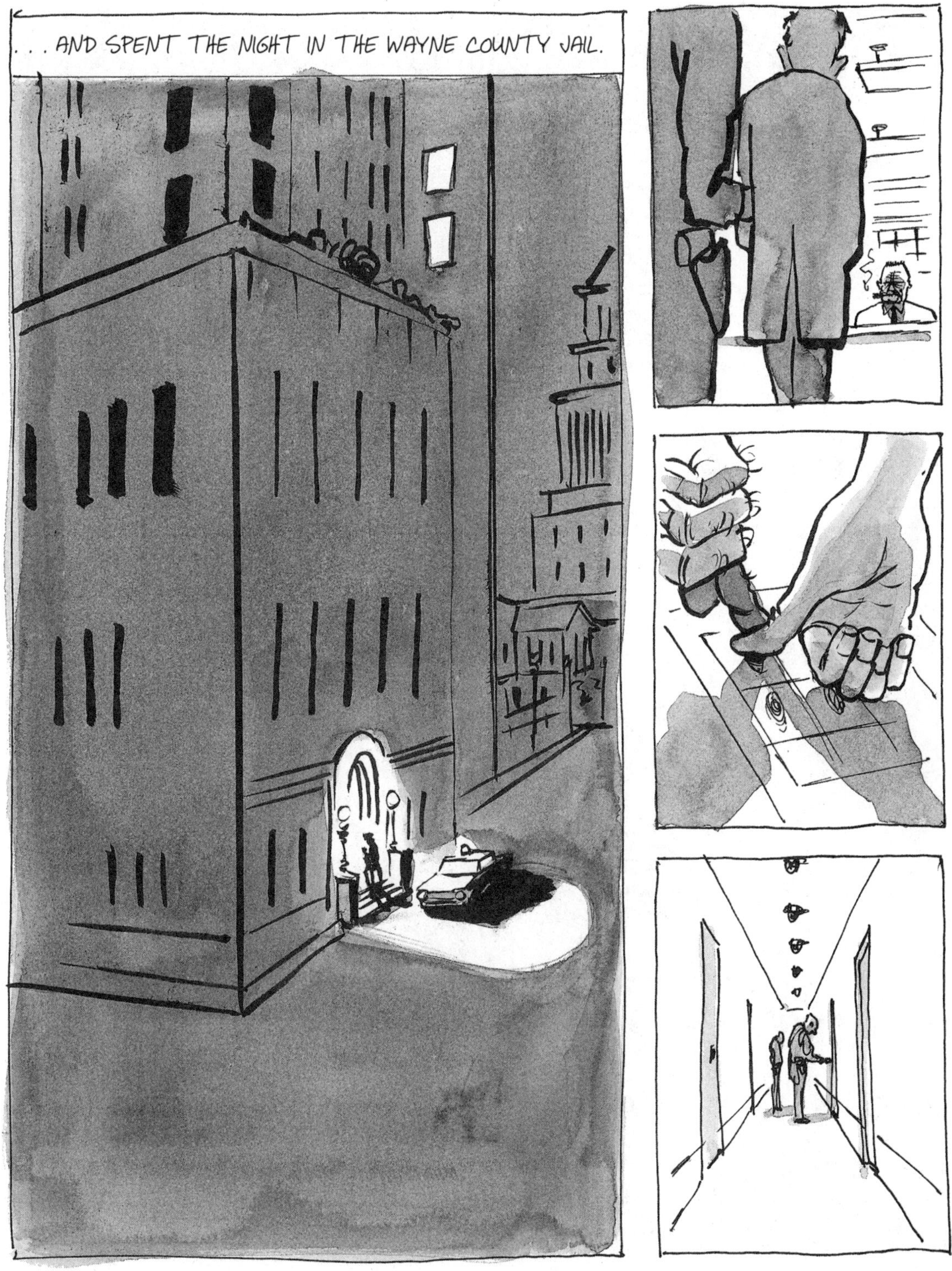
. . . AND SPENT THE NIGHT IN THE WAYNE COUNTY JAIL.

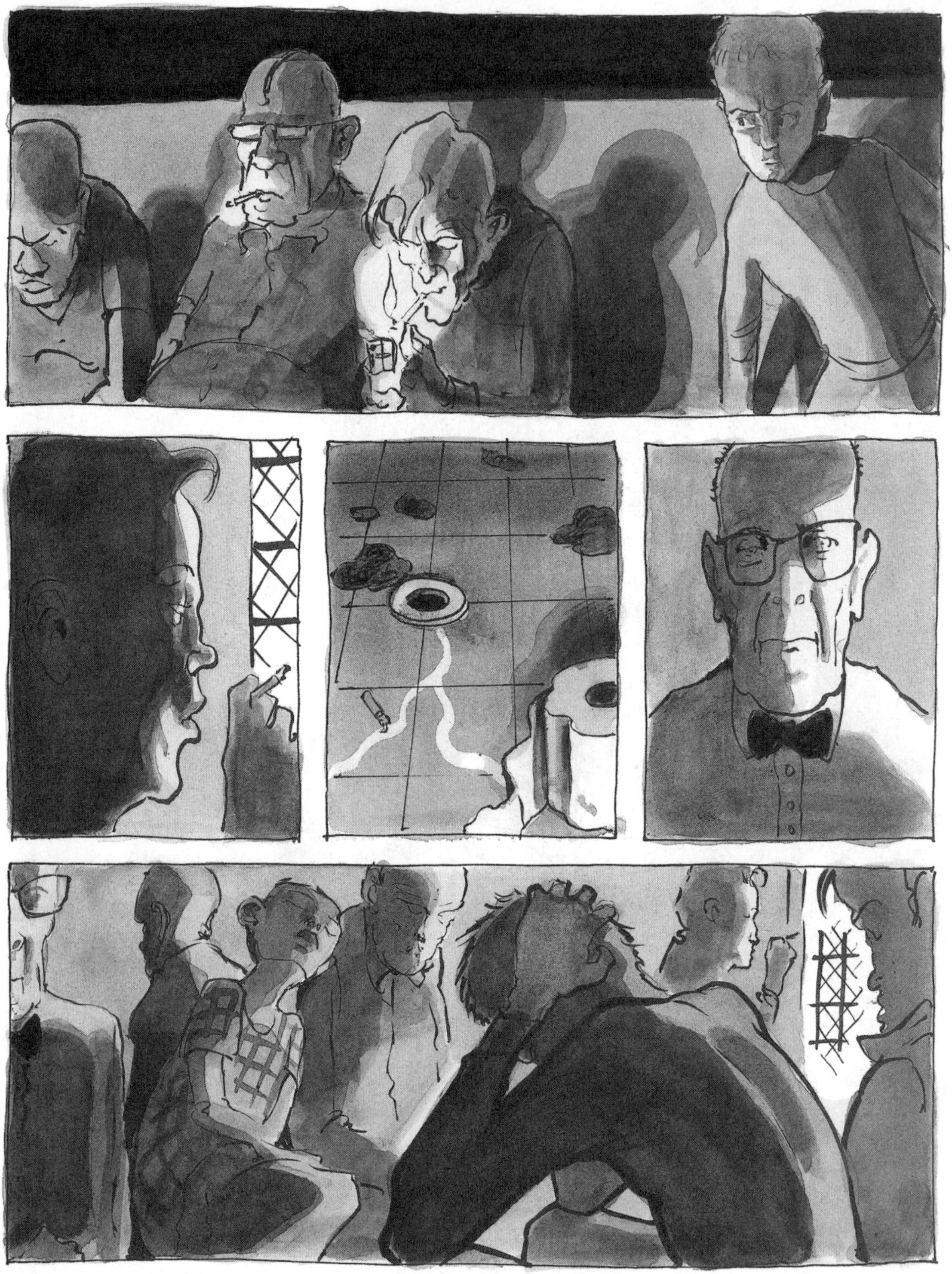

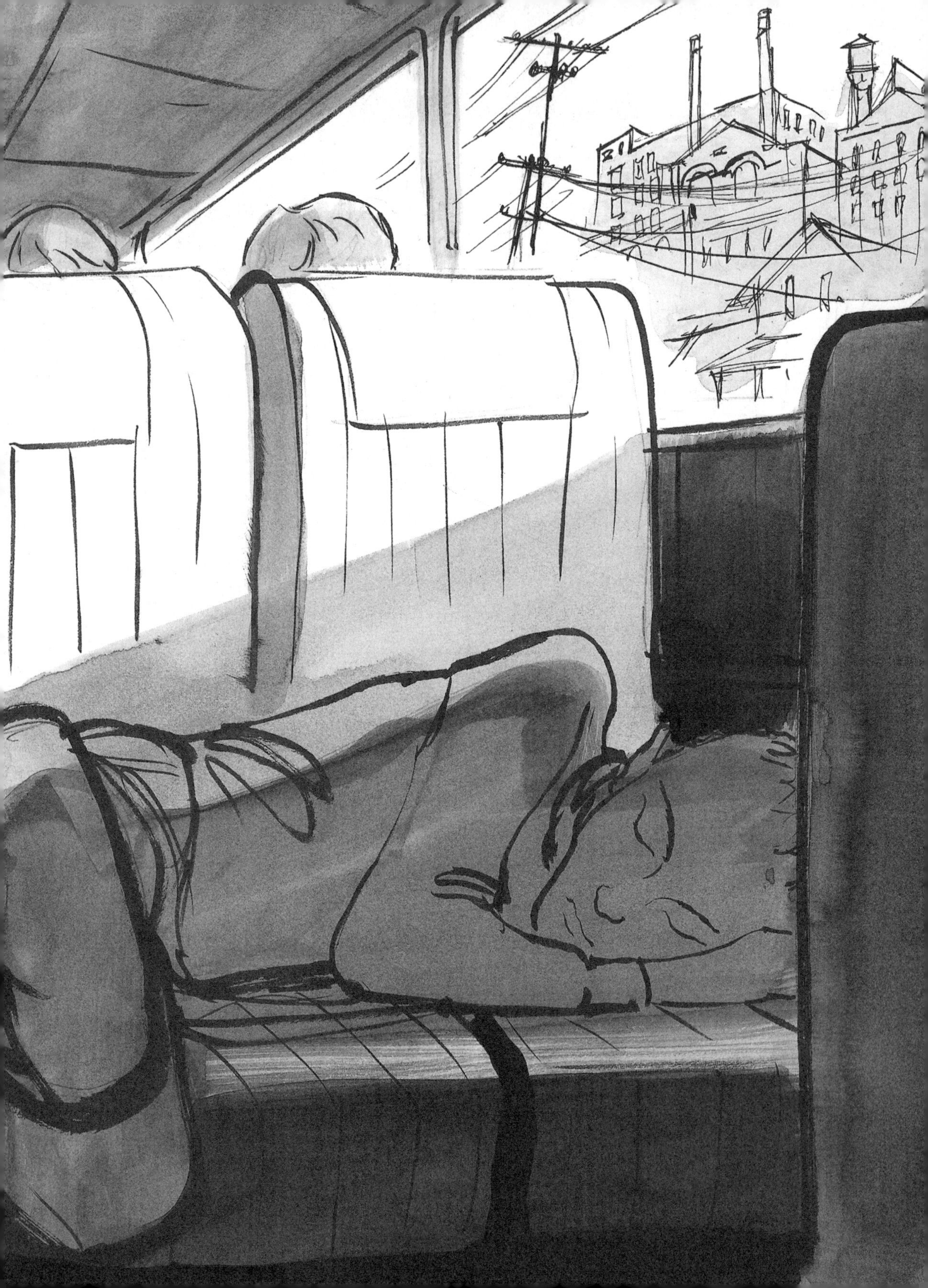

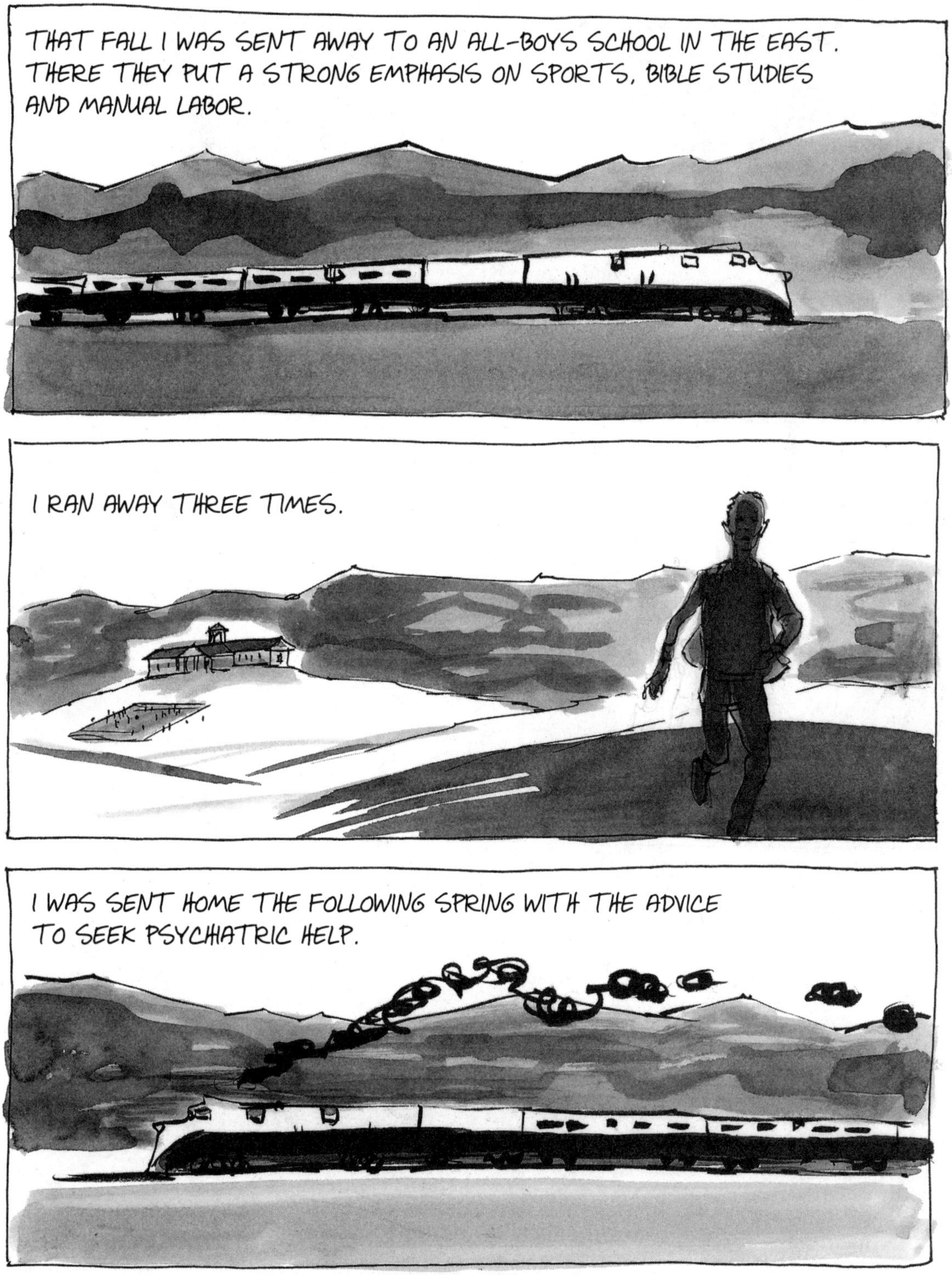
THAT FALL I WAS SENT AWAY TO AN ALL-BOYS SCHOOL IN THE EAST. THERE THEY PUT A STRONG EMPHASIS ON SPORTS, BIBLE STUDIES AND MANUAL LABOR.
I RAN AWAY THREE TIMES.
I WAS SENT HOME THE FOLLOWING SPRING WITH THE ADVICE TO SEEK PSYCHIATRIC HELP.

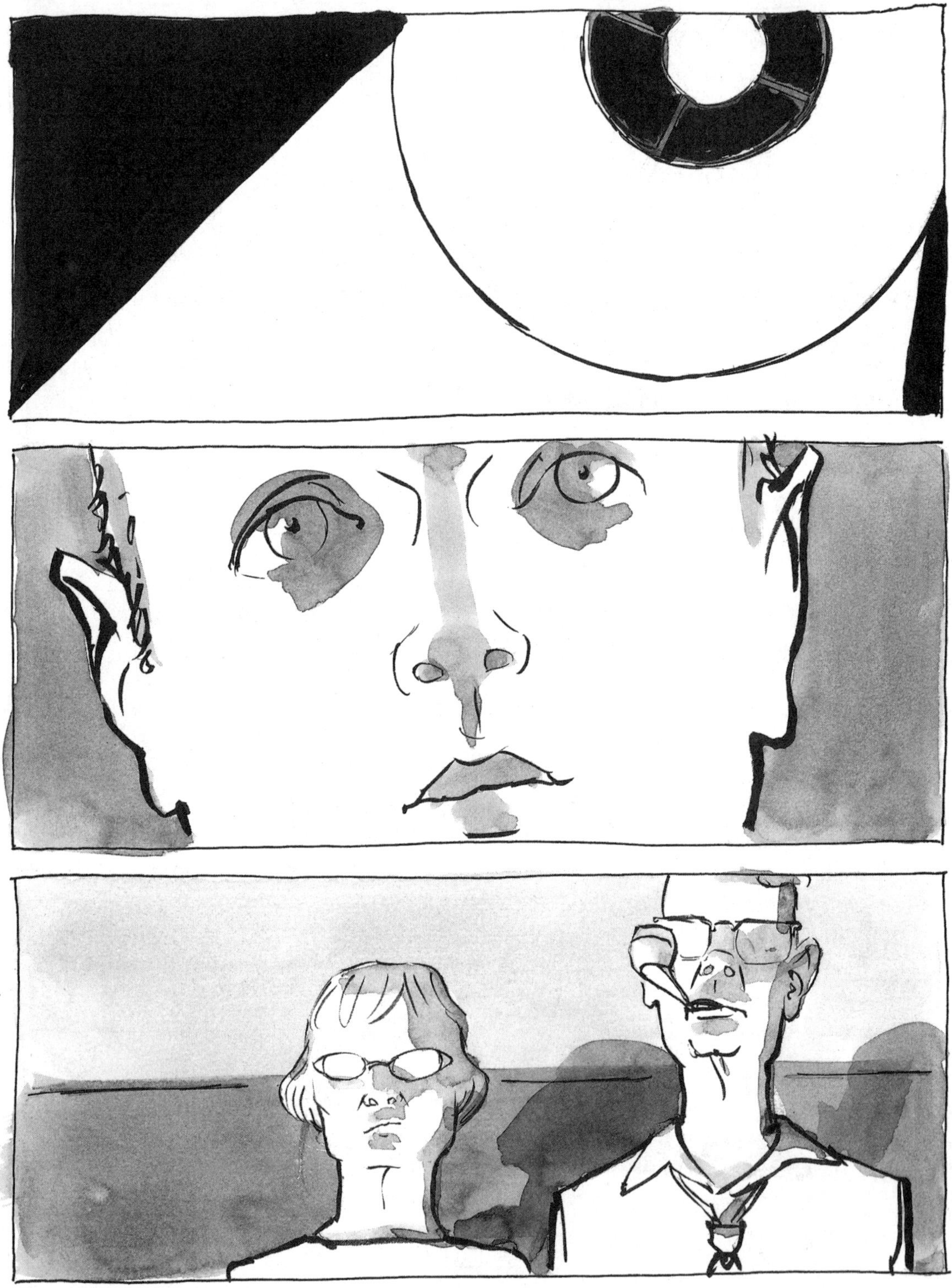

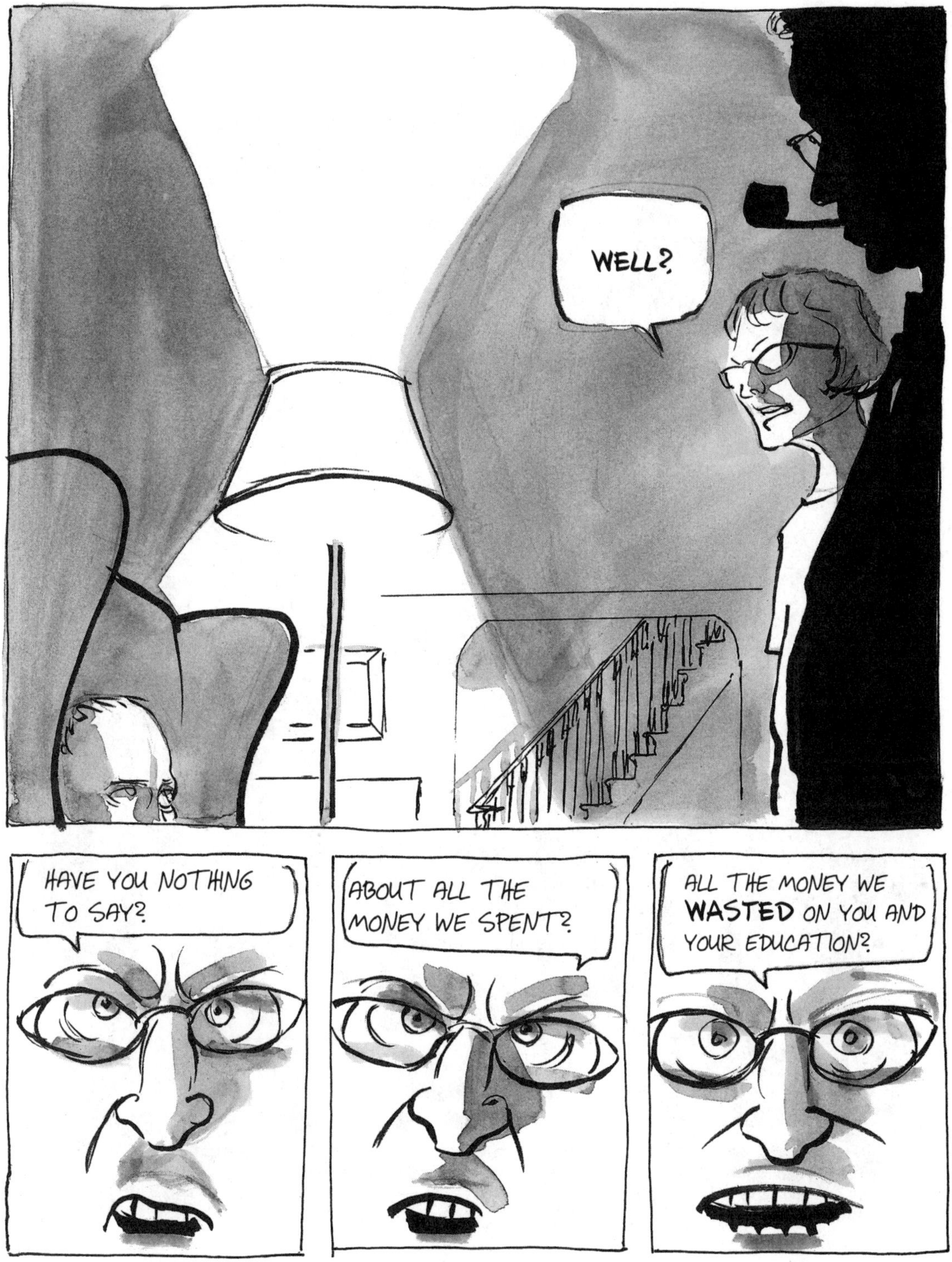
WELL?
HAVE YOU NOTHING TO SAY?
ABOUT ALL THE MONEY WE SPENT?
ALL THE MONEY WE **WASTED** ON YOU AND YOUR EDUCATION?

HOW I WANTED TO RESPOND:

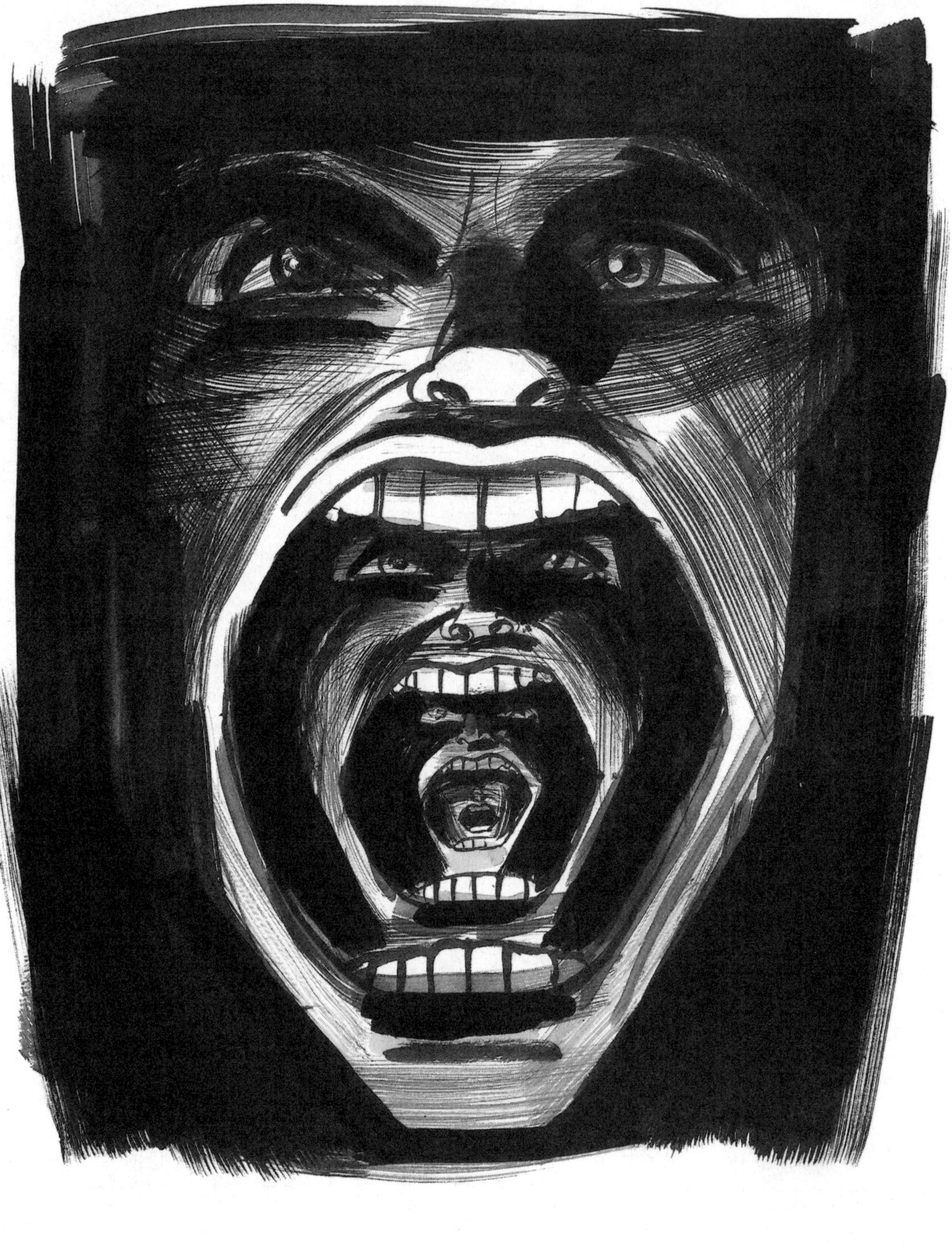

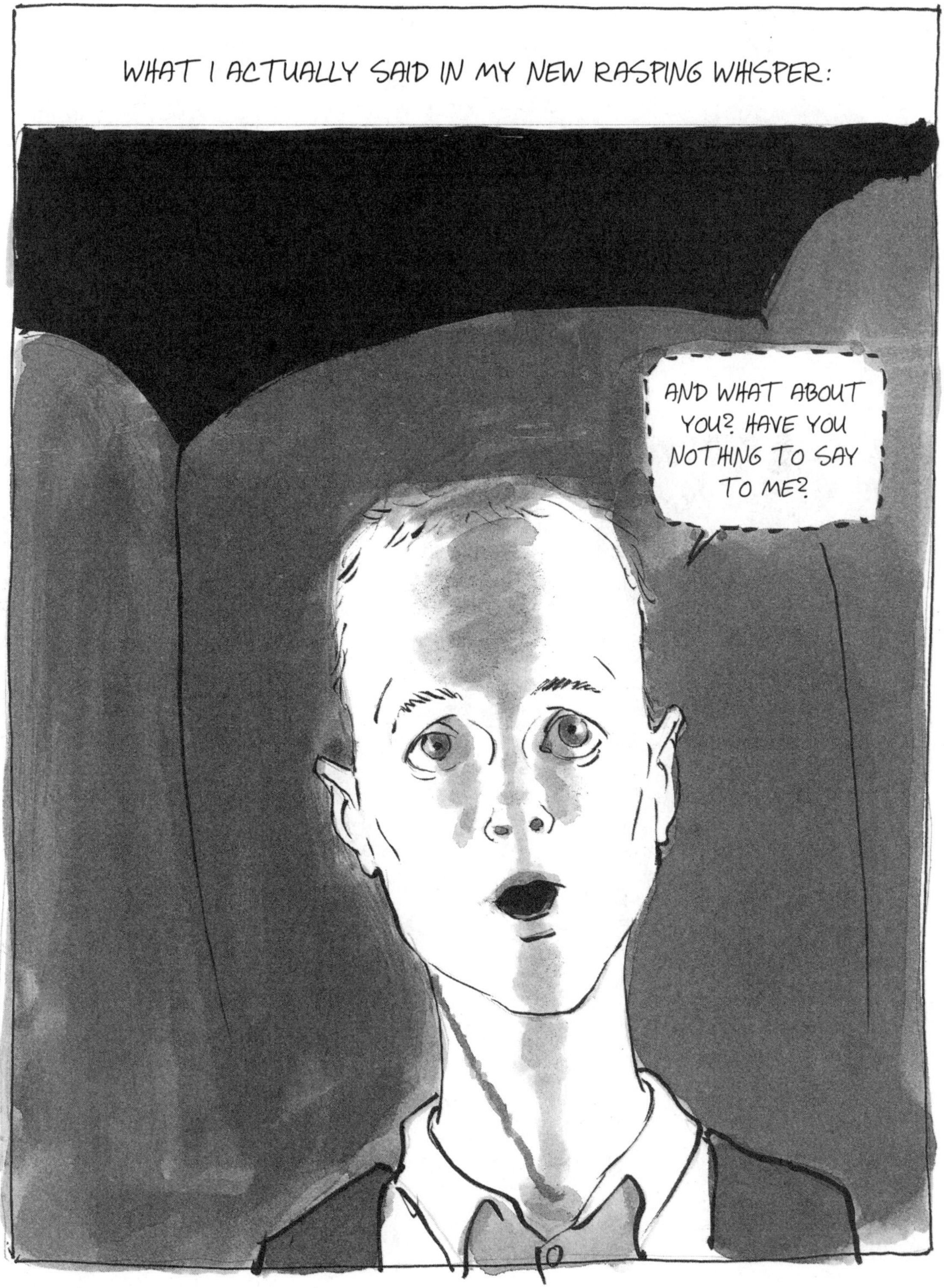
WHAT I ACTUALLY SAID IN MY NEW RASPING WHISPER:
AND WHAT ABOUT YOU? HAVE YOU NOTHING TO SAY TO ME?

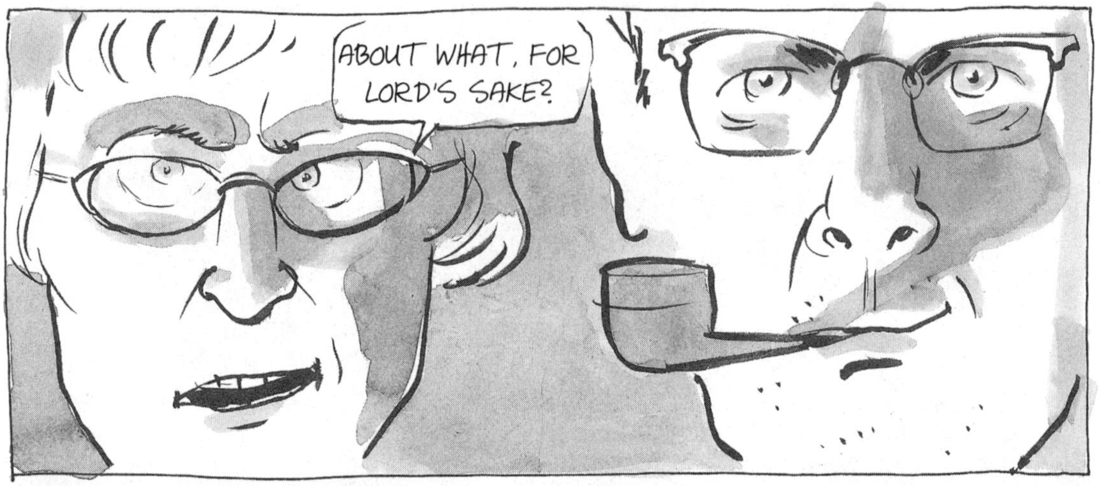
ABOUT WHAT, FOR LORD'S SAKE?

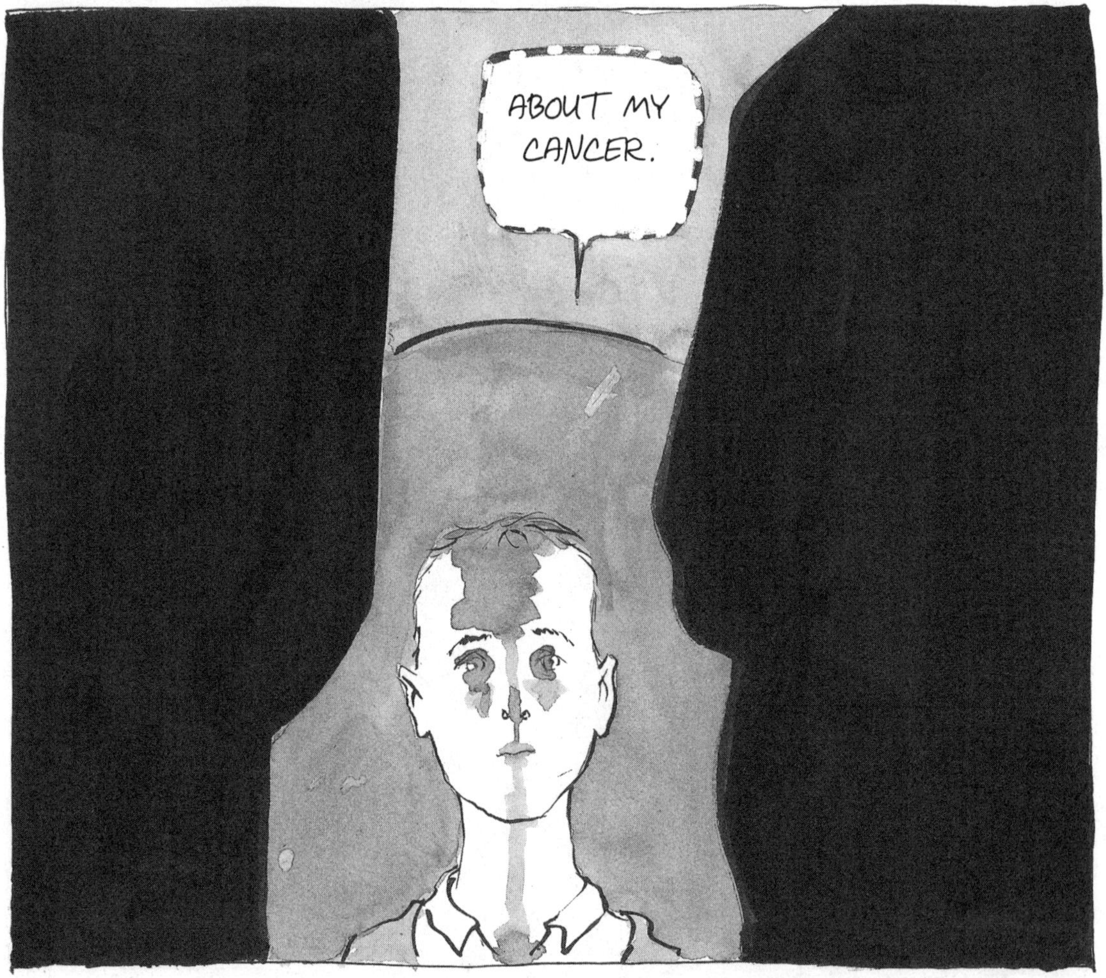
ABOUT MY CANCER.

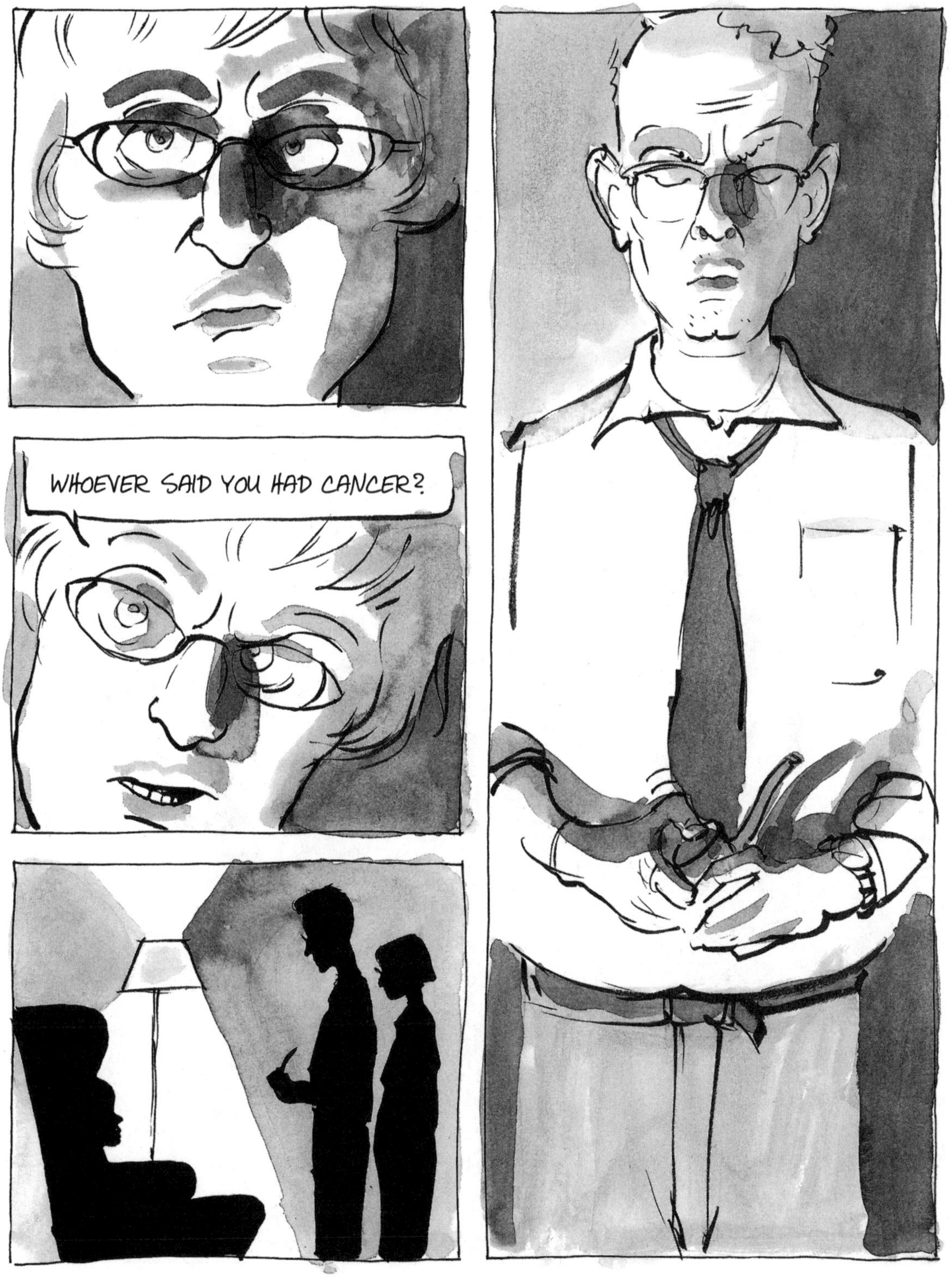
WHOEVER SAID YOU HAD CANCER?

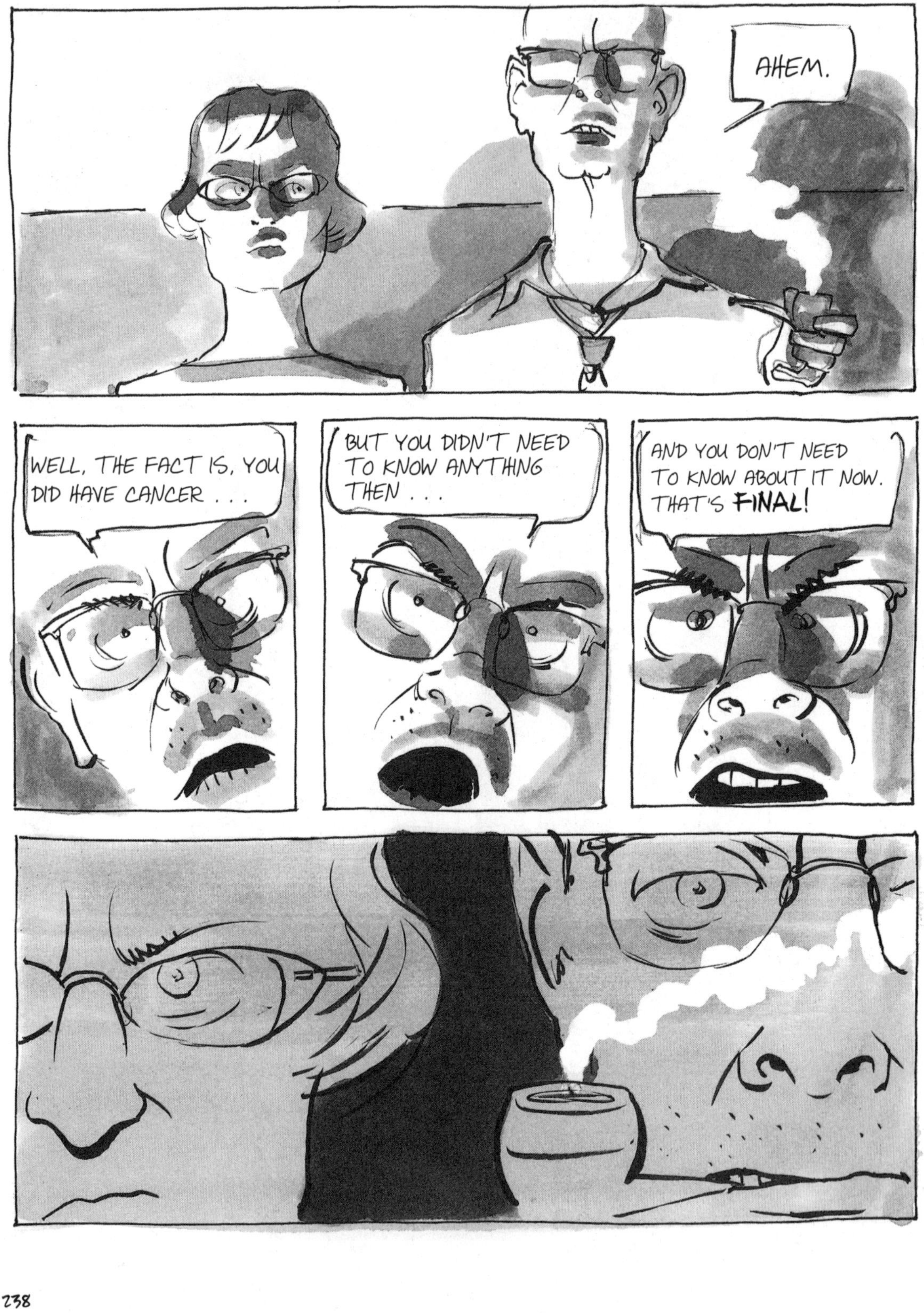
AHEM.
WELL, THE FACT IS, YOU DID HAVE CANCER . . .
BUT YOU DIDN'T NEED TO KNOW ANYTHING THEN . . .
AND YOU DON'T NEED TO KNOW ABOUT IT NOW. THAT'S FINAL!

THE ODD THING ABOUT RECURRING DREAMS IS THAT, NO MATTER HOW MANY TIMES YOU DREAM THE SAME THING, IT ALWAYS TAKES YOU BY SURPRISE.

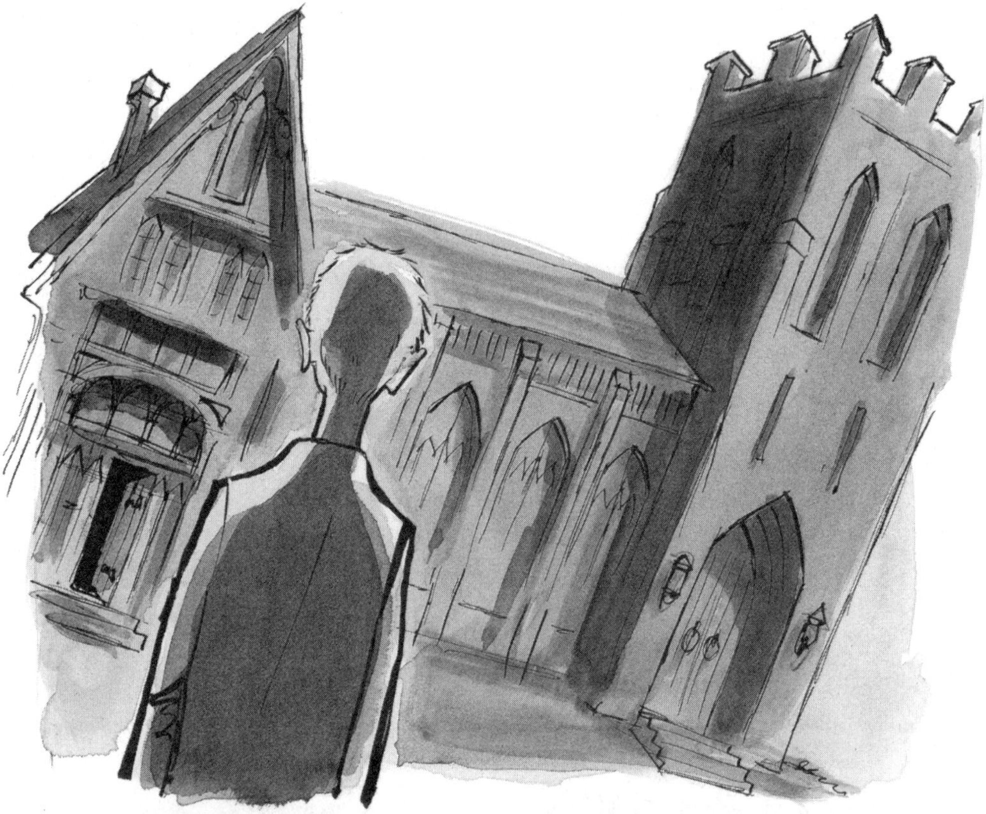

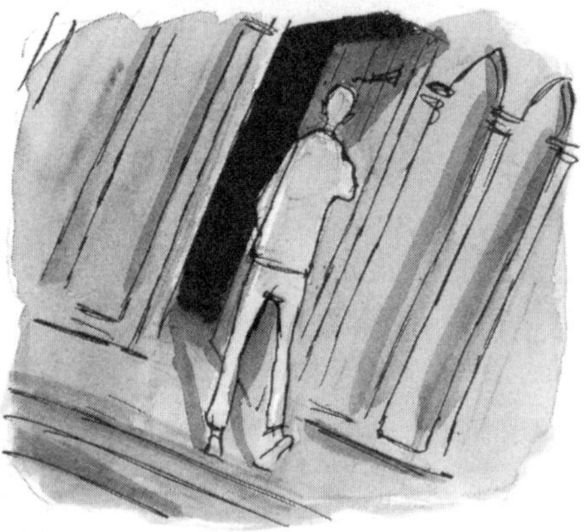

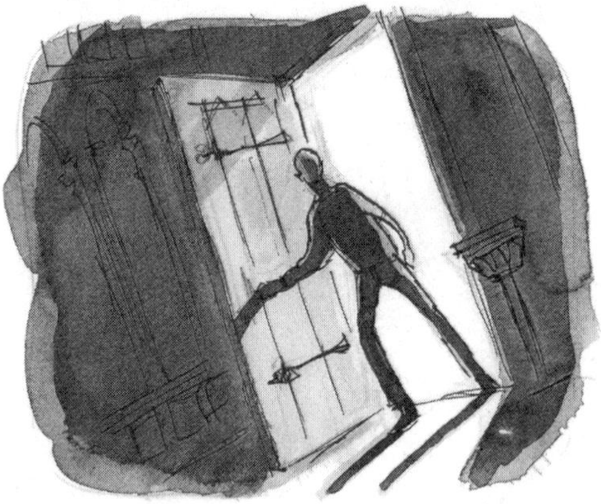

FOR A YEAR, SEVERAL NIGHTS A WEEK, I HAD TRAVELED THE SAME ROUTE, THROUGH THE SAME SUCCESSION OF ROOMS . . .

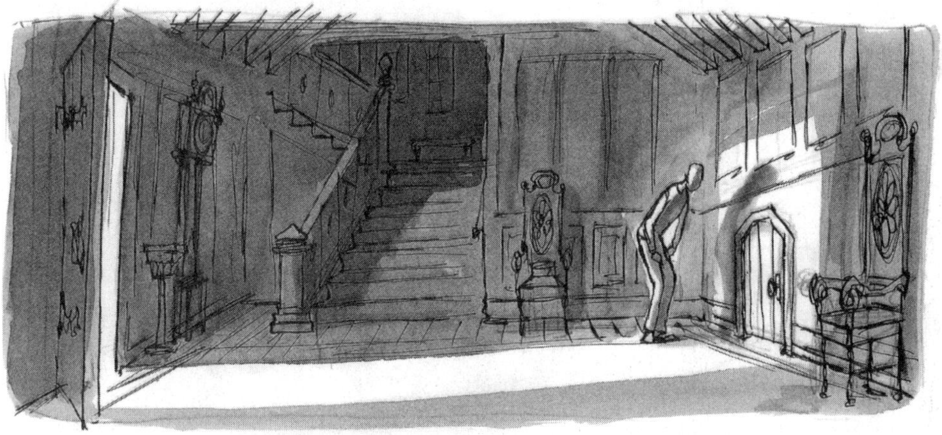

. . . NARROWING PASSAGEWAYS

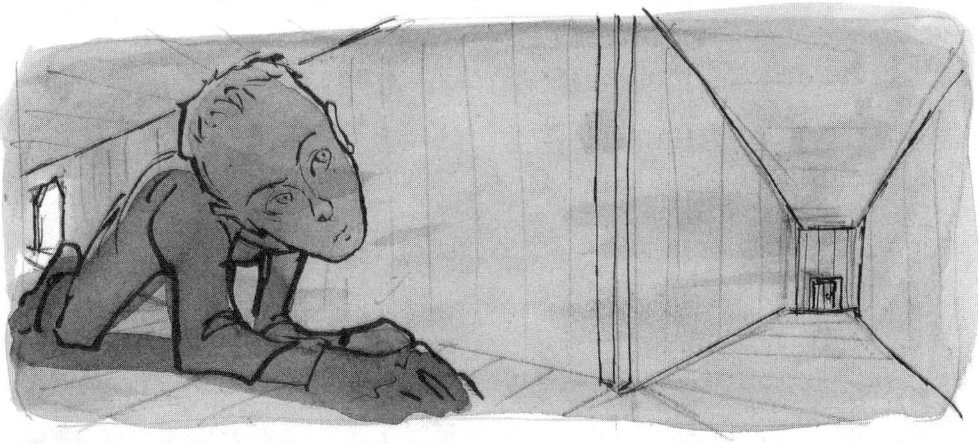

AND DOORS OF DIMINISHING SIZE . . .

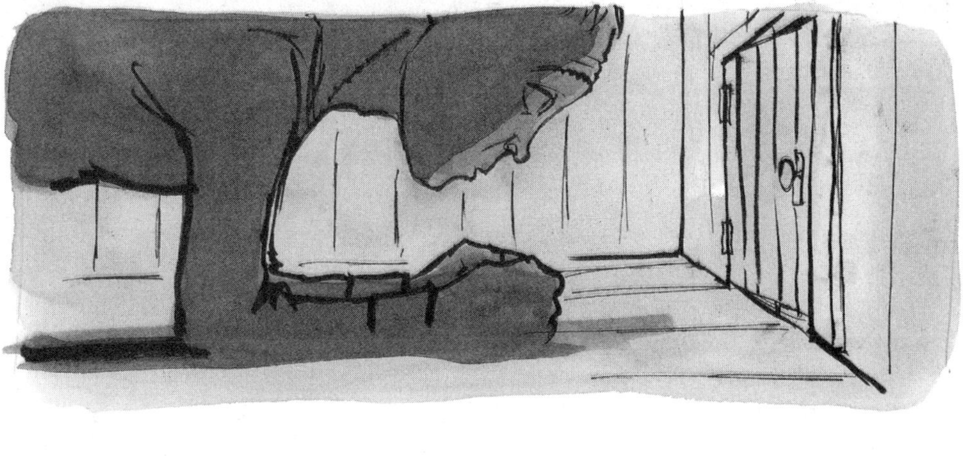

. . . EMERGING EACH TIME, WITH THE SAME SENSE OF DISBELIEF AND DESPAIR, INTO THAT TEMPLE WHOSE GUTS HAD BEEN BOMBED.

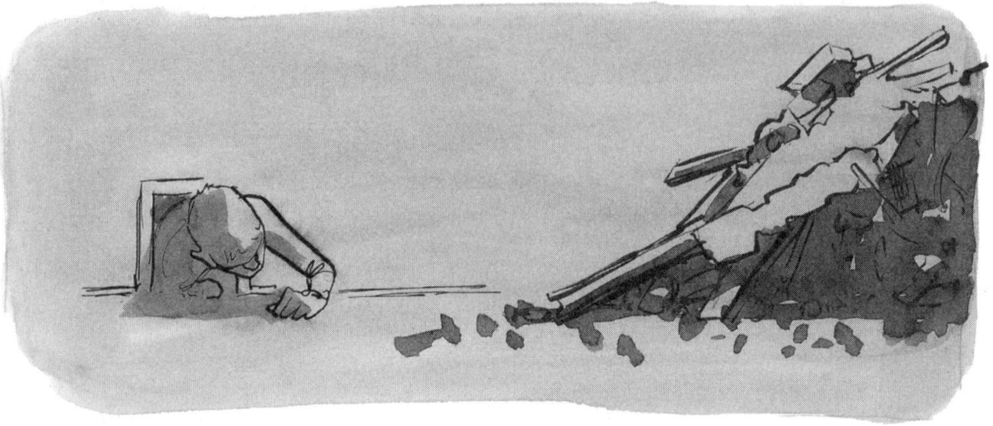

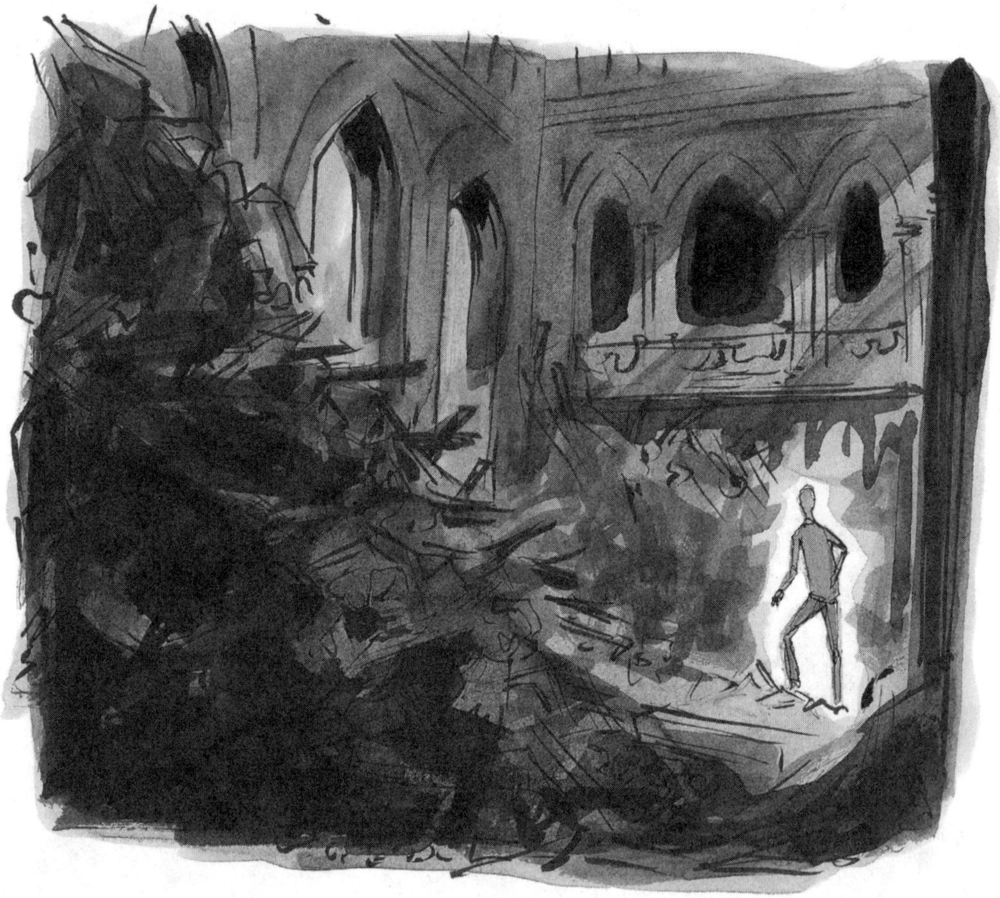

I WAS FIFTEEN

AUGUST 27
3 pm

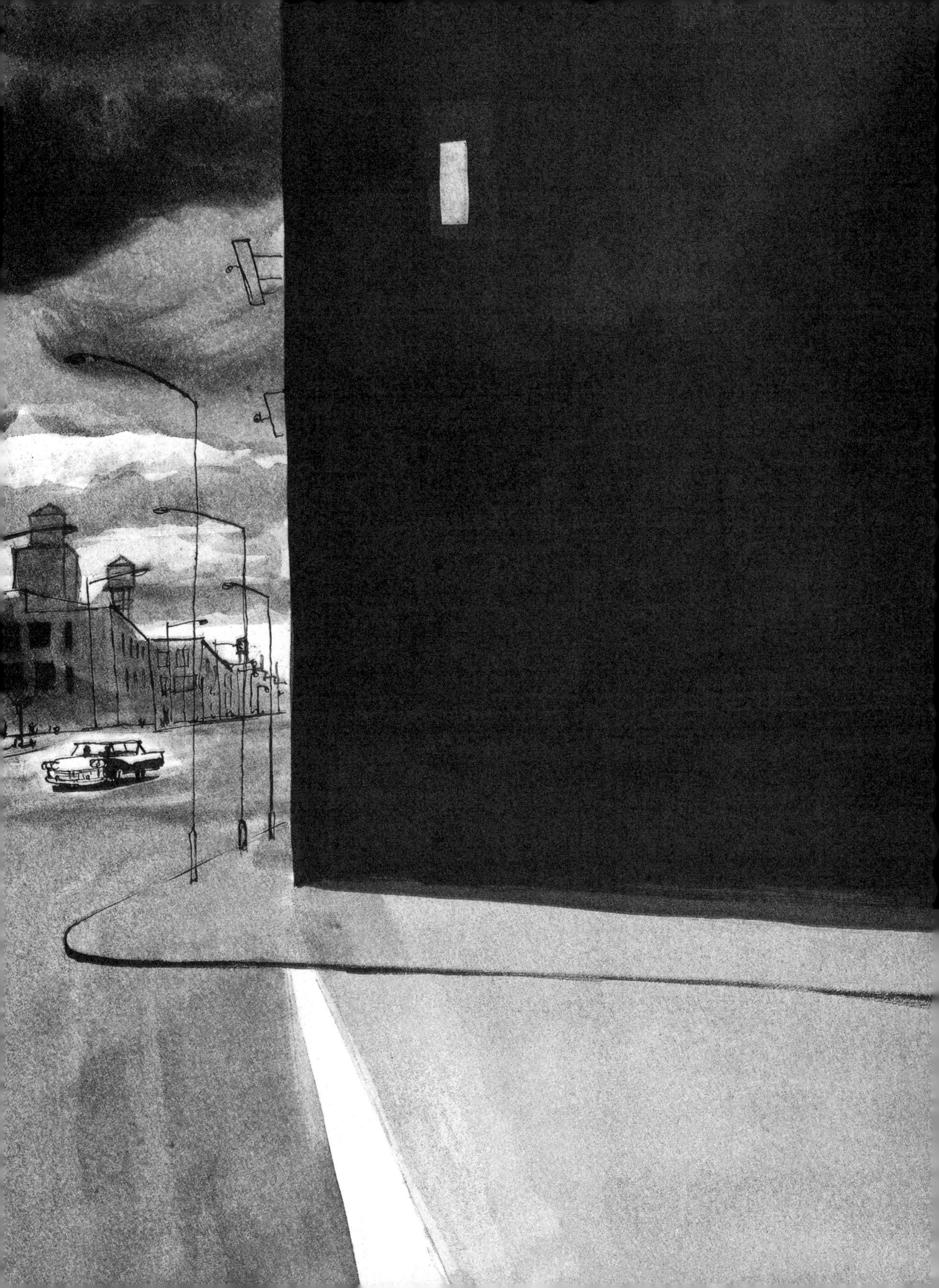

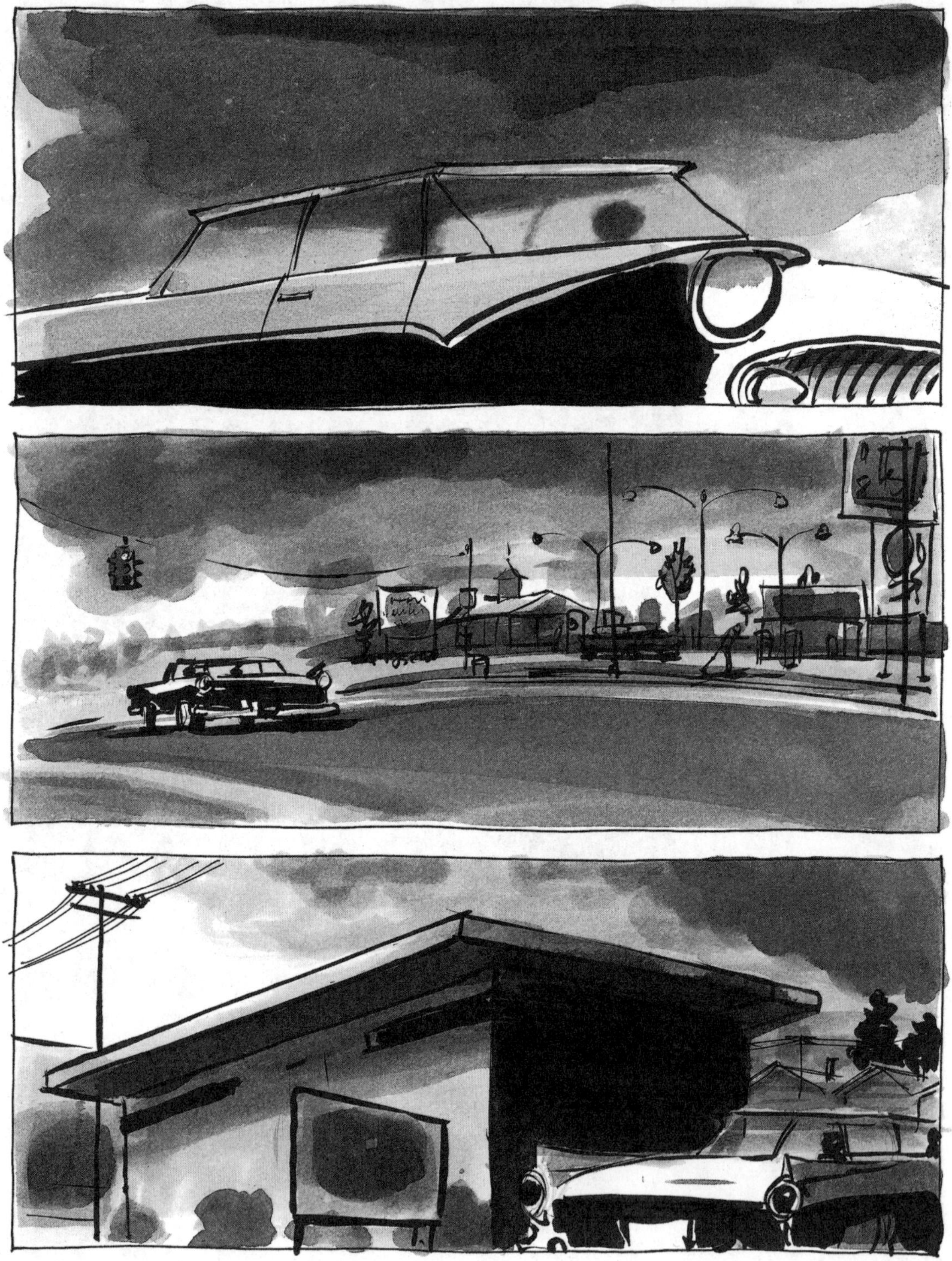

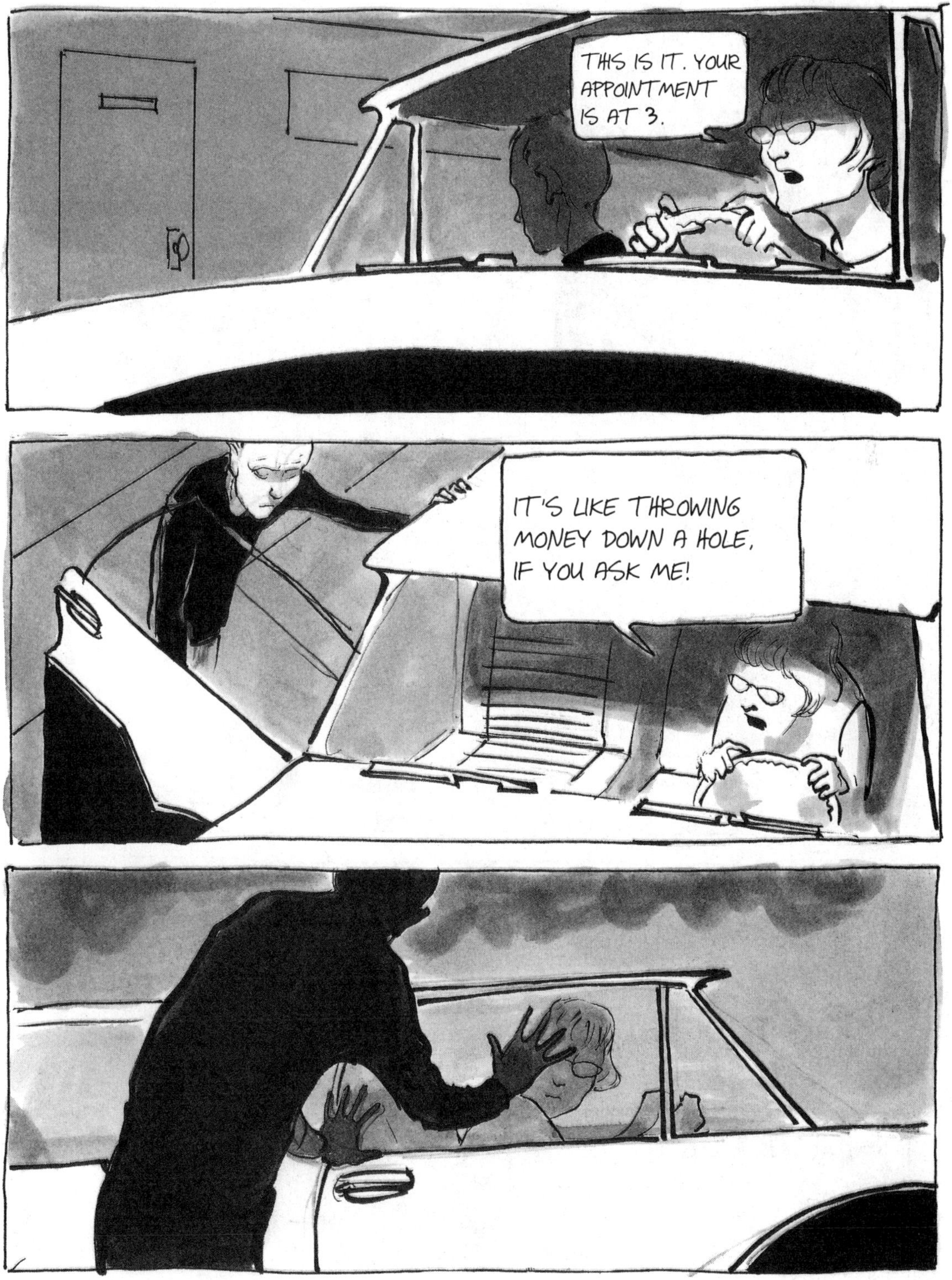
THIS IS IT. YOUR APPOINTMENT IS AT 3.
IT'S LIKE THROWING MONEY DOWN A HOLE, IF YOU ASK ME!

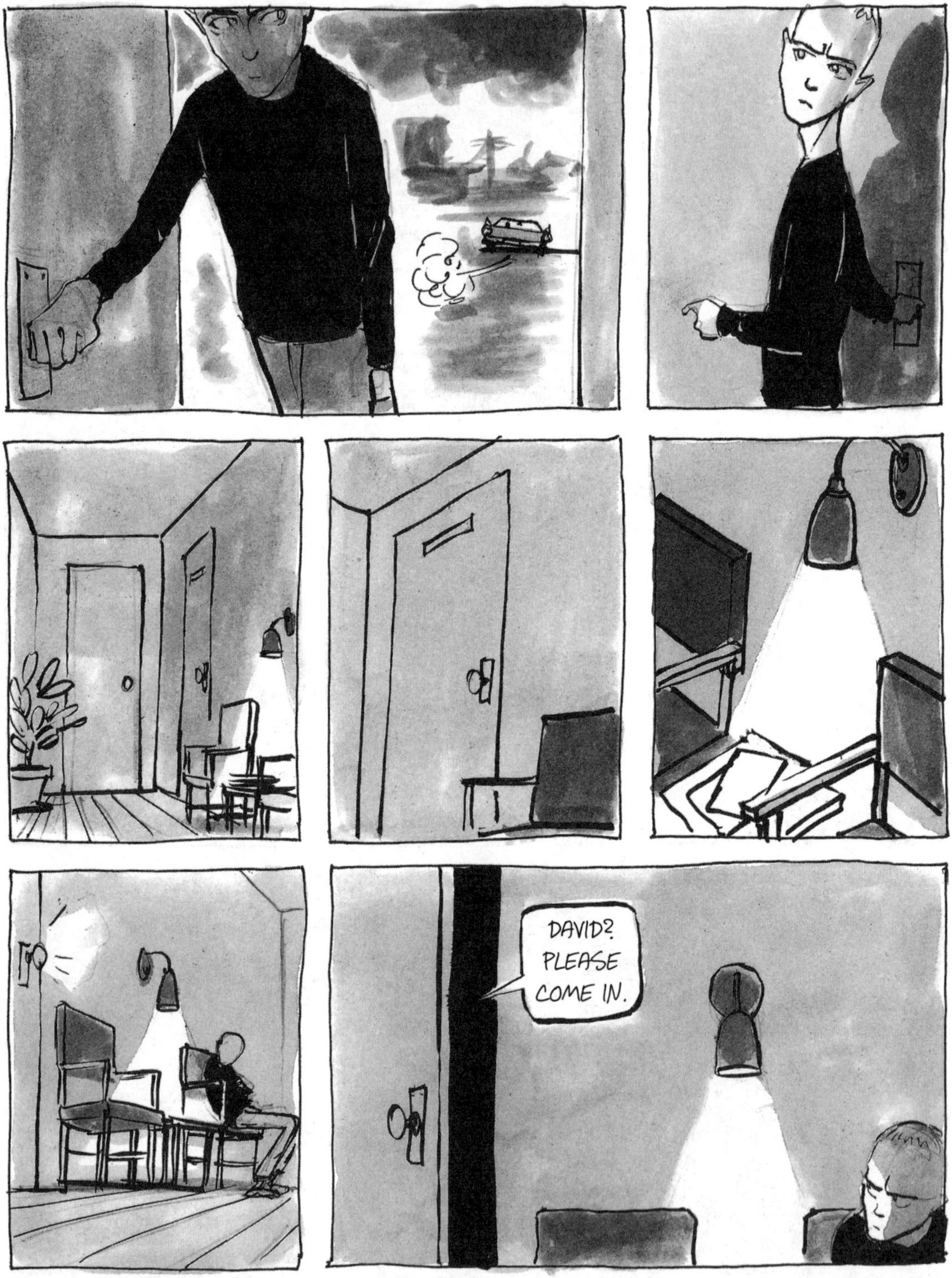
DAVID?
PLEASE
COME IN.

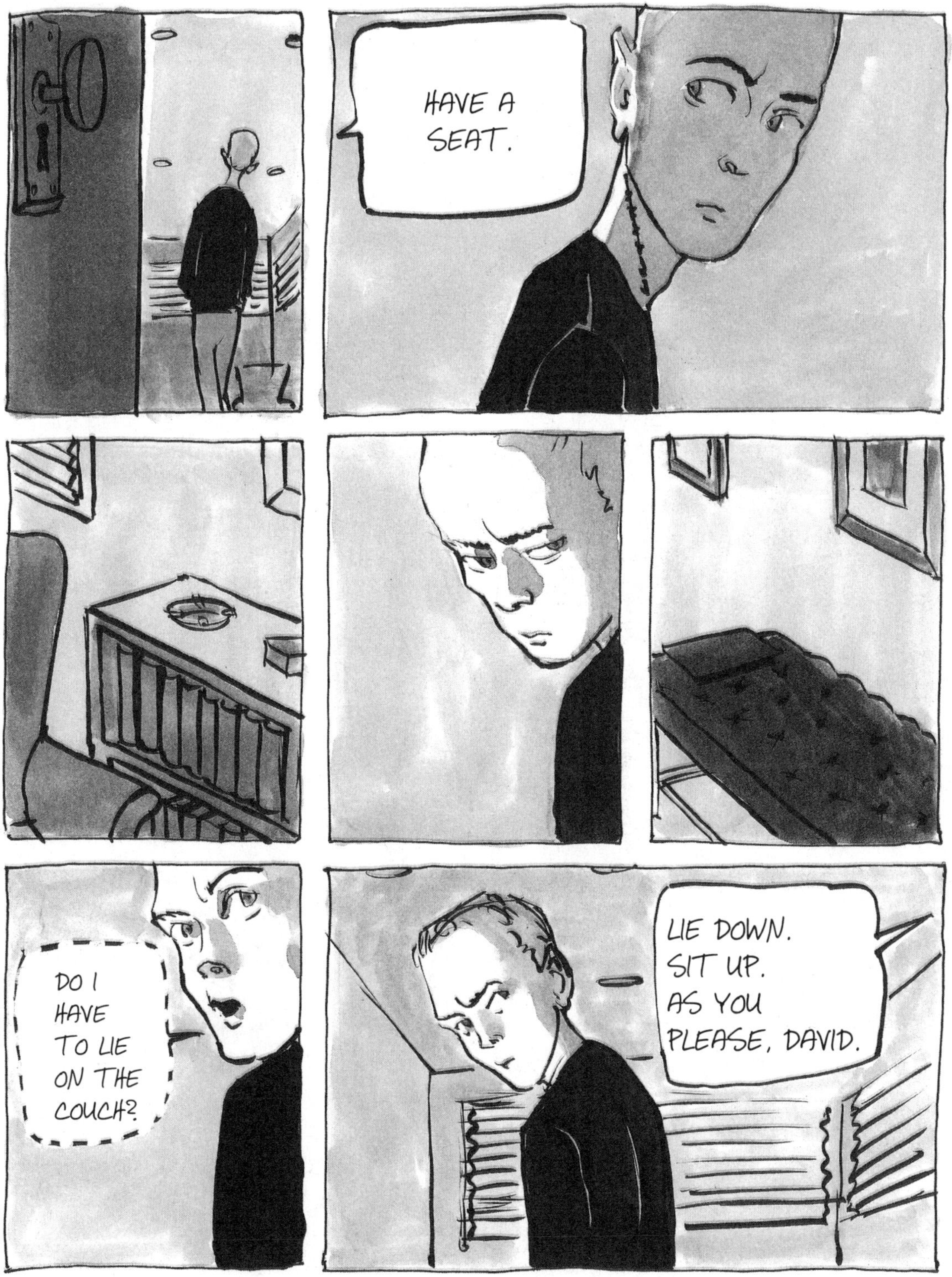
HAVE A SEAT.
DO I HAVE TO LIE ON THE COUCH?
LIE DOWN. SIT UP. AS YOU PLEASE, DAVID.

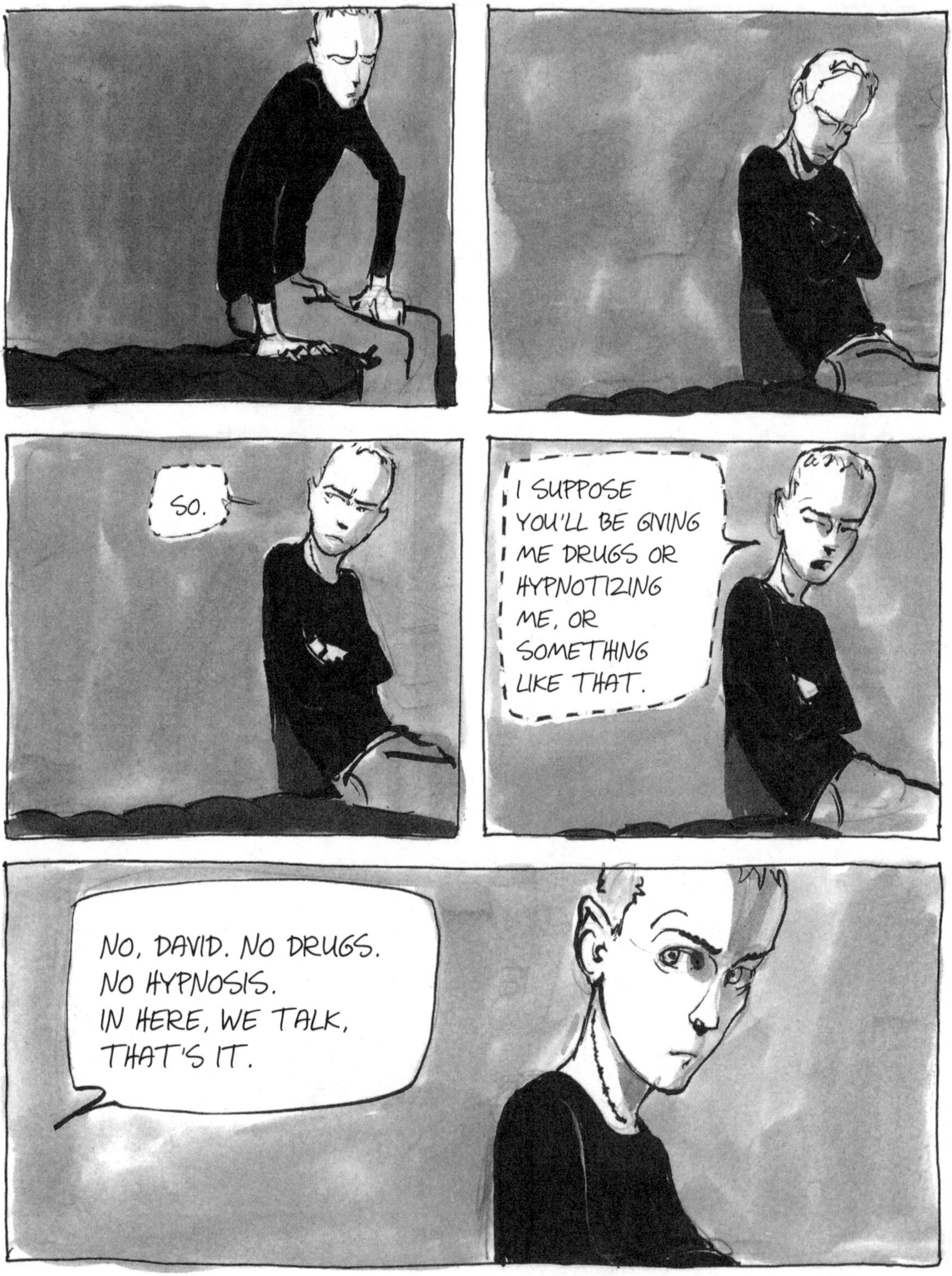
SO.
I SUPPOSE YOU'LL BE GIVING ME DRUGS OR HYPNOTIZING ME, OR SOMETHING LIKE THAT.
NO, DAVID. NO DRUGS. NO HYPNOSIS. IN HERE, WE TALK, THAT'S IT.

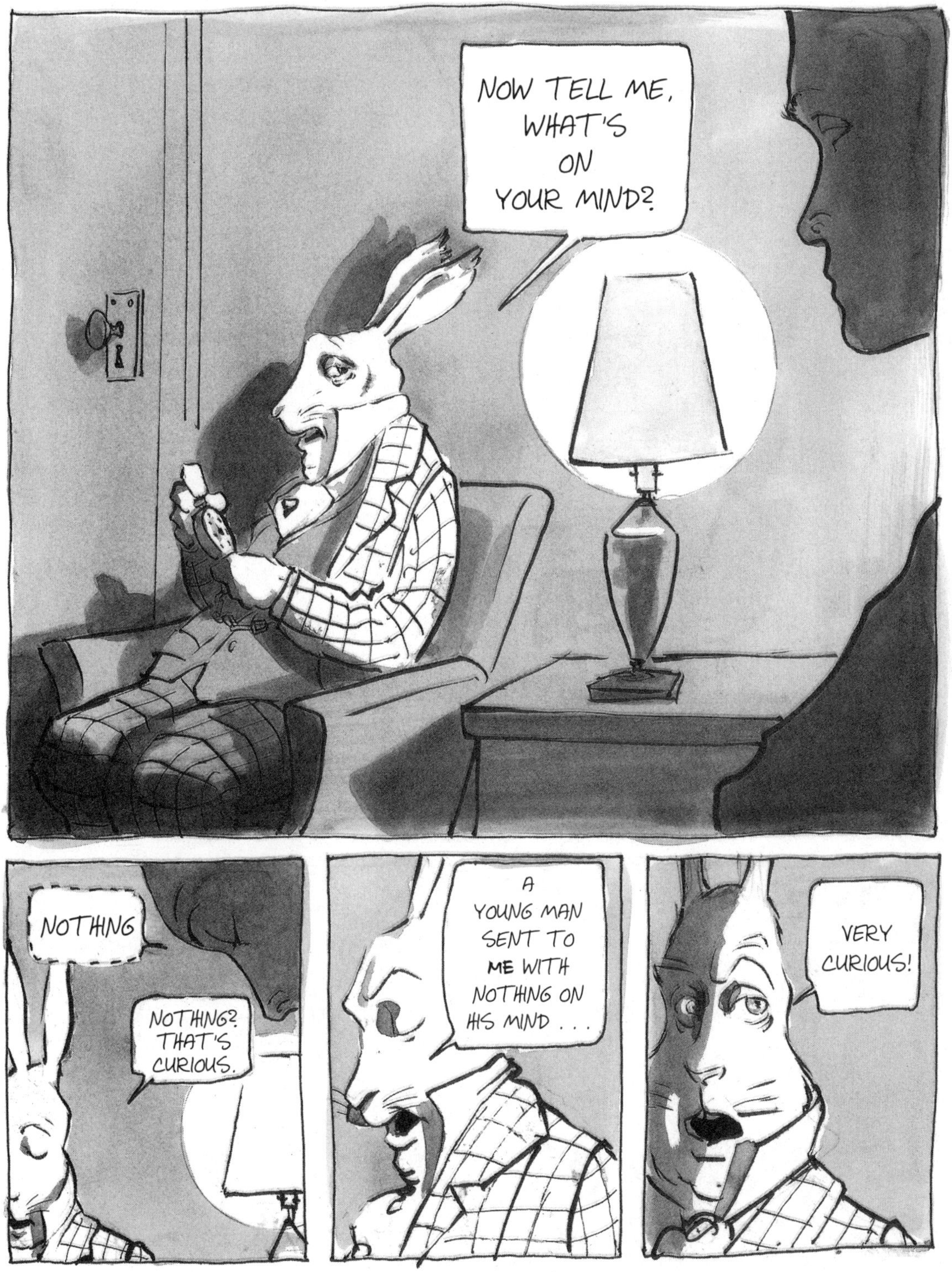
NOW TELL ME, WHAT'S ON YOUR MIND?
NOTHING
NOTHING? THAT'S CURIOUS.
A YOUNG MAN SENT TO ME WITH NOTHING ON HIS MIND . . .
VERY CURIOUS!

YOUR MOTHER SAYS YOU'VE BEEN ACTING CRAZY, DOING CRAZY THINGS. TRUE?

I GUESS SO.

NONSENSE.

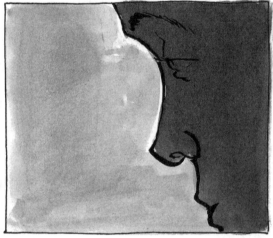

A BOY WHO HAS HAD CANCER . . . A BOY WHOSE PARENTS AND DOCTORS DID NOT TELL HIM HE HAD CANCER . . . A BOY WHO HAD TO FIND OUT THE TRUTH ON HIS OWN . . . IS THIS CRAZY?

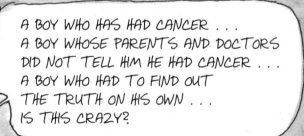

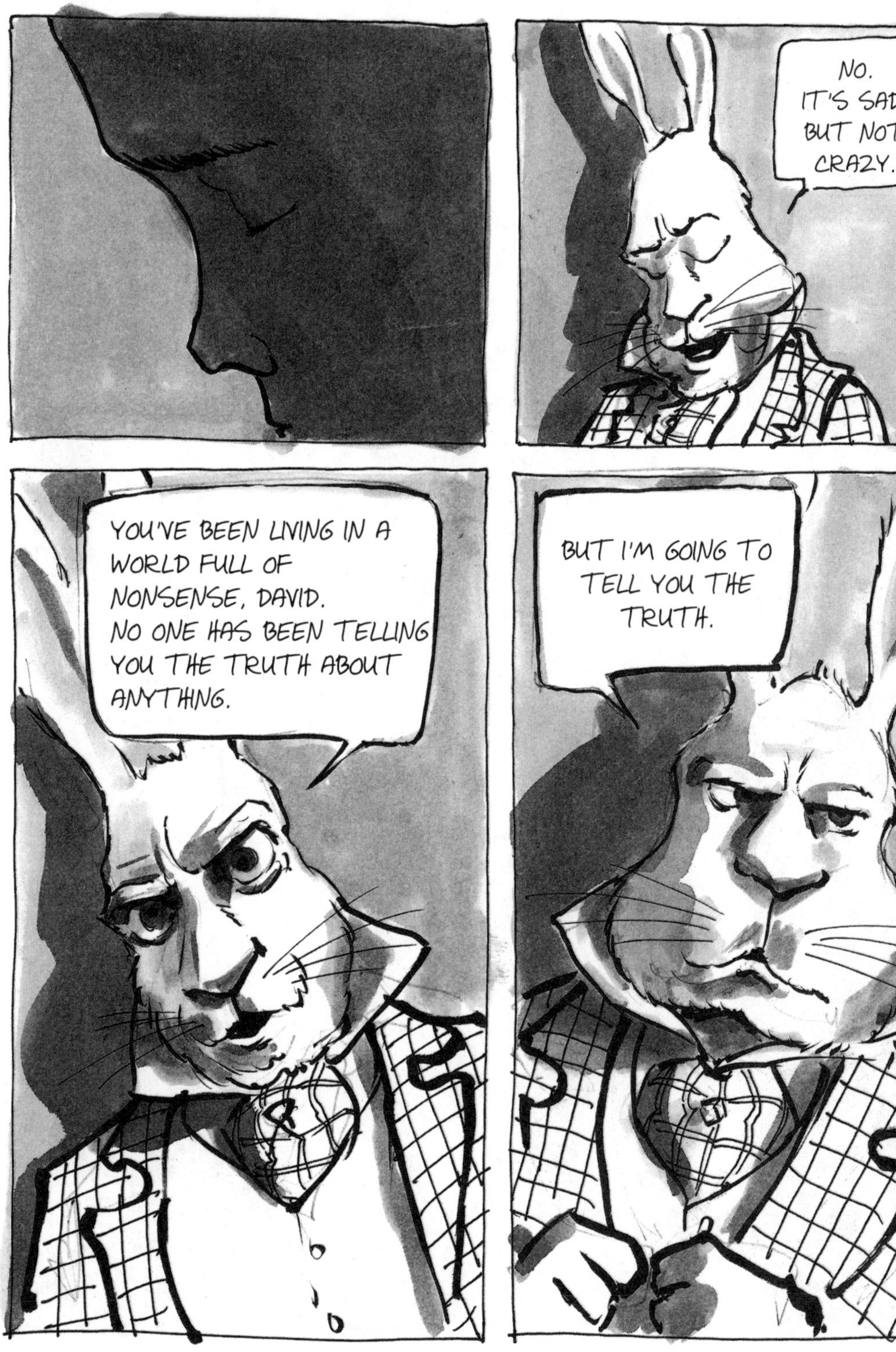
NO. IT'S SAD, BUT NOT CRAZY.
YOU'VE BEEN LIVING IN A WORLD FULL OF NONSENSE, DAVID. NO ONE HAS BEEN TELLING YOU THE TRUTH ABOUT ANYTHING.
BUT I'M GOING TO TELL YOU THE TRUTH.

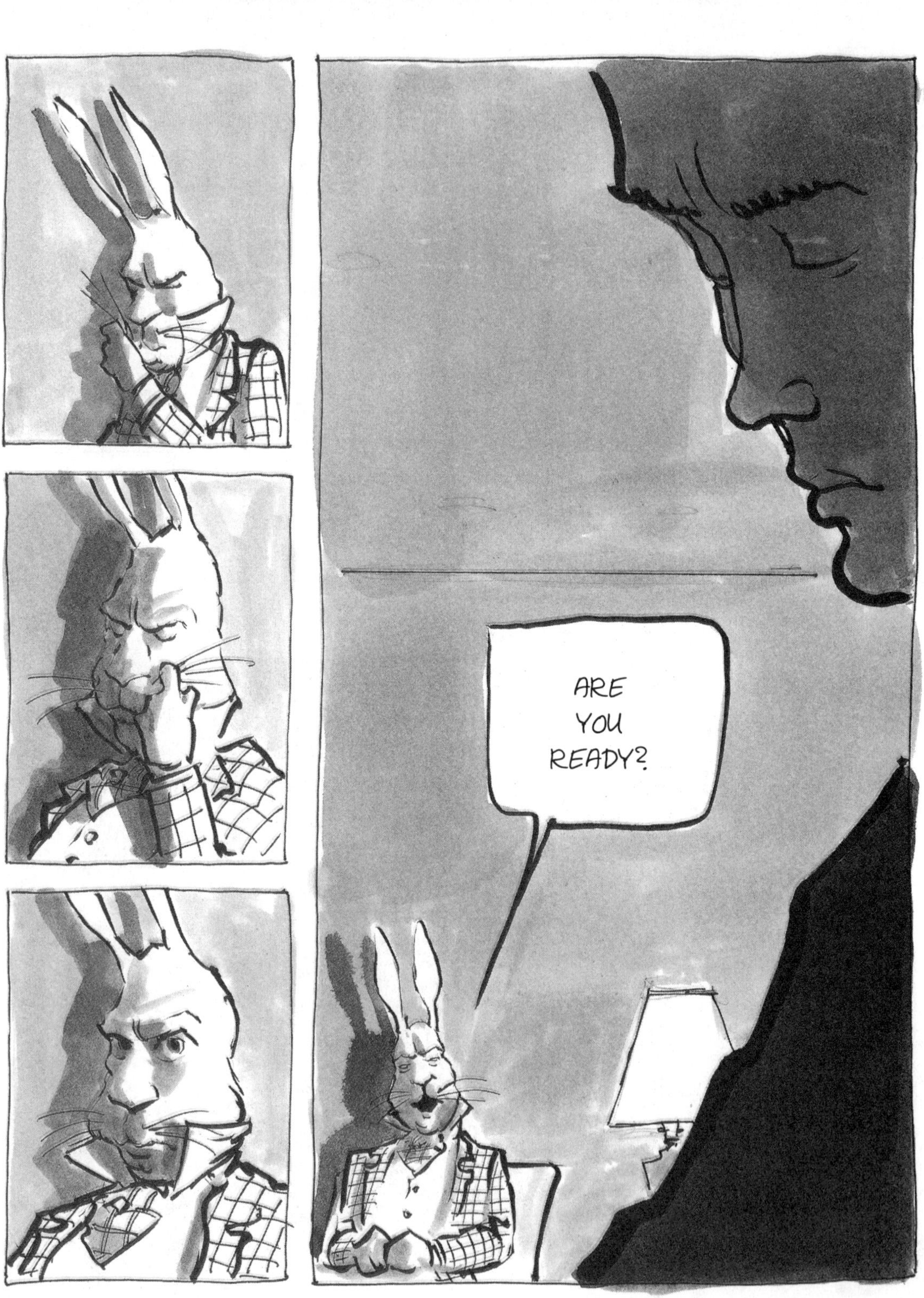
ARE YOU READY?

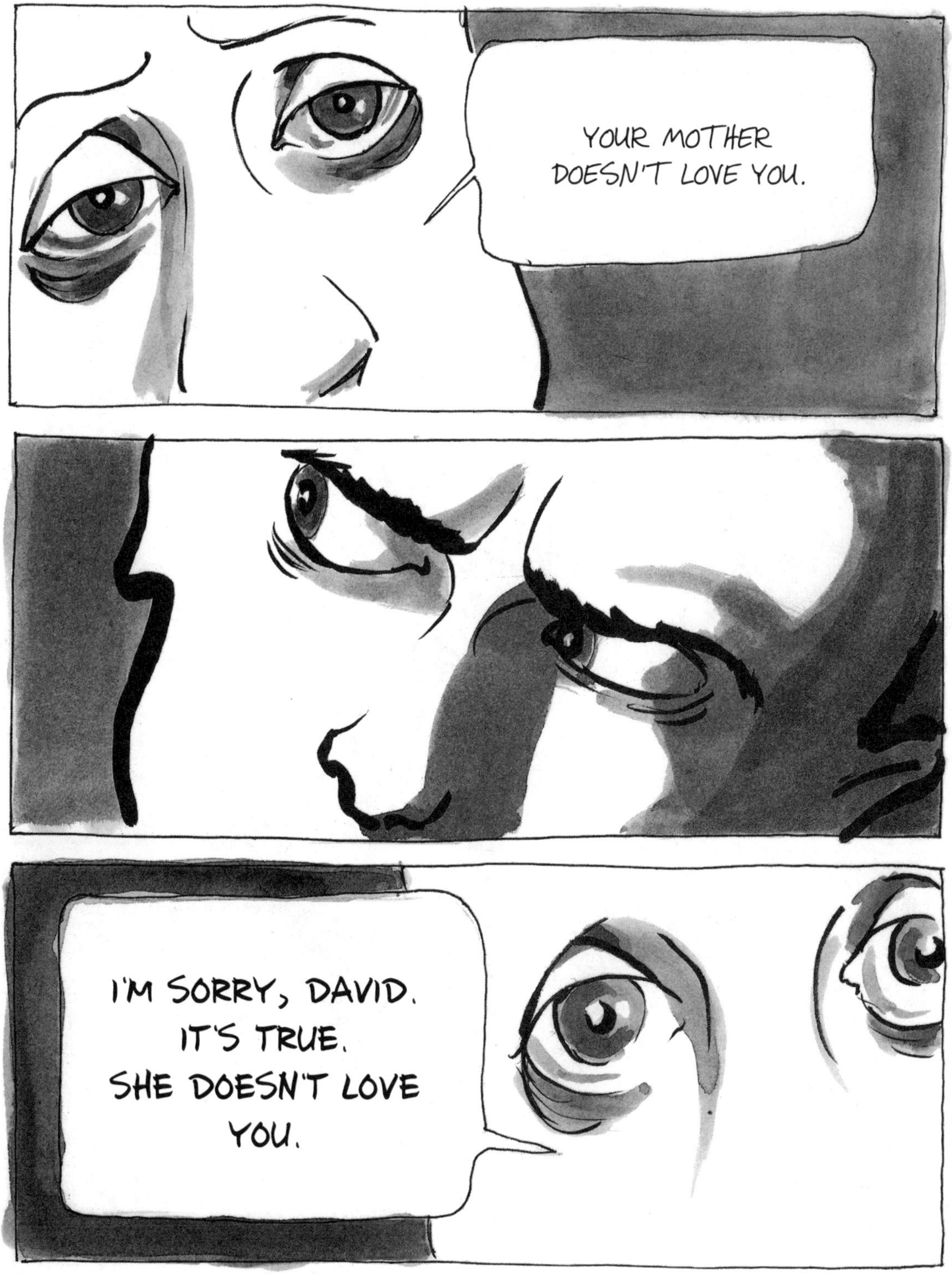
YOUR MOTHER DOESN'T LOVE YOU.
I'M SORRY, DAVID. IT'S TRUE. SHE DOESN'T LOVE YOU.

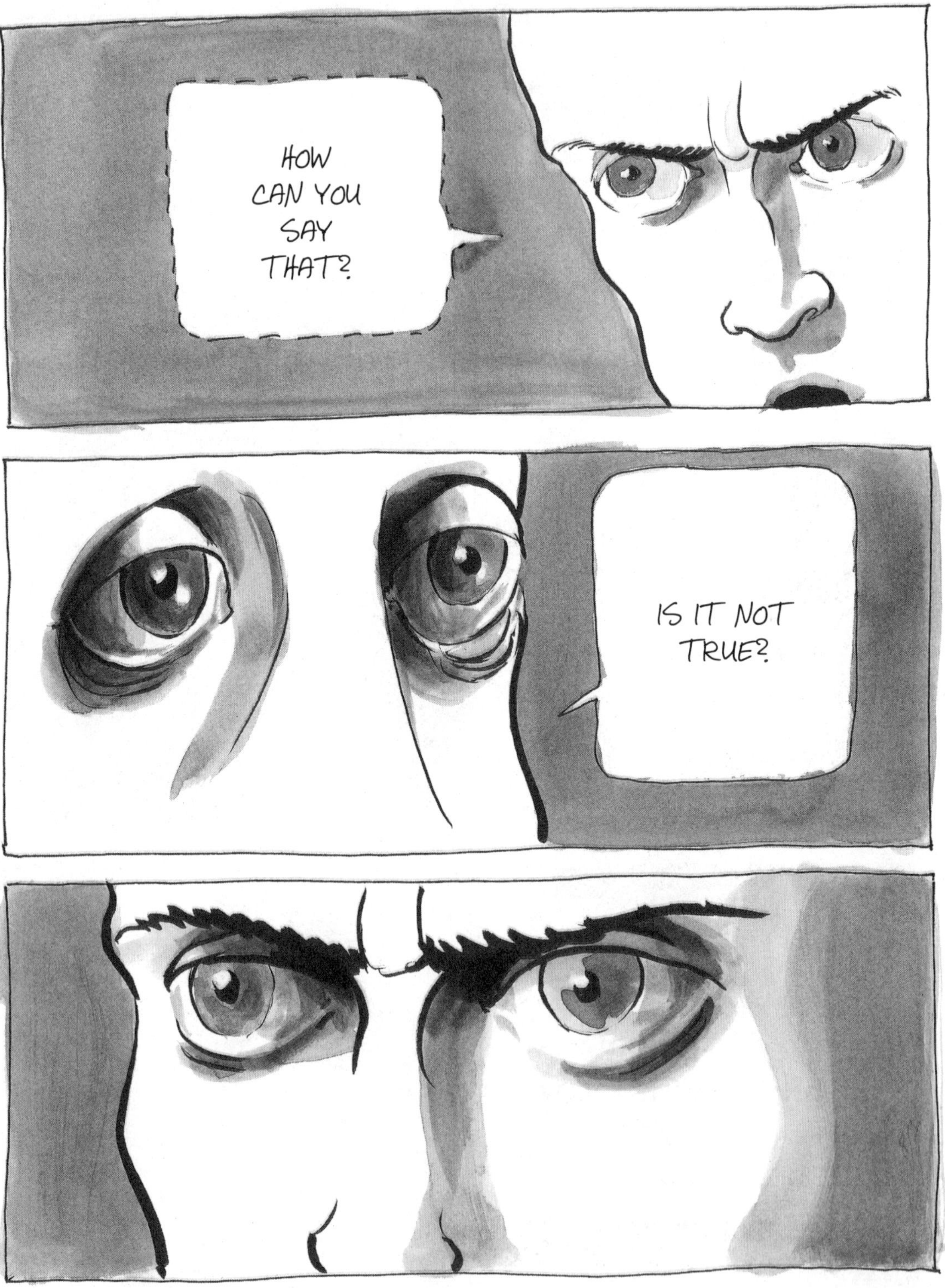
HOW CAN YOU SAY THAT?
IS IT NOT TRUE?

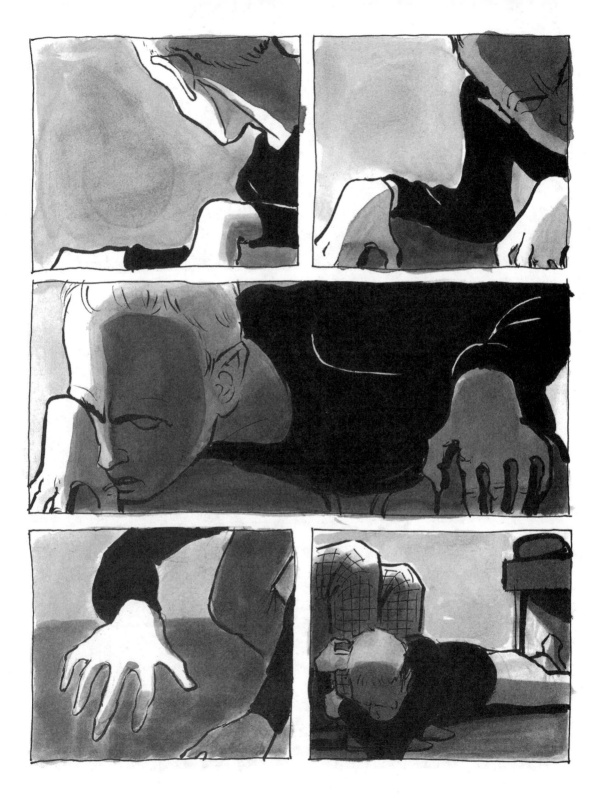

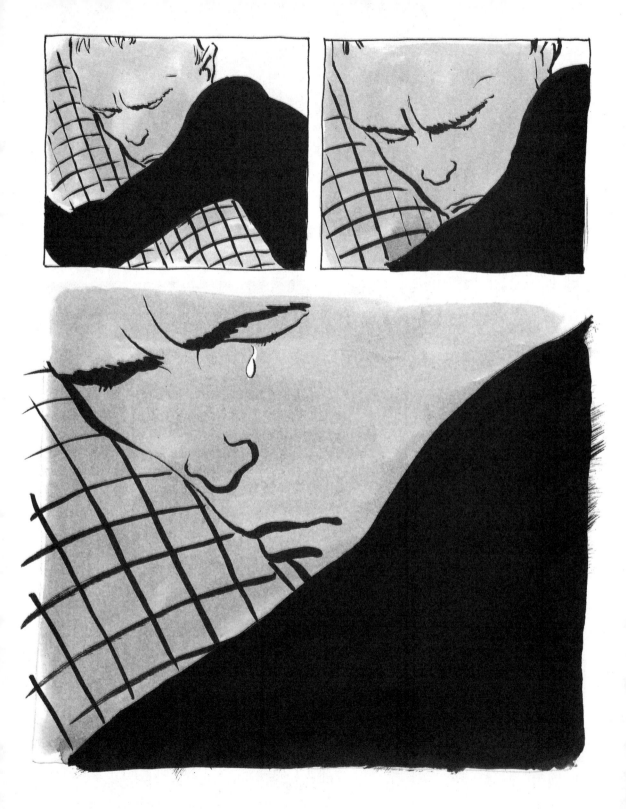

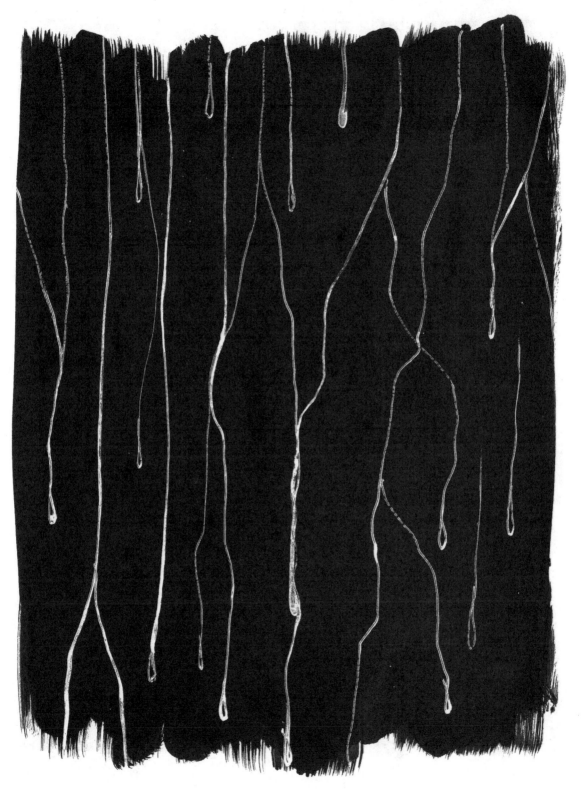

259

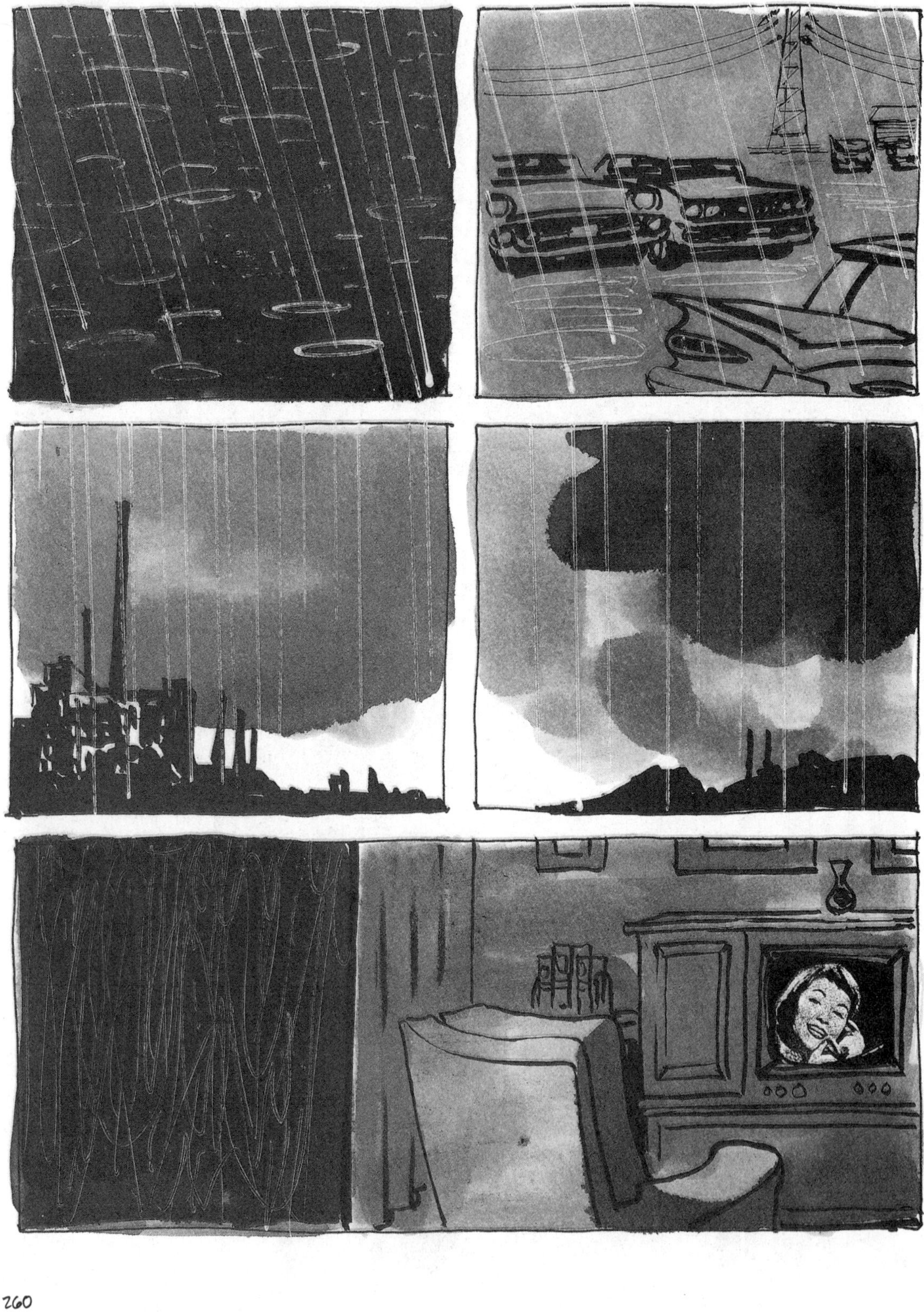

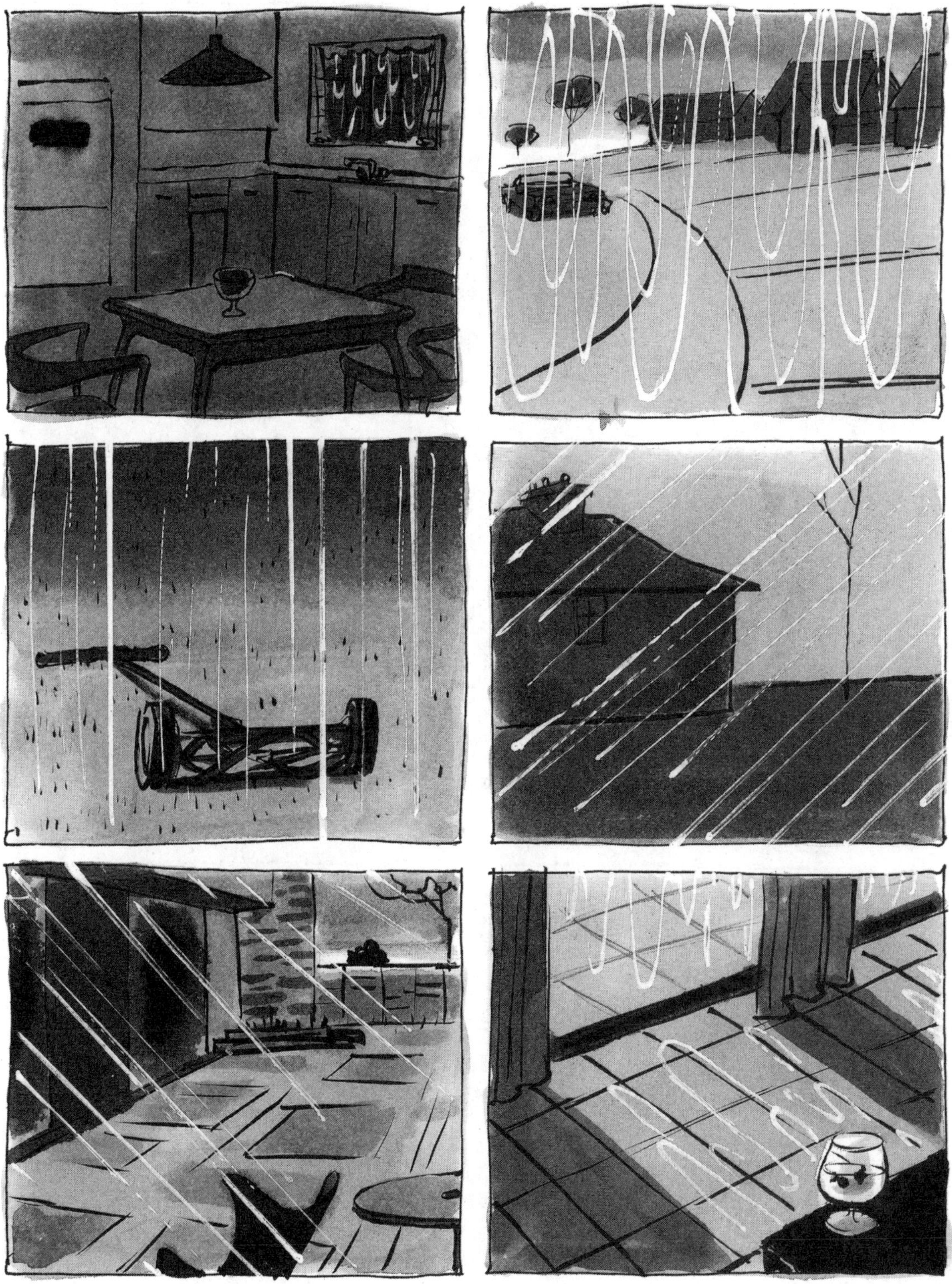

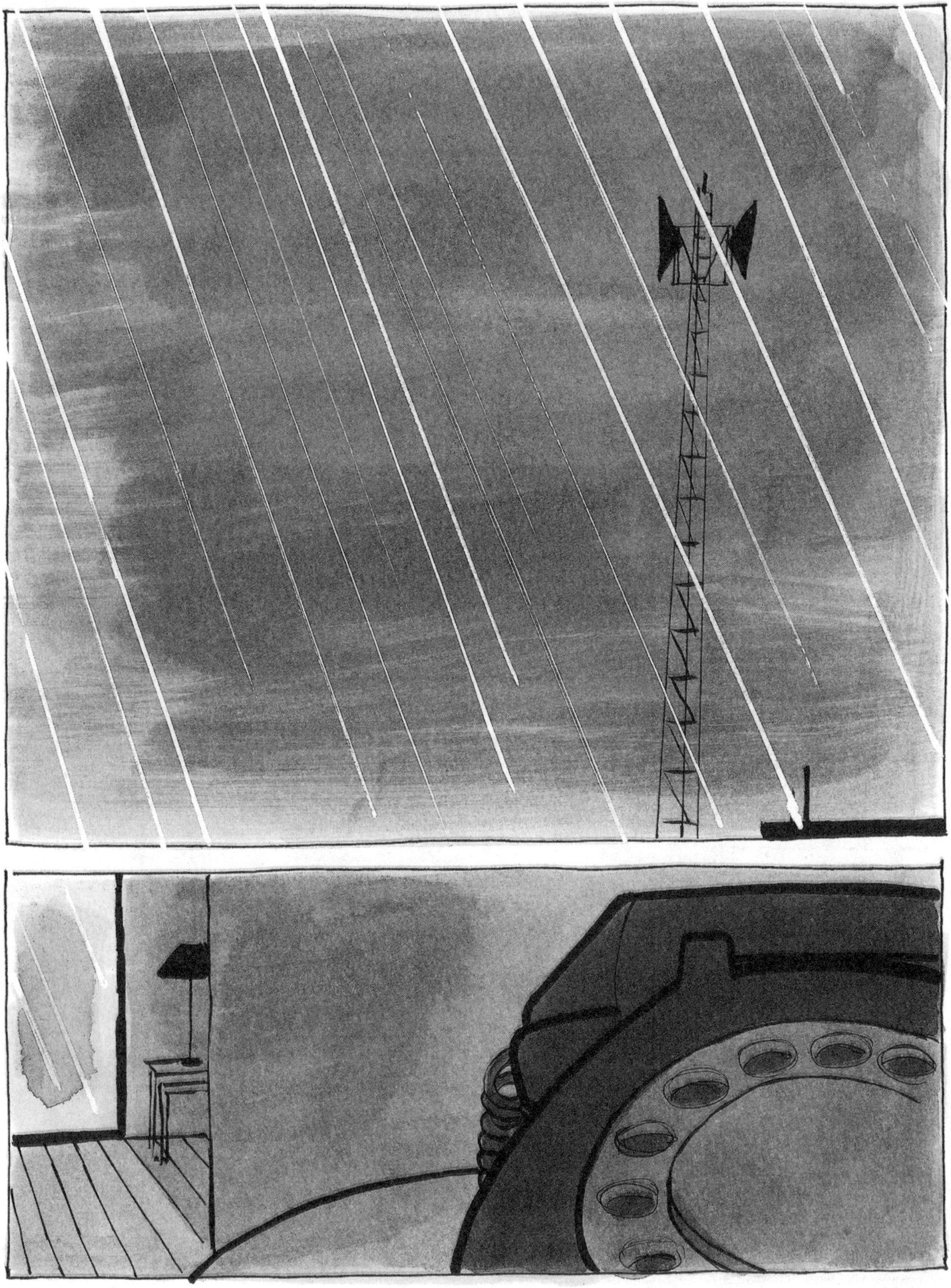

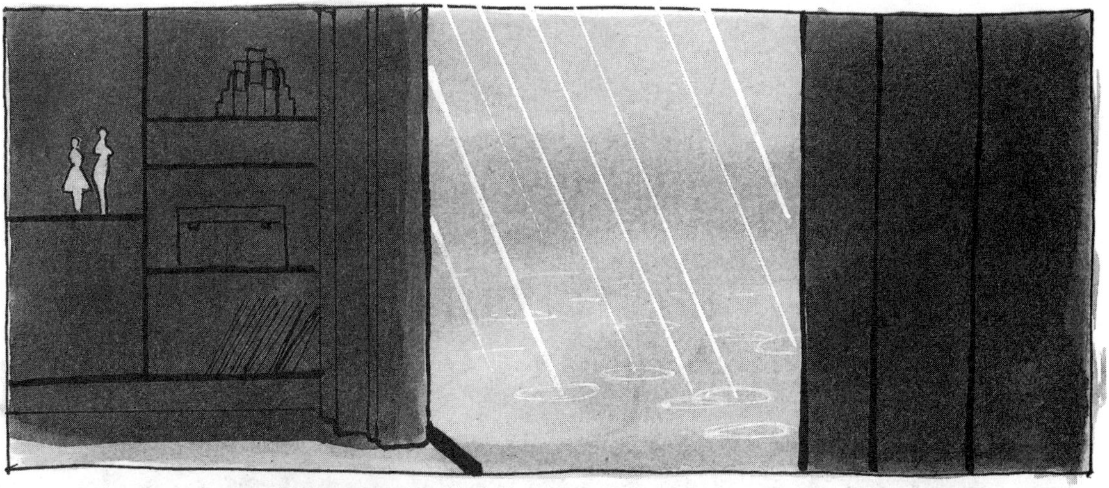

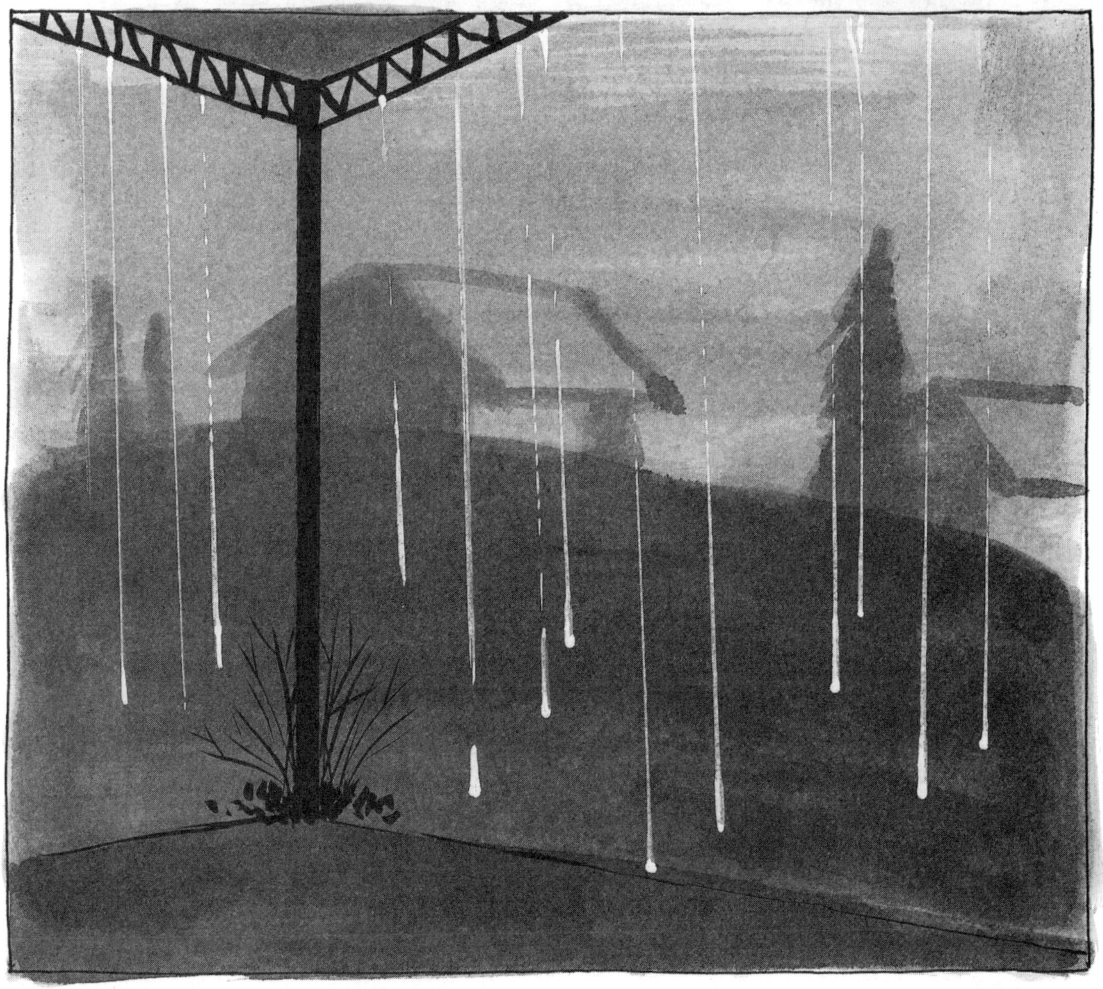

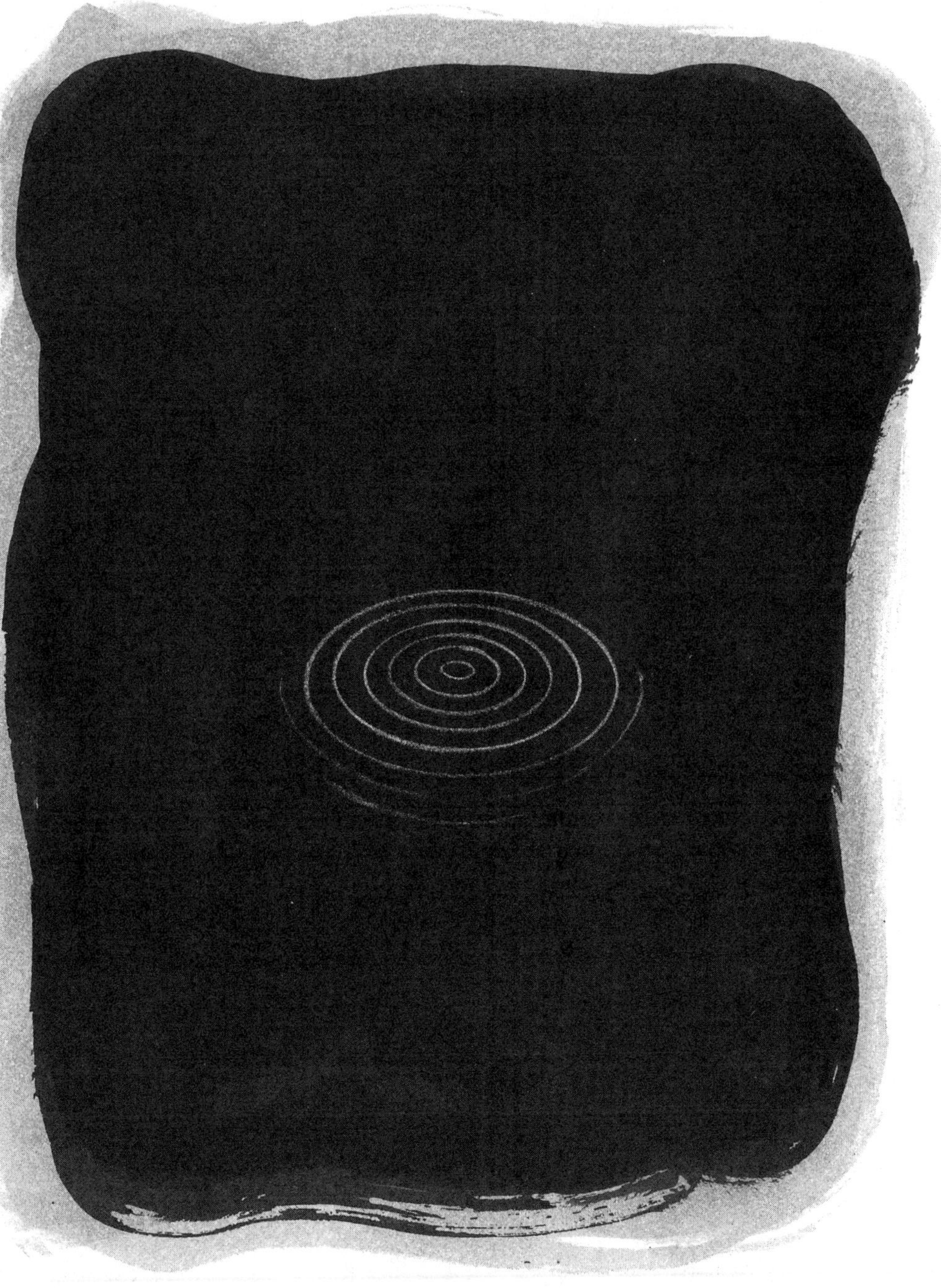

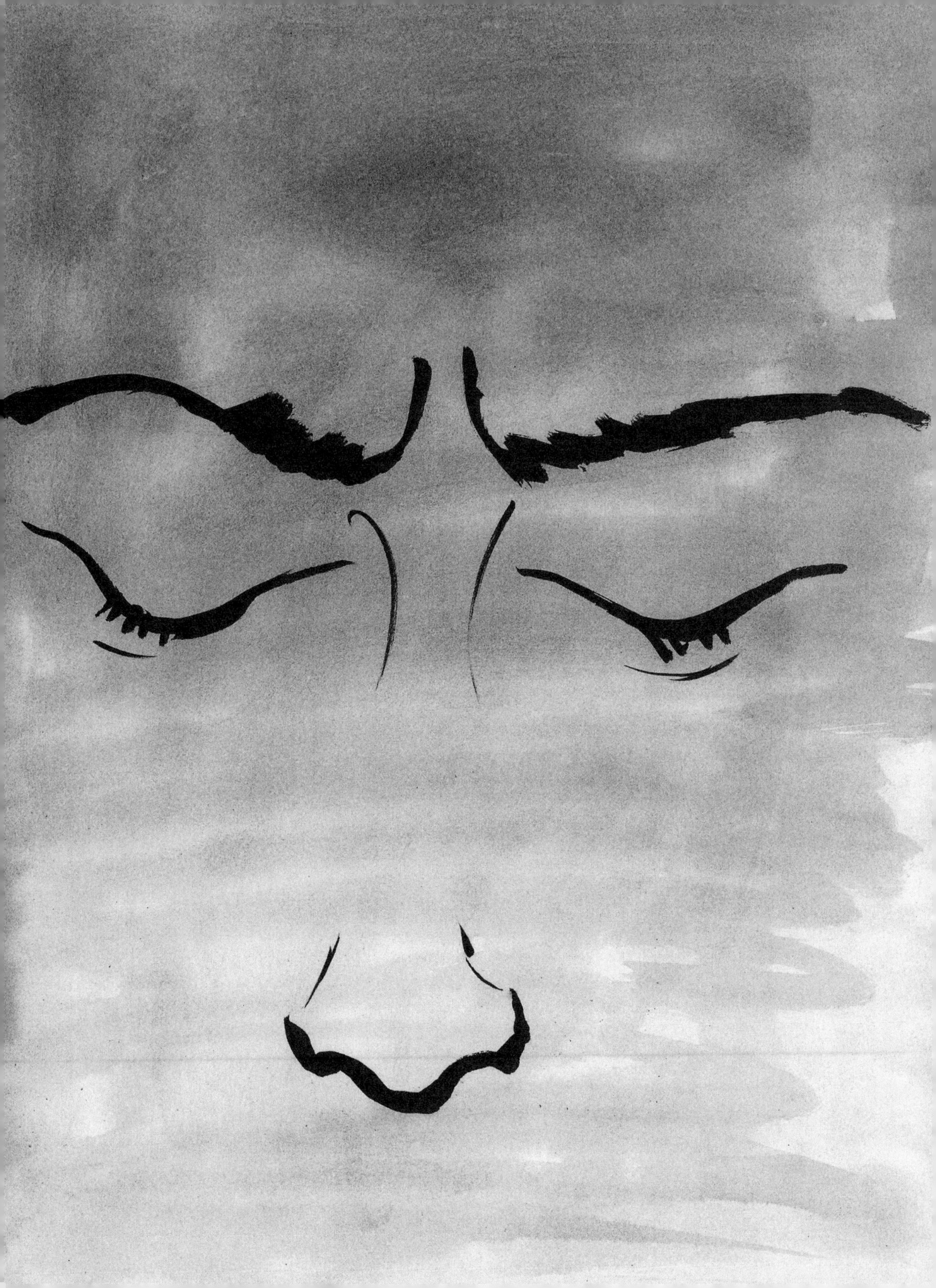

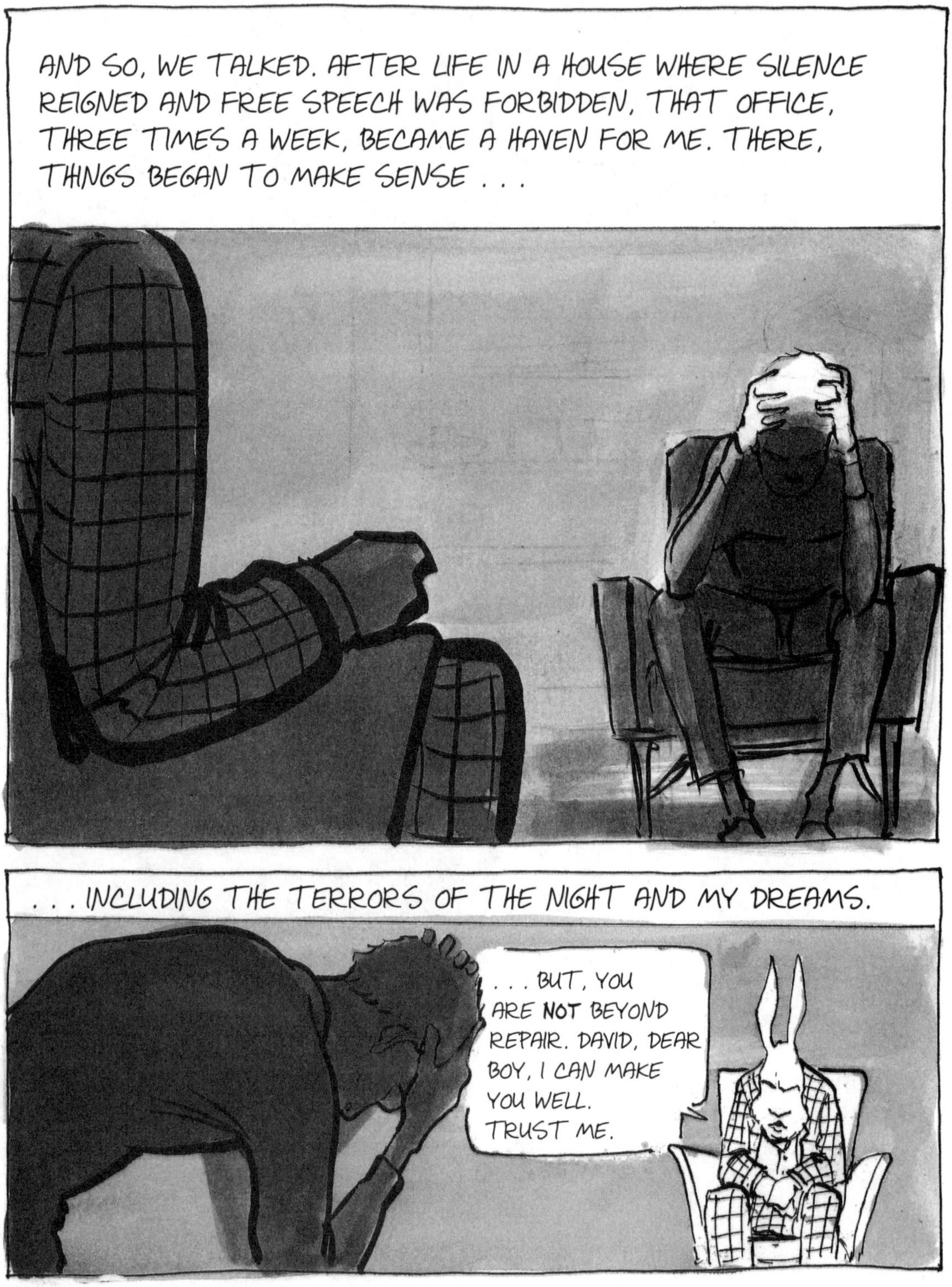
AND SO, WE TALKED. AFTER LIFE IN A HOUSE WHERE SILENCE REIGNED AND FREE SPEECH WAS FORBIDDEN, THAT OFFICE, THREE TIMES A WEEK, BECAME A HAVEN FOR ME. THERE, THINGS BEGAN TO MAKE SENSE . . .
. . . INCLUDING THE TERRORS OF THE NIGHT AND MY DREAMS.
. . . BUT, YOU ARE **NOT** BEYOND REPAIR. DAVID, DEAR BOY, I CAN MAKE YOU WELL. TRUST ME.

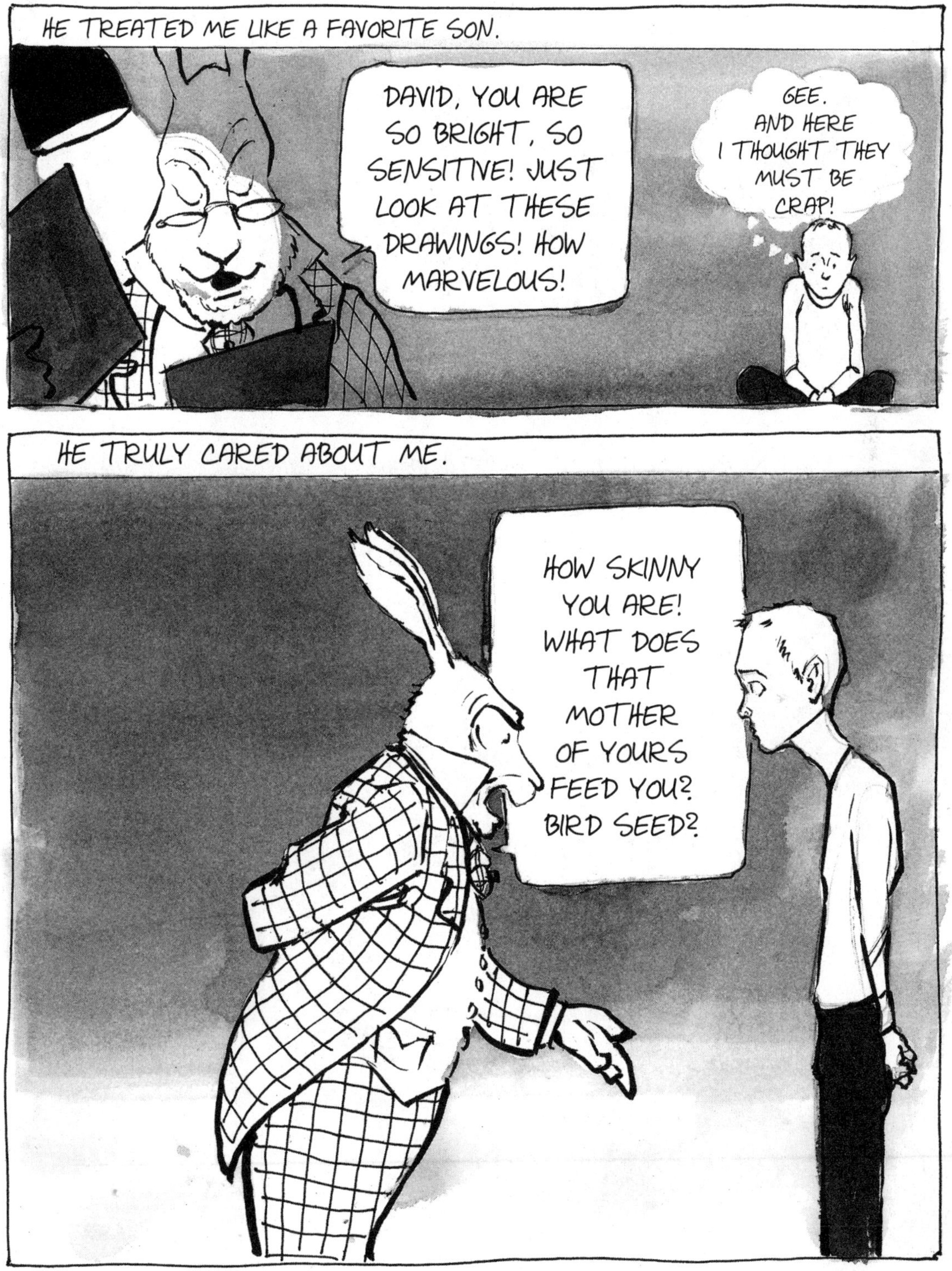
HE TREATED ME LIKE A FAVORITE SON.
DAVID, YOU ARE SO BRIGHT, SO SENSITIVE! JUST LOOK AT THESE DRAWINGS! HOW MARVELOUS!
GEE. AND HERE I THOUGHT THEY MUST BE CRAP!
HE TRULY CARED ABOUT ME.
HOW SKINNY YOU ARE! WHAT DOES THAT MOTHER OF YOURS FEED YOU? BIRD SEED?

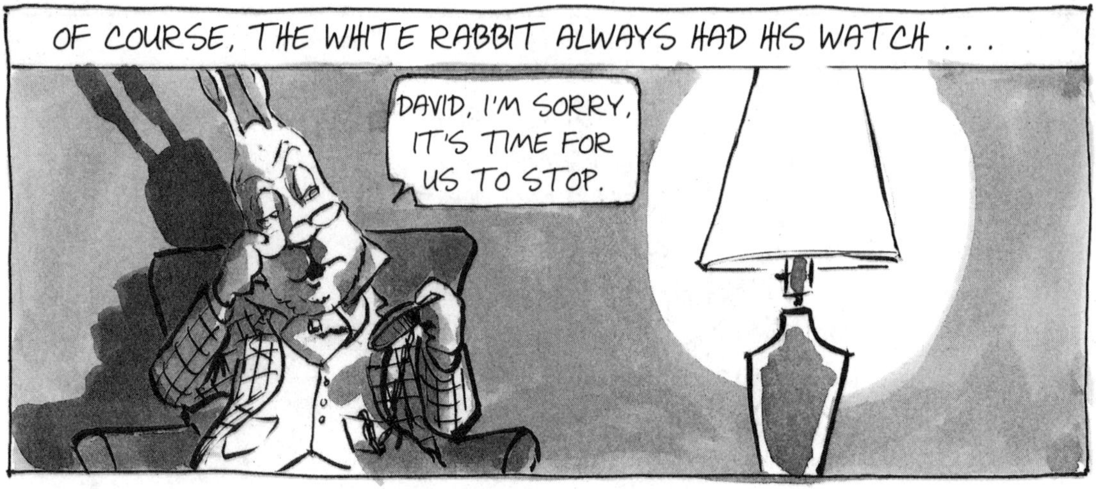
OF COURSE, THE WHITE RABBIT ALWAYS HAD HIS WATCH . . .
DAVID, I'M SORRY, IT'S TIME FOR US TO STOP.

. . . WHILE I ALWAYS HAD TO RETURN HOME, WHERE, AS I WAS SLOWLY BEGINNING TO PULL MYSELF TOGETHER, MY FAMILY SEEMED TO BE QUICKLY FALLING APART.

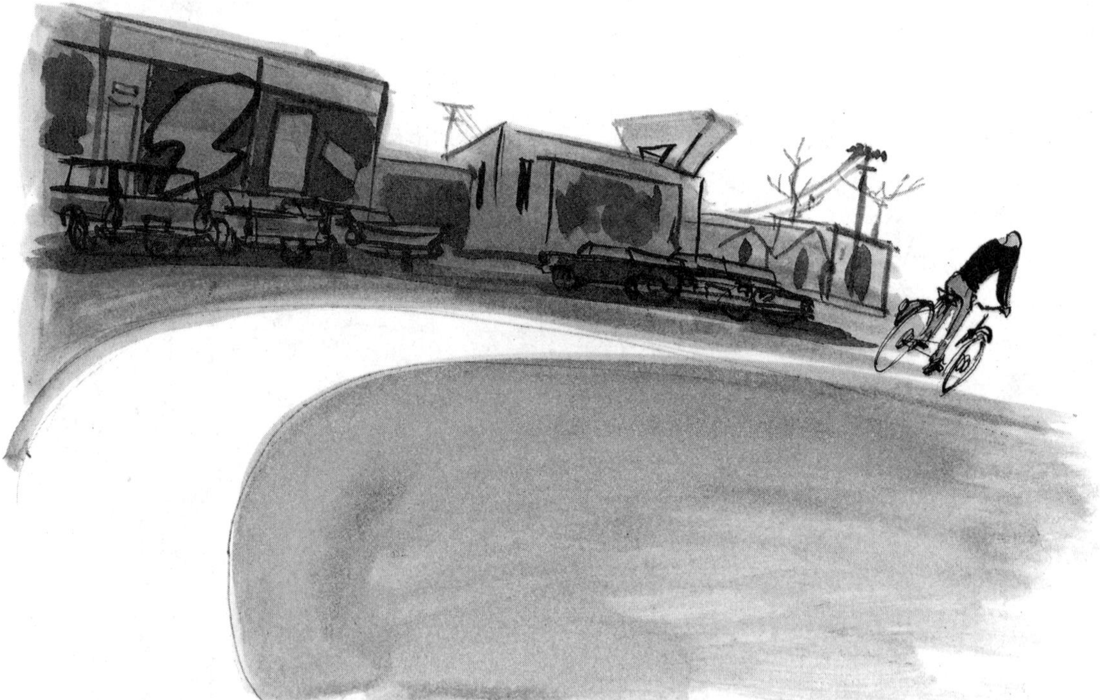

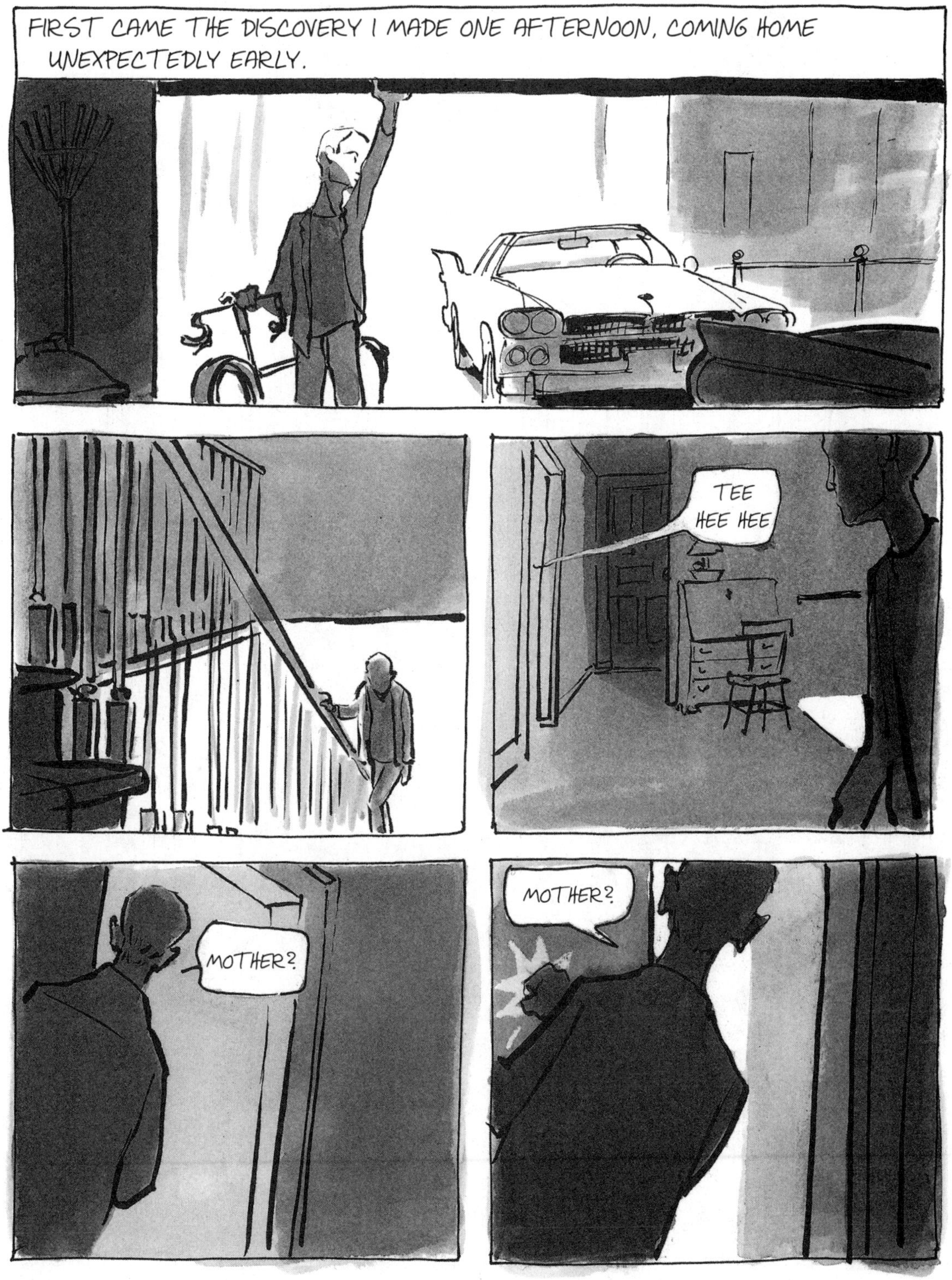
FIRST CAME THE DISCOVERY I MADE ONE AFTERNOON, COMING HOME UNEXPECTEDLY EARLY.
TEE HEE HEE
MOTHER?
MOTHER?

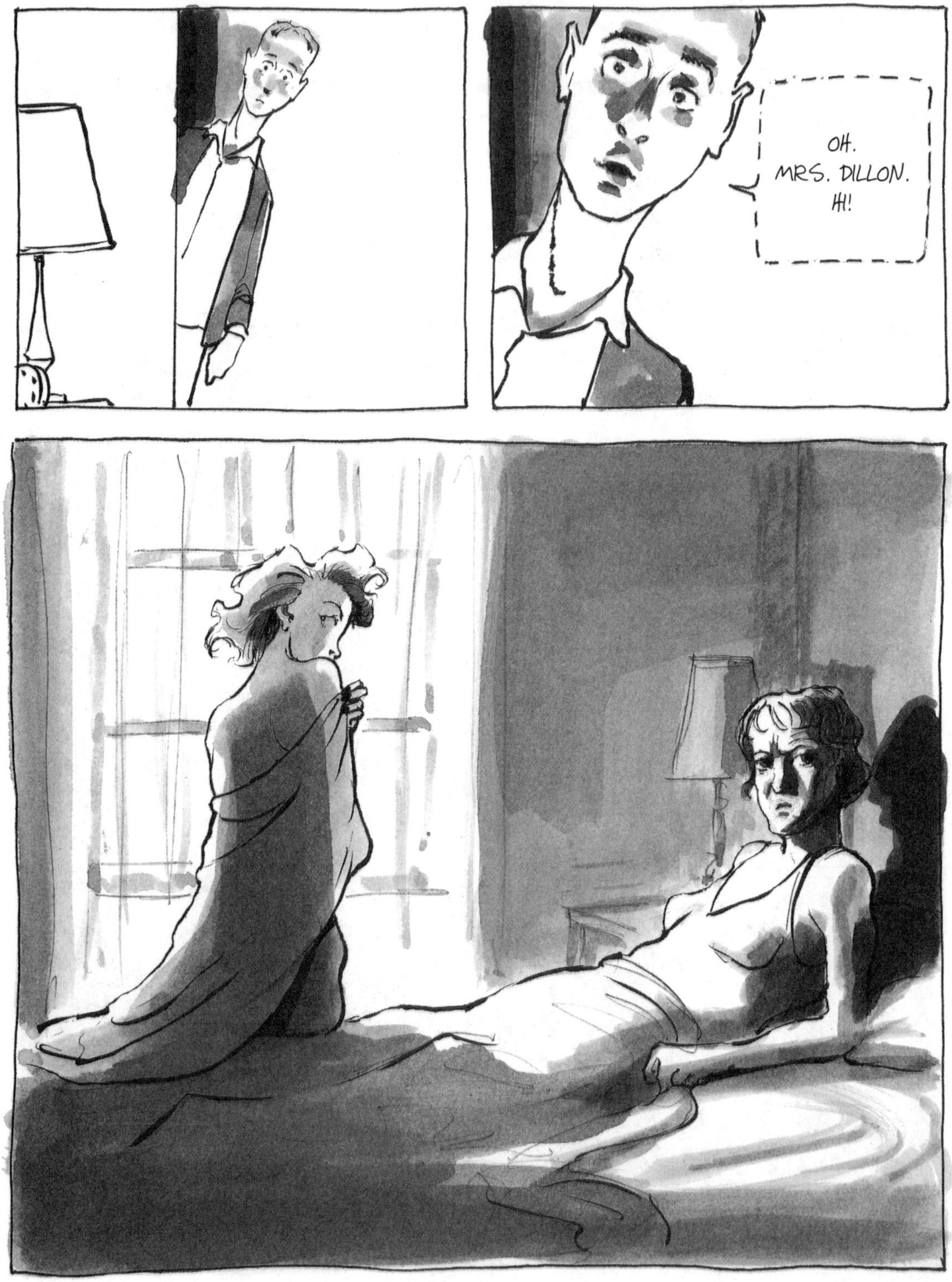
OH.
MRS. DILLON.
HI!

AFTER THAT AWKWARD MOMENT, WHILE MY OWN EMOTIONS
RICOCHETED BETWEEN EXTREMES OF BETRAYAL AND
FOOLISHNESS, ANGER AND CONFUSION, WHAT STAYED
WITH ME FOR THE LONGEST TIME WAS THE LOOK
MOTHER GAVE ME, ITSELF FULL OF COMPLEX FEELINGS,
FEW OF WHICH, I'D GUESS, HAD MUCH TO DO WITH ME.

I JUST HAPPENED TO BE THE ONE WHO
STUMBLED INTO THE ROOM AT THE WRONG
MOMENT, A MOMENT SHE MUST HAVE KNOWN
WAS COMING HER WHOLE LIFE.

THEN CAME THE NEWS FROM INDIANA.

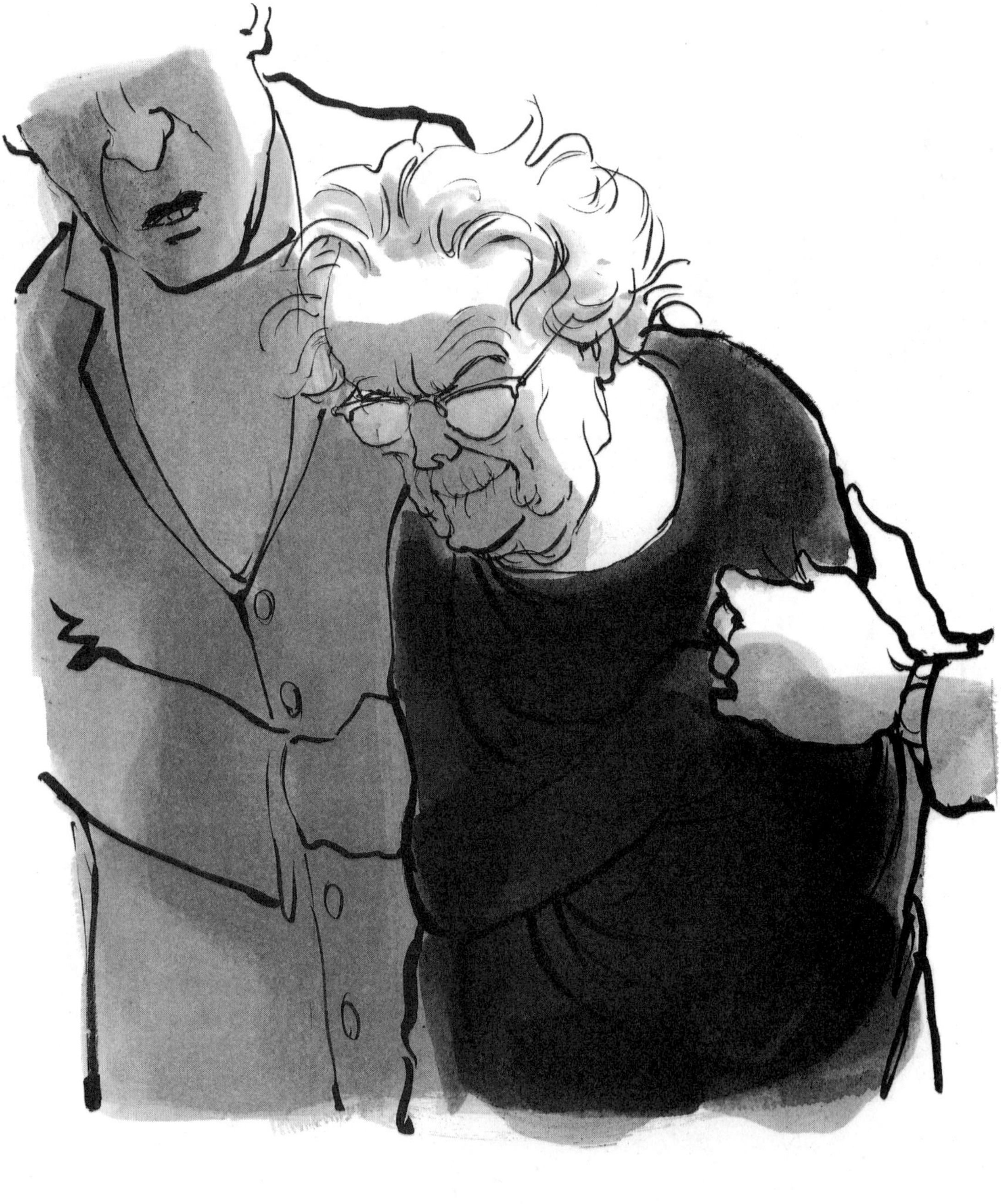

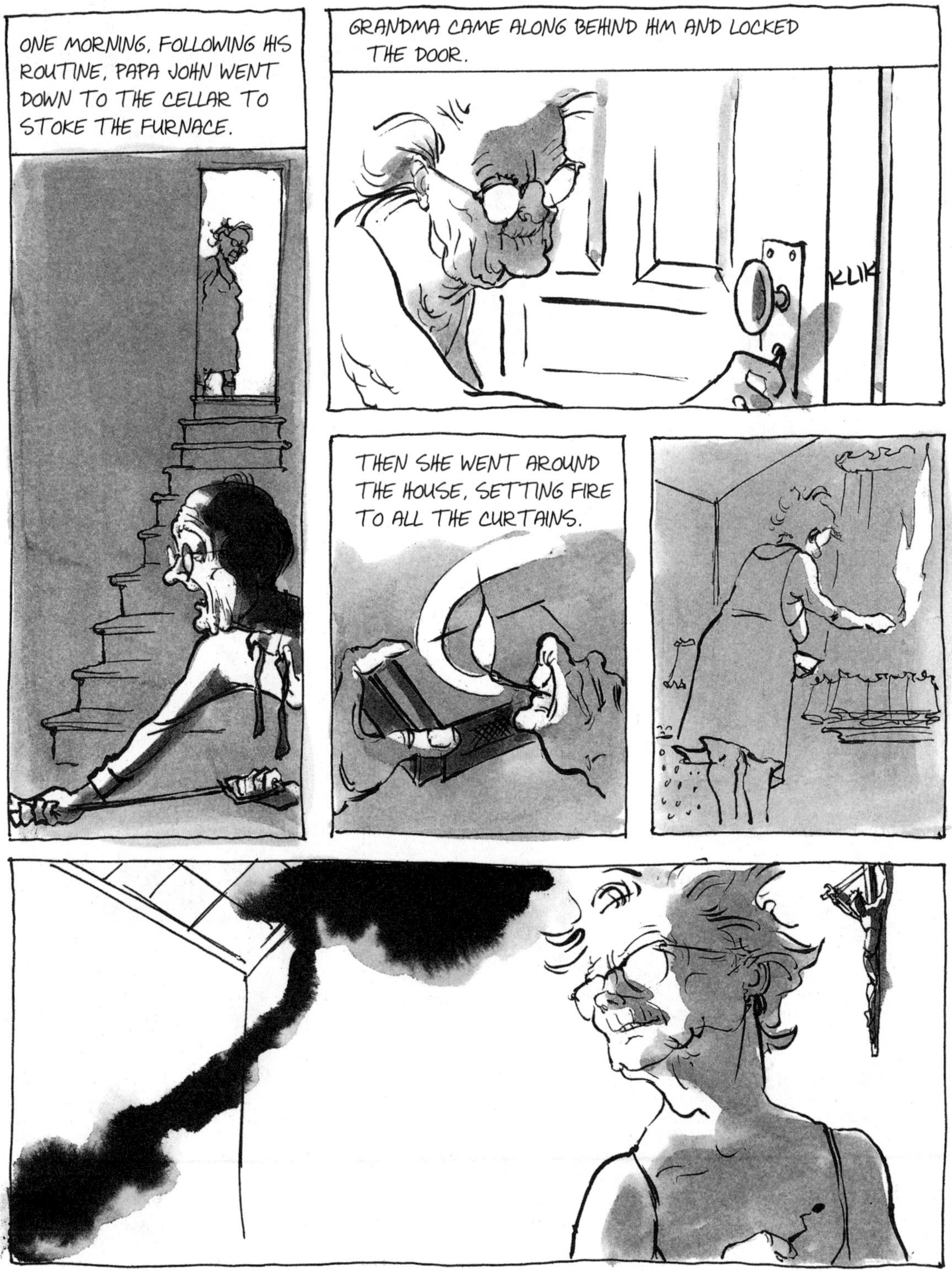
ONE MORNING, FOLLOWING HIS ROUTINE, PAPA JOHN WENT DOWN TO THE CELLAR TO STOKE THE FURNACE.
GRANDMA CAME ALONG BEHIND HIM AND LOCKED THE DOOR.
KLIK
THEN SHE WENT AROUND THE HOUSE, SETTING FIRE TO ALL THE CURTAINS.

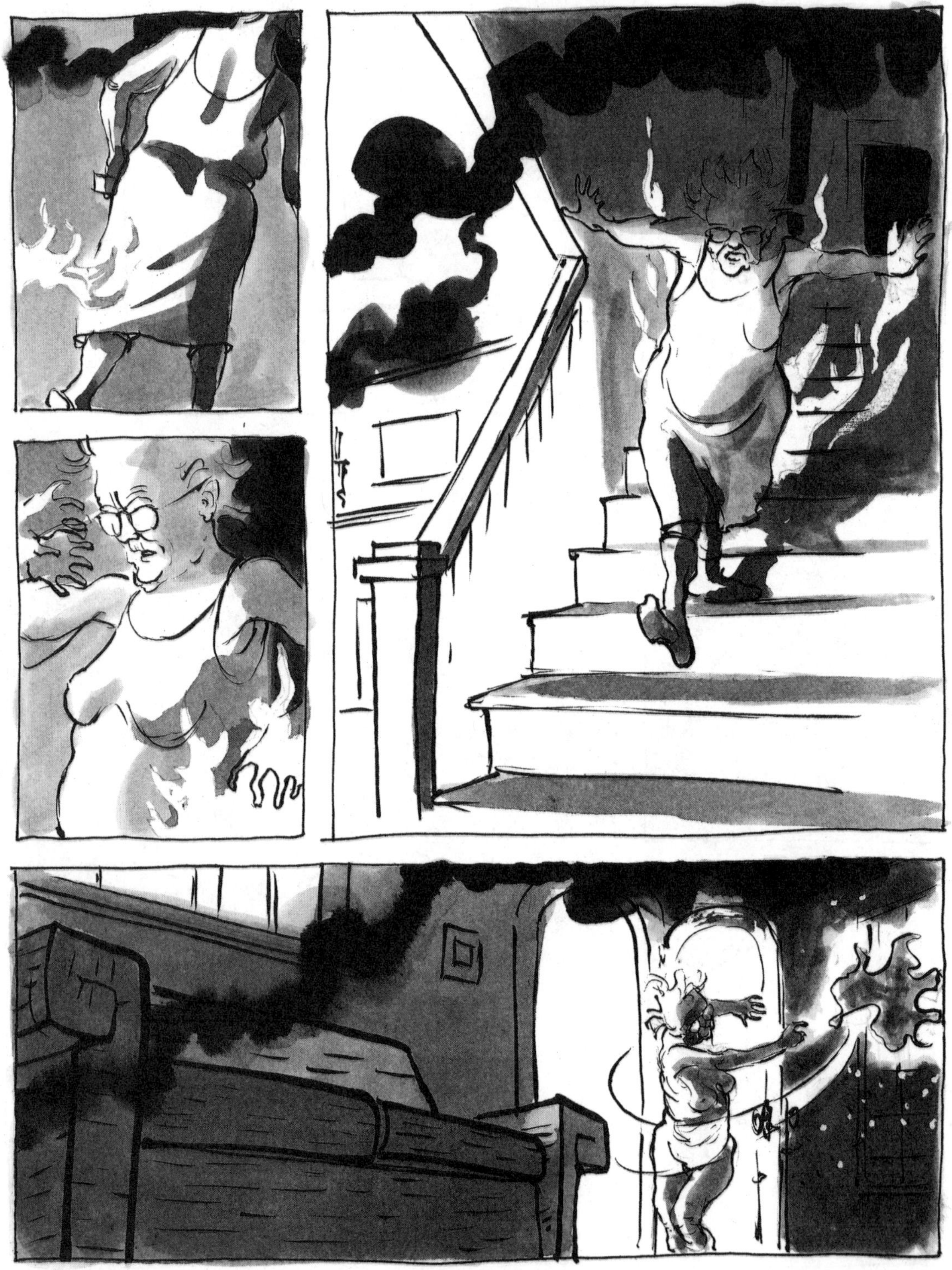

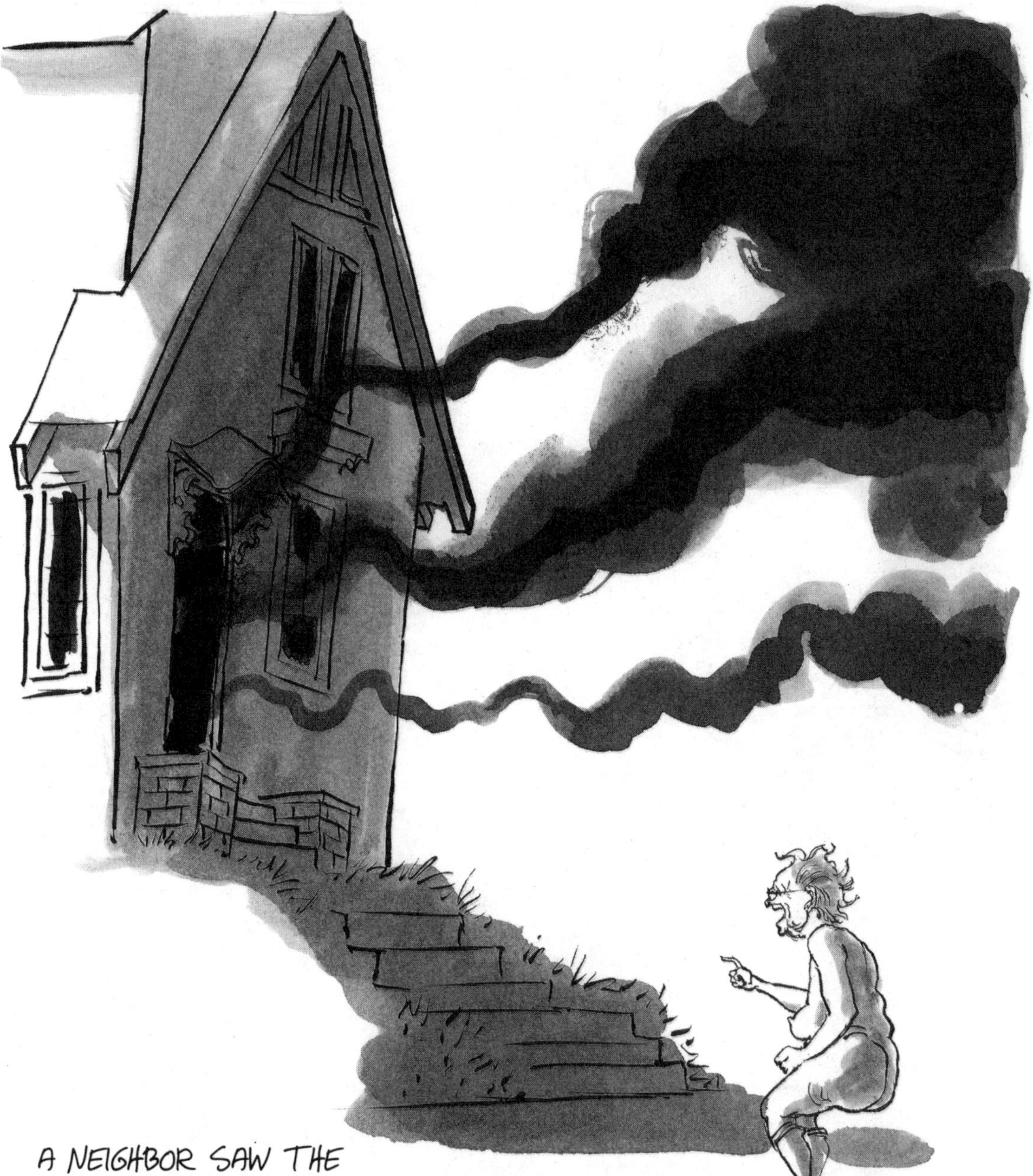
A NEIGHBOR SAW THE SMOKE, SAW HER DANCING AROUND AND PHONED FOR HELP. PAPA JOHN WAS SAVED AND GRANDMA WAS TAKEN AWAY TO THE STATE INSANE ASYLUM.

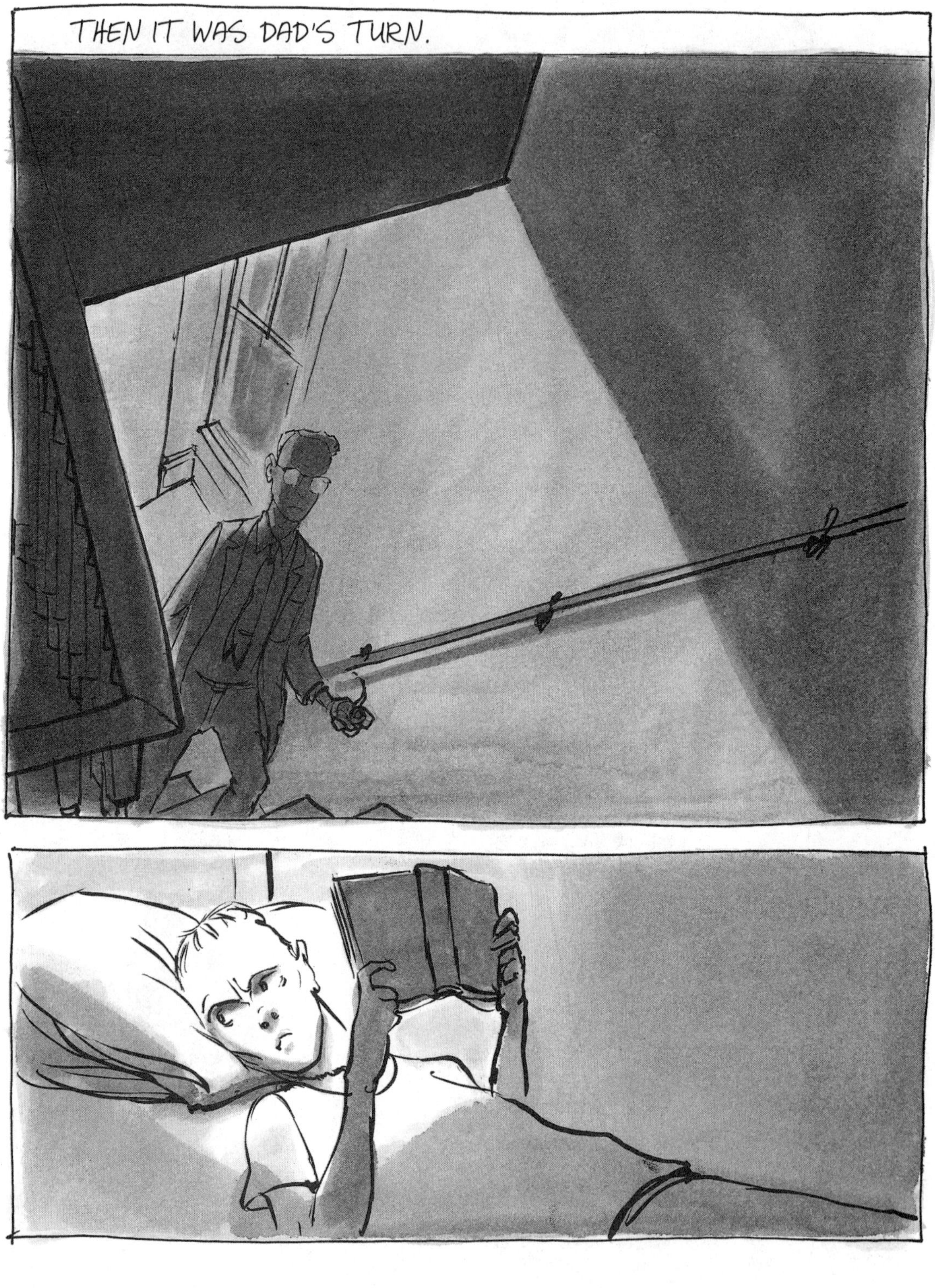
THEN IT WAS DAD'S TURN.

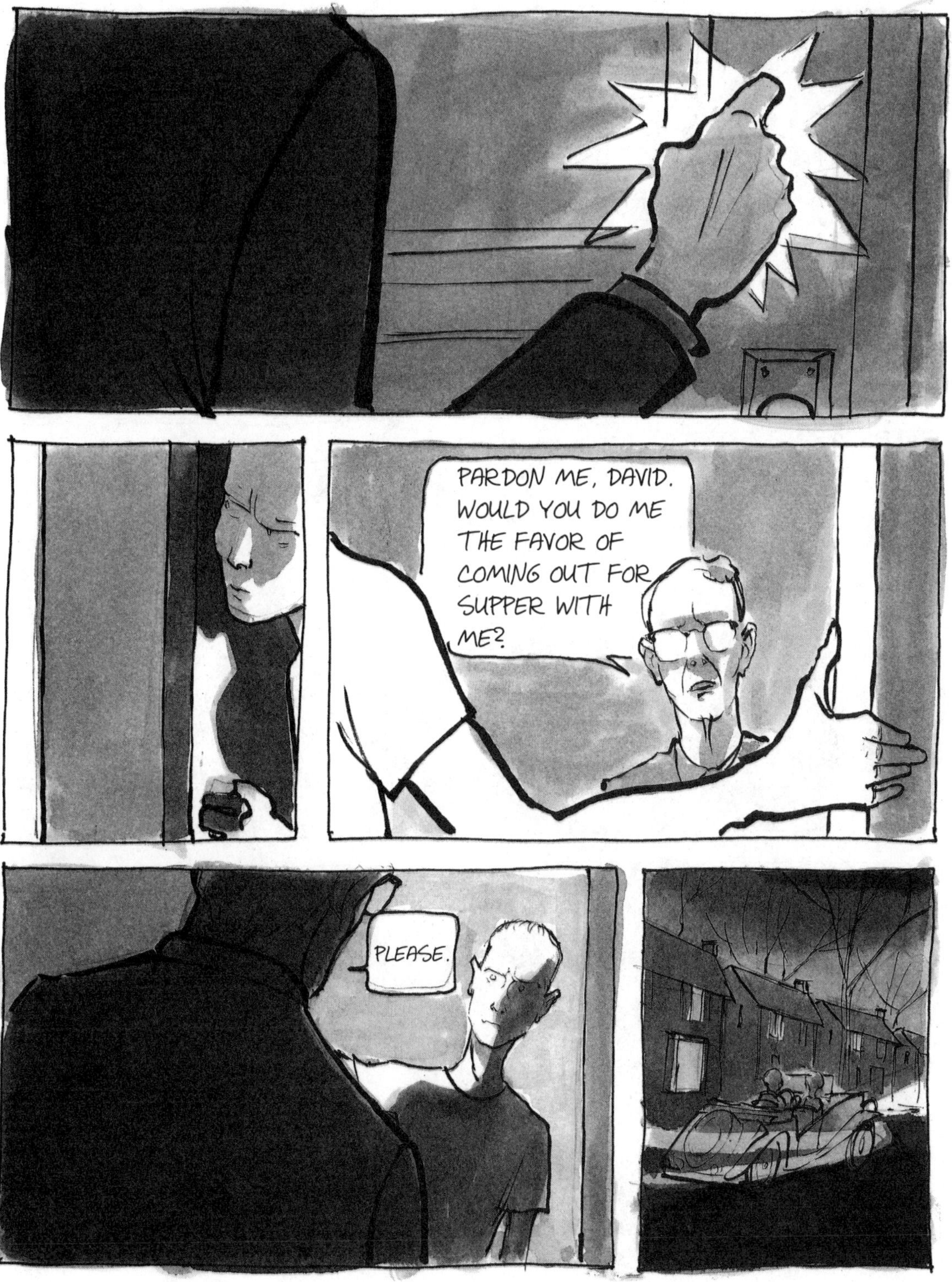
PARDON ME, DAVID. WOULD YOU DO ME THE FAVOR OF COMING OUT FOR SUPPER WITH ME?
PLEASE.

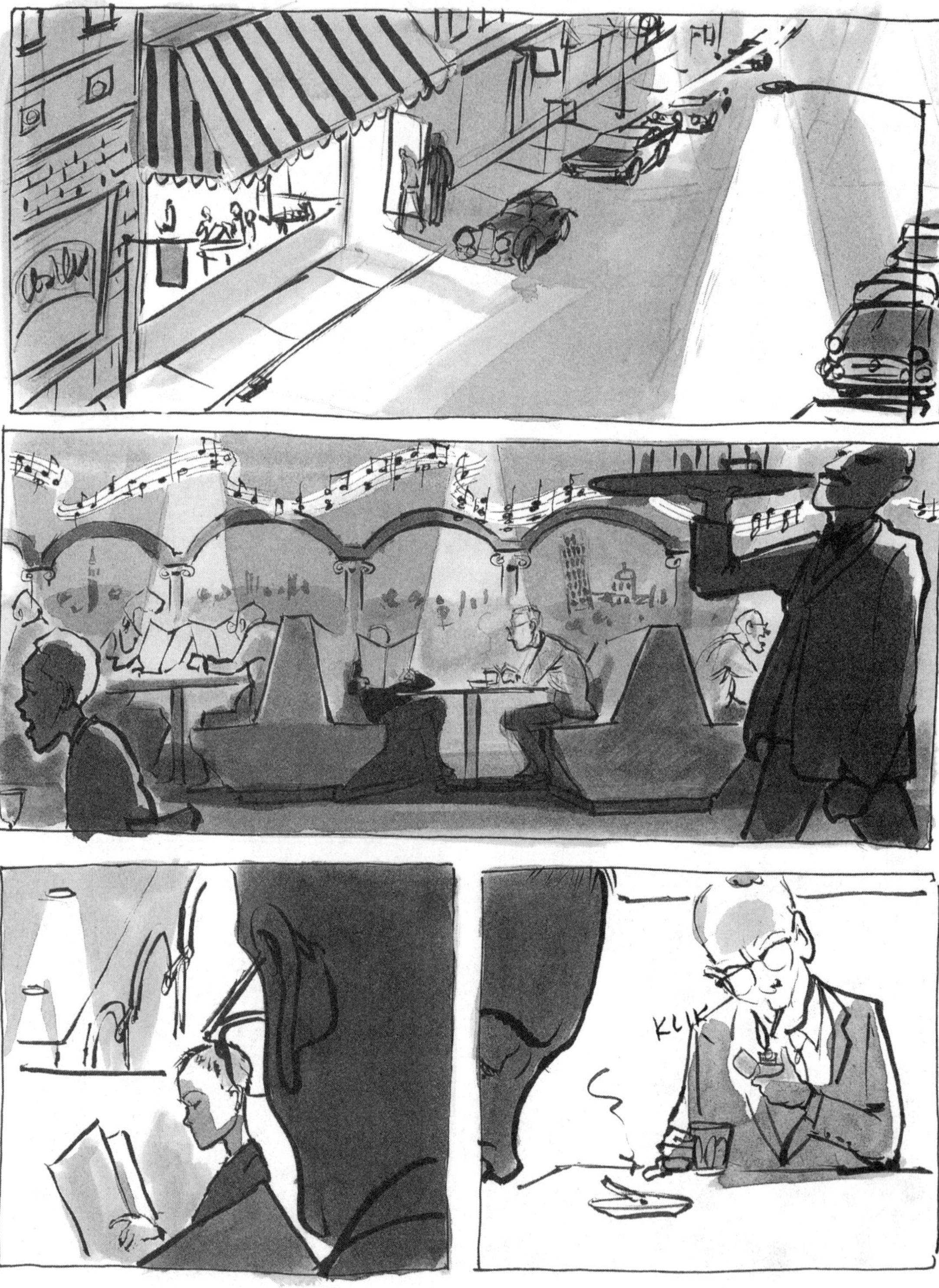
KLIK

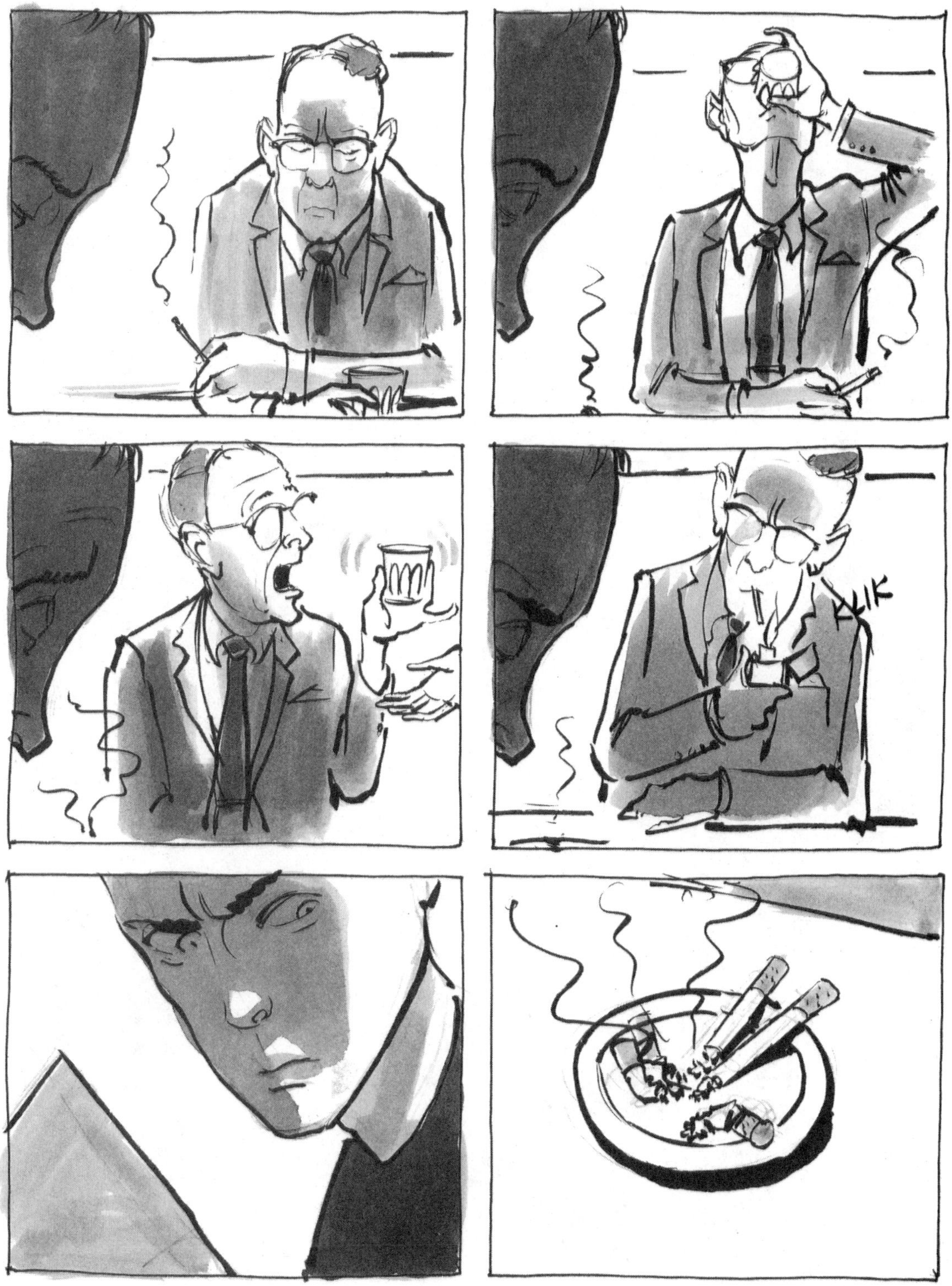
KLIK

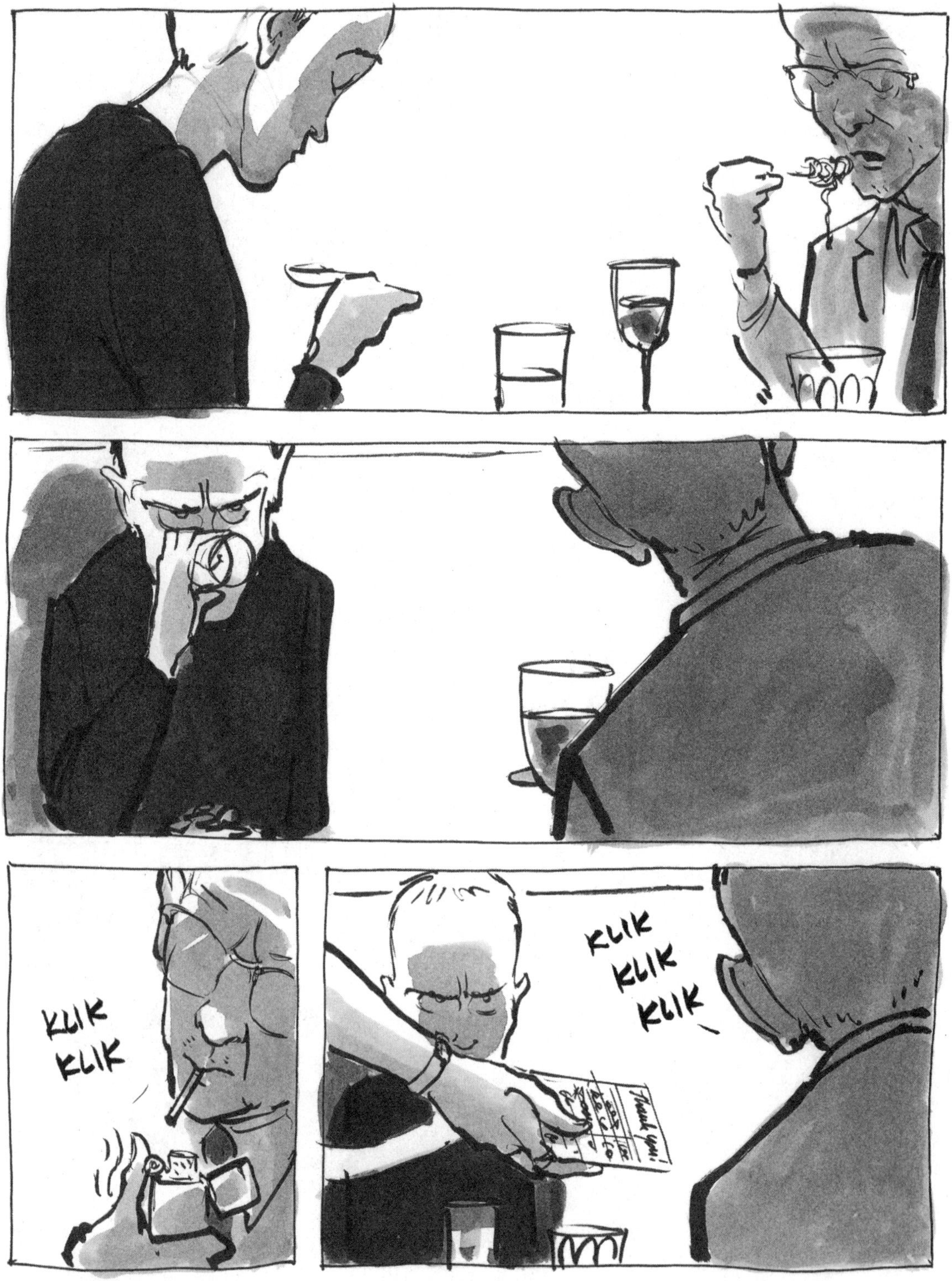
KLIK
KLIK
KLIK
KLIK
KLIK
Thank you!

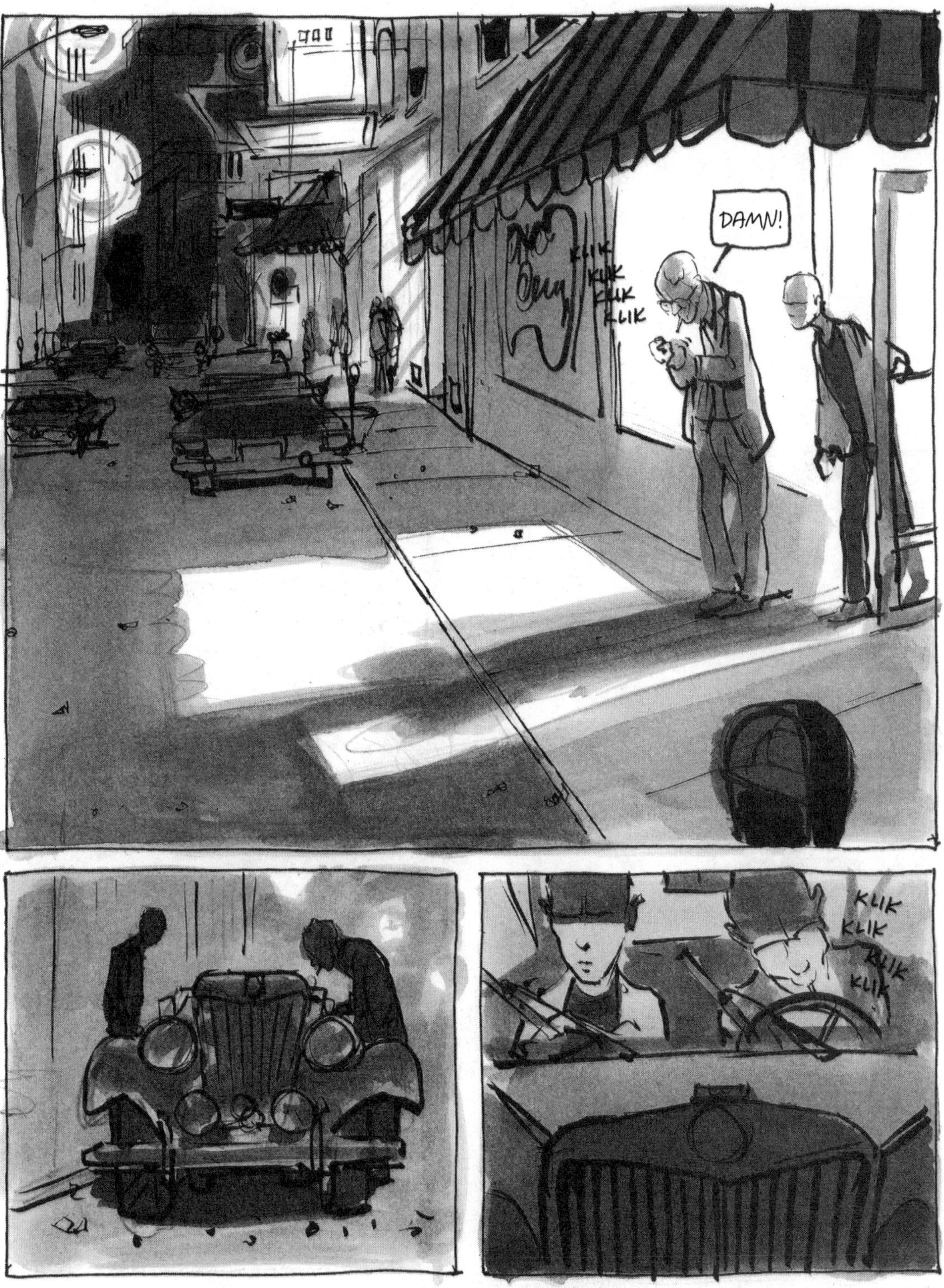
DAMN!
KLIK
KLIK
KLIK
KLIK
KLIK
KLIK
KLIK
KLIK

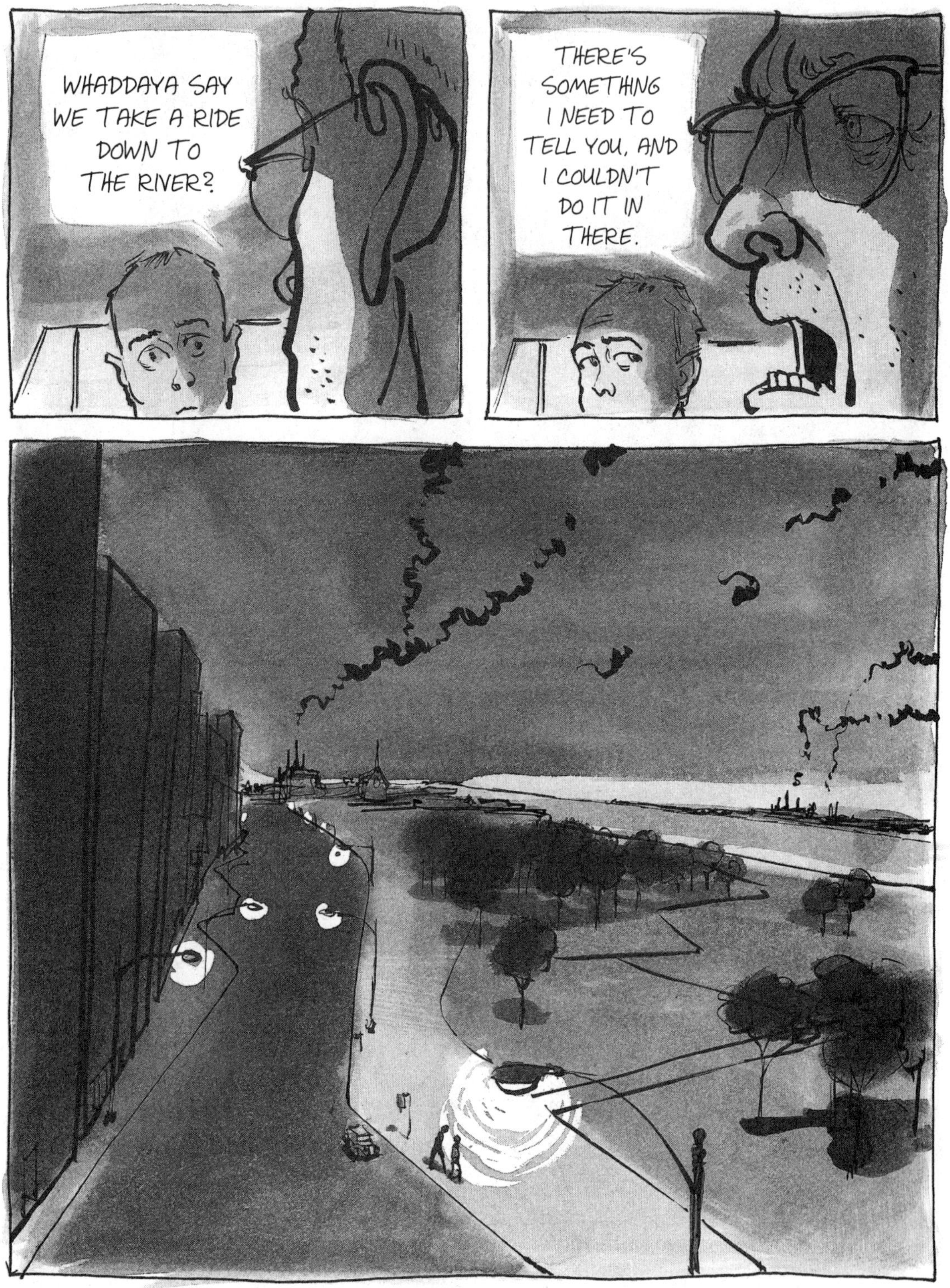
WHADDAYA SAY WE TAKE A RIDE DOWN TO THE RIVER?
THERE'S SOMETHING I NEED TO TELL YOU, AND I COULDN'T DO IT IN THERE.

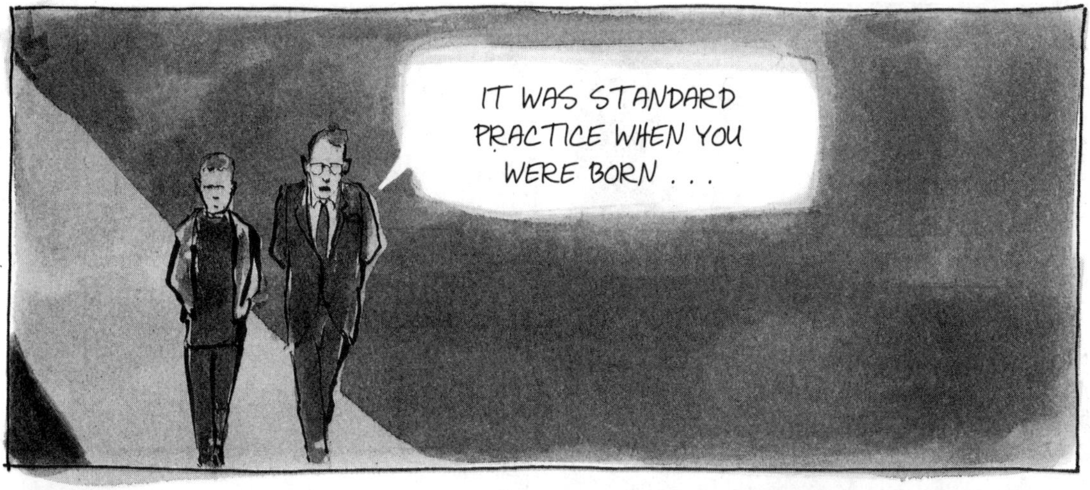
IT WAS STANDARD PRACTICE WHEN YOU WERE BORN . . .

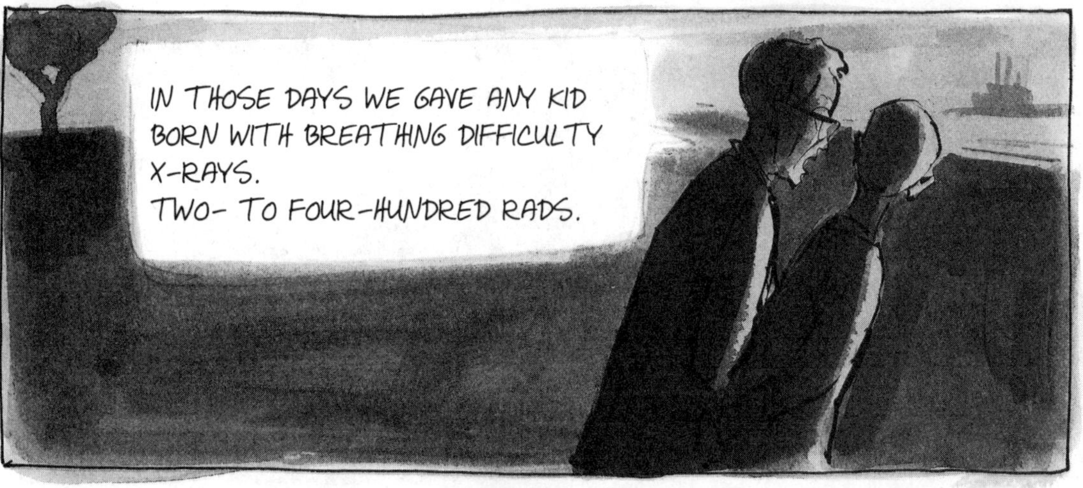
IN THOSE DAYS WE GAVE ANY KID BORN WITH BREATHING DIFFICULTY X-RAYS.
TWO- TO FOUR-HUNDRED RADS.

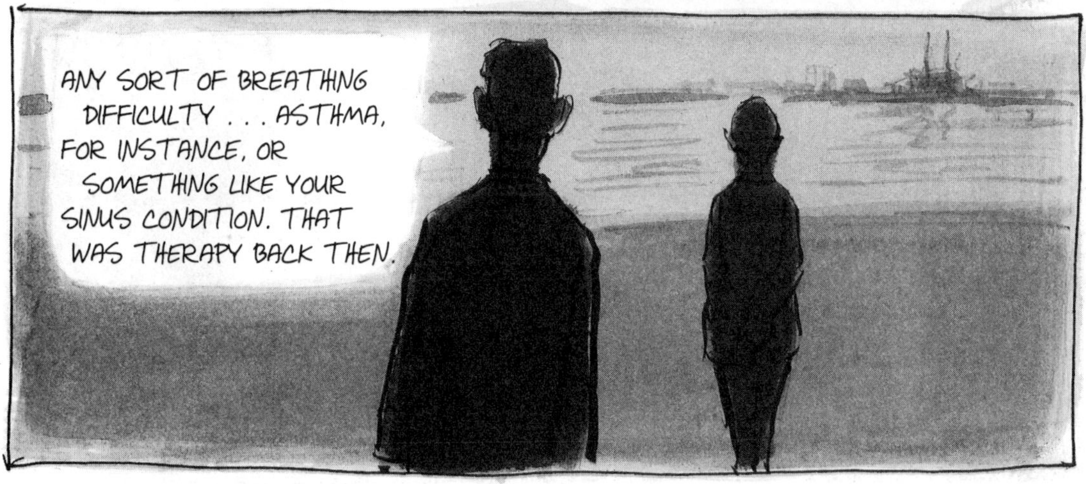
ANY SORT OF BREATHING DIFFICULTY . . . ASTHMA, FOR INSTANCE, OR SOMETHING LIKE YOUR SINUS CONDITION. THAT WAS THERAPY BACK THEN.

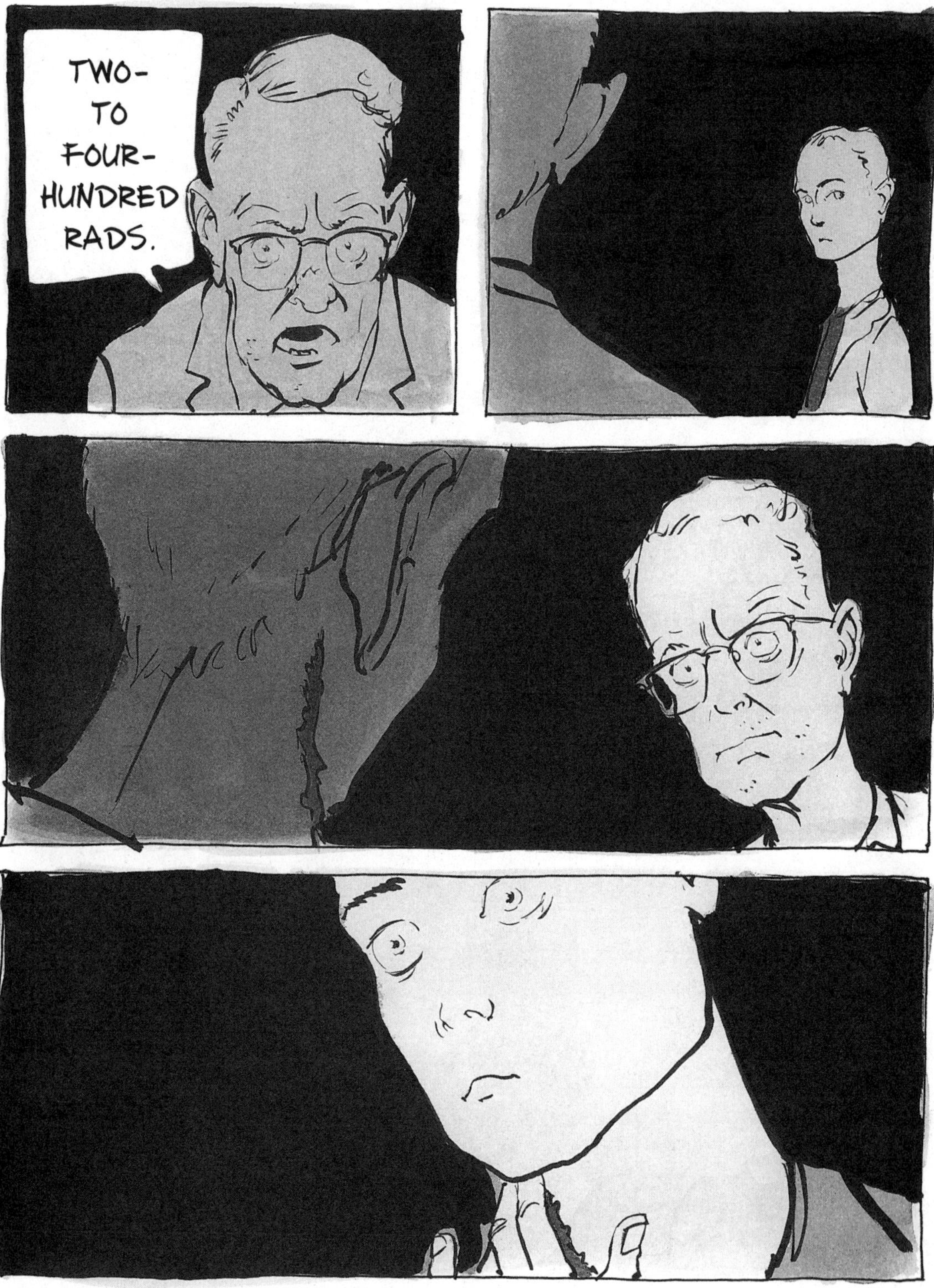
TWO- TO FOUR-HUNDRED RADS.

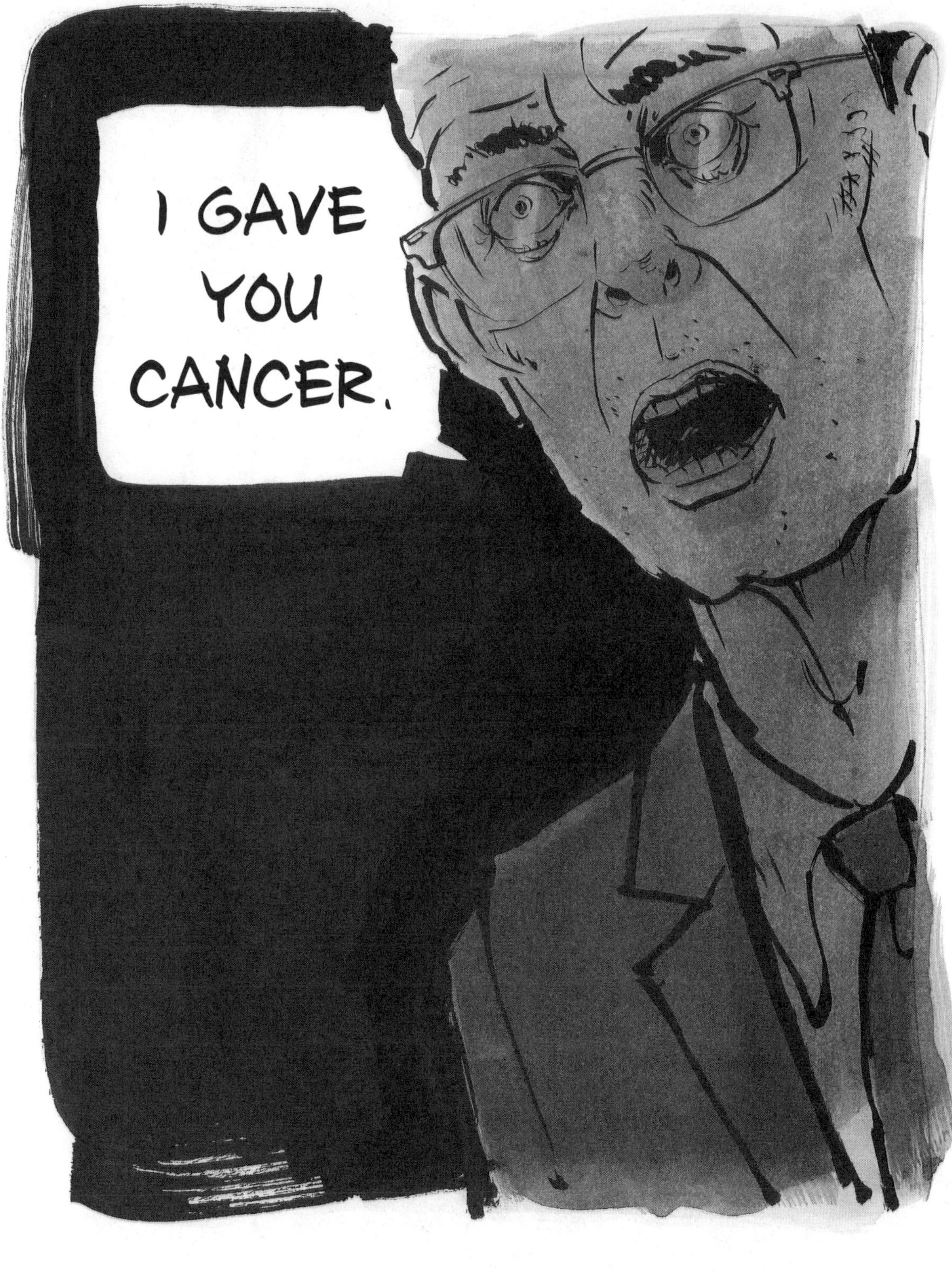
I GAVE YOU CANCER.

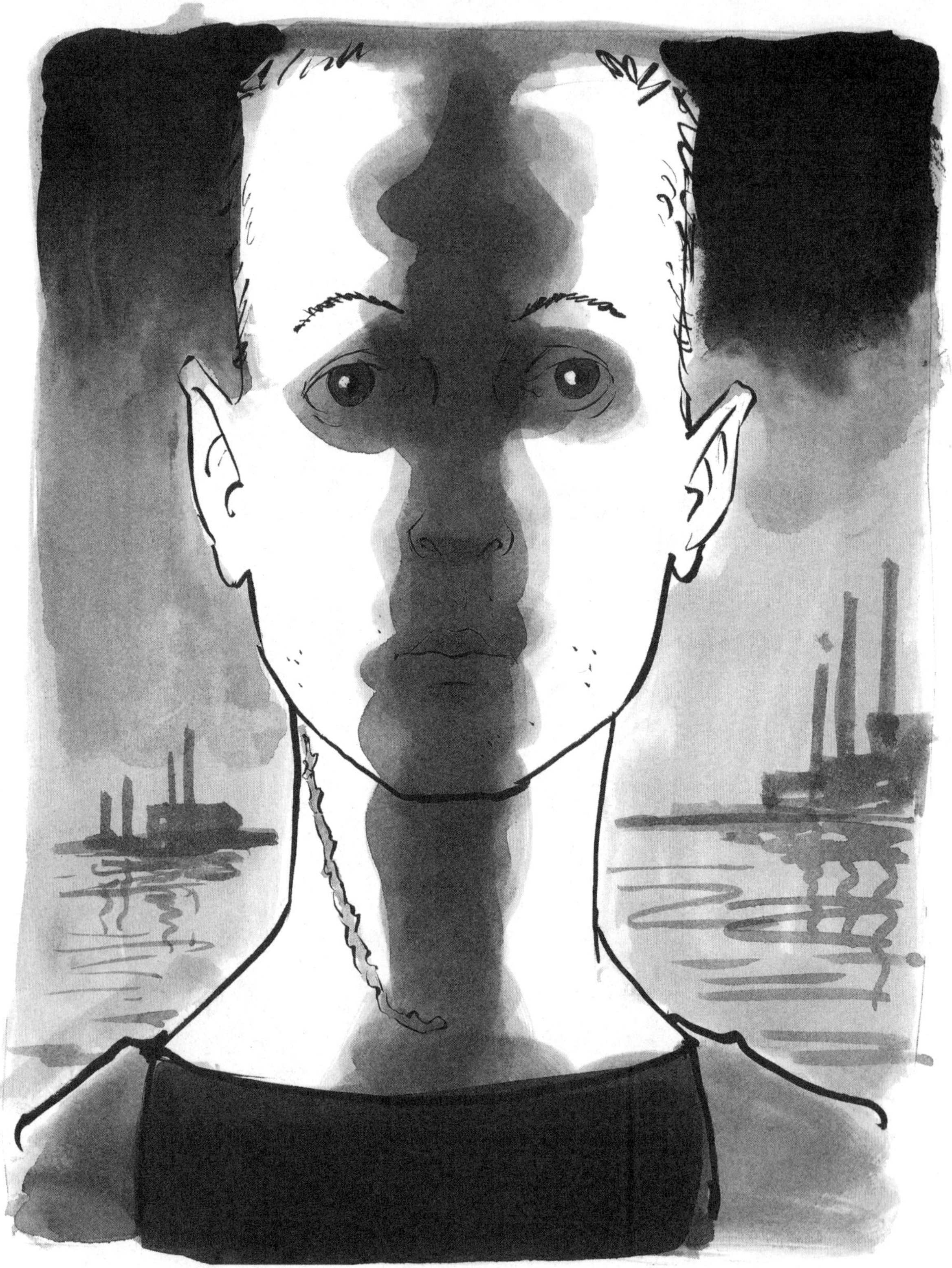

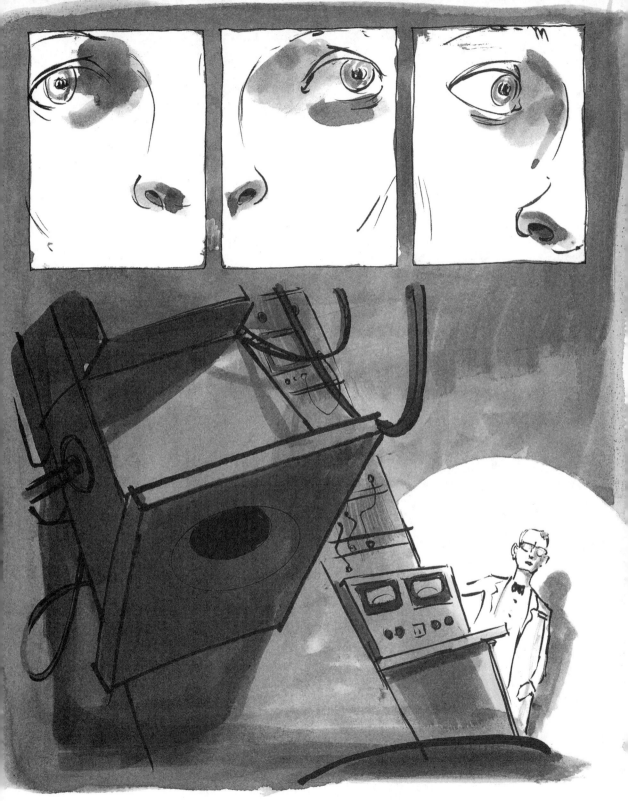

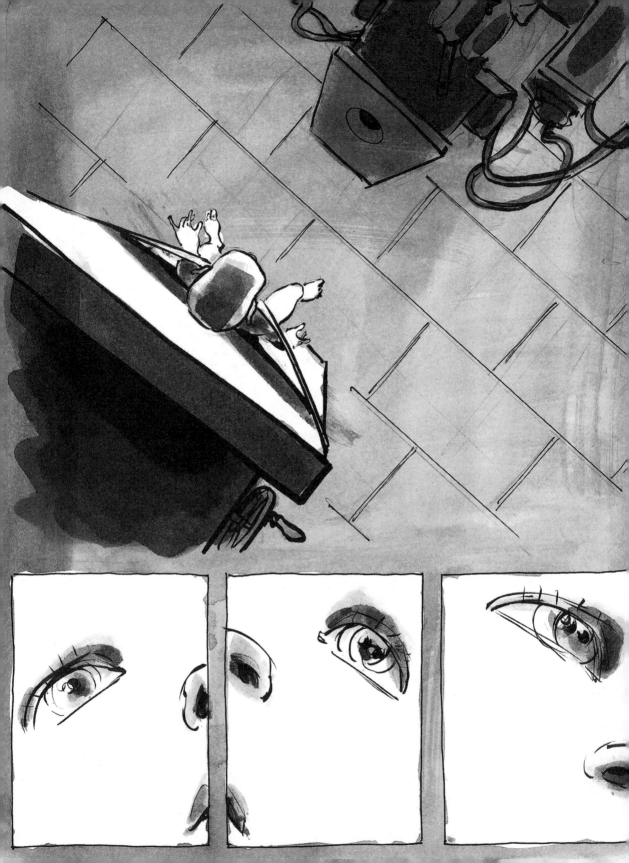

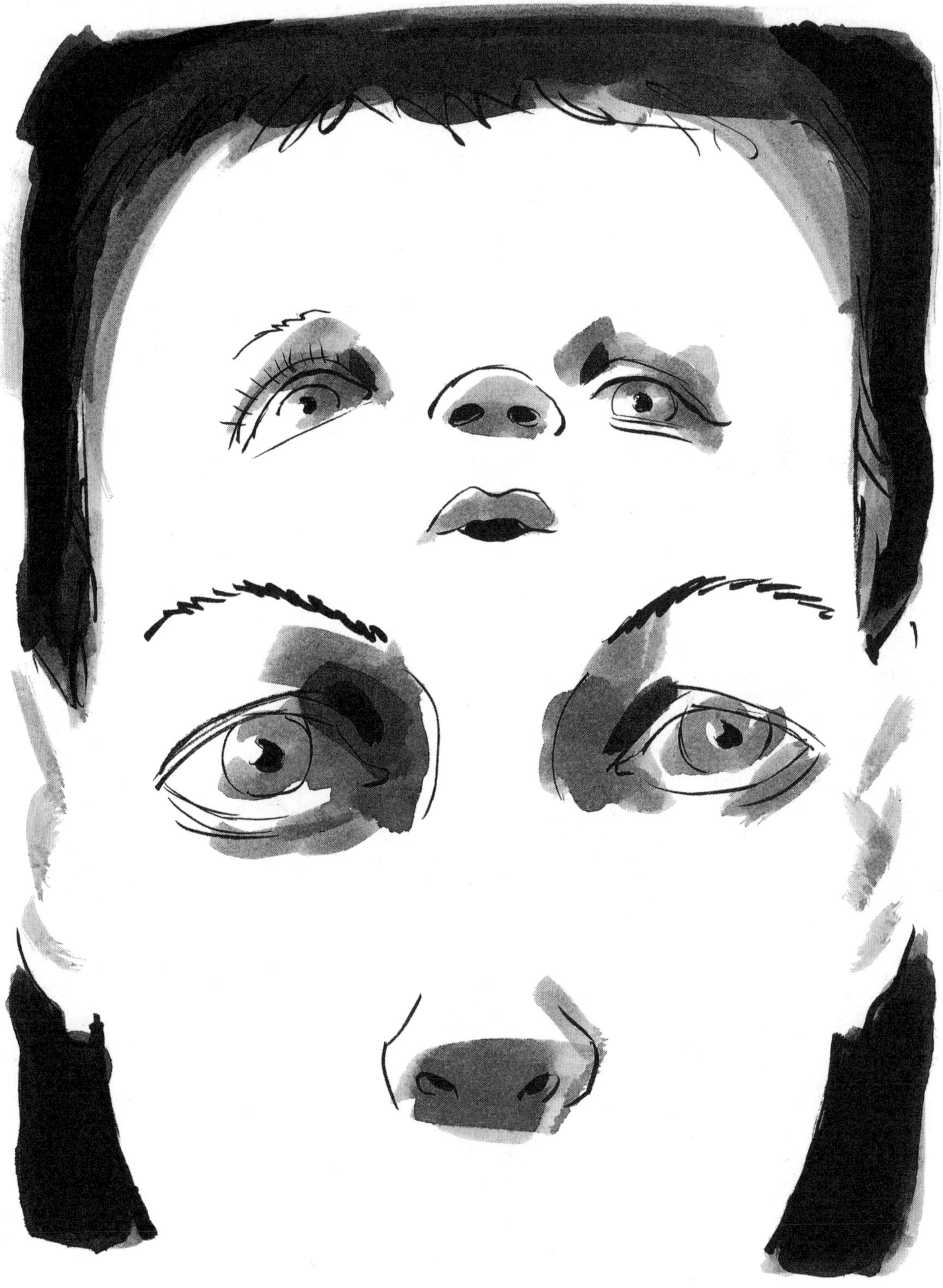

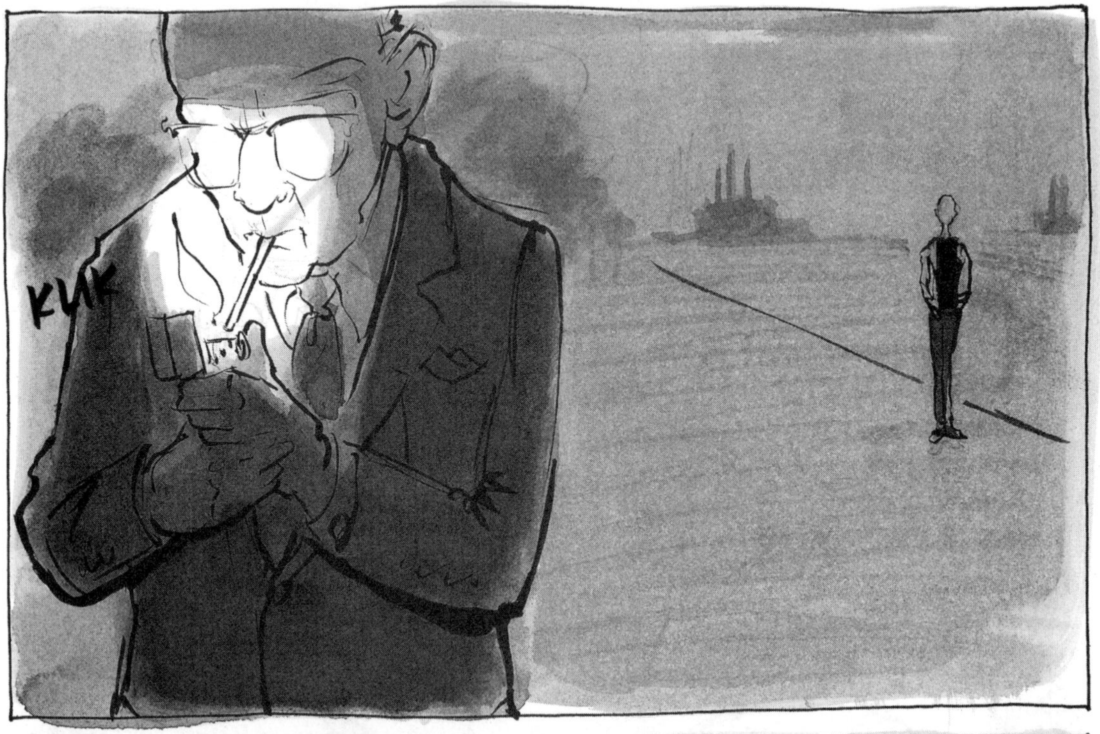
KLIK

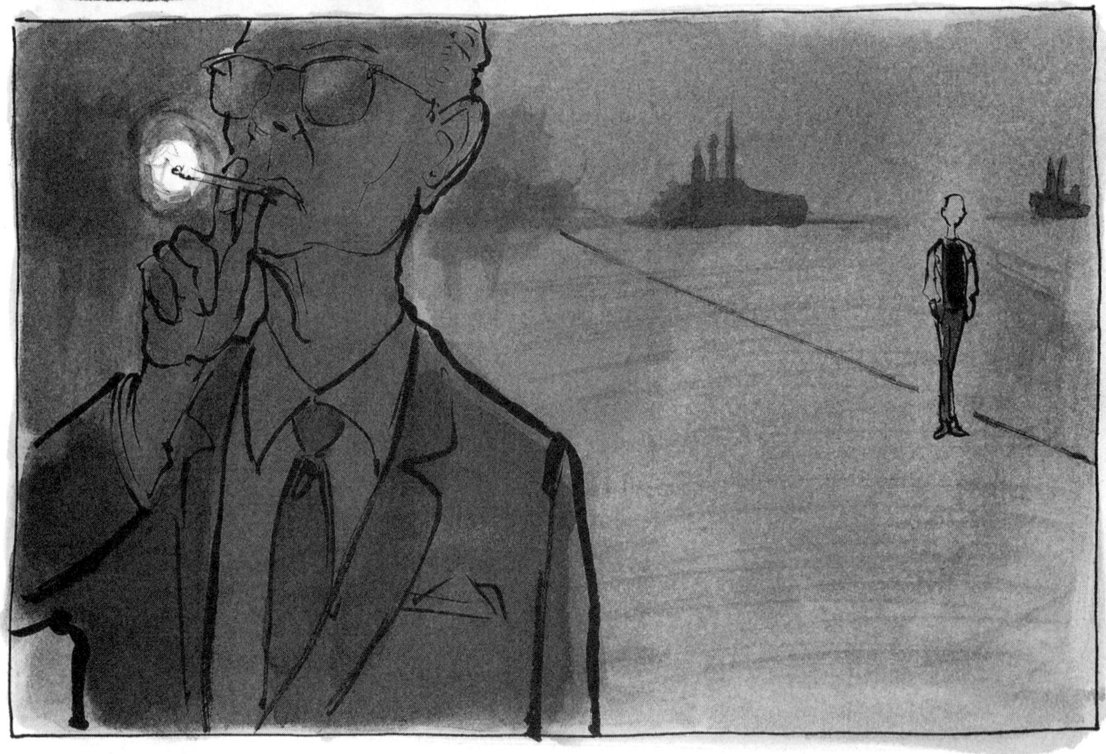

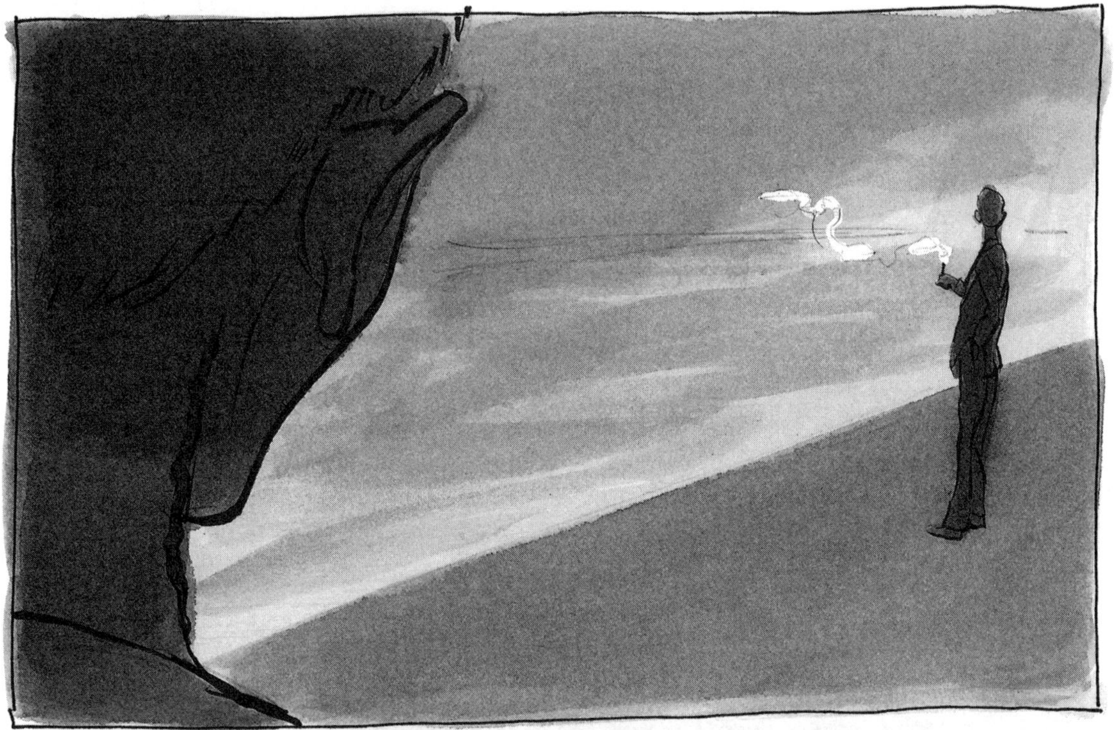

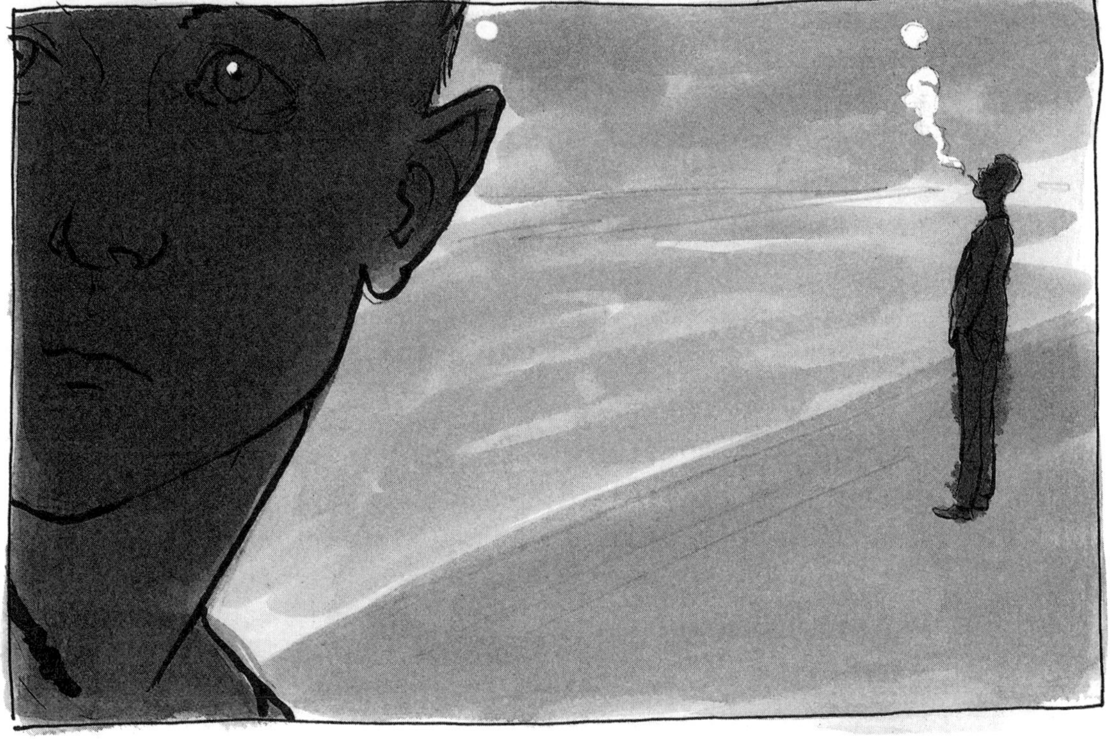

I MOVED OUT OF HOME WHEN I WAS SIXTEEN. STILL
A SENIOR IN HIGH SCHOOL, I RODE THE
BUS TO ATTEND CLASSES EACH DAY,
RETURNING EVERY AFTERNOON TO MY
ONE-ROOM APARTMENT IN DETROIT'S INNER
CITY.

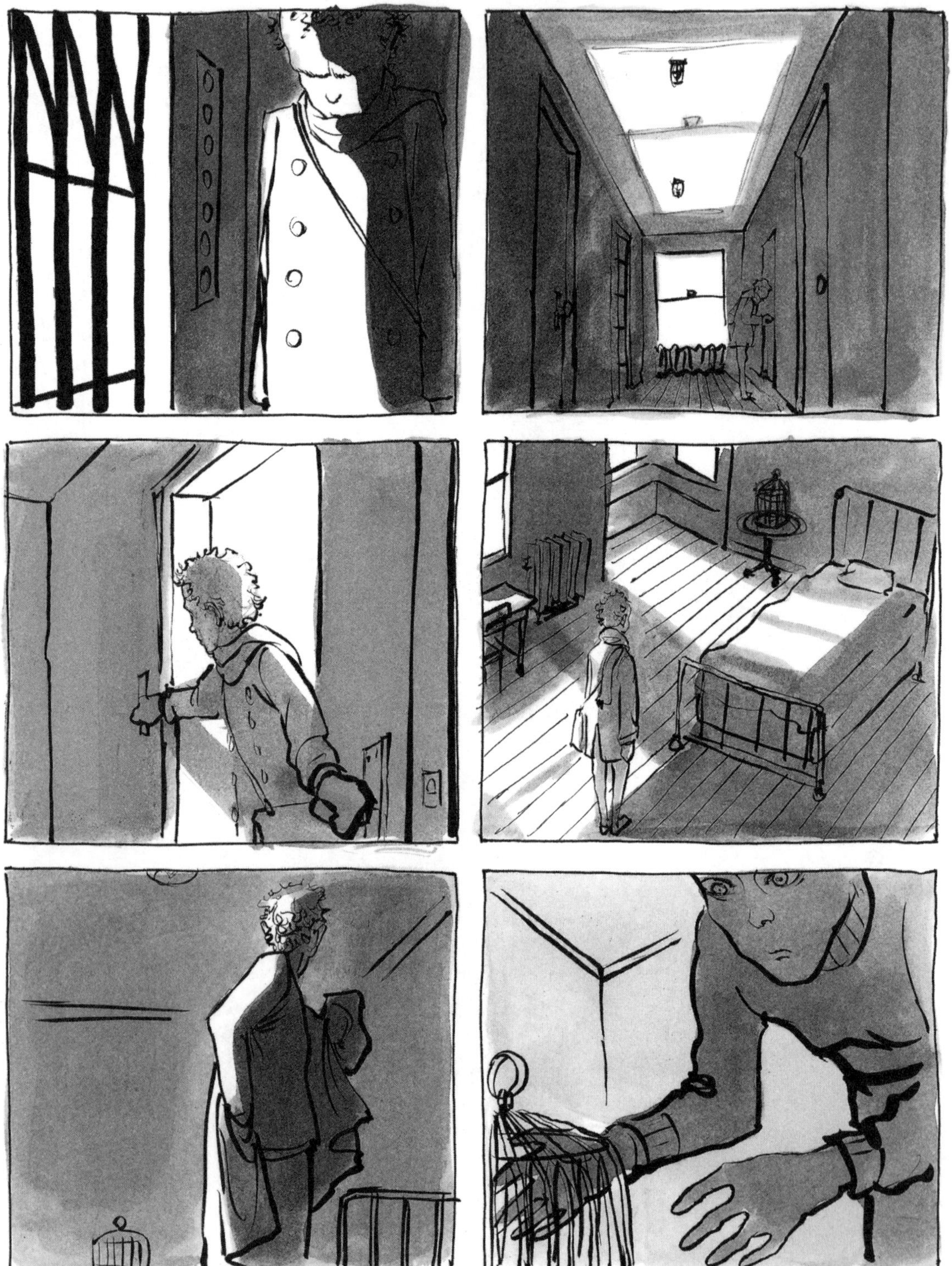

THE APARTMENT WAS TOO COLD FOR CANARIES, AND I WASN'T FARING MUCH BETTER. I WAS LONELY, OFTEN HUNGRY AND AFRAID OF THE NEIGHBORS. PLUS, MY ATTEMPTS AT BECOMING A WORLD-RENOWNED ARTIST WERE NOT GOING TOO WELL.

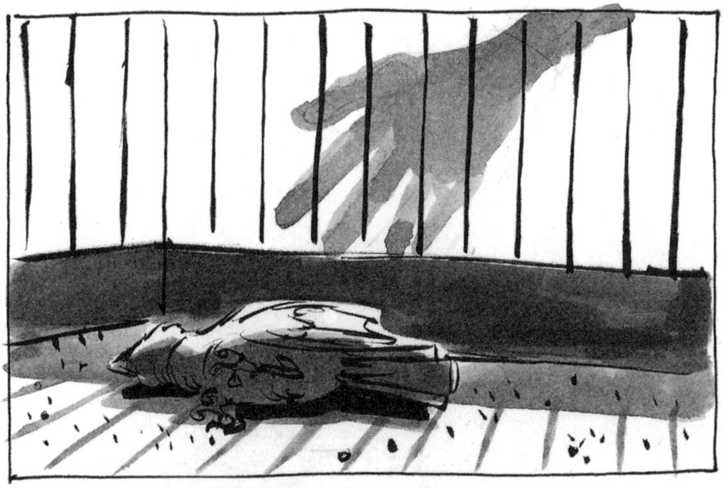

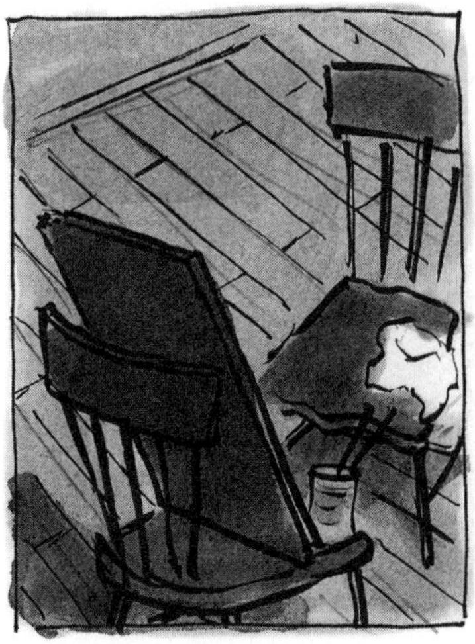

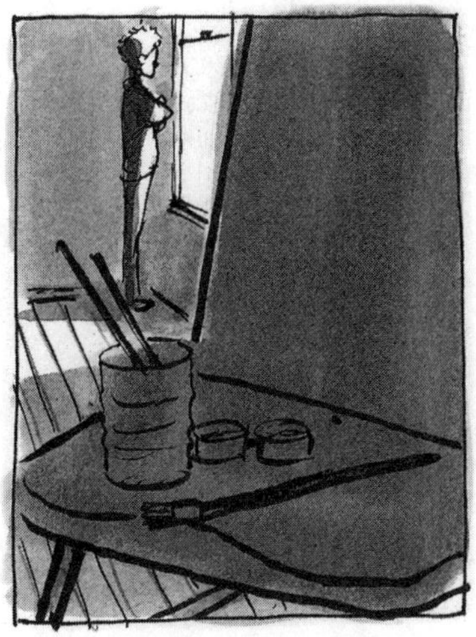

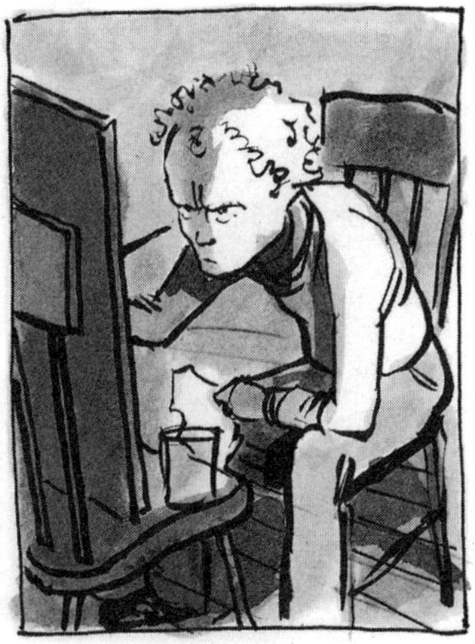

WITHOUT REALIZING HOW PERFECTLY THEY REPRESENTED MY BLOCKED STATE, I PAINTED A BRICK WALL AND A CLOSED DOOR.

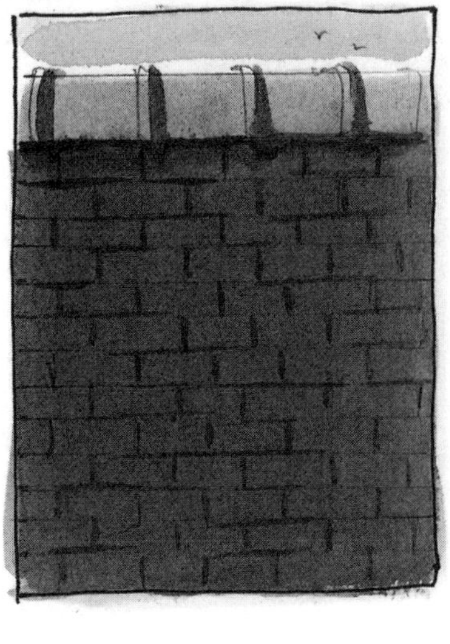

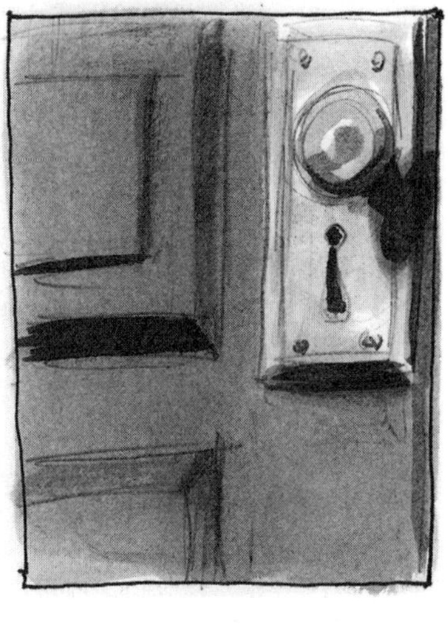

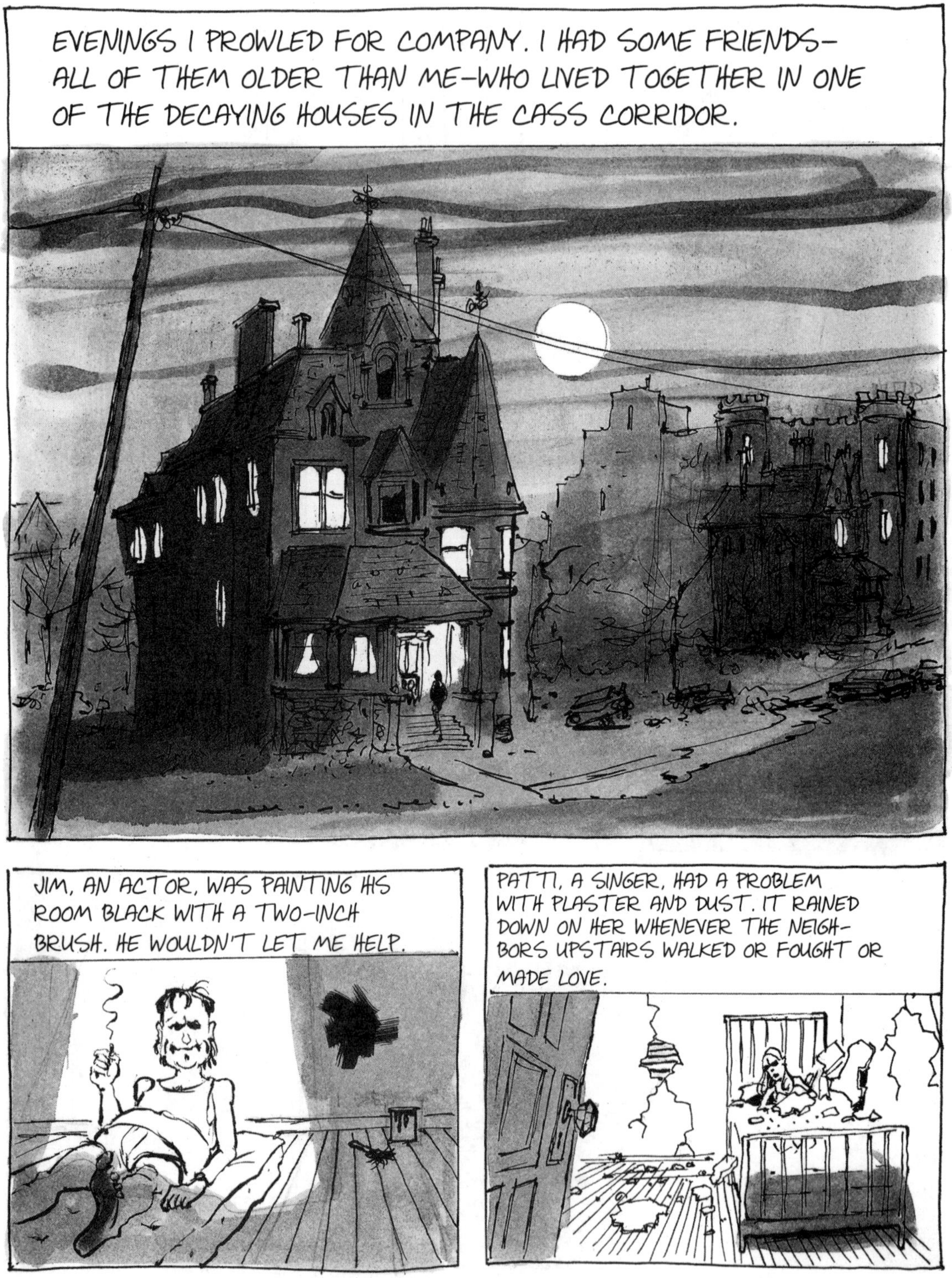
EVENINGS I PROWLED FOR COMPANY. I HAD SOME FRIENDS—ALL OF THEM OLDER THAN ME—WHO LIVED TOGETHER IN ONE OF THE DECAYING HOUSES IN THE CASS CORRIDOR.
JIM, AN ACTOR, WAS PAINTING HIS ROOM BLACK WITH A TWO-INCH BRUSH. HE WOULDN'T LET ME HELP.
PATTI, A SINGER, HAD A PROBLEM WITH PLASTER AND DUST. IT RAINED DOWN ON HER WHENEVER THE NEIGH-BORS UPSTAIRS WALKED OR FOUGHT OR MADE LOVE.

STAN AND LETITIA LIVED IN
THE UPSTAIRS BATHROOM. ONCE
THEY HAD LIVED IN A REGULAR
ROOM BUT THEY WERE BROKE
NOW AND FORCED TO DOWNGRADE.
THEY INSISTED IT WAS A FINE
PLACE TO LIVE: EXCELLENT
ACOUSTICS FOR STAN'S GUITAR,
GOOD LIGHT FOR LETITIA'S SELF-
PORTRAITS. AT NIGHT WE LIT
CANDLES AND PLAYED CHESS ON
THE TILE FLOOR.

BILL AND GINA LIVED IN THE
TOWER ROOM WHERE THE
FLOOR HAD COLLAPSED. THEY
LIVED AROUND THE EDGE OF THE
CRATER AND PITCHED THEIR
TRASH DOWN THE HOLE.

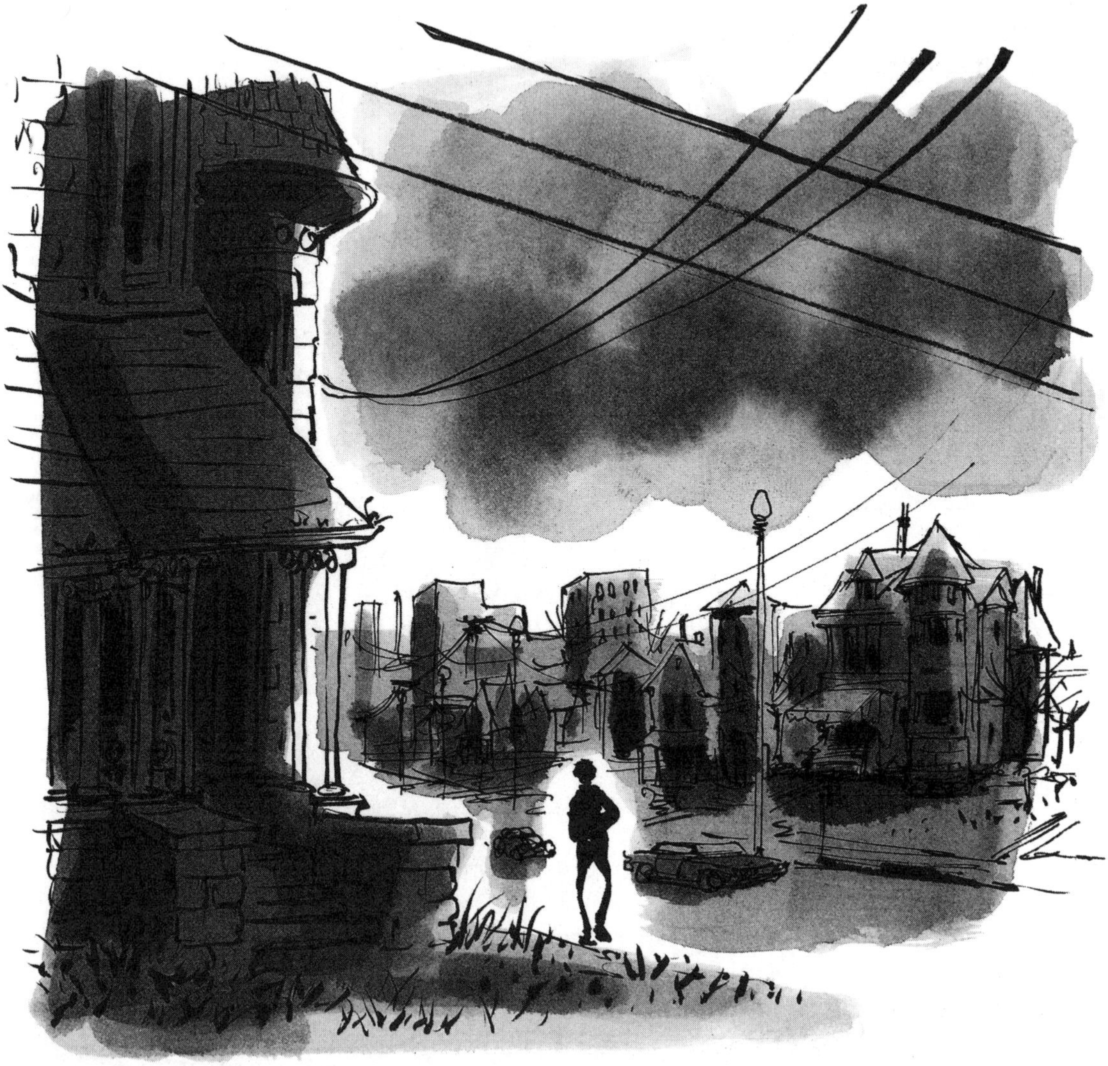

I LIKED THEM ALL. THEIR CIRCUMSTANCES AND BEHAVIOR WERE, BY ALMOST ANY STANDARD, BIZARRE, BUT I FELT MORE NORMAL AMONG THEM, AND LESS LONELY.

ALTHOUGH MY PARENTS TALKED SERIOUSLY ABOUT GETTING A DIVORCE, THEY NEVER DID.

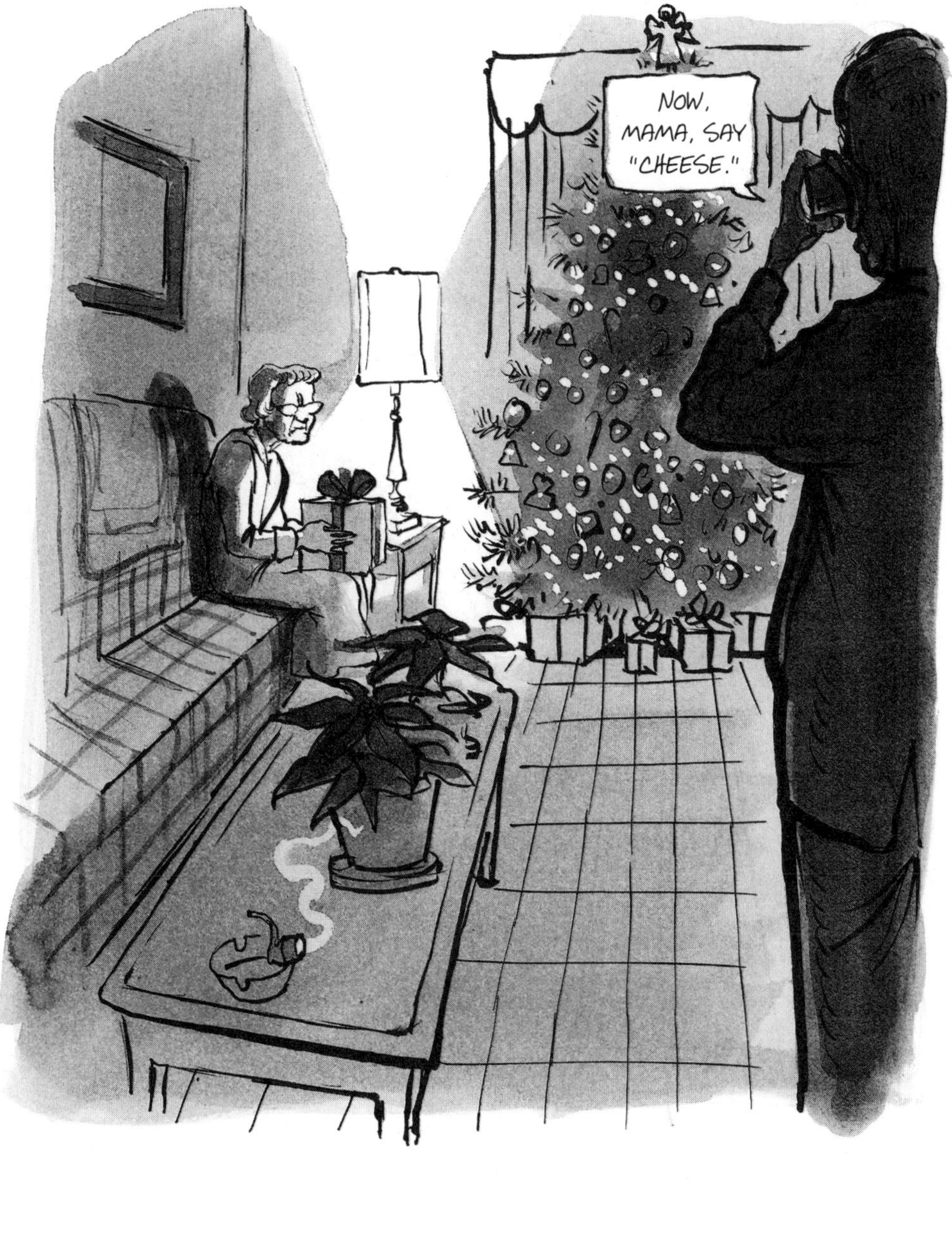
NOW, MAMA, SAY "CHEESE."

ART BECAME MY HOME.
NOT ONLY DID IT GIVE ME BACK
MY VOICE, BUT ART HAS GIVEN ME
EVERYTHING I HAVE WANTED
OR NEEDED SINCE.

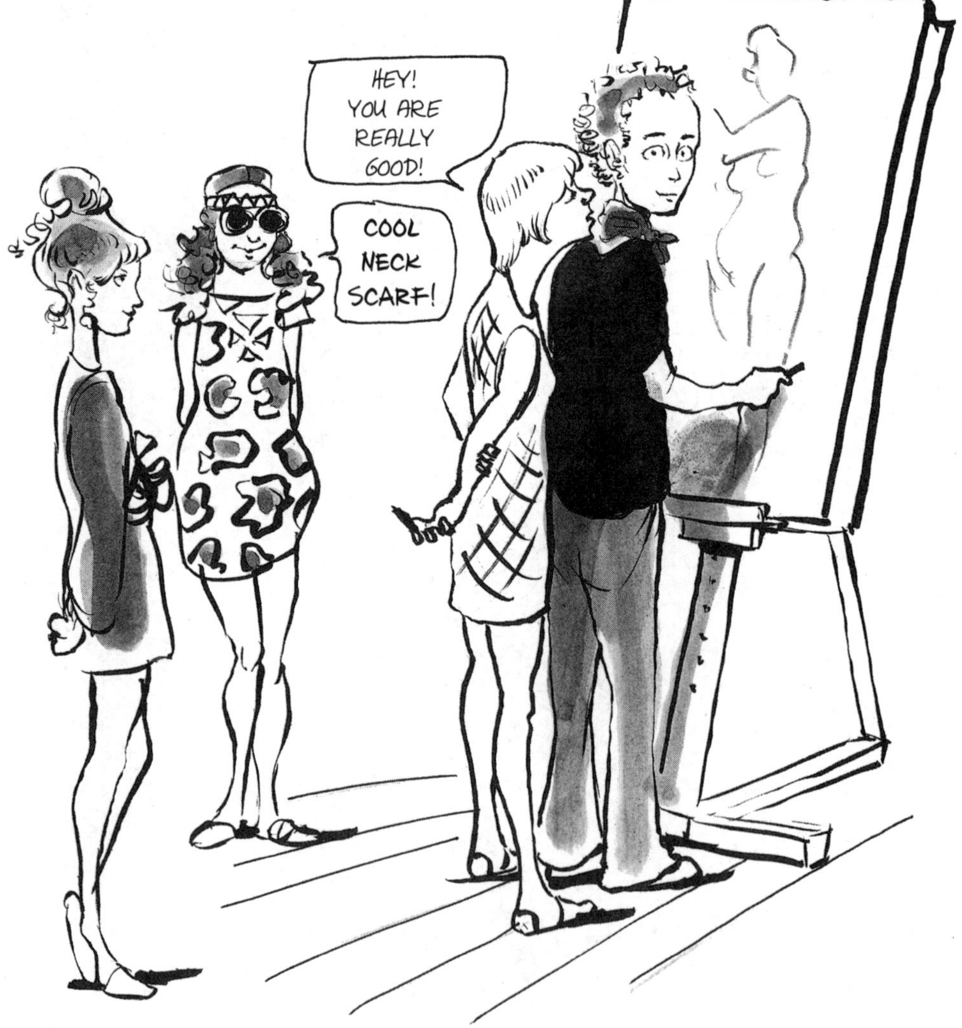
HEY! YOU ARE REALLY GOOD!
COOL NECK SCARF!

AT 30, WHEN I WAS TEACHING DRAWING
AT A COLLEGE IN UPSTATE NEW YORK,
DAD CALLED ONE NIGHT FROM DETROIT.
MOTHER WAS DYING, HE SAID. I SHOULD
COME QUICKLY.
ALONE IN THE CAR, I SCREAMED
ALL THE WAY BACK TO MICHIGAN.

I WASN'T SCREAMING IN ANGER OR RAGE OR
AT THE THOUGHT OF AN IMPENDING LOSS. I HAD
LEARNED THAT SCREAMING THICKENS UP THE
VOCAL CORDS. ALREADY THIS HAD GIVEN ME BACK
SOMETHING OF A VOICE. SO, I TOOK EVERY OPPOR-
TUNITY TO BE ALONE, TO SCREAM, OR SING
OR TELL MYSELF STORIES AS LOUDLY AS I COULD.

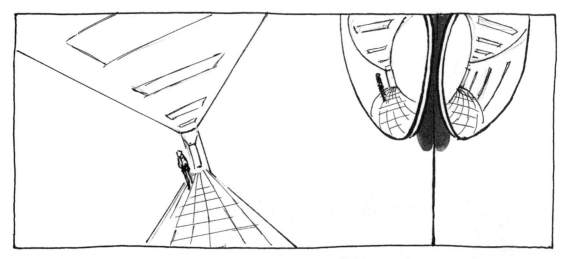

DING!

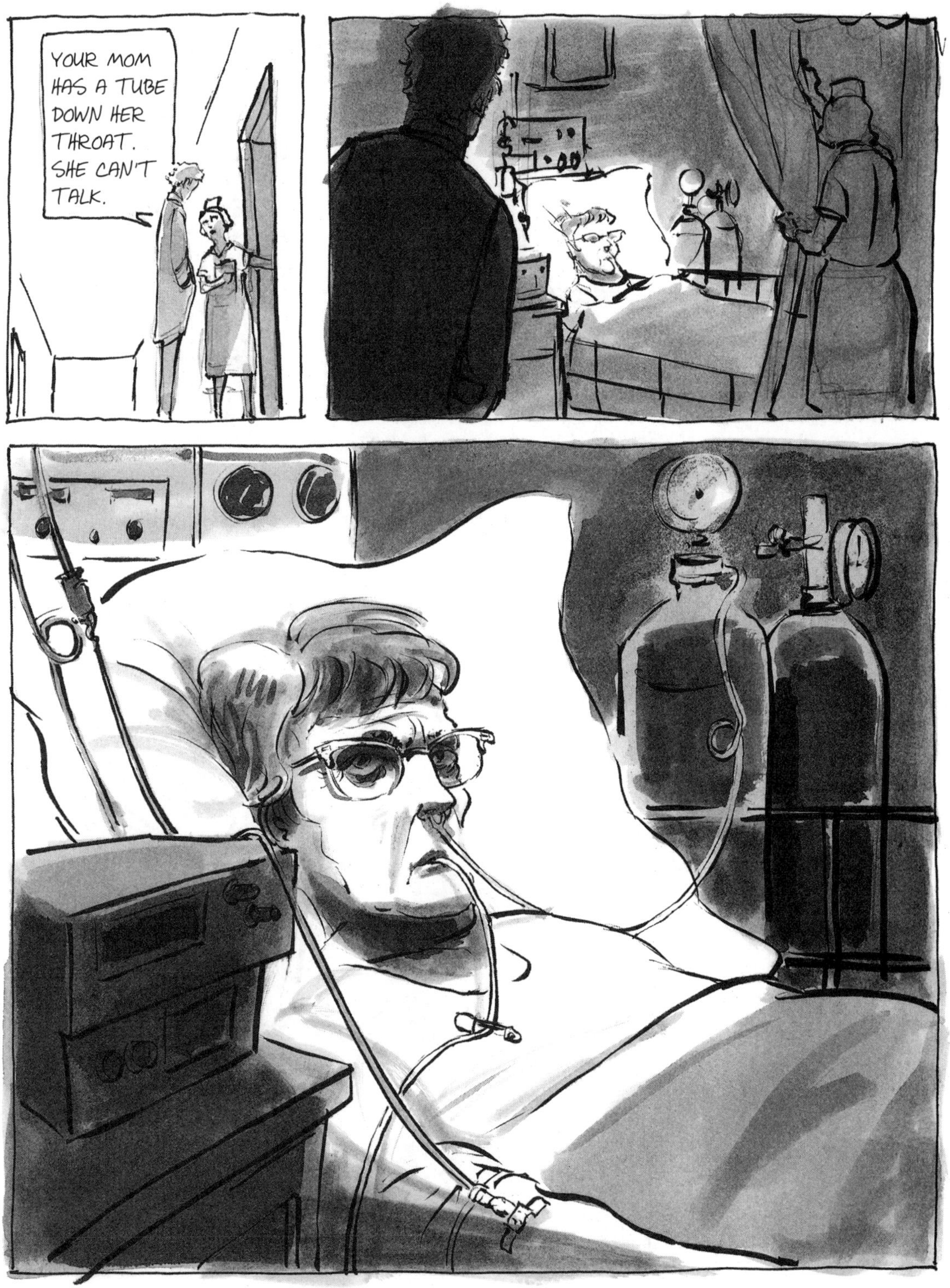
YOUR MOM HAS A TUBE DOWN HER THROAT. SHE CAN'T TALK.

SHE COULDN'T TALK
AND NEITHER COULD I.
I HAD BEEN SCREAMING
FOR SO MANY HOURS
THAT I, TOO, WAS
VOICELESS.

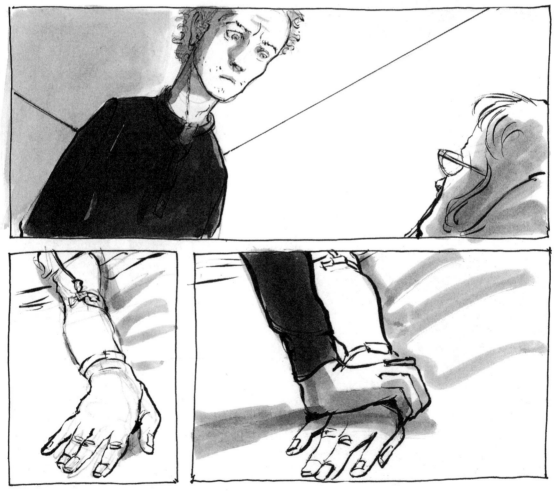

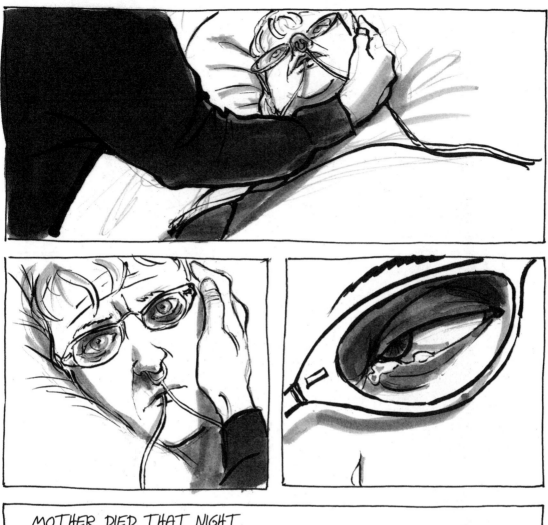

MOTHER DIED THAT NIGHT.

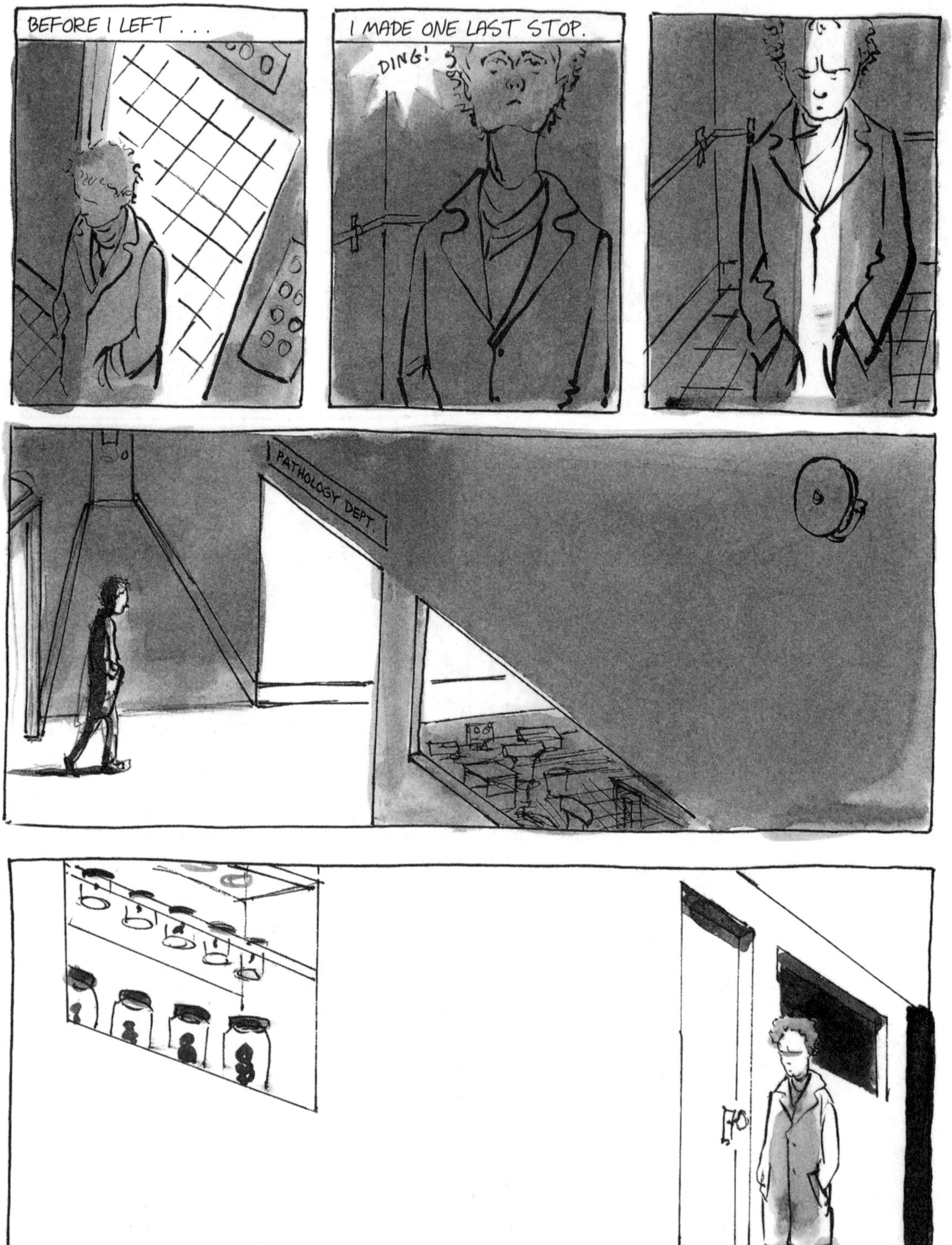
BEFORE I LEFT . . .
I MADE ONE LAST STOP.
DING!
PATHOLOGY DEPT.

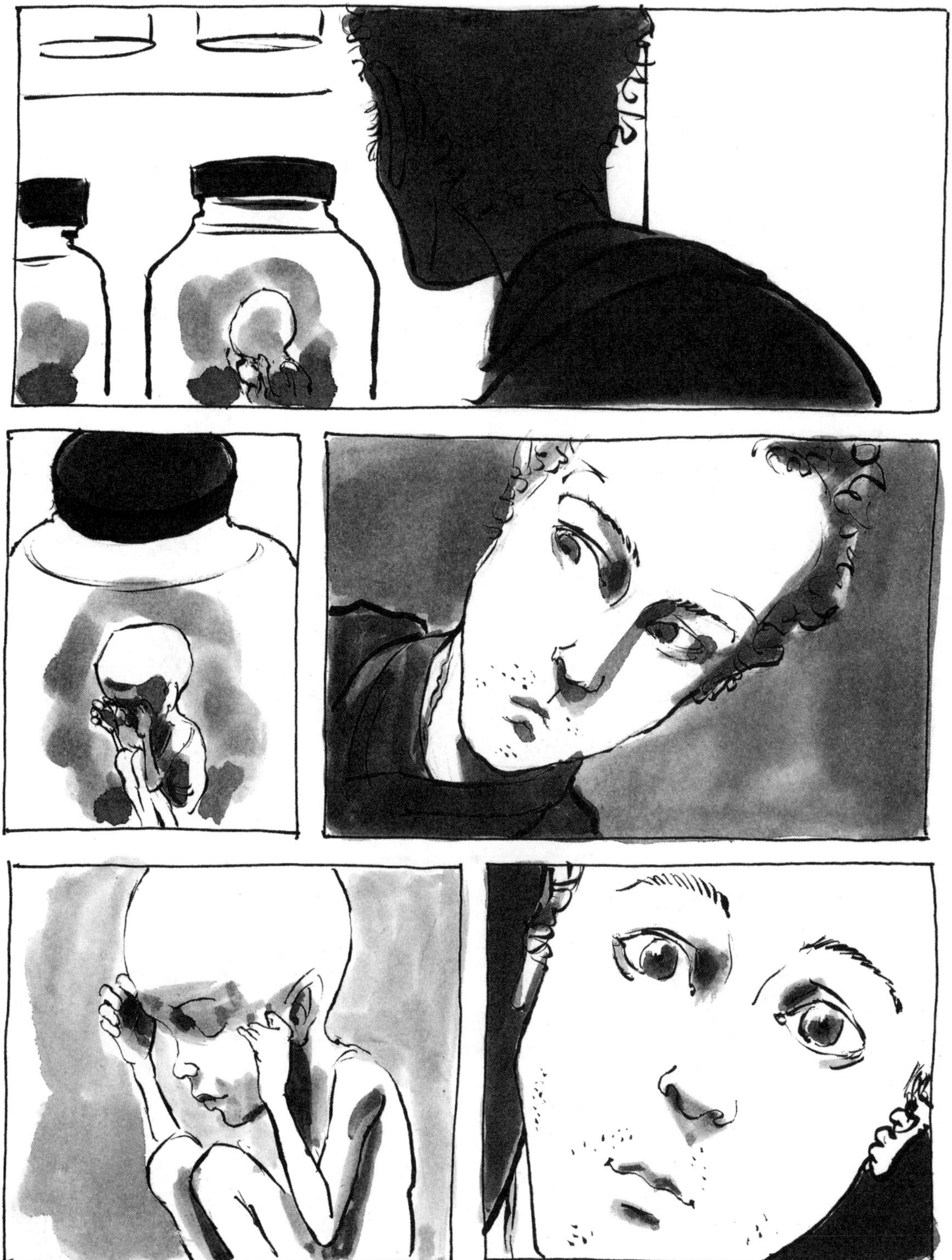

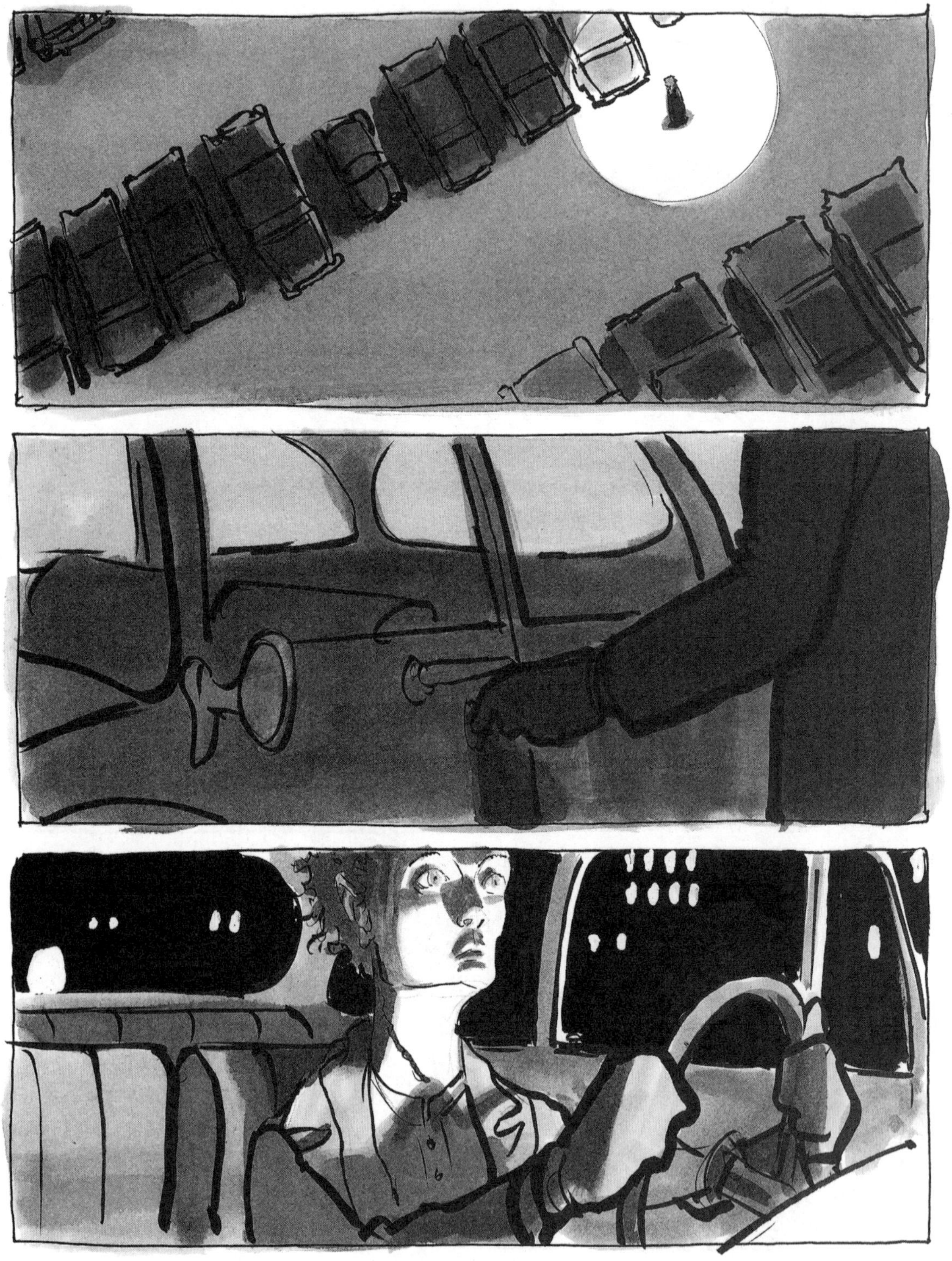

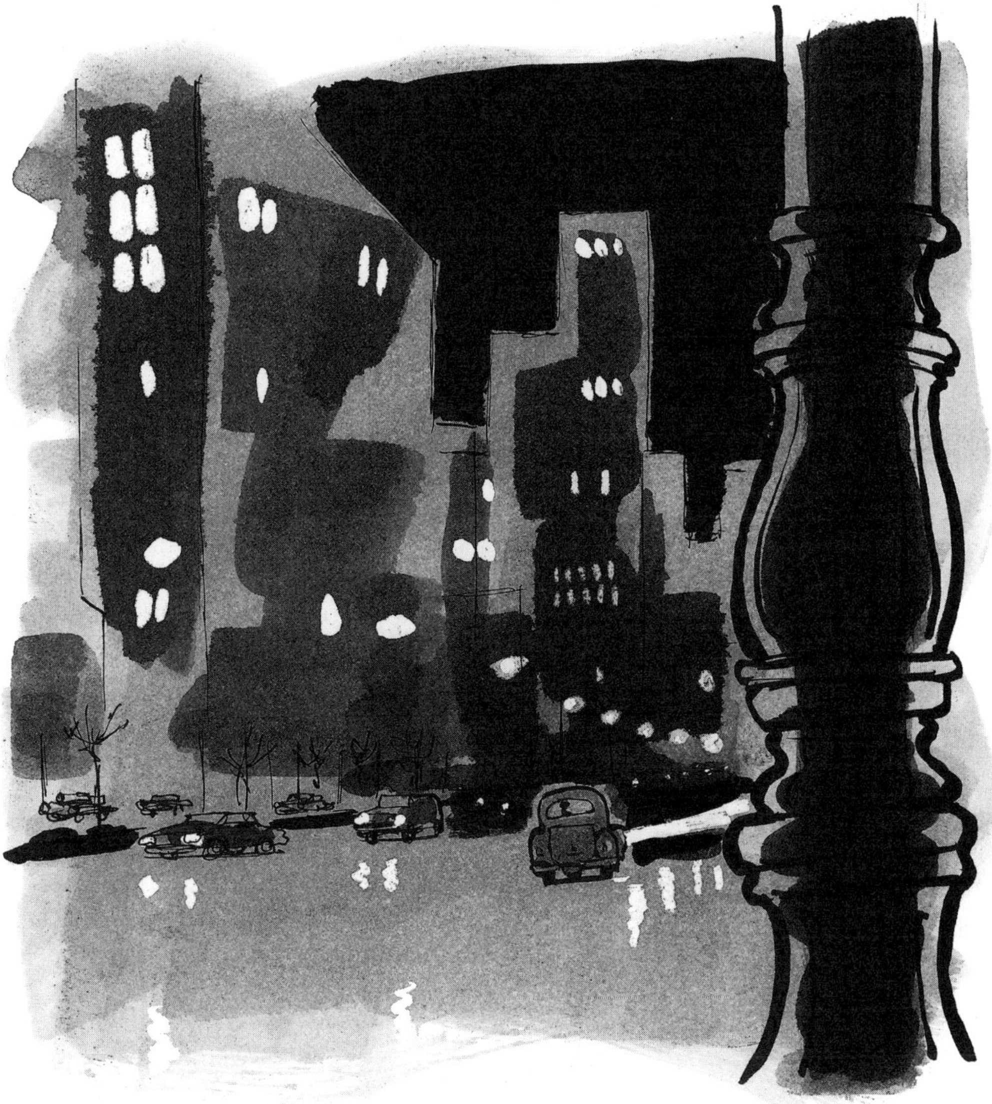

A FEW YEARS AGO
I HAD THE
FOLLOWING DREAM

IN THE DREAM
I WAS ONCE AGAIN
A BOY OF SIX . . .

A HOUSE, A GARDEN, A HIGH ENCLOSING WALL . . .

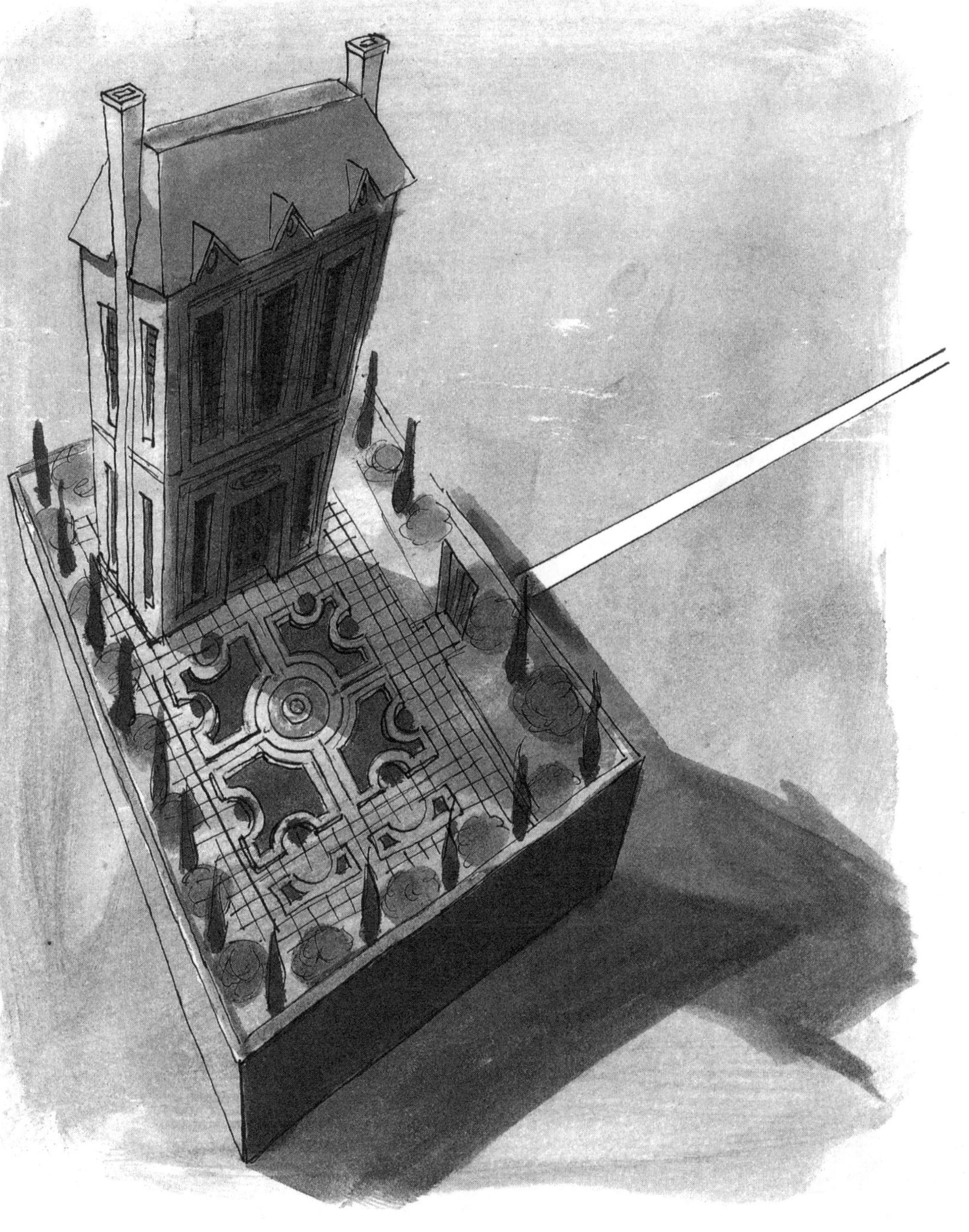

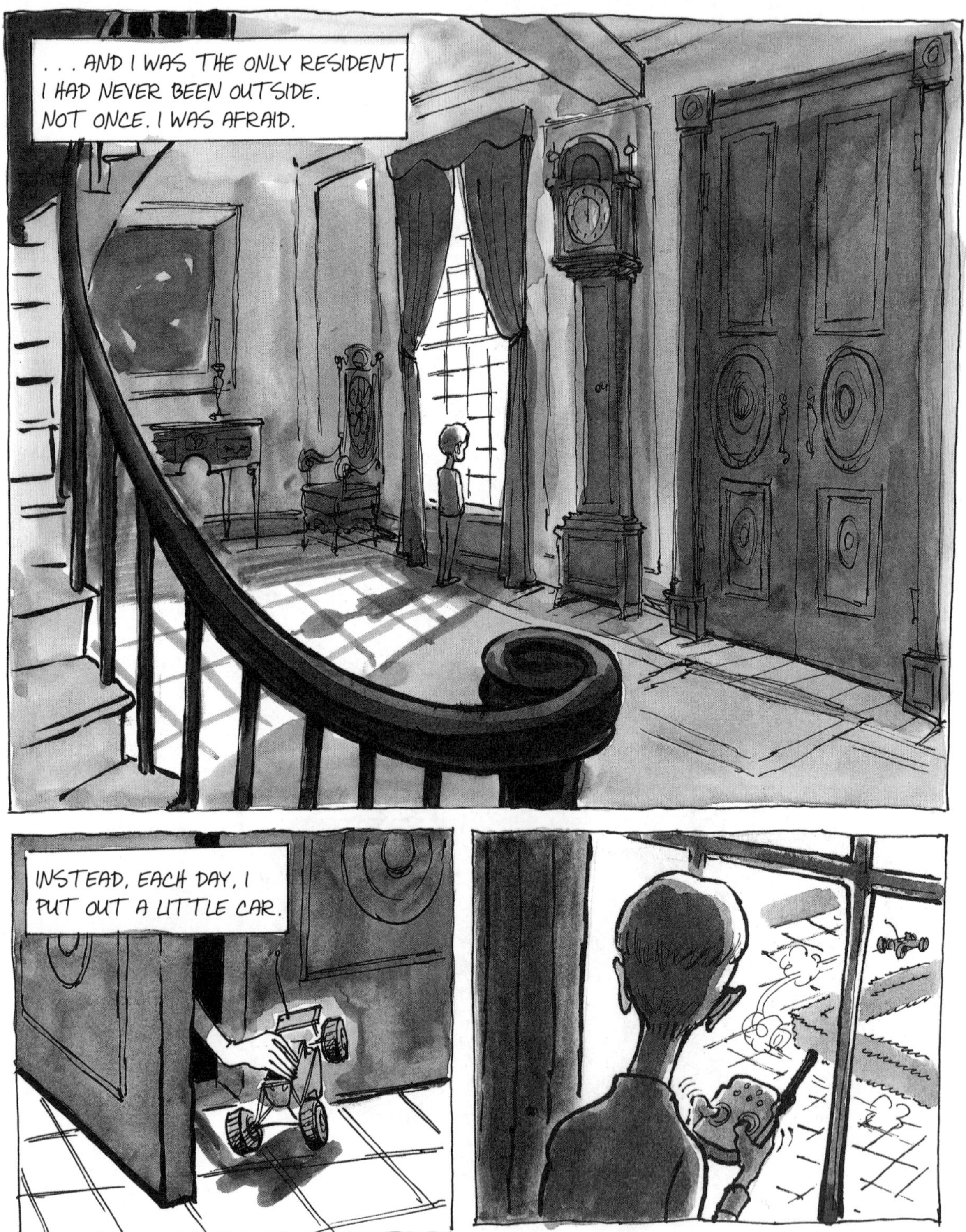
. . . AND I WAS THE ONLY RESIDENT. I HAD NEVER BEEN OUTSIDE. NOT ONCE. I WAS AFRAID.
INSTEAD, EACH DAY, I PUT OUT A LITTLE CAR.

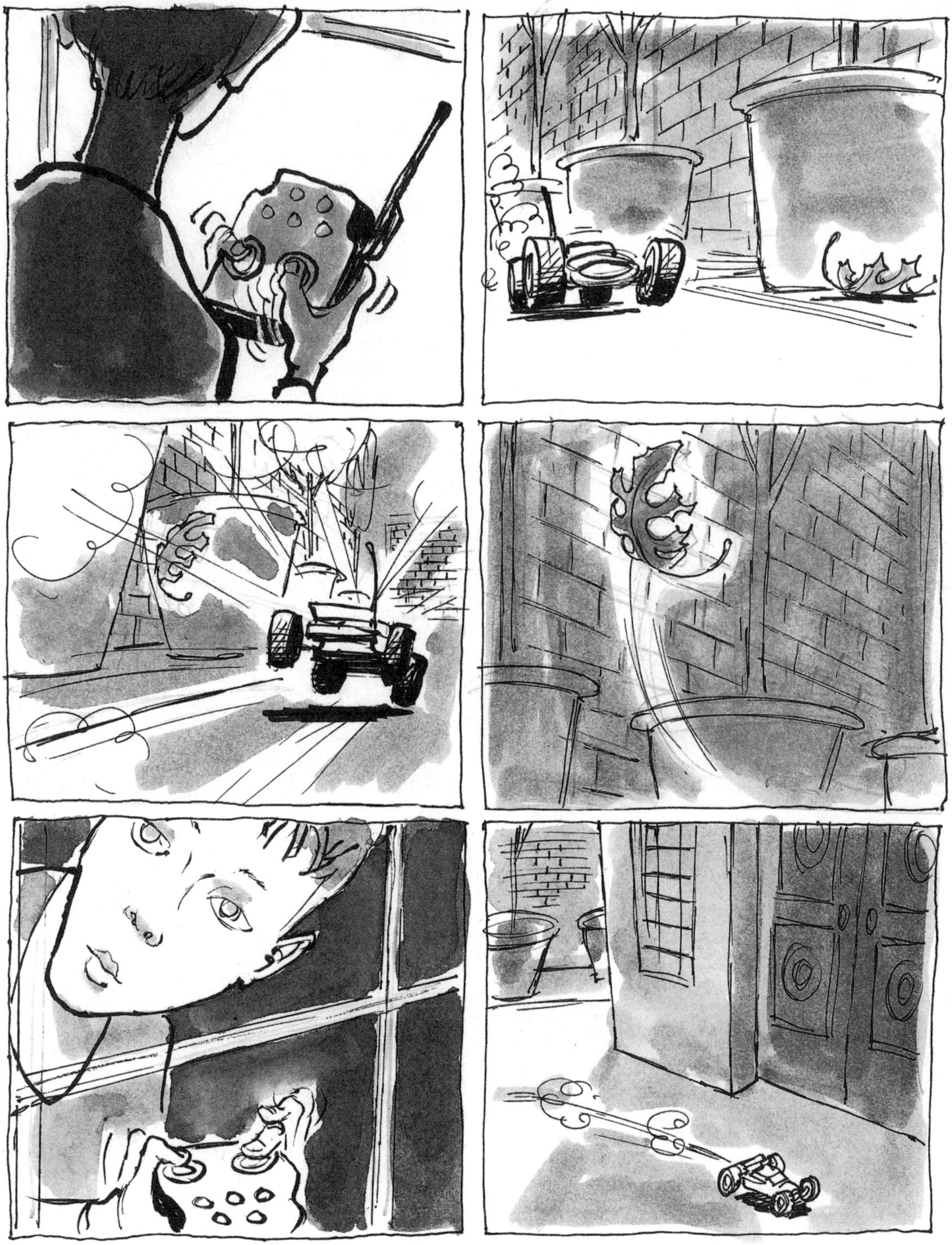

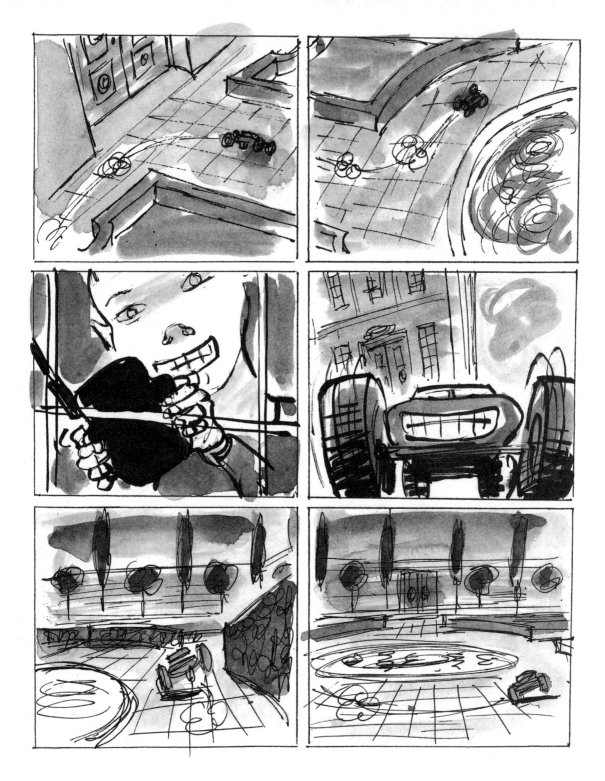

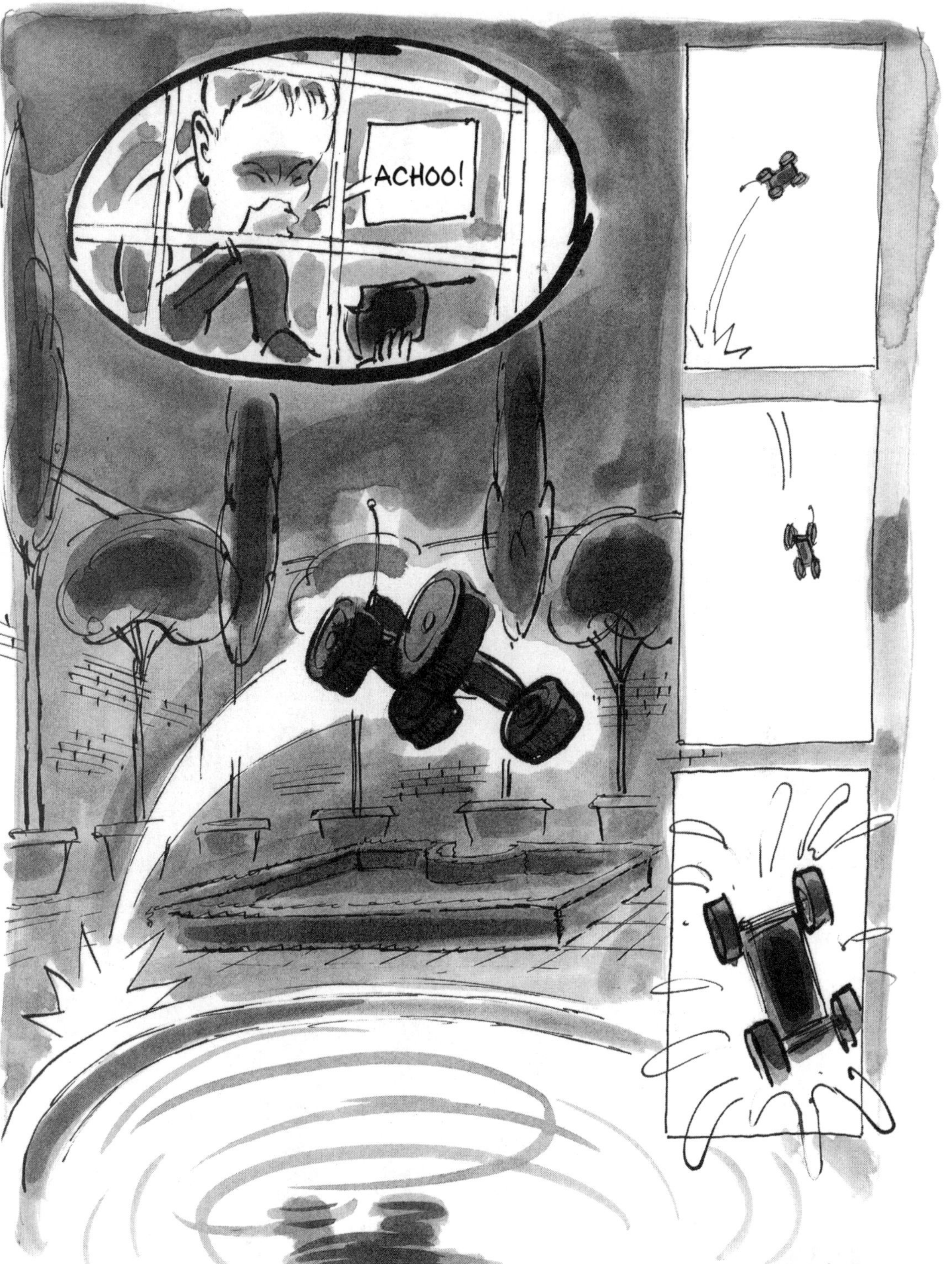
ACHOO!

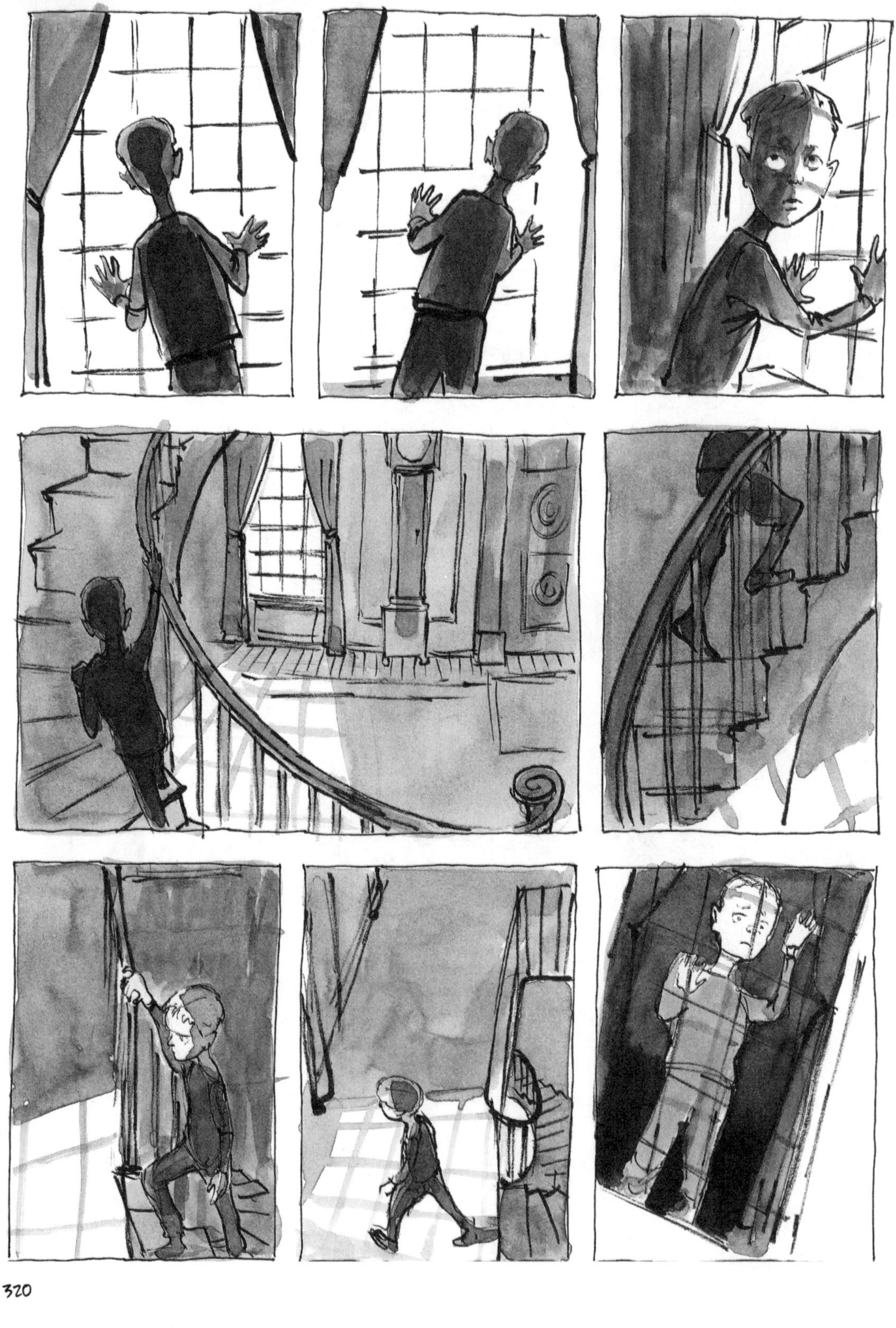

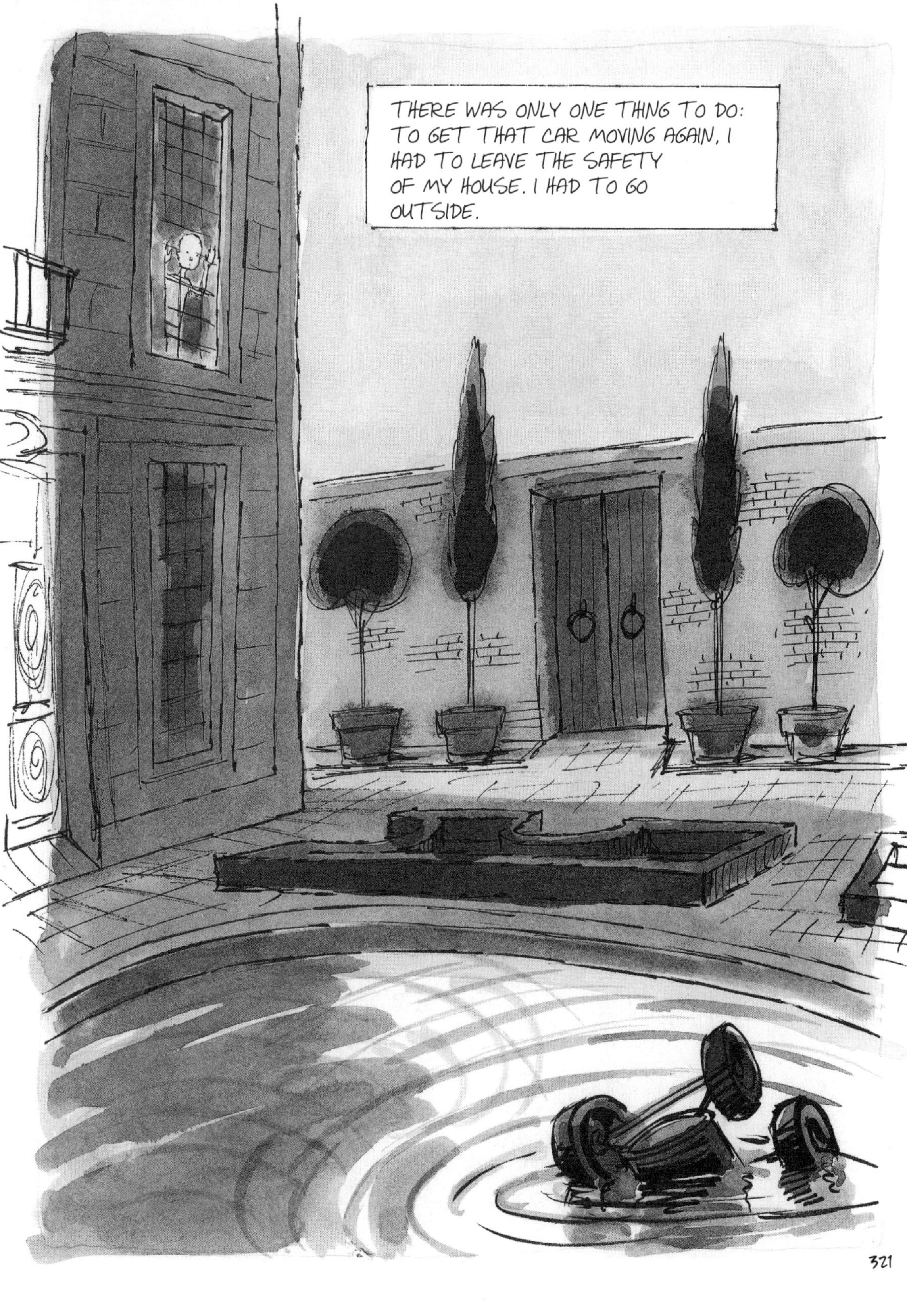
THERE WAS ONLY ONE THING TO DO: TO GET THAT CAR MOVING AGAIN, I HAD TO LEAVE THE SAFETY OF MY HOUSE. I HAD TO GO OUTSIDE.

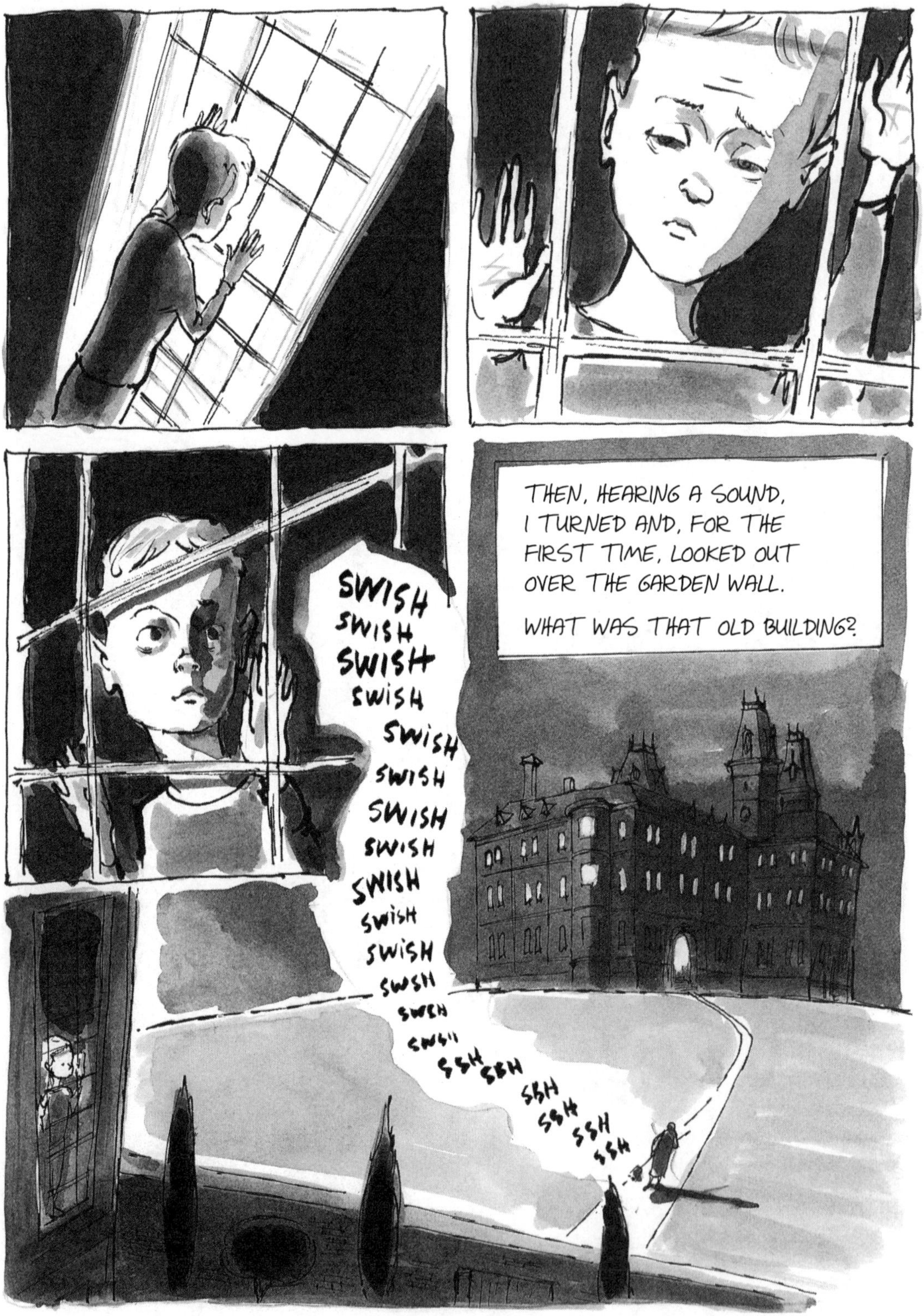
THEN, HEARING A SOUND, I TURNED AND, FOR THE FIRST TIME, LOOKED OUT OVER THE GARDEN WALL.
WHAT WAS THAT OLD BUILDING?
SWISH SWISH SWISH SWISH SWISH SWISH SWISH SWISH SWISH SWISH SWISH
SSH SSH SSH SSH SSH SSH

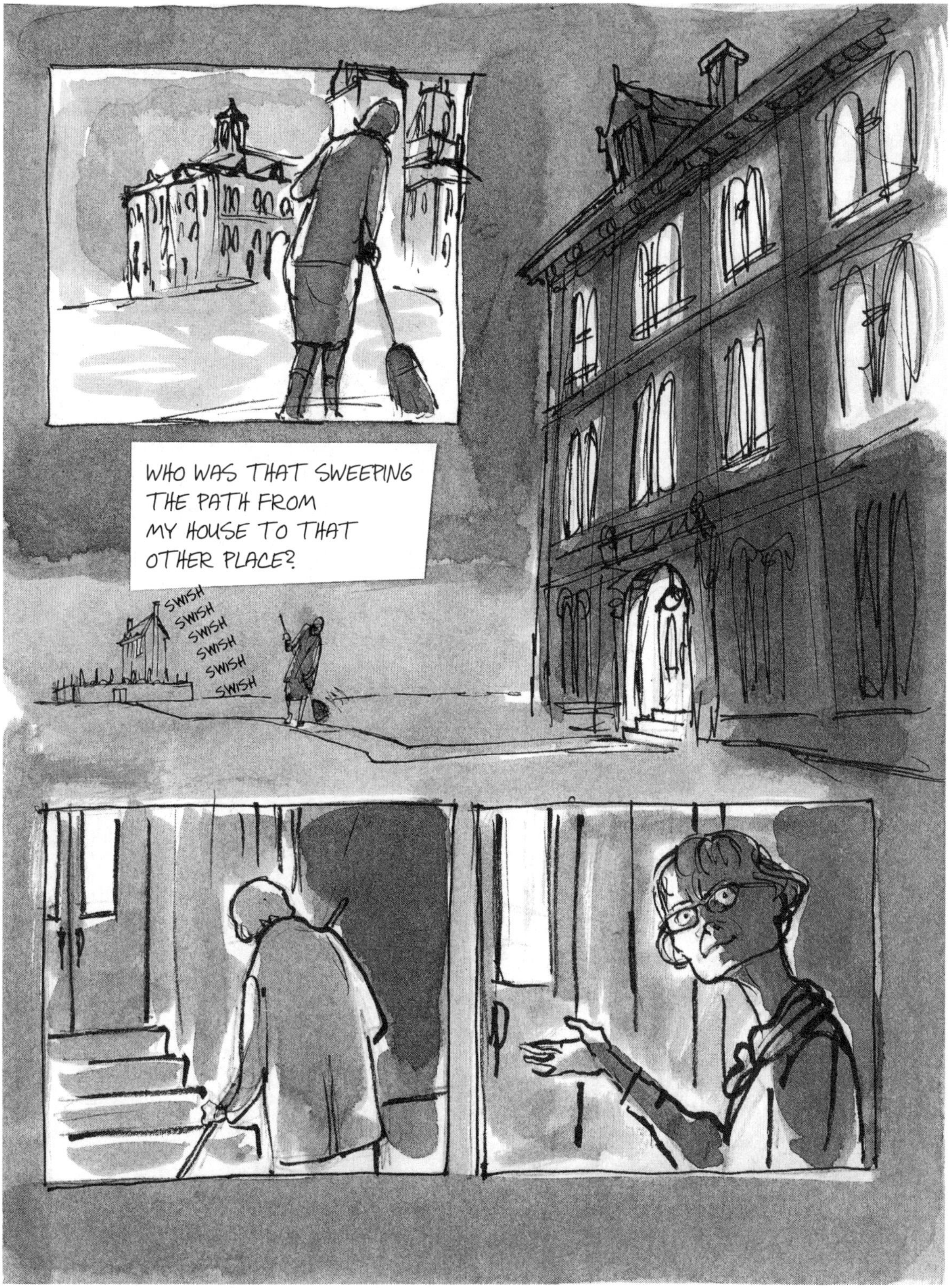
WHO WAS THAT SWEEPING THE PATH FROM MY HOUSE TO THAT OTHER PLACE?
SWISH
SWISH
SWISH
SWISH
SWISH
SWISH

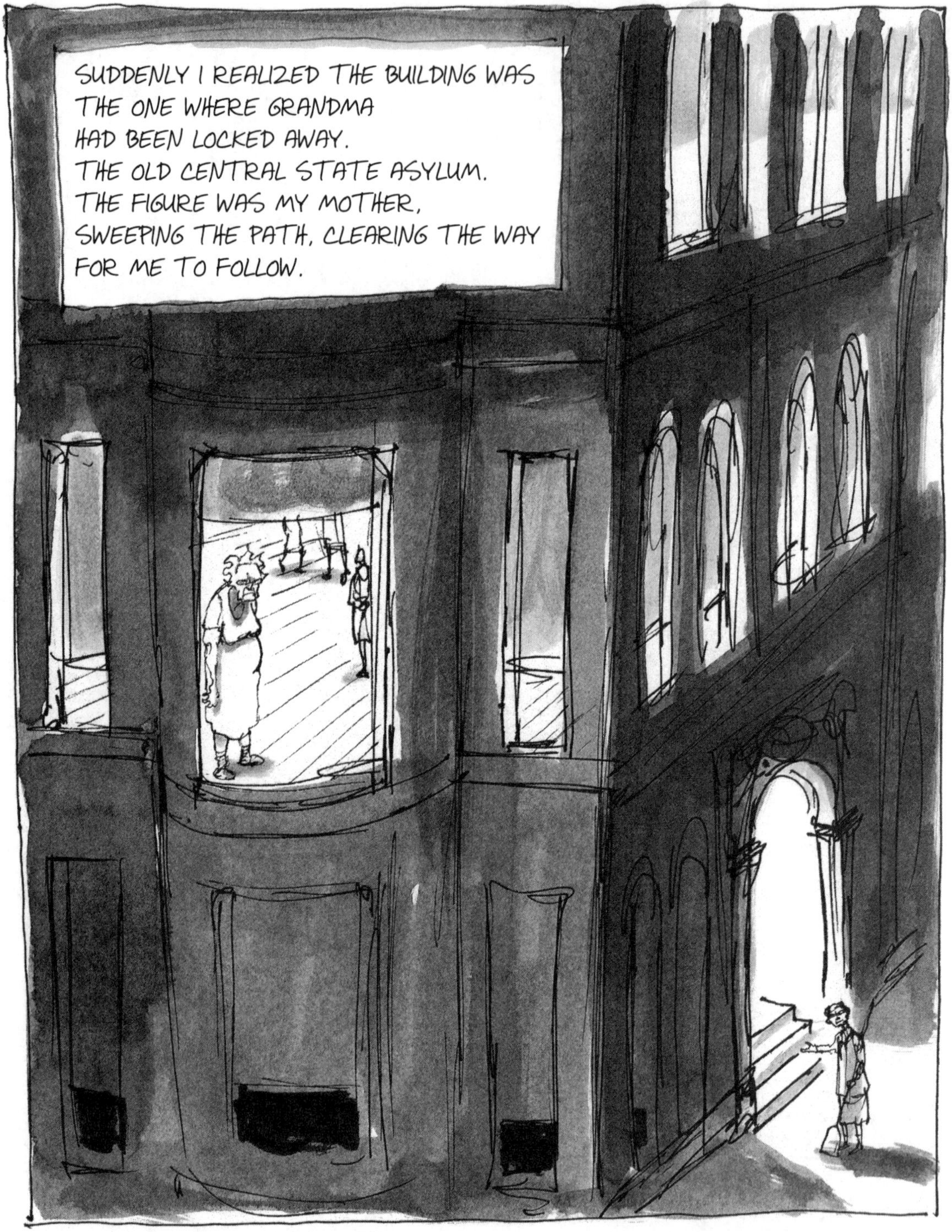
SUDDENLY I REALIZED THE BUILDING WAS THE ONE WHERE GRANDMA HAD BEEN LOCKED AWAY. THE OLD CENTRAL STATE ASYLUM. THE FIGURE WAS MY MOTHER, SWEEPING THE PATH, CLEARING THE WAY FOR ME TO FOLLOW.

I DIDN'T.

My mother died in 1970, age 58. Maturity, reflection and some family research have unearthed a few facts, which give a slightly different picture of this taciturn and difficult person. Her physical problems were beyond what I could imagine or understand as a child. Because nothing in our family was ever discussed outright, I only became aware of some of them years after her death.

Born with her heart on the wrong side of her chest, she suffered from multiple heart attacks toward the end of her life. She also had only one functioning lung.

If this had been her story, not mine, her secret life as a lesbian would certainly have been examined more closely.

I keep recalling a line from the novelist and poet Edward Dahlberg:

"Nobody heard her tears; the heart is a fountain of weeping water which makes no noise in the world."

A few years after my mother died, my father remarried—happily this time—and lived to the ripe old age of 84.

My brother, Ted, became a percussionist and for 30 years worked for the Colorado Symphony.

And here I am at 6 years old.

ACKNOWLEDGEMENTS

With love and grateful thanks to my dear friend/wife, Sarah Stewart, for—among countless other blessings—putting up with me through the whole ordeal of making this book; to my agent, Holly McGhee, who was the first to see the possibilities in *Stitches* and who worked tirelessly with me on its first dozen drafts; to my other pips at Pippin Properties, Emily Van Beek and Samantha Cosentino; to my patient and sagacious editor, Bob Weil, and his steady editorial assistant, Lucas Wittmann; to Paul Buckley, Ingsu Liu, Rubina Yeh, Anna Oler, and Sue Carlson for their inspired contributions to the design of this book; to my stepson Mark Stewart Guin for his always spot-on advice in both the language and visual departments; to my other stepson, David Stewart Andrews, for those last-minute edits; and to all those good friends who thought it sounded like a fine idea but really had no conception of what their encouragement meant: Brad Zellar, M. T. Anderson, François Place, Pierre Place, Pascal Lemaître, Stu Dybek, Joan Blos, Peter Blos, Kevin Brady, Robert Trenary, William Trenary, Paul Clemens, John Macabee, Kevin King, Walter Mayes, Alison McGhee, LeUyen Pham, Dan Potash, Michael Steiner, and, for his extraordinarily detailed and evocative memories of the people and places we used to know in Detroit, Steven Ligosky.

Lastly, my special thanks to Dr. Harold Davidson for pulling me to my feet and placing me on the road to the examined life.

ABOUT THE AUTHOR

David Small started his illustration career as an editorial artist working for national publications such as *The New Yorker, The New York Times, The Washington Post, Esquire,* and *Playboy.* He is best known as the author and illustrator of numerous picture books for children. His books have been translated into several languages, made into animated films and musicals, and have won many of the top awards accorded to illustration, including the 2001 Caldecott Medal for *So, You Want to Be President?* by Judith St. George; the 1997 Caldecott Honor and the Christopher Medal for *The Gardener,* written by his wife, Sarah Stewart; the Society of Illustrators' Gold Medal for *The Mouse and His Child* by Russell Hoban; the 2008 E.B. White Award and *Time* magazine's #1 Best Children's Book in 2007 for *When Dinosaurs Came With Everything* by Elise Broach.

For more information, please visit www.davidsmallbooks.com.